63

THE VICTOR BOOK OF

Operas

REVISED AND EDITED BY

Louis Biancolli

AND

Robert Bagar

SIMON AND SCHUSTER · NEW YORK
1949

ALL RIGHTS RESERVED
INCLUDING THE RIGHT OF REPRODUCTION
IN WHOLE OR IN PART IN ANY FORM
COPYRIGHT, 1929, BY VICTOR TALKING MACHINE CO.
COPYRIGHT, 1936, BY RCA MANUFACTURING COMPANY, INC.,
CAMDEN, NEW JERSEY, U.S.A.
COPYRIGHT, 1949, BY SIMON AND SCHUSTER, INC.
PUBLISHED BY SIMON AND SCHUSTER, INC.
ROCKEFELLER CENTER, 1230 SIXTH AVENUE
NEW YORK 20, N. Y.

MANUFACTURED IN THE UNITED STATES OF AMERICA
AMERICAN BOOK–STRATFORD PRESS, INC., NEW YORK

Publisher's Preface

For almost two generations now, music-lovers have regarded The Victor Book of the Opera *as a prime source of information on and entertainment from its subject—grand opera. Since 1912, when it was first issued by the Victor Company, over 600,000 copies have been sold, and this mounting volume is a testimony both to the merit of the work itself and to the increasing hold that opera has on the American public.*

The book, first issued anonymously by the Victor Talking Machine Company, was the work of various hands. It went through many editions, with changes chiefly in its listing of recordings and in pictures, and in 1939 it was re-edited for the tenth time by Charles O'Connell, author of The Victor Book of Symphonies. *It has now been completely revised and brought up to date, with the addition of many operas previously untreated, by Louis Biancolli and Robert Bagar, music critics of the* New York World-Telegram.

The book retains all the essential features that have so long made it the most popular book of its sort in America. These features include the detailed act-by-act stories of all the operas in the standard repertoire and scores of others less often heard; an outline history of opera; pictures of scenes from the operas and the world-famous singers of the past and present who are most closely identified with the great roles; complete listings of all the operatic recordings in the rich Victor catalogue; and introductory accounts of the composition and performance history of every opera. These last have been particularly re-edited and brought up to date, with careful verification of all the facts from musical histories, newspaper accounts, and especially that monument of musicological scholarship, the Annals of the Opera *by A. Loewenberg. In the odd and often*

v

stormy history presented by operatic performance, it is not always possible to be absolutely certain of the exact date of a première, *for the best of authorities often disagree. But every effort has been made in this, the eleventh edition of the book, to make it as reliable a reference work as is possible.*

With millions now listening regularly to operatic broadcasts, with even more millions regularly buying operatic recordings, and with the vast increase in the popularity of stage presentations of opera, it is the hope of the editors and the publisher that The Victor Book of Operas *will find an even firmer place than it had before in the hearts of the music-loving public.*

Contents

THE STORIES OF THE OPERAS
ARRANGED IN INDEX FORM
IN BOTH ENGLISH AND THE ORIGINAL LANGUAGE

Contents

Contents

ix

Contents

Suggested selling prices of RCA-Victor Red Seal records and albums are as follows:

12-inch Red Seal	$1.25
10-inch Red Seal	1.00
12-inch De Luxe (Vinylite)	2.00
12-inch Gold Label (Heritage Series)	2.50
10-inch and 12-inch albums	1.00
Recordrama albums	1.25

All prices quoted are list price, exclusive of Federal, state, and local excise taxes.

ACKNOWLEDGMENTS

AMONG the many who have co-operated generously in contributing the use of their pictures to this book, the following deserve special acknowledgment: Musical America, *The Metropolitan Opera Guild, The Metropolitan Opera Press Bureau, the* New York Times, *the San Francisco Opera Association, and Mr. Ronald Wise.*

An Outline History of Opera

ITALY

About the year 1580 a group of Florentine scholars and musical amateurs began discussing the possibility of adapting music to the drama. They believed that the ancient Athenians had performed their tragedies in a sort of musical declamation. This practice the Florentines endeavored to revive and from their attempts modern opera was born. For opera may be defined as a play in which the actors sing throughout, accompanied by an orchestra.

Avoiding the complex polyphony that was characteristic of the music of the period, the Florentines sought, instead, a style of solo music that would permit the words to be distinct—emotionalized speech rather than sustained song. The instrumental accompaniment was to be merely a support and background. The first application of this style of recitative to an entire play was made by Jacopo Peri and Giulio Caccini, who collaborated in setting Ottavio Rinuccini's *Dafne* (1597). In 1600 *Euridice*, another poetic drama by Rinuccini, was set to music by Peri, and again by Caccini.

The next step in the development of the new art was made by Claudio Monteverdi, whose *Orfeo* was produced at Mantua in 1607. Like his Florentine predecessors, Monteverdi emphasized dramatic expression but employed more elaborate musical means. His experiments led him to some of the boldest innovations in musical history. He called for a larger orchestra than had been previously demanded and made skillful use of it to intensify dramatic mood.

The next important step in the development of opera was taken by Alessandro Scarlatti (1659–1725). He emphasized the musical element of his works, sometimes at the expense of the dramatic, and was the first to make considerable use of the so-called *Da capo* aria (Provenzale is supposed to have been its inventor). In this form the first portion of an aria is repeated after a second has intervened, hence the Italian name, *da capo*, which means "from the beginning." Although satisfying musically, this device is not suitable to all dramatic situations. Yet so great was its musical appeal that it came to be used with increasing frequency. In his arias Scarlatti often attained a beauty and a poignancy that were new to melodic writing. Opera as he wrote it came to be known as *opera seria* (Italian for "serious opera") and became the prevailing fashion of the following century. Since Scarlatti's successors were for the most part men of less genius, an artistic decline soon set in. Accordingly, during the eighteenth century *opera seria* became stereotyped in form. The plots were almost always based on legends of classical antiquity. The libretti generally contained shallow and vapid verse, and the music was little more than a string of arias. The form and character of these arias were determined by fixed rules, and everything was arranged as a means of displaying the technical skill of the singers. Thus, the mechanics of singing attained its greatest perfection during this period. Although the innumerable operas written along such conventional lines have long disappeared from the stage, many arias from these early operas are still treasured for the haunting beauty of their melodies.

Side by side with the Italian *opera seria* there developed a humorous counterpart, *opera buffa*. Its closeness to real life saved this genre from degenerating into the formalism of *opera seria*. In earlier times the dialogue was spoken; later it was set to what was called a *recitativo secco*, or "dry recitative"—a lightly accompanied form of recitative particularly adapted to rapid or humorous dialogue.

Italian opera was infused with a new breath of life at the beginning of the nineteenth century through the work of Gioacchino Antonio Rossini (1792–1868), who wrote both serious and comic operas. In the invention of brilliant vocal melody he showed unrivaled genius. Rossini also gave added prominence to the orchestral accompaniment. His school was continued by Gaetano Donizetti (1797–1848) and Vincenzo Bellini (1801–1835). Both showed marked gifts in composing melody of a serene and limpid beauty.

Their successor, Giuseppe Verdi (1813–1901), one of the world's greatest dramatic composers, began his career with such works as *Oberto* (1839) and *Ernani* (1844), written in a style akin to that of Bellini and Donizetti, but already displaying greater vigor and dramatic force. Throughout his long career Verdi revealed a growing development of dramatic and orchestral power without any accompanying loss of musical inspiration. Evident, too, was a growing seriousness of purpose. Verdi's final works are remarkable for their depth of expression, clearness of characterization, freedom of form, and richness of harmony and orchestration. Indeed, many regard *Otello* and *Falstaff* as his crowning achievements.

The end of the nineteenth century was marked by the appearance of a new school of operatic composition, the *verismo*, paralleling the same movement in literature. This first appeared in Pietro Mascagni's *Cavalleria rusticana* (1890) and Ruggiero Leoncavallo's *Pagliacci* (1892), short masterpieces which established the world reputation of their composers. The aim here was to present dramas of real life, with all the interplay of violent passions, and set to music of realistic power.

The greatest genius in Italian opera since Verdi, and one of the most popular of all composers, was Giacomo Puccini (1858–1924). A gifted melodist, endowed with an uncanny flair for dramatic effect, Puccini was also noteworthy among Italian composers for his frequent use of exotic color and setting.

Recent Italian opera composers such as Umberto Giordano, Franco Alfano, and Italo Montemezzi have been influenced by the melodic style of Puccini and the methods of *verismo*, though their music also shows elements traceable to musical movements in France and Germany.

FRANCE

In France, opera had its rise in the ballet—elaborate spectacles performed for the entertainment of the seventeenth-century court. This may account for the interest in scenic effect that has characterized much French opera. When in 1645 an Italian opera troupe appeared in Paris for the first time, it gave fresh impetus to the musical phase of court performances. Jean Baptiste Lully (1632–1687), the first important composer of French opera, reflects the conventional life of the court for which he wrote; yet in his effort to make the words distinct and in the prominence which he gives to the visual elements of staging and pantomime, he set the pattern for the French opera of the future. Without altering the basic style, his successor, Jean Philippe Rameau (1683–1764), enriched it with a more varied harmony and greater orchestral prominence.

Meanwhile, a new form, *opéra comique,* was slowly evolving from the crude plays with interspersed songs which had long been popular with the French masses. Among the early writers of *opéras comiques* André Ernest Modeste Grétry (1741–1813) is outstanding. His works are notable for the vivacity and sparkle which enliven his formal eighteenth-century style. The aria *"La Fauvette"* from *Zémire et Azor* may be regarded as typical of his lighter vein.

Conventional Italian *opera seria* grew in favor in France during the eighteenth century, so that in the course of time two schools of thought arose—one preaching greater freedom and the importance of the dramatic and poetic side of opera, the other maintaining the superiority of *opera seria* with all its fixed formulas. The proponents of the former school found a powerful spokesman and standard-bearer in Christoph Willibald Gluck (1714–1787). Conscious of the inadequacy of the prevailing style, which he had used in many operas, Gluck attempted something of a reform in several of his later works. In this he met with little success, for Vienna, the scene of his first efforts, had wholly succumbed to the Italian school. Gluck then moved to Paris as a city that might prove more responsive to his theories.

Briefly stated, Gluck's thesis was that the music must always perfectly express the drama it accompanies. Nothing extraneous should be introduced for mere display, either vocal or orchestral. In his greater works Gluck attains an unprecedented dramatic force and expressive appeal.

Gluck's success, however, did not go unchallenged. His opponents brought to Paris the Italian Niccolà Piccinni, a composer of stereotyped *opera seria*. A sharp and acrimonious rivalry developed; indeed, so bitter was this "War of the Gluckists and Piccinnists" that it soon threatened to go beyond the purely verbal and aesthetic. The principles of Gluck finally triumphed, and even the embattled Piccinni was soon adopting his rival's manner, though with little success. Piccinni's music is today largely forgotten, but Gluck's *Alceste* and *Orfeo ed Euridice* are known to every music lover.

With the triumph of Gluck, Paris became for a time the center of European opera. During the next century a number of gifted operatic composers made it the scene of their greatest activity. Though many were of foreign birth, they soon adapted their native characteristics to the needs of French taste and style. Gasparo Spontini (1774–1851), whose *La Vestale* was a spectacular success, created a fashion for subjects of a heroic nature unfolded amid lavish scenic and orchestral color. In this he was followed by Halévy (1799–1862), composer of *La Juive*, and Meyerbeer (1791–1864), among whose best-known works are *L'Africaine*, *Les Huguenots*, and *Le Prophète*. The latter, a genius of vast theatrical resource, ranks among the greatest operatic innovators. Because of their gorgeous setting, large dramatic conception, and taxing demands for brilliant singing and acting, Meyerbeer's best works are truly "grand opera" in the most picturesque sense of the term. Admittedly, they are often marred by trivialities, pompousness, and an inability to exploit musical ideas to their fullest in artistic expression. But the man who could write Fides' aria, *"Ah, mon fils,"* in *Le Prophète* was an unquestioned genius of the first order.

The heroic grand-opera style was in time replaced by one of a simpler and more direct human appeal, as exemplified in Charles

Gounod's *Faust* (1859) and Georges Bizet's *Carmen* (1875), two of the enduring pillars of the world repertory. In both, the dramatic use made of accompanied recitative between the more formal vocal numbers again reveals the recurring French emphasis on the text. One of the most famous and prolific of later French composers was Jules Massenet (1842–1912). His style is marked by a suave melodiousness and refinement rather than by dramatic vigor. Gustave Charpentier, in his *Louise* (1900), presented a study of modern sociological problems and a picture of contemporary life. Written by a man of pronounced socialist sympathies, *Louise* has been called the first "proletarian opera." By the manner in which he makes the music cling inseparably to the mood and cadence of the text, Claude Debussy, in *Pelléas et Mélisande* (1902), again reverted to the principle of the original Florentine founders of opera.

GERMANY

In Germany we find the beginnings of opera dominated by Italian traditions. During the seventeenth and eighteenth centuries the court of every kingdom and principality maintained its own Italian or Italianized opera theater. During this period, however, there also emerged in the folk theaters a native product, the *Singspiel* (song play)—a light, often farcical or burlesque play in which spoken dialogue was interspersed with singing. Significantly, the characters were of humbler and less remote origin than those of court opera.

The first of the great German composers to write operas of lasting worth was Wolfgang Amadeus Mozart (1756–1791). Important as Mozart's work in the symphony, concerto, and string quartet was, his contribution to opera was perhaps even more significant. Two of his greatest works, *Le Nozze di Figaro* (1786) and *Don Giovanni* (1787) are written to Italian texts, with "dry recitatives." They are, in fact, magnificent descendants of the Italian *opera buffa*. On the other hand, *Die Zauberflöte* (1791) and *Die Entführung aus dem Serail* (1782) are set to German texts with spoken dialogue. Both these works show traces of the national style in their music and the influence of the *Singspiel* in the nature of their plots. Mozart ranks with the greatest of opera composers because of his unerring powers of characterization, his uncanny ability to express every shade of emotion, and his inexhaustible melodic invention.

If Mozart had learned much from his Italian and French predecessors, Ludwig van Beethoven (1770–1827) in turn learned much from Mozart and made significant advances of his own. For his one opera, *Fidelio,* shows the same profound originality and expressive individual power that mark his symphonic compositions. A consummate skill in using the orchestra to evoke atmosphere and depict the emotional turmoil of the characters is a striking feature of this sublime score. As in the *Singspiel,* spoken dialogue is used between the musical numbers.

Already foreshadowed in the work of Mozart and Beethoven, the romantic movement reached its operatic peak in the music of Carl Maria von Weber (1786–1826). The interest in the beauties of nature, the fascination for the terrors of the supernatural, the fanatic love of the exotic, whether European or Oriental, and the widespread enthusiasm for national folklore—all characteristic of the romantic movement in general—now found expression in the operas of this musical romantic. *Der Freischütz,* notable for its typically German folk story, characteristically national melodies, and ingenious tone painting in harmony and orchestration, is Weber's acknowledged masterpiece.

With the stupendous achievement of Richard Wagner (1813–1883), opera recalls once more the aims and ideals of the early Florentine group. For Wagner the quintessence of opera was drama. Music became increasingly a means of heightening the dramatic action and intensifying the illusion of life. Word and note were now indissolubly bound in a single unity of expression, and in this tremendous fabric Wagner's orchestra became a new instrument of massive power. No longer a mere accompaniment, it was now a running commentary on the events and emotions of the story unfolding on the stage; it caught every shifting nuance of feeling, it evoked memories and associations through a wondrous scheme of *Leitmotiven,* or leading themes. The orchestra was now alive to every suggestion of past happenings and every hint of the future, and throughout this complex web of tone one caught ominous strains of prophecy, often giving the entire score something of the tension and fatalism of Greek tragedy. Though Wagner had learned a great deal from Beethoven and Weber, his real forerunner in artistic outlook was Gluck, who had similarly stressed the pre-eminence of expression and drama in opera. This goal Wagner reached only after many years of groping, years during which his manner and style were partly imitative, as in *Rienzi*. And to the very end, he experimented with new devices of orchestral form and color, achieving what many regard as his most masterly synthesis of ideal and inspiration in *Parsifal*.

A faithful disciple of Wagner's was Engelbert Humperdinck (1854–1921), whose complete assimilation of the master's idiom is especially evident in the orchestral scoring of *Hänsel und Gretel*. This delightful fairy opera, of course, boasts a folksy spirit of childlike fantasy which owes nothing to Wagner.

It is Richard Strauss (1864–   ), however, who dominates the whole scene of post-Wagnerian opera in Germany. Like Wagner, Strauss has amplified and enriched the voice of the orchestra, creating, moreover, a whole emotional and pictorial language of his own. Strauss has shown a phenomenal versatility of style, from the barbaric splendor and realism of *Elektra* and *Salomé* to the delicious humor and nostalgia of *Der Rosenkavalier*. This remarkable gift of dramatic expression has also revealed itself in a series of powerful symphonic poems, notably *Don Juan* and *Death and Transfiguration*.

ENGLAND

In England opera has been largely dominated by foreign influences. The native-born Henry Purcell (1658–1695) showed a remarkable ability in his incidental music to various masques and plays, and especially in his one real opera, *Dido and Aeneas*. This work, produced in 1689 at a "boarding school for young gentlewomen,"

London, was subsequently given in concert versions, often quite mutilated, until its 1895 revival as a complete opera for the Purcell bicentenary. Later it obtained performances in both operatic and concert versions, a goodly number of which were of amateur sponsorship. It has been said, and with more reason than at once appears, that had Purcell not died prematurely, the history of opera in England might well have taken a different course.

With the death of Purcell English music, and with it opera, fell into a two-century period of stagnation. George Frederic Handel arrived in London, in 1710, and an era of opera in Italian, which had begun just previously, flourished in England, as elsewhere in Europe, excepting, perhaps, France, where the vernacular for operatic texts had strong supporters. Handel's *Rinaldo*, improvised within two weeks of his arrival, was a great success. More and more works for the lyric theater came from his pen, and he enjoyed, because of these, as well as compositions in other forms, a huge vogue.

Handel's stage music is not strictly of Italian derivation, since it combines elements from several schools. With the increasing popularity of works in the classical Italian tradition by Hasse and Porpora, Handel's operatic works, for all their estimable qualities, presently suffered a decline. Finally he devoted himself almost exclusively to the oratorio, the field of his greatest attainment.

Of much less virility are the nineteenth century's contributions to the operatic form, one of the better examples being Balfe's *The Bohemian Girl*, an engaging work, although of no great moment. In keeping with the best English tradition for literary quality and musical solidity are most of the Gilbert and Sullivan operettas.

In the twentieth century Gustav Holst, Ralph Vaughan Williams, and Eugene Goossens composed operas of musical worth, yet none of them survives. Of late years Benjamin Britten has demonstrated an exceptional talent in the operatic form. His *Peter Grimes* has already won international distinction. And his chamber opera, *The Rape of Lucrece*, a later work, has also created considerable interest.

RUSSIA

In Russia the first definite break away from the Italian tradition was made by Mikhail Ivanovich Glinka (1804–1857). In his patriotic *A Life for the Tsar* and the legendary *Russlan and Ludmilla* he paved the way for Russian nationalism in music. His style is lyrical and obviously influenced by Italian forms, but the Russian flavor of his melody and harmony is unmistakable. His successor, Alexander Sergeivich Dargomijsky (1813–1869), is notable for his use of the declamatory style. The famous nationalist group of "The Five" (Balakirev, Rimsky-Korsakov, Mussorgsky, Borodin, and Cui), while heatedly disclaiming adherence to Wagnerian theories, yet seem to show something of the influence of his work. However, their major operas possess originality and a distinctly Russian quality. Certainly in Mussorgsky's *Boris Godunov* and *Khovantchina*, Borodin's *Prince Igor*, and Rimsky's *Le Coq d'Or* and *Sadko*, we have some of the most significant contributions to the modern operatic stage, irregularly as these works may be now scheduled for performance. And there is no question as to Tchaikovsky's gifts as an operatic composer, bearing in mind his *Eugene Onegin* and *Pique-Dame*.

In more recent times Russia claims two notable composers of opera, the discerning and precise Serge Prokofieff and the vigorous Dmitri Shostakovich, although neither has made the lyric theater his special field. Prokofieff's *The Love of Three Oranges* has been justly appreciated for its musical subtlety, and his *War and Peace*— up to this printing not yet heard, except fragmentarily, outside of Russia—has earned the unqualified approval of its Russian listeners. Shostakovich's *Lady Macbeth of Mzensk* is a forceful, blatantly ironic opera, which has had an unhappy career in Russia, first winning and soon losing the Soviet hierarchy's favor. Elsewhere it has obtained a most noteworthy success.

UNITED STATES

Opera in the United States has been given more or less with regularity since the eighteenth century, antedating, in fact, the formation of the Union. During the nineteenth century the popularity of opera was increased by the establishment of permanent opera houses: in New Orleans, the Théâtre d'Orléans (later destroyed by fire); New York, Academy of Music and Metropolitan Opera House; Chicago, Chicago Auditorium—all these in addition to other theaters in various cities which have not functioned continuously as opera houses. There have also been traveling companies, not excluding the post-season tours of the Metropolitan Opera Company and the Chicago Civic Opera Company (latterly discontinued), besides a host of brief operatic seasons, festivals, and single performances in major localities.

American opera itself has had a strenuous career. Some of the works by native composers or naturalized ones have caught the public fancy. And among these would certainly be included these four out of the half dozen operas by the Italo-American Gian-Carlo Menotti: *Amelia Goes to the Ball* (Metropolitan production, though obtaining its *première* under the auspices of the Curtis Institute of Music, Philadelphia, April 1, 1937), the NBC-commissioned radio opera, *The Old Maid and the Thief*, and two operas commissioned by the Alice M. Ditson Fund of Columbia University, *The Telephone* and *The Medium*, these later being presented as a double bill for a run on Broadway. Deems Taylor's *The King's Henchman* and *Peter Ibbetson* have both been prominent Metropolitan productions. Among the other composers who may claim productions at the Metropolitan are Reginald De Koven, Howard Hanson, Walter Damrosch, and Bernard Rogers (whose *The Warrior*, commissioned by the Alice M. Ditson Fund, was given its *première* by the Metropolitan Opera Company, January 11, 1947). Virgil Thomson has to his credit two operas, *Four Saints in Three Acts* (produced by the Society of Friends and Enemies of Modern Music—Hartford, Conn., 1934) and *The Mother of Us All* (commissioned by the Alice

M. Ditson Fund of Columbia University—Brander Matthews Theater of Columbia University, New York, 1947). George Gershwin's *Porgy and Bess* and Kurt Weill's *Street Scene* are two more works obtaining considerable success.

THE STORIES OF THE

Operas

New York Times

SCENE FROM METROPOLITAN OPERA PRODUCTION

The Abduction from the Seraglio
(DIE ENTFÜHRUNG AUS DEM SERAIL)

COMIC OPERA in three acts. Music by Wolfgang Amadeus Mozart. Libretto by Gottlieb Stephanie, actually an altered version of the text by Christoph Friedrich Bretzner for Johann André's opera *Belmont und Constanze oder Die Entführung aus dem Serail* (Berlin, May 25, 1781). First performance, Burgtheater, Vienna, July 16, 1782. First performance in the United States, German Opera House, Brooklyn, N. Y., February 16, 1860, presumably in German. Metropolitan *première*, December 18, 1946, in an English translation by Ruth and Thomas Martin, with a cast including Eleanor Steber as Constanza, Pierrette Alarie as Blonda, Charles Kullman as Belmonte, Deszo Ernster as Osmin, Hugh Thompson as Selim, John Carter as Pedrillo, and Ludwig Burgstaller as the Mute; the conductor was Emil Cooper.

This opera was Mozart's first major success. It obtained thirty-four performances in Vienna beween 1782 and the decline of the *National-Singspiel* at the Burgtheater in 1788. The score is a particularly charming one, each of the principal characters being furnished with typifying music. In addition, there are several concerted numbers, among which is the specially effective quartet that closes **Act II**.

CHARACTERS

SELIM, *Pasha*	Speaking part	PEDRILLO, *Belmonte's servant*	*Tenor*
CONSTANZA, *beloved of Belmonte*	Soprano	OSMIN, *overseer of the Pasha's*	
BLONDA, *Constanza's maid and*		*country place*	*Bass*
beloved of Pedrillo	Soprano	A MUTE	
BELMONTE, *a Spanish nobleman*	Tenor	JANISSARIES, SLAVES, GUARDS	

The action takes place in Turkey in the sixteenth century

ACT I

Belmonte, a young Spanish nobleman, is eager to get a glimpse of Constanza, his beloved, who has been kidnaped, together with her maid Blonda, and brought to the seraglio of the Pasha Selim. Pedrillo, Belmonte's servant, as it happened, was with the girls when they were spirited away, so that he, too, is in the Pasha's toils, although he has managed, by artful maneuvering, to become the gardener at the Pasha's country place.

Osmin, the Pasha's overseer, testily refuses to give Belmonte much satisfaction, since he suspects him of being in league with Pedrillo, who has become a particular hate of his. Belmonte and Pedrillo, however, chance to meet, and they are overjoyed. The servant discloses that Constanza is unharmed, though, he says, it is the Pasha's plan to make her his favorite, much as she is repulsed by the idea. Belmonte tells Pedrillo that he has a ship lying outside the harbor and that everything is in readiness for an escape.

In the meantime, the Pasha and Constanza are seen, as Belmonte hides himself. While the Pasha, left alone, is walking in the garden, Pedrillo approaches him with the suggestion that a certain gentleman whom he knows would make a very good architect for His Excellency; and the Pasha promises to give this person an audition on the morrow. The Pasha departs, and Osmin joins Belmonte and Pedrillo in a lively trio which ends with the pair's slipping by him to get into the palace.

ACT II

After discouraging Osmin's ludicrous love-making, Blonda is joined by the distracted Constanza, whom she tries to console. As Blonda leaves, the Pasha enters, protesting his love for this new girl. In rebuttal Constanza sings the beautiful and brilliant aria, *"Martern aller Arten"* ("Tortures unabating"), in which she says that no amount of torture or agony can make her love him. With that she exits, leaving the Pasha to wrangle with his thoughts. Blonda appears, and she is a little disappointed in finding both Constanza and the Pasha gone. Can they have come to some *rapprochement,* she wonders. As she thinks of such things, Pedrillo the ubiquitous bustles in, telling her of Belmonte's arrival and the plans they have laid to abduct the naturally willing ladies, and also that she is to inform Constanza of all this. Left alone, Blonda muses on the new state of things and expresses her pleasure in the joyous aria, *"Welche Wonne, welche Lust"* ("What delight, what freedom!").

As soon as she leaves the stage, Pedrillo comes in, later joined by Osmin. The two engage in a comical scene, in which the overseer is given copious draughts of wine to drink, with the logical consequence of his becoming quite tipsy and, therefore, manageable. Pedrillo, developing superhuman strength,

New York Times

ELEANOR STEBER AS CONSTANZA

takes this mammoth on his back and drags him off, soon returning alone, to make the fourth in a quartet with Constanza, Belmonte, and Blonda, which is one of the score's high points.

ACT III

At night, in an open area before the palace, Pedrillo is seen making arrangements for the escape, and, after a few moments, is joined by Belmonte, whom he urges to sing a serenade, because Pedrillo has been singing to Blonda for so long, of nights, that it would create suspicion if no song were sung that evening. Belmonte obliges him by delivering the lengthy aria, *"Ich baue ganz auf deine Stärke"* ("I dedicate my all").

3

The singing awakens Constanza, who is in her quarters. She looks out, and when Belmonte sees her he ascends a ladder, and in a few moments both are seen making their escape through the palace door. Pedrillo, left behind, delivers his signal serenade and, presently, runs up the ladder to Blonda's room. However, the voices have shaken a mute from out of his sleep, and he immediately awakens Osmin. The latter, still under the influence of the wine, comes to a sudden realization of the proceedings when he sees the ladder before Blonda's house. In his clumsy manner he climbs to the window, arriving there just as Blonda and Pedrillo come to it from inside. The lovers, however, flee through the door, only to be brought back in company with Belmonte and Constanza under guard.

In the final scene, which takes place in a hall of Selim's palace, the Pasha censures Constanza for her apparent perfidy, although she assures him that Belmonte is the man to whom she has long been betrothed. Belmonte, at this point, declares that his father will be glad to pay any ransom for their freedom. And when the Pasha discovers that Belmonte's father is Lostados, a Commandant of Oran and his greatest enemy, he gloats with a particularly malignant pleasure. However, he relents, admonishing Belmonte to tell his father that he, Selim, releases the son of Lostados willingly, finding the greater satisfaction in returning good for evil. The joy of Constanza and Belmonte is increased when both Blonda and Pedrillo are also freed, over the stormy protests of Osmin. The opera closes with the ensemble singing a song of praise to the Pasha.

THE RCA-VICTOR RECORDS
(Sung in German unless otherwise noted)

OVERTURE: *Sir Thomas Beecham, Bart., and the London Philharmonic Orch.*
11-9191, 12″

Vienna Philharmonic Orch., Clemens Krauss, Cond. 11142, 12″

ACT I

WER EIN LIEBCHEN HAT GEFUNDEN (When a Maiden Takes Your Fancy): *Alexander Kipnis, Bass, with Orch.*
1738, 10″

ACT II

DURCH ZÄRTLICHKEIT (Avec de la tendresse) (With Tenderness and Coaxing): *Lily Pons, Soprano, with Orch. In French* 2110, 10″
(In Album M-702)

WELCHER KUMMER HERRSCHT IN MEINER SEELE (What Conflicting Feelings Rule My Soul): *Margherita Perras, Soprano, with Orch.* 12328, 12″

MARTERN ALLER ARTEN (Tortures Unabating): *Eleanor Steber, Soprano, with Orch. In English* 11-9773, 12″
(In Album M-1157)

DOCH DICH RÜHRT KEIN FLEHEN (Firm Is Thy Decision): *Eleanor Steber, Soprano, with Orch. In English*
11-9773, 12″
(In Album M-1157)

Gerardi

ACT III—DON PEDRO'S VESSEL (SETTING FOR THE VERONA FESTIVAL)

L'Africana

(L'AFRICAINE—THE AFRICAN)

OPERA IN five acts. Music by Giacomo Meyerbeer. Libretto by Eugène Scribe. First produced at the Paris Opéra, April 28, 1865. First London performance (in Italian), July 22, 1865. First American performance (also in Italian), December 1, 1865, at the New York Academy of Music.

Although he worked on this opera intermittently for twenty-five years, Meyerbeer never saw it produced. He died the day after he had applied the finishing touches to the score, and it was not till one year later that L'Africaine was finally produced. Meyerbeer had begun work on it in 1838. Differences with Scribe over the libretto delayed completion of the opera. Geography and background were constantly modified, and Vasco da Gama, the Portuguese navigator, only joined the dramatis personae as an afterthought. Long before L'Africaine was finished, reports of its contents had excited high expectation among operagoing Parisians. It is possible that Meyerbeer, who looked on the new opera as his masterpiece, died the victim of his own unremitting toil in revising and polishing it for the planned première at the Opéra. While neither he nor Scribe pretended to adhere to authentic ethnic and historical material in recounting the romantic exploits of Portugal's great explorer, L'Africaine breathes an exotic magic of its own. And Meyerbeer's powerful sense of theatrical display is everywhere apparent. Though a French opera with a French text, L'Africaine is better known to American operagoers in its Italian version, L'Africana.

CHARACTERS

VASCO DA GAMA, *officer in the Portuguese Navy*	Tenor	INEZ, *daughter of Don Diego*	Soprano
DON PEDRO, *King's Councilor*	Bass	ANNA, *her attendant*	Contralto
DON DIEGO, *member of the King's Council*	Bass	SELIKA, *a captive African queen*	Soprano
DON ALVAR, *member of the King's Council*	Tenor	NELUSKO, *a slave*	Baritone
		GRAND INQUISITOR	Bass

5

COUNCILORS, PRIESTS, SAILORS, SOLDIERS, ATTENDANTS, AND CAPTIVE SLAVES

The action occurs at the end of the fifteenth century and the beginning of the six-teenth, during the time of the daring voyages of conquest and exploration made by Portuguese mariners. The scene shifts from Lisbon to Don Pedro's ship at sea and the island of Madagascar.

ACT I

SCENE: *The Council Chamber of the King of Portugal.* During a session of the Royal Council, it is reported that the latest expedition of Admiral Diaz has met with disaster off the coast of South Africa. All are believed lost, in-cluding the great navigator, Vasco da Gama. Chief among the mourners is Inez, daughter of Don Diego, a member of the Royal Council. Vasco and she were to have been married on his return from the fabled new lands of the East. Don Diego now seeks to marry his daughter to Don Pedro, a powerful and unscrupulous schemer. It develops that one officer—still unnamed—has survived the reported shipwreck. As the council meeting proceeds, word is brought that the officer has arrived. It is Vasco himself, miraculously saved, and accompanied by two dark-skinned captives. He presents the pair—Selika and Nelusko—as living proof of the wondrous land he has discovered. Vasco also tells of a new route to the East, of untold treasures awaiting Portu-gal's bold adventurers, and he proves this with maps. Strong new ships and abundant funds are needed for this new exploit, Vasco informs the Council. But his plea falls on deaf ears. Don Pedro, after stealing a document from Vasco's papers, denounces him as a fraud and a heretic, and when Vasco replies with a bitter tirade against the assembly, he is seized and thrown into prison.

ACT II

SCENE: *The Prison of the Inquisition.* For a month now Vasco has been languishing in prison. As he sleeps, Selika watches over him fondly. Though a captive slave, unknown to Vasco she is really a queen in the land of her origin. But the proud Selika has fallen in love with her captor, and now jealousy mounts in her breast as she recalls Vasco's avowed love for Inez. Yet she saves Vasco from the dagger thrust of Nelusko, to whom Selika is not only queen but the woman he loves. As Vasco awakes, Selika declares her love and reveals the long-sought secret of a safe route to the mysterious land of his dreams. Vasco jubilantly pledges lifelong devotion to Selika, and they embrace warmly. Unexpectedly, the prison door opens, and Inez and Don Pedro appear. Inez's first thought is that the court gossip about Vasco and Selika is true. Haughtily she tells Vasco that he is free, that the price of his freedom has been her marriage to Don Pedro. Stunned, Vasco attempts to prove his innocence by making her a gift of his two slaves. Selika is crushed by this swift change in Vasco, while Nelusko scowls and grimly plots revenge. As a final blow, Vasco is told that Don Pedro will lead a new expedition with the help of Selika and Nelusko. In the project he recognizes the plan outlined by him in the stolen document.

ACT III

SCENE: *Aboard Don Pedro's Ship at Sea.* Secretly nursing plans of revenge on all Portuguese, Nelusko is steering Don Pedro's vessel toward shipwreck on the reefs. Some Portuguese officers begin to voice suspicion of treachery. Two ships of Don Pedro's fleet have already been lost, and there is fear that the flagship will be next. A storm begins to rise as Nelusko, in a mood betraying his vengeful design, intones an impassioned invocation to Adamastor, "Ruler of Ocean."

As the storm grows in fury, a ship is seen approaching, flying the Portuguese flag. The dauntless Vasco da Gama has caught up with Don Pedro's expedition! He has followed the exploring fleet to warn Don Pedro about Nelusko and to save Inez from impending disaster. Don Pedro scorns the warning and orders Vasco put in irons. Nelusko's plot succeeds. The storm overwhelms the ship, which crashes on a reef. At a summons from Nelusko wild natives board the vessel, liberate their queen, Selika, and kill most of the Portuguese. A few, including Vasco, are taken captive. In the turmoil Inez disappears.

Mishkin
BENIAMINO GIGLI AS VASCO

ACT IV

SCENE: *The Island of Madagascar—a Temple of Brahma on One Side, a Palace on the Other.* Amid a setting of barbaric luxury and riotous splendor Selika occupies her recovered throne. While the people pay homage to their returned ruler, the priests set up a cry for the death of the Portuguese captives. Vasco, meanwhile, has grown enamored of this island paradise. As he views its warm, exotic expanse, he sings an aria—*"O Paradiso"*—expressing this mood of rapture and enchantment—an aria that is regarded as Meyerbeer's melodic masterpiece. While the woodwinds supply a shimmering background, Vasco's voice rises to exalted fervor as he dwells on the wealth and glory this new land will bring his country.

Vasco escapes execution when Selika informs the priests that she is his wife; that if he is condemned she, too, must die. She appeals for help to Nelusko, who, loving his queen more than he loathes the Portuguese, confirms her statement. Preparations are being made to solemnize the marriage in native fashion, when an outcry is heard. It is the voice of Inez, whom Vasco had thought lost in the shipwreck and massacre, the voice of Inez pleading for help. Vasco is horror-struck as he realizes that she is about to be slain.

ACT V

SCENE 1: *The Queen's Garden* (often omitted in performance). Certain now that Vasco still loves Inez, Selika resolves to order her rival's death. Magnanimously, she changes her mind, when she becomes convinced of Inez's unselfish devotion to Vasco. Her one thought now is to see the lovers reunited after all their hardships. With Nelusko's help she contrives to set them free and even provides for their safe passage home.

SCENE 2: *A Promontory by the Sea.* As Vasco's ship slowly disappears from view, Selika watches it from a promontory overlooking the sea. Above her spread the branches of the deadly manchineel tree, and as she catches one last, lingering glimpse of the receding sails, she grasps some manchineel blossoms and inhales their poisonous fragrance. Nelusko finds her dying and, faithful to the end, he too breathes in the lethal odor of the tree.

THE RCA-VICTOR RECORDS
(Sung in Italian)

ACT III

ADAMASTOR, RE DELL' ONDE PROFONDE
(Adamastor, Ruler of Ocean) : *Robert Merrill, Baritone, with Orch.*
11-9384, 12″

Titta Ruffo, Baritone, with Orch.
7153, 12″

Mario Sammarco, Baritone, with Orch.
15-1018, 12″
(Acoustical Recording)

ACT IV

O PARADISO (O Paradise!) : *Ferruccio*

Tagliavini, Tenor, with Orch.
12-0071, 12″
(In Album MO-1191)
18-0107, 12″
(Vinylite) (In Album VO-13)

Jan Peerce, Tenor, with Orch.
11-9295, 12″

Jussi Bjoerling, Tenor, with Orch.
12150, 12″

Enrico Caruso, Tenor, with Orch.
14234, 12″

Beniamino Gigli, Tenor, with Orch.
7109, 12″

ACT II, SCENE 2—THE TEMPLE OF VULCAN (DESIGNED BY A. PASQUALI)

Aïda

OPERA IN four acts. Music by Giuseppe Verdi. Libretto by Antonio Ghislanzoni, aided by the composer, from the French of Camille du Locle, after a prose sketch by the Egyptologist Mariette Bey. First produced, Opera, Cairo, Egypt, December 24, 1871. First United States performance, Academy of Music, New York, November 26, 1873.

Ismail Pasha, Khedive of Egypt, approached Verdi through intermediaries, in 1869, suggesting that he compose an opera for the new Cairo theater, to celebrate the opening of the Suez Canal. Not only did Verdi refuse the commission, but he successfully resisted, for a time, the arguments presented by his friend, Camille du Locle, who may or may not have been the Khedive's choice for librettist. The Suez Canal was duly opened in 1869 and, too, the new theater in Cairo, but *Aïda* was not the work to signalize the dual event.

Du Locle, a persistent individual, whose blandishments had thus far proved unavailing, finally sent Verdi a four-page sketch of an opera plot based on an Egyptian subject (allegedly authentic), which the distinguished Egyptologist, Mariette Bey, had done. On seeing it, Verdi could scarcely hold his excitement, and from the rough draft a scenario was contrived by du Locle and himself. So, with contractual arrangements completed, Ghislanzoni chosen to versify the scenario in Italian, and January, 1871, picked as the date for the *première* in Cairo, the composer set to work on his music.

In this manner, piece by piece and with much detailed correspondence between composer and librettist (which serves to prove Verdi's important contribution to the libretto), grew the story of the Egyptian hero who spurns the hand of a princess for the love of a slave—the captive daughter of a hostile sovereign—wherein jealousy and patriotism unite to bring destruction to the lovers.

As so often in his career, international affairs and politics interfered with the first performance of Verdi's *Aïda*. This time it was the Franco-Prussian War. Costumes and scenery, which had been designed under the expert eye of Mariette Bey, remained in beleaguered Paris until the close of the war, thus necessitating a postponement. But the opera was at last given its *première*, and from all accounts it was a huge triumph. The chief singers were Pozzoni (Aïda), Grossi (Amneris), Mongini (Rhadames), Costa (Amonasro), and Medini (Ramfis). When *Aïda* was first given at La Scala, Milan, February 8, 1872, Verdi himself conducted. He was recalled thirty-two times amid a tumult of applause, and was presented with an ivory baton and a diamond star with the name *Aïda* in rubies and *Verdi* in other precious stones.

Musically, *Aïda* is of enormous interest in that it is the first work in Verdi's "mature" style, that is to say, a style revealing a new harmonic sense, sudden and surprising modulations, a greater richness of orchestral scoring. Verdi was accused by some of having imitated Wagner, which, of course, he did not do, although he would have been totally insensitive to the advances made by the German composer had he not profited by some of them, while, in the main, adhering to the Italian tradition. He composed no numbers for exhibiting the technical skill of singers in florid runs and trills, but wrote instead music that is always appropriate to the action of the drama, yet music that is always melodious and congenial to the voice. The orchestra is not treated in the complex symphonic style of Wagner, but it is more colorful than that previously known in Italian opera, still without ever submerging the singers. In keeping with his subject, Verdi created effects in his music that are plausibly Oriental, although *Aïda* is as Italian an opera, from one end to the other, as he ever wrote. Realizing that presenting the life of ancient Egypt called for much pageantry, he wrote rousing choruses for crowds of people and also rather exotic dances to enhance the Oriental aspects of the whole. The characterizations are all skillfully drawn—Rhadames, bold and romantic; Amneris, in varying moods, imperious and angry and jealous, or in terror; Aïda, simple and loving; Amonasro, crafty; Ramfis, stern and pompous; characters that are revealed in music as well as in words. All these features combine to make *Aïda* the absorbing music drama it truly is, and they help explain its enduring popularity.

World Wide
GIOVANNI MARTINELLI
AS RHADAMES

BLANCHE THEBOM
AS AMNERIS

CHARACTERS

AÏDA, *an Ethiopian princess*	*Soprano*	AMONASRO, *King of Ethiopia*	*Baritone*
THE KING OF EGYPT	*Bass*		
AMNERIS, *his daughter*	*Contralto*	RAMFIS, *high priest*	*Bass*
RHADAMES, *captain of the guard*	*Tenor*	A MESSENGER	*Tenor*

PRIESTS, PRIESTESSES, MINISTERS, CAPTAINS, SOLDIERS, OFFICIALS, ETHIOPIAN SLAVES AND PRIESTS, PRIESONERS, EGYPTIANS, ETC.

The action takes place at Memphis and Thebes during the epoch of the Pharaohs

ACT I

SCENE 1: *A Hall in the Palace (through the great gate at the rear may be seen the pyramids and the temples of Memphis).* After a calm prelude based on a brief theme that recurs several times during the opera, since it typifies the gentle Aïda, the curtain rises, revealing a hall in the palace of the King (or Pharaoh) of Egypt. The high priest of Isis, Ramfis, is telling Rhadames that the enemy Ethiopians are reported to be on the outskirts of Thebes and the Valley of the Nile. In reply to Rhadames' questions, he adds significantly that the goddess Isis has appointed a certain brave young warrior leader of the army that will be sent against the invaders. Left alone, Rhadames ponders over this news, occasional fanfares of trumpets creating a martial atmosphere. He dreams of himself as the "brave young warrior" and of the glory that would be his to return at the head of his victorious forces, in the recitative beginning *"Se quel guerriero io fossi"* ("If I were that warrior"). Then he dwells with pleasure on thoughts of Aïda, as the music changes from the warlike to the ardent and loving, with Rhadames now wholly committed to his womanly ideal in the famous aria *"Celeste Aïda* ("Heavenly Aïda").

Rhadames' ecstasy is interrupted by the entrance of Amneris. She does not know—nor does anyone else at court—that her slave Aïda is the daughter of the Ethiopian king, Amonasro. Curious about Rhadames and his love musings, she questions him guardedly, secretly hoping that she is the object of his passion. When Rhadames, merely to cover his confusion, answers that he was dreaming of heading the Egyptian armies in the coming campaign, Aïda appears, and, by the glance that flashes between the other two, Amneris learns where Rhadames' heart lies. The Egyptian princess, cautious and wily, takes Aïda aside with a show of friendship, asking her the reason for her anxious demeanor. Aïda says simply that she has been disturbed by the news of the war between her country and Egypt. Rhadames, meanwhile, suspects that Amneris has guessed the true state of things, and the varied emotions of these three personages are expressed in the dramatic trio they now sing.

The King enters with his entourage and a messenger arrives with the tidings that the Ethiopians are approaching the city under their king, Amonasro. *"Mio padre!"* ("My father!") Aïda exclaims in an aside. The Pharaoh nominates Rhadames leader of the army, and Amneris presents him with a banner. Then, having been charged by the King to defend the Nile, the Egyptians depart, exclaiming, *"Guerra! Guerra!"* ("War! War!").

Emotionally transported by the sentiments, Aïda cries with the others, *"Ritorna vincitor"* ("Return victorious"). But presently alone, she suddenly realizes the significance of her words. And in the remarkable aria that begins with the very phrase she has just shouted, she expresses her dismay, and prays for death.

SCENE 2: *The Temple of Vulcan.* Through the long rows of massive Egyptian pillars in the dim temple of Vulcan, we see in the distance a great altar, illuminated by a soft light from above. Statues of deities abound, and from golden tripods rises the smoke of burning incense. Ramfis stands at the altar, dominating this ceremony of prayer and dedication, while, outside, priestesses sing an eerie incantation. The deeper voices of the priests join in, and soon Ramfis and the whole assemblage invoke blessings on the expedition. A stately sacred dance is performed by the priestesses, while Rhadames enters and receives the consecrated veil. Now Ramfis presents Rhadames with the consecrated sword and armor. The music rises to a great climax, as all turn to the altar. Rhadames exhorts the god Vulcan to protect Egypt.

TRIUMPHAL SCENE—METROPOLITAN OPERA PRODUCTION

ACT II

SCENE 1: *A Hall in the Apartments of Amneris.* Reclining languorously on a couch in her quarters, Amneris is surrounded by slave girls who are singing a song in praise of her beloved. She occasionally cries ecstatically, *"Vieni, amor mio"* ("Come, my love"). Then she falls back indolently on the couch, while the Moorish slave boys entertain her with a sprightly dance.

Aïda approaches, and Amneris bids her other slaves depart. Left alone with the Ethiopian princess, she slowly gains her confidence. Then, studying her closely for any possible telltale sign, she leads Aïda to believe that Rhadames has been slain in battle. The spurious words are electrical, and Aïda gives a great cry of pain. And now that Amneris knows the truth about the love between Aïda and Rhadames, she announces that Rhadames lives and that she herself, "the daughter of the Pharaohs," is Aïda's rival.

Aïda is helpless. She implores mercy, and makes no attempt, now, to conceal her love, but Amneris promises her only death for her temerity. The sound of festival music outside, announcing the return of the victorious Egyptians, suggests a further idea of revenge. Aïda, the Egyptian princess says, shall witness Rhadames' triumphal procession and his obeisances to Amneris, as she sits beside her father the King.

SCENE 2: *Outside the City Walls.* A great throne has been erected at the city gates to welcome the conquering army. The King and his court, the priests, and the people are all there assembled. A majestic hymn, *"Gloria all' Egitto e ad Iside"* ("Glory to Egypt and to Isis"), is intoned. The Egyptian troops enter, preceded by musicians who play on long, brazen trumpets. Then fol-

Crimelli

TRIUMPHAL SCENE (SETTING BY A. PASQUALI)

low dancing girls who wave aloft welcoming palms. Presently the dancers perform their colorful ballet to music that mounts in excitement.

The song of praise is resumed, and still other troops enter. The soldiers carry war banners, while slaves bear sacred vessels and effigies of the gods. Finally, as the music swells to a stupendous climax, Rhadames appears in a horse-drawn chariot. He descends, at the height of the jubilation, and the King steps down from his throne and embraces him, declaring, "Savior of the country, I salute thee!" Rhadames kneels before Amneris, as she places the crown of victory on his head, and the King swears by his crown that Rhadames shall have any boon he desires. Rhadames, however, asks first that the prisoners be brought in. Thereupon the captives enter, and among them is Amonasro, who is unrecognized in his plain officer's garb. Aïda knows, though, and she rushes to him, unable to restrain herself. He cautions her not to reveal his rank, and, summoned by the Pharaoh, he acknowledges his daughter, admitting the enormous defeat and, lying in a convincing manner, describes how the "King of the Ethiopians" (himself), pierced by countless wounds, died at his feet. In a bluff and soldierly manner, which commends itself to the King, Amonasro begs pityingly that the prisoners be freed. The populace joins in the plea in a surge of compassion. Last, Rhadames, reminding the Pharaoh of his promise, asks for the life and liberty of his captives. The priests, led by Ramfis, object, but the King overrules them, though with the stipulation—at their insistence—that all be liberated save Amonasro and Aïda, who shall be kept as hostages. And at a rousing moment in the intensifying drama, the King declares that Rhadames shall have his daughter's hand in marriage as a reward for the brilliant victory.

The finale of this act involves a number of different sentiments expressed in musical threads that are beautifully interwoven in a great pattern: Amonasro swears to avenge himself; Amneris is exultant; Aïda reflects tearfully on the futility of her life; Rhadames spurns the throne of Egypt as not being "worth the heart of Aïda"; the King and the priests and the populace join in singing the glory of Egypt and Isis, and all these form a powerfully dramatic and musical climax to the scene.

ACT III

SCENE: *The Banks of the Nile: Moonlight (the temple of Isis can be seen behind the palm trees).* The mysterious mood of this scene is evoked by the long, sustained measures of the strings, which make the background for a wistful melody by the oboe. Sounds of voices, softly chanting a hymn, can be heard from within the temple. Soon Amneris and the high priest alight from a boat and proceed to the temple, there to invoke blessings of the gods on the union between the princess and Rhadames. As they disappear, Aïda enters for her secret tryst with Rhadames. She sings of vague fears, wondering if this is to be their last farewell. Should that be so, she says, the waters of the Nile will be her grave and give her, perhaps, peace and oblivion. Soon her thoughts go to her childhood, to those carefree days in her beloved homeland, and with a deep longing for it all she sings *"O patria mia"* ("O my native land").

Aïda's reverie is interrupted by her father, who declares forthwith that Rhadames' love for her may yet provide their means of escape and also that of victory over these "infamous Egyptians." Adroitly he puts Aïda through a variety of emotions, maneuvering, playing on her simplicity, and all the time persuading her to draw the secret of the Egyptians' military plans from Rhadames. At first she recoils at the thought, but after being denounced as a "slave of the Pharaohs" and the sole cause of the miseries visited on the Ethiopians, she tearfully consents. Rhadames, at this point, is approaching, and Amonasro—with a last warning to his daughter—runs off to hide among the palms. Rhadames enters and embraces Aïda, singing *"Pur ti riveggo, mia dolce Aïda"* ("I see you again, my sweet Aïda"). But urged by her father's injunction to work on Rhadames' love, she asks that he prove his devotion by fleeing with her. The scene is a notable dialogue in music, the pleading accents of the girl contrasting with the hero's agitation. Rhadames resists her, for a time, but the enchantment of the Oriental night, the allurement of her presence, and the desperate prospect of an enforced marriage to Amneris all weaken his resolve.

Under the bewitching influence of Aïda, Rhadames goes as far as to paint a glowing picture of life for them in some foreign land—maybe Ethiopia. And while he is in that blissful state, Aïda strategically puts the question, "By what road shall we avoid the Egyptian hosts?" He lets slip the information that the army will not take to a certain path until the morrow, even disclosing the name of the place. Here Amonasro appears out of the dark, and, with a fierce joy, repeats Rhadames' words, besides revealing his own identity, the "King of the Ethiopians."

Rhadames is horrified, and he agitatedly speaks of the dishonor he has brought upon himself. It is pointed out to him with subtle casuistry by Amonasro that he is guiltless; it is fate that has betrayed him. He is assured that happiness awaits them all in Ethiopia. Moreover, he dare not stay, but must make good his escape with Aïda and himself.

Amneris, coming from the temple, has overheard. Mad with jealousy, she rushes out and denounces the three, her wrath blazing forth with especial virulence against Rhadames, the betrayer of his country, his gods, and herself. Amonasro and Aïda escape, but Rhadames, filled with remorse, remains behind to yield himself to the high priest.

Lande

ACT I, SCENE 2—CONSECRATION SCENE

15

ACT IV

SCENE 1: *A Room in the Palace (one side, a door leading to Rhadames' prison cell).* Amneris is desperate; her rival has escaped, and the one object of her passion is about to be tried as a traitor. "Could he only love me," she exclaims, "I would save him!" She decides to try, and the accused man is brought in. Exerting all her powers, she tries to persuade him to promise never to see Aïda again. He refuses. The music reaches a climax of great and passionate beauty as he declares that death is a blessing, if it is for Aïda's sake. The love and pity of Amneris are transformed into hate, and she calls on the gods for revenge.

Guards conduct Rhadames to the judgment room, while Amneris is left to suffer alone as she hears the punishment she has herself brought about pronounced on the man she loves. As she turns she sees Ramfis and the priests solemnly entering the judgment hall, and she cries, "Behold the fatal ministers of death—do not let me behold those white-robed phantoms!" But the law is stronger than the will of Amneris. Her lamentation, the stern voices of Ramfis and his priests conducting the trial in the room below, combine to produce a doubly tragic sense of foreboding. Amneris, in torture, covers her face with her hands; but she cannot shut out the terrible voices of Rhadames' accusers. Through it all, he remains silent. Finally, the voice of Ramfis pronounces the sentence—death by burial alive beneath the temple of the god whom Rhadames has offended. The priests re-enter and again file impassively across the room, before the despairing eyes of Amneris. In a paroxysm of mingled wrath and anguish she denounces them, saying, " 'Tis they who offend heaven with their cruelty," but the priests sternly answer: "He is a traitor, he shall die!"

SCENE 2: *The Interior of the Temple of Vulcan (above, the temple proper, where the chanting priests intone their endless litanies; below, under the very statue of Osiris, the deity of the nether world, is the tomb where Rhadames has been condemned to die.)* The hero believes himself alone, and his reflections are embodied in the incomparable music of the aria *"La fatal pietra sovra me si chiuse"* ("The fatal stone upon me now is closing").

His thoughts soon turn from his own miserable fate to Aïda, and he prays that happiness may be hers. He is startled by the thought that in the shadow of the tomb he sees Aïda. He is not mistaken, it is she! She says that she has come to share death with him. Her father slain, his troops scattered, she has crept to earth like a stricken animal, her heart foreseeing the sentence to be passed upon Rhadames. Overwhelmed by the thought of her enormous sacrifice, Rhadames tries in vain to move away the heavy stone sealing the tomb. He sings, *"Morir! si pura e bella!"* ("To die! so pure and lovely"),

ROSE BAMPTON AS AÏDA

and Aïda repeats the melody, singing of the "ecstasy of an immortal love."

Meanwhile the priests above in the temple are going through their mysterious rites, solemnly chanting, "O mighty Phtha."

Together the lovers resign all hopes on earth and unite in a great duet, singing *"O terra, addio"* ("Farewell, O earth"). The melody is in broad, calm phrases, suggestive of the limitless sweep of infinity, and peaceful as eternity. It is sung in unison—even the close blending of the voices being a symbol of the absorption of the lovers into an unending union free from all things earthly. Amneris, repentant and disconsolate, enters the temple above to weep and pray over the tomb of her beloved. Below, in the oppressive darkness of the tomb the lovers, clasped in one final, passionate embrace, sing their farewell to earth and its sorrows and together await eternity.

THE RCA-VICTOR RECORDS

(Sung in Italian unless otherwise noted)

COMPLETE RECORDING: *Maria Caniglia, Soprano; Ebe Stignani, Mezzo-soprano; Beniamino Gigli, Tenor; Gino Bechi, Baritone; Tancredi Pasero, Bass; Italo Tajo, Bass; Adelio Zagonara, Tenor; Maria Huder, Mezzo-soprano; with Chorus and Orchestra of The Opera House, Rome; Tullio Serafin, Cond.*

DM-1174 (Vol. 1) (11-9921-
11-9930), 10-12"

DM-1175 (Vol. 2) (11-9941-
11-9950), 10-12"

M-1174 (Vol. 1) (11-9911-11-9920)

M-1175 (Vol. 2) (11-9931-11-9940)

COMPLETE RECORDING: *Dusolina Giannini, Soprano; Irene Minghini-Cattaneo, Mezzo-soprano; Aureliano Pertile, Tenor; Giovanni Inghilleri, Baritone; Luigi Manfrini, Bass; Guglielmo Masini, Bass; Giuseppi Nessi, Tenor; with Chorus and Orchestra of La Scala, Milan; Carlo Sabajno, Cond.*

DMC-100 (DM-54) (Vol. 1)
(13447-13456), 10-12"

(DM-54) (Vol. 2)
(13457-13465), 9-12"

MC-100 (M-54) (Vol. 1) (9488-9497)
(M-54) (Vol. 2) (9498-9506)

HIGHLIGHTS: Celeste Aïda; Ritorna vincitor; Grand March; Ballábile; Quest' assisa ch' io vesto; O patria mia; Fuggiam gli ardori; L'abborrita rivale; La fatal pietra; O terra, addio.

Enrico Caruso, Tenor; Dusolina Giannini, Soprano; Rosa Ponselle, Soprano; Giovanni Martinelli, Tenor; Aureliano Pertile, Tenor; Elisabeth Rethberg, Soprano; with various orchestras.

M-303 (1744 & 1745, 8993 & 8994,
11897 & 11898), 2-10"
4-12"

ACT I

CELESTE AÏDA (Heavenly Aïda): *Jussi Bjoerling, Tenor, with Orch.*
12039, 12"

Enrico Caruso, Tenor, with Orch.
7770, 12"

Enrico Caruso, Tenor, with Orch.
6000, 12"
(Acoustical Recording)

Giovanni Martinelli, Tenor, with Orch.
14206, 12"
(In Album M-329)

RITORNA VINCITOR (Return Victorious!):
Zinka Milanov, Soprano, with Orch.
11-9288, 12"
(In Album M-1074)

Rosa Ponselle, Soprano, with Orch.
7438, 12"

Elisabeth Rethberg, Soprano, with Orch.
7106, 12"

TEMPLE SCENE—*Nume, custode e vindici* (God, Guardian and Avenger): *Ezio Pinza, Bass; Giovanni Martinelli, Tenor; Metropolitan Opera Chorus; with Orch.*
8111, 12"

ACT II

GRAND MARCH: *Boston "Pops" Orchestra, Arthur Fiedler, Cond.*
11885, 12"

BALLÁBILE (Ballet): *Boston "Pops" Orchestra, Arthur Fiedler, Cond.*
11985, 12"

ACT III

O PATRIA MIA (O CIELI AZZURRI) (My Native Land): *Elisabeth Rethberg, Soprano, with Orch.*
7106, 12"

Celestina Boninsegna, Soprano, with Orch.
15-1006, 12"
(Acoustical Recording)

ACT IV

LA FATAL PIETRA (The Fatal Stone): *Rosa Ponselle, Soprano; Giovanni Martinelli, Tenor; with Orch.*
1744, 10"
(In Album M-303)

O TERRA, ADDIO (Farewell, O Earth): *Rosa Ponselle, Soprano; Giovanni Martinelli, Tenor; with Orch.*
1745, 10"
(In Album M-303)

SCENE FROM STATE OPERA PRODUCTION, BERLIN

Alceste

OPERA IN TWO ACTS, often given in three. Music by Christoph Willibald von Gluck. Libretto, in Italian, by Raniero de' Calzabigi, after Euripides. First produced in Vienna on December 26, 1767. Two years later the score was published, prefaced by a dedicatory epistle to the Grand Duke of Tuscany, later Emperor Leopold II. This proved an epoch-making document. Librettist and composer made a strong plea for naturalness, simplicity, and directness in operatic writing. The statement was an attack, too, on the decorative excesses of Italian opera. Gluck had begun his famous reform of opera. A new fusion of action and music had come about, and *Alceste* exemplified it. But the Viennese public was cold to this austere grandeur of style. "If that is the sort of thing the court opera is to provide, good-by," they said. "We can go to church without paying two gulden." After the *première* Gluck left the theater a disillusioned man. "*Alceste* has fallen," he bemoaned to a friend, who replied: "Yes, fallen from heaven!" Gluck's innovations won readier response in Paris when *Alceste*, in a new French version by Gand-Leblanc, Bailli du Roullet, was produced there on April 23, 1776. Pauline Viardot-Garcia proved a sensation in the title role when the Paris Opéra revived *Alceste* on October 21, 1861. The opera reached the United States only on January 24, 1941, when the Metropolitan Opera Company staged it with Marjorie Lawrence in the main part.

The issues raised by *Alceste* plunged Gluck into an artistic war with Niccolò Piccinni, standard-bearer of the conventional Italian style. The famous clash of the Gluckists and Piccinnists was allegedly touched off by Marie Antoinette in a search for new thrills. Soon all Paris had taken sides in this battle royal.

CHARACTERS

ADMETOS, *King of Pharae*	*Tenor*	APOLLO, *the Greek sun-god*	*Baritone*
ALCESTE, *his wife*	*Soprano*	APOLLO'S HIGH PRIEST	*Bass*
EVANDER, *a messenger*	*Tenor*	THANATOS, *god of death*	*Bass*
HERCULES, *ancient Greek hero*	*Bass*		

PRIESTS, PRIESTESSES, ATTENDANTS, AND THE PEOPLE OF PHARAE

Alceste

The action takes place in Pharae, in ancient Thessaly

The tragic breadth may be readily sensed in the Overture to *Alceste*. The action of the opera is eloquently foretold in the alternating themes of fate and pleading, in the dark colors of the orchestra, in the poignant phrases of noble feeling.

ACT I

SCENE: *The Temple of Apollo*. The people of Pharae learn with dismay that their king, Admetos, is dying. Accompanied by her children, Alceste enters the temple of Apollo to entreat the gods to spare her husband's life. The people join their prayers with hers, and suddenly the voice of Apollo is heard: Admetos can be saved, but on one condition—someone must die in his place. All except Alceste draw back in dread, but the Queen offers herself. The priests consult Apollo, who gives his consent. In an outburst of majestic power Alceste invokes the gods of the nether world in the magnificent aria, *"Divinités du Styx."*

ACT II

SCENE: *The King's Palace*. Again the people of Pharae are lamenting. Admetos has recovered, but now he has resolved to follow his devoted wife to the next world. At this point the Greek hero Hercules steps into the picture. Fresh from great exploits, Hercules comes to the feast at his friend Admetos' table. When he hears of Alceste's fate, he swears he will snatch her from the very gates of Hades. Alceste, donning a sacrificial veil, prepares to receive death. Admetos appears, determined to stop Alceste or die with her. The pair exchange tender avowals, as Thanatos steps forward to claim his prey. Hercules rushes in and snatches Alceste from Thanatos. The couple are reunited with great rejoicing, and Apollo, moved by such devotion, blesses them.

SCENE FROM METROPOLITAN OPERA PRODUCTION

20

ROSE BAMPTON AS ALCESTE

THE RCA-VICTOR RECORDS
(Sung in French unless otherwise noted)

OVERTURE: *BBC Symphony Orchestra, Adrian Boult, Cond.*   12041, 12″

NON, CE N'EST POINT UN SACRIFICE (No, It Is Not a Sacrifice): *Rose Bampton, Soprano, with Orch.*   18218, 12″

ACT I

DIVINITÉS DU STYX (Divinities of the Styx): *Helen Traubel, Soprano, with Orch.*   17268, 12″

ACT II

AH, MALGRÉ MOI (Against My Will): *Rose Bampton, Soprano, with Orch.*   18218, 12″

Amelia Goes to the Ball

OPERA BUFFA in one act by Gian-Carlo Menotti. Libretto written in Italian by the composer and Englished by George Meade. First performance, in English, Academy of Music, Philadelphia, April 1, 1937, under the auspices of the Curtis Institute of Music. First New York performance, same auspices, also in English, New Amsterdam Theater, April 11, 1937. Metropolitan *première*, March 3, 1938, again in English. First performance in the original Italian, San Remo, Italy, April 4, 1938. Given in Swedish at Stockholm, December 30, 1939.

Gian-Carlo Menotti has composed, besides *Amelia Goes to the Ball*, several other operas, each to his own English libretto. These include the tragedy *The Island God*, commissioned by the Metropolitan Opera Association; *The Old Maid and the Thief*, a radio work commissioned by the National Broadcasting Company; another tragedy, *The Medium*, and the comic piece, *The Telephone*. He has composed music in other forms, notably for the ballet, but his chief fame is owing to his efforts in the operatic field. Menotti has been called a born composer for the lyric theater, a description which would not seem inappropriate. He has shown a remarkable versatility in being able to create equally well for comic and for serious situations.

Amelia Goes to the Ball, in the opinion of many, is his most able work, although *The Medium* has been highly praised for the facility and the descriptive powers of the score and the astute development of the dramatic idea. However, in *Amelia* Menotti follows in the path of the celebrated Italian composers of *opera buffa*, to which he seems to take naturally. The music is vivid, bright, and expressive in this work, and the orchestration most adroit.

CHARACTERS

AMELIA	Soprano	THE CHIEF OF POLICE	Bass
THE HUSBAND	Baritone	TWO CHAMBERMAIDS	Mezzo-sopranos
THE LOVER	Tenor	THE CHORUS	Crowd of passers-by and
THE FRIEND	Contralto		neighbors

The action takes place in Milan, one evening in the year 1910

The Overture to the opera is in itself an excellent piece of composing, sparkling with melody, richly hued, and swiftly paced.

SCENE: *Amelia's Well-Appointed Bedroom (a large window, opening on a balcony, is seen in the background).* As the curtain rises, Amelia is being dressed for the season's first ball. In the middle of her preparations her husband enters menacingly. He accuses her of having a lover whose letter he has intercepted. More because she fears she will miss the ball than because of her husband's vengeance, Amelia is quite distressed.

Asking her to name her lover, the husband receives little information. She says, however, that she will tell all if he will but take her to the ball. The lover lives upstairs, she reveals, and the husband makes a dash for the stairs, ready to kill him at sight.

Amelia's disappointment at not going to the ball would be insupportable, and in order to prevent that she calls to her lover from her own balcony, exhorting him to flee. He slides down, instead, and suggests that they elope. This, of course, Amelia will not do, still set on going out, and asks him to come back later with the same suggestion. The husband is heard returning, and the lover conceals himself. There is little left for the husband to do now, but take Amelia to the ball, and he agrees to do so, although he informs her that had he found the home-wrecker he would have dealt with him promptly.

At these words the lover emerges from his hiding place and demands satisfaction. On seeing a much younger and much more vigorous man before him, the husband chooses the path of discretion, attempting to right matters by a discussion of love and the proprieties. Meanwhile, Amelia is quite bored with all this, and insists that she be taken to the ball, the husband and the lover being totally indifferent to her arguments. At one point the husband, shouting stentorian "No's" to her pleadings, is suddenly struck on the head with a sizable vase, adroitly maneuvered by Amelia herself. He falls to the floor, unconscious, and Amelia now cries for help, while the lover tries vainly to revive him.

Amelia's shouts attract a crowd of people, neighbors, passers-by, and so on, and soon the Chief of Police comes on the scene, together with several policemen. There is an investigation, in which Amelia accuses the lover of being a robber who, caught by the husband, yet managed to wriggle free only to bring down a vase upon her husband's head. This explanation seems satisfactory to all, excepting the lover, and despite all his protests he is manacled. A stretcher is brought in for the unconscious man, and he is carried out on it. And suddenly Amelia is overtaken by a fit of weeping.

The Chief of Police tries to console her, telling her, "Why despair for so little? After all, your husband will soon recover." Amelia's desolation, however, is that she will not now be able to go to the ball. But the Chief, ever the gallant, suggests a solution to the problem by offering to take her there himself. It requires but a second to convince Amelia, and presently she is again in the midst of preparations for the all-important function. The bystanders, meanwhile, make appropriate comments on the situation, lauding the Chief for his graciousness and Amelia for the attainment of her desire. There is a moral, and the people, who are really in the tradition of the ancient Greek chorus, conclude the opera with the words, "If woman sets her heart upon a ball, the ball is where she'll go!"

THE RCA-VICTOR RECORDS

OVERTURE: *The Philadelphia Orchestra, Eugene Ormandy, Cond.*   15377, 12″

R. *Strohmeyer*   ACT II—SAN FRANCISCO OPERA PRODUCTION

Andrea Chénier

OPERA IN four acts by Umberto Giordano; libretto by Luigi Illica. First produced at La Scala, Milan, March 28, 1896. First American performance at the New York Academy of Music, November 13, 1896. First performance at the Metropolitan Opera House, March 7, 1921, with a cast headed by Claudia Muzio and Beniamino Gigli. Giordano, flourishing during the Italian period of *verismo* (a form of naturalism), called his opera a *dramma di ambiente storico* (drama with historical setting). André de Chénier (1762–94), a gifted poet of French-Greek descent who combined classic breadth and romantic fervor in his work, was executed in the years of terror and intrigue following the French Revolution. Before going to his death he wrote a last poem in prison. Illica, with a librettist's license, naturally romanticized the poet's career, making shrewd use of Chénier's prison poem, and creating a drama of personal conflict that ends in a typical operatic situation: the lovers are reunited in death at the guillotine. Dramatic arias, fervid declamation, and the unusual setting of a revolutionary upheaval have combined to make *Andrea Chénier* Giordano's best-known opera. None of his other subsequent operas, among them *Fedora*, *Madame Sans-Gêne*, and *La Cena delle beffe*, has rivaled it in popular appeal.

CHARACTERS

ANDREA CHÉNIER, *poet*	*Tenor*	THE ABBÉ	*Tenor*
CHARLES GÉRARD, *a revolutionary*		A SPY	*Tenor*
leader	*Baritone*	FOUQUIER-TINVILLE, *public prose-*	
COUNTESS DE COIGNY	*Soprano*	cutor of the Revolution	*Bass*
MADELEINE, *her daughter*	*Soprano*	ROUCHER, *Chénier's friend*	*Bass*
BERSI, *Madeleine's maid*	*Mezzo-soprano*	FLEVILLE, *a writer*	*Tenor*
MADELON, *an old woman*	*Soprano*	SCHMIDT, *a jailer*	*Bass*
MATHIEU, *a revolutionary*	*Baritone*		

GUESTS, SERVANTS, PEASANTS, SOLDIERS, REVOLUTIONARIES, JUDGES, PRISONERS

The action of Andrea Chénier *occurs in Paris before, during, and after the French Revolution*

24

ACT I

SCENE: *The Ballroom of the Château de Coigny*. Preparations are being made for a ball. Gérard, a servant, bitter at the sight of his aged and ailing father, bewails the lot of the poor and denounces the wasteful rich. Impatiently he awaits the outbreak of revolution in France, partly because he is secretly in love with the Countess' daughter, Madeleine, who herself longs for freedom—freedom from a life of dull aristocratic routine. When the guests have finally gathered, a court pastoral with idealized shepherds and shepherdesses is enacted. Music suggesting the countryside is sung, and a ballet pantomime is staged in the stately style of an eighteenth-century idyl. Among the guests is the poet-patriot Andrea Chénier, famous for his gifts of poetic improvisation. The Countess urges Chénier to improvise on some theme of his own choosing. Chénier at first refuses, but yields when Madeleine coquettishly cajoles him, even venturing a suggestion: "Let Chénier improvise on the subject of love." The poet begins, but soon he reverts to the grave theme of oppression. The song—*"Un dì all' azzuro spazio"* ("Once o'er the azure fields")—becomes an impromptu tirade against tyranny and a burning plea for the relief of the poor. Bitterly, Chénier flails the pride and apathy of the rich, the wrongs inflicted on the subject classes.

A chorus of indignation greets the fiery idealism of Chénier's *improvviso*. Only Madeleine, drawn by the poet's zeal, is stirred by this new creed. To bring back the festive mood, the Countess commands the musicians to play dance music. Suddenly a clamor is heard outside the ballroom. The door flies open, and a band of ragged men and women burst in, led by Gérard. The intruders are ejected, and Chénier follows them.

R. Strohmeyer   ACT III—SAN FRANCISCO OPERA PRODUCTION

ACT II

SCENE: *The Café Hottot in Paris.* The Revolution an accomplished fact, Chénier has now come under suspicion for opposing Robespierre. Spies have been ordered to watch him, and Roucher has come to warn his friend to flee before it is too late. Bersi, Madeleine's maid, has meanwhile been conversing at a near-by table with a spy. There is an ominous moment as a death cart rolls by on its way to the guillotine. Bersi has handed Chénier a letter from a mysterious unknown, pleading for help and a rendezvous. Chénier refuses to heed his friend's warning and awaits the stranger. The lady, of course, is Madeleine. They declare their love for one another and prepare to flee together. Word, however, has reached Gérard, now a revolutionary functionary, of the rendezvous. Gérard bursts in on the love scene and attempts to seize Madeleine. As the rivals draw swords, Roucher hurries Madeleine away. Gérard is wounded and nobly exhorts Chénier to save himself and Madeleine from their enemies. When Gérard's friends arrive, they demand the name of the assailant. Gérard pretends not to have recognized him.

ACT III

SCENE: *The Revolutionary Tribunal.* Recovered from his wound, Gérard now appears before a revolutionary tribunal with a fervent plea for money for France. A collection is taken up, and jewels are contributed by the women. Madelon, an old woman, steps forward and volunteers her son to the defense of France against her enemies. Amid the mounting mood of patriotism the crowd sings *"La Carmagnole."* A spy enters to report Chénier's arrest to Gérard, who thus has a chance to dispose of a rival and win Madeleine for himself. Yet, as he prepares the official denunciation of Chénier, Gérard hesitates. He recalls the poet's stirring verses, his espousal of the cause of the poor, his flaming nobility. This man an "enemy of his country" (*"Nemico della patria"*), he asks himself sardonically. Can he sacrifice a friend to satisfy his passion for Madeleine? Gérard broods over the problem in music throbbing with the conflict of honor and desire. Almost cynically the orchestra chants a fragment of *"La Marseillaise."* Finally, Gérard yields and signs the fatal document. At this moment Madeleine appears. She learns of Chénier's arrest, and in a touching aria—*"La mamma morta"*—she tells of her mother's death and offers herself to Gérard in exchange for Chénier's freedom.

Madeleine's entreaties having won Gérard over, he vows to help the man she loves. As the trial proceeds, the crowd grows increasingly furious over the charges made against Chénier. There are loud cries of "Death to the traitor!" and against this surging wrath, the poet's own defense is of no avail. Even Gérard's eloquent plea that the charges are false proves futile.

ROSE BAMPTON AS MADELEINE

Gérard embraces the doomed poet, who is dragged away to the crowd's cries of *"À la lanterne!"* (To the scaffold!")

ACT IV

SCENE: *The Prison of Saint-Lazare.* It is midnight in the gloomy cell. Chénier, awaiting execution, is writing his last poem, *"Come un bel dì di Maggio"* ("As some soft day in May"). As he sings, the poet's firm belief in truth and beauty seems to mock the prison walls. Roucher listens attentively to his friend's farewell verses. Madeleine and Gérard now appear. Preferring death with her lover to life without him, she has bribed the jailer to substitute her name for that of another condemned woman. Together the lovers await the last ride together in the death wagon.

THE RCA-VICTOR RECORDS
(Sung in Italian unless otherwise noted)

ACT III

Monologo—Nemico della patria (The Enemy of His Country?): *Robert Merrill, Baritone, with Orch.* 11-9384, 12"

John Charles Thomas, Baritone, with Orch. 17639, 12"

Titta Ruffo, Baritone, with Orch. 7153, 12"

Armide

OPERA IN FIVE acts. Music by Christoph Willibald von Gluck. Book by Philippe Quinault, after an episode in Torquato Tasso's *Jerusalem Delivered*. First produced at the Paris Opéra, September 23, 1777. First American performance at the Metropolitan Opera House, under the direction of Arturo Toscanini, on November 14, 1910—the opening night of the season—with a cast headed by Olive Fremstad, Louise Homer, Enrico Caruso, and Pasquale Amato. Gluck was only one of many composers attracted by the story of the pagan temptress in Tasso's great epic poem of crusading chivalry in the Middle Ages. In fact, he used substantially the same libretto that Quinault had written for Jean-Baptiste Lully's *Armide* of almost a century earlier. Yet, though Lully, a native Florentine, was strictly the French stylist in his opera, Gluck, a German by birth, combined Italian and French trends in his own. At least half a hundred other *Armide*s were composed, chief among them the operas of Handel (*Rinaldo*) (1711), Sacchini (1772), Haydn (1784), and the highly successful one of Rossini (1817).

The action takes place in and near Damascus in 1099

Armide, an Oriental queen and enchantress, has found all the Crusaders in the neighborhood of Damascus easy prey except one—Renaud. Invincible, the saintly knight repels all her magic allurements. Arontes, whom Armide will marry if he conquers Renaud, arrives wounded, and the populace joins Armide in swearing vengeance upon the Crusader. Meanwhile, Artemidore has warned Renaud of the queen's wiles, but the fearless knight ventures into an enchanted wood, where he is soon lulled to sleep by the siren voices of naiads in a near-by stream. The vengeful Armide aims an arrow at the slumbering knight, but, miraculously, as she gazes at the man's beauty, her hatred turns to love. A fearful conflict now rages in Armide's heart. She summons the Spirit of Hate to free her from her passion, but she relents and orders the demon away. Renaud, awakening, is himself entranced by Armide and soon is established at the court at her side. When two fellow knights come to fetch him back to camp, they, too, momentarily succumb to the blandishments of the magic realm. Finally, Renaud shakes off the spell and prepares to leave. Armide pleads with him to remain, and, when she fails to hold him, gives a cry of despair and orders her enchanted palace burned to the ground.

Among the most gripping pages of the opera are Armide's impassioned invocation to the Spirit of Hate, "*Venez, venez, haine implacable*" ("Come, come, implacable hate"), the tender air of a shepherdess in the scene of the enchanted wood, and the touching duet of Armide and Renaud, "*Aimons-nous*" ("Let us love each other"), in the last act. The broadly classical Overture to *Armide* is virtually the same as the one Gluck wrote for his earlier opera, *Telemaco*.

THE BARBER OF SEVILLE

The Barber of Seville
(IL BARBIERE DI SIVIGLIA)

COMIC OPERA in two acts by Gioacchino Antonio Rossini; libretto by Cesare Sterbini, after Beaumarchais' comedy. *Première* at the Teatro Argentina, Rome, February 20, 1816; first New York performance (in English), Park Theater, May 3, 1819; New York *première* in Italian, given during Manuel García's initial American season, Park Theater, November 29, 1825.

This opera of Rossini's boasts a star-studded record of interpreters, among them the famous Garcías, Manuel, the elder, Manuel, the younger, María (later known as María Malibran), as well as such celebrated singers as Adelina Patti, Marcella Sembrich, Nellie Melba, Luisa Tetrazzini, María Barrientos, Amelita Galli-Curci, and Lily Pons (all Rosinas); Alessandro Bonci, Tito Schipa (Almavivas); Giuseppe Campanari, Mario Ancona, Riccardo Stracciari, Pasquale Amato, Titta Ruffo, and Giuseppe de Luca (Figaros); Charles Gilibert, Salvatore Baccaloni (Bartolos), Édouard de Reszke, Feodor Chaliapin, and Ezio Pinza (Basilios).

The Barber of Seville was a failure at its first performance, the reasons ascribed to that being many and varied. Chief of these, however, was that Rossini had dared to compose an opera on a subject that had been successfully treated by the esteemed Paisiello ten years before Rossini was born. It is because of this, in fact, that *The Barber* was first produced under the title *Almaviva, ossia l'inutile precauzione* (*Almaviva, or The Useless Precaution*). Another reason for the failure was the singing by García (as Almaviva) of a serenade of his own composing, which, as he tuned his guitar on the stage, earned gales of laughter. On the second night Rossini's charming serenade, "*Ecco ridente*," replaced it, and the public received this and the whole opera with respect and enthusiasm not shown the evening before.

The story is told of Rossini's imperturbable calm as his work, on opening night, was experiencing hisses, catcalls, and sneering shouts. He sat quietly at the piano, apparently unconcerned by it all, and when the performance was ended he went home and to bed, where a singer, come to console him, found him fast asleep!

R. Strohmeyer   ACT I—SAN FRANCISCO OPERA PRODUCTION

CHARACTERS

COUNT ALMAVIVA	*Tenor*	BASILIO, *a music teacher*	*Bass*
BARTOLO, *a physician*	*Bass*	FIGARO, *a barber*	*Baritone*
ROSINA, *his ward*	*Soprano*	BERTA, *a maid*	*Mezzo-soprano*

The action takes place at Seville, during the seventeenth century

The opera is preceded by a gay and springly overture, although it is not the one heard at the *première*. It is supposed that the overture used then was an original one based on Spanish themes. The Overture heard in our time also stems from a previous opera of Rossini's, *Elisabetta, regina d'Inghilterra,* though it had served also as curtain raiser for Rossini's *L'Equivoco stravagante* and *Aureliano in Palmira.*

ACT I

SCENE 1: *A Street in Seville.* The young and handsome Count Almaviva is deeply in love with Rosina, the ward of the mean and suspicious old Dr. Bartolo. In the gray light of dawn, he comes with a band of musicians to serenade his beloved. The musicians play a ditty for her; then the Count himself sings to the accompaniment of their mandolins, *"Ecco ridente in cielo"* ("Dawn with her rosy mantle").

He pays his musicians, evidently generously, for they are moved to express their gratitude with such enthusiasm that surely they must waken

R. Strohmeyer   ACT II—SAN FRANCISCO OPERA PRODUCTION

the sleeping Rosina, if the Count's very lovely serenade has failed to do so. He seems inclined to linger near his loved one's house, even though she does not come out to thank him for the charming song, and as someone else seems to be coming down the street toward the house, making a great deal of noise for such an early hour, Almaviva conceals himself to see who this might be. The newcomer is none other than Figaro, the gay barber of Seville. But besides being a barber, he is a sort of jack-of-all-trades, a so-called factotum, whose profession gives him entry to the homes of people of all stations; and thus he is a convenient instrument for the execution of the intrigues of young lovers as well as of old rogues. He displays his loquacious character and the very gay life he leads, in the brilliant and exceedingly rapid aria, *"Largo al factotum"* ("Room for the factotum").

Oh! what a happy life, ready all hours of the night, and, by day, perpetually in bustle and motion. Razors, combs, lancets, scissors—behold them, at my command! All call me! all want me!—dames and maidens—old and young. My wig! cries one—my beard! shouts another—tend me! cries this—a love letter! whispers that. Figaro, Figaro! Heavens, what a crowd! Figaro, Figaro! Heavens, what a rush! One at a time, for mercy's sake! Figaro here, Figaro there, Figaro above, Figaro below. Always in a hurry— quick as lightning—the factotum of the town. Oh, what living! A little work, but lots of fun, and a pocket always full of coin—what I get for my reputation. It's like this: without Figaro there's not a girl in Seville will marry; to me the little widows have recourse for a husband; I, under excuse for my comb by day, and under favor of my guitar by night, endeavor to please all in an honest way. Oh, what living! What living!

The Count, recognizing him, accosts Figaro and asks him to arrange a meeting with the fair Rosina, adding that his rank must not be known, for he does not wish the girl to be influenced by the glamour of it. He has assumed the name of Lindoro. Again he serenades the favored one, this time at Figaro's insistence, and in the tender, haunting strain, a tune of lovelorn youth, *"Se il mio nome"* ("If my name you would know"), he tells her he is Lindoro and that he loves her.

The two plotters hide for a moment as Dr. Bartolo comes from his house. He gives strict orders to the servant that no one is to be admitted except the music master, Basilio. The doctor hopes, with Basilio's aid, to arrange to marry Rosina this day, appreciating, as he does, the girl's dowry as much as the girl. After he disappears down the street, the Count and Figaro finish their plan. Troops are coming to the city, and Almaviva, disguised as a dragoon, must arrange to be billeted on the unwilling Bartolo!

SCENE 2: *A Room in Bartolo's House.* Rosina, reading a note from her Lindoro, is, naturally enough, rather agitated, and gives vent to her feelings in the delightful and brilliant coloratura aria, *"Una voce poco fa"* ("A little voice I hear").

Almost every resource known to the coloratura singer's art must be called upon to render this glittering number. Rapid scales and arpeggios united with contrasts of rhythm and dynamics express with a bubbling gaiety the tender emotions of the girl in words that in the Italian seem to have wings.

When the highly spirited Rosina has run from the room, the guardian, Bartolo, enters with Basilio, the music master, who is also a not inconsiderable master of intrigue himself. Bartolo is telling the music master that he wishes to marry Rosina himself—news doubtless already well known to Basilio, who informs him that the noble Almaviva has been haunting the neighborhood, and both immediately conclude that he is the mysterious serenader. Basilio suggests that they start some disgraceful rumor that will make Rosina reject the Count. He explains, in the broadly humorous aria, *"La Calunnia"* ("Slander's Whisper") that a calumny begins like a tempest howling through dreary forest caverns, until, its full fury gathered, it falls, a terrific lightning flash, on its helpless victim.

This description of the devastating effect of gossip is set to music that grows in an amazing crescendo to a climax of fury; yet the music contains an element of humor suggesting that, in the mouth of Basilio, these words are rather a travesty.

Rosina returns accompanied by Figaro, who tells her that her guardian

Leon Elzin, New York   JOHN CHARLES THOMAS AS FIGARO

plans to marry her himself. Laughing at the idea, she coyly inquires about the young man she has seen from the balcony. Figaro admits he is an excellent youth, who has, however, one failing. "A failing?" cries the girl. "Yes, a great one," answers the factotum blandly, "he is dying of love." The girl, greatly interested, plies him with other questions. Figaro finally slyly admits that the youth's adored one is named Rosina. "You are mocking," she cries, and the two make merry in a rollicking duet.

Rosina is impatient to see him, and Figaro assures her that her lover awaits only a line from her, then he will come. "I blush to do it," says the coy maiden. "Hurry," answers Figaro, "write him a little note, hurry!" "Oh, here's one," she confesses, "I had already written it—how stupid!"

When Figaro has left with the letter, Bartolo enters in hopes of finding out about the serenader of that morning. He suspects that Figaro may be carrying messages between his ward and this stranger. The girl's blushes and the ink marks on her fingers betray her; she answers that she has used the ink as a salve for a small cut. He calls attention to a freshly trimmed quill pen and a missing sheet of paper: she replies that she used the paper to wrap up some sweets for a girl friend and the pen to design a flower for her embroidery. The old man's rage and the girl's impertinent answers are characterized in the music of this scene, one of whose features is the song *"A un dottor della mia sorte"* ("To a doctor of my standing"), in which Dr. Bartolo cautions his young ward to forgo matching wits with a doctor of his rank.

A loud knocking is heard at the door—the Count, in his soldier's guise, pretending to be drunk. The old doctor, suspicious of the disguise, indignantly resists the order for the quartering of soldiers and pretends to go off to hunt for a license he has that grants him exemption from such imposition. This gives the lovers a brief moment to exchange words, and Almaviva manages to slip a note to Rosina. There is a grand to-do of sly intrigue amid much excitement in a quintet involving Rosina, Berta, Bartolo, Almaviva, and Figaro. Soon soldiers summoned by Bartolo arrive, and they arrest this peace-disturbing intruder, but immediately release him when he secretly reveals his identity to the astonished officer.

ACT II

SCENE: *A Room in Bartolo's House*. Though the soldier scheme has fallen through, Figaro soon invents another. As the curtain rises, we find the old doctor wondering if the drunken soldier may not be an emissary of Count Almaviva. He is interrupted by a stranger, none other than the Count himself pretending to be a Don Alonzo, a music teacher. He explains that Don Basilio is ill, and that he has come in his place to give Rosina her music lesson. He makes his entrance in a greeting that is musically superb for its oiliness and polite sarcasm, *"Pace e gioia"* ("Peace and joy").

ACT II—THE MUSIC LESSON

35

To allay the suspicions that begin to arise in Bartolo's mind, the Count, in a bold stroke, produces the note written by Rosina to her charming Lindoro. Asserting that he found it at the inn where Count Almaviva is staying, he offers to make Rosina believe she is the Count's dupe. The idea pleases Bartolo; in producing such a bit of slander, this strange music master has proved himself a worthy pupil of Don Basilio! Rosina enters for her lesson. Rossini wrote at this place a song for mezzo-soprano, the original Rosina voice. But when Rosina became a coloratura soprano, it was not used. The artist singing the role of Rosina now usually interpolates an air of her own choosing, a privilege which some singers have exercised to the point of extreme anachronism.

Figaro arrives, declaring, in spite of Bartolo's remonstrance, that this is the day he must shave him. When Bartolo gives him his keys to go fetch some linen, Figaro steals the key to the balcony, saving it for future use. Don Basilio, the real music teacher, appears, and the Count, reminding Bartolo of their scheme to deceive Rosina, points out that the matrimonial agent-music teacher must be disposed of. Dr. Bartolo immediately asks the startled Basilio how he comes to be walking abroad in a fever! When the Count slips a purse in his hand, the wondering Basilio is convinced that they all want him to behave as if he were, and diplomatically takes hasty leave. The lovers plot their elopement while Figaro detains Bartolo at shaving with generous splashes of soap in his eyes. Finally, the suspicious Bartolo approaches the preoccupied lovers and discovers that he is again being duped. The three conspirators laugh at him and run out, followed by the doctor, purple with rage.

Bartolo, driven to play his last card, shows Rosina the note, saying that her supposedly devoted Lindoro is conspiring to give her up to Count Almaviva. Justly infuriated, Rosina offers to marry Bartolo at once, reveals the plan to elope, and bids him have Lindoro and Figaro arrested when they arrive. As soon as he has gone to bring the police and the marriage broker, the Count and Figaro enter by means of the stolen key. Rosina greets them with a storm of reproaches, accusing Lindoro of pretending to love her in order to sacrifice her to the vile Count Almaviva. . . . The Count, delighted that Rosina, unaware of his identity, should prefer a true though poor lover to a scheming nobleman, now reveals himself, and the lovers are soon embracing amid a shower of blessings from Figaro.

They are interrupted by Don Basilio, who has returned in the office of notary and marriage broker, to unite Rosina and Bartolo, but with the aid of a pistol he is persuaded to marry Rosina to the Count instead. When Dr. Bartolo arrives a few minutes later with the police, it is too late, for the marriage contract has been signed, and Rosina is the wife of the distinguished Count Almaviva. The doctor decides to accept his hard luck philosophically, while the irrepressible Figaro bestows on all present his garrulous good wishes.

The Barber of Seville

De Bellis Studios
NINO MARTINI
AS COUNT ALMAVIVA

Lumière
AMELITA GALLI-CURCI
AS ROSINA

NORMAN CORDON
AS DON BASILIO

THE RCA-VICTOR RECORDS
(Sung in Italian unless otherwise noted)

RECORDRAMA: *Carlos Ramirez, Baritone; Hilde Reggiani, Soprano; Bruno Landi, Tenor; John Gurney, Bass; Lorenzo Alvary, Bass; Lucielle Browning, Mezzo-soprano; Wilfred Engelman, Baritone; with Orch. and Chorus, Giuseppe Bamboschek, Cond.*
DM-898 (11-8198-11-8205), 8-12″
M-898 (11-8190-11-8197)

OVERTURE: *Arturo Toscanini and the NBC Symphony Orchestra* 11-9066, 12″
(In Album M-1037)
18-0005, 12″
(Vinylite) (In Album V-2)

Arturo Toscanini conducting the Philharmonic-Symphony Orchestra of New York 11-9229, 12″
(In Album M-1063)

ACT I

ECCO RIDENTE IN CIELO (Dawn with Her Rosy Mantle): *Tito Schipa, Tenor, with Orch.* 1180, 10″

LARGO AL FACTOTUM (Room for the Factotum): *Leonard Warren, Baritone, with Orch.* 11-8744, 12″
John Charles Thomas, Baritone, with Orch. 15860, 12″
(In Album M-645)

Lawrence Tibbett, Baritone, with Orch. 14202, 12″
(In Album M-329)
7353, 12″

Luboshutz and Nemenoff (Duo Pianists) 11-8987, 12″

Robert Merrill, Baritone; RCA-Victor Orchestra, Jean Paul Morel, Cond. 12-0450, 12″

SERENATA—SE IL MIO NOME SAPER (Shall I Tell Thee the Name of Thy Lover?): *Tito Schipa, Tenor, with Orch.* 1180, 10″

ACT II

CAVATINA—UNA VOCE POCO FA (A Little Voice I Hear): *Miliza Korjus, Soprano, with Orch. In German* 13807, 12″
(In Album M-871)

Lily Pons, Soprano, with Orch. 8870, 12″

Amelita Galli-Curci, Soprano, with Orch. 7110, 12″

Luisa Tetrazzini, Soprano, with Orch. 7883, 12″

LA CALUNNIA (Slander's Whisper): *Feodor Chaliapin, Bass, with Orch.* 6783, 12″

ACT III

DUNQUE IO SON (Can It Be?): *Lily Pons, Soprano; Giuseppe de Luca, Baritone; with Orch.* 17233, 12″
(In Album M-702)

Nat'l Photo. & Adv. Co.   ACT I—METROPOLITAN OPERA PRODUCTION

The Bartered Bride
(PRODANÁ NEVĚSTA)

COMIC OPERA in three acts. Music by Bedřich Smetana. Libretto by Karel Sabina. First performance, National Theater, Prague, May 30, 1866. First United States performance, Metropolitan Opera House, New York, February 19, 1909, in a German translation by Max Kalbeck, with the title *Die verkaufte Braut*. A spirited, amusing opera that teems with comical situations, *The Bartered Bride* established Smetana as the first "national" composer of Bohemia (later Czechoslovakia). And it is said he was practically driven to that high office by a chance remark of Johann Franz von Herbeck's (noted Viennese conductor) to the effect that Czechs "were simply reproductive artists," a challenge which Smetana met willingly and, as he proved, successfully. The work is strongly folk in feeling, possessing a brilliant score with a flow of rich melody from overture to finale.

Originally *The Bartered Bride* was in two acts, consisting of twenty musical parts connected with spoken dialogue. Smetana divided his first act into two complete ones; he augmented his score with an aria for the heroine, a male chorus, and a dance number, and later he converted the spoken dialogue into recitative, with all of which he brought the opera to the form we know today.

Outstanding among the opera's musical numbers are the very comical duet between Hans and Kezal in Act II, which was a high point of the production in English given by the Metropolitan in 1936; a sextet in Act III, and the Overture, a melodious, sparkling, gay, and charming piece heard often in the concert hall.

CHARACTERS

KRUSCHINA, *a peasant*	Baritone	HANS, *Micha's son by a first marriage*	Tenor
KATHINKA, *his wife*	Soprano	KEZAL, *a marriage broker*	Bass
MARIE, *their daughter*	Soprano	SPRINGER, *manager of a theatrical troupe*	Bass
MICHA, *a landowner*	Bass		
AGNES, *his wife*	Mezzo-soprano	ESMERALDA, *a dancer*	Soprano
WENZEL, *their son*	Tenor	MUFF, *a comedian*	Tenor

COMEDIANS, CIRCUS PERFORMERS, VILLAGERS

38

The Bartered Bride

The action takes place in Bohemia, in the nineteenth century

An overture bristling with good humor and pretty melody precedes the opera. It is an excellent piece which, oddly enough, was played in this country some twenty years before the opera's arrival here.

ACT I

SCENE: *A Public Square Before an Inn.* Hans and Marie sit rather disconsolately at a table, discussing the obstacles in the path of their love. For today, on the anniversary of the consecration of the village church, Marie must accept a suitor of her parents' choice. Hans, suddenly emboldened, assures her that she will marry no one but him. He departs, on hearing approaching footsteps, and soon the marriage broker, Kezal, together with Marie's parents, enters. They talk with her about a prospective suitor, Wenzel, a rather silly rustic, whom she will hear none of, insisting that she loves Hans. Be all that as it may, her father writes out a promise to Micha that, no matter what happens, Marie will marry Micha's son.

ACT II

SCENE: *Within the Inn.* Young Hans and Kezal are tilting convivial glasses. There is an argument, in which Hans, romantic that he is, expounds on the joys of love, whereas his companion, a very practical man, insists that love is nothing at all without money. A moment later, Marie and Wenzel have a bit of an interview. He, a little on the sotted side, listens, as she explains that she loves another man; also that she knows of a girl he could really care for. Wenzel, quite affected by her interest, agrees to give up the idea of marrying Marie.

In the meantime, Kezel, a little distracted by the headstrong Marie, attempts to bribe Hans. At first the latter will hear none of it, but, as a crafty idea strikes him, he finally agrees only on condition that Marie shall marry no other man but Micha's son. He makes this very clear, and Kezel, overwhelmed by his success, draws up a contract, which Hans signs. They go to Marie's parents, who are also happy now that all seems to have been so easily arranged.

ACT III

SCENE: *A Public Square Before an Inn (as in Act I).* A traveling troupe of circus performers puts on a show. Among them is the tightrope dancer, Esmeralda, and she seems most desirable to Wenzel. He dons a bear costume and goes through several tricks at the instigation of the troupe's manager, who just picks out anyone at all, since his regular man is intoxicated.

Wenzel's parents come along and, finding him in the middle of this droll performance, try to bring him to Marie. But well briefed, as he had been by the young woman, and fearing her just a little bit, he refuses to marry her. But his parents finally persuade him, and they head for Marie's house.

There Kezal informs Marie, rather gloatingly, that Hans has relinquished all claims on her—for money, of course. She disbelieves him, but he shows her the proof, the contract signed by Hans, calling for a consideration of three hundred crowns. After some moments of confusion for Marie, Hans, the son of Micha by an earlier marriage, is found acceptable not only to Marie, as he always was, but also to her parents. All ends very happily for them, but Kezal, who has lost his three hundred crowns, is a much sadder man.

NORMAN CORDON AS KEZAL

THE RCA-VICTOR RECORDS
(Sung in Czech unless otherwise noted)

COMPLETE RECORDING: *Jan Konstantin, Baritone; Marie Pixová, Soprano; Ada Nordenová, Soprano; Zdenek Otava, Bass; Marta Krasova, Soprano; Jaroslav Gleich, Tenor; Vladimir Tomš, Tenor; Emil Pollert, Bass; Karel Hruška, Tenor; Otta Horakova, Soprano; Vaclav Marek, Tenor; with Chorus and Orchestra of the National Opera, Prague, Otakar Ostrčil, Cond.*

DMC-117 (DM-193) (Vol. 1) (13345-13352) 8-12"
(DM-193) (Vol. 2) (13353-13359) 7-12"
MC-117 (M-193) (Vol. 1) (11617-11624) (M-193) (Vol. 2) (11625-11631)

OVERTURE: *Chicago Symphony Orchestra, Désiré Defauw, Cond.* 12-0018, 12"
Boston "Pops" Orchestra, Arthur Fiedler, Cond. 4498, 10"
Chicago Symphony Orchestra, Frederick Stock, Cond. 1555, 10"

Griffith Pk. outdoor theatre - 195?

Kaufmann & Fabry Co., Chicago

ACT I

La Bohème

OPERA IN four acts. Music by Giacomo Puccini. Text by Giuseppe Giacosa and Luigi Illica. Based on episodes from Henri Murger's *Scènes de la vie de Bohème*. First produced at the Teatro Regio, Turin, February 1, 1896, under the direction of Arturo Toscanini. First performance in the United States at Los Angeles, October 14, 1897. First performance at the Metropolitan Opera House on December 26, 1900. *La Bohème* aroused quick public response, thanks to its heart-warming melodies and absorbing drama. Many early critics, however, objected strongly to its story, its music, even its romantic freedom. Turinese writers bemoaned what they called a decline in Puccini's powers; some dubbed the new work a mere potboiler, others dismissed it as an *operina* or operetta, and here in New York the *Tribune* critic flailed the new work as "foul in subject and fulminant and futile in its music." In due course, however, even the critics were won over by the bubbling verve and intense fervor of the music. Today most operagoers would rank *La Bohème* among their ten favorite operas.

Much of Puccini's early life went into this fervid tale of struggling young artists. Puccini remembered those frugal conservatory days in Milan when a sumptuous banquet in his dingy garret consisted of "soup, cheese, and half a liter of wine," when wood and coal had to be smuggled past a watchful landlady for a bit of forbidden home cooking. The landlady is said to have wept over the thought of her indigent young boarder who preferred music to food. Years later when Puccini dwelt at Torre del Lago, he became the center of an artistic coterie that met in a near-by villa. The group of painters, poets, and composers discussed art, played cards, joined in harmless pranks on the neighbors. At times Puccini would dash in excitedly with fresh manuscript. He would rush to the piano, and the Club Bohème of Torre del Lago would be the first to shed tears over little Mimi's pathetic fate. Through Puccini's opera, which they watched take shape with eager interest, the friends all fell in love with the ailing attic waif. In *La Bohème* Puccini wondrously transmutes those bleak early years in a Milanese attic and the gay camaraderie of the Club Bohème into a nostalgic picture of the Latin Quarter of Paris in the third decade of the nineteenth century.

CHARACTERS

RODOLFO, *a poet*	*Tenor*	BENOIT, *a landlord*	*Bass*
SCHAUNARD, *a musician*	*Baritone*	MIMI, *a maker of artificial flowers*	*Soprano*

41

MARCELLO, *a painter*	*Baritone*	ALCINDORO, *a state councilor*	*Bass*
COLLINE, *a philosopher*	*Bass*	MUSETTA	*Soprano*
PARPIGNOL, *a toy vendor*	*Tenor*	A CUSTOM-HOUSE SERGEANT	*Bass*

STUDENTS, WORKING GIRLS, CITIZENS, SHOPKEEPERS, STREET VENDORS, SOLDIERS, RESTAURANT WAITERS, BOYS, GIRLS, ETC.

The action takes place in Paris in the mid-nineteenth century

ACT I

SCENE: *In the Attic.* The cold, bleak garret dwelling of the inseparable quartet, Rodolfo, poet; Marcello, painter; Colline, philosopher; Schaunard, musician, is certainly large enough to accommodate such a family. The sparse furniture makes it seem doubly spacious. For the fireplace—devoid of fire—the few chairs, the table, the small cupboard, the few books, the artist's easel, appear like miniatures in this immense attic. Marcello, busily painting at his never-finished canvas—*The Passage of the Red Sea*—stops to blow on his hands to keep them from freezing. Rodolfo, the poet, gazes through the window over the snow-capped roofs of Paris. Marcello breaks the silence by remarking that he feels as though the Red Sea were flowing down his back, and Rodolfo answers the jest with another. When Marcello seizes a chair to break it up for firewood, Rodolfo halts him, offering to sacrifice the manuscript of one of his plays instead. The doomed play now goes into the flames, act by act, and as it burns, the friends feast their eyes on the blaze, but gain scant warmth from it. The acts burn quickly, and Colline, who now enters stamping with cold, declares that since brevity is the soul of wit, this drama was truly sparkling.

Accompanied by errand boys, the musician Schaunard bursts in cheerfully, bringing wood for the fire, food and wine for the table, and money—plenty of it, from the way he flashes it. To his enraptured companions he relates how a rich English amateur has been paying him liberally for music lessons. The festivities are cut short by the arrival of the landlord Benoit, who begins to demand his long overdue rent, when he is mollified by the sight of money on the table. As he joins the comrades in several rounds of drinks, he grows jovial and talkative. The young men feign shock when the tipsy landlord begins to boast of his affairs with women in disreputable resorts, protesting that they cannot tolerate such talk in their home; and he a married man, too! The gay quartet seize the landlord and push him out of the room.

Rodolfo remains behind to work as his companions go off to the Café Momus to celebrate. He promises to join them in five minutes. He now makes several fruitless attempts to continue an article, and a timid knock at the door finally interrupts his efforts. Rodolfo opens, and a young girl enters shyly.

ACT II

While explaining that she is a neighbor seeking a light for her candle, she is suddenly overcome by a fit of coughing. Rodolfo rushes to her side to support her as she begins to faint and drops her candle and key. He gives her some water and a sip of wine. Rodolfo recovers the candle, lights it, and, after accompanying her to the door, returns to his work. A moment later Mimi re-enters. She has suddenly remembered the key and pauses at the threshold to remind Rodolfo of its loss. Her candle blows out, and Rodolfo offers his, but that, too, soon goes out in the draft. Left in the dark, they grope together along the floor for the lost key. Rodolfo finds it and quietly pockets it. Slowly he makes his way toward his visitor, as if still searching for the key, and sees to it that their hands meet in the dark. Taken unawares, the girl gives a little outcry and rises to her feet. "Thy tiny hand is frozen" (*"Che gelida manina"*), says Rodolfo tenderly; "let me warm it for you."

Rodolfo assists the girl to a chair, and as he assures her it is useless to hunt for the key in the dark, he begins to tell her about himself. "What am I?" he chants; "I am a poet!" Not exactly a man of wealth, he continues, but one rich in dreams and visions. In a wondrous sweep of romantic melody he declares she has come to replace these vanished dreams of his, and now he dwells passionately on her eyes, eyes that have robbed him of his choicest jewels. As the aria ends, Rodolfo asks his visitor to tell him about herself. "Who are you?" he asks.

Simply, modestly, the girl replies: "My name is Mimi," and in an aria of touching romantic sentiment, she confides that she makes artificial flowers for a living. Meanwhile she yearns for the real blossoms of spring, the meadows, the sweet flowers that speak of love.

R. Strohmeyer   ACT III—SAN FRANCISCO OPERA PRODUCTION

Rodolfo is entranced by the simple charm and frail beauty of his visitor and sympathizes with her longing for a richer life. The enchanted mood is broken by the voices of Marcello, Colline, and Schaunard, calling Rodolfo from the street below. As Rodolfo opens the window to answer, the moonlight pours into the room and falls on Mimi. Rodolfo, beside himself with rapture, bursts out with a warm tribute to her beauty, and soon the two of them unite their voices in impassioned song, *"O soave fanciulla"* ("O lovely maiden"). Mimi coquettishly asks Rodolfo to take her with him to the Café Momus, where he is to rejoin his friends. They link arms and go out the door, and as they go down the stairs their voices are heard blending in the last fading strains of their ecstatic duet.

ACT II

SCENE: *A Students' Café in the Latin Quarter.* It is Christmas Eve. A busy crowd is swarming over the public square on which the Café Momus stands. Street vendors are crying their wares, and students and working girls cross the scene, calling to one another. Patrons of the café are shouting their orders to waiters, who bustle about frantically. The scene unfolds in a joyful surge of music, blending bits of choral singing, snatches of recitative, and a lively orchestral accompaniment. Rodolfo and Mimi, walking among the crowd arm in arm, stop at a milliner's, where the poet buys her a new hat. Then the lovers go to the sidewalk table already occupied by Colline, Marcello, and Schaunard.

Parpignol, a toy vendor, bustles through the crowd with his lantern-covered pushcart, trailing a band of squealing and squabbling children, who pester their mothers for money to buy toys. As the children riot around him,

La Bohème

Wide World Studio

ACT III—METROPOLITAN OPERA PRODUCTION

Parpignol flings his arms about in despair and withdraws with his cart. Meanwhile the Bohemians have been ordering lavishly, when suddenly there is a cry from the women in the crowd: "Look, look, it's Musetta with some stammering old dotard!" Musetta, pretty and coquettish, appears with the wealthy Alcindoro, who follows her slavishly about. Musetta and Marcello had been lovers, had quarreled and parted. Noticing Marcello with his friends, the girl occupies a near-by table and tries to draw his attention. Marcello at first feigns indifference, and when Mimi inquires about the attractive newcomer, Marcello replies bitterly: "Her first name is Musetta, her second name is Temptation!" In an access of gay daring, Musetta now sings her famous waltz, *"Quando me'n vo soletta per la via,"* in which she tells how people eye her appreciatively as she passes along the street.

The melody floats lightly and airily along, a perfect expression of Musetta's lighthearted nature. Presently the voices of the other characters join in—Alcindoro trying to stop her; Mimi and Rodolfo blithely exchanging avowals of love; Marcello beginning to feel a revived interest in Musetta; Colline and Schaunard commenting cynically on the girl's behavior. Their varied feelings combine with Musetta's lilting gaiety in an enchanting fusion of voices. Musetta now pretends her shoe hurts, that she can no longer stand, and Alcindoro hurries off to the nearest shoemaker. The moment he disappears from sight, she rushes to Marcello. The reunited lovers kiss, and Musetta takes a chair at Marcello's table. The elaborate supper ordered by Alcindoro is served to the Bohemians along with their own. As distant sounds of music are heard, the crowd runs excitedly across the square to meet the approaching band. Amid the confusion the waiter brings in the bill, the amount of which staggers the Bohemians. Schaunard elaborately searches

45

for his purse. Meanwhile as the band comes nearer and nearer, the people along the street grow more and more excited. Musetta rescues her friends from their plight by instructing the waiter to add the two bills together and present them to Alcindoro when he returns. A huge crowd now rushes in to watch as the patrol, headed by a drum major, marches into view. Musetta, lacking a shoe, hobbles about, till Marcello and Colline lift her to their shoulders and carry her off triumphantly to the rousing cheers of the crowd. Panting heavily, Alcindoro runs in with a new pair of shoes for Musetta, and as he slumps dejectedly into a chair he receives the collective bill.

ACT III

SCENE: *A Gate to the City of Paris (the Barrière d'Enfer).* A bleak, wintry dawn at one of the toll gates to the city. At one side of the snow-blanketed square stands a tavern, over the entrance of which, as a signboard, hangs Marcello's picture of the Red Sea. From within the tavern come sounds of revelry. Outside the gate a motley crowd of scavengers, dairy women, truckmen, and farmers have gathered, demanding to be let through. One of the customs officers warming themselves at a brazier saunters over to the gate and admits the crowd. From the tavern comes the sound of Musetta's voice. Peasant women pass through the gate, declaring their dairy products to the officials. From a side street leading out of the Latin Quarter comes Mimi, shivering with cold. A violent fit of coughing seizes her as she asks one of the officers where she can find Marcello. The officer points to the tavern, and Mimi sends a woman in to call him. Marcello, rushing to her side, greets her warmly with a cry of "Mimi!" "Yes, it is I; I was hoping to find you here," she replies weakly. Marcello tells her that he and Musetta now live at the tavern: he has found sign-painting more profitable than art, and Musetta gives music lessons. Mimi tells Marcello she needs his help desperately, for Rodolfo has grown insanely jealous and the constant bickering has made life unbearable. In a tender duet with Mimi, Marcello expresses his sympathy, and her frequent coughing only deepens his concern.

When Rodolfo comes from the tavern to call Marcello, Mimi slips behind some trees to avoid being seen. Now Mimi overhears Rodolfo complaining to Marcello about their quarreling. Just as he announces his decision to give her up, Mimi reveals her presence by another coughing fit, and Rodolfo rushes to embrace her, his love returning at the sight of her pale, fragile beauty. But she breaks away, and sings a touching little farewell song, in which she says she bears him no ill will, that she will now return to her little dwelling, that she will be grateful if he will wrap up her few things and send them to her.

Meanwhile Marcello has re-entered the tavern and caught Musetta in the act of flirting. This brings on a quarrel, which the couple continue in the street. As Mimi and Rodolfo bid each other good-by—*"Addio, dolce svegliare alla matina"* ("Farewell, a sweet awakening in the morning")— their friends almost reach the point of blows in their quarrel. The music vividly mirrors the difference in temperament of the two women—Mimi, sad, gentle, ailing; Musetta, bold and belligerent—as well as the different response of the two men. "Viper!" "Toad!" Marcello and Musetta shout to each other as they part. "Ah, that our winter night might last forever," laments Mimi. Their resolve to part weakens in the new mood of tenderness, and as they leave the scene Rodolfo sings, *"Ci lascieremo alla stagion fiorita"* —"We'll say good-by when the flowers are in bloom."

ACT IV

SCENE: *In the Attic (as in Act I)*. Rodolfo and Marcello, having again broken off with their mistresses, are back in their garret, living lonely, melancholy lives. Rodolfo is at his table, pretending to write, while Marcello is at his easel, also pretending. They are obviously thinking of something else —of their happy times with Mimi and Musetta. When Rodolfo tells Marcello that he passed Musetta on the street looking happy and prosperous, the painter feigns lack of interest. In friendly revenge, he tells Rodolfo he has seen Mimi riding in a sumptuous carriage, looking like a duchess. Rodolfo tries, unsuccessfully, to conceal his emotions, but a renewed attempt to work proves futile. While Rodolfo's back is turned, Marcello takes a bunch of ribbons from his pocket and kisses them. There is no doubt whose ribbons they are. Rodolfo, throwing down his pen, muses on his past happiness. "Oh, Mimi, you left and never returned" (*"Ah, Mimi, tu più"*), he sings; "O beautiful bygone days; O vanished youth." Marcello joins in reminiscently, wondering why his brush, instead of obeying his will, paints the dark eyes and red lips of Musetta.

Their mood brightens momentarily as Colline and Schaunard enter with a scant supply of food. With mock solemnity the friends apply themselves to the meager repast as if it were a great feast. When a dance is proposed, Rodolfo and Marcello begin a quadrille, which is quickly cut short by Colline and Schaunard, who engage in a fierce mock duel with fire tongs and poker. The dancers encircle the duelists, and just as the festive mood reaches its height, Musetta bursts in. She brings sad news: Mimi, who is with her, is desperately ill. The friends help Mimi into the room and place her tenderly on Rodolfo's bed. Again Rodolfo and Mimi are in each other's arms as past quarrels are forgotten. When Musetta asks the men to give Mimi some food, they confess gloomily there is none in the house, not even coffee. Mimi asks for a muff and Rodolfo begins rubbing her hands, which are stiff with cold. Musetta gives her earrings to Marcello, telling him to sell them to buy medicine and summon a doctor. Then, remembering Mimi's request, she goes to get her own muff. Spurred by Musetta's example, Colline resolves to sell his beloved overcoat to make some purchases for Mimi. In a pathetic song he bids farewell to the coat, and departs with Schaunard to find a buyer. Rodolfo and Mimi are now alone. Faintly her voice is heard: "Have they gone? I pretended to be sleeping so that I could be with you. There is so much to say."

The lovers unite their voices in a duet of poignant beauty as they recall the days spent together, of the first time they met, of how she told him her name was Mimi. Reminiscent strains of melody are spun by the orchestra as the couple dwell on their attic romance. Mimi wants to know if Rodolfo still thinks her beautiful. "Like dawn itself!" he exclaims ardently. Suddenly Mimi, coughing and choking, sinks back in a faint. Rodolfo cries out in alarm, as Schaunard enters and asks excitedly what has happened. Mimi, reviving, smiles wanly and assures them everything is all right. Musetta and Marcello enter quietly, bringing a muff and some medicine. Mimi eagerly seizes the muff, which Musetta insists Rodolfo has purchased for her. Growing weaker and weaker, Mimi at last falls asleep—or, so it seems. Marcello heats the medicine; the other men whisper together, and Musetta begins to pray. Rodolfo has fresh hope, now that Mimi is sleeping so peacefully. Schaunard tiptoes over to the bed. Mimi is not asleep—she is dead! Shaken, he whispers the news to Marcello. Rodolfo, having covered the window to keep out the light of dawn, notes the sudden change in his friends at the other end of the room. As he realizes the truth, the orchestra pounds out fortissimo chords full of tragic impact. Musetta kneels at the foot of the bed, Schaunard sinks into a chair, Colline stands rooted to one spot, dazed, while Marcello turns away to hide his grief. Rodolfo rushes across the room, flings himself on Mimi's bed, lifts her up, and sobs brokenly, "Mimi! . . . Mimi! . . . Mimi!"

THE RCA-VICTOR RECORDS
(Sung in Italian unless otherwise noted)

COMPLETE RECORDING: *Beniamino Gigli, Tenor; Licia Albanese, Soprano; Tatiana Menotti, Soprano; Afro Poli, Baritone; Duilio Baronti, Bass; Aristide Baracchi, Baritone; Carlo Scattola, Bass; Nello Palai, Tenor; with Chorus and Orchestra of La Scala, Milan, Umberto Berrettoni, Cond.*
DMC-107 (DM-518) (Vol. 1)
(12727-12733) 7-12″
(DM-519) (Vol. 2)
(12734-12739) 6-12″
MC-107 (M-518) (Vol. 1)
(12385-12391)
(M-519) (Vol. 2)
(12392-12397)

THE HEART OF "LA BOHÈME": *Beniamino Gigli, Tenor; Licia Albanese, Soprano; Tatiana Menotti, Soprano; Afro Poli, Baritone; Duilio Baronti, Bass, etc.; with Chorus and Orchestra of La Scala, Milan, Umberto Berrettoni, Cond.*
DM-980 (11-8689-11-8693) 5-12″
M-980 (11-8684-11-8688)

ACT I

RACCONTO DI RODOLFO—CHE GELIDA MANINA (Rudolph's Narrative—Your Tiny Hand Is Frozen): *Jussi Bjoerling, Tenor, with Orch.* 12039, 12″
(In Album M-633) 15820, 12″

JUSSI BJOERLING AS RODOLFO

ACT II

VALZER DI MUSETTA (Musetta's Waltz):
Lucrezia Bori, Soprano, with Orch.
1333, 10″

ACT III

ADDIO DI MIMI (Mimi's Farewell): *Dorothy Kirsten, Soprano, with Orch.*
11-9694, 12″
QUARTET—ADDIO, DOLCE SVEGLIARE (Farewell, Sweet Love): *Enrico Caruso, Tenor; Geraldine Farrar, Soprano; Gina Viafora, Soprano; Antonio Scotti, Baritone; with Orch.*
16-5001, 12″
(Acoustical Recording)
(In Album M-953)

MI CHIAMANO MIMI (My Name Is Mimi):
Grace Moore, Soprano, with Orch.
17189, 12″
Dorothy Kirsten, Soprano, with Orch.
11-9694, 12″
Lucrezia Bori, Soprano, with Orch.
14206, 12″
(In Album M-329) 6790, 12″
O SOAVE FANCIULLA (O Lovely Maiden):
Jussi Bjoerling, Tenor; Hjoerdis Schymberg, Soprano; with Orch.
11-8440, 12″

R. Strohmeyer
LICIA ALBANESE AS MIMI

ACT IV

O MIMI, TU PIÙ (Ah, Mimi, False One!):
Beniamino Gigli, Tenor; Giuseppe de Luca, Baritone; with Orch. 8069, 12″
Jan Peerce, Tenor; Leonard Warren, Baritone; with Orch. 11-9767, 12″
(In Album M-1156)
John McCormack, Tenor; Mario Sammarco, Baritone; with Orch.
(Acoustical Recording) 15-1009, 12″
DEATH SCENE—SONO ANDATI (Have They Gone?); O DIO, MIMI (O God! Mimi!): *Lucrezia Bori, Soprano; Tito Schipa, Tenor; with Orch.*
8068, 12″

JARMILA NOVOTNA AS MIMI

ACT I, SCENE 3—ZÜRICH STATE THEATER PRODUCTION

Boris Godunov

OPERA IN four acts (now given in three). Music by Modest Moussorgsky. Libretto, after
Pushkin and Karamzin, by the composer. First uncut performance on February 8, 1874,
at the Maryinsky Theater (Imperial Opera House), St. Petersburg. First performance
in the United States (in Italian), March 19, 1913, at the Metropolitan Opera House,
New York, with Arturo Toscanini conducting and a cast headed by Adamo Didur
(Boris), Louise Homer (Marina), and Paul Althouse (Dmitri). On December 9, 1921,
Feodor Chaliapin, singing in Russian while the rest of the cast used Italian, presented
his overpowering portrayal of Boris for the first time at the Metropolitan.

Boris Godunov is the acknowledged masterpiece of a strange, erratic genius whom
many regard as the greatest name in Russian music. Poor, sickly, addicted to drink and
drugs, and compelled to work at distasteful tasks, Moussorgsky somehow managed to
leave the world a legacy of beauty and power. Undisciplined in many ways, Moussorgsky
left much of his work incomplete and amorphous. Yet, he was a man of emphatic principles in art and adhered to an unwavering ideal of truth and sincerity. Despite the
pressure of tradition and politics, he pursued his path toward a new naturalism and
honesty in music. In Boris Godunov he chose a theme frowned upon by the authorities
and employed a style flouted by the academicians. In making the Russian people the
true protagonist of Boris Godunov, Moussorgsky expounded a democratic creed, and in
using a technique of realism he alienated the champions of a strict classicism. Thus,
Boris Godunov is not only the greatest of "national" music dramas but also the fiery
manifesto of a new operatic order.

Boris Godunov at first seems nothing but a sequence of episodes, a historical panel
drawn from a tangled epoch in Russian history. Actually there is remarkable unity. The
continuity is deep and psychological, linking the destiny of a man and a nation in a

wondrous polyphony of idea. Moussorgsky ruled out irrelevances. For standard contrivances like set arias and vocal display one must look elsewhere. The melodic line is governed not by accepted form and pattern, but by the expressive needs of the moment, the mood and emotional crisis of a situation. Since the people dominate the drama the choral outbursts are prominent and powerful. And the orchestra here, as in Wagner, becomes an integral part of the fabric, heightening atmosphere, accenting feeling, setting a scene pictorially and emotionally. What makes *Boris Godunov* national becomes equally apparent in the shape of the melodies, the occasional use of folk motives, the modal devices of Russian liturgy. A Russian folk song weaves through the massive web of the "Coronation Scene," and for local color Moussorgsky even resorts to authentic Polish dance rhythms in the scenes set in Poland. Nor does Moussorgsky overlook the effect of recurring themes in his delineative scheme.

After Moussorgsky's death, Rimsky-Korsakov drastically revised and reorchestrated *Boris Godunov*. It was then generally agreed the opera was too long and in places too crude. Rimsky deleted whole scenes, altered passages, smoothed out the rugged orchestration. In a word, he brought order where he thought he found disorder, brilliance where there was harshness, glitter where there was rawness. Such was the version regularly used from then on, in and outside Russia. At length the Moussorgsky original was divulged to the world, and startling discrepancies were noted. Rimsky had done a supreme job of polishing, there was no doubt. But in his excessive zeal he had almost stifled the daring and freshness of Moussorgsky's harmonies and colors. A heated controversy arose. Rimsky's supporters insisted on the superior merits of the revised version. Their opponents flailed Rimsky as a bungler and vandal, and held out for the untampered original, in all its jagged, corrosive, even primitive power. Recently Dmitri Shostakovich, often referred to as composer laureate of the Soviet Union, revised the opera afresh, this time strictly and avowedly in keeping with Moussorgsky's ideas. Needless to say, Rimsky's revision, whatever its misdemeanors, was the conscientious act of a friend and admirer of that troubled genius who gave the Russian people a collective voice that was heard around the world.

It should be noted that scholars have recently acquitted the historic Boris Godunov of the murder which motivates the central tragedy of the opera. Moussorgsky, like the poet Pushkin and the historian Karamzin, accepted Boris' guilt as an undisputed fact.

R. F. Schmiedt, Hamburg   ACT II, SCENE 2—HAMBURG PRODUCTION

CHARACTERS

BORIS GODUNOV	*Bass*	PIMENN, *a monk and chronicler*	*Bass*
XENIA, *his daughter*	*Soprano*	STCHELKALOV, *secretary of the*	
FEODOR, *his son*	*Mezzo-soprano*	*Duma*	*Baritone*
MARINA, *daughter of the*		INNKEEPER'S WIFE	*Mezzo-soprano*
Voyevode of Sandomir	*Mezzo-soprano*		
PRINCE SHUISKY	*Tenor*	POLICE OFFICIAL	*Bass*
GREGORY, *a novice, afterwards*		RANGONI, *a Jesuit monk*	*Baritone*
the Pretender Dmitri	*Tenor*	A NURSE	*Mezzo-soprano*
VARLAAM and MISSAIL,			
vagabond monks	*Bass and Tenor*	AN IDIOT	*Tenor*

TWO JESUITS, CHORUS OF BOYARS AND PEOPLE, ETC.

The action takes place in Russia and Poland, 1598–1605

ACT I

Dmitri, younger brother and only heir of Tsar Feodor, has been assassinated at the instigation of Boris Godunov, one of the Tsar's privy councilors. When Feodor himself dies, Boris cleverly masks his royal ambitions by retiring to the Novodievich monastery near Moscow. Secretly, however, he has given instructions to herd the people into the square before the monastery and force them to demonstrate in favor of himself as their next Tsar.

SCENE 1: *A Public Square Before the Novodievich Monastery Near Moscow.* After a brief orchestral prelude built on a recognizably Russian theme, the curtain rises. A crowd, goaded by police officers, is kneeling before the monastery, imploring Boris to accept the crown. "Why do you abandon us? Have mercy upon us, O Father!" they chant in a ringing appeal. Stchelkalov, secretary of the Duma, emerging from the monastery, silences the populace by announcing gravely that Boris remains unyielding. He urges them to beseech God to intercede for the good of Russia. With the glow of the setting sun falling across the square, a band of chanting pilgrims is heard in the distance. As the pilgrims approach and begin to distribute amulets, they, too, lift their voices in entreaty, urging more and more prayer. Then they withdraw, and with them their song, "Great Is Your Glory," dies away in distant whispers.

SCENE 2: *A Cell in the Monastery of the Miracles.* Pimenn, an old monk and chronicler, is bent over his monastic tome, inscribing the dire events of recent years. Gregory, a novice, asleep on a cot, suddenly wakes from a nightmare. Pimenn counsels prayer to the novice, and as he goes on to narrate the murder of Dmitri, the novice listens breathlessly. When he learns that the slain boy was his own age, a sudden thought crosses his mind. Pimenn leaves, and Gregory utters his thought: he will spread the report that Dmitri

FEODOR CHALIAPIN AS BORIS

53

R. Strohmeyer   ACT I, SCENE 1—SAN FRANCISCO OPERA PRODUCTION

still lives! Thus, Gregory, the false Dmitri, will become Tsar of Russia, avenge the boy's death, and outwit the assassin usurping the throne.

SCENE 3: *The Great Square Between the Cathedral of the Assumption and That of the Archangels in Moscow.* The curtain rises on a brilliant scene, rich and picturesque in color, sound, and movement. Giant bells are pealing. In the background, gleaming brightly, are the cathedral domes. The square is thronged with festively garbed people. Gay-colored banners flutter among them. Against this picture the wealthy boyars begin their stately procession toward the Cathedral of the Assumption, and, rising in their midst, is the stately figure of Boris, the new Tsar. From the portico of the Cathedral Prince Shuisky shouts, "Long live Tsar Boris!" and the people take up the cry in a burst of acclamation, "Glory to Tsar Boris!" In an eloquent address, Boris assures the people that though he will always have their cause and Russia's at heart, he is yielding to their will with great sadness. Doubts and fears for Russia and himself weigh upon his mind, he confesses, and now, invoking the aid of God, he asks the people to join with him in a prayer.

ACT II

SCENE 1: *An Inn at the Lithuanian Border.* Spurred by his mad ambition, Gregory has fled the monastery. With two companions he arrives before an inn at the Lithuanian border. Varlaam and Missail, clad in monkish robes, enter first, startling the innkeeper's wife, who has been singing a tender, folk-like melody. Gregory, a farm boy's clothes replacing his monastic garb, follows the friars into the inn. The others explain that they met Gregory on the road and that he is anxious to cross the border into Lithuania. Bottle in

R. Strohmeyer

ACT I, SCENE 3—SAN FRANCISCO OPERA PRODUCTION

hand, Varlaam, a boisterous and worldly soul, now sings a lively drinking song, a song rich in earthy humor and grim realism, with a sweeping *élan* that is peculiarly Russian. With fiendish glee it tells of the great Ivan the Terrible, how he once smashed a rebellion of the Tartars of Kazan by exploding mines in their midst. His song completed, Varlaam falls into a drunken sleep. Gregory's plan is to cross the frontier and, if his luck holds, to raise an army in Poland. But government officials, apprized of his flight, have warned the border patrol. Soldiers now enter the inn and eye the odd trio with suspicion. Gregory gives out the description of the fugitive from an officer's warrant, but he rephrases the wording to describe Varlaam. In the confusion following Varlaam's slowly spelled-out reading of the warrant, Gregory makes his getaway through a window.

SCENE 2: *The Tsar's Apartment in the Kremlin.* Boris' children, Feodor and Xenia, are together with their old nurse. Xenia is grieving over the death of her lover. To distract her, the nurse first sings a simple children's song, and then begins a game with handclapping obbligatos, in which Feodor, raising his head from a huge map of Russia he is studying, joins. The game stops abruptly as Boris enters. Observing the map which Feodor had been poring over, he affirms proudly that some day this knowledge will be of use to him. When the children have left, his face darkens as he muses on the future, and he delivers a magnificent monologue in which he reveals the great stress he is under. The greatest power is now his, yet he never knows peace of mind. Six long years he has been Tsar, and still the same haunting memory obsesses him. He cannot escape the vision of the murdered Dmitri;

day and night it plagues him. There is a frenzied rise of horror as Boris implores God to have mercy on him.

When the monologue ends, Prince Shuisky is admitted into the chamber and brings more bad news. A wild rumor is circulating that the slain Dmitri is still alive and open rebellion is brewing among the people. Shuisky tells the shaken Tsar that the Poles will back the Pretender, that he must mobilize his forces at once. Iago-like in his treachery, Shuisky now plays on Boris' superstitious nature. Possibly a miracle has come to pass, he suggests. Perhaps this is no false Dmitri, but the real one, the Dmitri whose body, he now remembers, showed no signs of decay several days after his death. Boris is frantic with a ghastly sense of certainty. Might not a murdered child rise from his grave to avenge the evildoer? When Shuisky departs, Boris falls back in his chair, shattered by an agony of remorse and terror. At this point the orchestra sets up a sinister throb, as of the ominous march of fate, measured in a relentless clocklike beat. Tortured by the burning memory of his deed, Boris shrinks back in horror as Dmitri's apparition looms before his deluded senses. Boris is at the peak of his wild seizure, his conscience searing him like a brand. Exhausted and broken, he sinks to his knees, praying, "God have mercy on the guilty soul of Boris!"

SCENE 3: *The Garden of a Polish Palace.* The Jesuit priest Rangoni has persuaded Marina, the daughter of a Polish nobleman, to serve her country by helping the false Dmitri, who is in love with her, to seize the throne of Russia. As Gregory waits for Marina among the deep shadows of her palace garden, the festive sounds of a banquet reach him from inside the palace. The guests stream out into the garden, and the orchestra strikes up a courtly but vivacious polonaise. As the ranks form and the stately, swaying patterns of the polonaise take shape, the guests sing: "Forward against Moscow . . . to vic-

R. Strohmeyer   ACT IV, SCENE 1—SAN FRANCISCO OPERA PRODUCTION

tory!" The dance ends, and as the music fades away, the guests re-enter the palace. Marina now appears. She rushes to Dmitri, and they join in a beautiful duet. Marina begins to taunt Dmitri gently on his lack of ambition, soon adding scorn to her taunts. Then she plays softly on his love for her, and in a great flourish Dmitri finally succumbs. He will himself lead the attack against Moscow; he will seize the throne from the usurper Boris; he will make Marina his queen! With its seductive mazurka rhythm, the music of this duet is a unique blend of romantic fervor and national color.

ACT III

SCENE 1: *In the Forest of Kromy*. Peasants and vagabonds drag in a boyar who has fallen into their hands. He is bound and gagged, and the crowd gathers around him in the clearing and begins to heap taunts and insults upon him. As they raise their voices in unison, their actions become clear; they are cursing Tsar Boris, the boyars who support him, and all they stand for. "Glory to this great boyar and to his Tsar Boris!" they chant in mock hallelujah. A village fool approaches, followed by a troop of jeering children. The simpleton seats himself on a rock, and, swaying idiotically, sings a plaintive song which is soon lost in the shrill mockery of the children, "Hail to our great Fool!" A fresh note of rebellion is added as Varlaam and Missail are heard some distance off, voicing a chantlike tirade at the cruel Boris. This provokes the crowd to more excited utterance, and we hear a stupendous chorus attesting loyalty to Dmitri and a thirst for revenge. "Death to the regicide!" the cry rings out. Two luckless Jesuits, wandering in at this point, join in hymning Dmitri, this time in Latin, *"Domine, salvum fac Regem Demetrium Moscoviae, Regem omnis Russiae!"* ("God save Dmitri, King of Moscow! King of all Russia!") Neither the people nor the friars, however, seek interference from Rome. The two Jesuits are seized, bound, and led off

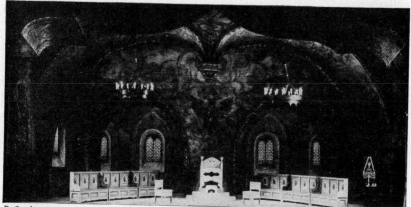

R. Strohmeyer

ACT IV, SCENE 2—SAN FRANCISCO OPERA PRODUCTION

to be hanged. Martial music is heard as troops file past the clearing, and the crowd sets up a fervid cheer. Dmitri—the false Dmitri—appears. "Glory unto our lawful Tsar!" the peasants shout. As he rides by, the Pretender promises them protection from oppression. In jubilant spirits, the crowd follows him into the forest. It is now snowing. The idiot, alone in the gathering dusk, observes a red glow in the distance, an indication that the rebels have already begun their work. Simply, yet with profound tragic import, he mourns the grievous state of Russia's people and the great calamities still to come:

> *The foe will come and blood will flow;*
> *Let thy tears flow, poor, starving people!*

SCENE 2: *In the Palace of the Kremlin.* The Duma is discussing measures to be taken against the Pretender Dmitri and the rebellious peasantry. Shuisky tells the assembled nobles of the secret agony of Tsar Boris which he has witnessed, but this only adds to their confusion, for Shuisky's insinuation is clear to all. The excited talk is cut short by the sudden entrance of Boris. There is a deathlike silence, as the self-tortured Tsar, muttering incoherent denials of guilt, stalks through the hall to the throne. As he seats himself, he momentarily regains his majestic calm. Shuisky begs Boris to grant audience to an aged monk who waits outside. In a forlorn hope that this man of God may bring peace to his tormented soul, Boris assents. Pimenn, the old monastic chronicler, enters and tells a strange story. In the dead of night an old shepherd who had long been blind had come to the monastery to report a marvelous experience: a childlike voice had counseled him in a dream to kneel in prayer at the tomb of the slain Dmitri. This the shepherd had done, and a miracle had happened! He had been cured of his blindness! Boris listens with growing horror and finally gives a wild shriek of terror and collapses.

When Boris regains his strength, he asks to be left alone with his son. And to Feodor he addresses a farewell full of agony and pathos, rising at times to poignant tenderness. "Farewell, my son," he sings; it would be wiser for Feodor not to inquire how his father had gained the throne; let him rule justly and fearlessly, and defend their faith. With fatherly solicitude Boris asks him to watch over their beloved Xenia, and with his hands resting on the boy's head, he prays God for forgiveness.

The solemn tolling of bells is heard as the voices of the people outside the palace rise in prayer for the soul of their sovereign. In musical intensity and panoramic breadth this final scene has no equal in opera. Russian choral music reaches its summit here. Against it surges the growing terror and agony of the haunted Tsar, reaching a climax of stupendous power. Boris, growing ever weaker, cries out, "Lord, grant Thy mercy . . . forgive this my deed . . . O death!" Priests join the nobles in a funereal procession through the hall. Boris rises in a final access of majesty, exclaiming: "Wait! I am still your Tsar!" Then, clutching at his heart, he sinks into a chair, writhing in a powerful death agony. The words, "God, have mercy!" come from his trembling lips; then summoning up his remaining strength, he points to his son and cries: "Behold your new Tsar!" One last spasm of a giant anguish, a cry of "Mercy!" and death at last brings him peace as the nobles stand by murmuring, heads bowed as if in prayer.

ALEXANDER KIPNIS AS BORIS

THE RCA-VICTOR RECORDS
(Sung in Russian unless otherwise noted)

RECORDRAMA: *Alexander Kipnis, Bass; Ilya Tamarin, Tenor; with Chorus and Orchestra, Robert Shaw, Choral Director; Nicolai Berezowsky, Cond.* DM-1000 (11-8768-11-8772), 5-12"
M-1000 (11-8763-11-8767)

SYMPHONIC SYNTHESIS (arr. Stokowski): *Leopold Stokowski and the Philadelphia Orchestra*
DM-391 (16542-16544), 3-12"
M-391 (14546-14548)

PROLOGUE—SCENE II

CORONATION SCENE: *Feodor Chaliapin, Bass, with Chorus and Orch. Chaliapin in Russian, Chorus in Italian*
11485, 12"

Luboshutz and Nemenoff (Duo Pianists)
2084, 10"

ACT I—SCENE II

COME NOW, COMRADES, FILL UP YOUR GLASS: *Alexander Kipnis, Bass, with Orch.* 11-9285, 12"
(In Album M-1073)

ACT II

MONOLOGUE—I HAVE ATTAINED THE HIGHEST POWER; CLOCK SCENE—AH! I AM SUFFOCATING: *Feodor Chaliapin, Bass, with Orch.* 14517, 12"

ACT III—SCENE II

FAREWELL, MY SON; I AM DYING; DEATH OF BORIS—HARK! THE PASSING BELL!: *Alexander Kipnis, Bass, with Orch.* 11-8925, 12"
Feodor Chaliapin, Bass, with Orch.
15177, 12"
6724, 12"

59

Cambridge — Wonderful Opera — Grandpa Bailey was lead-boy in march scene to bull-fight with Caruso as Don Jose —

Castagneri   ACT I—THE PUBLIC SQUARE IN SEVILLE

Carmen

OPERA IN four acts. Music by Georges Bizet. Libretto by Henri Meilhac and Ludovic Halévy, based on the novel of Prosper Merimée. World *première* at the Opéra-Comique, Paris, March 3, 1875. First American performance, Academy of Music, New York, October 23, 1878 (in Italian). In English it was given at Haverly's Fifth Avenue Theater, March 2, 1881. The opera entered the repertory of the Metropolitan on January 9, 1884, in Italian.

Bizet died on June 3, 1875, the night of the opera's twenty-third performance in ninety days at the Opéra-Comique, yet it has been suggested that heartbreak over its failure brought about his untimely demise. This theory is further refuted by the fact that in the same season fifty performances were given the work. Actually, although the ultrarefined sensibilities of the Parisian critics of the 1870's were somewhat stunned by the opera's rather stark realism for those days, the public, for its part, found the piece interesting and even exciting. By the time eleven years had passed, *Carmen* boasted its five hundredth showing at the Opéra-Comique, on October 23, 1891; its thousandth performance took place there thirteen years later, on December 23, 1904, and its twenty-five hundredth performance occurred in June, 1947.

On the basis of *Carmen*, Bizet has come to be ranked among the greatest of operatic composers. Though successful in winning the famous Prix de Rome at the Paris Conservatory, where he studied, he cannot be said to have had a financially profitable career. He was always hard pressed for funds, and, like Wagner, he was once compelled to waste valuable time in making cornet arrangements of popular tunes. Nevertheless, his talents won recognition among fellow musicians, including Liszt, who, it seems, was always able to recognize genius.

. In *Carmen* Bizet found a perfect subject for displaying his masterly ability in portraying local color musically—an ability that he had also revealed in *Les pêcheurs de perles*, and the glowing incidental music to Daudet's drama, *L'Arlésienne*. Yet in *Carmen*, despite his talent for local color, he never pauses to paint pretty though unessential tone pictures. Through all the lively scenes and the gay, reckless melodies that constitute a suitable and well-nigh indispensable background for the plot, one

60

feels a sense of foreboding, of impending disaster, that grows in intensity until the final curtain. Only a master of musical dramatics would be able to create with his sure, deft touches this steady crescendo of emotion.

Carmen is, moreover, one of the few operas that win nearly universal approval. The man in the street whistles and loves its melodies; the operagoer is thrilled by its swiftly moving scenes and tensely emotional music; the opera star is enthusiastic over its possibilities for singing and acting; the dramatic critic commends its carefully delineated characterizations; the musician admires its well-conceived and masterfully handled musical numbers, its thorough musicianship and excellently wrought orchestration.

On a canvas crowded with movement and colorful personalities, Carmen is the dominating figure. She does not live according to the conventions of the village-bred Micaëla; a life of that sort is entirely unknown to her. Her milieu has always been that of smugglers, bandits, and outlaws, with whom wildness and audacity are the true "conventions." They are gamblers who play with life and liberty, who stake a fat purse against a bloody death, who know no greater disgrace than to fail to pay their own strange debts of honor. If these are conventions, then Carmen is as conventional as the rest. She, too, is a gambler, taking gamblers' chances with what cards are dealt her. Her cards are her own audacious beauty, her wild coquetry, the dangerous fires of human passion; against the prize—the hearts of men—she can stake only herself. If we do not accept this as the basic psychology of Carmen's nature, the last act of the opera becomes meaningless. Why should she face Don José alone when she might have gone into the bull ring, or commanded a bodyguard of her own friends? She knows that Don José, a ruined man, is desperate and fearless when aroused. Yet she chooses to stay deliberately. According to gypsy law, she is his until the union is broken by mutual consent. Her "gamble" has been that he will weary of her when she wearies of him; and she has lost. Well, she will pay. None can accuse her of fear or falsehood. Thus conforming to gypsy convention, she stands alone and "faces her man."

This ardent drama, skillfully evolved from Prosper Merimée's story, is portrayed with felicity and distinction in Bizet's music—music in which every scene, every character, is clearly reflected. The "Fate" motive which sounds so ominously just before the brilliant scene of the first act is echoed again and again through the score, changing its form in a dozen ways. In the card scene it flickers through and through, like an angry tongue of flame in a bank of smoke. At the end, when the tragedy is done, it blazes forth luridly. Of this so-called "Fate" motive a story of supposed Oriental origin is told: when, according to Mohammedan tradition, Satan was cast from Paradise, he remembered only one strain of the music he had heard there. This, known as "Asbein," or the "Devil's Strain," Bizet used with fine symbolic as well as perfect musical fitness.

CHARACTERS

DON JOSÉ, *a brigadier*	*Tenor*	LE REMENDADO	*Tenor*
ESCAMILLO, *a toreador*	*Baritone*	MICAËLA, *a peasant girl*	*Soprano*
ZUNIGA, *a captain*	*Bass*	FRASQUITA ⎱ gypsies,	*Soprano*
MORALÈS, *a brigadier*	*Baritone*	MERCÉDÈS ⎰ *friends of Carmen*	*Soprano*
LE DANCAIRE	*Tenor*	CARMEN, *a cigarette girl, and a gypsy*	*Mezzo-soprano*

AN INNKEEPER, GUIDE, OFFICER, DRAGOONS, CIGARETTE GIRLS, GYPSIES, SMUGGLERS

The action takes place at Seville, Spain, about 1820

The Prelude brings before us, with a sudden stir of gay commotion, a vivid picture of the colorful crowd that we will see pouring into the ring at Seville, in the last act. Magnificent, dark Spanish beauties with their lace mantillas and heavily embroidered silken garments . . . their escorts in gala attire, even more brilliant . . . the excitement of the bull fight that is about to take place. This high-spirited music is interrupted, for a time, by the proud, steady beat of the world-famous "Toreador Song," gorgeous in its orchestral version.

For a moment the orchestra sounds the "Fate" motive, ominously—then the curtain rises on

ACT I

SCENE: *A Square in Seville*. It is the noon hour and the square is filled with townspeople, girls who work in the adjoining cigarette factory, and soldiers from the near-by guardhouse. Through this scene of activity comes a simple peasant girl. She tells the soldiers she is hunting for a corporal named José. He will not be there till the time the guard changes, they say; then, beginning to flirt, they ask her to remain till José comes. She runs away like a timid animal that has been frightened.

An intriguing little march tune is heard, played by fifes and trumpets, at first distant, then growing nearer. It is the change of guard that arrives, preceded by a troop of street urchins imitating the step of the dragoons who follow armed with their lances. Captain Zuniga and Corporal José are among them. The urchins and grownups watch with excited admiration the military ceremony of changing guard.

When that is over, some of the soldiers gather around Corporal José and jokingly tell him of the fair-haired girl who asked for him. "Micaëla," he explains, then adds, "I love her." Indeed, there are some beauties among the girls who have been watching the guard change, but José has not given them one glance. Now he sits astride a chair, preoccupied in trying to join the links of a small chain that has broken.

The bell of the cigarette factory strikes the hour for work, and the cigarette girls wedge through the crowd toward the factory gates, loitering on the way to make eyes at the soldiers and young men who lounge around the square. The languorous calm of the noon hour and the coquettish charm of these Spanish girls are beautifully pictured in the music.

Suddenly there is a stir among the people, the "Fate" motive is heard in the orchestra, and a shout goes up, "Carmen!" A girl darts through the way that the crowd makes for her. "Love you?" she calls insolently to the men who swarm around her with their attention. "Perhaps tomorrow, but not now!" Then, to the swaying, insinuating rhythm of a habañera, she begins to sing, an enticing gleam in her eyes.

While singing, she glances often at José, and many times dances so near that she almost touches him; moreover, by insinuating inflections of her voice she seeks to win his attention. Apparently unaware of her presence, perhaps fortified against her attractions by thoughts of Micaëla, the handsome soldier is occupied busily, almost obstinately, with the broken chain.

Geoffrey Landesman   ACT I—CLEVELAND ORCHESTRA PRODUCTION

"But if I love you, beware!" she sings, and tearing a blood-red flower from her bodice, she throws it boldly at him. He springs to his feet, seemingly about to rush madly at her. Instead he meets the look in her eyes and stands petrified on the spot. Carmen, with a cold, jeering laugh and a toss of the head, runs into the factory, followed by the other cigarette girls.

José stoops hesitatingly, as if against his will, and picks up the flower lying at his feet. He presses it to his nostrils, inhaling its mysterious perfume in a long, enchanted breath. Then, as if unconscious, he thrusts the flower under his blouse, over his heart.

At this very instant, Micaëla returns and runs to José with exclamations of joy. She brings news from home, and money from his mother's savings. His mother has also sent him a kiss. This, too, Micaëla delivers, but most shyly and modestly. She cannot remain long, but her coming brings a welcome change of thought. José exclaims to himself, "Who knows of what a demon I was nearly a prey!" Alarmed at hearing this, Micaëla asks what the peril may be. He replies that it is nothing, and they sing a nostalgic duet.

When Micaëla has gone, he takes Carmen's flower from under his blouse and is about to throw it away. Just then there are screams of terror in the cigarette factory, and a minute later the square is crowded with frightened girls, soldiers, and townspeople. From the agitated exclamations of the cigarette girls it is learned that Carmen has quarreled with one of them and stabbed her with a knife. The soldiers drive away the crowd, and Carmen is brought out and questioned. She answers insolently with a gay "Tra la la la" in a most flirtatious manner.

The officer loses patience at her conduct, orders her hands tied behind her back, and enters the guardhouse to write a warrant.

José is left alone to guard Carmen. Pacing back and forth across the square, he seems to be avoiding her. "Where is the flower I threw at you?" she coquettishly asks. Then she begins softly to sing the song known as the "*Seguidilla*," in which she tells him they will meet at the tavern of Lillas Pastia, near the wall of Seville.

"Keep still!" interrupts José, but Carmen continues unabashed, and the tormented dragoon knows that she is making the vulgarest of love to him, for purposes of her own; yet he cannot resist her beauty and her song. She murmurs to him insinuatingly, and turns, holding toward him her bound wrists. He loosens the knot quickly, but leaves the rope so that it still appears to be tied.

A minute later the captain comes from the guardhouse with a warrant for Carmen; following him are the soldiers; and the crowd, drawn by curiosity, fills the square. The captain orders José to take Carmen to prison. She is placed between two dragoons, and under the command of José the party starts. As they reach some steps at the back of the square, Carmen quickly frees her hands, pushes aside the soldiers, and, before they realize what has happened, dashes away, amid the gleeful shouts of the onlookers.

ACT II

SCENE: *The Tavern of Lillas Pastia.* The second act is preceded by a brief orchestral introduction, the steady-rhythmed music of the dragoons of Alcalá. At the inn of Lillas Pastia, gypsy smugglers from the mountains, joined by some officers and soldiers, have been having a feast. Now, the table in confusion, some of them sit back to smoke, others play the guitar, while a few begin to dance. Carmen sits watching the dancers, heedless of the attentions of Zuniga; then, suddenly, she rises and begins a song of gypsy life, whose measures increase speed, as Frasquita and Mercédès join in; and, finally, with the ballet doing a gypsy dance, the scene takes on a roistering, swirling abandon.

The energetic, forward-moving rhythm, the piquant lilt of the melody, the surprising colors of the harmony, and the delicacy of the orchestration are made more vivid by the impetuous clashing of the gypsies' tambourines. Carmen joins the dance, which grows faster and more impulsive.

It is about time for the inn to close, and while all are hurriedly preparing to leave, one of the officers conveys to Carmen the valuable information that the handsome young corporal, who has been under arrest since the time he allowed her to escape, has just been released from prison.

Suddenly, from outside come shouts, "Long live the toreador! Hail Escamillo!" The famous bullfighter, victor of the ring at Granada, enters

LAWRENCE TIBBETT AS THE TOREADOR

65

and, joining in their toast, sings a fiery tale of the bullfight, a glowing description of quick action, reckless daring, bloodshed, shouts of a great crowd ... and love, the "Toreador Song." The melody, a rousing delineation of all this, also reveals to us, more forcibly than words, Escamillo's character, brave to the point of recklessness, self-confident, and boastful.

Escamillo's gay, carefree manner, his fame, his flashing uniform, all impress Carmen greatly. And she, too, seems to strike his fancy. But her heart is still set on José.

The toreador departs, followed by the excited, cheering crowd. Zuniga tries to induce Carmen to go with him, but she refuses. He says he'll come back later. It is growing late, and the innkeeper again begins to close up, and Carmen remains with her gypsy girl friends, Frasquita and Mercédès. Two of the smugglers approach them. They need the help of the girls in "vamping" the coast guard into forgetting duty. In a rollicking quintet they spontaneously express their amusement at the idea.

The men are anxious for the girls to start at once, but Carmen wishes to wait; she confesses she expects José, and, as luck would have it, his voice is heard in the distance, singing a military air, the theme of the interlude before this act. The gypsies peer through the shutter and admire his appearance, suggesting that Carmen persuade him to join their band. Enthusiastic over this idea, she hurries them from the room just before José enters.

Castagneri   ACT II—THE INN OF LILLAS PASTIA

Castagneri
ACT III—THE SMUGGLERS' MEETING PLACE

She welcomes him with joy, then at once makes him jealous by telling him that Moralès and the officers made her dance for them. But now she will dance for José alone.

She begins to dance, to an odd little tune of her own composing and the clicking of her own castanets. José is absorbed in her motions. From the distance a bugle call is heard . . . "retreat," summoning all soldiers back to quarters. José stops the dance; he must go. Carmen laughs at the idea and resumes her dance. The sound of the bugle call draws nearer, passes by, and fades away in the distance, mingling with the melody of Carmen's song. Again, with an effort, José tears himself away from the fascination of her actions. "You don't understand," he cries, "I have to go back to quarters."

"What a dunce I am!" exclaims Carmen sarcastically. "I wear myself all out trying to entertain this gentleman . . . I thought he loved me . . . the bugle calls, and he runs off!" Then in a sudden fury she hurls his cap and saber at him and shouts, "There! go, my boy, directly to the barracks!"

Greatly hurt and humiliated, José seizes her by the arm, declaring, "You *must* hear me, Carmen!" He takes from his uniform the flower she gave him that fateful day in the square at Seville. To a hauntingly lovely melody that grows by degrees to an impassioned climax, he tells her how he kept this flower with him during his dreary life in prison, as he sings *"La fleur que tu m'avais jetée"* ("This flower you gave to me").

Carmen seems to be touched, but she is more determined than ever that

67

José shall go off with her to the freedom of the gypsies' life . . . the adventures, dangers, and escapes, the long nights under the free winds and the stars. . . . José is nearly won, as he murmurs to her tenderly, "Carmen!" Then he starts up with a sudden realization, "A deserter of my flag . . . be shamed, dishonored!" He rushes toward the door and answers her "Good-by" with "Farewell forever!"

At this very instant there is a knocking at the door, and a second later Zuniga, the officer who had been so struck with Carmen, bursts in. He stops suddenly as he sees José, and says coldly to Carmen, "Your choice isn't so good . . . you don't do yourself justice to take a mere soldier when you might have his officer!" He brusquely orders José to go. The soldier, naturally, refuses; the officer strikes him, and José, mad with rage, draws his saber. Carmen, to prevent bloodshed, screams to her companions for help. Officer and soldier are overpowered and separated. Some of the gypsies lead Zuniga away under close guard. For José the life of a law-abiding subject and loyal dragoon is done. Guilty of insubordination and of an attempt upon the life of a superior, he can only join the gypsies, become a deserter and an outcast . . . and the lover of Carmen.

ACT III

SCENE: *A Mountain Pass.* An interlude of great beauty precedes the third act. A pastoral melody, simple, but most exquisitely graceful, is first heard in the liquid tones of the flute and then taken up in imitation by other instruments; meanwhile the harp adds color and motion to the background. The tranquil purity of this interlude is a relief from the emotional strain of the preceding act. This piece stems from the incidental music Bizet composed for the play, *L'Arlésienne.*

The smugglers are gathering at their meeting place, a wild, desolate spot in the heart of the mountains. First one smuggler appears on a lofty pinnacle of rock in the distance, then several, finally the entire band, scrambling down over the barren rocks toward their camp. Their gradual arrival and stealthy movements are vividly pictured in music.

Carmen and José are among them. José is not happy in this mode of life. Just now he is obsessed by thoughts of his mother; she still believes he is an honest man.

"If you don't like our way of living here, why don't you go?" Carmen asks sarcastically.

"And leave you! Carmen! If you say that again . . ." he mutters and places his hand menacingly on his dagger.

Carmen merely shrugs her shoulders and calmly replies, "You may kill me, what does it matter? I will die as fate dictates." José sulks away, and

Byron

ACT IV—THE DEATH OF CARMEN

Carmen watches Frasquita and Mercédès, who are telling their fortunes with cards. These girls are having a gay time, for the cards predict love, wealth, and happiness. She seizes a pack of cards and coolly begins to tell her own fortune. In silence she shuffles and draws: "Spades!—a grave!" she exclaims darkly, under her breath. She recoils as from some unseen hand that threatens her. From the orchestra is heard the terrifying "Fate" theme. "First I, then he!" she adds, indicating José, then continues to shuffle the cards, while she sings the "Card Song."

Her spirit of bravado does not desert her, however, and when the leader of the band of smugglers announces that it is a favorable time to attempt the mountain pass with their contraband goods, she is all activity in helping prepare for the departure. After José has been stationed behind some rocks to watch for any surprise attack, the smugglers set out through the pass, singing joyfully at their anticipated conquest of the guard.

A guide comes from behind a cliff toward the camp, then quickly withdraws. It is Micaëla whom he has directed to this haunt of desperate characters. She comes seeking José and she sings a tuneful air, praying for heaven's protection, *"Je dis que rien ne m'épouvante"* ("I am not fainthearted").

A sudden shot rings out, and in terror she hides among the rocks. José has fired at a stranger coming up the pass. He might indeed have fired again, but the carefree manner in which the man waves his hat and exclaims, "An inch lower and it would have been all over with me!" causes José to put down his gun and go to meet him. It is Escamillo. In a moment the men recognize each other as rivals. Daggers flash, soldier and bullfighter struggle together. Escamillo falls, José's dagger at his throat. But the smugglers have returned, attracted by the sound of the shot. Like a flash, Carmen is between the two men and seizes José's arm. Escamillo rises, gallantly thanks Carmen for having saved his life, then with his usual bravado invites them all to the bull-fight at Seville, and calmly takes his leave. José again rushes after the toreador, but is restrained by the gypsies. Just then Micaëla is discovered and brought in. She begs José to return to his mother. Carmen interrupts and tauntingly says that he should go, this life is not for him. He turns to her excitedly, replying, "You tell me to go with her, so that you may run after your new lover."

The gypsies also advise him to leave, but he is firm. Then Micaëla pleads: "One last word, José, your mother is dying!" Now repentant and alarmed, José will go. He turns back for a moment, however, and calls darkly to Carmen, "Be happy . . . I'm going . . . but we'll meet again!"

As José leaves with Micaëla, the toreador is heard in the distance, singing his boastful song. Carmen listens, as if enchanted, and would run after him; José menacingly bars the way.

ACT IV

SCENE: *A Square in Seville.* A third intermezzo indicates the changed scenes of the opera—a rapid, impetuous dance, tones of plaintive longing mingled with impassioned gypsylike phrases grow to a tumultuous climax, then die away with a pleading phrase in the oboe and a few runs and chords by other woodwind instruments—a mood of vague foreboding.

A brilliantly dressed crowd is waiting in the square before the bull ring in Seville for the procession into the arena. Street hawkers with oranges, fans, cigarettes, and wines are vigorously shouting their wares. Soldiers, citizens, peasants, aristocrats, bull-ring loafers, black-haired, black-eyed women, Spanish beauties with towering combs, floating mantillas, and embroidered silken shawls; all these, a many-colored throng, move excitedly about the scene. From the orchestra rings out the bright, vivacious theme of the Prelude to the opera. The procession is approaching, and the crowd cheers and applauds the divisions of the parade that go by and enter the arena. "The *alguacil*, the *chulos*, the *bandilleros*, all in green and spangles, waving their crimson cloths! The picadors with their lances! Now, Escamillo! Hail! Bravo! Escamillo!"

A thunderous shout goes up as the toreador enters, Carmen on his arm. She is stunningly brilliant in her Spanish dress, and appears to be radiantly happy. Escamillo now takes leave of her, saying that if she loves him she soon will have reason to be proud. Completely won, Carmen vows that her heart could hold no other love.

A blare of trumpets and a march in the orchestra announce the entry of the alcalde. During this, two of Carmen's gypsy friends approach. They warn

GLADYS SWARTHOUT AS CARMEN

71

her to leave the place. José is hiding among the crowd, they say, and he appears to be desperate. Carmen calmly replies that she is not afraid; she will stay, wait for him, talk to him.

When the alcalde has entered the arena, the entire crowd follows, the brilliant music of the procession dies out in the distance, and Carmen is left face to face with Don José. She looks at him fearlessly and says, "I was told that you were here, warned." José is haggard and wan; from his sunken eyes glows a dangerous light. "Carmen," he begs hoarsely, "come, let's go far from here, begin life again. I adore you!" "It's useless for you to keep repeating that you love me," she answers impatiently, "I don't love you any longer." "But I, I love you, I worship you!" he pleads and threatens at the same time. "What's the use, superfluous words!" is her indifferent answer. "Well," he urges, "if I can win your love, I'll be a smuggler, anything you wish, all—but don't leave me, don't forget our past, how we loved each other!"

Her freezing answer is, "Carmen never will yield, free was she born, free shall she die!"

A sudden fanfare is heard from the arena; there are loud shouts of "Hurrah! Hail to the toreador!" At the shout of victory Carmen lets escape a little cry of pride and joy. During this Don José has had his gaze fixed on her. She starts to run toward the entrance; driven insane with jealousy, he bars her way.

In a sinister tone he mutters, "This man they are shouting for, he's your new lover!"

She defies him with, "Let me pass."

"On my soul! you'll never pass! Carmen, come with me!"

"Leave me, Don José."

"You're going to meet him ... you love him?"

"Yes, I love him! Even before death, I'd repeat, I love him."

Again there is a fanfare of trumpets and a shout of "Viva, toreador!"

Carmen again tries to enter the arena. José stops her violently. His voice hoarse with despair and jealousy, he again threatens: "And so I've sold my soul so that you can go to his arms and laugh at me!" The "Fate" theme sounds turbulently in the orchestra. From the arena is heard another fanfare, then the song of the crowd acclaiming Escamillo victor. With a defiant cry, Carmen throws away José's ring and darts toward the entrance of the amphitheater; there José overtakes her. A dagger flashes . . . Carmen falls. The crowd comes pouring from the arena, singing praises of the toreador. Leading the crowd is Escamillo, flushed with the victory he has won for his beloved. And he stops suddenly; she is lying at the gate, dead. There also stands Don José; he declares himself the guilty one and, bending over the lifeless form, cries out, "Carmen ... my adored Carmen."

Carmen

THE RCA-VICTOR RECORDS
(Sung in French unless otherwise noted)

GABRIELLE BESANZONI AS CARMEN

COMPLETE RECORDING: *Gabriella Besanzoni, Mezzo-soprano; Maria Carbone, Soprano; Piero Pauli, Tenor; Ernesto Besanzoni, Baritone; Nerina Ferrari, Soprano; Tamara Beltacchi, Soprano; Enrico Spada, Bass; Attillio Bordonalli, Baritone; Nello Pauli, Baritone; E. Venturini, Tenor; with Chorus and Orchestra of La Scala, Milan; Carlo Sabajno, Cond. In Italian*

DMC-104 (DM-128) (Vol. 1)
        (13360-13369), 10-12"
    (DM-128) (Vol. 2)
        (13370-13378), 9-12"
MC-104 (M-128) (Vol. 1)
        (11839-11848)
    (M-128) (Vol. 2)
        (11849-11857)

RECORDRAMA: *Gladys Swarthout, Mezzo-soprano; Licia Albanese, Soprano; Ramon Vinay, Tenor; Robert Merrill, Baritone; Anthony Amato, Tenor; George Cehanovsky, Baritone; Thelma Votipka, Soprano; Lucielle Browning,*

Mezzo-soprano; with RCA-Victor Choral and Orchestra; Robert Shaw, Choral Director; Erich Leinsdorf, Cond.
    DM-1078 (11-9323-11-9328), 6-12"
    M-1078 (11-9317-11-9322)

MUSIC FROM "CARMEN" (Orchestral): *Leopold Stokowski conducting the New York City Symphony Orchestra*
    DM-1002 (11-8799-11-8802), 4-12"
    M-1002 (11-8795-11-8798)

ACT I

HABAÑERA—L'AMOUR EST UN OISEAU REBELLE (Love Is Like a Wood Bird): *Gladys Swarthout, Mezzo-soprano, with Orch.*   14419, 12"

Gladys Swarthout, Mezzo-soprano, with RCA-Victor Choral; Robert Shaw, Choral Director; Erich Leinsdorf, Cond.   11-9289, 12"
    (In Album M-1074)

Emma Calvé, Soprano, with Orch.
    18144, 12"
    (Acoustical Recording)
    (In Album M-816)

Hartsook
GERALDINE FARRAR AS CARMEN

(Cousin of Francis husband)

Jeanne Gerville-Réache, Contralto, with Orch. 15-1008, 12"
(Acoustical Recording)

ACT II

SEGUIDILLA—PRÈS DES RAMPARTS DE SÉ-VILLE (Near the Walls of Seville): *Gladys Swarthout, Mezzo-soprano, with Orch.* 14419, 12"

ENTRANCE OF THE TOREADOR; CHANSON DU TORÉADOR (Toreador Song); EXIT OF THE TOREADOR: *Robert Merrill, Baritone; RCA-Victor Choral and Orch.* 11-9794, 12"

CHANSON DU TORÉADOR (Toreador Song): *Leonard Warren, Baritone, with Orch.* 11-8744, 12"

Lawrence Tibbett, Baritone; Metropolitan Opera Chorus; with Orch. 14202, 12"
(In Album M-329) 8124, 12"

AIR DE LA FLEUR—LA FLEUR QUE TU M'AVAIS JETÉE (Flower Song—This Flower You Gave to Me): *Jussi Bjoerling, Tenor, with Orch.* 12635, 12"

Enrico Caruso, Tenor, with Orch. In Italian 14234, 12"

Charles Dalmorès, Tenor, with Orch. 18141, 12"
(Acoustical Recording)
(In Album M-816) 15-1013, 12"
(Acoustical Recording)

James Melton, Tenor, with Orch. 10-1329, 10"

ACT III

AIR DE MICAËLA—JE DIS QUE RIEN NE M'ÉPOUVANTE (Micaëla's Aria—I Am Not Fainthearted): *Eidé Noréna, Soprano, with Orch.* 14742, 12"

Licia Albanese, Soprano, with Orch. 12-0014, 12"

Mishkin
ENRICO CARUSO AS DON JOSÉ

Shrine LA, Oct 52. Very lovely opera.
S.F.O. Company.
3-18-4- L.A op Co - An event to remember, - wonderful.

THE METROPOLITAN OPERA HOUSE SETTING

Cavalleria Rusticana
(RUSTIC CHIVALRY)

OPERA IN one act. Music by Pietro Mascagni. Libretto by G. Targioni-Tozzetti and G. Menasci, based on a short story by Giovanni Verga. World *première* at the Teatro Costanzi, Rome, May 17, 1890. American *première* at the Grand Opera House, Philadelphia, September 9, 1891. A few weeks later Rudolph Aronson and Oscar Hammerstein raced to produce the New York *première* first, Aronson winning with a matinee dress rehearsal at the Casino Theater on October 1, and Hammerstein claiming a technical victory with a regular performance that night at the Lenox Lyceum. The Metropolitan Opera Company first produced the spectacular novelty the following December 30. Emma Eames was the Santuzza and Valero the Turiddu. The performance was in Italian, unlike the Aronson and Hammerstein versions, which were in English. Eames, though vocally superb, was regarded as temperamentally unsuited for the part of the volcanic Sicilian heroine. It was Emma Calvé who brought fire and power to the role at her Metropolitan debut on November 29, 1893. A still more sensational performance was that directed by Arturo Toscanini on December 17, 1908, when the cast consisted of Emmy Destinn, Maria Gay, Marie Mattfeld, Enrico Caruso, and Pasquale Amato.

Mascagni was an impoverished music teacher, living at times on a meager plate of macaroni a day, till his one-act masterpiece brought him fame and fortune. The son of a Leghorn baker, he had been obliged to study music secretly as a boy, as his father intended him for a career as lawyer. The timely intervention of a sympathetic uncle and the sponsorship of a wealthy titled amateur settled the issue. Pietro went to the Milan Conservatory. There, however, the routine of study plagued him. The encouragement of a man like Ponchielli proved futile, and soon the boy ran away from school. After some arduous years with a traveling opera company, he married and settled down in Cerignola. Marriage only added to his financial woes, and his income from teaching and odd conducting jobs in town was scant. One day in 1889 the music publisher Son-

75

zogno offered a prize for a one-act opera. Mascagni promptly set to work, having discovered an excellent libretto in the realistic tale of Verga, standard-bearer of the Italian school of *verismo*. Utterly dissatisfied with the score, Mascagni put it aside. Luckily his wife, whose faith in the opera was stronger than her husband's, stole off secretly to the post office one afternoon and mailed it. The little opera won first prize.

When it was produced at the Teatro Costanzi in Rome, its success was immediate. The audience was wild with excitement, clamoring for the young unknown who had suddenly moved to the forefront of Italy's new composers. The composer's fame was made. Medals were struck in his honor, the city of Cerignola greeted him with torchlight processions on his return; and Mascagni relates in his memoirs that the entrance to his home was so jammed with cheering townspeople that it was necessary to haul him up to the first-story balcony on a knotted bedsheet. Later the King bestowed the Order of the Crown of Italy upon him—an honor that had not come to Giuseppe Verdi till late in life. A whole new chapter in naturalistic opera writing opened with *Cavalleria rusticana*, and people warmed to it instantly wherever it was played. Its rich, Latin melody, its dramatic impact, its pulsing passion combined to establish it securely in the repertories of the world. The compactness and unity of the story were ideal for a one-act opera, and even as a stage play, Eleanora Duse showed how this simple, passionate conflict in the lives of Sicilian peasants could become a drama of poignant power.

CHARACTERS

SANTUZZA, *a village girl in*		ALFIO, *a teamster*	*Baritone*
love with Turiddu	*Soprano*	MAMMA LUCIA, *mother of*	
LOLA, *wife of Alfio*	*Mezzo-soprano*	*Turiddu*	*Contralto*
TURIDDU, *a young soldier*	*Tenor*	CHORUS OF PEASANTS AND VILLAGERS	

The action takes place in a Sicilian village in the latter part of the nineteenth century

An orchestral prelude introduces us to the drama of stormy passions we are to witness. The music evokes a folkish background of warm color, and ominous phrases are heard hinting at Santuzza's fateful jealousy and the tragedy it will bring. But soon the music grows romantic in mood; from it blossoms the beautiful "Siciliana" of Turiddu, *"O Lola, bianca come fior di spino,"* a serenade with guitarlike accompaniment heard from behind the curtain. It is an avowal of undying love to Alfio's wife and Turiddu's former sweetheart. "White as a flower," Turiddu calls Lola, swearing that if he were to die and go to heaven, he would refuse to enter if she were not there too. (It is important to know at the start of the opera that Turiddu and Lola were once engaged to be married.)

At the end of the prelude and "Siciliana," the curtain rises. It is Easter morning in the square of a Sicilian village. On one side stands a church; on the other a wineshop and the dwelling of Mamma Lucia. Church bells are ringing, and in the distance voices are heard, singing, as peasants gather for the Easter Mass. The orchestra gives out a bright and joyous melody in typical folk vein, expressing the carefree holiday mood of the people as they stream into the square. The women are singing of Eastertime, of tender love. The men join in, hymning the charms of women and their industrious ways. Some of the villagers enter the church; others form little groups, and then walk off in different directions. As their voices fade away in the distance,

LOLA ENTERS THE CHURCH

Santuzza appears. She approaches Mamma Lucia's dwelling and calls out to her. "What is it?" asks the old woman. "Where is Turiddu?" the girl asks anxiously, repeating her query over and over. Mamma Lucia evades answering: "Do not ask me. I do not know. I want no trouble!" Santuzza now pleads with her with mounting ardor, "Tell me, for God's sake, where is Turiddu hiding himself?" Mamma Lucia replies finally that Turiddu has gone to Francofonte to buy wine. "That's not so," Santuzza cries. "Last night he was seen in the village." The mother's suspicions are aroused, for she has not seen her son. When she invites Santuzza to enter the house with her, the girl shamefacedly reminds Lucia that she cannot enter, that she is an outcast, excommunicated (*"Non posso entrare in casa vostra. Sono scomunicata"*). The moral law of the Sicilian village forbids her entering Mamma Lucia's home. "What of my son?" the mother asks, alarmed.

Before Santuzza can reply, the cracking of whips and the jingling of bells are heard. Alfio, the village carrier, is approaching, and as he reaches the square he sings a lively song in praise of the teamster's career, adding some words of eulogy for his beautiful and loving wife, Lola, who is home, waiting for him. A crowd follows him and joins in his song. Alfio asks Mamma Lucia if she can sell him some of her fine wine. "Not just now," she replies. "Turiddu has gone to buy a fresh supply of it." Astonished, Alfio exclaims, "But Turiddu is here in town. I saw him myself this very morning. He was standing not far from my cottage." Mamma Lucia is about to express surprise, when Santuzza checks her and Alfio departs. From inside the church now come the voices of a choir singing the *"Regina Coeli"*

("Queen of Heaven"). The crowd outside joins in with "Hallelujahs." The peasants then kneel in prayer and sing the Resurrection hymn, *"Innegiamo, il Signor non e morto,"* led by the voice of Santuzza. Reflected in this joyful music of Easter is a pastoral simplicity typical of the religious feelings of the Sicilian peasantry.

The people now enter the church, and Lucia and Santuzza are again alone. The mother asks Santuzza why she motioned her to keep silent when Alfio spoke of seeing Turiddu in the village. Santuzza now gives us the needed background to the drama developing among them. She reminds Mamma Lucia that her son was once engaged to Lola, that while he was away serving in the army Lola forgot him and married Alfio. Then Turiddu returned. Crushed when he learned the truth, he proceeded to console himself with Santuzza, whose reputation he ruined. Now, Lola, weary of Alfio, has enticed Turiddu back and is jealous of Santuzza. Mamma Lucia now learns from the distraught girl that during Alfio's frequent absences Lola and Turiddu have been together. This is all divulged, with mounting passion and pathos, in Santuzza's great aria, *"Voi lo sapete"* ("Well you know, good mother"), which reaches a pitch of frenzied despair at the point where the girl reveals that Lola and Turiddu love one another again.

Shaken by Santuzza's anguished confession, Mamma Lucia heeds her plea to go into the church to pray for her. As she does so, Turiddu enters the square, also on his way to church. Surprised at seeing Santuzza outside of church on Easter day, he tries to avoid talking to her, but she insists on speaking to him. She upraids him for lying that he has been to Francofonte. He was seen near Lola's house by her husband, she shrieks; he still loves her! Turiddu denies it, and Santuzza is suddenly frightened when he hints that his life will be in danger if Alfio learns the truth about his visits to Lola. Raising his voice, Turiddu cries that he will not be the slave of Santuzza's wild jealousy. "Strike me, insult me," she sobs in mingled love and desperation; "I forgive you, but my suffering is too much for me!"

Lola's voice is now heard in the distance, singing a lighthearted song about a radiant flower, the mood of which suggests the coquette. As Lola enters she grasps the situation at a glance, and the two women exchange words bristling with irony and innuendo. Turiddu is left almost speechless with confusion. With a shrug, the flirtatious Lola enters the church, beckoning her lover to follow. But Santuzza detains him, pleading vehemently, "Do not leave me, Turiddu!" "Why do you follow me around?" retorts Turiddu. "Why do you spy on me at the church door?" Turiddu's anger mounts as the girl's desperate frenzy grows, and finally, as Santuzza shouts, "Betrayer," he flings her roughly to the ground. As he strides defiantly into the church, Santuzza hurls a furious curse after him: "May this Easter bring you bad luck!" and falls, sobbing frantically.

THE DEATH OF TURIDDU

When she looks up again, Alfio is approaching. "God himself has sent you!" she exclaims to him. "At what part of the Mass are they?" he asks calmly. "It is rather late," Santuzza replies, adding significantly, "Lola went with Turiddu." Alfio, in surprise, asks, "What did you say?" and Santuzza blurts out the whole story: that while he earns an honest living his wife is betraying him with Turiddu, Turiddu who is rightfully hers, Santuzza's. Alfio's voice rises in wrath, as he listens dumfounded. "If you are lying, I'll rip your heart open!" he threatens. But he is convinced and, after a pause, thanks Santuzza and vows to have his revenge that very day. Leaving Santuzza dazed and fearful of the tragedy her jealousy is bringing on, Alfio stalks off, uttering cries of *"Vendetta!"*

Santuzza leaves, and the square is deserted for a few moments. It is time for a pause in this seething frenzy of dramatic outcries and clashes. A calm, devotional mood rises from the orchestra now, as the *"Regina Coeli,"* earlier sung by the choir, returns to remind us it is Easter, a day of peace and piety. In contrast, there follows a haunting melody, tense with religious fervor, but suggesting, too, the hot, searing passions of the previous scenes. This orchestral episode is the famous "Intermezzo," a favorite concert piece the world over, and the number that has carried the name of Pietro Mascagni and the title of his masterpiece into homes and hamlets where "grand opera" is still a remote and legendary term.

As the strains of the "Intermezzo" soar to a climax and finally die away,

people begin to emerge from the church. A crowd is now assembled outside
Mamma Lucia's wineshop. Turiddu is in high spirits, for Lola is with him
and Santuzza is nowhere about to plague him. Turiddu invites his friends to
partake of his mother's wine. Glasses are filled, and he leads them in singing
an infectious drinking song, in which the sparkling magic of wine is hymned
in jubilant tones. As Alfio enters, all greet him cordially. Turiddu offers him
a glass, but Alfio gruffly refuses it. "Your wine would become poison in my
stomach!" he snarls at Turiddu. Turiddu retorts, "At your pleasure," and
empties the glass on the ground. Lola is frightened, and several women con-
fer hastily, approach Lola, whisper to her, and take her away with them. The
two men exchange a few sharp words, and then give a challenge in the Sicilian village fashion of the time: the men embrace and Turiddu bites Alfio's
ear in token of acceptance.

After Alfio leaves for the place appointed for the duel, Turiddu calls
out to his mother. With mounting alarm, the mother listens to him as he begins an aria pulsing with tragic import and filial love, *"Mamma, quel vino è
generoso"* ("Mother, that wine is generous"). He is going away, he says, and
may not return. "If I should not come back, be a mother to Santuzza, the girl
I vowed to marry," he pleads. To quiet her fears he assures her that it is only
the wine that makes him talk this way. Then he kisses her and rushes off with
a farewell sob. Mamma Lucia follows him for a few steps, shouting his name
in despair. Santuzza enters and throws her arms about her. The square now
begins to fill again. A nervous expectancy is in the air. The taut excitement
grows as a murmur of voices is heard in the distance. Then the cry of a
woman rises shrilly, "They've murdered Turiddu!" Confused voices are
heard approaching. Terrified women rush into the square, one of them taking
up the cry, "They've murdered Turiddu!" Santuzza gives an anguished
shriek and collapses. Women rush to Mamma Lucia's side as she too reels
and faints. The stupefied crowd looks on in horror.

THE RCA-VICTOR RECORDS

COMPLETE RECORDING: *Beniamino Gigli,
Tenor; Lina Bruna Rasa, Soprano;
Gino Bechi, Baritone; Giulietta Si-
mionato, Contralto; Pietro Mascagni
conducting the Orchestra del Teatro
della Scala di Milano.* In Preparation

SICILIANA—O LOLA: *James Melton, Tenor;
RCA-Victor Symphony Orchestra,
Wilfred Pelletier, Cond.*   18365

SANTUZZA AND TURIDDU DUET: *Dusolina
Giannini, Soprano, and Beniamino
Gigli, Tenor; Orchestra of La Scala,
Milan, Carlo Sabajno, Cond.*   17697

INTERMEZZO: *Boston "Pops" Orchestra,
Arthur Fiedler, Cond.*   4303

VOI LO SAPETE: *Zinka Milanov, Soprano;
RCA-Victor Orchestra, Frieder Weissmann, Cond.*   11-8927

VIVA IL VINO SPUMEGGIANTE (BRINDISI):
*Beniamino Gigli, Tenor; Metropolitan
Opera Chorus and Orchestra, Giulio
Setti, Cond.*   8222

ADDIO ALLA MADRE: *Jussi Bjoerling,
Tenor; with Orchestra, Nils Grevillius, Cond.*   11-9387

Le Cid

OPERA IN four acts. Music by Jules Massenet. Libretto by Adolphe d'Ennery, Louis Gallet, and Édouard Blau, after the play by Corneille of the same name. First produced at the Paris Opéra, November 30, 1885. American *première* in New Orleans, on February 23, 1890. Though altered considerably by Massenet's librettists and the playwright Corneille before them, the story of *Le Cid* is based on historical fact. A great warrior and champion of the common people, Rodrigo Díaz de Bivar acquired the title of *El Cid Campeador* ("The Fighting Conqueror") in his struggles against the Moors in Spain. Later he became the hero of Spanish balladry and epic, and soon fabulous legends were woven about his memory. Outstanding in the opera are Chimène's beautiful aria, "*Pleurez, pleurez, mes yeux,*" and the fetching ballet music, in which Massenet sought to evoke eleventh-century Spain through the use of national rhythms and melodic turns. The Spanish equivalent of *Le Cid* is *El Cid*, deriving from the Arabic *el seid*, meaning "the conqueror."

CHARACTERS

CHIMÈNE	*Soprano*
COUNT DE GORMAS, *her father*	*Baritone*
RODRIGO *(the Cid)*	*Tenor*
DON DIEGO, *his father*	*Bass*
THE KING	*Baritone*
THE INFANTA	*Soprano*
MOORISH ENVOY	*Bass*
DON ARIAS	*Tenor*
DON ALONZO	*Bass*
SAINT JAMES	*Baritone*

A. Dupont
EMMA CALVÉ AS CHIMÈNE

The action takes place in Burgos, Spain, during the eleventh century

ACT I

SCENE 1: *The House of Count Gormas in Burgos.* Returned from his battles with the Moors, a conquering hero, Rodrigo (the Cid), is celebrating at the house of Count Gormas, where he learns that the King is planning to knight him. Chimène, the Count's daughter, is in love with the Cid and is overjoyed when she is told that both her father and the King approve of the match. However, it soon develops that the Infanta is also secretly in love with the Cid, but has renounced him because he is not of royal blood.

SCENE 2: *A Gallery Leading to the Cathedral.* The King confers the sword of knighthood on the Cid, who addresses it in a fervent avowal of loyalty. Then as the Cid departs for the chapel, the King bestows on Don Diego, the Cid's father, a governorship expected by Count Gormas. In a moment of rage, the Count insults Don Diego, and then strikes him. Being too old to fight himself, Don Diego appeals to his son to uphold the family honor. The Cid vows to do so, but is grieved to learn the name of his adversary.

Le Cid

ACT II

SCENE: *A Street in Burgos*. The Count accepts the Cid's challenge, and they fight. More by accident than design the Count is slain, and Chimène, rushing frantically toward her father's body, vows revenge on the Cid. There is a change of scene to the great square of Burgos, where a festival is in progress before the King's palace. Merrymakers are dancing, and the Spanish rhythms grow in dash and animation. As the crowd looks on in mounting excitement, the dancing unfolds to a richly colored sequence of warm melodies, mirroring swift changes of mood from a soft, sinuous languor to headlong gaiety, all in the fiery spirit of a Spanish carnival. In the midst of the revelry Chimène appears. Approaching the King, she passionately pleads for revenge upon the Cid for the death of her father. As the King and his courtiers weigh her plea, news arrives that the Moors have declared war. The King requests Chimène to await the outcome of the battle. Chimène agrees.

ACT III

SCENE 1: *Chimène's Chamber*. The Cid has come to bid farewell to Chimène, whom he finds in tears, ready to forgive him. Spurred by her patriotic fervor, he departs, happy in the thought of reconciliation and eager, now, for the coming fight with his country's foes.

SCENE 2: *The Cid's Camp*. The battle is going against the Spaniards. The Moors have surrounded them, and the Cid chides his soldiers on their faintheartedness. As defeat seems near, and some of the men desert, the Cid falls to his knees and prays. Saint James suddenly appears before him in a vision, assuring him of victory.

ACT IV

SCENE 1: *A Hall in the King's Palace*. Deserters from the Cid's army bring the King news of his defeat and death. Chimène, grief-stricken, collapses. Presently a second report is brought in, denying the first: the Cid is alive and the Spaniards have won!

SCENE 2: *The Palace Court*. The Cid has returned victorious, but Chimène again demands that he be punished. The shrewd King consents, but commands her to pronounce sentence herself. As Chimène hesitates, the Cid draws his dagger and offers to end his life by his own hand. He seeks only forgiveness for his deed. Chimène relents and rushes into her lover's arms.

THE RCA-VICTOR RECORDS

BALLET MUSIC—ACT II (Castillane; Andalouse; Aragonaise; Aubade; Catalane; Madrilène; Navarraise): *Boston "Pops"* Orchestra, Arthur Fiedler, Cond.
DM-1058 (10-1233-10-1235), 3-10″
M-1058 (10-1230-10-1232)

White   ACT III—ARRIVAL OF KING AND QUEEN

Le Coq d'Or
(THE GOLDEN COCKEREL)

OPERA IN three acts. Music by Nikolai Rimsky-Korsakov. Libretto by Vladimir Bielsky, after the poem by Pushkin. First performance given at Zimin's Private Theater, Moscow, October 7, 1909. American *première*, Metropolitan Opera House, March 6, 1918, in French, when it was produced as an opera-pantomime in the stage version devised by Mikhail Fokine for Diaghilev's Ballet Russe. In this version the members of the ballet enacted the movements of the personages of the drama on the center of the stage, while singers, in academic cap and gown, were ranged in jury boxes on either side. A revival at the Metropolitan, February, 1937, was in the work's purely operatic form, the singers enacting their own roles. In the cast were Ezio Pinza as King Dodon and Lily Pons as the queen.

This, the last and most popular of Rimsky-Korsakov's operas, was at first banned from the stage by the Russian censor, owing to a particular element of satire in the story, which, it has since been assumed, was aimed at Russia's conduct of the war against Japan.

At the height of his powers when he composed this work, Rimsky-Korsakov surmounted many unusual difficulties in his musical treatment of the libretto. Learned professor and author of erudite musical treatises and contrapuntal pieces, the composer, by the beauty of his melody, the opulence and daring of his harmony, and the brilliance and originality of his orchestration successfully met the challenges like the superb craftsman he truly was, in a score both acid and humorous and thoroughly in the spirit of the fantastic tale.

CHARACTERS

KING DODON	*Bass*	AMELFA	*Contralto*
PRINCE GUIDON } *his sons*	*Tenor*	THE ASTROLOGER	*Tenor*
PRINCE APHRON	*Baritone*	THE QUEEN OF SHEMAKHA	*Soprano*
GENERAL POLKAN	*Bass*	THE GOLDEN COCKEREL	*Soprano*

The action takes place in a mythical land

83

ACT I—METROPOLITAN OPERA PRODUCTION

PROLOGUE

A muted trumpet intones a characteristic motive of the Cockerel. Then bizarre melodies and harmonies are heard from the orchestra, and an ancient Astrologer appears before the curtain. He tells us that through his magic he will show us a fable of olden times; he suddenly disappears, and the curtain rises.

ACT I

SCENE: *The Council Chamber of King Dodon.* King Dodon sits in council of state; he is harassed by many cares, for warlike neighbors insist on attacking his country. He would much prefer peace, for he is lazy and gluttonous and would not have his feasting disturbed. His sons, the Princes Guidon and Aphron, propose various absurd plans of attack, but the wise old general, Polkan, disagrees with their suggestions, and soon the assembly is in an uproar. Now the Astrologer enters and offers Dodon a Golden Cockerel which will always give warning when danger is near. The ruler is delighted and says that he will give the Astrologer as a reward anything that he may desire, whereupon the Astrologer remarks, with a certain cynicism, that treasures and honors bring only worry, but he accepts the monarch's word with thanks. Reassured by the gift, Dodon is put to bed in great state. His regal dreams are interrupted by the Cockerel sounding the alarm; the enemy is invading the country, and Dodon sends his two sons, each in command of

Le Coq d'Or

Wide World Studio   ACT III—METROPOLITAN OPERA PRODUCTION

half an army. Again his slumbers are disturbed by a signal of danger. The King, accompanied by Polkan, sets out in command of an even greater army.

ACT II

SCENE: *A Narrow Mountain Gorge.* By the faint moonlight a desolate mountain gorge is seen. Dodon arrives with his troops. He finds the bodies of his sons and their men slain—they have been fighting one another. He sheds a few formal tears. Day begins to break over the mountain, and, as the mist rises, a brilliantly decorated tent is perceived near by, apparently the enemy's. Dodon and his men prepare to attack. A cannon is brought up, but just as it is ready to be fired, the folds of the tent tremble, and the soldiers run away. The sun is now rising from behind the mountains, and there appears from the tent the beautiful Queen of Shemakha. Raising her arms as in prayer, she salutes the sun with a song—an exotic melody, colored with extraordinary chromatics and strange modulations, known as the "Hymn to the Sun."

Dazed and fascinated by her beauty and her singing, Dodon falls in love with her. She in turn ridicules the old monarch, luring him on to sing and dance, much to the amusement of her courtiers, for his voice is broken and his step doddering. Finally, summoning his courage, he makes his awkward proposal. She seems to hesitate and then yields, only on condition that General Polkan shall be executed.

85

ACT III

SCENE: *A Street in Dodon's Capital.* Dodon and the new Queen are welcomed back to the capital in the most extravagant splendor. The bride is already bored by her quavering husband. The Astrologer appears and demands as his reward—the Queen! Dodon begs him to accept, instead, riches or power. The Astrologer is firm; Dodon becomes angry and strikes him with his scepter. The Astrologer drops dead. There is a sudden thunderstorm, the scene grows dark, and the Golden Cockerel is heard crowing. The bird flies at Dodon, pecks him on the head, and the old ruler falls lifeless. The Queen is heard laughing, and when daylight returns she has vanished. The people sing a weird lament . . . who now will be their King?

EPILOGUE

As the curtain falls, the Astrologer again appears and, reminding us that this is merely a fairy tale, says—quite enigmatically—that in Dodon's kingdom only himself and the Queen are mortal.

THE RCA-VICTOR RECORDS
(Sung in French unless otherwise noted)

Morton & Co.
ACT I—SAN FRANCISCO OPERA PRODUCTION

ORCHESTRAL SUITE: *London Symphony Orchestra, Eugene Goossens, Cond.*
DM-504 (12748-12750), 3-12″
M-504 (12347-12349)

ACT II

HYMNE AU SOLEIL (Hymne an die Sonne) (Hymn to the Sun) : *Patrice Munsel, Soprano, with Orch.*   11-8886, 12″

Milizia Korjus, Soprano, with Orch. In German   12021, 12″

Lily Pons, Soprano, with Orch.
17232, 12″
(In Album M-702)

Fritz Kreisler, Violinist, with Piano
15487

ACT III

CORTÈGE DES NOCES (Bridal Procession): *San Francisco Symphony Orchestra, Pierre Monteux, Cond.*
18161, 12″
(In Album M-820)

Boston "Pops" Orchestra, Arthur Fiedler, Cond.
11-8509, 12″
(In Album M-797)

Ezra Stoller   SCENE FROM JUILLIARD SCHOOL OF MUSIC PRODUCTION

Così Fan Tutte

(SO DO THEY ALL)

COMIC OPERA in two acts. Music by Wolfgang Amadeus Mozart. Libretto by Lorenzo da Ponte. The original title of this work was *Così fan tutte, o sia La Scuola degli amanti* (*So Do They All, or The School for Lovers*). First performance, Burgtheater, Vienna, January 26, 1790. American *première*, Metropolitan Opera House, March 24, 1922. Given in English by the opera department of the Juilliard School of Music, February 28, 1940.

Whether owing to da Ponte's rather weak text or because of the subject itself, *Così fan tutte* has not become a staple of the operatic repertoire. It is generally accepted as being an entertaining work, though not always up to Mozart's best standards. Anyway, audiences, in so far as one can tell, have always seemed to enjoy its frivolous plot and substantially good and occasionally brilliant score. The libretto has had all sorts of revisions, alterations, and, in general, "treatments." Yet none of these has had anything approaching the longevity of the original itself, which, whatever its faults, whether of improbability, shallowness, or what else, has proved to be, in the final analysis, the text best suited to Mozart's music.

CHARACTERS

FIORDILIGI, *a lady of Ferrara*	Soprano	GUGLIELMO, *an officer, in love with Fiordiligi*	Baritone
DORABELLA, *her sister*	Soprano or Mezzo-soprano	DON ALFONSO, *a cynical old bachelor*	Basso buffo
DESPINA, *their waiting maid*	Soprano		
FERRANDO, *an officer, in love with Dorabella*	Tenor		

SOLDIERS, SERVANTS, MUSICIANS, BOATMEN, WEDDING GUESTS, ETC.

The action takes place in Naples during the eighteenth century

The Overture to *Così fan tutte* contains only one motive from the opera, that which is sung by Don Alfonso and the two young men toward the close of Act II to the words *"Così fan tutte."* After a short, slow introduction, there appears a gay, bubbling sequence, typical of Mozart in his lightest moments, interspersed with rapid exchanges between leading instruments. When this has been developed to a certain extent, the *"Così fan tutte"* motive returns, and presently the Overture comes to a close.

ACT I

SCENE 1: *A Café*. Ferrando, Guglielmo, and **Don Alfonso** are sitting together at a table, having a general discussion about the constancy of women. Ferrando, very much in love with Dorabella, gets quite personal about it, mentioning the great trust he reposes in his own young lady, Dorabella, whose loyalty is the equal of her beauty. Not to be outdone, Guglielmo rushes to Fiordiligi's defense, and, for a moment, it begins to look as if the conversation will turn into a free-for-all. Don Alfonso, an aging bachelor, calm and very cynical, takes all of this zeal in stride, quite poised and assured in his knowledge of the world and its ways, a knowledge obtained, doubtless, from a lifetime of experience.

At any rate, the discussion soon comes to the point where a wager is made—the stake, one hundred sequins, and the terms, Ferrando's and Guglielmo's complete agreement to do everything Don Alfonso prescribes for the next twenty-four hours. But, he cautions, nothing of this must be communicated to their "Penelopes," as he ironically refers to the young women. So certain are Ferrando and Guglielmo of winning that they begin to speculate how they will spend the money, and, finally, all three drink a toast to the wager.

SCENE 2: *A Garden Overlooking the Bay of Naples*. Dorabella and Fiordiligi, seated in the garden of their house, are gazing with ecstasy on medallions of their lovers. And to music of expressive beauty, contrasting with the kittenish quality of the textual lines, the sisters almost try to outdo one another in praise of their respective heroes.

Thus, as they are carrying on in rhapsodic mood, Don Alfonso appears on the scene. He is quite agitated, the orchestra depicting this to perfection, and after a few seconds of time in which he seems to regain his composure, he tells them that the worst has happened—Ferrando and Guglielmo have been ordered off to the wars. So desolate are they, he continues, that they have not the courage to bid their loves good-by in person, but that if the young women could withstand a painful interview of parting, they might come. He signals at once, and the two officers appear, as if by magic.

The ensuing quintet concluded, there is heard a drum roll, announcing the imminent departure of the officers' ship. A regiment of soldiers marches by, the usual crowd of townspeople dogging its steps, while they sing of the glories of the martial life. There is a tearful farewell between the lovers, during which even Don Alfonso, cynic though he is, does not remain unmoved. The ship leaves, and Don Alfonso joins the ladies in a prayer for a safe voyage. But when they leave he is again the detractor of womankind, and sings smugly to that effect.

SCENE 3: *An Anteroom in Fiordiligi's and Dorabella's House.* Despina, maid to the two sisters, enters with a tray containing cups of chocolate which she has prepared for her mistresses. Before their arrival she launches into a diatribe against domestic service. She is the typical servant-comedienne of broad farce, complaining, rather shrewd, impudent, and, in the long run, loyal.

Fiordiligi and Dorabella come into the anteroom and almost immediately indulge in an exaggerated show of their grief. Dorabella is heard in a recitative, *"Ah! scostati"* ("Ah! begone!"), and an aria, *"Smanie implacabili"* ("Implacable wrath"), descriptive of her rebellious mood. Despina, meanwhile, counsels the young women—through purely self-arrogated powers—to do as their heroes are probably doing, that is, have a good time. And in the aria *"In uomini, in soldati"* ("In men, in soldiers") she expresses her contempt for all males and their philandering traits. At this the two ladies bounce up and leave the scene in righteous indignation.

To add to the confusion, Don Alfonso now appears and bribes Despina to aid him in his scheme. With him are two spurious Albanian noblemen, who, of course, are Ferrando and Guglielmo in more or less comic disguises. The scheme is to supplant the ladies' lovers with these two likely gentlemen, who are not recognized by Despina. So, placing Don Alfonso in a hiding place, Despina summons her mistresses, who, as can be imagined, are horrified at the presence of two men in their house, and at such a time. When Don Alfonso enters, with due formality, he is agreeably surprised at finding these gentlemen, who, he declares, are good friends of his, and he makes much of his joy at seeing them again.

It is the lovers' job to be as ardent as possible, a little matter which, to be sure, is wildly magnified. The ladies at first protest mightily at this improper turn of events, and Fiordiligi sings, in what must naturally be assumed to be a serious vein, a lengthy protestation of her faithfulness. This is all contained, however, in a recitative followed by the well-known burlesque aria, *"Come scoglio"* ("Like a rock"). Guglielmo's answer to that is *"Non siate ritrosi"* ("Don't be so shy"), a subtle and truly charming piece.

Nevertheless, the girls depart very haughtily, and the two masqueraders practically collapse from laughter, pointing the finger of ridicule at Don Alfonso and the apparent failure of his antifemale theories. He says, pointedly, however, *"E voi ridete"* ("And you laugh"), reminding them that the twenty-four hours of the wager are not yet over. Now Ferrando is given an aria, *"Un' aura amorosa"* ("A breeze of love"), a sentimental song all about the theory that love brings love, and such.

The disguised officers depart, leaving Don Alfonso alone with Despina, and in the ensuing colloquy their little scheme to break down the ladies' resistance is further advanced.

SCENE 4: *The Garden of Fiordiligi's and Dorabella's House.* The two young women, in moods of melancholy reflection, sing the duet *"A, che tutta"* ("Ah, what a destiny"). Barely have they finished when Ferrando and Guglielmo rush in, each of them holding up, so that all may see, a bottle containing, we are told, a poison of which both have taken a draught. Don Alfonso, following on their heels, and Despina set out for the doctor. In the meantime, the young men go through all sorts of fraudulent contortions, and the ladies, not unsympathetic now, gently minister to the youths.

Don Alfonso returns with the "doctor," who is none other than Despina in a grotesque getup, and, after much mumbo-jumbo with a magnet, she seems to restore them to health. As the officers come to, they renew their amorous tactics, whereupon the sisters again leave in disapproval.

ACT II

SCENE 1: *A Room in Fiordiligi's and Dorabella's House.* Still quite indignant, the sisters are briefed by Despina, now as herself again, on the possible attractions offered by the two "Albanian noblemen," and on how, perhaps, the sorrows they bear may now be in some measure compensated in an interesting manner. Alone, the sisters discuss this new and provocative suggestion, discovering that they might find some amusement in the company of these undeniably personable strangers, provided, however, that all is done with care and propriety. So, Dorabella selects the dark one (Guglielmo) for herself, and Fiordiligi, of course, the other. And they come to this important decision in the engaging duet, *"Prenderò quel brunettino"* ("I'll take the dark one"). After this Don Alfonso enters, and invites them to the garden, where a surprise awaits them.

SCENE 2: *The Garden.* Ferrando and Guglielmo, still in their disguises, are on a barge moored to the landing place. There are singers and players, and the two men sing a duet serenade to the ladies. When the latter appear, Ferrando and Guglielmo continue their courtship. There are some conventional remarks, and Guglielmo, left alone with Dorabella, manages to soothe her enough to place around her neck a heart on a chain, which, he says, is a token of his great esteem for her, removing, at the same time, a necklace with a miniature of Ferrando. Ferrando, on the other hand, returns from a short walk among the trees with Fiordiligi not entirely successful with his wooing. Presently, Ferrando and Guglielmo discuss their respective experiences, and, in summation later with Don Alfonso, it is rather agreed that thus far, at least, half the bet has been won by him. The latter, not content with half a wager, would still prove to Guglielmo that Fiordiligi is as vulnerable as the other lady has shown herself to be.

SCENE 3. *A Room in the House.* Dorabella receives congratulations from Despina on her sensible behavior. And when Fiordiligi comes in, with an apparent air of displeasure, we learn that she disapproves of her sister's behavior, while, at the same time, envying her a bit. And at this point Dorabella gives her a talk on being practical about things, and when Dorabella leaves, Fiordiligi decides to take a step in the only honorable direction. She orders Despina to fetch the officers' uniforms of Ferrando and Guglielmo (although it is not made clear just how these came to be reposing in the sisters' wardrobe). Her idea is that there is but one way in which she and her sister may retain their honor, and that by both donning the uniforms and joining their men at the front. But Ferrando, still the Albanian, rather unpropitiously enters, and with increasing ardor on his part and proportionally diminishing resistance on Fiordiligi's he succeeds in getting her admission that she loves him. To all of this both Guglielmo and Don Alfonso have been witness, and now it is Guglielmo's turn to eat humble pie. At first the young men would seek all sorts of redress for the faithlessness of their sweethearts, but Don Alfonso counsels them, in the song *"Tutti accusan le donne"* ("All blame the women"), that all women would act as they have done, and it is best to marry them, as they had originally planned, for they are no different from others. Besides, he adds, the men love them, don't they? Here Despina appears, saying that the sisters have made up their minds to marry their Albanian swains, and have, therefore, sent for the notary.

SCENE 4: *A Large Room in Fiordiligi's and Dorabella's House.* The wedding feast is being prepared, under the watchful direction, of course, of Don Alfonso. The four protagonists enter, and soon a company of townspeople join them, singing a chorus of good wishes. The sisters and the officers, still garbed as Albanian noblemen, thank Despina for her part in making their happiness possible. And when the guests have departed, the two couples drink toasts all around.

In the midst of this ironic jubilation Despina appears, this time in the costume of a notary. With due (and grotesque) courtesy the contract arrangements are agreed upon and signed. Just then a distant drum roll is heard, and Don Alfonso, who has run to the window, announces that Ferrando's and Guglielmo's regiment has returned from the wars, and, alas, that both young men are with it.

The spurious Albanians are rushed out of the room, in the great turmoil that follows. Don Alfonso consoles the terrified and, understandably, very penitent sisters, while the young men hastily redon their original uniforms. As the real Ferrando and Guglielmo now, they return and express surprise at the rather tame response of their sweethearts and also at the presence of a notary. Besides, Ferrando has picked up the marriage contract, which Don Alfonso seems to have dropped, not without purpose.

To add to the sisters' consternation, Don Alfonso now asks the young men to look in the other room, which they do, and after some seconds for a quick change emerge as the Albanians. Guglielmo now gives to Dorabella the miniature of Ferrando, and both men sarcastically shower praise on the "doctor" who saw them safely through a dose of poison.

Now that the sisters know everything, they are completely humiliated. However, it is Don Alfonso who patches up things, with the thought that it was all done for the good of the lovers. The opera ends with a lively finale whose gist is to take things as they come.

THE RCA-VICTOR RECORDS
(Sung in Italian)

COMPLETE RECORDING: *Ina Souez, Soprano; Luise Helletsgruber, Soprano; Heddle Nash, Tenor; Willi Domgraf-Fassbaender, Bass; John Brownlee, Baritone; Irene Eisinger, Soprano; with Chorus and Orchestra of the Glyndebourne Festival Co.; Fritz Busch, Cond.* (Recorded in the Glyndebourne Opera House, Glyndebourne, England)

DMC-113 (DM-812) (Vol. 1)
(13718-13724), 7-12″

(DM-813) (Vol. 2)
(13732-13738), 7-12″
(DM-814) (Vol. 3)
(13745-13750), 6-12″
MC-113 (M-812) (Vol. 1)
(13711-13717)
(M-813) (Vol. 2)
(13725-13731)
(M-814) (Vol. 3)
(13739-13744)
OVERTURE: *BBC Symphony Orchestra, Adrian Boult, Cond.* 18084, 12″

L'Art du Théâtre

ACT V—THE RIDE TO HELL

La Damnation de Faust
(THE DAMNATION OF FAUST)

A "DRAMATIC LEGEND" in four parts. Music by Hector Berlioz. Libretto by Berlioz and Gandonnière, after Gérard de Nerval's French version of Goethe's *Faust*. First produced, in oratorio form, at the Paris Opéra-Comique on December 6, 1846. Adapted as an opera by Raoul Gunsbourg and produced at Monte Carlo on February 18, 1893. Dr. Leopold Damrosch conducted the American *première* of the oratorio version on February 5, 1880. The Metropolitan Opera Company produced it as an opera on December 7, 1906, with Geraldine Farrar, Charles Rousselière, and Pol Plançon in the chief roles. The New York Philharmonic-Symphony revived *The Damnation of Faust*, in concert form, on December 19, 1942, when Artur Rodzinski conducted, and the chief soloists were Jarmila Novotna, Frederick Jagel, and Ezio Pinza. Berlioz's mastery of orchestral color marks not only the famous "Rákóczy March," but the two other excerpts usually bracketed with it on symphonic programs: the "Minuet of the Will-o'-the-Wisps" and the "Dance of the Sylphs." The rest of the score, though less familiar, is remarkable for evocative beauty and delineative power. Berlioz is said to have transported Faust to Hungary for the opportunity to introduce his exciting arrangement of the Hungarian march. When the German critics protested, Berlioz retorted, "I was not bound to follow Goethe's plan."

CHARACTERS

MARGUERITE	*Soprano*	MEPHISTOPHELES	*Baritone or Bass*
FAUST	*Tenor*	BRANDER, *a student*	*Bass*

PEASANTS, STUDENTS, SOLDIERS, SYLPHS, INFERNAL SPIRITS, AND CELESTIAL SPIRITS

The action takes place in a German village in the sixteenth century

PART I

SCENE: *Plains of Hungary.* It is dawn as Faust, wandering through the fields, voices a tender tribute to spring. An orchestral passage in pastoral mood follows, interspersed with hints of the Hungarian march. Presently a group of villagers break in on Faust's meditations and join in a "Dance of the Peasants Under the Linden Tree." The scene soon shifts to another part of the Hungarian plain, where an army is advancing. As Faust, untouched by any patriotic fervor, draws away, the "Rákóczy March," with its bold and stirring rhythms, rings out brilliantly.

PART II

SCENE 1: *Faust's Study in North Germany.* Alone in his study, Faust is musing gloomily on suicide. As he lifts a cup of poison to his lips, the Easter hymn, "Christ Is Risen," sung in six-part chorus, is heard from a near-by church. Toward the close Faust joins in the singing, but then breaks off brusquely with a cry of blasphemy. At this outburst Mephistopheles suddenly appears, mocking him on his lost piety. Cleverly he inveigles Faust to sign over his soul, promising wealth, fame, and "boundless joy."

SCENE 2: *Auerbach's Cellar.* A group of students lift their voices in a brisk drinking song and then urge Brander, who is drunk, to contribute one of his own. Brander does so with a facetious ballad about a rat who grew fatter and fatter in his tiny home in the cellar larder. Gaily the students join in at the final words and thereupon improvise a mock-scholastic fugue on the word "Amen," using the melody of Brander's song. (In the manuscript appear Berlioz's words, later scratched out, "If one fears to wound the feelings of a pious audience or an audience that admires scholastic fugues on the word 'Amen,' a cut of the following ten pages may be made.") When Mephistopheles congratulates them on the style and sentiment of their fugue, the students bid him sing a selection of his own. The fiend obliges with a weird ballad about a king who had, as pet, a big black flea. As the students applaud wildly, Faust becomes disgusted and proposes to Mephistopheles that they leave this "brutal company." The fiend makes an ironic gibe about Faust's delicate taste and the two spread their mantles and take flight to the banks of the Elbe.

SCENE 3: *The Banks of the Elbe.* Mephistopheles urges his young companion to fall asleep among the flowers. As Faust follows his advice, a chorus of sylphs and gnomes weaves a fascinating web of sound about him. This is followed by the fine-spun orchestral reverie in waltz time, "Dance of the Sylphs." While dreaming, Faust utters the name of Marguerite, and as the sylphs flutter away, he awakes with her name still on his lips. Mephistopheles now promises to take Faust to Marguerite's chamber. The two join a column of soldiers and students marching to town. As the soldiers intone a rousing chorus the others join in a Latin student song, *"Jam nox stellata velamina pandit"* ("Now the starry night spreads out its coverlets").

PART III

SCENE: *Marguerite's Chamber*. It is evening. Drums and trumpets are heard in the distance. Faust, entering Marguerite's bedroom, expresses his longing in a tender song. As Marguerite nears, Mephistophéles cautions Faust to conceal himself behind the curtains and make the most of his opportunity. Marguerite enters, carrying a lamp. As she undresses, she recounts a vision she has had of a handsome lover. This is followed by the beautiful ballad of the "King of Thule," which, Berlioz explained, was to be sung by Marguerite "simply as an old tale that she had heard in childhood, and which she now absently hums." As part of the plan of seduction, Mephistopheles invokes the aid of the "Will-o'-the-Wisps." As he orders the "fiddlers of hell" to play their best, the orchestra spins the wondrous gossamer web of the "Minuet of the Will-o'-the-Wisps." Then he sings a short serenade and, ordering the invoked spirits back to their flaming pits, turns his attention to Faust and Marguerite, who have been ardently confessing their love to one another. Mephistopheles breaks in on their rapturous duet with the warning that the neighbors have learned of Faust's secret visit and are now shouting the news scornfully at the mother's window. As the neighbors approach, Faust and Marguerite vow to see one another again, and Mephistopheles hurries off with his young companion.

PART IV

SCENE 1: *Marguerite's Chamber*. Alone in her room, Marguerite pours out her heart in the passionate words of Goethe's *"Meine Ruh' ist hin"* ("My peace of mind is gone"). As the song ends, drums and trumpets sound, and the singing of soldiers and students is heard in the distance.

SCENE 2: *A Forest*. Faust delivers a fiery invocation to nature in the forest. Only here, he exclaims, can his troubled soul find repose. With the last phrase of his outburst, hunting calls are heard and Mephistopheles breaks in on Faust's nostalgic mood. He startles him with the news that Marguerite has been condemned to death for poisoning her mother, explaining that Marguerite had inadvertently given her mother an overdose of a sleeping potion. To buy her salvation Faust now signs an oath to serve Mephistopheles in all things.

SCENE 3: *A Cave*. There follows a "Ride to Hell" episode, with Faust and Mephistopheles mounted on two black horses. They hurry past terrified peasants kneeling before a crucifix. Cries of terror come from a group of women and children huddled in the road. In mounting dread Faust notes the legions of ghastly skeletons dancing on all sides of them as they speed along.

The ground rocks. Blood rains down upon the earth. Mephistopheles shouts exultantly that Faust is now beyond redemption. With a final gasp of horror from the youth, the two plunge into the Abyss.

A chorus of the Spirits of Hell welcomes them with a shrieking torrent of strange sounds, *"Has! Irimiru karabrao! Has! Has!"* said by the mystic Swedenborg to be the speech of the demons and the damned. The orchestra whips up a fiendish turmoil here. When Mephistopheles informs the Princes of Darkness that he is Lord and Master of this "proud mortal," an infernal orgy begins in celebration of Mephistopheles' triumph. As the Spirits of Hell dance around him, they chant their wild gibberish: *"Diff diff Astaroth, diff diff Belzebuth Belphegor Astaroth Mephisto sat sat rayk ir kimour!"*

EPILOGUE

SCENE 1: *On Earth*—SCENE 2: *In Heaven*. In the epilogue on earth the Princes of Darkness tell of Faust's awesome end in the seething lakes of fire and brimstone. In the final scene in heaven, seraphim plead to the Almighty for the salvation of Marguerite, and as a Voice calls out her name, the girl is absolved and led into heaven to the jubilant chanting of angels.

THE RCA-VICTOR RECORDS
(Sung in French)

ACT I

Marche hongroise (Rákóczy March) (Hungarian March): *Boston Symphony Orchestra, Serge Koussevitsky, Conductor*   14230, 12″
      11-9232, 12″
(In Album M-1063)
Leopold Stokowski and the Philadelphia Orchestra   6823, 12″

ACT II

Danse des sylphes (Dance of the Sylphs) (Presto and Minuet): *Boston Symphony Orchestra, Serge Koussevitsky, Cond.*   14230, 12″

ACT III

Menuet des feux-follets (Minuet of the Will-o'-the-Wisps): *Boston Symphony Orchestra, Serge Koussevitsky, Cond.*   14231, 12″

ACT IV

D'amour l'ardente flamme (Romance of Marguerite): *Rose Bampton, Soprano, with Orch.*   12-0015, 12″

From an Old Print   AENEAS RELATING HIS STORY TO DIDO

Dido and Aeneas

OPERA IN three acts. Music by Henry Purcell. Libretto by Nahum Tate, after Virgil's *Aeneid*. First produced in England, about 1689, by Josias Priest's Boarding School of Chelsea. American *première* unknown, probably an unchronicled amateur or school performance. Nahum Tate was Poet Laureate of England at the time of his collaboration with Purcell. The text of *Dido and Aeneas* was a second remove from Virgil's great epic, being based directly on Tate's own play, *Brutus of Alba*, which had been performed at Dorset Garden ten years before. The text, while scarcely a literary glory, is eminently singable. Tate, a third-rate poet, was not attempting to match his powers with those of the Latin Homer. *Dido and Aeneas* is Purcell's masterpiece, yet it was long regarded as "a chamber opera for amateurs," and the earliest amateurs to stage it were the elegant young ladies of the Chelsea School run by Josias Priest, a dancing teacher who periodically served the London theaters as *maître de ballet*. Purcell achieves great expressive beauty in *Dido and Aeneas*. The mark of individual genius is inscribed on every page. Yet, outside influences are apparent, too—the Italian cantata style, the French Lully's technique of dance music, and the English masque. Even in the miniature prelude to the opera Purcell borrowed a pattern from Lully—the slow introduction followed by an allegro built on fugal lines. As for Dido's celebrated "Lament," that alone would keep the memory of Purcell and his opera alive.

CHARACTERS
(as the parts are assigned in modern productions)

DIDO, *Queen of Carthage*	*Contralto*	AENEAS, *prominent in the de-*	
BELINDA, *a lady in waiting*	*Soprano*	*fense of Troy and legend-*	
ATTENDANT	*Mezzo-soprano*	*ary founder of Rome*	*Baritone*
SORCERESS	*Contralto*	SPIRIT, FIRST WITCH, SECOND WITCH, COURTIERS, SAILORS	

The action takes place in ancient Carthage

The tragic story of the Queen of Carthage is drawn from the fourth book of Virgil's *Aeneid*. Tate, of course, made some necessary modifications. Since

97

the opera was intended for performance at a girls' school, Dido's death had to be altered. Instead of committing suicide, the queen is made to die of a broken heart. Anna—Dido's confidante and sister—becomes Belinda. And Tate, following a common practice of the London stage, introduced witches as a set of malign, fateful symbols. Having fled devastated Troy, Aeneas is bound for Latium, where the gods are preparing an empire for him. A storm overtakes Aeneas' fleet, forcing him ashore at Carthage. There he and his men are feted by the widowed queen, Dido, who promptly falls in love with him. Though Aeneas returns her love, the gods frown on this union. Reminding Aeneas of his destiny to found a new nation in Italy, they order his departure from Carthage. With a heavy heart Aeneas sails away. Dido utters her great "Lament" and dies. This moving threnody rises to sublime heights through the simplest means. The technique is miraculously just in mirroring the intensity of Dido's anguish.

Recitative: *Thy hand, Belinda, darkness shades me,*
On thy bosom let me rest.
More I would, but Death invades me,
Death is now a welcome guest.

Aria: *When I am laid in earth, may my wrongs create*
No trouble in thy breast;
Remember me, but ah! forget my fate.

THE RCA-VICTOR RECORDS
(Sung in English)

ORCHESTRAL SELECTIONS (Arr. & Orchestrated by Caillet): *The Philadelphia Orchestra, Eugene Ormandy, Cond.* M-647 (15863-15864), 2-12″

ACT III
DIDO'S LAMENT—WHEN I AM LAID IN EARTH: *Marian Anderson, Contralto, with Orch.* 17257, 12″

Samuel H. Gottscho SCENE FROM JUILLIARD SCHOOL OF MUSIC PRODUCTION

Dinorah

(LE PARDON DE PLOËRMEL)

OPERA IN three acts. Music by Giacomo Meyerbeer. Libretto by Jules Barbier and
Michel Carré. First produced at the Paris Opéra-Comique, April 4, 1859. The
American *première* occurred at the French Opera House, New Orleans, on March 4,
1861, in French. It reached New York, in Italian, at the Academy of Music on
November 24, 1862, and was first staged at the Metropolitan Opera House on
January 29, 1892, again in Italian, with a cast headed by Marie van Zandt as Dinorah
and Jean Lassalle as Hoël. Amelita Galli-Curci was the Dinorah in the brilliant
Metropolitan revival of January 22, 1925, and Giuseppe de Luca was the Hoël. The
performance was once more in Italian. Seldom performed now, *Dinorah*—originally
produced under its French title, *Le Pardon de Ploërmel*—was a great favorite with
an earlier generation of operagoers. The opera shows the restless Meyerbeer turning
from romance and history to a new field of weird Breton fantasy and superstition.
The *pardon* of the original title means a "pilgrimage" in the sense of an act of piety.
The opera is saved from oblivion today largely because of the brilliant coloratura
aria, "The Shadow Song," and the compactly dramatic overture.

CHARACTERS

HOËL, *a goatherd*	*Baritone*	A HUNTER	*Bass*
CORENTIN, *a bagpipe-player*	*Tenor*	A REAPER	*Tenor*
DINORAH, *Hoël's fiancée*	*Soprano*	TWO GOATHERDS	*Sopranos*

The action takes place in Brittany

ACT I

SCENE: *A Wild and Desolate Mountain Place.* Before the opera starts,
a thunderstorm has destroyed Dinorah's cottage and interrupted her
marriage to the goatherd Hoël. In despair, Hoël seeks the help of a
village sorcerer, who makes him a proposition: if the goatherd will spend
a year of trial in a remote and desolate glen, he will reveal to him the
secret of a hidden treasure. However, there is a stern warning: the first
to touch the buried fortune will die. Hoël agrees and takes with him
Corentin, a half-witted bagpipe-player. Corentin, he schemes, will be the
first to place his hands on the booty.

When the curtain rises Dinorah, half crazed by the belief that Hoël
has deserted her forever, is wandering in the mountains, searching for a
stray goat. Recovering the lost goat, she sits down and sings an eerie
lullaby and then makes her way to Corentin's hut, which is located near
by. When the bagpiper returns he starts in fear, mistaking Dinorah for
the sinister Lady of the Meadows. Dinorah, playing on his fears, commands him to play music while she dances, and finally whirls him into her
frenzied dance, till they both fall exhausted. Shortly after Dinorah leaves,
Hoël appears and informs Corentin that the sorcerer has instructed him
to look for a white goat which will lead him to the treasure. Hoël hears

the tinkling of a goat bell and goes in pursuit, dragging the terrified idiot along.

ACT II

SCENE: *A Forest of Birch Trees in the Moonlight.* Dinorah has come to an open place in the woods where the weird shadows in the moonlight heighten her mood of mad fantasy. As she catches her shadow outlined sharply on the ground, she flings her arms out as if to embrace it as a long-lost friend. Beginning a wild dance in the moonbeams, she now sings the celebrated "Shadow Song," with its fitful play of florid fancy and waltzlike lilt. Pathetically, she tells the shadow of Hoël's love for her and begs it never to leave her.

The scene changes to a desert plain, with the sea in the distance. A violent storm is raging. Hoël is still seeking the treasure. Corentin, seized with terror, has become suspicious of Hoël's designs. To save himself, he persuades the crazed Dinorah to go down into the gorge where the treasure is hidden. While Dinorah is crossing a bridge, a dam bursts in the mountains and the rising waters carry her away. Hoël, who recognizes her from a broken necklace he has picked up, plunges into the flood to rescue her.

ACT III

SCENE: *A Rural Spot.* A morning calm has followed the storm. As the curtain rises, Hoël appears, bearing the unconscious Dinorah. As hunters and goatherds gather about them, Hoël, believing her dead, reproaches himself bitterly. Gradually, however, Dinorah comes back to life. She instantly recognizes Hoël and her reason returns. Hoël vows to abandon the treasure hunt, and assures Dinorah that her frightful experience was only a dream. As the lovers are reunited, the chorus intones a grateful "Hymn to the Virgin," recalling the *pardon*, or pilgrimage, of Ploërmel.

Matzene
AMELITA GALLI-CURCI AS DINORAH

THE RCA-VICTOR RECORDS

OMBRE LÉGÈRE (Schattentanz) (Shadow Song): *Miliza Korjus, Soprano, with Orch. In German*
13807, 12"

(In Album M-871)

Lily Pons, Soprano, with Orch. In French
11-8225, 12"

Bassani, Milan

ACT II, SCENE 2—LA SCALA PRODUCTION, MILAN

Don Carlos

OPERA IN five acts. Music by Giuseppe Verdi. Libretto by François Joseph Méry and Camille du Locle, founded on a tragedy by Schiller. First performance at the Opéra, Paris, March 11, 1867, in French. United States *première* at the Academy of Music, New York, April 12, 1877, in Italian. Also in Italian, *Don Carlos* entered the Metropolitan repertory on December 23, 1920, with Rosa Ponselle, Margarete Matzenauer, Giovanni Martinelli, Giuseppe de Luca, Adamo Didur, and Marie Sundelius in the principal roles. Feodor Chaliapin first sang the role of Philip II at the Metropolitan on December 2, 1922.

    Don Carlos belongs to an intermediate stage of Verdi's career as a composer. Coming after the magnificent successes of *Il Trovatore, La Traviata,* and *The Masked Ball,* it shows Verdi reaching out toward the fuller, richer style with which he was later to become associated in *Aïda.*

    Schiller's highly dramatic tragedy inspired Verdi to compose some thrilling operatic music. Moreover, the fact that he was writing for the French lyric theater may have influenced him to follow, somewhat, the example of Meyerbeer in conceiving his work on a grandiose scale.

    Sixteen years or so after the world *première* of *Don Carlos* Verdi, apparently finding its libretto a bit cumbersome, gave Antonio Ghislanzoni authority to shorten it to four acts, he himself revising the score. Although he considered this abbreviated version musically stronger with the excision of Act I, a third edition reinstated Act I, retaining, however, several alterations in the previous revision.

CHARACTERS

PHILIP II OF SPAIN	*Bass*	PRINCESS EBOLI	*Mezzo-soprano*
DON CARLOS, *Infante of Spain*	*Tenor*	THEOBALD, *Elizabeth's page*	
RODRIGO, *Marquis of Posa*	*Baritone*		
GRAND INQUISITOR	*Bass*	COUNTESS OF AREMBERG	
A FRIAR	*Baritone*	COUNT OF LERNA	
ELIZABETH OF VALOIS	*Soprano*	A ROYAL HERALD	

FLEMISH LADIES, INQUISITORS, GENTLEMEN AND LADIES OF THE COURTS OF FRANCE AND SPAIN, MEMBERS OF THE POPULACE, PAGES, GUARDS, FAMILIARS OF THE HOLY OFFICE, SOLDIERS, MAGISTRATES, DEPUTIES FROM THE VARIOUS PROVINCES CONSTITUTING THE SPANISH EMPIRE

The action takes place in France and Spain in the sixteenth century

Don Carlos, son of Philip II, King of Spain, is in love with the beautiful Elizabeth de Valois, daughter of Henry II, of France. She returns his affection, but for reasons of state is compelled to marry not Don Carlos, but Philip II himself; thus the young prince finds himself in love with his own stepmother. He confides in his friend, Rodrigo, who advises him to leave the Spanish court and obtain a commission from his father to go to the Netherlands and relieve the Flemings from some of the cruelties inflicted on them by their Spanish rulers. Don Carlos meets with Elizabeth, to gain her influence in obtaining the object of this request from Philip. But as the King is secretly in favor of the method of rule of the Spanish tyrants, the request only angers him and helps estrange father and son. Moreover, as a result of this meeting, the former passion between Don Carlos and Elizabeth returns with even greater intensity.

Don Carlos has a dangerous admirer in Princess Eboli, who learns that the Queen has by no means ceased to love him, and, overcome by jealousy, informs Philip of the state of affairs. At the beginning of the last act, we see the King alone in his library, thinking of his unhappy, loveless state. It is dawn, and his weary eyes long for sleep. "Yet," he meditates, "I shall sleep only in my royal mantle when the day of my doom shall have come," and sings the beautiful aria beginning with the words *"Dormirò sol nel manto"* ("I shall sleep").

Acting on the advice of the Grand Inquisitor, he orders Don Carlos to be thrown in prison. Princess Eboli repents her rash act and confesses to the Queen. Elizabeth orders her to leave the court . . . death or exile! Left alone, the Princess pours forth her grief in the air *"O don fatale"* ("Oh, fatal gift"), a melody of great beauty and dramatic force.

Rodrigo visits Don Carlos in prison and there is shot by order of the King, who suspects him of aiding the Flemings. He bids farewell to earth in the beautiful melody, *"O Carlo, ascolta."*

Carlos is freed, but, in keeping a tryst with Elizabeth before the tomb of Charles V in the Monastery of Yuste, is discovered by the King, and handed over to the officers of the Inquisition. However, a monk steps forth from the tomb, and, dressed as he is in the habit of the Emperor, all present take him for an apparition. In their surprise the officers release Don Carlos, who is led away by the strange figure into the monastery.

JOEL BERGLUND AS PHILIP II

ALEXANDER KIPNIS AS PHILIP II

THE RCA-VICTOR RECORDS
(Sung in Italian)

ACT IV

O DON FATALE (Oh, Fatal Gift): *Sigrid Onegin, Contralto, with Orch.*
7191, 12"

Marian Anderson, Contralto, with Orch.
14745, 12"

O CARLO, ASCOLTA (O Carlos, Listen to My Plea): *Giuseppe de Luca, Baritone, with Orch.*
1591, 10"

SIGRID ONEGIN AS PRINCESS EBOLI

R. Strohmeyer   ACT I, SCENE 1—SAN FRANCISCO OPERA PRODUCTION

Don Giovanni
(DON JUAN)

OPERA IN two acts. Music by Wolfgang Amadeus Mozart. Libretto by Lorenzo da Ponte, partly founded on Bertati's *Don Giovanni, o sia Il Convitato di pietra* (*Don Juan, or The Stone Guest.*) The complete title of the Mozart-da Ponte opera is really *Il Dissoluto punito, o sia Il Don Giovanni* (*The Reprobate Punished, or Don Juan*). First performance, National Theater, Prague, October 29, 1787. First American performance given at the Park Theater, New York, May 23, 1826, in Italian. Metropolitan *première* took place on November 29, 1883, with a cast including Emmy Fursch-Madi, Christine Nilsson, Marcella Sembrich, Italo Campanini, Giuseppe Kaschmann, and Mirabella.

The Don Juan theme, whose origin has been traced to legends out of Spanish monasteries no longer in existence, was first treated by Tirso de Molina (Gabriel Tellez) in a dramatic play, dating from 1630, which, more or less, is the source for da Ponte's libretto. Other dramatists who have utilized the legend have been Molière, for his comedy *Don Juan, ou Le Festin de pierre* (*Don Juan, or The Stone Guest*), 1665, and Thomas Shadwell, in his *The Libertine.* The legend has received numerous treatments by many men of literature, and the composers who have turned to it for inspiration number among them, besides Mozart and Gazzaniga (who did the setting for Bertati's libretto), Gluck, who composed a ballet based on it, and Dargomijsky, who wrote a four-act opera on the theme to a libretto by Alexander Pushkin.

Don Giovanni is one of the comparatively few great operas that were successful from their very first performance. It is at once popular with the operagoing public and beloved and admired by connoisseurs. Such widely varied geniuses—to name only a few—have all testified to its greatness: Beethoven and Rossini, Wagner and Gounod! For well-nigh a century and a half it has been an inexhaustible treasure house of melody.

This great opera began its career as an *opera buffa*, but Mozart was so carried away with the dramatic possibilities of the story that his music makes of it something much greater. For the opening and closing scenes he composed some of the most remarkable dramatic music ever written. The intermediate scenes, although treated in spirit of comedy, are invested with music charming and gloriously beautiful. Through his melodies, at first seemingly so attractively naïve, Mozart delineates the characters of his drama in a most subtle manner. Where later composers might have required involved harmonies, polyphonic treatment of themes, and elaborate orchestration for a thorough exposition of the dramatic ideas, Mozart uses his incomparable melodies, and with his simple means attains an equally great effect.

Don Giovanni

The story is told that at the first rehearsal of this opera, Mozart, who was directing, was not satisfied with the way in which the actress playing the part of Zerlina gave her cry of terror from behind the scenes. He left the orchestra, and, ordering a repetition of the finale of the first act, concealed himself on the stage behind the wings. There stood Zerlina, awaiting her cue. When it came, Mozart quickly reached from his hiding place and pinched her. She gave a piercing shriek. "That's the way I want it," exclaimed the composer, returning to the orchestra, while the actress in her amazement both laughed and blushed.

It is said that on the eve of the general rehearsal, that is to say, two nights before the *première*, friends of Mozart reminded him that the overture was still unwritten. The composer pretended to grow nervous about it, and went to his room. About midnight he began work. His wife was at his side and kept him awake with stories and with punch. At seven in the morning when the music copyists came, the work was done.

CHARACTERS

DON GIOVANNI, *a licentious young nobleman*   Baritone (or Bass)

DON PEDRO, *the Commandant*   Bass

DON OTTAVIO, *betrothed to Donna Anna*   Tenor

LEPORELLO, *his servant*   Bass

MASETTO, *a peasant*   Bass (or Baritone)

DONNA ANNA, *his daughter*   Soprano

DONNA ELVIRA, *a lady of Burgos*   Soprano

ZERLINA, *betrothed to Masetto*   Soprano

De Bellis Studios
ELEANOR STEBER AS DONNA ELVIRA

PEASANTS, MUSICIANS, DANCERS, DEMONS

The action takes place at Seville, in the middle of the seventeenth century

The Overture begins with the solemn music of the banquet scene, which takes place at the end of the opera, when the Commandant's statue, accepting Don Giovanni's invitation, visits him during his dinner. This is followed by music of much gayer and brighter quality, a characterization of the bold, pleasure-seeking Don.

ACT I

SCENE 1: *A Courtyard of the Commandant's Palace in Seville.* Leporello, wrapped in his cloak, is waiting in a garden outside a house in Seville. He complains that he has rest neither by night nor day, and he adds, "Gaily he within is sporting, while I must keep off all intrusion." The complaining servant quickly conceals himself as his master, Don Giovanni, comes excitedly from the house, pursued by Donna Anna. The sounds of their voices

ACT II. SCENE 3

bring the Commandant, Donna Anna's father, to the scene. A duel soon follows, and the gray-haired Commandant falls dying from a stroke of the agile
Don, who at once flees with Leporello. Donna Anna has run for aid, and
when she returns she is grief-stricken to find her father dead. With her is her
betrothed, Don Ottavio. Noble youth that he is, he endeavors to calm her
despair and joins with her in swearing vengeance upon the unknown assailant
and murderer.

SCENE 2: *A Lonely Square Outside of Seville.* While fleeing along a desolate
road, Don Giovanni and his inevitable Leporello espy a woman approaching
who seems to be weeping bitterly. Giovanni says that he will go to console
her. "As you've done eighteen hundred others," murmurs Leporello. But
on drawing nearer the Don starts back in surprise. It is Donna Elvira, whom
he has deserted even while eloping with her. She berates him for his deceit-
fulness. Giovanni attempts to explain his sudden disappearance. If she will
not believe him, let her hear what Leporello says about it. While the servant
holds her attention for a moment, the deceiver quickly slips away. When
Donna Elvira turns to Giovanni, he is gone! Leporello tells her to be comforted, singing the celebrated "Catalogue Song," "*Madamina, il catalogo è
questo*" ("Dear lady, this is the catalogue"). What comfort Donna Elvira
may receive from Leporello's arch enumeration of the Don's philanderings
is hard to imagine. This sprightly patter song is a splendid example of
Mozart's musical felicity with words.

ACT II, SCENE 1—ELVIRA, LEPORELLO, AND THE DON

After giving her this cynical comfort, Leporello goes in pursuit of his master. And Donna Elvira, like Donna Anna, is now, too, seeking revenge.

SCENE 3: *A Country Spot Near Don Giovanni's Castle.* In the country, villagers are making merry with singing and dancing, in honor of the forthcoming marriage of Zerlina and Masetto. Don Giovanni joins the gathering and, having cast covetous eyes upon the village bride, orders Leporello to invite all to his castle, then cleverly detains Zerlina.

The maiden is greatly flattered by the Don's gallantry and his offer of marriage. The courtly grace of Giovanni and the hesitant yielding of Zerlina are admirably expressed in the duet *"Là ci darem la mano!"* ("Thy little hand, Love"). Just as Giovanni seems to have succeeded, Donna Elvira appears, and by her denunciation shows the noble's real character to Zerlina, who at once hurries to her betrothed. Donna Anna and Don Ottavio also come upon the scene. To them, Don Giovanni so far is merely an acquaintance not associated with any of the dark deeds of the former evening. Donna Elvira's accusations, however, begin to raise suspicions, and in Giovanni's parting words Donna Anna recognizes the voice of her father's murderer. She leaves Don Ottavio, who renews, to himself, his vow to avenge her wrongs, for to him she is all happiness. He sings of his love for her in the exalted beauty of the aria *"Dalla sua pace!"*

SCENE 4: *The Garden of Don Giovanni's Palace.* Don Giovanni has ordered a festival at his palace that evening. In the garden, together with other peas-

ants, Masetto and Zerlina are still quarreling over the Don's amorous overtures to her. The youth upbraids the girl for her faithlessness in yielding so
easily to Giovanni, and tells her to go away forever. She pleads with him,
singing the wistful and lovely aria *"Batti, batti, o bel Masetto"* ("Scold me,
dear Masetto"), in which she seeks his forgiveness.

Upon hearing such a plea, Masetto, of course, forgives her. Don Giovanni now approaches, and after an attempt to smooth things over with the
jealous husband-to-be, he invites all into the palace. Leporello opens a window for a moment, and we hear the strains of the minuet that is being danced
within. As he stands there enjoying the evening air, three masked figures
enter the garden, and Leporello, in accordance with the custom of the time,
invites them to the festivities. When they have accepted, Leporello goes to
admit them. The masked characters are none other than Donna Anna, Donna
Elvira, and Don Ottavio, who, before entering the palace, pause to pray for
heaven's aid in achieving vengeance, their voices joining in the solemn trio,
"Protegga, il giusto cielo" ("May heaven aid our cause").

SCENE 5: *Don Giovanni's Palace.* In Don Giovanni's palace the festivities
are progressing merrily. The graceful and courtly minuet is danced to the
incomparable music of Mozart.

During the minuet Giovanni has contrived to lead Zerlina to an adjoining room. Suddenly the dance is interrupted by her screams for help, and a
moment later, the Don comes in, sword in hand and dragging Leporello. But
this ruse fails to convince anybody of Giovanni's innocence. Donna Anna,
Donna Elvira, and Don Ottavio unmask and confront Giovanni; but he,
ignoring their accusations, draws his sword and, forcing a passage through
the crowd, escapes.

ACT II

SCENE I: *Before Donna Elvira's House.* At the rise of the curtain, we find
Don Giovanni and Leporello in front of Donna Elvira's house. Leporello
complains about his recent treatment by Don Giovanni, and the latter placates
him with money. Donna Elvira then comes to the window, and, since she cannot quite forget her love, she is still vowing revenge. She has taken Zerlina
into her care, and it is this magnet that draws Giovanni to Elvira's house.
The Don changes cloaks with Leporello, and with the help of darkness and
this disguise, the servant succeeds in luring away Donna Elvira, who rejoices
that her lover has returned. Meanwhile Giovanni serenades Zerlina in a most
ingratiating air, *"Deh, vieni, alla finestra"* ("Come to the window").

Masetto approaches, and Giovanni, trying to conceal his identity, assumes the manner of Leporello. Masetto is hunting for Giovanni to kill him,
or at least give him a good beating, but the clever Don administers the drub-

bing to Masetto instead. Thus Zerlina finds her betrothed lying in the street in a rather amusingly sore and battered condition. She asks if he is badly hurt, and he replies that he is wounded not only in body, but in heart. Zerlina prescribes a balm in the engaging aria, *"Vedrai, carino"* ("Dearest, shall I tell you").

Bruno

ROSE BAMPTON AS DONNA ANNA   JAMES MELTON AS OTTAVIO

SCENE 2: *The Garden of the Commandant's Palace.* Leporello does so well with his ludicrous impersonation of Don Giovanni that he cannot get away from Donna Elvira. Before the house of Donna Anna, however, the pair are confronted by the various persons whom Don Giovanni has wronged; Leporello is forced to reveal himself and flee from their wrath. Don Ottavio, who is present, again affirms his intentions of bringing justice upon Giovanni; he then sings the great aria, *"Il mio tesoro intanto"* ("To my beloved"), a difficult piece of florid *bel canto*.

SCENE 3: *Before the Statue of the Commandant in the Graveyard.* In fleeing from his master's accusers, Leporello chances upon Don Giovanni. It is now long past midnight, and as they grope about in the darkness they come upon a statue erected to the memory of the Commandant. Giovanni orders Leporello to invite it to supper with him at his palace. The statue nods acceptance; Leporello trembles, but his master is undaunted.

SCENE 4: *In the Commandant's Palace.* Before the final scene, we have a touching one between Don Ottavio and Donna Anna. He implores her to forget her sorrows, for the villain will soon be apprehended and be punished for his deeds. And he asks her to marry him. But her answer, tender and considerate, is that she cannot while still in the grasp of her recent sorrows. How-

New York Times
TITO SCHIPA AS DON OTTAVIO

ever, she continues, she does love him and assures him that they will marry in time, as she sings the magnificent aria, *"Non mi dir"* ("Beloved mine, do not say").

SCENE 5: *A Banquet Hall in Don Giovanni's Palace.* In the palace a banquet is spread. While Giovanni eats, his own private orchestra plays airs from operas of the day. Leporello, looking on rather nervously, comments on the music that is being played. "That's a song I've heard too often!" he says concerning a Mozart number, which is *"Non più andrai"* from *The Marriage of Figaro.*

The musicians take their leave. Donna Elvira unceremoniously enters and, on her knees, entreats Giovanni to change his ways. He is firm—cold in his refusal. She leaves, hopeless. In the corridor she screams; she re-enters the room and runs out through another door. Giovanni orders Leporello to see what it is; the servant comes back trembling, "The man in stone!" He refuses to open the door. Giovanni boldly takes a candle, draws his sword, and goes into the corridor. A moment later he backs into the room; there follows him, with slow, heavy footsteps, accompanied by fearsome music, the statue of the Commandant. "You have invited me . . . I am here!" it says. Leporello has sought refuge under the table. Giovanni coolly orders him to serve the meal. "Don Giovanni, I have been your guest, will you be mine?"

"Yes!" replies the Don, still fearless. The statue grasps his hand, to seal the bargain, and the Don is held in its stony grip. Wrenching himself free, Don Giovanni spurns the suggestion of repentance. A fiery pit opens, and the Don disappears in flames, brave to the end.

To impart to the opera a "happy ending," there is generally added a finale in which Donna Anna, Donna Elvira, Zerlina, Don Ottavio, Leporello, and Masetto take part. Leporello tells them of Don Giovanni's fate, after which they all rejoice, for their cause has been righted.

Don Giovanni

THE RCA-VICTOR RECORDS
(Sung in Italian unless otherwise noted)

COMPLETE RECORDING: *John Brownlee, Baritone; Ina Souez, Soprano; Luise Helletsgruber, Soprano; Roy Henderson, Baritone; David Franklin, Bass; Koloman von Pataky, Tenor; Salvatore Baccaloni, Bass; Audrey Mildmay, Soprano; with Chorus and Orchestra of the Glyndebourne Festival Co.; Fritz Busch, Cond.* (Recorded in the Glyndebourne Opera House, Glyndebourne, England):

DMC-106 (DM-423) (Vol. 1)
              (16426-16433), 8-12"
      (DM-424) (Vol. 2)
              (16434-16440), 7-12"
      (DM-425) (Vol. 3)
              (16441-16448), 8-12"
MC-106 (M-423) (Vol. 1)
              (14747-14754)
      (M-424) (Vol. 2)
              (14763-14769)
      (M-425) (Vol. 3)
              (14777-14784)

ACT I

MADAMINA, IL CATALOGO (The Catalogue Aria): *Joel Berglund, Baritone, with Orch.*   10-1346, 10"

LÀ CI DAREM LA MANO (Thy Little Hand, Love): *Elisabeth Rethberg, Soprano; Ezio Pinza, Bass; with Orch.*
                     2154, 10"
         (In Album M-783)
Margherita Perras, Soprano; Gerhard Hüsch, Baritone; with Orch. In German   4374, 10"

OR, SAI CHI L'ONORE (Vengeance Aria): *Rose Bampton, Soprano, with Orch.*
                11-8466, 12"

FINCH' HAN DAL VINO (For a Carousal): *Ezio Pinza, Bass, with Orch.*
                   1467, 10"

BATTI, BATTI, O BEL MASETTO (Scold Me, Dear Masetto): *Lucrezia Bori, Soprano, with Orch.*   14614, 12"
         (In Album M-405)
Eleanor Steber, Soprano, with Orch.
                11-9114, 12"

MINUET: *Victor Band*   20990, 10"

ACT II

SERENATA—DEH VIENI ALLA FINESTRA (Open Thy Window): *Ezio Pinza, Bass, with Orch.*   1467, 10"

VEDRAI, CARINO (Dearest, Shall I Tell You): *Lucrezia Bori, Soprano, with Orch.*   1846, 10"
         (In Album M-405)

IL MIO TESORO (To My Beloved): *Richard Crooks, Tenor, with Orch.*
                 15235, 12"
James Melton, Tenor, with Orch.
               11-8929, 12"
         (In Album M-1013)
John McCormack, Tenor, with Orch.
               15-1015, 12"
   (Acoustical Recording)

NON MI DIR, BELL' IDOL MIO (Beloved Mine, Do Not Say): *Rose Bampton, Soprano, with Orch.*   11-8466, 12"

EZIO PINZA AS DON GIOVANNI

111

ACT I, SCENE 1—METROPOLITAN OPERA PRODUCTION

Don Pasquale

OPERA BUFFA in three acts. Music by Gaetano Donizetti. Libretto by the composer and "Michele Accursi" (pseudonym of Giacomo Ruffini, a political exile from Italy, whose real name appears in later editions of the score), based on Angelo Anelli's libretto for Stefano Pavesi's opera, *Ser Marc' Antonio*. First performance, *Théâtre-Italien*, Paris, January 3, 1843. American *première*, New York, Park Theater, March 9, 1846, in English. The initial performance in the United States, in Italian, occurred at the Astor Place Opera House, November 29, 1849. An important revival at the Metropolitan on April 5, 1913, offered Lucrezia Bori, Umberto Macnez, Antonio Scotti, and Antonio Pini-Corsi in the principal roles, with Arturo Toscanini conducting. With Salvatore Baccaloni as the Don, the opera obtained another auspicious revival at the Metropolitan on December 21, 1940, the others including Bidu Sayao and Nino Martini.

This delightful work shows Donizetti's excellent gifts for comedy. His music sparkles with verve and good humor, in which respects it matches the gaiety of the libretto itself. Latterly it has been one of the Metropolitan's most ably presented operas.

CHARACTERS

DON PASQUALE, *an old bachelor*	*Bass*	DR. MALATESTA, *a physician*	*Baritone*
ERNESTO, *his nephew*	*Tenor*	A NOTARY	*Bass*
NORINA, *a young widow*	*Soprano*	VALETS, CHAMBERMAIDS, DRESSMAKERS, ETC.	

The action takes place in Rome, early in the nineteenth century

A gay little overture brings forward a few of the melodies of the opera proper. They serve admirably to set the mood for the work.

ACT I

SCENE 1: *A Room in Don Pasquale's House.* Don Pasquale is displeased with his nephew Ernesto, and particularly with the latter's devotion to the charming young widow, Norina. Yet Dr. Malatesta, the Don's friend and physician, is in perfect sympathy with the lovers, and promises to aid them.

112

He starts forthwith by singing the praises of a fictitious sister of his to Don Pasquale, who by this time has become completely enamored of the mysterious lady, decides to marry her sight unseen, and thus cut Ernesto entirely out of his will. His enthusiasm is depicted in the song *"Ah! un fuoco insolito"* ("Unwonted fire"). In fact, when Ernesto appears, presently, he is roundly scolded and given the information about the Don's decision to marry, and especially irate does he become when he discovers that it was his friend Malatesta who contrived the evildoings. And he sings of his despair in the aria *"Sogno soave e casto"* ("Fond dream of love").

SCENE 2: *In Norina's House.* The next scene reveals Norina, the lady in the case, who is disliked by Don Pasquale and loved by Ernesto. She is discovered in her room, reading a romantic novel, and she laughs merrily, for, as she says in the lively *"So anch' io la virtù magica"* ("I, too, know the magical craft"), the tricks and tears and wiles of accomplishing a man's enslavement are known to her. Norina knows that Malatesta has a plan for deceiving Don Pasquale, and he now tells her of it. It requires that Norina shall masquerade as the sister of Malatesta and so plague the Don that he will sicken of the idea of marriage and probably force Norina to marry his nephew, Ernesto, which is, of course, exactly what Norina and Ernesto desire. They rehearse the part Norina is to play when she meets Don Pasquale.

ACT II

SCENE: *Don Pasquale's House.* After a brief prelude, the curtain rises, disclosing Ernesto, who is still bemoaning his sad fate. He soon departs, and Don Pasquale enters, arrayed in his finest. He is awaiting the arrival of his future bride, who appears, heavily veiled, escorted by Malatesta. She is exceedingly shy and coy, and Don Pasquale, of course, has no idea of her true identity. In any case, he is delighted with her, and proposes marriage, to which, after some high-pressure salesmanship on the Don's part and a studied restraint on hers, she consents. The Notary is brought in, and Don Pasquale, with much legal verbiage, dictates the terms of the marriage contract and signs it. Just as Norina is also about to sign it Ernesto is heard without. He enters, recognizes Norina, but by frantic gestures and whisperings is persuaded to remain silent and to act as witness to the marriage contract. As soon as this is done, Norina abandons her affected timidity and turns instantaneously into a vicious termagant. She will have nothing to do with Pasquale and announces her intention to retain Ernesto as usher in her house. The Don objects to this, and Norina ferociously reproves and even threatens him. Then in the presence of Pasquale she summons the household staff and outlines a scheme of living so extravagant that her husband-to-be is choked with rage and declares he will not pay her bills.

ACT III

SCENE: *The Same.* Norina, marvelously gowned, is giving orders to a troop of servants, while Pasquale is contemplating the huge pile of unpaid bills his marriage has produced. He attempts forcefully to dissuade Norina from going to the theater and for his pains has his ears soundly boxed by his vigorous lady. As she goes on her way she drops a letter, which Pasquale discovers to be an appointment for a rendezvous. With jealousy added to his other troubles, he is in complete despair, and the plotters now feel that Pasquale has been sufficiently tortured. Malatesta offers to correct matters if Pasquale will give him carte blanche. This the Don is glad to do, with the condition that Norina leave his house at once. Ernesto comes to serenade Norina, who presently joins him, and while they are talking, Pasquale and Malatesta approach. Ernesto withdraws.

Don Pasquale accuses Norina of secreting a lover in the house. She denies this, and Pasquale's search for the miscreant is fruitless. The solution comes when Pasquale calls Ernesto and promises him a liberal allowance if he will marry Norina and get out of his house. This Ernesto is only too glad to do, and presently it is discovered that Dr. Malatesta's spurious sister and Norina were the same person; that the marriage of Don Pasquale was a mock marriage, and all his misfortune is the result of a mischievous scheme. But the old man is so happy to extricate himself from his troubles that he sends his nephew and the bride away with his blessings.

THE RCA-VICTOR RECORDS
(Sung in Italian)

BIDU SAYAO AS NORINA

COMPLETE RECORDING: *Tito Schipa, Tenor; Ernesto Badini, Baritone; Afro Poli, Baritone; Adelaide Saraceni, Soprano; Giordano Callegari, Bass; with Chorus and Orchestra of La Scala, Milan, Carlo Sabajno, Cond.*
DMC-116 (DM-187) (Vol. 1)
      (13330-13337), 8-12"
   (DM-187) (Vol. 2)
      (13338-13344), 7-12"
MC-116 (M-187) (Vol. 1)
      (11563-11570)
   (M-187) (Vol. 2)
      (11571-11577)

ACT I
SOGNO SOAVE E CASTO (Fond Dream of Love): *Tito Schipa, Tenor, with Orch.* 1282, 10"
ACT III

NOTTURNO—TORNAMI A DIR CHE M'AMI (Once Again Let Me Hear Thee): *Amelita Galli-Curci, Soprano; Tito Schipa, Tenor; with Orch.* 1755, 10"

Apex

SAN CARLO OPERA COMPANY SETTING

Don Quichotte
(DON QUIXOTE)

OPERA IN five acts. Music by Jules Massenet. Libretto by Henri Cain, based on Jacques Le Lorrain's play, in turn based on the novel by Cervantes. First produced at Monte Carlo, February 19, 1910, with Feodor Chaliapin in the title role. American *première* in New Orleans on January 27, 1912. Le Lorrain's play deeply impressed Raoul Gunsbourg, manager of the Monte Carlo Opera. He communicated his enthusiasm to Massenet, who promptly saw possibilities of adding *Don Quixote* to his growing operatic gallery of historical and literary figures. Le Lorrain gave his consent, but died shortly after. Henri Cain was then engaged to write the libretto. In the opera the tragicomic knight retains the noble pathos and chivalric fantasy of the Spanish classic, but the wild buffoonery is reduced to a minimum. The rural siren, Dulcinea, becomes a rich courtesan, and Sancho Panza remains his faithful, practical self. The ramifications of the plot are the work of the French authors rather than of Cervantes, who is, of course, solely responsible for the famous episode of the windmills.

CHARACTERS

DON QUIXOTE	Baritone	GARCIAS, *a burlesquer*		Soprano
LA BELLE DULCINEA, *a courtesan*	Soprano	RODRIQUEZ		Tenor
SANCHO PANZA	Baritone	JUAN		Tenor
PEDRO, *a burlesquer*	Soprano	TWO VALETS		Baritones

The action takes place in Spain

115

ACT I

SCENE: *A Public Square Before Dulcinea's House.* Don Quixote is paying court to the courtesan Dulcinea. As he proposes marriage, in flowery language, Dulcinea's many other admirers deride the Don and his rustic retainer, Sancho. The amused courtesan prevents a duel between the deluded knight and another suitor, and agrees to marry the Don if he recovers for her a precious necklace stolen by the brigand Tenebrun.

ACT II

SCENE: *Before the Windmills.* The Don and Sancho begin their search for the necklace. Mounted on Rosinante and a donkey, they approach some windmills, which the Don mistakes for giants stretching menacing arms toward them. The Don charges.

ACT III

SCENE: *The Camp of the Brigands.* Seized as they arrive at the camp of the brigands, the companions are bound and threatened with death. But the Don's strange talk and grave bearing awe his captors; his gentleness and lofty ideals almost move the bandits to tears. Finally they permit him to go his way unharmed, and as a token of their feelings they even surrender the stolen necklace to the Don.

ACT IV

SCENE: *A Salon in Dulcinea's House.* A fete is in progress in Dulcinea's house as the misguided knight returns with his faithful follower, Sancho. Solemnly he restores the jewel to Dulcinea, who, overjoyed, embraces the Don. But when he again proposes marriage, she recoils and mocks him. She is only a courtesan, she confesses, unworthy of so noble a husband. The Don and Sancho leave gloomily to the derisive laughter of Dulcinea's guests.

ACT V

SCENE: *A Path in the Forest.* It is a starlit night. Sancho is leading his brokenhearted and disillusioned master along a forest path. They stop, and Sancho watches over the Don as he rests against the trunk of an oak. The music that follows is overwhelming in its pathos and beauty, and Chaliapin, differentiating the voices of the Don and Sancho, communicates all its majesty in his celebrated recording. The orchestra plays very softly a wistful melody, and Sancho sings a prayer for the repose of his master's soul. The Don now awakens. His voice is feeble, and he knows that death is upon him. Sancho cries out in grief when the Don announces they must part. The woodwinds discourse a soft pastorale as the knight recalls the village of his childhood. Now he must die. Sancho gives a sob of anguish. In a final surge of strength the Don rises, and to a bold orchestral accompaniment the great knight-errant declares that he had always fought the good fight for the weak and helpless. Then he remembers a promise to Sancho, a promise of castles in Spain, yes, even of an island. Take that island, says the Don; it is all I can give—an enchanted island of infinite wonders, an island of dreams! As the Don's strength gives out, he gasps a last wish to Sancho to say a prayer for him. The voice of Dulcinea is heard from afar, singing a farewell to happiness and love. The Don throbs with joy at the sound of her voice. It is the voice of his beloved calling to him, and he will go. The Don dies, and Sancho disconsolately sobs out his grief.

Mishkin
FEODOR CHALIAPIN AS DON QUICHOTTE
AND GIUSEPPE DE LUCA AS SANCHO PANZA

THE RCA-VICTOR RECORDS
(Sung in French)

ACT V

MORT DE DON QUICHOTTE (Death of Don Quixote) : *Feodor Chaliapin, Bass; Olive Kline, Soprano; with Orch.* 6693, 12″

Elektra

TRAGEDY IN one act (after Sophocles). Music by Richard Strauss. Libretto by Hugo von Hofmannsthal. This, incidentally, was his first collaboration with Strauss. First performance, Dresden Hofoper, January 25, 1909, with a cast comprising Anna Krull as Elektra; Margarete Siems as Chrysothemis; Ernestine Schumann-Heink as Clytemnestra, and Karl Perron as Orestes. Ernst von Schuch conducted. The work was first given in the United States at the Manhattan Opera House, New York, February 1, 1910, in a French translation by Henri Gauthier Villars, the cast consisting of Mariette Mazarin, Alice Baron, Jeanne Gerville-Réache, Gustave Huberdeau, and Jean Duffault (Aegisthus), with Henriquez de la Fuente conducting. Revived at the Metropolitan in the original German, December 3, 1932, with Gertrude Kappel, Göta Ljunberg, Karin Branzell, Friedrich Schorr, and Rudolf Laubenthal. Later performances that season presented Ljunberg as Elektra, Dorothee Manski as Chrysothemis, and Maria Olszewska as Clytemnestra.

Richard Strauss' score for this work is emotionally powerful; it teems with extraordinary realistic effects, and further displays his remarkable orchestral imagination. It is a quite singable score, in spite of its often violent qualities, and as examples of that there are Elektra's invocation of Agamemnon, some of the music assigned to Clytemnestra, and those passages of tender beauty which follow the scene of recognition between Orestes and Elektra.

There is one set, which shows the rear of the palace in Mycenae. Adjacent are the servants' quarters. King Agamemnon, murdered by his wife Clytemnestra and her lover Aegisthus, lies in a visible grave, over which his daughter Elektra mourns his death. Both she and her sister Chrysothemis have been reduced to being servants by their despotic, evil mother, as well as by Aegisthus, who now rules in the slain king's place. Orestes, brother of Elektra, has made good his escape from Mycenae.

In the meantime, Elektra mourns and prays for revenge, invoking her father's spirit and vowing that his children will one day dance in joy upon his grave. Her only concern is how to obtain this revenge, for she herself feels unequal to the task.

Clytemnestra, a quite horrid and sinister figure, appears during one of her daughter's lamentations. The queen remarks on her inability to sleep, and inquires of Elektra, whom she flatters as being "wise," what blood rituals or sacrifices may be made, that her serenity and untroubled sleep may be restored. The answer to all this is scorn and mockery from Elektra, as she predicts in a scathing attack the dire events that will overtake Clytemnestra and her paramour. Fear-stricken before this avenging figure, the queen recoils, but when one of her confidantes rushes in to whisper something to her, suddenly Clytemnestra's mood changes to rapture. Mystified, Elektra is soon informed of the reason for the transformation, for Chrysothemis comes to her sister with the tragic, though wrong, information that their brother is dead.

There is a scene in which Elektra tries to persuade her sister to commit the retributive act, but Chrysothemis says that she is incapable of it, and with that she departs.

Elektra

In the shadow of the gate we see a stranger, and we know it is Orestes, although neither Elektra nor her brother knows the other at first. When recognition finally comes Elektra again launches into a tirade against her mother and Aegisthus, but she finds in Orestes one who is most eager to avenge Agamemnon, and his sister's ecstasy is unconfined.

Accompanied by his old tutor, Orestes rushes into the palace, and from the cries within of Clytemnestra we know that she has been struck down. Aegisthus enters the yard through the gate, and Elektra detains him with a mock servility. Soon he makes his way into the palace, where he, too, meets his fate. There is a great rushing about of women, as Elektra embraces her sister and together with her sings a frenetic duet of their liberation. Then Elektra, as she had promised, dances triumphantly on her father's grave until she falls, lifeless.

Wide World Studio
ROSA PAULY AS ELEKTRA AND IRENE JESSNER AS CHRYSOTHEMIS

THE RCA-VICTOR RECORDS
(Sung in German)

EXCERPTS: *Erna Schleuter, Soprano; Walter Widdop, Tenor; Paul Schoeffler, Baritone; Ljuba Welitsch, Soprano; Ernst Erbach, Bass; Sir Thomas Beecham, Bart., conducting the Royal Philharmonic Orchestra and Chorus.*
M-1247 (12-0471-12-0474), 4-12" DM-1247 (12-0475-12-0478)

Carlo Edwards ACT I—METROPOLITAN OPERA PRODUCTION

L'Elisir d'Amore
(ELIXIR OF LOVE)

OPERA BUFFA in two acts. Music by Gaetano Donizetti. Libretto by Felice Romani, after Scribe's *Le Philtre*. First performance, Teatro della Canobbiana, Milan, May 12, 1832. In the United States it was given first in English at the Park Theater, New York, June 18, 1838, and later in Italian, at Palmo's Opera House, New York, May 22, 1844. This excellent *opera buffa* has obtained numerous performances at the Metropolitan Opera House, where such celebrated tenors as Enrico Caruso, Beniamino Gigli, and Tito Schipa have appeared as the hero Nemorino. It was at a presentation by the Metropolitan, given in the Brooklyn Academy of Music, December 11, 1920, that Caruso first showed signs of the illness which was later to cause his death.

L'Elisir d'amore is one of the brightest pieces in the category of comic opera. Donizetti is said to have composed the score in exactly fourteen days. Its clever and amusing plot provided the composer with many opportunities to display his creative facility with subjects of a light and carefree nature. Also, he composed for this work the expressive aria, *"Una furtiva lagrima,"* which has been a favorite of tenors ever since.

CHARACTERS

ADINA, *a wealthy and independent young woman* Soprano

NEMORINO, *a young peasant, in love with Adina* Tenor

BELCORE, *a sergeant of the village garrison* Bass

DR. DULCAMARA, *a traveling quack doctor* Bass

A LANDLORD, A NOTARY, PEASANTS, SOLDIERS, VILLAGERS

The action takes place in a little Italian village during the nineteenth century

ACT I

SCENE: *The Homestead of Adina's Farm.* It is a glorious summer's day, and Adina sits surrounded by her friends, reading a romance. From a distance the lovesick Nemorino gazes at her with rapture and expresses his feelings in the aria *"Quanto è bella"* ("How lovely she is").

A burst of laughter from Adina startles everyone. She reads the legend of Tristan and Isolde, in which the knight wins the lady's affection by means of a wonderful elixir. Nemorino sees no mirth in the tale and sighs wishfully for some of the magical draught.

Martial music is heard, and the dashing Sergeant Belcore appears with a bouquet for Adina. She has but few smiles for him, and Nemorino, somewhat encouraged, renews his suit as soon as Belcore departs. Adina, though respecting this worthy young fellow, finds him rather dull and tells him to go visit his sick uncle, and that his suit is useless.

A commotion among the villagers is heard, and Dulcamara, a quack doctor, riding in a splendid carriage, appears. He has a whole trunkful of wonderful nostrums whose virtues he extols in the comic aria *"Udite, udite, o rustici"* ("Hear me, good folk"). To Nemorino, the doctor seems heaven-sent, and he immediately petitions him for some love elixir. Although a bit puzzled, the doctor loses no time in producing a bottle of strong wine which he says is the coveted potion. Nemorino gives the doctor his last coin, and, as soon as he sees him depart, drinks the elixir.

Nemorino feels exalted and begins to sing and dance, and Adina, coming in, is astonished to see her lovesick swain so merry. Feeling sure that the potion will bring the lady to his feet, he pays no attention to her, which piques her so much that when the sergeant arrives and renews his suit, she consents to wed him in three days. Nemorino laughs loudly at this, which so enrages the lady that she sets the wedding for that very day. This, in turn, sobers Nemorino, who fears that the marriage may take place before the potion works, and he begs for delay, singing his heartfelt plea, *"Adina credimi."* Adina and the others only laugh at him and begin preparations for the wedding.

ACT II

SCENE: *Interior of the Farmhouse.* There is a great wedding-day feast. The notary arrives, and the party goes to an inner room to sign the contract. Dulcamara, however, remains loyal to the table. To him comes Nemorino, whose uncle is dying, and whose sweetheart is marrying another. And the elixir did not work! Dulcamara produces another bottle, but pockets it when Nemorino is unable to pay for it. Belcore appears, and Nemorino desperately confides his misery to him. Belcore suggests that he enlist as a soldier, for which he will receive twenty crowns.

This colloquy takes the form of a wonderfully melodious duet in which the sly sergeant cajoles the hesitating swain with promises of pay and renown. Finally, Nemorino signs the articles, and each sings of what is uppermost on his mind.

Nemorino takes the money, runs in search of the doctor, and drinks the second bottle of love potion! The peasant girls, having heard that the death of Nemorino's uncle has just made him rich, begin to pay him attention. Adina capitulates when she sees her now freshly heartened lover approach, surrounded by sixteen girls. Nemorino is thus convinced that the elixir has worked and, moved to compassion at the sight of Adina's tears, sings the romance *"Una furtiva lagrima"* ("A furtive tear"), a remarkably beautiful melodic inspiration.

Adina soon returns, bringing the soldier's contract, and says that Nemorino must not go away. All misunderstandings are now cleared, and Belcore arrives to find his bride-to-be embracing another. He considers the situation with true soldierly philosophy, saying, "There are other women." As he goes off, the villagers tell Adina and Nemorino of the latter's good fortune. The doctor claims credit for the reconciliation, and the curtain falls as he is relieving the peasants of their wages in return for bottles of his wonderful elixir of love.

White   ACT I—DULCAMARA EXPOUNDING THE ELIXIR

THE RCA-VICTOR RECORDS
(Sung in Italian)

ACT II

ROMANZA—UNA FURTIVA LAGRIMA (A Furtive Tear): *Enrico Caruso, Tenor, with Orch.*
11-8112, 12"
6016, 12"
(Acoustical Recording)

Ferruccio Tagliavini, Tenor, with Orch.   (In Album MO-1191) 12-0070, 12"
18-0106, 12"
(Vinylite) (In Album VO-13)

Richard Crooks, Tenor, with Orch.   15235, 12"
Beniamino Gigli, Tenor, with Orch.   7194, 12"

LAWRENCE TIBBETT AS THE EMPEROR

The Emperor Jones

OPERA IN two acts and a prologue. Music by Louis Gruenberg. Libretto by Kathleen de Jaffa, after the play by Eugene O'Neill. First performance, Metropolitan Opera House, New York, January 7, 1933, with Lawrence Tibbett in the title role. Tullio Serafin conducted.

CHARACTERS

BRUTUS JONES, *a former Pullman porter*	*Baritone*	AN OLD NATIVE WOMAN *Soprano*
HENRY SMITHERS, *a cockney trader*	*Tenor*	CONGO WITCH DOCTOR *Dancer*

SOLDIERS, CONVICTS, FORMLESS FEARS, PLANTERS, SLAVES

The action takes place on an island in the West Indies

The opera is based on the story of the powerfully built Negro convict Jones, in the toils of the law for the murder of a friend in a crap game. While working in a chain gang, Jones kills a guard, escapes, and stows away on a ship which eventually lands him on a West Indies isle. Here his superior sophistication enables him to dominate the natives; he becomes "Emperor" of a tribe, and this position of eminence gives him opportunity to loot, ravish, and otherwise use the credulous natives. He has a revolver, in which the last bullet is a silver one—the only one potent enough, he tells his subjects, to kill the Emperor Jones. This bullet he will use when, as, and if he finds it

123

necessary, but as the opera begins, Jones foresees no imminent need for the silver bullet. In the prologue, however, we are permitted to observe what the Emperor Jones has not yet perceived—that his subjects are weary of his overbearing and cruel rule, and that they are preparing his downfall. "He mus' die, he mus', he mus'," they chant; "he steal our money, he steal our women, he make us bump our heads on de ground to him lik' a god. Huh!"

ACT I

In the first act Jones confides to Henry Smithers, a cockney trader with whom he is in league, that he is planning to abandon the tribe, and escape to the coast with much treasure. He says he has cached food and other supplies along the trail, and that he will find his way without difficulty to a coastal point where a French gunboat will pick him up.

Smithers indicates it is high time for this escape, for already the tribe is in revolt. Jones scoffs at this, but finds it alarmingly true when he summons his ministers and court, and no one answers. At this Jones "resigns de job of Emperor" and plans departure immediately. There is an interlude during which the voices of the tribe are heard, savage, determined, and threatening.

ACT II

The second act deals with Jones' attempted flight through the forest. He is pursued by his own fears and by the ever-louder, closer, and persistent drums of his savage subjects. Frightened by shadows and by his conscience, the Emperor wearies himself in the tangled ways of the jungle. His gorgeous uniform is in rags; his feet are tortured in his fancy boots, and tortured more terribly when he runs barefoot. Hallucinations bedevil him, and cause him to shoot wildly at shadows, using up all but the silver bullet and incidentally revealing his position to his pursuing enemies. At length the last shred of bravado leaves him, and he breaks down in a plea to the Almighty for mercy in the "Standin' in de Need of Prayer."

He confesses his murders and his lesser crimes, and begs mercy—but it is too late. The ghosts of his victims appear to him; he seeks cover, then runs desperately here and there. It is no use; and when, as a final terror, he is confronted by the witch doctor of the tribe, who summons the avenging natives, Jones, with a last scream of supplication, fires the fatal bullet into his head, and dies. The tribesmen dance in a frenzy of triumphant vengeance, and at length disappear in the forest. The stage is left to Smithers, who, inspecting the body of the Emperor Jones, mutters, "Dead as a 'erring. Well, God blimey, yer died in a grand style, anyhow."

THE RCA-VICTOR RECORDS
(Sung in English)

Standin' in de Need of Prayer: *Lawrence Tibbett, Baritone, with Orch.*   7959, 12"

Larcher

ACT I—ELVIRA'S APARTMENT

Ernani

OPERA IN four acts. Music by Giuseppe Verdi. Libretto by Francesco Piave, after Victor Hugo's play, *Hernani*. First produced at the Teatro la Fenice, Venice, March 9, 1844. United States *première*, in the original Italian, at the Park Theater, New York, April 15, 1847. First Metropolitan performance on January 28, 1903, with a cast headed by Marcella Sembrich, Emilio de Marchi, Antonio Scotti, and Édouard de Reszke. In the Metropolitan revival of December 8, 1921, Rosa Ponselle and Giovanni Martinelli sang the parts of Elvira and Ernani.

When Victor Hugo's flamboyant *Hernani* was first produced in Paris it was at once seized upon as a fiery manifesto of romanticism. Two schools clashed over it, the romantics and the classicists. The fervent rhetoric of the play, its unrestrained passions and ringing bombast suited the heightened mood of the day, and Parisians went through the streets chanting or mocking its surging Alexandrines. It was a day when problems of art broke up friendships. True romantic that he was, Giuseppe Verdi was also swept off his feet by the impetuous rush of Hugo's lines. And the opera shows it, in the high-pitched emotionalism, the melodramatic outcries, the melodic sweep. This is the young Verdi, the Verdi of the first of the four periods of a magnificent development, pouring out inexhaustible melody with youthful abandon and a lordly unconcern for the considered unity and balance that were to come later. As with several other operas by Verdi, *Ernani* ran into trouble with the authorities. The rebellious mood of the Italian people made their Austrian rulers doubly vigilant of the stage. The conspiracy in *Ernani* had to be modified. Hotheaded Italians might be incited, the censors contended. Objection was also raised against the undignified use of a hunting horn on the stage, but Verdi's protest prevailed here. Hugo himself was anything but flattered by the opera. When it reached Paris, he fumed against what he regarded as a travesty of his play, even insisting on the characters being transformed into Italians! Nevertheless, *Ernani* did for Verdi what the play had done for Hugo: it brought him prestige and recognition outside his own country. And even today listeners throb to the power of the young giant that surges through this vibrant score.

CHARACTERS

DON CARLOS, *King of Castile*	Baritone	ERNANI, *a bandit chief*	Tenor
DON RUY GOMEZ DE SILVA, *a grandee of Spain*	Bass	ELVIRA, *betrothed to Don Silva*	Soprano
		JUANA, *her nurse*	Mezzo-soprano

ESQUIRES, ATTENDANTS, MOUNTAINEERS, BANDITS, FOLLOWERS OF DON SILVA, FOLLOWERS OF THE KING, SPANISH AND GERMAN NOBLES AND LADIES, ELECTORS, AND PAGES

The action takes place in Aragon, Aix-la-Chapelle, and Saragossa, in 1519

ACT I

SCENE 1: *A Mountain Retreat in Aragon.* John of Aragon, a Spanish duke who was deprived of his wealth and placed under a ban by the King, has become the bandit Ernani. In the mountain camp of his band he is meditating gloomily on the approaching marriage of Elvira, the woman he loves, to the elderly grandee, Don Ruy Gomez de Silva. Resolved to prevent this loveless union, he asks his followers to pledge their help in abducting the woman whose beauty he now describes in a tender aria. Ernani and his men depart in the direction of Silva's castle.

SCENE 2: *Elvira's Chamber in the Castle.* Elvira is alone, brooding over her coming marriage, which she is powerless to prevent. Grief-stricken, she thinks of her long-lost lover, Ernani, and calls on him to rescue her. With the words *"Ernani, involami"* ("Ernani, fly with me"), she begins a coloratura aria of great brilliance that combines vocal display with a touching expression of despair. Don Carlos, King of Castile, who is also enamored of Elvira, enters the room disguised and makes violent love to her. Elvira repulses him, and he is about to drag her off by force when a secret panel opens and Ernani steps forth. Don Carlos recognizes him and exclaims: "You are Ernani, assassin and bandit!" The ensuing quarrel grows bitter and menacing, with Elvira trying to protect Ernani. Suddenly the door flies open, and Don Silva appears. One can picture his astonishment as he discovers two men fighting over his bride on the eve of their wedding. Wrathfully, he bids his soldiers bring his armor and sword, but his attitude abruptly changes: he has recognized the King and, though secretly enraged, now bows in deference. Don Carlos urges Ernani to depart, but Ernani indignantly refuses till Elvira adds her own plea. In the confusion that follows Ernani escapes.

ACT II

SCENE: *A Hall in Don Silva's Castle.* Elvira and Don Silva are about to be married. Ernani has disappeared, and reports have reached Elvira that he is dead. A squire announces that a holy man is outside seeking the hospitality of the nobleman. Don Silva, believing the pilgrim will bring happiness to the household sheltering him, instructs the squire to let him in. The holy man enters, thus entitling himself to Don Silva's protection as a guest. This is no pointless formality, for the holy man enters and, as Elvira enters in her bridal attire, he promptly throws off his disguise, revealing himself as Ernani. The bandit chief demands to be turned over to the King, preferring death to life without Elvira. At that moment the King's arrival is announced. Don Silva, bound to shield his guest, conceals Ernani in a secret passage.

The King enters and orders Don Silva to surrender the bandit, but Don Silva haughtily refuses, and the King orders the castle searched. Finding no

ACT III—THE TOMB OF CHARLEMAGNE

trace of Ernani, he carries off Elvira as hostage. Don Silva now summons
Ernani from his hiding place, and, taking down two swords, challenges him
to a duel. Ernani is compelled to refuse, for his host has just risked his life
for him. Don Silva taunts him, flinging the word "Coward!" at him. Ernani
decides to fight, but asks for one last look at Elvira. When Don Silva tells
him the King has carried her off, Ernani berates him: "Fool, the King is our
rival! He wants her for himself!" He thereupon proposes that he and Don
Silva join forces against the King, and the grandee consents. Once Elvira is
saved, Ernani swears to give himself up, as a pledge of which he gives Don
Silva a hunting horn. Once the horn is blown, Ernani vows by the memory
of his father that he will kill himself.

ACT III

SCENE: *A Vault in the Aix-la-Chapelle Cemetery.* Don Carlos is led to the
gloomy catacombs of Aix-la-Chapelle, the tomb of the Emperor Charlemagne, having been informed that the conspirators intend to meet here. The
solemn atmosphere of the place induces a mood of reverence in him for his
great ancestor. Hiding himself, he overhears the talk of the conspirators.
Ernani, joyous at the chance of avenging his father's death, is chosen to as-
sassinate Don Carlos. A sudden booming of cannon announces that Don
Carlos has been proclaimed Emperor. As electors and courtiers enter from
a secret door, Don Carlos orders the plotters arrested and put to death. When
Elvira begs for mercy, he countermands the order and sets them all free, including Ernani. As a further gesture, he unites the long-divided lovers, and
all now raise their voices in a magnificent tribute to the new Emperor's mag-
nanimity—*"O sommo Carlo"* ("O noble Carlos")—all except the vengeful
Don Silva, whose sinister mutterings come fitfully through the stirring chorus
of praise.

ACT IV

SCENE: *A Terrace of the Palace in Aragon.* Elvira and Ernani are together on the terrace, rapturous in their new-found happiness, when suddenly a horn sounds, the fatal horn that reminds Ernani of his pledge. Don Silva has neither forgotten nor forgiven! Sinister as death itself, he arrives and solemnly demands fulfillment of the oath. Don Silva, deaf to Elvira's pleas for her husband's life, offers his enemy the choice of a dagger or a cup of poison. Ernani bids Elvira a touching farewell and then seizes the dagger and drives it into his heart. Elvira faints over his lifeless body, and Don Silva is left gazing with evil triumph upon his terrible revenge.

THE RCA-VICTOR RECORDS
(Sung in Italian unless otherwise noted)

ACT I

CAVATINA — ERNANI, INVOLAMI (Ernani, Fly with Me): *Miliza Korjus, Soprano, with Orch. In German*
12603, 12″

INFELICE, E TU CREDEVI (Unhappy One!): *Ezio Pinza, Bass, with Orch.*
7552, 12″

ACT III

O SOMMO CARLO (O Noble Carlos): *Giu-* seppe de Luca, Baritone; Alfredo Tedesco, Tenor; Grace Anthony, Soprano; Metropolitan Opera Chorus and Orch. 8174, 12″

Mattia Battistini, Baritone; Emilia Corsi, Soprano; Luigi Colazza, Tenor; Aristodemo Sillich, Bass; with Chorus and Orch. 18144, 12″
(Acoustical Recording)
(In Album M-816)

Palm Springs.
2-19-85 - Beautiful.

ACT II—THE BALL IN HONOR OF TATIANA

Eugene Onegin

OPERA IN three acts. Music by Peter Ilyich Tchaikovsky. Libretto by the composer and Konstantin Shilovsky, after the romantic poem of Alexander Pushkin. First produced by the students of the Imperial College of Music at the Little Theater, Moscow, March 29, 1879. Its first public performance occurred in Moscow, January 23, 1881. The opera was introduced to the United States in concert form by the Symphony Society of New York (in English), February 1, 1908. The Metropolitan *première* took place, in Italian, on March 24, 1920.

Eugene Onegin is the most successful of Tchaikovsky's operas, although none of his stage works is consistently performed in the repertoires of the world's major opera houses, save, perhaps, in Russia. However, Tchaikovsky's music, although not a typical operatic score, since it shows little development of dramatic ideas, is yet sympathetic in its portrayal of the leading characters. These, however, are mirrorings of himself, more or less, defeated, frustrated, utterly subjective personages. The score offers three particular pieces, Lensky's melancholy aria, Tatiana's "Letter Song," and the waltz, which have been for many years concert-hall favorites.

CHARACTERS

MME. LARINA, *a landowner*	Mezzo-soprano	LENSKY, *his friend*	Tenor
TATIANA} *her daughters* OLGA }	Soprano Contralto	PRINCE GREMIN	Bass
EUGENE ONEGIN, *a young dandy*		TRIQUET, *a Frenchman*	Tenor
	Baritone	FILIPIEVNA, *a nurse*	Mezzo-soprano

The action takes place on an estate near the city of St. Petersburg, and also in it, during the nineteenth century

A short orchestral prelude features a motive which is connected with Tatiana.

ACT I

SCENE 1: *A Garden Adjoining Mme. Larina's House.* To Mme. Larina's house, near St. Petersburg, come her daughter Olga's fiancé, Lensky, and his friend Eugene Onegin, a Russian gallant, rather bored, and particularly so by rural scenes. Olga's romantic sister, Tatiana, falls in love with Onegin at first sight.

SCENE 2: *Tatiana's Room.* Tatiana is sleepless that night. She asks Filipievna to tell her a story, one to soothe her, and the nurse does so, as she relates the story of her own wooing and marriage, a long time ago. In a moment of candor Tatiana reveals her love for Onegin, and she bids the nurse fetch her pen, ink, and paper and then depart. In her youthful ingenuousness she writes to Onegin, expressing all that she had not dared say in his presence, and she asks him to meet her.

SCENE 3: *The Garden.* Onegin meets Tatiana, as requested, but spurns her confession of love, saying that he has neither time nor inclination for affairs of the heart. Tatiana runs away in utter dejection, overcome with shame.

ACT II

SCENE 1: *A Living Room in Mme. Larina's House.* A ball is being given in honor of Tatiana's birthday. And here is heard the charming and brilliant waltz. Eugene, who is present, ignores Tatiana, and pays deliberate court to her sister instead. This arouses Lensky's jealousy, who challenges Onegin to a duel.

SCENE 2: *A Mill by a Wooded Stream.* Lensky awaits Onegin at the place appointed. He looks over the desolate winter landscape, and thinking of his youth, which seems so remote, and of death, which seems so near, he sings the piece known as "Lensky's Aria." Presently, his opponent appears, the duel takes place, and Lensky falls, as Onegin, realizing his folly, is overwhelmed with remorse.

ACT III

SCENE 1: *Hall in the Palace of Princess Gremina (Tatiana), six years later.* Onegin is among the guests at a reception given by Prince Gremin, Tatiana's husband. There he is astonished to find Tatiana the wife of a man of distinction and in high favor with the Tsar. He now realizes that he loves her, resolving to win back her affection.

SCENE 2: *Tatiana's Boudoir.* Tatiana enters, bearing a message from Onegin, in which he begs to see her. Confused by the turn of events, firm in her resolve to remain true to the man she has married, yet apprehensive concerning her feelings toward Onegin, Tatiana awaits his coming. He enters right in the middle of her thoughts, and, aware that she is weeping, rushes in and falls down at her feet. The interview is a most unhappy one, Tatiana reminding him of his cruelty that day in the garden of her mother's home, yet admitting that she has forgiven him. Slowly she says that she still loves him. Together they sing of the happiness that was once so close to them, and the futility of their present plight. Tatiana, recovering, finally bids him on his honor to depart, and leaves him standing silently for a moment. And then, with a final cry of anguish, he departs, as the curtain falls.

THE RCA-VICTOR RECORDS
(Sung in Russian)

ACT I

PRINCE GREMIN'S AIR: *Alexander Kipnis, Bass, with Orch.*   11-9284, 12"
(In Album M-1073)

ACT II

WALTZ: *Sir Thomas Beecham, Bart., and the London Philharmonic Orchestra*
11-9421, 12"
Boston "Pops" Orchestra, Arthur Fiedler, Cond.   4565, 10"

Indianapolis Symphony Orchestra, Fabien Sevitzky, Cond.   12-0044, 12"
(In Album M-1189)

ACT III

POLONAISE: *Sir Thomas Beecham, Bart., and the London Philharmonic Orchestra*   11-9421, 12"
Boston "Pops" Orchestra, Arthur Fiedler, Cond.   12429, 12"
(In Album M-554)

Bains
GIUSEPPE DE LUCA
AS EUGENE ONEGIN

Euryanthe

ROMANTIC OPERA in three acts. Music by Carl Maria von Weber. Libretto by Helmina von Chézy, founded on a thirteenth-century French romance, *L'Histoire de Gérard de Nevers*. First produced at the Kärntnertor-Theater, Vienna, October 25, 1823. Reputed American *première*, Wallack's Theater, New York, 1863. First performance by the Metropolitan Opera Company, December 23, 1887. The most recent Metropolitan revival was during the season of 1914–15, when Arturo Toscanini conducted, and Frieda Hempel sang the title role.

The eccentric wife of a noted French Orientalist and Sanskrit scholar, Helmina von Chézy, is responsible for the inane libretto of Weber's *Euryanthe*. Thus handicapped, the opera survives today largely through its overture, a masterpiece of fervid romantic writing in chivalric mood. The lady librettist was similarly unlucky with another play, *Rosamunde*, which is remembered today because a then obscure young composer named Franz Schubert wrote the incidental music for it. The Chézy libretto was concocted in an emergency. The spectacular success of Weber's earlier opera, *Der Freischütz*, prompted Barbaia, the Vienna impresario, to commission another. Weber cast about frantically for an appropriate book. By chance the erudite Frau von Chézy had just unearthed an old French tale, the same that had probably inspired Boccaccio's story of the merchant Bernabo's wife in the *Decameron* (second day, ninth novella). The offer was made and accepted, and in a short time the facile von Chézy pen had completed the three acts. The score was ready in August, 1823, and the *première* followed two months later. The length of the opera, its gnarled libretto, its bizarre background and lack of dramatic impact combined to make the production a failure. All praised the music, however, all except Schubert, who objected to its "striving after effect." The theme of tested fidelity in *Euryanthe* is an old one, probably going back to old Greek balladry. In the Middle Ages it went through many variations, especially in the literature of chivalry. After Boccaccio and the European folk ballads had absorbed it, the story returned in its finest version in the wager made by Posthumus and Iachimo in Shakespeare's *Cymbeline*.

CHARACTERS

LOUIS VI	Bass	LYSIART, *Count of Forêt*	Baritone
ADOLAR, *Count of Nevers*	Tenor	EGLANTINE DE PUISET, *captive daughter*	
EURYANTHE OF SAVOY, *his bride*	Soprano	*of a mutineer*	Mezzo-soprano

The action takes place at the Castle Premery and burg of Nevers in the early twelfth century

The Overture to *Euryanthe* opens with a fiery exordium, after which the first subject is announced, based on Adolar's phrase in Act I, *"Ich bau' auf Gott und meine Euryanthe"* ("I build on God and my Euryanthe"). The lyric second theme, changed by the first violins, is from Adolar's second act aria, *"O Seligkeit, dich fass' ich kaum"* ("O Holiness, I scarcely grasp you"). The largo passage brings in an episode in eerie mystery, evoking the ghost of Emma and a tomblike solemnity. Finally the note of chivalry and victory returns in the brilliant development and coda.

ACT I

SCENE 1: *A Hall in the King's Palace.* Adolar, Count of Nevers and Rethel, engages in an argument with Lysiart, Count of Forêt and Beaujolais, on the fidelity of women. Adolar believes them faithful and trustworthy, Lysiart, differing, cynically ridicules him, boasting that he could even win the saintly Euryanthe. Adolar, furious, makes a rash wager: he will stake his life and all his possessions on Euryanthe's virtue. The challenge is accepted.

SCENE 2: *The Palace Garden of Nevers.* Euryanthe innocently ensnares herself. Becoming friendly with Eglantine, who is in love with Adolar, she confides the secret of her sister Emma's suicide, and tells of a mysterious ring hidden in the girl's tomb. Eglantine, seeking to ruin her trusting friend, now sees a way to attain her aim.

ACT II

SCENE 1: *The Palace Garden of Nevers.* Eglantine has acquired the telltale ring. When Lysiart confesses to her that he has given up hope of winning the wager, Eglantine gives him the ring and narrates the story behind it.

SCENE 2: *A Hall in the King's Palace.* The courtiers have assembled. Adolar and Euryanthe are together as Lysiart enters with a smile of triumph. In a grand flourish he exhibits the ring as proof that Euryanthe has yielded to him, and claims the stakes. Deprived of his possessions and convinced of his bride's guilt, Adolar stalks out of the palace.

ACT III

SCENE 1: *A Forest.* Euryanthe has caught up with Adolar. He is on the point of killing her but restrains himself in an access of love and remorse. As Adolar again abandons her, the King's hunting party appears, and for the first time Euryanthe reveals the story of the ring and Eglantine's part in it.

SCENE 2: *The Palace Garden of Nevers.* Eglantine is about to marry Lysiart, when the ghost of Emma appears to her. Maddened by terror, she begins to give away the whole plot against Euryanthe, when Lysiart draws a dagger and kills her. As Lysiart is led away to execution, Adolar, his possessions restored to him, is reunited to Euryanthe, who forgives him for his lack of faith.

THE RCA-VICTOR RECORDS

Overture: *BBC Symphony Orchestra, Adrian Boult, Cond.*   12037, 12"

3-11-4 - Bright costumes — Dull music — no single pleasant aria —

New York Times   ACT III, SCENE 1—METROPOLITAN OPERA PRODUCTION

Falstaff

LYRIC COMEDY in three acts. Music by Giuseppe Verdi. Libretto by Arrigo Boïto, after Shakespeare's *Merry Wives of Windsor* and *King Henry IV*. First performance, Teatro alla Scala, Milan, February 9, 1893. Initial production in the Western Hemisphere, Buenos Aires, July 8, 1893. *Première* in the United States at the Metropolitan, February 4, 1895.

It has been said that Verdi's muse was essentially a tragic muse, yet with this work, composed in his eightieth year, he proved to some critics (Rossini, now dead, had been one of them) that he could write with great wit and an almost Mozartian boyishness. His music brightly illuminates the story of "Fatpaunch," as the character emerges out of Boïto's libretto, and, further, shows no lessening of the technical skill he had possessed all during his career.

Reading the *Gazzetta musicale*, one day, Verdi came upon an article by one Dupré, in which the author quoted Rossini as saying once that Verdi could not compose a comic opera. Rather irritated, Verdi wrote to his publisher, Ricordi, "I have read in your paper Dupré's description of our first meeting and the judgment of Jupiter Rossini (as Meyerbeer used to call him). But look here! I have been searching for twenty years for a comic-opera libretto and, now that I have practically found one, you with your article instill into the public an unreasonable desire to condemn my opera in advance, thus prejudicing your interests and mine."

It is not known for certain that Verdi meant the libretto for *Falstaff* in his letter, although there was proof before this that he had been considering a comic opera. In any case, *Falstaff* might not have been written if it had not been for the combined urgings of the Mayor of Milan, Signora Verdi, Boïto, and others whose influence finally prevailed; although, as for Verdi himself, he had said something to the effect that with *Otello* he had "fired his last cartridge."

Verdi did not, as formerly, compose ten, but two hours a day, while working on *Falstaff*. Still the opera made good progress. And one evening, in November, 1890, Boïto virtually informed the world of what was going on by proposing a toast to "Fatpaunch."

Fifty-three years had passed since Verdi had composed a comic opera. The earlier one had been *Il Finto Stanislao*, and that, for all the gaiety of some of its music, is

134

scarcely a true comedy, for its very involved libretto stood in the way. But in *Falstaff* the aged composer was dealing with as ingenious and orderly a libretto as he had ever known, and a richly comic one, besides. Boïto, despite the many liberties he had taken with the original story of *The Merry Wives of Windsor*, and the borrowings from *Henry IV*, supplied the composer with a concentrated book, beautifully balanced in every way, the dialogue of which is highly literary in quality.

In the music of *Falstaff* Verdi departs from traditions to which he had held so long. Here we do not find, as in *Aïda* or *La Traviata* or even in *Otello*, arias and duets and trios and ensembles packed with drama and emotional excitement. In fact, the music, being a definition of the comedy and the characters, is light and airy and almost as casual as a breeze. At least, it sounds that way, although it required an immense technique to achieve that. For the *Falstaff* music is episodic, fragmentary in essence, which it obviously needed to be, thanks to the mercurial quality of the libretto. However, by an accumulation of such fragments, such bubbly and delicately tinted character and plot identifications—never, as in Wagner, depending on psychological development or thematic extension—the general impression is hardly that of a scattering of clever things, but of a tightly knit, extremely well-ordered score.

What a wonder that Verdi, after composing a long line of tragic operas, should end his career with a comedy! That this work should be, in addition, a masterpiece, taking its rightful place beside Mozart's *Marriage of Figaro*, Wagner's *Die Meistersinger*, and Rossini's *Barber of Seville*, is a tribute to the versatility of his genius.

Of particular interest, in a score that teems with interesting matters, are Falstaff's monologue on honor, the quartet by the women in the garden, Ford's soliloquy, Falstaff's song, *"Quand' ero paggio del Duca di Norfolck"* ("When I was the Duke of Norfolk's page"), and the concerted finales of each act.

CHARACTERS

FALSTAFF	*Baritone*	PISTOL		*Bass*
FENTON	*Tenor*	MISTRESS FORD		*Soprano*
FORD	*Baritone*	ANNE FORD		*Soprano*
DR. CAIUS	*Tenor*	MISTRESS PAGE		*Mezzo-soprano*
BARDOLPH	*Tenor*	MISTRESS QUICKLY		*Mezzo-soprano*

The action takes place in Windsor, England, in the fifteenth century

ACT I

SCENE 1: *A Room in the Garter Inn.* The jovial, fat old rogue, Falstaff, is with his friends Bardolph and Pistol at the Garter Inn, where Sir John quaffs his huge draughts as his friends look on. Dr. Caius rushes in and quarrels with the knight and his two men, but he is soon thrown out, and Falstaff, reflecting on the low state of his financial resources, writes two famous letters— one to Mistress Page, the other to Mistress Ford—by which he hopes to make a profitable liaison with the wives of two rich burghers.

SCENE 2: *In Ford's Garden.* In Ford's garden the two women compare the letters and, discovering them to be alike, plan revenge. In this they are joined by the men, Ford, Fenton, and Dr. Caius; even Bardolph and Pistol will help, for they too, having smarted under Falstaff's gibes, want vengeance. Fenton is on hand because he is in love with Mistress Ford's daughter, Anne, even though Ford himself plans to have her marry Dr. Caius. Dame Quickly is

New York Times ACT I, SCENE 2—METROPOLITAN OPERA PRODUCTION

sent to invite Falstaff to an interview with Mistress Ford, and meanwhile the men arrange to have Ford introduced to Falstaff under an assumed name.

ACT II

SCENE 1: *A Room in the Garter Inn.* Dame Quickly delivers her message, and having flattered old Sir John almost to distraction, she leaves. Bardolph now introduces Ford as Signor Fontana (in Shakespeare he is called Brook), the latter begging Falstaff, with offers of gold, to intercede for him with Mistress Ford. Thereupon the knight declares his pleasure with the task and, in high glee, goes out to dress himself in his best attire, while Ford, in his jealousy, delivers his famous soliloquy on the faithlessness of women. When Falstaff returns, decked out in extraordinary finery, there is a little scene of amusing effect, as Falstaff and Ford (or Fontana) do an Alphonse-and-Gaston act before going out the door, and finally decide to exit together arm in arm.

SCENE 2: *A Room in Ford's House.* Falstaff arrives at Ford's house, but before he can proceed very far with his interview, Ford is heard coming. Falstaff quickly hides behind a screen. Ford enters with the other men and, hoping to find the rakish knight, begins a search of the house. As soon as the men are out, the women hurriedly conceal Falstaff in a large laundry basket they have thoughtfully provided, pile soiled clothes over him, and fasten down the lid. A moment later Ford returns, having thought of the screen. Even as he enters he hears back of it a sound suspiciously like a kiss—Fenton and Anne are having an unrehearsed love scene of their own! Ford rushes out, more enraged than ever. Thereupon his wife has the servants empty the basket into the Thames, which flows below. Ford returns in time to be shown the knight climbing clumsily from the water, laughed at by all who see him.

ACT III

SCENE 1: *Before the Inn.* Falstaff is back at the inn, sad and disillusioned. He reviles the wickedness of the world, and as he gulps down his mulled wine gradually begins to regain his courage and, of course, his ego. This transformation is accompanied by the orchestra in a brilliant passage which, beginning with a pianissimo trill, grows into a fortissimo, indicative of the rebirth of his faith in himself. Dame Quickly appears and, after a rebuff or two, succeeds in restoring the knight's confidence in her. She arranges another meeting between him and Mistress Ford. He is to disguise himself as the Black Huntsman and await the lady by Herne's Oak in Windsor Park at midnight. As the two go into the inn, in order to discuss the plans more privately, the conspirators come forward and go over their plot to give Sir John his final blow.

SCENE 2: *Herne's Oak in Windsor Park.* It is a moonlit night, and everyone is disguised. Falstaff and Mistress Ford meet, and the knight begins his awkward love-making. Immediately eerie sounds are heard; Mistress Ford runs away in mock terror, while Falstaff throws himself face down on the ground, for it is fatal to gaze upon supernatural beings! The whole company enter,

Knesing

FALSTAFF AND MISTRESS FORD

disguised as fairies. They seem to stumble upon Falstaff accidentally, then give this "impure mortal" a sound thrashing, until he promises to mend his ways. Ford has definitely agreed to give Anne in marriage to Dr. Caius, but the women, set on helping Fenton's cause, have confused the men in their disguises. Thus, when masks are suddenly removed, Dr. Caius finds that he has been making love to Bardolph. In the laughter that follows Ford agrees to the union of Fenton and Anne, and all ends happily—save for Falstaff, who, at least, can laugh at the discomfiture of Ford, even though it is not the one he had expected. And the opera ends in a magnificent fugue by voices and orchestra on the theme, first stated by Falstaff, that "all the world's a jest."

LEONARD WARREN
AS FALSTAFF

Wide World Studio
ALESSANDRO DE PAOLIS AS BARDOLFO
AND NORMAN CORDON AS PISTOL

THE RCA-VICTOR RECORDS
(Sung in Italian)

ACT II

MONOLOGO DI FORD—È SOGNO? O REALTÀ?
(Ford's Monologue—Am I Awake?
Or Do I Dream?) : *Leonard Warren,
Baritone, with Orch.* 18293, 12"

Maurice Seymour
DUSOLINA GIANNINI AS MISTRESS FORD

La Fanciulla del West

(THE GIRL OF THE GOLDEN WEST)

OPERA IN three acts. Music by Giacomo Puccini. Libretto by Guelfo Civinini and Carlo Zangarini, after David Belasco's play, *The Girl of the Golden West*. First performance, Metropolitan Opera House, New York, December 10, 1910, Puccini and Belasco both being present. Arturo Toscanini was the conductor, and Emmy Destinn was the Minnie, Enrico Caruso the Dick Johnson, and Pasquale Amato the Jack Rance.

The plot is concerned with rather melodramatic happenings during the days of the California gold rush in '49. While remaining true, in general, to his usual melodious style, Puccini adapted his score to a rapidly moving conversational dialogue. He also showed that he was aware of the musical progress of the times by his use of consecutive and unresolved seventh chords somewhat in the manner of Ravel, and in the employment of Debussian augmented triads. Moreover, for the sake of local color, he introduced melodies and rhythms characteristic of the South and Southwest—of plantations, Mexicans, and Indians. Yet the music, for all that, is unmistakably Italian.

CHARACTERS

MINNIE, *owner of the Polka bar*	*Soprano*	SONORA	*Baritone*
		TRIN	*Tenor*
JACK RANCE, *sheriff*	*Baritone*	SID	*Baritone*
DICK JOHNSON (RAMERREZ)	*Tenor*	HANDSOME	*Baritone*
		HARRY *miners*	*Tenor*
NICK, *bartender at the Polka*	*Tenor*	JOE	*Tenor*
ASHBY, *Wells-Fargo agent*	*Bass*	HAPPY	*Baritone*
BILLY JACKRABBIT, *an Indian*	*Bass*	LARKEN	*Bass*
WOWKLE, *his squaw*	*Mezzo-soprano*	JOSÉ CASTRO, *member of Ramerrez's gang*	*Bass*
JAKE WALLACE, *a traveling camp minstrel*	*Baritone*	A POSTILION	*Bass*
		MEN OF THE CAMP	

The action takes place at the foot of Cloudy Mountain, in California, during the days of the gold fever, about 1849–50

ACT I

SCENE: *Interior of the Polka Barroom.* Ashby, agent of the Wells-Fargo Company, enters the "Polka" barroom and, joining the miners there assembled, says that he is close on the track of Ramerrez, chief of the band of Mexican outlaws who have recently committed a big robbery. The sheriff, Jack Rance, in talking with the men, boasts of his love affair with the "girl," Minnie, and says that he is going to marry her. One of the miners disputes his claim, and a brawl results. Minnie herself enters and stops it. Minnie owns and runs the Polka, for she is the orphaned child of the founder of this establishment, and also acts as mother and guardian angel to the miners and cowboys who frequent the place. When Rance proposes to her in his crude fashion, she spurns him and holds him at bay with a revolver.

A stranger enters and gives his name as Dick Johnson of Sacramento.

The sheriff is suspicious of him, but Minnie takes his part, saying that she has met him before. Johnson is in reality none other than the hunted Ramerrez, and he has come for no better purpose than to rob the saloon. Unaware of this, Minnie recalls with Dick the time they first met and fell in love with one another. The men all go in search of Ramerrez, leaving their gold with Minnie. She declares that if anyone is to steal the gold he must do so over her dead body. Johnson has become more and more enamored of her and relinquishes his plan of robbery; now he admires her courage. She invites him to visit her in her cabin when the miners shall have returned.

ACT II

SCENE: *Minnie's Dwelling.* Johnson and Minnie meet at her "shack" and idyllically sing of their love. Suddenly shots are heard outside in the darkness—the men are again searching for Ramerrez. Not wanting to be found with her lover, Minnie conceals Johnson, then admits the men, who are hunting, they say, for Dick Johnson, much to her dismay. Minnie declines their offered protection, and they leave. Then she turns upon Johnson with the revelations that she has just heard. Dick acknowledges their truth, but goes on to tell how he was compelled by fate to become a bandit. Since meeting her he had resolved to give up his old life, and had prayed in vain that she would never know of his past. The tense dramatic atmosphere is reflected in somber chords in the orchestra.

But Minnie cannot forgive him for having deceived her after confessing his love and sends him out into the night. A moment later shots are heard, Minnie runs to the door, opens it, and drags in Johnson, seriously wounded. She hides him in a loft under the roof. The sheriff soon enters, hot on the trail. Minnie has almost overcome his suspicions when a drop of blood falls from the loft, revealing the wounded Dick's whereabouts. Knowing that the sheriff is a desperate gambler, Minnie, as a last resort, offers to play a game of poker with him, the stakes to be her own hand and Johnson's life, or else her own and the prisoner's freedom. Minnie is constrained to cheat, but wins the game and her lover.

ACT III

SCENE: *The Great California Forest.* Johnson, nursed back to life by Minnie, is about to be hanged by Ashby's men. He asks one last request. Let her believe that he had gained his freedom and gone away to live the nobler life she had taught him. He touchingly apostrophizes her as the "star of his wasted life." This last request of Johnson's is sung to the most famous melody in the opera, *"Ch'ella mi creda libero"* ("Let her believe that I have gained my freedom").

Just as the lynchers are about to draw the rope taut, Minnie rushes in on horseback. She at first holds the crowd at bay with her drawn revolver, then appeals to them eloquently, reminding them of her faithful care of their needs; they should not fail her now. The "boys" relent and, in spite of Rance's protests, release the prisoner. Johnson and Minnie bid them farewell and go away together to begin life anew.

THE RCA-VICTOR RECORDS
(Sung in Italian)

ACT III

CH'ELLA MI CREDA LIBERO (Let Her Believe That I Have Gained My Freedom): *Jussi Bjoerling, Tenor, with Orch.* 4408, 10"

EDWARD JOHNSON
AS DICK JOHNSON

JUSSI BJOERLING AS FAUST

Morton & Co.

ACT II—SAN FRANCISCO OPERA PRODUCTION

Faust

OPERA IN five acts. Music by Charles François Gounod. Libretto by Jules Barbier and Michel Carré, based on Goethe's dramatic poem, *Faust*. First performance at the Théâtre-Lyrique, Paris, March 19, 1859. Reputed American *première*, in German, in Philadelphia, November 18, 1863. Produced one week later, November 25, at the New York Academy of Music, in Italian. In the original French the opera was probably first performed in America in New Orleans on April 27, 1881. *Faust* opened the Metropolitan Opera House on October 22, 1883, with a cast headed by Christine Nilsson, Sofia Scalchi, Italo Campanini, Giuseppe del Puente, and Franco Novara. Performances of *Faust* later became so numerous there that the music critic William J. Henderson, with the Bayreuth *Festspielhaus* in mind, once referred to the Metropolitan as the *Faustspielhaus*, a pun that is frequently quoted when Gounod's popular opera is discussed by critics.

The origins of the *Faust* legend are buried in historical mists. Ballads, folk tales, and dramas were inspired by Faust's sinister pact with the devil. Variations multiplied, and each poet contributed some fresh touch or new character. Christopher Marlowe's *Dr. Faustus* enshrined a famous vision of Helen of Troy, she of "the face that launched a thousand ships." It was Goethe's poem that achieved the final synthesis of poetry and philosophy. Thereafter Faust became an international obsession. Overtures, symphonies, and tone poems, even an oratorio and several ballets, sprang from Goethe's masterpiece. Operas based on episodes from it soon became legion. Bertin, Spohr, Zöllner, Boïto, and Busoni are among the composers who conceived *Faust* in terms of sung drama. And in 1925, in Soviet Russia, Marxists carried the legend one step further and staged Gounod's *Faust* in satiric modern guise, with the hero an American millionaire living sumptuously in a Berlin hotel.

If Goethe's poem gave universal shape to this winter's tale of the Middle Ages, Gounod's version, which uses the Faust-Marguerite episode as basis, became its musical counterpart in the affections of operagoers the world over. Yet, the opera achieved scant success at its first performance in Paris, and even less in Milan. Soon, however, it caught on and became an international craze, possibly the greatest opera craze in history. At Paris alone, performances reached a grand total of 2,000 on the night of December 31, 1934. In the late 1860's *Faust* was flourishing briskly in England, for a while even threatening to crowd all other operas out of circulation. The opera was a great favorite of Queen Victoria's. Shortly before her death she summoned a group of French singers to

Windsor Palace. Though old and weak and sick, she listened happily to her beloved music from *Faust*. Each time a familiar phrase was sung the Queen's lips parted in a smile of recognition. A veritable furore greeted *Faust* on its arrival in America. In the twenty years preceding the opening of the Metropolitan Opera House the opera had already built up a huge following here. Thus, the choice of opening opera for the new house was a fairly easy one for its first impresario, Henry Eugene Abbey. And for the title role Abbey brought over Italo Campanini, the great Italian tenor who had earlier proved quite a sensation as Faust in London.

Despite this subsequent acclaim, *Faust* had been anything but a bed of roses for Gounod. In setting the greatest poem in German literature to music he invited the acid gibes of the critics, especially the pompous savants across the Rhine. Then Carvalho, the director of the Théâtre-Lyrique of Paris, insisted on assigning the role of Marguerite to his wife, though Gounod had the soprano Ugalde in mind. Moreover, objection was raised against the way the love scene followed the church scene. Gounod again yielded and shifted the scenes. Shortly before the *première* officials objected to the cathedral scene. Finally, the tenor caught a bad cold. Add the lukewarm reception of the opening night, and everyone was ready to agree the production was a fiasco. But soon the power and beauty of Gounod's music, the human drama and spectacle of fantasy and sorcery, worked their charm on the public. Before the season was over, there were fifty-seven performances. For the subsequent London production of *Faust* Gounod wrote an additional aria for the celebrated baritone, Sir Charles Santley. This was Valentine's *"Avant de quitter ces lieux."* It was felt Sir Charles deserved greater attention than the score already accorded his role.

CHARACTERS

FAUST	*Tenor*	MARGUERITE	*Soprano*
MEPHISTOPHELES	*Bass*	SIEBEL, *a youth, in love with*	
VALENTINE, *Marguerite's*		*Marguerite*	*Soprano*
brother	*Baritone*	MARTHA, *friend of Marguerite*	
WAGNER, *a student*	*Baritone*		*Mezzo-soprano*

PEASANTS, TOWNSPEOPLE, SOLDIERS, STUDENTS, PRIESTS, BOYS, ETC.

The action takes place in Germany in the sixteenth century

The brief prelude to *Faust* gives little more than a clue to the drama about to unfold. The mood of portent is sounded in the fateful single note heard from the full orchestra and then in the sinister chords in the strings. The pace quickens to an episode suggesting Faust's anguish of mind, followed by Valentine's beautiful melody, *"Avant de quitter ces lieux."* The prelude ends in stately and solemn fashion.

ACT I

SCENE: *Faust's Studio*. Faust, a philosopher and alchemist of note, is seen in his dismal study. Hoary and bent with age, he is poring over a huge volume that lies open on the table. Half discernible in the flickering light of a lamp are the strange tools of medieval necromancy scattered about the room. Musty parchment rolls are seen on all sides. The expiring lamp is a symbol of the despair and weariness in the heart of this learned man. Life and the pursuit of knowledge have finally disillusioned him, and the universe remains an unsolved riddle. Tired of the struggle to find a meaning in it all, Faust

Boyer and Bert ACT II—THE KERMESSE—PARIS OPERA PRODUCTION

resolves on suicide. He fills a goblet with poison and raises it to his lips. Outside his murky chamber day has been dawning. Faust pauses as a cheerful song of young women passing by in the street comes through his window. He goes to the window, and as his rage and envy mount at the sight of gay humanity, he curses life and calls aloud to Satan for help.

There is an eerie flash of light, and Mephistopheles, in gallant attire, appears. By turns gay, cynical, and ingratiating, he proposes a compact. In return for wealth and power, Faust shall sign away his soul! The philosopher spurns riches and glory and demands the gift of youth instead. Mephistopheles agrees. Youth and love shall be Faust's as long as he pledges his soul. As Faust falters at the awful prospect, the fiend now tempts him with a glowing vision of the lovely Marguerite seated at a spinning wheel, her beautiful blond braids falling down her back. In rapture Faust gazes at this picture of youth and loveliness, and as the orchestra weaves a shimmering web of magic, he addresses the vision, *"O merveille"* ("Oh, wonder"), in ecstatic song. Faust, ready now to pawn his immortal soul, in one determined gesture seizes the proffered potion, raises it in a toast to the vision, and gulps it down.

The evocation vanishes, and Faust undergoes a magic transformation. As the light returns, the gray beard and scholarly garb have disappeared. In place of the bent and wearied philosopher there stands an elegantly clad cavalier, eager for adventure. Mephistopheles promises he shall see Marguerite that very day. There is a spirited duet, and Faust impetuously dashes out of the study, followed by the grinning fiend.

ACT II

SCENE: *The Public Square of a German Town.* A crowd has gathered to celebrate the *kermesse,* or village fair. Students, soldiers, burghers of all ages are milling about in gay confusion. There is drinking, talking, flirting, and quarreling. A lively chorus, differentiating the moods and manners of each group, pictures the colorful scene: soldiers are heard chanting martially; women set up a gay bantering chatter; gossiping old men shriek in facetious falsettos. Toward the end, the groups unite in a chorus of six parts, a magnificent piece of ensemble writing. Among the crowd is Valentine, Marguerite's brother. About to leave to join his country's army, Valentine reveals to his friends how troubled he is about leaving his orphan sister alone. In a beautiful and tender melody (*"Avant de quitter ces lieux"*—literally, "Before leaving this place") he asks heaven to watch over her. Siebel, his young friend, secretly in love with Marguerite, generously assures Valentine that during his absence he will see that no harm comes to her. The student, Wagner, wishing to banish the solemn mood of the moment, mounts a table before an inn and begins to sing a ribald ditty concerning a rat.

Mephistopheles, pushing through the carnival crowd, breaks in on Wagner's song, and proposes to sing one of his own. This is the *"Veau d'or"* ("The Calf of Gold"), a bold and sinister hymn in praise of Mammon, cynically describing how men are drawn by gold to evil, and ending in a weird dance led by Mephistopheles himself. Vastly entertained, the crowd looks on in amazement as the Evil One proceeds to execute feats of magic. As he tells fortunes and reads palms, the simple peasants are left gaping. In a moment of playful malice Mephistopheles seizes Siebel and swears that whatever flower he touches will wither in his hands. Wagner, enchanted by the newcomer's gifts, proposes a toast. Wine is brought, but Mephistopheles tastes it and hurls it down in disgust. He will give them a finer wine to drink, he says. As he strikes the barrel of Bacchus used as a sign over the inn, wine gushes out copiously. All are permitted to name their favorite vintage and drink at this magic source.

Mephistopheles offers a toast to Marguerite. Valentine, enraged at hearing his sister's name publicly flaunted, draws his sword and lunges at the devil. Mephistopheles instantly traces a magic circle about himself, and as Valentine's blade crosses it, it breaks in half. Valentine, promptly realizing what he is contending with, in approved medieval fashion holds aloft the crosslike hilt of his broken sword. Mephistopheles recoils in terror from the Christian symbol as the soldiers follow Valentine's example in raising their swords hilt-up and join in a noble chant, rich and sonorous in its growing fervor. The solemnity of the moment quickly subsides in the revival of the festive spirit. The crowd now takes up a dance, the *"Kermesse* Waltz,"

Boyer and Bert   ACT III—GARDEN SCENE—PARIS OPERA PRODUCTION

which swirls with lifting exuberance from the orchestra as they sing another melody expressing their holiday joy.

In the midst of this merrymaking Marguerite approaches, making her way timidly through the whirl of dancers. Prayer book in hand, she is returning from church. Siebel wishes to join her, but each time he starts toward her, he is blocked by the suave yet ominous figure of Mephistopheles. Meanwhile Faust has reached her side. Respectfully he offers to escort the "highborn and lovely maid" home. Confused and blushing, Marguerite modestly refuses, pointing out that she is neither highborn nor lovely, and in any case can find her way alone. As she walks on, Faust watches her blissfully. The orchestra sets up a romantic accompaniment to this scene, beginning with a tender peacefulness and mounting to rapturous brilliance. Mephistopheles, observing the coy rebuff, laughingly suggests to Faust that perhaps his aid will be needed in winning Marguerite. The crowd now resumes the waltz, and the square is again an animated scene of whirling dancers lost in care-free gaiety.

ACT III

SCENE: *The Garden Before Marguerite's House*. Trees, shrubs, and flower beds surround Marguerite's dainty little cottage. Siebel enters the garden and begins gathering some roses and lilies for the girl he has promised Valentine to watch over. As he sings a sweet melody of love (*"Faites-lui mes aveux"*—

"Gentle flow'rs in the dew"), the flowers suddenly fade in his grasp. Mephistopheles' dire prophecy has come true! Suddenly a happy thought comes to Siebel. He goes to a near-by font of holy water, dips his hand in, and once more touches the flowers. The fiend's power is now unavailing, and Siebel resumes his delicate air. Presently he disappears among the shrubs, returning with a bouquet of flowers which he fastens to the door of the cottage. Then he hurries off.

From behind the bushes Faust and Mephistopheles have been observing Siebel. Faust gazes ardently at Marguerite's garden, and as Mephistopheles leaves him with the promise to bring back the treasure to go with these flowers, he begins a tenderly romantic cavatina, addressed to Marguerite's humble cottage, *"Salut, demeure chaste et pure"* ("All hail, thou dwelling"). What true wealth amid such poverty! sings Faust ecstatically. Mephistopheles returns with a casket of jewels which he places near Siebel's bouquet. The intruders scurry for cover as Marguerite suddenly enters the garden. Dreamily, her thoughts on her recent encounter, she seats herself at the spinning wheel and begins to sing, at first wondering softly who the stranger was. Then she turns to a simple song of long ago (*"Le Roi de Thulé"*), quaint and charming, telling of the faithful King of Thule who had had a cup of gold made in memory of the woman he loved. Thoughts of Faust again intrude. The spinning stops, the song is broken off, and Marguerite once more wonders what his name was. Impatient with herself, she resumes the song, then stops her spinning, and walks toward the house. The bouquet catches her eye, and she guesses it is from Siebel. Then she starts as her eye catches the casket. Throbbing with expectancy, she opens it and is dazzled by the brilliance within. Jewels! Marguerite begins to try on the sparkling gems, and as she looks at herself in a mirror she bursts out into the famous "Jewel Song" (*"Air des bijoux"*), an aria sparkling with girlish rapture and coquettish delicacy.

Martha, the old gossip, now enters the garden and gushingly compliments Marguerite on her handsome appearance. Her rapture is cut short by Mephistopheles, who appears and salutes her gallantly. From him Martha learns of her husband's death, but her grief is brief, for this elegantly sinister stranger has already caught her fancy. Faust offers his arm to Marguerite, and the four now promenade through the garden, which is growing dim in the gathering dusk. The couples pass one another, and at times their voices blend in bright, rich harmonies. Martha grows more and more interested in the red-robed cavalier, as Marguerite is slowly becoming enamored of Faust. As it begins to grow dark, she entreats Faust to leave. He embraces her ardently, but she slips out of his grasp and flees into the shadows of the garden, Faust in pursuit. Meanwhile Mephistopheles, wearied of Martha's attentions, eludes her, and, safely alone, launches into a solemn "Invocation"

(*"Il était temps!"*), in which he calls upon the night and the flowers to con-
spire with bewitching shadows and soft perfumes in his diabolical designs on
Marguerite's soul. The evil incantation ended, he slinks off into the night.

Marguerite and Faust return. Remarking that it is growing late, the girl
gently bids farewell, but Faust pleads to remain at his beloved's side. The
night's enchantment is beginning its subtle work. Marguerite plucks a flower
and removes its petals one by one in an age-old game, finally exclaiming joyously, "He loves me!" "Believe the flower!" Faust cries out, drawing nearer.
As he utters the phrase, *"D'une joie éternelle"* ("Of joy everlasting"), a
wondrous love duet begins with their combined echo of the word *éternelle*.
Music of sensuous beauty and deep, vibrant passion now follows, subtle orchestral colors blending softly with the voices of the lovers. At length Marguerite breaks away from her lover and runs into the house. She pauses at the
door to throw him a kiss and promises to meet him the following day.

Mephistopheles again steps into the picture, taunting Faust on his innocence. "Wait till you hear what she tells the stars!" he counsels him. Marguerite opens her casement window, and as Faust listens enchanted she sings
her song of rapture to the night, *"Il m'aime"* ("He loves me"). The melody
soars in passion, and Marguerite finally cries out, "Ah, hurry back to me,
my beloved!" Faust rushes to the open window, and with a strangled cry of
"Marguerite!" clasps her to him. The lovers are lost in the deepening night,
through which comes the sardonic, triumphant laughter of the fiend.

From the Painting by Kreling
ACT I—FAUST WEARIES OF LIFE

EZIO PINZA AS MEPHISTOPHELES

ACT IV

SCENE 1: *Marguerite's Room.* Marguerite is alone in her room, busily spinning, and brooding over her betrayal. Siebel, ever faithful, approaches her, swearing vengeance on Faust. Marguerite stops him with the declaration that she still loves the man who deserted her, and Siebel assures her of his eternal fealty. Then Marguerite reveals that though all spurn her now, at least the church is still open, and there she will go to pray for her child . . . and for him.

SCENE 2: *A Church.* A few women cross the scene and enter the church. Marguerite follows them and kneels. In reply she hears the mocking voice of Mephistopheles, reminding her of her sins. A choir of demons jeeringly calls out her name. Prayer is useless, says the fiend. And Marguerite's despair grows as the church choir awesomely chants of the Day of Judgment. Terrified, she rushes from the church, the fierce cry of Satan, *"À toi l'enfer!"* ("You are damned!"), ringing in her ears.

SCENE 3: *A Square Before the Church.* At one side of the square is the church from which Marguerite has fled in a frenzy of terror and remorse. At the other side is Marguerite's home. Martial music is heard as the troops return home victorious. Valentine greets Siebel, who, confused, evades his questions about Marguerite. The assembled troops now voice the joy of their home-coming in the famous "Soldiers' Chorus" (*"Gloire immortelle de nos aieux"*—"Immortal glory of our ancestors"). Ready to die are we like our brave forebears, they sing, but now it is peace and time to return to loving arms. The jubilant crowd disperses. Valentine, alarmed over Siebel's evasive remarks, rushes into the cottage. A cynical little theme is heard in the orchestra. Mephistopheles approaches, followed by Faust. The fiend is ready to enter, but Faust, torn with grief over his shameful conduct, restrains him. Mocking him, Mephistopheles stations himself below Marguerite's window and, strumming a guitar, sings an insulting serenade (*"Vous qui faites l'endormie"*—"You who pretend to be slumbering"), each stanza of which ends in a taunting laugh. Against a snarling, eerie accompaniment of plucked strings and chuckling woodwinds, the fiend chants his ballad of mocking innuendo.

Outraged, Valentine bursts from the house, sword in hand. Mephistopheles retorts scornfully to Valentine's angry charges, and the brother challenges them. Faust reluctantly raises his sword in defense. Mephistopheles applies his black magic, and Valentine falls, mortally wounded, as the murderers flee. The noisy quarrel has drawn townspeople to the square, and they find Valentine writhing on the ground. As he dies he mournfully tells his friends it is too late now to give him any help. In words of biting harshness he curses his sister for the shame and tragedy her love for Faust has brought them. The crowd pleads with him to relent and show mercy, but it is too late. Valentine dies, and Marguerite falls at her brother's feet, sobbing frenziedly. The people kneel and pray for the peace of his soul.

ACT V

SCENE 1: *The Brocken in the Harz Mountains.* (This scene is usually omitted in performances outside France. The ballet music was written by Gounod for the production of the Paris Opéra.) In search of further adventure Mephistopheles brings Faust to witness the revels of Walpurgis Night. These were held, according to medieval legend, on the eve of May first on the Brocken, the highest peak of the Harz Mountains, in Germany. On this desolate height, wrapped in ghostly mists, witches and demons hold their unholy orgy. Lightning flashes luridly over the gruesome scene. At a summons from Mephistopheles the shades of the great courtesans of history appear to the strains of sensuous ballet music. Lais, Cleopatra, Helen of Troy, Phryne are evoked in the dazzling vision. Suddenly, amid the wanton revelry there rises the image of Marguerite, crushed as if by the blow of an ax. Faust starts back abashed. He demands that Mephistopheles take him to her side.

SCENE 2: *A Prison.* Marguerite, her mind almost shattered, is awaiting death for killing the child she has borne Faust. Mephistopheles and Faust have come to rescue her. They must work fast, for this is the morning of her execution. As Marguerite lies asleep on a straw bed in her dingy cell, Faust orders Mephistopheles to leave, for fear he will add to the poor girl's anguish. Marguerite awakens when Faust calls softly to her. Delirious, she seems at first unaware of his presence. As in a dream she sings quietly of their first meeting, of the night in the garden. Tenderly, dimly, as from afar, the music of the *kermesse* and the garden scenes returns in wistful, nostalgic echoes. Faust frantically urges her to come with him. As Marguerite raves on, her broken mind unable to cope with reality, Faust, in despair, realizes he cannot reach her.

Mephistopheles calls out impatiently that they must hurry. The horses are ready for their escape, he shouts, as the pulsating accompaniment of the orchestra suggests the sounds of trampling and neighing, with the song of the "Calf of Gold" heard in the basses. Marguerite suddenly draws back in fear as her vision clears and she sees Mephistopheles. She calls out to God for protection, her voice soaring in angelic purity, as she seems to glimpse the joy of heaven and forgiveness. Faust and Mephistopheles struggle vainly against her vision, but Marguerite has found the strength to fight the tempting voices of Faust and his demon friend. Her last words to Faust damn him forever: "Why those bloody hands? Go, you fill me with horror!" In a joyous choiring of seraphic voices, Marguerite's soul is borne to heaven, as Mephistopheles, with a gloating cry of "Condemned!" drags his victim off to perdition. Gounod rises to sublime heights in this final trio and "Apotheosis," vividly contrasting the opposing forces of good and evil, and massing great organlike sonorities for the moment when the prison walls open and Marguerite's tormented soul is given its final repose.

From a Lithograph
ACT III—THE QUARTET

LEONARD WARREN AS VALENTINE

DOROTHY KIRSTEN AS MARGUERITE

Faust

THE RCA-VICTOR RECORDS
.(Sung in French unless otherwise noted)

COMPLETE RECORDING: *Mireille Berthon, Soprano; César Vezzani, Tenor; Marcel Journet, Bass; Marthe Coiffier, Soprano; Louis Musy, Baritone; Mme. Montfort, Alto; Henri Cozette, Tenor; with Chorus and Orchestra of the Opéra, Paris, Henri Büsser, Cond.*
DMC-102 (DM-105) (Vol. 1)
(13411-13420), 10-12″
(DM-105) (Vol. 2)
(13421-13430), 10-12″
MC-102 (M-105) (Vol. 1)
(11000-11009)
(M-105) (Vol. 2)
(11010-11019)

ACT II

INVOCATION—AVANT DE QUITTER CES LIEUX (Dio possente) (Even Bravest Heart May Swell): *Lawrence Tibbett, Baritone, with Orch.* 8452, 12″

Leonard Warren, Baritone, with Orch. 18420, 12″

Giuseppe de Luca, Baritone, with Orch. In Italian 7086, 12″

Mario Ancona, Baritone, with Orch. In Italian 15-1002, 12″
(Acoustical Recording)

LE VEAU D'OR (The Calf of Gold): *Feodor Chaliapin, Bass; Henri Cozette, Tenor; Chorus and Orch.* 7600, 12″

Ezio Pinza, Bass; Metropolitan Opera Chorus and Orch. 1753, 10″

VALSE (Arr. Orch.): *Boston "Pops" Orchestra, Arthur Fiedler, Cond.* 10-1009, 10″

(Arr. Sarasate): *Erica Morini, Violinist, with Piano* 10-1011, 10″

ACT III

FAITES-LUI MES AVEUX (Flower Song— Gentle Flow'rs in the Dew): *Gladys Swarthout, Mezzo-soprano, with Orch.* 11-8280, 12″
(In Album M-925)

CAVATINE—SALUT! DEMEURE (All Hail, .Thou Dwelling): *Jussi Bjoerling, Tenor, with Orch.* 13790, 12″
Richard Crooks, Tenor, with Orch. 15542, 12″
(In Album M-585)

BALLADE—IL ÉTAIT UN ROI DE THULÉ (Ballad of the King of Thule): *Jeanette MacDonald, Soprano, with Orch.* 2050, 10″

Elisabeth Rethberg, Soprano, with Orch. 7179, 12″

AIR DES BIJOUX (Jewel Song): *Jeanette MacDonald, Soprano, with Orch.* 2050, 10″

Eidé Noréna, Soprano, with Orch. 15821, 12″
(In Album M-633)

Elisabeth Rethberg, Soprano, with Orch. 7179, 12″

Blanche Arral, Soprano, with Orch. 15-1016, 12″
(Acoustical Recording)

ACT IV

CHOEUR DES SOLDATS (Soldiers' Chorus): *The RCA-Victor Choral, with Orch., Robert Shaw, Cond.* 11-9289, 12″
(In Album M-1074)

(Arr. Band): *Arthur Pryor's Band* 35804, 12″

MEPHISTO'S SERENADE—VOUS QUI FAITES L'ENDORMIE (You Who Pretend To Be Slumbering): *Feodor Chaliapin, Bass, with Orch.* 7600, 12″

ACT V

BALLET—NUIT DE WALPURGIS (Walpurgis Night): *Boston "Pops" Orchestra, Arthur Fiedler, Cond.* 13830, 12″

PRISON SCENE—ALERTE! ALERTE! (Leave Her): *Joan Cross, Soprano; Webster Booth, Tenor; Norman Walker, Bass; Sadler's Wells Chorus and Orchestra. In English* 36235, 12″

Geraldine Farrar, Soprano; Enrico Caruso, Tenor; Marcel Journet, Bass; with Orch. 16-5003, 12″
(Acoustical Recording)
(In Album M-953)

Nellie Melba, Soprano; John McCormack, Tenor; Mario Sammarco, Baritone; with Orch. 15-1019, 12″
(Acoustical Recording)

153

ACT IV—THE DEATH OF LEONORA

La Favorita

OPERA IN four acts. Music by Gaetano Donizetti. Libretto by Alphonse Royer and Gustave Vaëz (also Agustin Eugène Scribe), adapted from the drama *Le Comte de Comminges* by Baculard-d'Arnaud. First performance, Opéra, Paris, December 2, 1840, in French. (This work originally consisted of three acts, was entitled *L'Ange de Niside*, and was scheduled for production at the Théâtre de la Renaissance.) First American performance, New Orleans, Théâtre d'Orléans, February 9, 1843, also in French. Metropolitan *première*, November 29, 1895, in Italian. A notable Metropolitan revival, November 29, 1905, boasted Edyth Walker, Jeanne Jomelli, Enrico Caruso, Antonio Scotti, and Pol Plançon in the principal roles.

Although not so well known as *Lucia di Lammermoor*, this opera of Donizetti's contains much music that is prized by singers, and especially the mezzo-soprano aria, "*O mio Fernando*," which is a favorite of recitalists. The music, dramatic, always fluent, and very melodious, requires above all else exquisite singing. The libretto is considered a good example, in comparison to others of its time, of ironic tragedy, and the tragedy, like that of Hardy's *Tess of the d'Urbervilles*, centers on the grim detail of a heroine's letter failing to reach her lover.

CHARACTERS

ALFONSO XI, *King of Castile*　　Baritone

LEONORA DE GUZMAN, *his mistress*
　　　　　　　　　　Mezzo-soprano

FERNANDO, *a monastic novice*　　Tenor

BALTASAR, *prior of the Monastery of St. James*　　Bass

DON GASPARO, *officer of the King*　　Tenor

INEZ, *confidante to Leonora*　　Soprano

The action takes place mostly in Castile, in the year 1340

154

ACT I

SCENE: *The Cloister of the Monastery of St. James of Compostella.* Fernando, a novice, is sitting with Baltasar, the prior, in a cloister, ancient and grass-grown even in this, the year 1340. Fernando wishes to renounce his novitiate, for he has fallen in love with a beautiful unknown who passes by the monastery. "Do you not know her?" asks Baltasar, and Fernando exclaims, "I know her not, yet I love her." At this Baltasar sternly bids him go and not profane the sacred place; and Fernando, unhappy at having to leave the monastery, pleads for forgiveness, but sets out on his search for the mysterious beauty.

The scene changes to the island of Leon, where Leonora (the Favorite) lives and whence she has sent for Fernando. He is led blindfolded to his destination by a fair guide who refuses to reveal the identity of the lady who has sent for him. Leonora now appears, and a tender love scene follows; but the Favorite is anxious, fearing that Fernando will learn she is the King's mistress. She commands him to leave her forever, and gives him a parchment which she says will insure his future. He wishes to remain, but Inez enters, whispering to Leonora that the King is at the villa. As Fernando leaves, he recognizes the monarch, and his hopes fall, for—he reasons, not knowing of their relationship—how can a recreant monk now aspire to her hand with a King for a rival. He looks at the parchment—his commission as an officer in the army of the King!

ACT II

SCENE: *The Gardens of the Alcázar.* The King has just installed himself with Leonora at the Alcázar, newly regained from the Moors. Here he is sought out by Baltasar, who threatens him with a papal interdiction for deserting his legal wife, an interdiction that will apply to all the court if the King does not drive Leonora from him. The King, torn between love and fear of the Church, hesitates; he is tempted to brave the papal denunciation.

ACT III

SCENE: *The Hall of the Palace.* Fernando, returning victorious from the wars, is offered by the grateful King any reward he may desire. The hero asks only for the hand of Leonora, who enters at this very moment. This is a request the King is rather happy to grant, for it will relieve him of any further fear of ecclesiastical curses. With the cruelest irony that only Fernando is not in a position to grasp, the King bestows the hand of Leonora on the conqueror. Left alone, Leonora meditates on the tragedy of her position; she sings a sustained, melancholy air in which she declares her willingness to sacrifice everything for Fernando's sake, and these thoughts are expressed in the lofty and melodious aria *"O mio Fernando."*

She sends her attendant, Inez, to reveal the truth to him in a letter telling all. At the King's order, Inez is intercepted, and the wedding takes place at once; then Fernando's wrath is aroused by the cold looks and sneers he and his bride receive from the courtiers. Overcome with rage, he draws his sword, and bloodshed would soon follow were it not that Baltasar arrives and the shameful truth is revealed to Fernando.

ACT IV

SCENE: *A Cloister of the Monastery.* Fernando has fled from the world and now seeks consolation in the monastery. Baltasar and a chorus of monks musically reflect upon the joy and serenity of penitence and salvation, in *"Splendon più belle"* ("In heavenly splendor").

Before entering the chapel for the final rite which will make him one of the order, he soliloquizes on his unhappy fate. The phantom of love and its illusions are left behind—only memories remain, pale, tranquil, tender, and ineffably sad, and he sings of this in the romanza *"Spirito gentil"* ("Spirit so fair").

Leonora, stricken unto death, follows him even here and, disguised as a novice, gains admittance. She is found on the chapel steps by Fernando when he comes from the service making him one of the order, and as he lifts her forgivingly in his arms, she dies.

THE RCA-VICTOR RECORDS
(Sung in Italian)

ACT III

A TANTO AMOR (Thou Flower Beloved): *Mattia Battistini, Baritone, with Orch.* 15-1010, 12"
(Acoustical Recording)

O MIO FERNANDO (Oh, Dearest Ferdinand): *Sigrid Onegin, Contralto, with Orch.* 7191, 12"

Nan Merriman, Mezzo-soprano, with Orch. 11-9793, 12"

ACT IV

SPLENDON PIÙ BELLE IN CIEL (In Heavenly Splendor): *Ezio Pinza, Bass; Metropolitan Opera Chorus and Orch.* 7552, 12"

Fedora

OPERA IN three acts. Music by Umberto Giordano. Libretto by Arturo Colautti, after Sardou's drama. First produced, Teatro Lirico, Milan, November 17, 1898. First performance in the United States, Metropolitan Opera House, December 5, 1906, when Lina Cavalieri made her debut in this country in the title role. The cast also included Enrico Caruso, Bella Alten, and Antonio Scotti. The Metropolitan's revival on December 8, 1923, had, as its chief singers, Maria Jeritza, Giovanni Martinelli, Queena Mario, and Scotti.

CHARACTERS

PRINCESS FEDORA ROMAZOV	Soprano	BOROV, a doctor		Baritone
COUNTESS OLGA SUKAREV	Soprano	GRECH, a police officer		Bass
COUNT LORIS IPANOV	Tenor	LOREK, a surgeon		Baritone
DE SIRIEX, a diplomat	Baritone	BOLESLAV LAZINSKI		Mime
DMITRI, a groom (boy)	Contralto	DR. MÜLLER		Mime
DÉSIRÉ, an attendant	Tenor	MARKA, a waiter		
BARON ROUVEL	Tenor	BASIL, a domestic		
CYRIL, a cook	Baritone	IVAN, a detective		

ACT I

SCENE: *The House of Count Vladimir Andreyevich.* Count Vladimir, the betrothed of the beautiful Princess Fedora, is brought home mortally wounded. It is hinted that Count Loris has committed this murder as part of a Nihilist plot. Fedora swears vengeance.

ACT II

SCENE: *Fedora's House in Paris.* A magnificent reception is being held at Fedora's house in Paris. She uses all her skill in fascinating Count Loris, in the hope that she will find proof of his guilt. He has already fallen madly in love with her, and when they happen to be left together for a few minutes she leads him on coquettishly, until, growing poetic under her enchantment, he tenderly declares that his love is so great and strong that it compels her to love him. Even now she has pushed him away. Yet her hand is searching his; and while her lips deny it, her eyes confess that she loves him. The melody of this avowal of love, *"Amor ti vieta"* ("My love compels"), is a sustained cavatina; the orchestra supplies a glowing accompaniment.

Outside, police are waiting to seize Loris after the guests have departed. Loris weepingly confesses to the murder, and reveals, moreover, that his wife was betrayed and brought to her untimely death by Vladimir. On learning this, Fedora, who herself has fallen in love with Loris, embraces him, and saves him from the police.

Fedora

ACT III

SCENE: *Fedora's Villa in Oberland.* Although Loris and Fedora are living happily together in Switzerland, he is followed by a police spy. News comes that because of Loris' deed his brother was put into prison, where he died, his mother then dying of the shock. A message also comes bearing Loris' pardon, and with the same mail comes a letter revealing that it was Fedora who set the detectives after him. In sudden blind anger, Loris is about to kill her, but she quickly swallows poison. Then he implores her to live. It is too late: she dies in his arms.

THE RCA-VICTOR RECORDS
(Sung in Italian)

ACT II

ARIOSA DI LORIS—AMOR TI VIETA (My Love Compels): *Richard Crooks, Tenor, with Orch.* 2063, 10"

Alessandro Ziliani, Tenor, with Orch. 1735, 10"

Rembrandt

FINALE OF THE OPERA

Fidelio

OPERA IN two acts. Music by Ludwig van Beethoven. Libretto by Josef Sonnleithner and Georg Friedrich Treitschke, after a French play by Jean Nicolas Bouilly, entitled *Lénore, ou L'Amour conjugal* (*Lénore, or Conjugal Love*), said to be based on a "historical fact." First produced, in three acts, at the Theater an der Wien, Vienna, on November 20, 1805. On the following March 29, the work was revived in a cut version condensed to two acts. Further revision was done in the years following, and on May 23, 1814, it was produced at the Kärntnertor-Theater in Vienna, enjoying its first emphatic success. The American *première* occurred at the Park Theater, New York, September 9, 1839, the language being English. A German version followed in 1856 at the Broadway Theater, and the young Metropolitan Opera Company first staged it on November 19, 1884, with the phenomenal Marianne Brandt making her local debut as Leonora and Leopold Damrosch conducting.

Fidelio was Beethoven's only opera. In the self-sacrificing heroine Leonore may be found a companion portrait to the ideal hero enshrined in the "Eroica" Symphony. For the fearless and devoted Leonore is a symbol of freedom and valor fighting despotism. Although the original title of the opera was *Leonore* it was found necessary to substitute *Fidelio* since there had been at least two earlier operatic settings of the same play, with the same title, one by a Frenchman, Pierre Gaveaux, the other by an Italian, Ferdinando Paer, who was *Kapellmeister* at Dresden.

The problem of an overture to *Fidelio* so worried Beethoven that he composed, in all, four complete specimens. The first was discarded. The next was used for the world *première* of *Fidelio* in 1805 and is now known as "Leonore" Overture No. 2. The following one—"Leonore" Overture No. 3—was composed for the Viennese revival four months later. The one that is now used regularly to open the opera was written for the 1814 revival. It is known simply as the Overture to *Fidelio*. Gustav Mahler introduced the practice at the Metropolitan Opera House of inserting the "Leonore" Overture No. 3 between the two scenes of Act II. All three "Leonore" overtures differ sharply from the *Fidelio* Overture, which, unlike them, is more in the nature of a true prelude, built around a single musical idea rather than reflecting a whole drama. The "Leonore" Overture No. 3 ranks first in popularity because of its brilliant exposition and resounding presto finale. The "Leonore" Overture No. 2 is more in the nature of a tone poem, a sequence of shifting moods in a dramatic plan. Beethoven altered the third to bring it closer to sonata structure. This may be noted in the reprise of the allegro section. To make room for this and the fully worked-out coda, Beethoven deleted much of the adagio and allegro material of the "Leonore" Overture No. 2. In both cases the first section of the overture is built on Florestan's despairing song, "*In des Lebens Frühlingstagen*" ("In the springtime of life"). After the brilliant allegro section, Beethoven shows his shrewd dramatic sense. There is a sharp halt, and trumpet calls sound offstage. This gives the signal for freeing Florestan and Leonore from Pizarro's clutches. As for preferences regarding the overtures, it was Romain Rolland who suggested, "Let us prefer both!"

CHARACTERS

FLORESTAN, *a Spanish nobleman*　*Tenor*

LEONORE, *his wife, who disguises herself and takes the name of* FIDELIO　*Soprano*

DON FERNANDO, *Prime Minister of Spain and friend of Florestan*　*Bass*

PIZARRO, *governor of the prison, and enemy of Florestan*　*Bass*

ROCCO, *chief jailer*　*Bass*

MARCELLINA, *Rocco's daughter*　*Soprano*

JACQUINO, *Rocco's assistant, in love with Marcellina*　*Tenor*

PRISONERS, GUARDS, SOLDIERS, AND PEOPLE

The action takes place in the eighteenth century at a fortress used for the confinement of political offenders, near Seville, Spain

ACT I

(Following the tradition of Gustav Mahler, this act is often divided into two scenes, the first taking place in Rocco's kitchen. According to the libretto, however, the entire act takes place in the courtyard of the prison.)

SCENE: *Courtyard of the State Prison.* The story of *Fidelio* centers in an episode of political despotism. Florestan, a valiant fighter for freedom, is imprisoned in a dark dungeon by his ruthless enemy, Pizarro, governor of the state prison. There he is slowly starving to death. Meanwhile, reports have reached his wife, Leonore, who does not know his whereabouts, of his death. Frantic, she clings to the hope that this is some villainous game of Pizzaro's. As a last desperate measure she resolves to search out Pizarro's prison, find her husband, and free him. To do so, she disguises herself as the youth Fidelio and secures employment as assistant to the jailer Rocco. To complicate matters, Rocco's daughter, Marcellina, falls in love with the handsome lad, thus arousing the jealousy of Jacquino, Rocco's turnkey, who is planning to marry the girl. Leonore encourages the romance as a way of gaining information about the vaguely mentioned prisoner in the dungeon below, whom Pizarro is slowly starving to death. The curious romantic tangle involving Marcellina's misplaced feelings is brought out with wondrous delicacy in the canonical quartet, "*Mir ist so wunderbar!*" ("It is so wonderful!")

When Pizarro appears, the music promptly alters in color to the sinister hues of impending evil. Florestan's implacable enemy has heard that the

Prime Minister is planning to visit the prison. This will be awkward, with a deliberately starved prisoner, and a guiltless one at that, languishing in a foul, unlighted dungeon. We glimpse the man's vile nature, its depths of savage hate, in the fearsome aria, *"Ha! welch' ein Augenblick!"* ("Ha! what a moment!") Pizarro, resolved to slay Florestan before the expected arrival of the Minister, orders Rocco to prepare a grave. But Rocco recoils at the thought of murder, and Pizarro decides to commit the deed himself.

Leonore overhears the whole plot; and when the two men depart, she leaves her hiding place and pours out her outraged feelings in one of the most dramatic *scenas* in all opera, *"Abscheulicher! wo eilst du hin!"* ("Thou monstrous fiend"), begins the impassioned recitative. Leonore wrathfully speculates on what fresh villainy Pizarro is planning. She is scathing in her wrath, and then, as an aria of sublime beauty and repose begins, she appeals to God for strength and hope to carry out her purpose. A moving scene follows Leonore's outcry. At her request, Rocco allows the prisoners to file out into the courtyard for a breath of fresh air and a glimpse of the sun. The men rub their eyes as they behold the world again in great wonder and join in a magnificent chorus—*"O welche Lust!"* ("Oh, what joy!")—expressive of their thirst for freedom and their thwarted joys. Eagerly Leonore scans their faces, but Florestan is not among them. However, Leonore's hopes revive as she learns that she must accompany Rocco down into the dungeon.

ACT II

SCENE 1: *A Dark Subterranean Dungeon.* Florestan is revealed alone in the bleak depths of Pizarro's prison, chained and fastened to the wall. Soon he begins a poignant monologue on his grievous state. In the beautiful aria following the recitative he recalls his days of youth and spring and freedom, *"In des Lebens Frühlingstagen"* ("In the springtime of life"). For loving liberty, for being innocent of any crime, he has been condemned to this endless torment. In his frenzy he has a vision of Leonore and cries out ecstatically to it. Rocco and Leonore now appear. With some difficulty Leonore recognizes her husband in this broken and ragged man. She says nothing, but helps Rocco to dig the grave. When Pizarro at length appears and tries to stab the defenseless prisoner, Leonore rushes to shield him. "Kill his wife first!" she shouts defiantly. Florestan, dazed with joy, shouts out, "My wife! Leonore!" Pizarro, in a burst of savage rage, attempts to slay them both, but Leonore is ready for him. She whips out a pistol and levels it at him, shouting, "One step more, and you die!" Suddenly a trumpet call sounds: the anxiously awaited Minister has finally arrived. Florestan and Leonore, saved and reunited, join their voices in a throbbing outburst of rapture, *"O namenlose Freude"* ("O nameless joy").

Fidelio

SCENE 2: *The Courtyard of the State Prison* (same as Act I). Florestan's fellow prisoners have been released by the Minister, and Leonore herself removes the chains from Florestan. Marcellina, fully recovered from her infatuation, consents to marry the turnkey Jacquino. Pizarro is arrested and led away by Don Fernando's men, and the chorus sings a final tribute to the devoted wife whose valor rescued her husband from certain death.

THE RCA-VICTOR RECORDS
(Sung in German)

FIDELIO OVERTURE: *BBC Symphony Orchestra, Bruno Walter, Cond.*
11809, 12"

LEONORE OVERTURE NO. 1, IN C MAJOR, OPUS 138: *BBC Symphony Orchestra, Arturo Toscanini, Cond.*
15945, 12"

LEONORE OVERTURE NO. 3, IN C MAJOR, OPUS 72A: *Arturo Toscanini and the NBC Symphony Orchestra*
DM-1098 (11-9450 & 11-9451), 2-12"
M-1098 (11-9448 & 11-9449)

Vienna Philharmonic Orchestra, Bruno Walter, Cond.
DM-359 (13826 & 13827), 2-12"
M-359 (11958 & 11959)

ACT I

MIR IST SO WUNDERBAR (It Is So Wonderful): *Erna Berger, Soprano; Marcel Wittrisch, Tenor; Willi Domgraf-Fassbaender, Baritone; Henriette Gottlieb, Soprano; with Orch.*
11826, 12"

ABSCHEULICHER! WO EILST DU HIN! (Thou Monstrous Fiend): *Kirsten Flagstad, Soprano; the Philadelphia Orchestra, Eugene Ormandy, Cond.* 14972, 12"

Rose Bampton, Soprano; Arturo Toscanini and the NBC Symphony Orchestra 11-9110, 12"

O WELCHE LUST (Oh, What Joy!) (Prisoners' Chorus): *The Metropolitan Opera Chorus and Orch.* 11249, 12"

Wide World Studio
KIRSTEN FLAGSTAD AS FIDELIO

ACT II

ER STERBE, DOCH ER SOLL ERST WISSEN (He Dies, But First Shall Know His Slayer): *Henriette Gottlieb, Soprano; Walter Ludwig, Tenor; Willi Domgraf-Fassbaender, Baritone; Walther Grossmann, Bass; with Orch.*
11826, 12"

THE PHANTOM SHIP

Der Fliegende Holländer
(THE FLYING DUTCHMAN)

OPERA IN three acts. Music by Richard Wagner. Text by the composer, founded on Heine's version of an old legend which he took from a Dutch drama. Produced at Dresden, January 2, 1843. First performed in the United States at the Philadelphia Academy of Music, in Italian, under the translated title *Il Vascello fantasma*, November 8, 1876. Metropolitan *première*, in German, November 27, 1889, with Theodor Reichmann, Sophie Wiesner, Paul Kalisch, and Emil Fischer, the conductor being Anton Seidl. Seidl also conducted when the work was given at the same theater in Italian, with Jean Lassalle, Emma Albani, Montariol, and Édouard de Reszke.

The North Sea, seldom gentle, was in one of its wildest moods when Wagner crossed it in 1839. The ship was nearly wrecked three times, and once was compelled to put up in a Norwegian harbor for safety. During the stormy voyage, Wagner recalled Heine's account of the legend of the Flying Dutchman, who had been condemned to sail the seas until doomsday unless he should find a woman who would be true to him till death. Wagner was at that time exceedingly unhappy, bankrupt, and without work. The story of the unfortunate Dutchman appealed to him greatly—became a symbol of his own wretched condition. The Norwegian harbor and the song of the Norwegian sailors enter into the opera; but, above all, it is the sea that dominates, the unceasingly restless ocean.

When Wagner finally arrived in Paris, he set to work to write a libretto for his opera; in order to relieve his strained circumstances, he sold a scenario of this libretto to Léon Pillet, manager of the Paris Opéra, the latter turning it over to a pair of librettists, Foucher and Révoil, and their libretto was set by another composer, Pierre Louis Philippe Dietsch, a conductor at the Opéra. This work, long since forgotten, was actually produced a few months before Wagner's.

With the money he received from the sale of the libretto, Wagner set himself up in a quiet apartment and began writing the music of his own opera. *Rienzi* had achieved a great success at Dresden; accordingly, the management of the opera there agreed to produce *The Dutchman*. After the dazzling, brilliant earlier work, the somber beauty of *The Dutchman*, more psychological and introspective, was a disappointment to the first audience. The opera, nevertheless, marks a great step forward in the development of Wagner's musical and dramatic style; here he first uses leading motives—*Leitmotive* —to an appreciable extent, and the orchestra is treated in the symphonic manner. The genius is beginning to find himself!

CHARACTERS

DALAND, *a Norwegian sea captain*	*Bass*	DALAND'S STEERSMAN	*Tenor*
THE DUTCHMAN	*Baritone*	SENTA, *daughter of Daland*	*Soprano*
ERIC, *a huntsman, a lover of*		MARY, *Senta's nurse*	*Contralto*
Senta	*Tenor*		

SAILORS, MAIDENS, HUNTERS, AND VILLAGERS

The action takes place in a Norwegian village in the eighteenth century

The Overture is in itself a vivid picture of the entire story: the stormy sea, portrayed as no other composer has ever succeeded in doing; the gloomy Dutchman, the curse upon him and his longing for redemption; the tranquil motive of Senta, who shall bring about that redemption; for a moment of relief, the gay song of the Norwegian sailors, soon overwhelmed in the storm; and finally the crashing of the Curse motive, displaced by the theme of Senta, glorified and radiant, as it will be heard at the end of the opera, when across the glow of the sunset the figures of Senta and the redeemed Dutchman are seen rising from the sea heavenward.

ACT I

SCENE: *A Norwegian Harbor.* The legend, as told both by Heine and by Wagner, relates to a Dutch sea captain who once swore that in spite of storms and contrary winds he would round the Cape of Good Hope, even in spite of all hell. As a punishment for his impious vow he was condemned to sail the seas until the crack of doom. But once in seven years this "Flying Dutchman" was permitted to land; if then he could find a maiden who would be faithful unto death, she would bring release from the curse. At the opening of the opera, this Dutchman, Vanderdecken, is driven by a storm to seek shelter in the same harbor where Daland, a Norwegian sea captain, has also been compelled to put up. Daland is rather impressed by this gloomy stranger, who is master of a ship with black masts and blood-red sails, and no less so by his apparent wealth. The Dutchman offers to pay well for lodgings, which Daland is quite agreeable to supply him. Suddenly, and almost bluntly, Vanderdecken asks his host-to-be whether or not he has a daughter. Daland says yes, and the Dutchman, without frill or fuss, immediately sues for her hand. This, not altogether surprisingly, delights Daland, who straightway invites the striking individual to be his guest. Presently the weather becomes more favorable, and both ships weigh anchor, headed for Daland's home.

ACT III

ACT II

SCENE: *A Room in Daland's House.* The second act shows Senta, Daland's daughter, at home with a crowd of girls who are spinning very busily. They sing, meanwhile, a most charming chorus, as the orchestra accompanies them with occasional imitation of the whirring wheels. Senta, however, has a specific aim in life, which is to be the cause of the Flying Dutchman's salvation. She sits dreamily in her armchair, gazing at the portrait of the Dutchman, in dark beard and black Spanish attire, which hangs over the entrance. Her companions quite cheerily tease Senta about her reveries, and she answers that she will sing them a much better song, a ballad about the Flying Dutchman, in which she discloses that she would be the savior of this harried man by her love.

The piece is known as "Senta's Ballad." It begins with the mariner's wild cry of "Yo-ho-ho, Yo-ho-ho." And as the orchestra vividly depicts the raging ocean, she sings of the Dutchman's attempt to round the Cape, of his oath and the curse hurled upon him, and of how he is driven hopelessly across the seas in a ship with "blood-red sails." Then continuing—to the peaceful theme first heard in the Overture—she sings of his possible salvation, if anywhere on earth he can find a woman who will be faithful unto death. And in growing agitation she adds that such a woman there is and, quite oblivious of her surroundings, declares passionately that she is the one —she will save him from his unhappy fate.

With this Eric, who loves her, enters and vainly attempts to dissuade her from her mad dream. She can give him no hope, however, and he darts out in despair. Senta's eyes are held fast by the picture and, suddenly and dra-

165

matically, she espies the Dutchman standing in the doorway, having just come in with her father. Senta and the dark mariner exchange a long, searching look, as Daland sings of their respective attributes—Vanderdecken's wealth and Senta's charms and virtues. They scarcely hear Daland, who, nettled by the lack of attention, leaves them. An ornate duet of mutual avowal takes place, following which Daland returns to confirm their betrothal.

ACT III

SCENE: *The Bay Near Daland's Home.* Daland's house is seen on one side, and the ships of Vanderdecken and Daland are also partly visible. There are high cliffs rising from the sea some distance away. Senta is observed rushing out of her house and onto the beach. In swift pursuit is Eric, who comes to reproach her for her faithlessness. This declaration is heard by the Dutchman, who, coming on the scene unnoticed, reflects upon the words and comes to the conclusion that if Senta is capable of being untrue to one man, she can be untrue also to another—himself. Whereupon he believes that once again he has been led almost to the point of his redemption only to be disillusioned, and now he must sail the seas for another seven years. He boards his ship swiftly, heading it straight out to sea, where a storm begins to rage. But the frantic Senta, stunned only for a moment by the swift turn of circumstances, climbs speedily up one of the cliffs and, shouting after him, "Here stand I, faithful unto death!" flings herself into the ocean. And then a miracle takes place; the bleak and ghostly ship sinks at once from sight, as, rising heavenward, the figures of Senta and the Dutchman are clasped in an eternal embrace.

THE RCA-VICTOR RECORDS
(Sung in German)

ACT I

Steuermannslied—Mit Gewitter und Sturm (The Steersman's Song) : *Lauritz Melchior, Tenor, with Orch.*
17725, 12"
(In Album M-749)
11-8678, 12"
(In Album M-979)

Wie oft in Meers tiefsten Schlund (How Oft' in Ocean's Deepest Cave) : *Friedrich Schorr, Baritone, with Orch.* 7269, 12"

Die Frist ist um (The Term is Past) : *Joel Berglund, Baritone, with Orch., Leo Blech, Cond.*
12-0532, 12"

KIRSTEN FLAGSTAD AS SENTA

ACT III, SCENE 2—CHICAGO OPERA PRODUCTION

La Forza del Destino
(THE FORCE OF DESTINY)

OPERA IN four acts. Music by Giuseppe Verdi. Libretto by Francesco Maria Piave, after the Spanish play, *Don Alvaro, o La Fuerza del sino*, by Angel de Saavedra, Duke of Rivas. First performance, Imperial Italian Theater, St. Petersburg, November 10, 1862. First New York performance, Academy of Music, February 24, 1865. A revised version of the text, done by Antonio Ghislanzoni, was first heard at the Teatro alla Scala, Milan, February 20, 1869. The second version is described here, that being the one followed generally in present-day performances.

In *La Forza del destino* we find the composer making an advance in musical style over the successes just preceding it, *Trovatore* and *Traviata*. While in a general sense equally melodious, the music seems possessed of a greater seriousness and depth of purpose. The orchestral accompaniment is at once more full-bodied and colorful; the harmonies are richer and more varied. Seldom has Verdi charged a scene with a more genuine feeling of the dramatic, of tragic foreboding, almost "atmospheric" in character, than he has done in the second scene of Act II of this opera.

CHARACTERS

THE MARQUIS OF CALATRAVA		*Bass*	PADRE GUARDIANO, *an abbot*		*Bass*
DONNA LEONORA	} *his children*	*Soprano*	FRA MELITONE, *a friar*		*Baritone*
DON CARLO		*Baritone*	CURRA, *Leonora's maid*		*Mime*
DON ALVARO, *a young nobleman*		*Tenor*	AN ALCALDE		*Bass*
PREZIOSILLA, *a gypsy*		*Mezzo-soprano*	A SURGEON		*Tenor*

SPANISH AND ITALIAN PEASANTS, SOLDIERS, FRANCISCAN FRIARS, ETC.

The action takes place in Spain and Italy, about the end of the eighteenth century

The Overture preceding the opera is appropriately dramatic. After a compelling blare of trumpets, a rather ominous, even sinister melody is

167

heard. Apparently it is meant to typify the unhappy nature of the work. This melody recurs frequently throughout the opera, at times bold and menacing, at others acting as a dark undercurrent to other themes. This is, more or less, a "fate" motive, which, having made its point in the Overture, is replaced by other motives—notably the pathetic, desolate air of Alvaro's plea, which appears in the third act, and the very beautiful melody of Leonora's prayer, sung during the second scene of Act II. Other themes from the opera enter into the scheme, and all combine in a compelling mood picture of the tragic events to follow.

ACT I

SCENE: *Drawing Room of the Marquis of Calatrava, in Seville.* Don Alvaro is the young prince of a distinguished foreign family, but this counts for so little in Spain that the beautiful Leonora, certain that her own family will never permit marriage, plans, instead, to elope with him. Her father, the Marquis of Calatrava, discovers them and, ignoring their protests, accuses them of shameful conduct. Assuming all the blame, Alvaro throws away his pistol and presents his bare chest to the aged noble's sword, but when the pistol strikes the floor it explodes and mortally wounds the Marquis. He dies, cursing his daughter.

ACT II

SCENE 1: *An Inn at Hornachuelos.* Leonora, in male disguise, has fled from Seville to this mountain hostelry; she is alone and in despair, having lost all trace of Don Alvaro since the fatal night. Her uneasiness increases when she recognizes among the motley crowd her brother, Don Carlo, who is masquerading as a student. She overhears his threats of vengeance. In the meantime, Preziosilla, a gypsy, urges all the men to go to Italy and join the fight against the Germans.

SCENE 2: *The Monastery at Hornachuelos.* Leonora has come to the door of the monastery, where, kneeling in the moonlight, she prays for the Virgin's protection, in the aria *"Madre, pietosa Vergine"* ("Mother, merciful Virgin"). She knocks and, confessing all, begs for protection from the kindly abbot, Padre Guardiano. He tells her of a deserted cave in the mountains where she may abide as a "hermit" in safety. The doors of the monastery chapel swing open, revealing in the distance the brilliantly lighted great altar. The deep tones of the organ unite with the solemn supplication of the kneeling monks and Padre Guardiano, who prays that a curse descend upon any person who should ever intrude upon or seek to learn the identity of this stranger. Then Guardiano bids Leonora depart to the mountain retreat; there none shall disturb her, for she will be under the protection of the monastery. She sings, together with the holy men, the simple and affecting prayer, *"La Vergine degli angeli"* ("May Angels guard thee").

ACT II, SCENE 2—METROPOLITAN OPERA PRODUCTION

ACT III

SCENE 1: *A Wood Near Velletri, Italy*. Don Alvaro, believing Leonora dead, has enlisted in the Spanish army under the name of Don Federico Herreros. He is tormented by memories of his past, and to a tender and melancholy air he soliloquizes, *"O tu che in seno"* ("Oh, thou heavenly one").

His reveries being interrupted by a cry of distress, he goes out and finds a wounded man—Don Carlo, his sworn enemy! Since they have never before met, and since both are going under assumed names, neither recognizes the other, and they become close friends.

Later, Don Alvaro, seemingly mortally wounded in battle, begs Carlo to swear to perform his last request. Carlo, torn with pity, swears that he will do his bidding. Alvaro begs him to search in his effects for a package of letters which he wishes burned without opening. Then, Alvaro says he will die happy, and to a poignant melody sings farewell, while his friend replies with words of comfort—a duet of the most intense emotional fervor—*"Solenne in quest' ora"* ("Swear in this hour").

Destiny, however, cannot be thwarted, and although Carlo does not open the package, he discovers elsewhere in the wounded man's effects a picture of Leonora, and, in the aria *"Ah, egli è salvo"* ("Ah, he is saved"), he promises to deal with him.

SCENE 2: *A Military Camp Near Velletri.* Alvaro, now restored to health, strives to convince Don Carlo that he is guiltless of wrongdoing and worthy of Leonora. Intent on avenging his father's death, Don Carlo will not believe him, and insists they fight it out. Alvaro refuses until Carlo threatens to search out Leonora and take her life instead; then Alvaro consents and, in the duel that follows, he wins. Believing that he has killed a second man, he decides to take holy vows and end his days in a monastery, for he cannot go to Leonora with the blood of both her father and her brother on his hands.

ACT IV

SCENE 1: *The Monastery of Hornachuelos.* In the five years that have passed, Don Alvaro, now Father Raphael, has become noted for his immaculate life and his compassionate kindness toward all who suffer. Yet even to the sacred calm of this retreat, Don Carlo, who has recovered from his wound in the duel with Don Alvaro, comes seeking vengeance. While he awaits Alvaro, he sings, *"Invano Alvaro"* ("In vain Alvaro"), in which he remarks on the futility of Alvaro's retirement and of his "hypocrite's garb."

Don Alvaro naturally exclaims in surprise on beholding Carlo, whom he thought dead. Carlo coldly presents him with a sword: they must fight to the death. Alvaro bids him be gone: he is now a man of peace and cannot fight. To this Carlo replies, "Coward!" The friar, well schooled in ignoring his own feelings, answers, "Your menaces, wild and angry words, are cast to the winds." His lines are sung to the broken, pathetic little melody first heard in the Overture.

Alvaro tries hard to convince Don Carlo that vengeance lies with God. In return he receives the most venomous insults. In the music, the pleading accents of the priest are remarkably contrasted with the sinister threats of Don Carlo. Slowly, yet inevitably, the benevolent friar becomes again the fiery man of action; he prays for self-restraint. . . . Carlo strikes him insultingly. Alvaro seizes the weapon, and, the convent being no place to fight, the men rush away. The music swells with a tumult of wild passion.

SCENE 2: *A Wild Spot Near Hornachuelos.* As the curtain rises, we hear in the orchestra the agitated melody first played at the opening of the Overture. On this dark night Leonora, pale and worn, yet beautiful, has issued from her desolate cavern to pray, still tormented by memories of her ill-fated love. *"Pace, pace, mio Dio!"* ("Peace, peace, O my God!") she implores, to a melody of haunting sadness and loveliness that rises and rises as thoughts of Alvaro come crowding. In despair, she finally exclaims that her longing for peace is vain, and turns to re-enter her cave. Suddenly one hears the sounds of clashing swords.

Carlo is wounded, this time mortally. The dying man begs his enemy, as Father Raphael, to confess him and yield absolution. This Alvaro will not do, for he believes himself accursed. He hurries to summon the "hermit." Each having believed the other long since dead, the lovers cry out in horror on suddenly beholding one another. Leonora, finding her brother dying, rushes to embrace him; but Don Carlo, still unforgiving, stabs her even as her arms fold about him. Music of the utmost dramatic forcefulness accompanies these terrifying events; then as Leonora falls dying, shuddering chords, alternately loud and soft, are heard in the orchestra.

The kind Padre Guardiano has sought out the duelists and bids Don Alvaro cease his cursing against fate and humble himself before the Eternal. The heart-rending plaint of Leonora, the despairing lament of Don Alvaro, and the comforting voice of the Padre combine to make this one of the most moving scenes in all opera. There is a sudden cry of pain from Leonora, and she sinks to the earth.

"Dead," sobs Don Alvaro.

"Ascended to God," replies Guardiano.

The music dies away in ethereal harmonies.

ACT III, SCENE 1—*SOLENNE IN QUEST' ORA*

EZIO PINZA AS PADRE GUARDIANO

ZINKA MILANOV AS DONNA LEONORA

THE RCA-VICTOR RECORDS
(Sung in Italian)

OVERTURE: *Arturo Toscanini and the NBC Symphony Orchestra* 11-9010, 12"

ACT II

LA VERGINE DEGLI ANGELI (May Angels Guard Thee): *Rosa Ponselle, Soprano; Ezio Pinza, Bass; Metropolitan Opera Chorus and Orch.*
8097, 12"

ACT III

O TU CHE IN SENO AGLI' ANGELI (Thou Heavenly One): *Enrico Caruso, Tenor, with Orch.*
6000, 12"
(Acoustical Recording)

SOLENNE IN QUEST' ORA (Swear in This Hour): *Beniamino Gigli, Tenor; Giuseppe de Luca, Baritone; with Orch.* 8069, 12"

Jan Peerce, Tenor; Leonard Warren, Baritone; with Orch. 11-9767, 12"
(In Album M-1156)

Enrico Caruso, Tenor; Antonio Scotti, Baritone; with Orch.
8000, 12"
(Acoustical Recording)

ACT IV

INVANO ALVARO! (In Vain Alvaro!)

LA MINACCIE, I FIERI ACCENTI (Thy Menaces Wild): *Giovanni Martinelli, Tenor; Giuseppe de Luca, Baritone; with Orch.* 8085, 12"

Jan Peerce, Tenor; Leonard Warren, Baritone; with Orch. 11-9768, 12"
(In Album M-1156)

PACE, PACE, MIO DIO! (Peace, O My Lord!): *Zinka Milanov, Soprano, with Orch.* 11-8927, 12"

IO MUOJO! (I'm Dying!)

NON IMPRECARE (Blame Me Not): *Giovanni Martinelli, Tenor; Ezio Pinza, Bass; Rosa Ponselle, Soprano; with Orch.* 8104, 12"

White   SCENE FROM THE ORIGINAL PRODUCTION

Four Saints in Three Acts

OPERA IN a prelude and four acts. Music by Virgil Thomson. Libretto by Gertrude Stein ("An Opera To Be Sung"). First produced February 7, 1934, by The Friends and Enemies of Modern Music, Inc. (A. Everett Austin, Jr., president), at the auditorium of the Avery Memorial, Hartford, Conn., with an all-Negro cast including Beatrice Robinson Wayne, Bruce Howard, Edward Mathews, Embry Bonner, Altonell Hines, and Abner Dorsey. Costumes and sets by Florine Stettheimer; Alexander Smallens conducted.

Four Saints in Three Acts played for one week in Hartford; six weeks at the Forty-fourth Street and Empire theaters, New York; one week at the Auditorium Theater, Chicago. These performances were all conducted either by Alexander Smallens or the composer. In the spring of 1941, two concert performances of the opera were given—one at the Museum of Modern Art, New York, under the composer's direction, and one at Town Hall, New York, Alexander Smallens conducting. In June, 1942, an hour of the music was played over the Mutual Broadcasting System for the United States Treasury Department, the conductor being Alfred Wallenstein. In May, 1947, the entire work was performed over the Columbia Broadcasting System. The cast in all performances has remained substantially the same as that of the original production.

Although it is called *Four Saints in Three Acts*, the work actually presents some thirty or more saints in four acts.

The subject matter of the opera is the religious, or saintly, life. Saint Theresa and Saint Ignatius are shown in typical scenes, each surrounded by assistants and pupils. The four saints referred to in the title are Saint Theresa; her chief helper, Saint Settlement; Saint Ignatius; and his first lieutenant, Saint Chavez. The Compère and Commère, acting as commentators, converse with each other and with the saints and announce to the audience, as masters of ceremony, the progress of the play.

Mr. Thomson suggests that listeners should "not try to understand the words of this opera literally or to seek in the music of it any direct reference to Spain." And he continues, "If, by means of the poet's liberties with logic and the composer's constant usage of the simplest formulae in our musical vernacular, something is evoked of the gaiety and the mystical strength of lives consecrated to a nonmaterialistic end, the authors will consider their message to have been communicated."

A second opera by Virgil Thomson and Gertrude Stein, *The Mother of Us All*, was commissioned by the Alice M. Ditson Fund of Columbia University and given its *première* at the Brander Matthews Theater during Columbia University's 1947 festival of modern music.

CHARACTERS

SAINT THERESA I	*Soprano*	SAINT CHAVEZ	*Tenor*
SAINT THERESA II	*Contralto*	COMMÈRE	*Mezzo-soprano*
SAINT IGNATIUS LOYOLA	*Baritone*	COMPÈRE	*Bass*

DOUBLE CHORUS OF NAMED AND UNNAMED SAINTS AND SIX DANCERS

The Prelude ("A narrative of prepare for the saints") is a sort of choral overture, "To know to know to love her so. Four saints prepare for saints. It makes it well fish."

ACT I

SCENE: *The Steps of the Cathedral at Ávila* ("Saint Theresa half indoors and half out out of doors"). This act represents in the form of living pictures scenes from the religious life of Saint Theresa.

ACT II

SCENE: *A Garden Party or Picnic in the Country* ("Might it be mountains if it were not Barcelona"). The saints play games; the Compère and the Commère have a love scene, and a ballet depicts angels learning to fly. Toward evening the saints are vouchsafed a vision of the Celestial Mansions. "How many windows and doors and floors are there in it?" they reverently ask.

ACT III

SCENE: *Barcelona—Saint Ignatius and Jesuits Mending Their Nets* ("Saint Ignatius and one of two literally"). Saint Ignatius and the Jesuits are at their religious and military exercises. There are a vision of the Holy Ghost ("Pigeons on the grass alas and a magpie in the sky"), a ballet of Spanish girls with sailors, a storm, which Saint Ignatius quiets, and a foretaste of Doomsday ("around is a sound"). This is followed by a choral procession and an intermezzo, which leads into a brief fourth act, or epilogue.

ACT IV

SCENE: *The Saints in Glory* ("The sisters and saints reassembled and re-enacting why they went away to stay"). The saints recall their earthly lives and join in a communion hymn, "When this you see remember me." The Compère announces, "Last act!" The chorus replies, "Which is a fact!"

THE RCA-VICTOR RECORDS
(Sung in English)

CONDENSED RECORDING: *Altonell Hines, Contralto; Abner Dorsey, Bass; Edward Matthews, Baritone; Beatrice Robinson-Wayne, Soprano; Ruby Greene, Contralto; Charles Holland, Tenor; Inez Matthews, Soprano; David Bethea, Tenor; Randolph Robinson, Baritone; with Chorus and Orchestra conducted by Virgil Thomson.*

DM-1244, 5-12"

Fra Diavolo

OPÉRA COMIQUE in three acts. Music by Daniel François Auber. Libretto by Eugène Scribe. First produced at the Paris Opéra-Comique on January 28, 1830. American *première*, at New York, on October 17, 1831. First performed at the Metropolitan Opera House, at the New Theater, on February 4, 1910, with Edmond Clément as Fra Diavolo and Bella Alten as Zerlina. Alessandro Bonci, presented by Oscar Hammerstein at the Manhattan Opera House, numbered the gentleman-brigand among his favorite roles, and in recent years Tito Schipa has carried on the tradition of an authentic *opéra comique* style. The story of *Fra Diavolo* has a curious genealogy. Beginning as the theme of an opera by Lesueur, *La Caverne*, it was transformed into a ballet-panto-mime called *The Robber of the Abruzzi*, and reached final form in Auber's long-cherished comic opera.

CHARACTERS

FRA DIAVOLO, *disguised as the Marquis of San Marco*	Baritone	MATTEO, *an innkeeper*	Bass
		ZERLINA, *his daughter*	Soprano
LORD ALLCASH, *a traveling Englishman*	Bass	GIACOMO and BEPPO, *bandits*	Bass and Tenor
LADY ALLCASH	Mezzo-soprano	PEASANTS, DRAGOONS, AND BANDITS	
LORENZO, *an officer of the Roman dragoons*	Tenor		

The action takes place near Terracina, Italy, about 1830

Like so many other operas famous in their time, *Fra Diavolo*, out-side of France, is remembered today mainly because of its captivating Overture. The blend of gay adventure and intrigue is vividly reflected in this popular concert number. The mock military note is sounded at once in the opening drum roll and the march that follows. Horns and bassoons then take up a transitional episode, and the allegro section, typical of the classical overture, begins. This is engagingly developed around a gallant theme depicting the young lover Lorenzo and the jolly music of the merrymaking at the inn.

ACT I

SCENE: *Matteo's Inn.* Before the curtain rises, Lord and Lady Allcash have been held up and robbed on the road by the ubiquitous bandit, Fra Diavolo, who has so far eluded arrest through his clever disguises. When the opera opens, we are introduced to Zerlina, daughter of the innkeeper Matteo, and Lorenzo, a young officer in love with her. Lorenzo, who is unacceptable to Matteo because he is poor, sees a golden opportunity in the reward pro-claimed for the capture of Fra Diavolo. As the noble couple enter the inn and announce their encounter with the brigand, Lorenzo sets off with his dragoons to track him down. Traveling with Lord and Lady Allcash is the Marquis of San Marco, a suave gallant who annoys his lordship by openly flirting with his wife. Actually the Marquis is Fra Diavolo in one of his numerous masquerades. The flirtation with Lady Allcash is only a ruse, for Fra Diavolo is interested in greater stakes—the jewels the couple have suc-cessfully concealed from his men. Soon Lorenzo returns with the triumphant news that the bandits have been caught and slain, and Lord Allcash's stolen valuables recovered. Lorenzo is given a generous reward which will enable him to marry Zerlina.

ACT II

SCENE: *Zerlina's Bedchamber*. While Zerlina is showing the titled guests to their room, Fra Diavolo admits two of his confederates into the inn. The three bandits now steal into the girl's room and conceal themselves in a closet. The plan is to wait till all are asleep and then make off with Lord Allcash's jewels. Lorenzo and his soldiers return to the inn just as the brig-ands are discovered in Zerlina's room. Fra Diavolo, still in the guise of the Marquis, helps his men make their escape, and blandly confesses his designs on both Zerlina and Lady Allcash. Lorenzo and Lord Allcash are enraged, and the young officer demands satisfaction. A duel is arranged for the fol-lowing day.

ACT III

SCENE: *In the Mountains, Not Far from Matteo's Inn*. Fra Diavolo is hum-ming the charms of a highwayman's life. Meanwhile Beppo and Giacomo have been captured and, faced with the threat of death, have betrayed their chief. Fra Diavolo is presently ambushed and shot. In a last flourish of gal-lantry, he tells the truth about the episode in the bedroom, thus reuniting Lorenzo and Zerlina, who was on the point of marrying the rich peasant her father had selected for her.

Lande

Der Freischütz
(THE FREE-SHOOTER)

OPERA IN three acts. Music by Carl Maria von Weber. Libretto by Friedrich Kind, founded on a tale in the *Gespensterbuch*, edited by Apel and Laun. First performance, Schauspielhaus, Berlin, June 18, 1821. First performance in the United States, at Philadelphia, December, 1824, in English. In the Metropolitan Opera House revival of March 23, 1924, recitatives were composed by the conductor Artur Bodanzky, although he refrained from adding to the score in the scene of the Wolf's Glen.

Weber, the great pioneer of nationalism in German opera, endeavored, in *Der Freischütz*, to escape Italian influence by discarding plots of intrigue, and instead sought material for his opera in the legends of his own country. Thus he opened up the dual paths of romanticism and nationalism which led, eventually, to Wagner's monumental *Ring des Nibelungen*. Originally written with spoken dialogue and based on a native subject, *Der Freischütz* is a link between the old *Singspiel* and Wagner.

The title *Der Freischütz* means, literally, "free-shooter," a term applied to one who used magic bullets. The story of the opera is founded on an old tradition among huntsmen in Germany, to the effect that whoever should sell his soul to Zamiel, the Demon Hunter, would receive seven magic bullets, which would always hit the mark. But the seventh bullet was meant for himself, and he must thus yield up his soul to Zamiel if he has not in the meantime found another victim for the demon; for every convert his life will be extended and he will receive a fresh supply of bullets.

CHARACTERS

OTTOKAR, *a Prince of Bohemia*	Tenor	CASPAR, *first huntsman* ⎱ *in the*	Bass
KUNO, *head ranger to the Prince*	Bass	MAX, *second huntsman* ⎰ *service*	Tenor
		of Kuno	
AGATHE, *his daughter*	Soprano	ZAMIEL, *the Black Huntsman*	Speaker
ÄNNCHEN, *a relative and friend*		A HERMIT	Bass
of Agathe	Soprano	KILIAN, *a peasant*	Tenor

BRIDESMAIDS, HUNTSMEN, AND ATTENDANTS ON THE PRINCE, PEASANTS, MUSICIANS, SPIRITS, DEMONS, AND VARIOUS APPARITIONS

The action takes place in Bohemia, shortly after the termination of the Thirty Years' War

177

The Overture, long a concert favorite, is, in effect, a musical synopsis of the opera, presenting, as it does, the chief melodies from the score. It opens in religious calm, with a beautiful melody played by the horns. There creeps in the fearsome, sinister music of Zamiel and of the terrifying scene in the Wolf's Glen. Opposed to this baleful music is heard the triumphant outburst from Agathe's aria: "We shall meet in joy at last!" In the ensuing struggle between these forces of good and evil, thrillingly depicted in music, good is triumphant, and the Overture ends in a mood of rejoicing.

ACT I

SCENE: *A Forest Shooting Range.* Kuno, head ranger to Ottokar, a Bohemian prince, has two assistants, Max and Caspar, both excellent marksmen. Max is in love with Agathe, Kuno's daughter, who has promised to be his bride. He is, therefore, all the more eager to prove himself the best shot at a contest to be held before the Prince. The preliminary trial is won, however, by Kilian, a peasant. Max is found bewailing his bad luck by the dissolute Caspar, whose evil ways have led him to put himself into the power of Zamiel. Caspar sees in Max a chance to extend his own days of grace and induces him to come to the Wolf's Glen, there to receive some magic bullets which never miss their mark.

ACT II

SCENE 1: *In Agathe's House.* In the meantime, Agathe is anxiously awaiting her lover, much alarmed by his delay. She bids her cousin, Ännchen, retire, for her attempts at bringing cheer with a gay song are vain. Left alone, her thoughts revert to Max. She opens the window and, looking out at the beautiful starlit night, exclaims at the wonder of it, then sings her expressive prayer, *"Leise, leise"* ("Softly, softly").

Her lover finally arrives, but joy of their meeting is brief, for Max, a bit abashed, says he must bring to the Prince a stag he has shot near the

Wolf's Glen. Agathe begs him not to go near the haunted spot, but he disregards her warnings.

SCENE 2: *At the Wolf's Glen.* At the Wolf's Glen Max meets Caspar, and amid the most terrifying happenings, all in the very best manner of early-nineteenth-century German romanticism, they summon Zamiel and, after many hair-raising moments, cast the magic bullets.

ACT III

SCENE 1: *Agathe's Chamber.* Agathe has had an evil omen in a dream. Despite Ännchen's cheering words, and the arrival of the bridesmaids with the bridal wreath, she is extremely morose. Her apprehension further increases when, on opening the box, she finds, instead of the bridal wreath, a funeral one.

SCENE 2: *The Forest Shooting Range.* When the shooting contest is about to begin, the assembled foresters sing a rousing chorus in praise of hunting.

During the contest Max amazes all with his remarkable skill. At the final shot, Max's seventh bullet, the Prince points to a white dove he has observed hovering above a tree. At that moment Agathe appears from behind the tree and cries out to Max not to shoot, for she is that dove. But it is too late: Agathe sinks in a swoon, and Caspar falls mortally wounded from the tree whence he had been watching the contest. He had, in fact, planned to sacrifice Agathe to Zamiel, thereby being permitted to live longer. The demon appears, however, and claims Caspar. Thus the story of the magic bullets is revealed, and the Prince banishes Max for his wickedness. A strange hermit opportunely appears, however, revives Agathe, and pleads Max's cause, declaring that the prayer of Agathe has been answered, Providence using her to restore Max to truth and honor. The young man is therefore forgiven, and all ends happily.

THE RCA-VICTOR RECORDS
(Sung in German)

OVERTURE: *Arturo Toscanini and the NBC Symphony Orchestra* 11-9172, 12"

Boston "Pops" Orchestra, Arthur Fiedler, Cond. 12040, 12"

ACT II

LEISE, LEISE, FROMME WEISE (Agatha's Prayer—Softly, Softly): *Maria Jeritza, Soprano, with Orch.* 6588, 12"

THE "DYING" GIANNI—METROPOLITAN OPERA PRODUCTION

Gianni Schicchi

OPERA IN one act. Music by Giacomo Puccini. Libretto by Gioachino Forzano. First performance, Metropolitan Opera House, December 14, 1918, in a world *première* of three one-act Puccini works, the others being *Il Tabarro* and *Suor Angelica*. Together they are known as the *Trittico (Triptych)*.

The cast at the *première* consisted of Florence Easton, Lauretta; Giulio Crimi, Rinuccio; Giuseppe de Luca, Gianni Schicchi, and Adamo Didur, Simone. In the Metropolitan revival of season 1935–36, given in English, Lawrence Tibbett was the Schicchi; Hilda Burke, Lauretta; Nino Martini and Joseph Bentonelli alternated as Rinuccio. On January 6, 1944, Salvatore Baccaloni first appeared as Gianni at the Metropolitan, with Licia Albanese and Nino Martini as coartists. The performance was presented in Italian.

Gianni Schicchi is a shrewd but goodhearted Tuscan peasant of the thirteenth century. His daughter, Lauretta, loves Rinuccio, whose family is at present greatly disturbed because a relative, Buoso Donati, has just died, leaving his fortune to a monastery. Schicchi is consulted by the disappointed relatives in the hope that he may prove clever enough to suggest a plan for obtaining the property. As Donati's death has not yet been made public,

Schicchi suggests that he himself impersonate the old man and dictate a new will, leaving the estate to Rinuccio's family. Schicchi is placed in the dead man's bed, and a notary summoned. The latter takes down the new will; after leaving a few worthless trifles to the relatives, Schicchi bequeaths the bulk of the property to himself! The relatives are highly indignant, but they dare not expose him, for in so doing they would render themselves liable to punishment. A minute after the notary and witnesses have gone, they go after Schicchi with cries of "Robber! Traitor! Scoundrel!" But Schicchi seizes a stick and, though his nightgown is torn to shreds in the struggle, drives the cursing relatives from the house. The lovers, who eventually will be Schicchi's heirs, are happily united.

THE RCA-VICTOR RECORDS
(Sung in Italian)

O MIO BABBINO CARO (Oh, My Beloved   *with Orch.*   11-9115, 12″
Daddy): *Licia Albanese, Soprano,*

THE READING OF DONATI'S WILL—METROPOLITAN OPERA PRODUCTION

Apex   ACT II—ENZO'S VESSEL

La Gioconda

OPERA IN four acts. Music by Amilcare Ponchielli. Libretto by Arrigo Boïto (writing under the pen name of Tobia Gorrio), based on Victor Hugo's drama, *Angelo, tyran de Padoue* (*Angelo, Tyrant of Padua*). First performance at La Scala, Milan, April 8, 1876. United States *première*, at the Metropolitan Opera House, New York, December 20, 1883, with Christine Nilsson in the title role. Boïto, perhaps wisely, used his anagram *nom de plume* in signing the gnarled libretto of *La Gioconda*. A fabulously gifted man, he later wrote the text and composed the music for his own powerful opera, *Mefistofele*, besides supplying Verdi with model librettos for *Otello* and *Falstaff*. The prose play of Victor Hugo on which Ponchielli's opera is based also furnished texts for music dramas by Mercadante, César Cui, and Eugen d'Albert. Boïto, not without irony, entitled the gruesome libretto, *La Gioconda* (*The Joyous Girl*). *"Che* La Gioconda *ci giocondi entrambi!"* he punned in a letter to Ponchielli accompanying the completed text— "That *The Joyous Girl* may bring us both joy!" The phenomenal success of the opera bore out his hope. Few operas rival *La Gioconda* in variety of appeal. There are sumptuous spectacle and ceremony, a picturesque ballet, luscious arias and duets, and an almost unbroken pageant of violent and impassioned action. Stabbings and poisonings are frequent happenings here, while kidnaping, arson, and terrible acts of revenge form part of this high-pitched drama of Venetian intrigue. Ironically, the ever-popular ballet, "The Dance of the Hours," is intended to represent a triumph of good over evil, of light over darkness. *La Gioconda* is scarcely an illustration of this victory.

Ponchielli, who taught Giacomo Puccini, helped strengthen the role of the orchestra in Italian opera. The symphonic texture is rich and ample and closely adapted to the shifting action, and of course the melodic warmth of the whole score is one of its most appealing features.

CHARACTERS.

LA GIOCONDA, *a ballad singer*	Soprano	LAURA, *his wife*	*Mezzo-soprano*
LA CIECA, *her blind mother*	Contralto	ENZO GRIMALDO, *a Genoese noble*	*Tenor*
ALVISE, *an official of the State Inquisition*	Bass	BARNABA, *a spy of the Inquisition*	*Baritone*

182

A BOATMAN, A PUBLIC LETTER WRITER, A PILOT, AND CHORUS OF MONKS, SENATORS, SAILORS, LADIES, GENTLEMEN, POPULACE, MASQUERS, ETC.

The action takes place in Venice in the seventeenth century

ACT I

SCENE: *Street Near the Adriatic Shore, Venice.* The situation before the curtain rises is as follows: La Gioconda, a ballad singer, in love with Enzo Grimaldo, a Genoese noble and captain of a ship now in the harbor of Venice, supports her blind mother, La Cieca, by singing in the streets. Barnaba, an influential police spy, has become infatuated with her and is scheming to possess her.

The grand courtyard of the Ducal Palace is the scene of gay festivities. Sailors, shipwrights, townspeople, foreigners, peasants, in holiday attire, mingle freely. They raise their voices in chorus, shouting, *"Feste! Pane!"* ("Festivals and bread!"). Barnaba, who has been leaning against a pillar, moodily watching the lively scene, steps forward and announces that the regatta is about to begin. The merrymakers hasten to the shore, and Barnaba scornfully mutters after them, "Dancing over their graves," for the prisons of the Inquisition are underfoot. In a grim soliloquy we learn of his designs on La Gioconda, who now approaches, leading her sightless mother. Barnaba hides behind the column. The girl seats the helpless woman on the church steps and is about to follow the crowd when Barnaba stops her and boldly declares his passion. Shuddering with disgust, La Gioconda rebuffs him, and when he attempts to grasp her, she eludes him and rushes away. Barnaba resolves on a cruel revenge.

The crowd returns from the regatta, carrying the winner on their shoulders. Barnaba approaches the loser of the regatta and tells him that he owes his defeat to La Cieca, who is a witch. The defeated man and his friends rush to La Cieca and drag her from the church steps, crying, "Let's burn the witch!" At that moment Enzo, La Gioconda's friend, enters in disguise, as he is considered an enemy of Venice. He runs to the old woman's side and shields her from the savage mob. Against their shrill cries of "She is a witch!" he taunts them with attacking a defenseless blind woman.

As the music surges in tense, dramatic stress, the doors of the palace abruptly fly open and the Grand Duke Alvise and his wife Laura appear. Laura, formerly betrothed to Enzo, implores her husband to protect La Cieca against the mob's violence. The Duke intercedes, and La Cieca is freed. In gratitude she gives Laura her rosary, voicing her feelings in the beautiful aria, *"Voce di donna."* Meanwhile, the vigilant Barnaba has observed a telltale glance pass between Laura and her former lover. As the doors of St. Mark's swing open, the crowd enters the magnificent church. Enzo remains behind, thoughtfully gazing after Laura. Barnaba, his mind already afire

183

with a diabolical plan, approaches him. With the words of address, "Enzo Grimaldo," a dramatic dialogue ensues between the two men. Barnaba immediately wins his interest by mentioning Laura. Yes, he knows about them, says the crafty spy; how they loved one another, and still do. That very night, he assures the excited nobleman, while the Duke is busy with his Council, Laura will steal off and visit him on his ship. Rather shabbily, Enzo does nothing but utter a pious hope for the girl's safety when Barnaba divulges his own passion for La Gioconda. Enzo leaves to return to his ship.

Alone, Barnaba seeks the service of a public scribe. As he dictates aloud, La Gioconda and La Cieca enter and conceal themselves. Barnaba's anonymous letter is to the Chief of the Inquisition, informing him of the meeting to take place between his wife and Enzo Grimaldo. La Gioconda hears this with mingled emotions, shuddering at the thought of Enzo's danger and crushed by his betrayal. Filled with despair, mother and daughter enter the church.

ACT II

SCENE: *A Lagoon Near Venice.* Enzo's ship is shown at anchor. It is dark, and the orchestra weaves soft measures on the beauty of the Venetian night. There is even a hint of mystery in the music, of approaching tragedy. Sailors, chanting gaily, busy themselves about Enzo's ship as it rides at anchor. Down in the hold deep voices are heard singing of the terrors of the sea. They are answered cheerily by younger members of the crew perched along the rigging. Barnaba, disguised as a fisherman, appears in his boat, accompanied by the scribe. Hailing the Genoese sailors, he proceeds to sing a jolly ballad, full of rhythmic dash and melodic appeal—*"Ah, pescator, affonda l'esca"* ("Fisher boy, thy bait be throwing"). The friendly crew joins in at the refrain. The song ended, Barnaba commands the scribe to carry back a report on the strength of the crew, adding that he will remain and await developments.

Enzo appears and releases his men from duty with the announcement that he will keep watch himself. Stars are visible now in the beautiful Venetian sky above. As the moon comes out from behind a cloud, the waters in the lagoon begin sparkling. Enraptured by the scene and the prospect of seeing Laura soon, Enzo begins a warm soliloquy *"Cielo e mar!"* ("Heaven and ocean!"), in which he sings rapturously of the vision of the night and his love. A boat approaches. It is Barnaba bringing Laura. The lovers embrace ardently as the spy gives them his blessings and leaves. They resolve to sail away together when the wind rises. Enzo goes belowdeck to rouse the men, and Laura, already a prey to remorse, falls to her knees in prayer. At this moment La Gioconda, disguised, appears. The two women engage in a stormy quarrel over Enzo. La Gioconda is on the point of stabbing her rival, but

ZINKA MILANOV AS LA GIOCONDA   BENIAMINO GIGLI AS ENZO

relents as a boat quietly approaches. Laura immediately recognizes it as her husband's. Terrified, she prays to the Holy Virgin to help her, raising aloft her rosary, which La Gioconda promptly recognizes as her mother's token of thanks to the woman who saved her life. Determined now to aid Laura at all costs, La Gioconda enables her to escape in a boat. Enzo appears. Calling for Laura, he is unexpectedly faced by a vengeful and taunting Gioconda. The Duke's war galleys, led by the wily Barnaba, are moving on his ship. Desperate from the loss of Laura and the certainty of humiliating defeat, Enzo gives the order to fire the ship to prevent its being captured. To La Gioconda's further chagrin, the last word on his lips is "Laura," as the vessel sinks in flames.

ACT III

SCENE 1: *A Room in Alvise's Palace.* A festival is about to take place at the Ducal Palace as Alvise prepares a cold-blooded revenge on his faithless wife. In a fiendish aria he muses on the manner of her death. Not by a dagger thrust shall Laura die, but by poison, and, ironically, to the sounds of singing and dancing in the neighboring room. Laura enters and is promptly handed the flask of poison. This she must drink as the serenade ends in the grand ballroom of the palace, where the Duke is feting the gathered nobles of the land. With a scowl of contempt Alvise leaves Laura. But as she lifts the poison to her lips, La Gioconda, who has concealed herself in the room, rushes out and snatches the fatal flask from her. In place of the poison, she gives Laura a harmless drug that will produce a deathlike sleep. Laura now drinks. La Gioconda again hides as Alvise re-enters the chamber, notices the empty bottle, and cries: "Death has forever claimed her." As he leaves, La Gioconda reappears and remarks grimly, "I have saved her for him, for the one who loves her."

SCENE 2: *The Ballroom of Alvise's Palace.* For the entertainment of his noble guests Alvise has provided a sumptuous ballet, the famous "Dance of the Hours." This is perhaps the most ironic spectacle in the whole range of grand opera. For the dance is supposed to depict the triumph of right over wrong, a curious triumph in the light of the events in the adjoining funeral chamber. The "Hours" of the dance are merely symbols, acted by dancers in groups of six. The music begins by picturing the first faint glimmerings of dawn. Twitterings and shimmerings are heard in the violins and upper wood-winds, as the dancers enter in delicate tints. Slowly the music rises to a fierce climax. The rhythms become more energetic. It is high noon, and the brighter "Hours" of day swing into place on the stage. Evening approaches now, and the music grows serene, darker-hued, as the dancers tiptoe in, evoking the mood of twilight. There follow the somber "Hours" of night. Midnight approaches, and the music thins out to a few orchestral whispers. The harp gives out some lacy arpeggios, and in the languorous strains that follow a solo dance is enacted. Finally, all twenty-four "Hours" gather as a unit and plunge into a rival whirl of dancing. Victory goes to the "Hours" representing Light.

This edifying spectacle no sooner ends than the guests are invited to witness a whole pageant of actual horror. The scoundrelly Barnaba rushes into the palace, dragging La Gioconda's blind old mother. At the top of his voice he charges her with practicing witchcraft. La Cieca vows that she was merely praying for the souls of the dead. Enzo is among the masquers, and when a bell begins to toll solemnly, Barnaba whispers into his ear that it is tolling for Laura. Enzo throws off his mask and reveals himself as the noble-man Alvise had proscribed. "My country and my bride you stole," he shouts at Alvise. "Now complete your crime!" The Duke, sensing the moment has come for the ghastly climax of his revenge, flings back the curtains of the death chamber, and a cry of horror comes from the crowd. Extended on a bier is Laura's body. Enzo rushes at Alvise, brandishing a poniard and shouting, "Hangman!" But before he can reach the man, guards seize him.

ACT IV

SCENE: *A Ruined Palace on the Island of Giudeca, in the Adriatic.* To this deserted island not far from Venice, La Gioconda has succeeded in bringing the unconscious Laura. Two men carry the girl into the ruined interior of an abandoned palace. La Gioconda directs the men to place her on a bed and offers to pay them for their help. They reject the money, reminding her that they are her friends. La Gioconda suddenly grows alarmed about her mother and implores the men to search every highway and piazza of Venice for her. They assure her she can depend on them, and she clasps their hands in farewell. Left alone, she approaches the table and thoughtfully eyes the flask of poison upon it. There begins now the celebrated aria, *"Suicidio,"* an aria pulsing with dramatic fervor and feverish intensity. Suicide is her sole resource, the girl reflects. Since love, mother, all hope of happiness have vanished, let her die, and jealousy will torture her no longer. As she raises the flask, a devilish thought crosses her mind. What if Laura were dead, or, if alive, what if she were to disappear beneath the silent waters of the Adriatic? The aria reaches a frenzied pitch here as eerie voices reach her from the lagoon, telling of the dead in the Orfano Canal. La Gioconda recoils from her own thought. The tempest rages on in her soul, till, crying, *"O amore! amore! Enzo! Pietà!"* she throws herself down near the table, sobbing wretchedly.

At that moment Enzo, released from prison with Gioconda's aid, enters. He looks suspiciously at the distraught girl, wondering why she has summoned him to this ruin. "What do you want of me?" he asks coldly. "To give you back the sun, life, infinite liberty, joy in the future, love, and paradise," she replies to the baffled Enzo. Would he die for Laura? she asks. Yes, he would join his beloved in her tomb. "Laura's tomb is empty," La Gioconda retorts; "I have removed her!" Enzo is appalled. Convinced that Gioconda is lying, he forces her to swear on a crucifix. As she does so, he lunges at her with a dagger, when the cry, "Enzo!" comes from the alcove. It is Laura. Enzo, as in a dream, watches her approach, then rushes forward and embraces her. When Laura tells him that Gioconda saved her life, both fall on their knees before the girl and bless her. With Gioconda's help, the lovers now make their escape. Only she and one other know at what price Enzo's freedom has been purchased. Barnaba had named the price—herself.

Now, after Laura and Enzo leave, Gioconda again reaches for the poison, but before she can drink, Barnaba appears. He has come for his reward. Gioconda, terrified at first, recovers her courage and begins a grim game of pretense with the odious spy. Coquettishly she pleads for time to adorn herself properly with sparkling jewels. Barnaba assents. At length Gioconda cries: "I have kept my word. I have not lied and I have not fled. I have not betrayed you. You wanted me, you accursed demon! Take me!" As Barnaba rushes to embrace her, Gioconda stabs herself with a knife she had concealed in her dress. She falls to the floor. Barnaba, in a savage access of rage, bends over the girl and shrieks into her ear, "Yesterday your mother offended me. I have strangled her!" But Gioconda can hear no longer. Furiously he rushes from the room and disappears down the dark street.

La Gioconda

THE RCA-VICTOR RECORDS
(Sung in Italian)

ACT I

VOCE DI DONNA O D'ANGELO (La Cieca's Romanza): *Blanche Thebom, Mezzo-soprano, with Orch.*   11-9795, 12"

ENZO GRIMALDO, PRINCIPE DI SANTAFIOR (Enzo Grimaldo, Prince of Santa Fior): *Beniamino Gigli, Tenor; Giuseppe de Luca, Baritone; with Orch.*   8084, 12"

MONOLOGO—O MONUMENTO (Barnaba's Soliloquy): *Leonard Warren, Baritone, with Orch.*   18293, 12"

ACT II

BARCAROLA—PESCATOR, AFFONDA L'ESCA (Fisher Boy, Thy Bait Be Throwing): *Giuseppe de Luca, Baritone; Metropolitan Opera Chorus and Orch.*   8174, 12"

Leonard Warren, Baritone; RCA-Victor Choral and Orch.   11-9790, 12"

CIELO E MAR! (Heaven and Ocean!): *Jussi Bjoerling, Tenor, with Orch.*   12150, 12"

Beniamino Gigli, Tenor, with Orch.   7194, 12"

Jan Peerce, Tenor; RCA-Victor Orchestra, Erich Leinsdorf, Cond.
MO-1250   (12-0497-A)
VO-22   (18-0175-A)

ACT III

BALLET MUSIC—DANZA DELLE ORE (Dance of the Hours): *Boston "Pops" Orchestra, Arthur Fiedler, Cond.*   11833, 12"

Victor Symphony Orchestra   35833, 12"

Lou White, Organist   36225, 12"

ACT IV

SUICIDIO! (Yes, Suicide!): *Zinka Milanov, Soprano, with Orch.*   11-9293, 12"

Emmy Destinn, Soprano, with Orch.   15-1014, 12"
(Acoustical Recording)

Bain
GIUSEPPE DE LUCA AS BARNABA

I Gioielli della Madonna
(THE JEWELS OF THE MADONNA)

OPERA IN three acts. Music by Ermanno Wolf-Ferrari. Libretto by the composer, with verses by Carlo Zangarini and Enrico Golisciani. First performance, in German, at the Kurfürstenoper, Berlin, December 23, 1911. American *première*, in Italian, at the Chicago Auditorium, by the Chicago Opera Company, under the composer's supervision, January 16, 1912. The same company staged the new work at the Metropolitan Opera House on March 5, 1912. Wolf-Ferrari had come to be regarded as essentially a writer of comic opera before *The Jewels of the Madonna* allied him with the operatic school of violent realism. The wild terrors and passions of this opera were in marked contrast to the gay frivolities of *Le Donne curiose* and *Il Segreto di Susanna*. Many critics felt Wolf-Ferrari had ventured into an uncongenial field. A speedy return to the pleasanter realm of urbane comedy was urged. That the opera had power, despite its strained emotions and exaggerated motivation, no one, however, denied. One or two dramatic arias and duets stood out vividly, and the delicately spun intermezzi were to become favorite concert items. Then, the opera offered a colorful pageant of Neapolitan street life, melodramatic, to be sure, but evoking much of the motley magic and animation of the city through a rich fabric of folk song and dance.

CHARACTERS

GENNARO, *a young blacksmith, in love with Maliella*   Tenor

MALIELLA, *an adopted daughter of Carmela, in love with Rafaele*   Soprano

RAFAELE, *leader of the Camorrists, members of a secret criminal society*   Baritone

CARMELA, *Gennaro's mother*   Mezzo-soprano

BIAISO, *a public scrivener*   Tenor

CICILLO
ROCCO } *Camorrists*   Tenor / Bass

STELLA
CONCETTA } *women of the*
SERENA } *Camorrist circle*   Soprano / Soprano / Soprano

GRAZIA, *a dancer nicknamed "Blondine"*

TOTONNO, *a young Neapolitan*

VENDORS, MONKS, CAMORRISTS, PEOPLE OF NAPLES

The action takes place in Naples at the beginning of the nineteenth century

ACT I

SCENE: *A Public Square in Naples.* The festival of the Madonna is being celebrated in one of the poorer quarters of Naples. As the procession reaches the center of a public square, Maliella, the wayward foster daughter of the devout Carmela, dashes into the street in a prankish mood of coquetry and is given chase by Rafaele, a Camorrist gang leader. He catches the tantalizing little spitfire and in the act of kissing her shrieks with pain when she jabs him with a hatpin. Rafaele, stung to even greater ardor, boasts he is ready to risk everything for her. Maliella is horrified, but fascinated, too, when Rafaele swears to steal the jewels from the holy image of the Virgin which has just passed by. These he will hang about Maliella's pretty neck. Rafaele's reckless bravado is working on Maliella. Meanwhile, Gennaro, a simple young blacksmith also in love with Maliella, has overheard his rival's boasts and caught Maliella's greedy fascination. A mad design begins to form in his brain.

ACT II

An orchestral intermezzo, masterly in its delicate tinting and suave melodic texture, divides the two acts. Through a rich web of shrewdly adjusted colors one senses the soft, intense mood of a Latin night, the crossplay of seething passions. From the gathering music evolves a picture of a city where danger and superstition lurk, but where life has its gay, carefree moments of carnival and play.

SCENE: *A Garden.* Maliella, lingering among the shadows of her moonlit garden, listens scornfully to Gennaro's declaration of love. How can his love compare with that of Rafaele, who has promised her the Virgin's jewels? The taunt rouses Gennaro to grim determination. As Maliella returns to the house, he collects some tools and keys, wraps them up furtively, and steals off into the night. Rafaele and his Camorrist henchmen enter and begin serenading Maliella. Yielding to the gang leader's pleas, she promises to come to him the following day. Alone again, still thrilling to the memory of Rafaele's love-making, Maliella hears Gennaro returning. A horrible fear seizes her as Gennaro begins unwrapping the package he had concealed in his clothes. At once dazzled and terrified, she gazes at the booty that Gennaro worshipfully spreads out before her: the Madonna's jewels, sparkling magically in the moonlight. "For you!" cries Gennaro exultantly. Maliella's stare is fixed in a kind of mystic rapture on the glowing gems. Slowly she picks them up and adorns herself in glittering array. In the daze of the moment, with the thought of Rafaele still throbbing through her, she yields to Gennaro.

ACT III

A second intermezzo precedes the last act. This, too, is splashed with the local color of Neapolitan folk themes, more impetuous than the other in rhythmic drive and pulsing with a waltzlike verve. The basic melody is Rafaele's serenade, first heard in Maliella's garden.

SCENE: *A Hideout of the Camorrists in the Outskirts of Naples.* The intermezzo serves as a lively introduction to the revelry going on in the dingy den of the Camorrists. Candles are glimmering all through the room, and on one wall is a crude fresco of the Madonna di Monte Vergine. The Camorrists and their women companions are dancing the fiery tarantella and the more somber apache. In the midst of the merrymaking, Rafaele's voice rises, toasting Maliella as the girl who will succumb to him alone. At the height of the revels, Maliella, wearing a scarlet shawl, bursts like a madwoman into the room. Sobbing hysterically, she rushes to Rafaele, who forces the secret of Gennaro's success from her. The women laugh derisively, remembering Rafaele's boast. Burning with rage, the gang leader flings her violently to the ground. As the shawl slips from Maliella's grasp, the Madonna's jewels scatter over the floor. The crowd recoils in superstitious dread. To add to the fevered intensity of the scene, Gennaro rushes in, frenzied with remorse. Maliella points to him as the thief. Then as a stormy wind blows out most of the candles, leaving the den in a weird semidarkness, Maliella gives a frantic cry of "To the sea!" and rushes from the place to drown herself in the storm-tossed waters of the Bay of Naples. Wild with terror, the Camorrists disperse, and Gennaro, crazed now beyond hope, gathers up the jewels. Reverently he crawls toward the image of the Madonna on the wall, places the jewels before it, and drives a dagger into his heart. As he dies, he presses Maliella's discarded shawl to his trembling lips.

THE RCA-VICTOR RECORDS

ACT III

DANCE OF THE CAMORRISTI: *Boston "Pops" Orchestra, Arthur Fiedler, Cond.* 4330, 10"

ACT II—THE GARDEN SCENE

FINALE OF ACT I—D'OYLY CARTE OPERA PRODUCTION

The Gondoliers
(OR, THE KING OF BARATARIA)

COMIC OPERA in two acts. Music by Arthur Sullivan. Book by W. S. Gilbert. First produced at the Savoy Theatre, London, December 7, 1889. Like *The Mikado*, *The Gondoliers* offered Sullivan ample scope for the free play of his musical faculties. Occasions for a variety of set pieces and dances abounded in the book. Again the composer could not complain that the spotlight was mainly on the librettist. Gilbert's extravagant story inspired some of his gayest flights of melody. Here were places, too, for such fetching dances as fandangos, boleros, and cachuchas, and for the ensemble sequences Sullivan wrote choruses that have made *The Gondoliers* an enduring favorite of amateur choral societies. Many musicians and critics regard *The Gondoliers* as Sullivan's most brilliant score, and certainly in spontaneity of melody it ranks high in the hearts of all true Savoyards. With so much in its favor, it is not surprising to learn that the opening night of *The Gondoliers* brought Gilbert and Sullivan perhaps the "greatest triumph of their joint careers," as Deems Taylor has pointed out—the only possible exception being the *première* of *The Mikado*. Shortly after the first performance Gilbert wrote to his collaborator, "It gives one the chance of shining right through the twentieth century with reflected light." Sullivan, who was frequently troubled by the fear that Gilbert's lines commanded greater attention than his music, graciously replied: "Don't talk of reflected light! In such a perfect book as *The Gondoliers* you shine with an individual brilliancy which no other writer can hope to attain." Unfortunately, sharp clashes over problems and costs of production were soon to bring a final break between these two friends, the most successful team of collaborators in the history of operetta, if not of the theater.

CHARACTERS

THE DUKE OF PLAZA-TORO, *a grandee of Spain*	Baritone	DON ALHAMBRA DEL BOLERO, *the* Grand Inquisitor Bass
LUIZ, *his attendant*	Tenor	

MARCO PALMIERI		*Tenor*
GIUSEPPE PALMIERI	*Venetian*	*Baritone*
ANTONIO	*gondoliers*	
FRANCESCO		
GIORGIO		

THE DUCHESS OF PLAZA-TORO   *Contralto*
CASILDA, *her daughter*   *Soprano*
INEZ, *the King's foster mother*   *Contralto*

GIANETTA		*Soprano*
TESSA		*Contralto*
FIAMETTA	contadine—*literally,*	
VITTORIA	*"country-girls"*	
GIULIA		

CHORUS OF GONDOLIERS AND CONTADINE,
MEN-AT-ARMS, HERALDS, AND PAGES

LEONARD OSBORN AS MARCO
AND CHARLES DORNING AS GIUSEPPE

ACT I

SCENE: *The Piazzetta, Venice (Date, 1750).* The handsome gondoliers Marco and Giuseppe have completely turned the heads of the pretty *contadine* and flower girls of Venice. Their only problem now is whom to choose as their brides. They decide to settle the question by allowing themselves to be blindfolded while the lovesick girls and their other gondolier admirers dance around Marco and Giuseppe. In the ensuing game Marco blindly catches Gianetta, and Giuseppe, Tessa. The remaining *contadine* accept their fate and pair off with the previously ignored *gondolieri*. They all run off merrily to get married. As they disappear, a gondola stops before the steps of the Piazzetta. From it emerge the Duke and Duchess of Plaza-Toro, their daughter Casilda, and their suite, consisting of "His Grace's private drum," Luiz. The new arrivals are dressed as befits their noble station, though their clothes are a little the worse for wear. The Duke and Duchess have brought their daughter Casilda from Spain. The Duke promptly sends Luiz to demand an audience with Don Alhambra, the Grand Inquisitor. Turning to his daughter, he now reveals that when she was six months old she was married by proxy to the infant son of the wealthy King of Barataria. The King subsequently became a Wesleyan Methodist of a most bigoted and persecuting kind. So the Grand Inquisitor stole the youthful heir to the throne and conveyed him to Venice. A fortnight later the Baratarian King and his court were all killed in an insurrection. As a result Casilda is now Queen of Barataria. But the whereabouts of the new King is still a mystery. Casilda, moreover, is in love with someone else—none other than her father's "private drum," Luiz.

Don Alhambra, the Grand Inquisitor, now approaches and, after being introduced to Casilda, explains that when he stole the youthful Prince of

Barataria, he brought him to Venice and entrusted him to the family of a highly respectable gondolier, who had a son of the same age. The gondolier, being addicted to excessive drinking, muddled up the two children, so that when the Inquisitor went to fetch the royal child he found it impossible to tell which was which. This news is received rather philosophically. The only person who can possibly tell the youths apart is the foster mother of the Prince, Inez (who is Luiz's mother). Luiz is accordingly sent to fetch her. When Giuseppe and Marco return with their brides, Don Alhambra (whom they at first mistake for an undertaker) announces that one of them is the King of Barataria, and that until the mystery is unraveled they must take up the reins of government as one individual. Giuseppe and Marco may take all their friends with them—all, that is, except the ladies, who must stay behind. This is rather a blow to the newlyweds, but they are assured that the separation will be brief. A boat is summoned, and the gondoliers clamber aboard with Giuseppe and Marco. As they depart the *contadine* wave a tearful farewell.

ACT II

SCENE: *A Pavilion in the Court of Barataria (Three Months Later)*. Being idealists at heart, Marco and Giuseppe have reorganized the state along Utopian lines. The result is somewhat chaotic, but they seem to enjoy it, and as the act opens they are seen cleaning the royal crown and scepter while they sit on the royal throne, clad in magnificent robes. They have resolved that if they want anything done, they will do it themselves. In a delightful little song, "Of happiness the very pith," Giuseppe outlines his day's work as a monarch about the palace. Only one thing is missing, they confess: it is dull without female society. Scarcely have they made this confession when the *contadine* run in, led by Fiametta and Vittoria. Curiosity has prompted the invasion, though they know they are strictly forbidden to come. Tessa and Gianetta excitedly inquire if their husbands have anyone to mend the royal socks, and if it is known yet which of them is to be queen. In honor of their arrival Giuseppe and Marco now announce a grand banquet and dance.

In the middle of a brilliant cachucha there is an unexpected interruption as Don Alhambra enters. Astonished at the scene, he tries, by citing examples, to explain where their theories of government are wrong. Presently he announces the arrival of Casilda. The Grand Inquisitor now reveals that one of them, Marco or Giuseppe (whichever is the real King of Barataria), is married to the beautiful Casilda. Of course, this makes one of them an unintentional bigamist since he has married a *contadina* too. Poor Tessa and Gianetta are very upset, for one or the other is married and one is not. They burst into tears. Meanwhile Casilda is afraid that she will never learn to love her husband. But on this point the Duchess is firm. "I loved your father," she says, and proceeds to explain how she married and "tamed" him. The Duke, it now develops, has turned his social prestige to account by becoming a "limited company." This encourages Casilda to hope that when the King realizes what a shady family he has married into he will refuse to recognize the alliance. The Duke and the Duchess deny the charge that their transactions are shady, in a delightful duet, "To help unhappy commoners."

Marco and Giuseppe now proceed to describe the condition of the country and the attitude of their subjects toward them. The Duke, in the famous gavotte, "I am a courtier," instructs them on the correct demeanor of a king, which they try, very awkwardly, to adopt. Soon Marco and Giuseppe are tactfully left alone with Casilda, but Gianetta and Tessa come in, and they all discuss the highly complicated problem of exactly who is married and who is not. They are interrupted by Don Alhambra, who enters, accompanied by the Duke and Duchess and all the court of Barataria. Inez, the foster mother of the Prince, has been found, and is now brought forward to solve the mystery. To everyone's astonishment, she confesses that when an attempt

SYDNEY GRANVILLE AS DON ALHAMBRA

was made to steal the young prince placed in her care, she substituted her own little boy. The rebel bands never knew the difference, and the child she now called her "son" was none other than the King of Barataria. Luiz is therefore the King! Overjoyed, Casilda and Luiz are reunited, and everything ends legally, much to the great relief of Marco and Giuseppe and their brides.

DOROTHY GILL
AS THE DUCHESS

MARTYN GREEN
AS THE DUKE OF PLAZA-TORO

THE RCA-VICTOR RECORDS
(Sung in English)

COMPLETE RECORDING: *D'Oyly Carte Opera Company; Dr. Malcolm Sargent, Cond.; under the personal direction of Rupert D'Oyly Carte. (Cast includes: Bertha Lewis, Sybil Gordon, Beatrice Elburn, Winifred Lawson, Aileen Davies, Mavis Bennett, Derek Oldham, George Baker, Henry Lytton, Richard Walker, Arthur Hosking, Leo Sheffield.)*

DC-16 (13272-13283), 12-12"
C-16 (11188-11199)

VOCAL GEMS: *Light Opera Company, with Orch.*
36146, 12"
(In Album C-23)

From the Painting by Czackorski   HAMLET AND THE ACTORS

Hamlet

OPERA IN five acts. Music by Ambroise Thomas. Libretto by Michel Carré and Jules Barbier, after Shakespeare. First produced at the Paris Opéra, March 9, 1868 (French), and in the United States at the Academy of Music, New York, March 22, 1872 (Italian). The first production at the Metropolitan Opera House was also in Italian, March 10, 1884, when Giuseppe Kaschmann was the Hamlet and Marcella Sembrich the Ophelia. A later production at the Metropolitan first used the French text in this country on February 10, 1892, with Jean Lassalle as Hamlet and Marie van Zandt as Ophelia.

The libretto is neither very faithful to its source nor of any special literary importance. It has been called a parody of Shakespeare's tragedy, although that is not entirely fair to it. Some of the original circumstances of the plot have been altered, especially by the introduction into the opera of Hamlet's drinking song, which—not without reason—has been looked upon as ludicrous by strict Shakespeareans. Nevertheless, the essentials of the Bard's work are here. And among the musical numbers, two of them, the aforesaid drinking song and Ophelia's florid Mad Scene, are well-known concert pieces. The textual blemishes are in part compensated for by musical passages of beauty and dramatic force.

Only two months after the death of the King of Denmark, his widow has married his brother and successor, Claudius. Hamlet, son of the Queen and the deceased King, appears at the marriage festivities in deep mourning. Ophelia, his betrothed, worried at his strange behavior, wonders if he has ceased to love her. He reassures her, and on the departure of her brother, Laertes, promises to cherish and care for her.

Informed of a strange nocturnal visitor, Hamlet ascends the battlements of the castle at night, and there the ghost of his father comes to him with the dreadful information that he was murdered by Claudius at the instigation of the Queen. The ghost begs Hamlet to take revenge on Claudius but to leave his mother's punishment to heaven.

In order to watch his uncle more closely and to avoid suspicion because of his actions, Hamlet pretends to grow insane. He plans to have presented before the King a play so nearly in accordance with the murder as described by the ghost that the King will instinctively betray himself. He instructs the assembled players in the plot he has conceived; then calling for wine bids them make merry in the celebrated drinking sing, *"O vin, dissipe la tristesse"* ("O wine, this gloom dispel").

The vigorous rhythm of this song, and its attractive melody, first sung by Hamlet alone, then repeated by the troupe of actors, are the chief reasons for its unusual brilliance and effectiveness.

The playlet is given before the King, as Hamlet has planned. As the action progresses, the guilty monarch shows agitation, and finally in a rage orders the actors to stop and leave at once. Hamlet rushes forward and denounces the murderer, but no one will believe him—he is merely a madman!

When alone, Hamlet chides himself on his lack of decision; although he is certain of the King's guilt, he has done nothing to avenge his father. To avoid remorse he contemplates suicide. His mother and Ophelia enter and plead with him to give up these wild imaginings, but he maintains his old pose of insanity and, believing that Ophelia is involved in his mother's plot, treats her most harshly.

Hamlet's pretended insanity and his cruelty, however, bring upon Ophelia a madness that is all too genuine. She wanders to the shore of a lake where a crowd of peasants are making merry. An exquisite orchestral introduction accompanies her, a strange, wild figure, with flowing hair and torn white dress. Speaking to the amazed peasants, she tells them childishly of the lark which she heard at dawn, then launches into a brilliant display of birdlike trills and staccatos.

Ophelia turns to the shepherds and asks them to listen to her song, a sad melody, interrupted at intervals by wild laughter and weeping. Presently she seems to forget the others, and placidly plays with her flowers, until the magical siren's song is heard, luring her to the water's edge. She plunges in to her death, still singing of Hamlet's vow of love.

In the churchyard Hamlet meditatively watches the gravediggers prepare a last resting place for Ophelia, whose funeral train soon arrives. The ghost appears and, with his looks of reproach, stirs Hamlet to tremendous excitement. The Prince thereupon rushes at and stabs the guilty Claudius. The ghost then solemnly nominates him as successor to the throne, consigns the Queen to a convent, and disappears as the crowd acclaims Hamlet king.

THE RCA-VICTOR RECORDS
(Sung in French unless otherwise noted)

ACT II

CHANSON BACHIQUE (BRINDISI)—O VIN, DISSIPE LA TRISTESSE (Drinking Song—O Wine, This Gloom Dispel) : *Robert Merrill, Baritone, with Orch.*　　11-9291, 12"
John Charles Thomas, Baritone, with Orch.　　　　　　　　　　1639, 10"
Titto Ruffo, Baritone, with Orch. In Italian　　　　　　　　　18140, 12"
(Acoustical Recording)
(In Album M-816)

EMMA CALVÉ AS OPHELIA

Mario Sammarco, Baritone, with Orch.   15-1018, 12″
(Acoustical Recording)

ACT IV

SCÈNE DE LA FOLIE (Ophelia's Mad Scene): *Amelita Galli-Curci, Soprano, with Orch.*
In Italian   6562, 12″

THE HOME OF THE WITCH

Hänsel und Gretel
(HÄNSEL AND GRETEL)

OPERA IN three acts. Music by Engelbert Humperdinck. Libretto by Adelheid Wette, based on Ludwig Grimm's fairy tale. First produced at the Hoftheater, Weimar, Germany, December 23, 1893. American *première*, in English, at Daly's Theater, New York, October 8, 1895. First performed at the Metropolitan Opera House, in German, November 25, 1905, with a cast including Lina Abarbanell, Bella Alten, Otto Goritz, Marion Weed, and Louise Homer.

Humperdinck's delightful fairy opera was first destined for home performance. The composer's sister, Adelheid Wette, had written some verses based on Grimm's fairy tale which she sent to her brother to set to music for a Christmas celebration for her children. The holiday entertainment proved so successful that sister and brother elaborated it into a full-length opera. Composed in 1893, the work was warmly acclaimed at its Weimar *première*, and the ingratiating quality of the opera soon won a huge following the world over, the young of all ages being drawn by its childlike mood of enchantment. There is wondrous simplicity about Humperdinck's melodies, and the charm of folk music hovers about the score. But Humperdinck was also a supreme craftsman and an orchestrator of prodigious power. He had learned and absorbed much from Wagner, so much in fact that the master had engaged this worshipful disciple to supervise the epic task of preparing *Parsifal* for its world *première* at Bayreuth. Thus, along with a tender, homespun texture of theme one finds in *Hänsel und Gretel* contrapuntal power and orchestral color of vast range.

CHARACTERS

PETER, *a poor broommaker*	*Baritone*	THE WITCH	*Mezzo-soprano*
GERTRUDE, *his wife*	*Mezzo-soprano*	THE SANDMAN	*Soprano*
HÄNSEL, *their son*	*Mezzo-soprano*	THE DEWMAN	*Soprano*
GRETEL, *their daughter*	*Soprano*		

ANGELS AND GINGERBREAD CHILDREN

In its closely knit and colorful scheme, the Prelude marvelously reflects the course of the fairy tale. There are moods of childish frolicking and gaping terror, promptly sensed in Humperdinck's cleverly combined rhythms and colors. The material, drawn largely from the opera, is woven compactly into a deftly unified scheme. A prayer, chanted by horns and bassoons, opens the Prelude in a serene mood. After some development, the tempo quickens. A trumpet calls out brilliantly over a web of woodwinds and pizzicato strings. A new melody creeps in among the strings and woodwinds, ushering us into a spooky world of sorcery and mystery. The trumpet call rings out again, and a spirit of dancelike jubilation settles on the orchestra, which finally recovers its calm with a return of the prayer motif.

ACT I

SCENE: *At Peter's Home.* In a cottage by the woods dwells the family of Peter the broommaker. Both Peter and his wife Gertrude are away selling brooms, and when the curtain rises, the children, Hänsel and Gretel, are shown at work, Hänsel binding brooms and Gretel knitting. Soon they grow tired of their tasks, and Hänsel begins to complain of a gnawing hunger. The children begin a useless hunt about the house for food. Gretel tries to cheer her brother with singing and dancing, and Hänsel endeavors to join in the dance, but his clumsy movements only succeed in arousing Gretel's laughter. Gertrude, entering the hut, is furious at finding the children at play and goes to punish them. In her haste she breaks the pitcher of milk she had concealed for supper and then in despair sends the children out into the woods to pick strawberries. Worn and discouraged, Gertrude falls asleep. Soon Peter arrives. He is in a jolly mood, partly drunk and singing, for the day's sales have been good, and he has brought a basket of food. When he learns that the children have gone into the forest, he grows serious and fumes at his wife for sending them out. Maybe the fearful witch will seize them and turn them into gingerbread! Peter and Gertrude rush out to look for their children.

ACT II

SCENE: *In the Forest.* Hänsel and Gretel are wandering through the woods, gay and carefree. While Hänsel goes picking berries, Gretel sits under a fir tree and weaves a garland of roses, meanwhile singing a sweet little folk song of long ago, *"Ein Männlein steht im Walde"* ("There stands a little man in the wood"). The children now sit down together and avidly eye the basket of berries. Hänsel tries one berry, and Gretel follows suit; then they try another, and still another, and before long there are no more berries. Around them the shadows begin to gather. Night is falling, and fear seizes the children as they try in vain to find the way back to the hut. In her fright

Gretel cries out for her father and mother. The woods that had been so cheerful in daylight are now overrun with unknown terrors. Mysterious, ghostly sounds seem to come from the shadows around them. But the Sandman arrives, sprinkling sleep into their eyes to a tender little lullaby, *"Der kleine Sandmann bin ich"* ("The little sandman am I"). The children say their prayers together in a simple and childlike theme of soft-spun beauty, *"Abends will ich schlafen gehen, vierzehn Engel um mich stehn"* ("When I go to sleep at night fourteen angels stand around me"). As they fall asleep, the angels they have been singing about descend in a dream and form a circle around them to protect them against the evils of the forest. The tableau is heightened by the dreamy, gossamer web of the orchestra, which seems to catch all the wondrous glints of fairyland evoked by the children's sleep.

ACT III

SCENE: *The Witch's House.* The mist is clearing as the Dawn Fairy comes to shake dewdrops on the children, who rub their eyes and wake up. Excitedly they relate their dreams to each other, when suddenly they turn around and give a start. There before them, shining in the rays of the rising sun, stands a tempting little house made of cake. Surrounding it is a wall of gingerbread boys and girls. Forgetting all fear in their hunger, Hänsel and Gretel begin nibbling at the wall, dancing and singing the while. In the midst of their munching the Witch stalks out of the house. She tries to be friendly, but the children are frightened out of their wits. They are on the point of rushing away when a wave of the Witch's magic wand roots them to the spot. The Witch locks Hänsel in the cage and orders Gretel to do housework for her. Hänsel is now fed generously to make him more appetizing. In glee the Witch now grasps a broom, hobbles about the room with it, and sings a weird little song about the daily routine of witches (the so-called *Hexenritt*—the "Witches' Ride").

But while the Witch is busy fattening up her little victim, Gretel manages to steal the magic wand and, as the Witch's back is turned, frees her brother. The Witch now orders Gretel to look in the oven to see if the cakes are ready. Gretel pretends to be slow-witted and asks to be shown how it is done. As the Witch stoops in front of the open door, the children give a push together and slam the door shut. Jubilant now, Hänsel and Gretel express their joy in a delightful "Gingerbread Waltz." With a crash the oven falls apart. The spell is shattered, and all the captive children are freed from their gingerbread state. Peter and Gertrude, who have been searching the woods all night, arrive in time for the celebration. From the ruins of the oven the children extract a huge gingerbread figure—the Witch, thoroughly baked and harmless. All join in a joyous hymn of thanksgiving.

Hänsel und Gretel

ACT II—SLUMBER SCENE

THE RCA-VICTOR RECORDS
(Sung in German unless otherwise noted)

ABRIDGED RECORDING: *Junior Programs Opera Company; Saul Lancourt, Director; Victor Orchestra, Nathaniel Shilkret, Cond. In English*
P-38 (26701-26704), 4-10″

SELECTIONS (Barefoot Goslings; Sandman's Song; Gingerbread House): *Victor Orchestra* 22175, 10″

SELECTIONS (Children's Prayer; Witch's Ride; Waltz; Finale): *Victor Orchestra* 22176, 10″

OVERTURE: *BBC Symphony Orchestra, Adrian Boult, Cond.* 11929, 12″

ACT II

EIN MÄNNLEIN STEHT IM WALDE (There Stands a Little Man): *Elisabeth Schumann, Soprano, with Piano* 1948, 10″

LIED DES SANDMÄNNCHENS—DER KLEINE SANDMANN BIN ICH (Sandman's Lullaby—I've Shut the Children's Peepers): *Elisabeth Schumann, Soprano, with Piano* 1948, 10″

DREAM PANTOMIME: *National Symphony Orchestra, Hans Kindler, Cond.* 11-8948, 12″

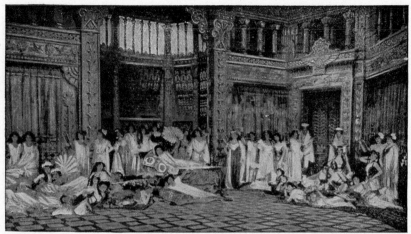

Larcher

ACT II, SCENE 1—THE CHAMBER OF HEROD

Hérodiade

OPERA IN four acts. Music by Jules Massenet. Libretto by Paul Milliet and Henri Grémont (Georges Hartmann), after an earlier Italian version by Zanardini, based on Gustave Flaubert's novelette, *Hérodias*, in turn based on the Biblical episode. First performance at the Théâtre de la Monnaie, Brussels, December 19, 1881, having been scheduled for *première* early that spring in Milan, but dropped. The opera, French to the core, did not reach the stage of the Paris Opéra till December 22, 1921! The United States *première* occurred in New Orleans, on February 13, 1892. *Hérodiade* was introduced to New York at Oscar Hammerstein's Manhattan Opera House on November 8, 1909—the opening night of its fourth and last season—with Lina Cavalieri as Salomé, Charles Dalmorès as John, Jeanne Gerville-Réache as Herodias, and Maurice Renaud as Herod. How popular Massenet had become with the American operagoing public may be seen in the fact that the Metropolitan Opera Company opened its Brooklyn season that night with the same composer's *Manon*.

When *Hérodiade* was first produced in London in 1904, it bore two alterations. The title was now *Salomé* and the locale was Ethiopia, a change made by order of the British censor. *Salomé*, of course, is also the title of Richard Strauss's opera, the antithesis of *Hérodiade* in style. To the gory scriptural episode Massenet brought the suave refinement and melodic delicacy of a cultivated French gentleman. Strauss, with fierce power of orchestral and psychological resource, evoked the tense, barbaric atmosphere of a morbidly degenerate court. Like their composers, the operas are worlds apart in color and treatment.

CHARACTERS

SALOMÉ	Soprano	VITELLIUS, *a Roman proconsul*	Baritone
HEROD, *king of Galilee*	Baritone	THE HIGH PRIEST	Baritone
HERODIAS, *his wife*	Contralto	A VOICE IN THE TEMPLE	Bass
PHANUEL, *a young Jew*	Bass	A YOUNG BABYLONIAN WOMAN	Contralto
JOHN THE BAPTIST	Tenor		

MERCHANTS, HEBREW SOLDIERS, ROMAN SOLDIERS, PRIESTS, LEVITES, TEMPLE SADDUCEES, ETHIOPIANS, NUBIANS, ARABS, ROMANS

The action takes place in Jerusalem about A.D. *30*

ACT I

SCENE: *The Courtyard of the Palace of Herod.* A great horde of merchants, traders, and slaves has gathered in the courtyard at dawn, bartering. The Pharisees and Sadducees among them soon begin to wrangle, and then come to blows. Phanuel, a young Jew serving as Herod's astrologer, attracted by the uproar, bids them cease, and the crowd disperses. As Phanuel muses gloomily on the fading chances of a strong Israel, with the people thus divided, his thoughts are interrupted by the entrance of Salomé. The beautiful girl is seeking John the Baptist, who had saved her in the desert as a child. While Phanuel listens sympathetically, she sings a graceful aria, *"Il est doux, il est bon"* ("He is kind, he is good"), in which the episode is narrated with great tenderness of feeling. Salomé, separated from her family years before, does not know that Herodias is her mother. As Salomé leaves, Herod enters, burning with desire for the mysterious beauty whom he has seen lurking about the palace grounds. Herodias breaks in on his romantic reverie to demand the head of John for publicly branding her a Jezebel. To Herodias' chagrin, Herod refuses, knowing that John's influence among the people is strong. Amid the woman's recriminations the majestic figure of John appears. He denounces them in such withering terms that Herod and Herodias rush out, terrified. As in a daze, Salomé approaches John and, flinging herself at his feet, declares her love. Gently and understandingly, John bids her turn to God and speak only of the purer love that is the gospel he preaches. Though impressed, Salomé is left puzzled by the distinction between the two kinds of love.

ACT II

SCENE 1: *Herod's Chamber.* Full of longing for Salomé, Herod lies restless on a sumptuous couch, attended by beautiful slave girls who sing and dance for him. Their presence irks him now, for his thoughts are elsewhere —with the girl who so tantalizingly eludes him. A mysterious potion is brought to him that will enable him to see in a vision the woman he most longs for. Suspecting this may be a ruse to poison him, Herod hesitates at first, but desire soon overcomes his scruples and he drinks. Instantly he beholds the promised vision of Salomé and into a famous aria, *"Vision fugitive"* ("Fleeting vision"), he pours all the ardent yearning that torments him. For her, he chants deliriously, he would gladly give up his soul. As the image vanishes, Herod tries to sleep. While he tosses about in a fever of obsession, Phanuel enters, bringing news of rebellious mutterings among the populace against the Roman occupation. A great cry for Herod is heard outside.

SCENE 2: *A Public Square in Jerusalem.* Messages reach Herod, assuring him of allies in the struggle against Rome, and local patriots come to him, pledging their allegiance in helping to set up Herod as independent ruler. Dreaming of new power, Herod now denounces Rome to the populace. He counts on the help of John, who detests Rome. Herodias laughs scornfully at the people who come swearing loyalty to Herod. Trumpets sound, and as Vitellius, the Roman proconsul, is announced, Herod suddenly changes his tune. He is the flunkey again, prostrating himself before the Roman. Only John remains standing, proud and defiant, and Vitellius, observing him, is struck by the man's fearlessness. To the tense populace Vitellius announces that Rome, desiring the friendship of the Jews, is prepared to restore the Temple of Israel. The proconsul carefully notes the respect shown to John by the people. Herod, meanwhile, has fixed his stare on Salomé, who is watching John with rapture, while Herodias, aware of the king's passion, eyes the girl jealously. Secretly she now warns Vitellius of John's growing influence over the people. At length, the Prophet steps forward to denounce the Romans and their envoy, predicting that their glory will vanish in the dust. Then, gathering his followers about him, the Prophet disappears.

ACT III

SCENE 1: *Phanuel's House.* Phanuel is alone at a window, gazing out over a city silent under the starry sky. The memory of John's last appearance in public comes to him, and the astrologer wonders if he is a man or a god. He calls upon the stars to give some sign, and prophesies a dread fate for the city that lies before him in the night. Herodias enters, seeking her horoscope. She rages at the thought of Salomé, crying, "Vengeance on the woman who has stolen Herod's love!" Phanuel proceeds to read her destiny in the stars, but he finds only blood there! A mysterious star hovers in the skies near her own, Phanuel adds, reminding Herodias of her long-lost daughter, whom she suddenly longs to see again. Phanuel takes her to the window and points to Salomé, who is about to enter the temple. Horrified, she cries, "That woman my daughter! Never!" And in a fresh surge of vengeful hatred adds, "She is my rival!"

SCENE 2: *Inner Court of the Temple.* At the entrance to the Temple prison, Salomé appears, half fainting. The news of John's arrest and imprisonment has reached her, and she has come to be near him. Herod enters and, on seeing Salomé, bursts into a fiery avowal of love, but Salomé repulses him with disgust, saying that she loves another. With an angry vow that he will find this man and destroy him, Herod now turns to the grim business of trying the Prophet. As John is brought in, the priests set up a clamor for his death. Herod offers John his life if he will aid him in ousting the Romans.

ACT III, SCENE 2—INNER COURT OF THE TEMPLE

John refuses. When the priests again demand his execution, Salomé rushes to him and flings herself at his feet. Herod, thunderstruck, now knows his rival. When Salomé shouts that she will die with the Prophet, Herod orders them both put to death, and the guards seize them and drag them away.

ACT IV

SCENE 1: *A Dungeon in the Temple.* In an underground vault of the Temple, John is praying for strength to face the ordeal to come and to resist the disturbing love of Salomé. Suddenly the girl appears. She has been released on Herod's orders, but she is obsessed by one thought: to die with John. Touched by the girl's devotion and remorseful over her sacrifice, John urges her to flee. When she refuses bitterly, John is convinced that their love is right, that heaven itself approves. Clasping each other in a despairing embrace, they sing, *"Il est beau de mourir en s'aimant"*—"It is beautiful to die loving." Priests enter the dungeon, and as Salomé, resisting frantically, is dragged off to Herod's palace, John is led away to execution.

SCENE 2: *The Great Hall of the Palace.* A brilliant festival in honor of the Roman Empire is under way in Herod's palace. To entertain the assembled dignitaries, Phoenician girls perform a sensuous Oriental dance. Salomé rushes to Herod and Herodias, imploring them to allow her to die with John, but Herod is adamant. Turning to the queen, Salomé pleads, "If you were ever a mother, have pity on me!" Herodias shudders at the words and for a moment seems about to yield. Just then the executioner appears in the rear of the hall, dripping sword in hand. "The Prophet is dead!" he announces solemnly. Salomé, catching Herodias' look of triumph, with a scream lunges at her with a dagger. "No! No!" shrieks the frightened queen; "I am your mother!" Salomé stops and draws back in horror, then, reflecting a moment, she grips the dagger and with the words, "If you are my mother, then take back your own blood with my life!" she stabs herself.

THE RCA-VICTOR RECORDS
(Sung in French)

ACT I

IL EST DOUX, IL EST BON (He Is Kind, He Is Good): *Grace Moore, Soprano, with Orch.*
11-8258, 12"
(In Album M-918)

Licia Albanese, Soprano; RCA-Victor Orchestra, Jean Paul Morel, Cond.
12-0525, 12"

ACT II

VISION FUGITIVE (Fleeting Vision): *Robert Merrill, Baritone, with Orch.*
11-9291, 12"

John Charles Thomas, Baritone, with Orch.
1639, 10"

ACT III

RECIT.—C'EN EST FAIT! (It Is Done!)

ARIA—SALOMÉ! SALOMÉ! DEMANDE (Salomé! Salomé! Ask): *John Charles Thomas, Baritone, with Orch.*
15859, 12"
(In Album M-645)

Cautin & Berger
EMMA CALVÉ AS SALOMÉ

L'Heure Espagnole

(THE SPANISH HOUR OR SPANISH TIME)

COMIC OPERA in one act. Music by Maurice Ravel. Text by Franc-Nohain (pseudonym of Maurice Le Grand), after his comedy of the same title. First performance, Opéra-Comique, Paris, May 19, 1911. Initial American performance, by the Chicago Civic Opera Company, Auditorium, Chicago, January 5, 1920, with Yvonne Gall as Concepcion and Alfred Maguenet as Ramiro, Louis Hasselmans conducting. Given for the first time in New York by the same company, Lexington Theater, January 28, 1920, with the same artists. Initial performance by the Metropolitan, November 7, 1925, with Lucrezia Bori as Concepcion and Lawrence Tibbett as Ramiro, Louis Hasselmans conducting. *L'Heure espagnole* was also presented by the Juilliard School of Music, March 9, 1936, in an English translation by Robert A. Simon.

The first of two operas by Ravel, the other being *L'Enfant et les sortilèges*, *L'Heure espagnole* has by far been the more successful. The composer wrote for it a score that is a marvel of orchestral effects and subtle colors, easily the equal of a libretto that has long been considered perfect in every way. The opera has been given on many French stages, and outside of France—besides Chicago and New York—at London, Brussels, Rotterdam, Basle, Prague, Hamburg, Stockholm, Turin, Budapest, Berlin, and other places, frequently in the local vernacular.

CHARACTERS

TORQUEMADA, *a clockmaker*	*Tenor*	GONZALVE	*admirers of*	*Tenor*
CONCEPCION, *his young wife*	*Soprano*	DON INIGO GOMEZ	*Concepcion*	*Bass*
RAMIRO, *a muleteer*	*Baritone*			

The action takes place in the shop of Torquemada, a clockmaker of Toledo, Spain, in the eighteenth century

After a short introduction, based on a calm theme played by the woodwinds in the early measures, the curtain rises on Torquemada's little shop, filled with all kinds of examples of his art. Ramiro, a muleteer, enters. He is a tall, athletic-looking young man, who asks the clockmaker to repair his watch. While Torquemada is examining the timepiece, his young wife, Concepcion, comes in, reminding him that this is the day when he must regulate the municipal clocks. She further reproaches him for not bringing one of the two grandfather clocks up to her bedroom. He complains about the size and weight of these clocks, and as his wife, in an aside, remarks disparagingly about his physical powers, he picks up his tools and departs, telling Ramiro to wait for him.

Considerably nettled by the presence of Ramiro, who is interfering with a tête-à-tête she had planned to have with the poet Gonzalve, Concepcion persuades the muleteer to carry one of the grandfather clocks upstairs, in order to get him out of the way. When Ramiro departs, with the clock easily balanced on his back, Gonzalve makes his entrance, and he is effusively greeted by Concepcion. But her joy is short-lived, however, for, in addition to Gonzalve's dilatory tactics, Ramiro soon returns, proudly announcing that he has completed the job. Yet, scarcely at a loss for ideas, Concepcion begs

Ramiro's indulgence for her mistake; it was another clock she wanted him to move.

Good-naturedly, the muleteer, with a remarkable nonchalance that has already impressed Concepcion, starts to put the second clock on his shoulders, but the lady changes her mind on a sudden impulse and asks him to bring down the first. Meanwhile, she urges Gonzalve to get into the second clock, the intention being to have Ramiro carry both that and Gonzalve upstairs, an ingenious arrangement, to say the least. Gonzalve falls in with this suggestion, for the unusual transportation will provide him with a new experience. As they talk, a cheery voice is heard outside, and Concepcion, hastily closing the door to Gonzalve's temporary prison, sees that the voice is that of Don Inigo, the banker, who is very amorously disposed. She tries to quiet him with the words that "clocks have ears." But this does not discourage the banker, for he continues to make advances, ceasing only when Ramiro and the first clock make their appearance.

Willing as ever, Ramiro picks up the second clock, Gonzalve and all, and is about to go up with it, when she decides to accompany him, fearing what the uneven trip may do to her cramped poet. Don Inigo, in the meantime, thinks of playing a trick on Concepcion, and how better to do that than secrete himself in one of those grandfather clocks. This he does, after some effort, for he is a corpulent person, and presently Ramiro returns. He is now joined by Concepcion, who, in assumed dismay, declares that she just cannot bear to have in her room a clock that acts as erratically as the one now upstairs. So, Ramiro, matter-of-fact as can be, heads for the upper story to oblige the lady.

While Ramiro is out, Don Inigo playfully imitates a cuckoo, from his hiding place, and Concepcion, at first nonplused, soon discovers the source of the sound. In a heated argument with Don Inigo, she is telling him off, when Ramiro comes down with the second clock, which still houses Gonzalve. The young Hercules takes it as his duty, now, to bring up the first clock again, and this he does, the heaviest of all the clocks, thus far (with the fat and weighty banker in it), not bothering him at all. More appreciation from the lady; in fact, it begins to take on a significant edge.

Gonzalve, despite Concepcion's order to get himself off, is loath to quit his little private niche, and they are talking, he poetically, she excitedly, when Ramiro returns. Gonzalve, who has heard his footsteps, hurries to his hiding place.

Ramiro, in his simple reasoning, guesses that Concepcion is angered by the latest clock disposal, so he tells her not to fret, that he will come back directly with the first clock. And he joyfully heads for his objective. During his absence Concepcion berates the poet, who can offer no other consolation than to spout verses. And when Ramiro reappears, with clock-plus-Don

Inigo, he asks if there are further orders from her. Concepcion, now deeply interested in this simple but ever so powerful youth, says yes, that he must go upstairs again. "With which clock?" he asks innocently. "Without a clock," she declares significantly, and the muleteer obediently follows her up the stairs.

While the muleteer and the girl are about their affairs, Gonzalve comes out of his hideout, but, seeing Torquemada about to enter the shop, tries to go back, only to open the door of the wrong clock, the one containing Don Inigo. And when Torquemada does enter both Gonzalve and Don Inigo are in full view. Torquemada, an ingenuous soul and hardly perturbed by their presence, believes, in fact, that they have come to do business with him, and he succeeds in selling to the two men the respective clocks. The banker, however, cannot get out of his narrow cell, thanks to his obesity, and although Gonzalve and Torquemada and, lastly, Concepcion, who has now returned, all put their strength to the job, it is Ramiro, all by himself, who pulls him out—so very easily.

The opera ends with an epilogue in the form of a quintet, in which each of the characters expresses his thoughts to the audience, Concepcion remarking that Ramiro, who passes her window every morning, shall be henceforth her only dependable chronometer.

Criterion Photocraft Co.
DESIGN BY BRUNO FUNARO FOR JUILLIARD SCHOOL OF MUSIC PRODUCTION

Gerardi ACT II—CASTLE AND GARDENS OF CHENONÇEAUX

Les Huguenots
(THE HUGUENOTS)

OPERA IN five acts. Music by Giacomo Meyerbeer. Libretto by Eugène Scribe and Émile Deschamps. First performance, Paris Opéra, February 29, 1836. First American performance, New Orleans, Théâtre d'Orléans, April 29, 1839. First performed at the Metropolitan Opera House during the season 1883–84, where it has since been sung in French, German, and Italian.

The most famous of Meyerbeer's operas, *Les Huguenots* has seven stellar roles, which impresarios have been only too eager to cast significantly. The part of the page has been done in two versions, for soprano and contralto, the latter converted especially for the contralto Marietta Alboni for the London production (in Italian) of July 20, 1848. At the Metropolitan in the 1890's prices for best seats were fixed at seven dollars to match the seven stars in the cast, who would be Jean de Reszke as Raoul, Édouard de Reszke as Marcel, Lilli Lehmann or Lillian Nordica or Félia Litvinne as Valentine, Sigrid Arnoldson or Nellie Melba or Marcella Sembrich as Marguerite, Sofia Scalchi or Eugenia Mantelli or Rosa Olitzka as the page, Jean Lassalle or Pol Plançon as St. Bris, and Victor Maurel or Mario Ancona as de Nevers. In 1905, a Metropolitan revival offered Enrico Caruso as Raoul, together with Marcel Journet, Nordica, Sembrich, Edyth Walker, Antonio Scotti, and Plançon. And in the revival there of 1912, the seven stars were Caruso, Adamo Didur, Emmy Destinn, Frieda Hempel, Bella Alten, Léon Rothier, and Antonio Scotti.

Meyerbeer has provided this dramatic story, written around the Massacre on the night of St. Bartholomew, with a very effective setting. There are some trite moments in the music, but the score, as a whole, is impressive, to say the least, when sung by a cast of capable artists. Richard Wagner, who could scarcely be called an admirer of Meyerbeer's, found in the music of *Les Huguenots* much that he could praise.

CHARACTERS

COUNT DE ST. BRIS } *Catholic*	*Baritone*	RAOUL DE NANGIS, *a Huguenot*	
COUNT DE NEVERS } *noblemen*	*Baritone*	*nobleman*	*Tenor*

212

MARCEL, *servant to Raoul*   Bass   VALENTINE, *daughter of St. Bris*   Soprano

MARGUÉRITE DE VALOIS, *betrothed*   URBAIN, *page to Marguérite*   Soprano or
   to Henry IV of Navarre   Soprano   *Mezzo-soprano*

LADIES AND GENTLEMEN OF THE COURT, BOTH CATHOLIC AND HUGUENOT; PAGES, CITIZENS,
SOLDIERS, THE NIGHT WATCH, STUDENTS, MONKS, AND THE PEOPLE

*The action of the opera takes place during 1572, the first two acts in Touraine, the
remainder at Paris*

ACT I

SCENE: *The Count de Nevers' House.* A group of Catholic noblemen are
dining as guests of the Count de Nevers. There is also present Raoul de
Nangis, a Huguenot, who, however, is treated with respect and politeness
because all present know that Marguérite de Valois, the betrothed of the
King, is eager to reconcile Catholic and Protestant, and that he who furthers
her purpose is likely to win royal favor. When Nevers toasts the ladies and
proposes that each tell of some adventure with the fair sex, Raoul, first to be
asked, willingly complies. In a romanza he tells them of an unknown beauty
whom he rescued this very morning from some drunken revelers. He does
not know her, but he is in love with her, he says.

    The applause which greets this romantic recital is interrupted by
Raoul's sturdy old Huguenot servant, Marcel, who distrusts his master's
Catholic friends and sings the Lutheran choral, "A Mighty Fortress Is Our
God." The guests accept Raoul's apologies for Marcel's act and ask the old
fellow to sing again. He responds with a vigorous Huguenot ditty against the
"snares of Rome."

Gerardi

ACT III—THE PUBLIC SQUARE

White

ACT I—THE GREAT BANQUET SCENE

The resulting rather constrained feeling is quickly forgotten when a servant announces that a veiled lady wishes to speak to Nevers, who at once retires to meet her, amidst the banter of his friends. All are curious about the lady, and Raoul himself joins in peeping behind a curtain. It is none other than the unknown beauty he rescued that morning; at once he believes that a liaison exists between this woman and Nevers.

Still another unexpected diversion occurs in the arrival of a page, who, in the very ornate but melodious "Page's Song," *"Nobles seigneurs, salut"* ("Noble sirs, I salute you"), informs them that one of their number is addressed with the unusual request to go blindfolded in a carriage wherever his guide may take him.

Raoul, though highly puzzled when he learns that the message is addressed to him, gallantly accepts. He also wonders at the sudden respect with which he is treated, for he does not realize that the seal on the letter is that of Marguérite de Valois.

ACT II

SCENE: *Castle and Gardens of Chenonçeaux.* Marguérite de Valois, surrounded by her maids of honor, rejoices, as she sings, *"O beau pays de la Touraine"* ("O lovely Touraine"), in the pleasant sunny field of Touraine after the stress of life at court. Valentine, daughter of the Count de St. Bris, enters and tells Marguérite news—she has succeeded in breaking her engagement to marry the Count de Nevers, news in which both rejoice, for Valentine does not love the man, and Marguérite has other plans for her.

From an Old Print   VIARDOT GARCIA AS VALENTINE AND MARINI AS MARCEL

Valentine and some of the ladies go away as Raoul is brought before Marguérite and the bandage removed from his eyes. Though astonished to find himself before her, he gallantly offers her his sword and service. She tells him of her desire for him to marry Valentine, and as he knows of Marguérite's ambition to reconcile Catholic and Protestant by this union, he consents. The nobles of the court are summoned, and when they appear they gather around the Queen and in commemoration of the union of Raoul and Valentine swear an oath of eternal truce between their parties. Valentine is brought in, to be presented to her betrothed. Raoul recoils in horror and exclaims, "I her husband?" for he recognizes in Valentine the woman who called secretly on the Count de Nevers. Misunderstanding his action, all present are filled with the greatest consternation; Valentine is overcome with shame, and St. Bris, furious at the insult to his daughter, joins with Nevers in swearing vengeance. Marguérite's presence does indeed prevent immediate bloodshed, but her hopes of reconciling the warring factions are forever shattered.

ACT III

SCENE: *A Square in Paris.* Near the entrance to a chapel on the banks of the Seine, a group of Catholic students has gathered about the doors of an inn; and at another inn across the way a number of Huguenot soldiers have met to drink and play dice. Townspeople of all sorts pass to and fro, their many-colored costumes adding glamour to the brilliant sunlight. A bridal procession passes—Valentine and Count de Nevers are to be married. While the bridal party is in the chapel, Marcel enters with a message for St. Bris, from Raoul. The wedding over, Valentine remains in the chapel to pray alone, and Marcel presents the message to St. Bris; it proves to be a challenge. The nobles re-enter the chapel.

Twilight falls, the curfew sounds, and the people disperse. Valentine comes from the chapel in deathly terror, for she has overheard the nobles plotting to kill Raoul. She finds Marcel waiting for his master, and warns him of the plan. It is too late for him to see Raoul before the hour of the duel, so he hastily gathers a group of Huguenot friends near by. The two parties prove to be evenly matched, a serious fray is threatened and, in fact, is prevented only by the arrival of Marguérite, who happens to be passing. Raoul also learns that he has deeply wronged Valentine, for her visit to Nevers was made at the request of the Queen merely to break off the engagement. His remorse comes too late, for now Valentine is married to this man she never loved, and a boat, gay with lanterns and music, has come up the Seine to take her to the Count's home.

ACT IV

SCENE: *A Room in Nevers' Castle.* Alone at her new home, Valentine still thinks of Raoul, who suddenly and unexpectedly appears. He so longs to see Valentine that he has entered the castle at the risk of his life; she warns him, but he insists on remaining and scarcely has time to hide behind the tapestry before St. Bris, Nevers, and other leaders of the Catholic party enter. Thus, the young nobleman overhears the whole ghastly plot for the massacre of the Huguenots. Nevers alone among them refuses to swear allegiance to the plan, and he is led away under guard. While all draw their swords, three monks who have entered bless them.

The crowd having departed, Raoul comes cautiously from his hiding place; he would run to warn his friends. Valentine meets him, and fearing he may kill her father she will not let him go. They sing a surpassingly beautiful duet, which is interrupted by the sinister tolling of the great bell of St. Germain, the preliminary signal for the slaughter. Raoul makes an effort to rush to the aid of his people; Valentine clings to him.

The Italian version ends here, as a fusillade of shots from the street kills the lovers.

ACT V

SCENE: *The Street Before Nevers' House.* But in the original version there is a fifth act, whose action takes place in the street during the massacre. After Valentine's protests that she would rather die with Raoul than return to her own faction, they go out into the night, and Raoul asks Marcel to act as priest and marry them, which he does. In their most ecstatic moment the lovers and Marcel are shot down by the soldiers of St. Bris, who, too late, discovers that they have killed his own daughter.

Mishkin
ENRICO CARUSO AS RAOUL

THE RCA-VICTOR RECORDS
(Sung in French)

ACT I

PIFF! PAFF! (Marcel's Aria) : *Marcel Journet, Bass, with Orch.* 15-1003, 12"
(Acoustical Recording)

CAVATINE DU PAGE—NOBLES SEIGNEURS, SALUT! (Page's Song—Noble Sirs, I Salute You!) : *Sigrid Onegin, Contralto, with Orch.* 7146, 12"
Louise Homer, Contralto, with Orch. 15-1011, 12"
(Acoustical Recording)

ACT I—D'OYLY CARTE OPERA PRODUCTION

Iolanthe

(OR, THE PEER AND THE PERI)

COMIC OPERA in two acts. Music by Arthur Sullivan. Libretto by W. S. Gilbert. First produced at the Savoy Theatre, London, November 25, 1882, as "an entirely new and original fairy opera." *Iolanthe* enjoys the distinction of being the first Gilbert and Sullivan operetta written especially for the splendid new Savoy Theatre constructed by Richard D'Oyly Carte for the exclusive performance of the works of this gifted team. As in *Trial by Jury*, Gilbert is again satirizing some solemn English institution. In the earlier work, it was the English court system. In *Iolanthe* it is the House of Lords. Yet in a larger sense, the absurdly worded lyrics are directed at all pretense and the unearned privilege of rank. With all that, *Iolanthe* has an ethereal charm of its own, in the glow and magic of its enchanted revels. While many consider it one of the less important works of Gilbert and Sullivan, so shrewd and discerning a Savoyard as Deems Taylor ranks *Iolanthe* with *Pinafore* and *The Mikado* as representing the peak of their achievement. To the American composer and critic the score is "one of the most spontaneous and ingratiating that Sullivan ever wrote, harmonically much more colorful than most of them and offering more rhythmic variety." And dwelling in similar vein on Gilbert's share, Mr. Taylor adds: "Nowhere in the entire Savoy repertoire are Gilbert's lyrics defter in rhyme or more captivating in meter. . . . Though, as some complain, Gilbert's characters are never quite human, they share one attribute with all the Little People who have no souls: they do not die."

CHARACTERS

THE LORD CHANCELLOR	Baritone	STREPHON, an Arcadian shepherd	Tenor
EARL OF MOUNTARARAT	Baritone	QUEEN OF THE FAIRIES	Contralto
EARL OF TOLLOLLER	Tenor	PHYLLIS, an Arcadian shepherdess	
PRIVATE WILLIS of the Grenadier		and ward in chancery	Soprano
Guards	Bass		

218

Royston - Herts England
Took part at Iolanthe -

Iolanthe

IOLANTHE, *a fairy,*
    Strephon's mother   *Mezzo-soprano*

CELIA ⎫
LEILA ⎬ *fairies*
FLETA ⎭

CHORUS OF DUKES, MARQUISES, EARLS, VISCOUNTS, BARONS, AND FAIRIES

ACT I

SCENE: *An Arcadian Landscape, in the Background a Stream.* At the rise of the curtain, the fairies enter. Led by Leila, Celia, and Fleta, they trip across the stage, singing as they dance. At the end of their chorus the fairies lament that ever since Iolanthe was banished twenty-five years ago, their revels have lacked any real spirit. According to the law, Iolanthe's crime—that of marrying a mortal—should have been punished by death. At this point in the conversation the Fairy Queen enters and finishes the story herself. The Queen, rather than let so dire a punishment be visited on a beloved fairy, had, instead, banished Iolanthe, on the condition that she never communicate with her husband. The Queen herself laments the loss of Iolanthe, to whom she is deeply indebted. For, though the Queen is built on the most generous proportions, it was Iolanthe who taught her to curl up inside a buttercup, to swing upon a cobweb, to dive into a dewdrop, to nestle in a nutshell, and to gambol upon gossamer! Leila remarks that Iolanthe certainly did surprising things.

The fairies all beg the Queen to restore Iolanthe to them, and the Queen, who is troubled by no small curiosity to know why, of all places, Iolanthe, when banished, chose to live in the bottom of the stream, now summons the exiled sprite. Iolanthe rises from the water. Clad in tattered and somber garments, she approaches the Queen with head bent and arms crossed. Miraculously her rags fall from her, and she now appears clothed as a fairy. The Queen places a diamond coronet on her head and embraces her. After the others have embraced her, the Queen asks why she chose to live in the bottom of the stream. Iolanthe replies that she wished to be near her son, who was born shortly after her banishment. All are curious to see this child, half fairy and half mortal, now grown to manhood.

At this moment this very youth, Strephon, approaches, singing and dancing, and playing on a flageolet. He does not see the fairies, who conceal themselves as he enters. From the conversation of Strephon and Iolanthe we learn that he intends to marry Phyllis this very day, even though the Lord Chancellor, whose ward she is, withholds his consent. The fairies and the Fairy Queen come forward and make Strephon's acquaintance before they leave. The Queen and the fairies trip away, Iolanthe going off last, after taking an affectionate farewell of her son. Phyllis enters, singing and dancing, and also accompanying herself on a flageolet. She grows serious as she recalls that the punishment for marrying a ward of the court without the Lord Chancellor's consent is penal servitude for life. She wonders now if they

219

should not wait two years until she becomes of age. But Strephon thinks that the House of Lords has become so attentive to her that delays are dangerous, and Phyllis agrees.

Trumpets herald the approach of the Peers. During the instrumental march, they enter in a procession in pompous dignity, wearing their gorgeous robes of state. The Earl of Mountararat and the Earl of Tolloller lead the parade. The Lords have been so powerfully affected by the beauty of Phyllis that they have petitioned the Chancellor to bestow her upon the one she selects. This is the reason for their visit here. The Lord Chancellor is grieved to have to confess that he is himself so attracted by the girl that he is wasting away under the strain of his position. For if he were to award her to himself, his action might be misconstrued. Thus, even though it pains him, he gallantly waives all claims for himself. Could he give his own consent to his own marriage with his own ward? Can he marry his own ward without his own consent? And if he did so, can he commit himself for contempt of his own court? It is indeed painful, the Chancellor avers, to have to sit upon a woolsack stuffed with such thorns as these.

Having gone to summon Phyllis, Lord Mountararat returns, followed by the young lady. The Peers depart, marching around the stage with much pomp. The Lord Chancellor separates Phyllis from Strephon and orders her away. Alone with Strephon now, the Lord Chancellor asks him what excuse he can offer for daring to disobey an order of the Court of Chancery. Strephon replies that he knows only nature's acts of Parliament. Since he loves Phyllis, all the voices of nature—from the brooks to the thunderstorms—have commanded that he marry her. "Are you also Chancellor of birds and trees?" Strephon asks. The Chancellor admits it's an intriguing point, but doubts whether the evidence is conclusive. An affidavit from a thunderstorm would of course be seriously considered. Strephon asks if he would apply the prosaic rules of evidence to so poetic a case. The Chancellor answers that he certainly would, for he owes his present distinguished position to the fact that he has always kept his duty before his eyes. When he has finished, the Lord Chancellor rushes away, leaving Strephon in tears over his hopeless predicament.

Iolanthe enters, and proceeds to comfort him, promising to seek help from the Fairy Queen. The Peers approach in the background, advancing unseen and on tiptoe. Lords Mountararat and Tolloller lead Phyllis between them, who at first listens in horror to what she hears, and then rushes forward and reveals herself. Iolanthe and Strephon are much confused. Strephon's avowal that Iolanthe is his mother is laughed at, and Phyllis has no choice but to believe him unfaithful. As Iolanthe clings for protection to Strephon, Phyllis sings of her distress, and despairingly gives her heart to one of two Lords, "I don't care which." Strephon calls the fairies to his aid. They troop in at his summons, and the situation is explained to them. The Peers and Lord Chancellor attempt to dismiss them, but the daring Fairy Queen will not budge till she has pronounced sentence on their stupidity. She threatens them in ominous tones and tells them their fate: Strephon shall be sent to Parliament, and every bill he proposes shall be passed by magic. The Peers, however, remain defiant.

ACT II

SCENE: *The Palace Yard, Westminster, Westminster Hall at the Left.* Private Willis is discovered on sentry duty. In the loneliness of night he muses on politics and its stupidity. The fairies enter, singing of the mischief Strephon has caused in Parliament. Meanwhile the Peers are greatly upset because Strephon is about to carry his bill to throw the peerage open to competitive examination. The fairies claim the honor for this, saying that by magic they compel the members to vote for any bill Strephon wishes. Lord Mountararat retorts, "This comes of women interfering in politics," adding that if there's any British institution not susceptible of improvement, it's the House of Peers. The Peers depart solemnly. Lords Mountararat and Tolloller remain with the fairies to plead with them to stop this mischief. The fairies refuse, although Leila has been much attracted by the Peers, and Celia, herself weakening, is moved to exclaim, "For self-contained dignity, combined with airy condescension, give me a British representative peer!"

Lords Mountararat and Tolloller go, and the fairies remain looking wistfully after them. The Fairy Queen enters and scolds them for their breach of the fairy law, reminding them of the death penalty for those who marry a mortal. They must control their weakness! The Queen admits that she is herself not insensible to the power of manly beauty. Pointing to Sentry Willis, who remains motionless at his post, she says he has the most extraordinary effect upon her. If she yielded to her impulse, she would fall down and worship him. But she stifles that inclination. Sorrowfully, the fairies go away, led by the Fairy Queen. Phyllis now enters in tears, for she finds herself engaged to two noblemen at once, neither of whom she loves. Lords Mountararat and Tolloller enter, each wanting to embrace her and claiming her as his own. Phyllis finds them equally wealthy and equally plain, so that there is no choice to make between them. She says that if one of them would forgo his title and distribute his estates among the Irish tenantry, then she could see a reason for accepting the other. But although they have been friends since boyhood, neither can quite persuade the other to make such a sacrifice. As they leave, the Lord Chancellor enters at this point, looking very miserable and sounding even worse in the celebrated "Nightmare Song."

During the last lines of the song, Lords Mountararat and Tolloller have re-entered. They gaze sympathetically upon the Lord Chancellor's distress.

At the end of the song they approach him and offer their condolences. His situation is admittedly most trying: first, he is Lord Chancellor, entrusted with the guardianship of Phyllis; second, he is her suitor. And he confesses, "In my latter capacity I am overawed by my dignity in my former capacity; I hesitate to approach myself—it unnerves me." The others urge him to take courage, and then go away, dancing together, arm in arm.

Phyllis and Strephon, wandering about disconsolately at this hour of the night, again appear. Phyllis' taunt about his young mother leads Strephon to explain that he is only half mortal. Phyllis bursts into tears, saying that she would rather have half a mortal she loves than half a dozen that she does not love. Strephon suggests that she had better stick to her mortals, for there would be too many difficulties with him. For one thing, his grandmother and his aunts look as young as his mother! Phyllis says that she understands: whenever she sees him kissing a young lady she'll know it's an elderly relative. So they agree to get married at once—before they change their minds— saying ". . . we'll get married first—and change our minds afterward." Iolanthe enters, and they ask her to intercede for them with the Lord Chancellor. That exalted personage also arrives on the scene, exulting over the great victory he has won with himself—he has at last succeeded in persuading himself to give his consent to his marriage with Phyllis! The young people withdraw, and Iolanthe appeals to the Chancellor on behalf of the lovers.

The Peers and Strephon enter. When the Queen raises her spear, the Lord Chancellor and Strephon beg her to be merciful. Leila and Celia rush forward, Leila crying, "Hold! If Iolanthe must die, so must we all, for as she has sinned, so have we!" And now it is revealed that all the fairies have married Peers! The Queen is forced to admit that she cannot "slaughter the whole company!" Yet, as she unrolls a scroll, she says the law is clear: "every fairy must die who marries a mortal!" But the keen legal mind of the Lord Chancellor is equal to the emergency. Let every fairy die who doesn't marry a mortal, he proposes. This pleases the Queen, and she alters the scroll. Then to save herself she happily asks Private Willis if he will marry her at once. True British soldier that he is, he declares himself ever willing to "save a female in distress." By Her Majesty's command, wings now spring from the shoulders of Private Willis and all the Peers. They too have become immortals! Triumphantly the Queen cries, "Away we go to fairyland!"

THE RCA-VICTOR RECORDS
(Sung in English)

COMPLETE RECORDING: *D'Oyly Carte Company; Dr. Malcolm Sargent, Cond.; under the personal direction of Rupert D'Oyly Carte. (The cast includes: Bertha Lewis, Alice Moxon, Beatrice Elburn, Nellie Briercliffe, Winifred* *Lawson, Nellie Walker, George Baker, Leslie Rands, Derek Oldham, Darrell Fancourt, Sydney Granville.)*

DC-10 (12905-12915), 11-12"
C-10 (9708-9718)

Manuel

THE JUGGLER SEES BONIFACE

Le Jongleur de Nôtre Dame

(THE JUGGLER OF OUR LADY)

OPERA OR, as in the French, "miracle" in three acts. Music by Jules Massenet. Libretto by Maurice Léna, after a story in Anatole France's *L'Étui de nacre* based on a medieval miracle play. First performance, Monte Carlo, February 18, 1902. First American performance, Manhattan Opera House, New York, November 27, 1908, with Mary Garden, Maurice Renaud, and Hector Dufranne.

This opera is said to owe its existence to the fact that a certain concierge in Paris fell ill and took a day off, thereby obliging M. Massenet to collect his own mail. Otherwise the libretto would have gone the way of hundreds of librettos continually showered upon the successful composer. For Massenet, it is a unique work; excepting the brief passage for angels, it is written entirely for men's voices. Massenet had written such a long line of heroine operas—*Thaïs, Hérodiade, Manon*—that he was accused of being an *effeminate* composer. Perhaps, as Mr. Henry T. Finck suggests, he was piqued at this, and wished to show his critics he could write an opera omitting the fair sex. If that be true, there is irony in the fact that he later adapted the role of the juggler for Mary Garden, and that since that date the work—like many another of Massenet's—has become familiar to American audiences as a prima-donna opera.

CHARACTERS

JEAN, *the juggler*	*Tenor or Soprano*	THE MONK MUSICIAN	*Baritone*
BONIFACE, *cook of the monastery*	*Baritone*	THE MONK POET	*Tenor*
THE PRIOR	*Bass*	THE MONK SCULPTOR	*Bass*
THE MONK PAINTER	*Baritone*		

AN APPARITION OF THE VIRGIN, TWO ANGELS, A KNIGHT, A JOVIAL FELLOW, A DRUNKEN MAN, A MONK CRIER, MONKS, KNIGHTS, CITIZENS, PEASANTS, MERCHANTS AND THEIR WIVES, CLERGYMEN, AND BEGGARS

The action takes place at Cluny, near Paris, in the fourteenth century

223

ACT I

SCENE: *A Square Before the Abbey of Cluny.* It is May Day at Cluny, and a merry crowd is gathered on this market day before the gates of the monastery. Jean, announcing himself as "King of Jugglers," haggard and worn from illness, and weak from lack of food, begs leave to entertain them. They scoff at his sorry appearance; nor do they wish his tricks; instead they demand his famous "Hallelujah of Wine," a sacrilegious mock litany. At the height of the performance, the prior of the monastery appears and wrathfully disperses the crowd. After threatening Jean with the torments of hell, he suggests that the mountebank enter the monastery. Although Jean loves his freedom, the sight of Boniface, cook at the abbey, leading home a mule heavily laden with good things for the table of the brothers, is too much; he is soon converted.

ACT II

SCENE: *The Hall of Study Within the Abbey.* Life in the abbey agrees with him physically, but his constant jests and gross delight in the things of the table scandalize as well as amuse his fellow monks. He strives to sing with the choir, but he cannot grasp the Latin; how should a poor juggler know the language of the saints? The monks, striving in vain to teach him their various arts, fall to quarreling as to which is the greater, painting or sculpture; the good prior is obliged to conduct them to the chapel, there to study art in a spirit of prayer and devotion. Poor Jean is grieved by his ignorance; to console him the cook tells him that anything done well is good in the sight of the Lord. To convince him of this he sings the "Legend of the Sage," in which he tells him of the devotion of a humble flower.

The eyes of the old monk soften as he tells the quaint story of the rose that refused to shelter the little child Jesus from the wrath of Herod for fear of staining its lovely petals, and the humble sage flower that undertook the task cheerfully and became blessed among flowers. Jean listens open-mouthed. Is it possible that even the low gift of the juggler may be acceptable in the eyes of the Blessed Virgin?

ACT III

SCENE: *In the Chapel of the Abbey.* Jean appears before the altar in the dim chapel. Dressed in his juggler's costume he performs his tricks and sings his villainous songs; finally, he breaks into a wild dance. The good Boniface, understanding the feverish earnestness of the juggler's manner, has, with difficulty, been restraining the horrified monks who have been looking on. As Jean collapses in prayer before the altar, Boniface points to a strange glow of light upon the face of the Virgin, who slowly stretches forth her hands in benediction. "A miracle!" cry the monks, devoutly sinking to their knees. The chapel is flooded with a mystic glow, and the face of Jean is transfigured. While the monks pray for the passing of a soul, from above floats the chanting of angels. "At last," cries the dying juggler, "at last I can understand Latin!"

MARY GARDEN AS THE JUGGLER

THE RCA-VICTOR RECORDS
(Sung in French)

ACT II

LÉGENDE DE LA SAUGE (Legend of the Sage) : *Marcel Journet, Bass, with Orch.* 6785, 12"

French Poster
DEATH OF THE JUGGLER

Morton & Co.   ACT I—SAN FRANCISCO OPERA PRODUCTION

La Juive
(THE JEWESS)

OPERA IN five acts by Jacques Halévy. Libretto by Eugène Scribe. First performance at the Paris Opéra, February 23, 1835. American *première*, Théâtre d'Orléans, New Orleans, February 13, 1844. First performance, in German, at the Metropolitan Opera House, with Leopold Damrosch conducting, during the season of 1884–85. First Metropolitan performance in French, with Enrico Caruso as Eléazar and Rosa Ponselle as Rachel, November 22, 1919. Eléazar was Caruso's last role. Moreover, the performance of *La Juive* of December 24, 1920, marked his farewell to the stage. The illness that forced him to stop singing proved fatal. Death came to the beloved tenor the following August 2 in his native Naples.

Rossini is said to have rejected the libretto of *La Juive*. Its appeal for Halévy, who had been reared in a devout Jewish home, was irresistible. This was an opportunity to give authentic and dramatic expression to a tragic and passionate theme, a chance to voice in enduring music the brave defiance of a fiery conviction, the ringing challenge of the Jew Eléazar in death. The celebrated French tenor, Adolphe Nourrit, was responsible for the fact that the role of the elderly Eléazar is written for tenor, rather than for baritone or bass. Weary of the saber-rattling gallantry of many tenor roles, he prevailed on Halévy to write the part for high voice. Moreover, the words of the greatest aria in the opera, Eléazar's *"Rachel! quand du Seigneur,"* are supposed to have been written by him. Great tenors like Mario, Caruso, and Martinelli have shown a special fondness for the role of the valiant Jewish goldsmith and have gone to great pains to observe faithfully every aspect of the religious issue involved. In studying the role Caruso consulted rabbinical authorities on the precise detail of dress and gesture. It is said that even the most devout Jew could not detect any lapse from orthodox form in his portrayal.

CHARACTERS

CARDINAL BROGNY, *presiding at the Council of Constance*	Bass	RACHEL, *his daughter*	Soprano
LEOPOLD, *prince of the realm*	Tenor	RUGGIERO, *chief bailiff of Constance*	Baritone
EUDOXIE, *the emperor's niece, and Leopold's betrothed*	Soprano	ALBERT, *an officer of the imperial guard*	Bass
ELÉAZAR, *a Jewish goldsmith*	Tenor	EMPEROR SIGISMUND	*(a silent role)*

226

COURTIERS, PRIESTS, SOLDIERS, POPULACE

The action takes place in Constance at the time of the historic Council in 1414

ACT I

SCENE: *The Square Before the Cathedral of Constance.* By order of Emperor Sigismund, a great festivity is in progress in the city of Constance for the recent victories of Prince Leopold in his battles with the Hussites. A *"Te Deum"* is being sung in the cathedral. Outside, an excited crowd is rejoicing over the news. All are jubilant, all except Eléazar, the Jewish goldsmith who plies his trade in a corner shop, oblivious of the festive atmosphere.

The sight of Eléazar hard at work on a holiday arouses the crowd's indignation. People rush to the shop and drag Eléazar and his beautiful daughter, Rachel, out into the street. Eléazar protests that the holiday really does not concern him, a non-Christian, that no disrespect was intended. But this only brings a warning of death from the chief bailiff, Ruggiero, and guards are summoned to lead the hapless couple away. The sudden appearance of Cardinal Brogny, who has just left the cathedral, quiets the irate mob. As the Cardinal approaches Eléazar, they recognize one another. From the whispers they exchange we learn that as a private citizen in Rome Brogny had instigated a pogrom in which Eléazar's two sons were slain; that later Brogny's wife and daughter were lost after their house in Rome mysteriously burned down. A prince of the Church now, Cardinal Brogny is in a position to order the crowd to release Eléazar and Rachel. To Eléazar he proposes that the past be forgotten and offers the goldsmith his friendship. This the aged Jew will not accept, for what he has suffered cannot be blotted out so easily. The Cardinal, in a solemn cavatina—extending over an extremely wide range—prays to heaven to pardon these nonbelievers and bring them to the true faith. The people applaud his pious hopes and soon disperse.

The square is now empty. Prince Leopold, disguised in simple, black garb, approaches. Masquerading as a Jewish painter named Samuel, he has been paying court to Rachel. The lovers meet, and Rachel asks him to come that night to her father's house to celebrate the feast of the Passover with them. Leopold agrees. Again the square is swarming with merrymakers. Innocently Eléazar and Rachel watch the festivities from the cathedral steps. Ruggiero, still scheming to destroy them, finds their presence offensive and incites the crowd to mistreat them. Leopold rushes to the aid of the couple, speaks a few commanding words, and the violence subsides. Rachel, marveling at this show of authority, is certain now that her fiancé is not what he pretends to be. The imperial procession passes through the square, accompanied by the cheers of the crowd, and presently the *"Te Deum"* sounds again. Meanwhile, Leopold, hiding his face, steals away.

La Juive

ACT II—SAN FRANCISCO OPERA PRODUCTION

ACT II

SCENE: *A Room in Eléazar's House*. The feast of the Passover is being celebrated in Eléazar's home. A group of faithful Jews, all friends of the goldsmith, are seated about the table, engaged in the ritual of the religious holiday. Eléazar leads in singing the prayer of the occasion, "O God, God of our
fathers!" Leopold is also present among the celebrants, having kept his
promise to Rachel, whom he cannot dismiss from his thoughts. When the
time comes in the ritual to eat the sacred bread, Leopold, to Rachel's horror,
lets his portion fall under the plate. Continuing his prayer, Eléazar raises
his voice in supplication: may God hear him and stretch out a mighty hand
to his afflicted people!

Suddenly there is a knock at the door, followed by a cry to open in the
name of the emperor. The gathered Jews start with fear and hastily put the
sacramental tableware out of sight. The door is opened, and the Princess
Eudoxie enters. In the weak candlelight of the room, she does not recognize
Leopold. Eudoxie has come to tell Eléazar that she wishes to purchase a very
special jewel for the victorious prince and requests him to deliver it the following day. After she departs, Rachel takes Leopold to one side and demands
an explanation of his strange conduct. When the feast is over and they are
alone, Leopold finally reveals to her that he has lied, that he is not Samuel,
the Jewish painter, but a Christian. Rachel is dazed at first, but her love is too
strong, and when Leopold proposes that they elope, she assents. At that moment Eléazar surprises them and grows furious on learning the truth about
Rachel's suitor. As he raises a dagger and makes for Leopold, Rachel intercedes. Eléazar relents as Rachel explains how much they love one another.

228

Finally, he agrees to their marriage, but at the word marriage, Leopold starts, cries out in anguish that he cannot wed a Jewess, and dashes out the door, barely escaping Eléazar's dagger thrust.

ACT III

SCENE: *The Great Hall in the Imperial Palace.* Prince Leopold, conqueror of the Hussites, is being feted in a huge hall glittering with decorations. The emperor and his nobles are at the banquet table, with the prince seated beside the Princess Eudoxie. Eléazar and Rachel enter, bringing a gold chain, the jewel ordered by the princess. As the prince kneels to have her place it about his neck, Rachel, recognizing him, rushes forward and wrenches the chain from her hands, screaming that Leopold is unworthy of such an honor. He has committed a grave offense, she tells the startled assembly—the crime of pledging eternal faith to a Jewess! That Jewess is . . . herself, Rachel, daughter of the goldsmith Eléazar! To music tense with terrifying drama, the Cardinal rises and, after calling down the curse of heaven upon all Jews, excommunicates Leopold. All three are condemned to death and thrown into prison. The Cardinal's dread malediction still rings in the ears of the horrified guests, "May their last remains be left without a tomb!"

ACT IV

SCENE: *A Hall in the Court of Justice.* Eudoxie has received the emperor's permission to have Rachel brought before her. The princess implores the

Franklin & Rognon   ACT III—SAN FRANCISCO OPERA PRODUCTION

girl to testify in Leopold's defense, and Rachel, thinking of the man she loves, yields to her pleas. She will take the guilt upon herself alone and clear the faithless Leopold. The Cardinal enters, and makes a new proposal: let Eléazar and his daughter become Christians and they will be saved from death. Eléazar wrathfully refuses. Whatever happens he will cling to the faith of his fathers. But he vows to the Cardinal that before he dies he will have his revenge. Does the Cardinal remember the horrible day in Rome when he lost his wife and daughter? Well, that daughter still lives, but only he, Eléazar the Jew, knows where she is. This much he can divulge—a Jew had saved her from death! The Cardinal, taken aback, pleads with Eléazar to reveal the name of this man, but Eléazar swears no power on earth will draw the secret from him. The Cardinal leaves, profoundly shaken by Eléazar's words. Alone, Eléazar now appeals to heaven for guidance. Must Rachel be sacrificed with him? Yes, she is the Cardinal's daughter, not his. But he, Eléazar, has brought her up as his own, loves her as his own flesh and blood. In a moving monologue, *"Rachel! quand du Seigneur"* ("Rachel! when the grace of God"), he ponders the plight of the helpless girl. Now he remembers how he had vowed to give her shelter and protection, and it is he, her guardian, who is yielding her to death. To add to his anguish, the piteous voice of Rachel seems to whisper, "No, Father, I am young; let me live! Set your daughter free!" Eléazar, wrenched by conflicting emotions, wonders whether he should reveal his secret. But outside, the crowd is clamoring for blood, demanding death for the Jews. Eléazar knows there is no salvation for either himself or Rachel.

ACT V

SCENE: *A Place of Execution in a Street in Constance.* A horrible death is being prepared for the condemned prisoners. In the center of the street stands a huge caldron of boiling oil. Eléazar and Rachel await their end with defiant fortitude. Leopold is nowhere to be seen, and Rachel now divulges her secret to Eléazar: she has saved Leopold by assuming sole guilt. Eléazar is horrified by this unexpected turn, though after a pause he reminds Rachel that there is still time to save herself by becoming a Christian. Rachel shakes her head. She would rather die in her faith by the side of her father. The Cardinal again beseeches Eléazar to reveal the whereabouts of his daughter, but Eléazar refuses. At length, as Rachel climbs the steps and is thrown into the seething caldron, Eléazar, in wild disdain, shouts to the horror-struck Cardinal, *"There* is your daughter!"

La Juive

Mishkin

GIOVANNI MARTINELLI AS ELÉAZAR

THE RCA-VICTOR RECORDS
(Sung in French)

ACT I

CAVATINE—SI LA RIGUEUR ET LA VEN-
GEANCE (Although Oppressed): *Ezio
Pinza, Bass, with Orch.* 1246, 10"

ACT II

PASSOVER SCENE—O DIEU, DIEU DE NOS
PÈRES (O God, God of Our Fathers);
SI TRAHISON (If Treachery or Trea-
son): *Jan Peerce, Tenor; Dorothy
Sarnoff, Soprano; with Chorus and
Orch.* 18401, 12"

DIEU, QUE MA VOIX TREMBLANTE (God,
May My Trembling Voice): *Giovanni
Martinelli, Tenor, with Orch.*
6545, 12"

ACT III

MALÉDICTION—VOUS QUI DU DIEU VIVANT
(You Who Have the Clemency): *Ezio
Pinza, Bass, with Orch.* 1246, 10"

ACT IV

RACHEL! QUAND DU SEIGNEUR LA GRÂCE
TUTÉLAIRE (Rachel, When the Grace
of God Entrusted You to Me): *Giovanni Martinelli, Tenor, with Orch.*
6545, 12"

Enrico Caruso, Tenor, with Orch.
(Acoustical Recording) 15-1004, 12"

*Jan Peerce, Tenor; RCA-Victor Orches-
tra, Erich Leinsdorf, Cond.*
MO-1250 (12-0498-A)
VO-22 (18-0176-A)

231

THE STRELTSY

Khovantchina

MUSICAL DRAMA in five acts. Music by Modest Moussorgsky, completed, revised, and orchestrated by Rimsky-Korsakov. Libretto by the composer and Vladimir Stassov, after Pushkin's play. First performance (amateur) by the Musical Dramatic Club, St. Petersburg, February 21, 1886. First public performance, Kiev, November 7, 1892. American *première*, in English, Philadelphia, April 18, 1928. New York *première*, March 7, 1931, in Russian.

Like *Boris Godunov, Khovantchina* has for the basis of its text events in the history of Russia, in this case the struggle between the old and the new that took place at the close of the seventeenth century. A variety of typical characters are brought into relief: Dositheus, the sincere and devout leader of the sect of Old Believers; Ivan Khovantsky, representative of the half-Oriental, fanatical, and conservative Russia; Galitzin, who strives for the introduction of European culture in his country; Marfa, the passionate and mystical Old Believer; the dissolute Andrei Khovantsky; Emma, the German girl; the fierce Streltsy; the down-trodden and suffering populace. The Old Believers, around whom much of the action centers, were a sect who, clinging to the old, though inaccurate version, broke away from the Orthodox Church when a revision of the Bible was introduced in 1655. Also during this period the Tsars were removing many of the privileges that had formerly been granted the nobility. This was resented and was fought against by the nobles. Hence the struggle of the Prince Khovantsky and his bodyguard, the Streltsy. The score was not quite complete at Moussorgsky's death, although it had already grown to monumental length. Rimsky-Korsakov therefore revised, completed, orchestrated, and reduced it to a length suitable for performance; tasks for which his great knowledge of orchestration, his practical stage experience, and his intimate friendship with the composer made him eminently fitted. Certainly, whatever the ultimate verdict on Rimsky-Korsakov's work as a reviser may be, none can deny him the deepest gratitude for having thus made available some of Moussorgsky's most beautiful and characteristic pages.

CHARACTERS

PRINCE IVAN KHOVANTSKY, *commander of the Streltsy*	*Bass*	THE BOYAR SHAKLOVITY	*Baritone*
		DOSITHEUS, *head of the Old*	
ANDREI KHOVANTSKY, *his son*	*Tenor*	*Believers*	*Bass*
PRINCE VASSILY GALITZIN, *a representative of Young Russia*	*Tenor*	MARFA, *a young widow*	*Mezzo-soprano*
		EMMA, *a young girl*	*Contralto*

ARCHERS, PERSIAN SLAVES, TOWNSPEOPLE, ETC.

The action takes place during the reign of Peter the Great (1682–1725)

The orchestra plays a brief prelude—a remarkable musical picture, thoroughly Russian in character, of dawn in Moscow.

ACT I

SCENE: *The Red Square in the Kremlin.* Here are gathered a group of Streltsy, one of whom, lying near a pillar, mumbles sleepily about an attack of the previous evening in which many deeds of violence took place. A scribe enters to take up his daily stand; after making a few gibes at his expense, the Streltsy leave. The Boyar Shaklovity enters and bribes the scrivener into writing a denunciation of the Khovantskys for plotting against the throne. In a short time the elder Khovantsky (Ivan) arrives and shows by his arrogant commands that he is indeed ambitious. After the crowd has departed, Emma runs in. This girl is hotly pursued by the younger Khovantsky (Andrei), whose attentions she in vain tries to avoid. At the climax of their scene, Marfa, a discarded love of Andrei's, enters, protects Emma from his unwelcome embraces, and in one of her strange trances prophesies his ultimate fate. The elder Khovantsky returns, takes a fancy to Emma, and orders his followers to arrest her. Father and son quarrel jealously over the girl. Fortunately, Dositheus enters at this moment, rebukes the men for their violence, and restores peace.

ACT II

SCENE: *The Prince Galitzin's Home.* Prince Galitzin, in spite of his European education, is superstitious and has Marfa summoned to tell his horoscope.

Marfa, having filled a silver goblet with water, calls upon the spirits of the underworld in the uncanny, mysterious first part of her "Divination." Then, gazing into the bowl, she foresees Galitzin's future: his power and riches will avail him naught, for he shall be overcome by poverty and sorrow. Galitzin is frightened at this and secretly orders a servant to drown Marfa in a marsh near by. Khovantsky enters, and their ensuing bitter dispute is quelled only by the timely arrival of Dositheus.

ACT III

SCENE: *A Street Near Andrei Khovantsky's Home.* Marfa, having escaped the drowning ordered for her, is seated near Andrei Khovantsky's home, and recalls her passion for him. Susan, a fanatic Old Believer, reproves her for singing shameless love songs and threatens to denounce her as a witch. Dositheus again restores peace. Night falls, and along the street, now deserted, comes Shaklovity. Gazing over the slumbering city, he exclaims: "Yes, the Streltsy are sleeping"; then, thinking of this harassed country, he continues, saying that while Russia sleeps her enemies waken, the enemies who would strike her down without mercy. Then, singing a broad, noble melody, he prays for divine guidance for his native land.

The Streltsy now enter and are encountered by their womenfolk, who soundly berate them for their conduct. The quarrel is interrupted by the scribe, running in breathlessly to report that the revolt of the Tsar's guard has been suppressed . . . foreign troops and Peter the Great's bodyguard have arrived—the cause of Old Russia is lost. The Streltsy kneel in prayer.

ACT IV

SCENE 1: *Ivan Khovantsky's Country House.* Prince Ivan Khovantsky is at his country house, being diverted by the songs of his serving maids and the wild, impassioned dances of his Persian slaves.

Shaklovity appears, summoning him to the Tsarina's council. As Prince Ivan, in his robes of ceremony, crosses the threshold, he is stabbed and drops dead.

Entr'acte: Before the curtain rises on Scene 2, the orchestra plays music of a mournful nature, as if it were accompanying an intensely solemn processional.

SCENE 2: *Square Before the Bizarre Church of Vassily Blajeny.* Forcing his way through the lamenting populace, Galitzin, under guard, is led to exile—Marfa's words are being fulfilled. The people follow the procession, the music dies away, and the square remains empty. The orchestral music of this scene is highly descriptive of the action.

Dositheus approaches, soliloquizing on Russia's unhappy condition. Marfa comes to him with the news that the foreign mercenaries have been ordered to trap the Old Believers in their meeting place and execute them. Dositheus declares that they would sooner immolate themselves; he charges Marfa to bring Prince Andrei among them. When, however, the Prince learns that Emma has been safely married to her lover, he curses Marfa as a witch and vainly attempts to summon the Streltsy to put her to death. Vainly, for the Streltsy, themselves condemned, enter, bearing axes and blocks for their own execution. At the last moment, however, word comes that the Tsar has pardoned them.

ACT V

SCENE: *A Wood Near Moscow*. The Old Believers have assembled by moonlight at their meeting place in the woods near Moscow. Dositheus urges them to remain faithful, and Marfa prays for the soul of her beloved Andrei, who, urged by her great devotion, mounts the pyre that the white-robed brethren have built for themselves. The soldiers are heard approaching, and Marfa lights the pyre. The soldiers recoil in horror at the sight of the self-immolation of the Old Believers, who continue their chant until overcome by the flames, while a blare of trumpets announces the passing of the old and the dawn of a new day for Russia.

THE RCA-VICTOR RECORDS

PRELUDE: *Boston Symphony Orchestra, Serge Koussevitsky, Cond.*   14415, 12″

Rialto Studio THE COURT OF KING EADGAR

The King's Henchman

OPERA IN three acts; music by Deems Taylor; libretto by Edna St. Vincent Millay. First produced, February 17, 1927, at the Metropolitan Opera House, New York.

Deems Taylor, born December 22, 1885, in New York, began his career, not as a musician, but rather as a journalist, connected with various New York newspapers. He had, however, studied piano, harmony, and counterpoint, and though self-taught in composition, several cantatas and orchestral works brought him a growing reputation as a composer, a reputation that developed into fame with the success of *The King's Henchman*, his first opera. Just credit must also be given to Edna St. Vincent Millay, one of the most distinguished of contemporary poets, for the librettist's share of this success. Miss Millay here shows her ability as a dramatic poet. The plot, said to be based on an early Anglo-Saxon chronicle, is appropriately narrated in an old Saxon style of language; there is effective characterization, an abundance of humorous detail, and genuine poetic beauty. Mr. Taylor has provided music, modern, though not ultramodern, in character, and splendidly orchestrated. His score is adapted closely to the action after the manner of Wagner, and, at times, of Debussy, and, particularly in the last act, is of great dramatic force.

CHARACTERS

EADGAR OF WESSEX, *King of England*	*Baritone*	THORED, *Master of the Household to Ordgar*	*Baritone*
ÆTHELWOLD, *Earl of East Anglia, friend and foster brother of Eadgar*	*Tenor*	HWITA, *cupbearer to Eadgar*	*Tenor*
		LORD GUNNER	*Tenor*
ORDGAR, *Thane of Devon*	*Bass*	LORD BRAND	*Baritone*
MACCUS, *Master of Horse to Æthelwold*	*Bass*	LORD CYNRIC	*Baritone*
		LORD WULFRED	*Baritone*
ÆLFRIDA, *Ordgar's daughter*	*Soprano*	LORD OSLAC	*Bass*
ASE, *her servant*	*Mezzo-soprano*	LADY GODGYFU	*Soprano*
		LADY HILDEBURGH	*Soprano*
DUNSTAN, *Archbishop of Canterbury*	*Tenor*	LADY LEOFSYDU	*Soprano*
		LADY OSTHARU	*Soprano*

EADGAR'S MEN-AT-ARMS, OTHER NOBLES AND LADIES, SERVANTS OF EADGAR'S COURT AND ORDGAR'S HOUSEHOLD, DEVONSHIRE VILLAGERS, ETC.

The action takes place in England in the tenth century

ACT I

SCENE: *Hall of King Eadgar's Castle at Winchester.* Great feasting and revelry are in progress at the court of King Eadgar. Maccus is singing a rugged old lay of warriors and battle and in return receives praises of the courtiers. King Eadgar, long a widower, has heard of a wonderful beauty, Ælfrida, who lives at Devon, and has determined to make her his wife and queen, should reports of her beauty be true. The kingdom is in such turmoil, however, because of an ecclesiastical disturbance, that Eadgar cannot well leave his court. He has therefore determined to send his friend and foster brother, Æthelwold, a brave warrior, but young and inexperienced in the ways of women. For this reason Æthelwold is reluctant, but finally, because of his affection for the King, promises to go. Eadgar and Æthelwold pledge friendship according to the old Saxon rite, both drinking from the same cup of wine. Day is beginning to break, and there is a sudden stir as the men of Æthelwold's retinue ride past the door. In the excitement of departure, Maccus begins a song, bold in melody and sturdy in rhythm; Æthelwold and the courtiers join in the refrain: "O Caesar, great wert thou!"

The song, while celebrating the prowess of various Caesars, concludes with the characteristic sentiment that Caesar's day is over while that of Britain has just begun. The song ended, Æthelwold and Maccus mount their horses and ride away, while the courtiers sing, "Farewell."

There is an orchestral introduction to the next act.

ACT II

SCENE: *A Devonsire Forest on Allhallows' Eve.* During a dense fog, Æthelwold and his trusted friend and servant, Maccus, become separated from their men and lost in the forest. They wander for hours mistakingly believing themselves far from their destination. Finally, Æthelwold lies down to sleep while Maccus continues searching for their followers.

Ælfrida approaches, a bit frightened, it is true, although she is accompanied by her serving woman, Ase. It is Halloween, and she has come to discover, by an ancient rune, who her future husband is to be. Having found a suitable spot near by, she sends Ase away, and sings an incantation. While she sings, the fog clears and she beholds Æthelwold asleep on the ground. The charm has worked! Trembling with fear, yet fascinated by this handsome youth, she bends over him and kisses him gently.

Æthelwold awakens, greatly startled, and likewise believes that this is some supernatural creature whom he sees, and whose presence has aroused a strange emotion in him. When the two have convinced one another that

237

they are both mortal, they find themselves already desperately in love. Their happiness in one another's arms is cut short, however, by Ase, who from a distance calls Ælfrida by name. Ælfrida hurries away for a moment, and Æthelwold, shaken with horror and dismay at learning her identity, would hurry off, never to return; but while he is yet near Ælfrida calls him. He is powerless to resist, and he bids Maccus go to the King and say that Ælfrida is indeed not beautiful, but rich, and that Æthelwold, who is poor, craves the King's consent to marry her.

ACT III

SCENE: *Hall of Ordgar's House on the Coast of Devonshire.* Though seeming to be happily married, Æthelwold is secretly tormented by thoughts of his treachery to his friend and King; and for Ælfrida the first charm of marriage has begun to fade; she is discontented in spite of her love for Æthelwold. She had expected that with the King's foster brother for a husband, she would at least go to the court, not remain thus buried at her father's house in Devonshire. Now, on this spring morning, Æthelwold yields to her entreaties and, with a show of his former decisiveness, promises he will take her away; they shall go to the great city of Ghent, in Flanders, a city of Ælfrida's dreams. Yet close upon this resolve, Maccus enters, saying that the King approaches with his retinue. In dismay, Æthelwold confesses his deception, and begs Ælfrida for the sake of their love to disguise herself as though she were both ugly and crippled, then to remain in her chamber under the pretext that she is ill; he will conduct Eadgar there to see her. Ælfrida is angry for a moment, knowing now that she might have had the King for husband. As things are, she will not even be seen by him in her real beauty! Yet, fearing for Æthelwold's safety, she promises. Ase, who has overheard their conversation, whispers to Ælfrida not to be so weak as thus to ruin her chances; but Ælfrida replies that she will keep her promise, and the two go to her room.

A crowd of villagers hurry in, excited at the thought of seeing the King. Soon after, Eadgar arrives with his retinue. He has come on a friendly visit, not even suspecting Æthelwold's deception. After a few words of greeting, Æthelwold tells his lord that Ælfrida is ill and may not leave her quarters. Presently they turn to go to Ælfrida's chamber. At that moment, the door opens, and before them stands Ælfrida, proud and radiantly beautiful in her fairest gown and jewels. Eadgar is at first dazed; then realizing the truth, grieves at his friend's faithlessness, while, in the deepest remorse, Æthelwold draws his dagger and stabs himself. As he falls dying, the faithful Maccus catches and gently supports him, while Eadgar, who has not stirred from the spot where he stood when first he beheld Ælfrida, solemnly walks over and, gazing down upon his friend, bids Maccus lay him down. He sings a noble threnody for the departed, "Doughty of heart was he." The people reply in a beautiful refrain. While they sing, the body of Æthelwold is taken up and borne away in great solemnity, but Ælfrida is left to follow alone, in contrition and despair.

THE RCA-VICTOR RECORDS
(Sung in English)

ACT III

NAY, MACCUS, LAY HIM DOWN: *Lawrence Tibbett, Baritone; Metropolitan Opera Chorus and Orch.*
11-8932, 12"
(In Album M-1015)

R. Strohmeyer   ACT I—SAN FRANCISCO OPERA PRODUCTION

Lakmé

OPÉRA COMIQUE in three acts. Music by Léo Delibes. Libretto by Edmond Gondinet and Philippe Gille, based on the romance, *Le Mariage de Loti*. First performance at the Paris Opéra-Comique, April 14, 1883. American *première*, in English, at the New York Academy of Music, with Theodore Thomas conducting, March 1, 1886. First performed by the Metropolitan Opera Company, in Italian, with Adelina Patti, April 2, 1890; in French, with Marie van Zandt (the original Lakmé), February 22, 1892. Among the great interpreters of Lakmé have been Adelina Patti, Marie van Zandt, Marcella Sembrich, Luisa Tetrazzini, Amelita Galli-Curci, and, in recent years at the Metropolitan, Lily Pons.

The story of *Lakmé* shows many points of similarity with other repertory operas. Like *Aïda*, *L'Africaine*, and *Madama Butterfly*, it is more or less Oriental in setting and color. Like Aïda, Lakmé is in love with her country's enemy. Nilakantha of *Lakmé* and Nelusko of *L'Africaine* have many vengeful traits in common. Both Lakmé and Selika (*L'Africaine*) poison themselves botanically, the former using the blossoms of the stramonium weed, the latter by inhaling the deadly perfume of the manchineel tree. Its resemblance with *Madama Butterfly*, of course, lies in the tragic denouement of a romance of East and West. Delibes wrote the role of Lakmé for van Zandt, the gifted and beautiful Brooklyn girl who had so fascinated the composer Massenet. A story still lingers in the gossip annals of opera that Marie van Zandt's career in Paris ended some years later when she appeared on the stage slightly wobbly from overdrinking. The story has been ascribed to the malicious jealousies of rival sopranos who tried to prevent her success in Lakmé. Despite the intrigues preceding the *première*, van Zandt's performance in Delibes' Hindu opera was a phenomenal triumph.

CHARACTERS

GERALD, *a British officer*	Tenor	ROSE, *her friend*	Soprano
FRÉDÉRIC, *his friend, also a*		MRS. BENSON, *governess of the*	
British officer	Baritone	young ladies	Mezzo-soprano
NILAKANTHA, *a Brahman priest*	Bass	MALLIKA, *slave of Lakmé*	Mezzo-soprano
HADJI, *a Hindu slave*	Tenor	A FORTUNETELLER	
LAKMÉ, *daughter of Nilakantha*	Soprano	A CHINESE MERCHANT	
ELLEN, *daughter of the Governor*	Soprano	A SEPOY	

240

Lakmé

HINDUS, MEN AND WOMEN, ENGLISH OFFICERS AND LADIES, SAILORS, BAYADERES, CHINAMEN, MUSICIANS, BRAHMANS, ETC.

The action takes place in India in the middle of the nineteenth century

ACT I

SCENE: *A Garden in India.* The fanatical Brahman priest, Nilakantha, stands before the temple he guards, exhorting the gathered worshipers to have courage and await the day when the English invaders will be driven from the land. From the temple is heard the voice of a maiden in prayer— *"Blanche Durga, pâle Siva, puissant Ganeça!"* ("White Durga, pale Siva, mighty Ganesa!"). It is Lakmé, Nilakantha's daughter. The Hindus prostrate themselves, echoing the prayer devoutly. The worshipers rise and leave.

Soon a party of English sight-seers approaches, drawn by the exotic beauty of the temple and the luxuriant foliage and flowers surrounding it. Though warned by the English officer, Frédéric, the party breaks down the frail fence surrounding the temple. As they enter the garden, the girls stop to marvel at the beautiful white blossoms. "Don't touch them!" Frédéric cries. "They're *Datura stramonium,* harmless in England, but under this sky fatally poisonous!" As the visitors presently come upon some jewels left by Lakmé, they feel increasingly conscious of trespassing and prepare to leave. Gerald, another British officer, announces he will remain to sketch the dazzling jewelry they have found. Ellen, his fiancée, joins the others. Left alone, Gerald gazes delightedly at the gems, expressing his pleasure in a charming air, *"Prendre le dessin d'un bijou, est-ce donc aussi grave?"* ("Is it such a grave thing to copy the design of a jewel?")

While Gerald is busy with his sketch and song, Lakmé returns and eyes the stranger with wonder. Fascinated by the beauty of this member of a race she has been taught to hate, she fails to summon the guards who would instantly kill him. Gerald, in turn, is enchanted, and is inclined to ridicule her proffered warning of danger. Lakmé keeps urging him to leave, but Gerald replies with a rhapsodic avowal of love. Lakmé is overwhelmed, but finally persuades him to leave before her father returns. Nilakantha enters, raging over the broken fence and the profaned temple. *"Vengeance! Il faut qu'il meure!"* he cries wrathfully—"Vengeance! This man must die!" As other Hindus take up the cry of revenge, Lakmé cowers in terror.

ACT II

SCENE: *A Public Square in an Indian City.* Nilakantha and Lakmé mingle with the motley crowd of a Hindu bazaar. Nilakantha is disguised as a beggar, Lakmé as a street singer. The fanatic priest, still searching the city for

241

Lakmé

R. Strohmeyer   ACT II—THE BAZAAR—SAN FRANCISCO OPERA PRODUCTION

the temple intruder, now plans a new stratagem to lure the culprit into betraying himself. Among the crowd appears the British party, conversing gaily, looking over the teeming wares of street merchants, and watching the exotic ballet of bayaderes, the sacred dancers of the priests of Brahma. Presently Nilakantha resorts to a fiendish piece of trickery. Knowing the profaner of his temple will step forward at the sound of Lakmé's voice, he commands his daughter to sing the legend of the pathetic pariah's daughter. At first reluctant, Lakmé consents when Nilakantha assures her Brahma does not permit his believers to forget an outrage. As the entrancing "Bell Song" begins, the crowd gathers about Lakmé. She sings: *"Où va la jeune hindoue, fille des parias, quand la lune se joue dans les grands mimosas?"* ("Where goes the young Hindu girl, daughter of the pariahs, when the moon plays among the huge mimosas?") The song is one of the glories of coloratura literature, making taxing demands on vocal agility, but rewarding in its splendor of fancy and its deft effects of pseudo-Oriental color. The bells blend charmingly with the staccato flights of the high soprano voice. And for Lakmé the song about the outcast maiden has a poignant parallel in her own predicament. As the song ends, Gerald rushes forward, his ardor reviving at the sight of the Hindu girl. But Lakmé is alarmed as Gerald rapturously greets her. Nilakantha now approaches, sneaks up on the British officer, and, driving a dagger into him, escapes. Lakmé gives a frantic cry, and rushes to Gerald. Observing that the wound is not fatal, her mood brightens and in her joy she exclaims, "You are mine forever! I shall live only for you! May God protect our love!"

LILY PONS AS LAKMÉ

ACT III

SCENE: *A Forest in India.* A hut stands under a huge tree deep in a tropical forest, with brilliant flowers blooming on all sides. Here Lakmé and her slave have carried the wounded Gerald, and while he lies on a bed of leaves, Lakmé watches over him, singing soothing melodies. Gerald finally opens his eyes and greets her ecstatically in a song of dreamy beauty, *"Je me souviens, sans voix, inanimée, je te voyais sur mes lèvres penchée"* ("I remember how I saw you bent over my lips, voiceless and still"). Gerald is more enamored than ever of the lovely Hindu maiden, who is nursing him back to health. Lakmé now goes to fetch water from a sacred spring, having solemnly assured Gerald that all who drink from this spring remain forever faithful in love. During her absence Frédéric, searching anxiously for Gerald, at last finds him and greets him warmly. When he realizes how much in love his friend is with Lakmé, he reminds him of his duty to his regiment, which has been ordered away. Soon Lakmé returns, and the lovers drink the magic water. While they do so, the sound of martial music comes from the distance, and Gerald starts up eagerly at the thought of his regiment. Observing this, Lakmé now knows that her hold on the British officer is broken. Secretly she culls a blossom of the deadly *Datura stramonium* and swallows it. Nilakantha enters. Furious at the sight of Gerald near his daughter, he commands his followers to kill him, but Lakmé restrains them. "If the gods demand a victim in expiation," she cries out to her father, "let them call me!" Terrified, Nilakantha watches her reel as she exclaims to Gerald,"You have given me the sweetest dream under heaven!" Lakmé dies with a smile on her lips, as Gerald gives an anguished cry of "Dead!" Raising his head, Nilakantha declares gravely, "She is now amid the splendor of the skies."

THE RCA-VICTOR RECORDS
(Sung in French unless otherwise noted)

ACT I

PRIÈRE—BLANCHE DURGA (*O Durga bionda, proteggici*) (Prayer—O Durga Fair): *Miliza Korjus, Soprano, with Chorus and Orch. In Italian*
12136, 12"

ACT II

AIR DES CLOCHETTES—OÙ VA LA JEUNE HINDOUE? (Bell Song): *Lily Pons, Soprano, with Orch.* 1502, 10"
Miliza Korjus, Soprano, with Orch. In Italian 12136, 12"

Apex ACT I—ARRIVAL OF LOHENGRIN—SAN CARLO OPERA PRODUCTION

Lohengrin

OPERA IN three acts. Music by Richard Wagner. Libretto by the composer, based upon medieval legends. First produced at Weimar, Germany, August 28, 1850, under the direction of Franz Liszt. First American production, Stadt Theater, New York, April 3, 1871, in German. It was given in Italian at the New York Academy of Music, March 23, 1874, with a cast including Christine Nilsson as Elsa, Annie Louise Cary as Ortrud, Italo Campanini as Lohengrin, Giuseppe del Puente as Telramund, and Nannetti as the King. It was in Italian also that Lohengrin entered the Metropolitan's repertoire, the principals in the cast being Nilsson, Emmy Fursch-Madi, Campanini, Giuseppe Kaschmann, and Franco Novara. This opera has been a very popular one at the Metropolitan; Elsa has been sung there by such artists as Lillian Nordica, Emma Eames, Milka Ternina, Johanna Gadski, Emmy Destinn, Maria Jeritza, Elisabeth Rethberg, Maria Müller, Lotte Lehmann, Kirsten Flagstad, and Helen Traubel; Ortrud has been embodied by Marianne Brandt, Marie Brema, Ernestine Schumann-Heink, Louise Homer, Edyth Walker, Margarete Matzenauer, Karin Branzell, Maria Olszewska, Gertrude Kappel, Marjorie Lawrence, and Kerstin Thorborg; among the Lohengrins have been Jean de Reszke, Albert Saléza, Heinrich Knote, Lauritz Melchior, and Set Svanholm; the Telramunds include Jean Lassalle, David Bispham, Anton van Rooy, Clarence Whitehill, Friedrich Schorr, Herbert Janssen; the part of the King has had such interpreters as Édouard de Reszke, Pol Plançon, Karl Braun, Michael Bohnen, Paul Bender, Ludwig Hofmann, Emanuel List, and Norman Cordon. And among the conductors have been Anton Seidl, Luigi Mancinelli, Emil Paur, Walter Damrosch, Alfred Hertz, Artur Bodanzky, Erich Leinsdorf, Karl Riedel, and Fritz Busch.

Wagner's Rienzi had been very successful when produced at the Dresden opera; The Flying Dutchman had been something of a failure, and Tannhäuser had appealed even less to early audiences. Thus Wagner could not succeed in having his next opera, Lohengrin, produced there, even though he held the post of royal conductor at that very theater. He had completed the orchestration in March, 1848, and when in 1849 the wave of social unrest that was sweeping over Europe reached Dresden, he joined the popular uprising, believing that a more democratic form of government might improve artistic conditions. This "May Revolution," apparently successful at first, was soon suppressed by the military forces, and Wagner was compelled to make his escape from the country. An exile in Switzerland, he wrote to Franz Liszt the following April and begged him to produce *Lohengrin*. It is hard to realize at the present time the moral courage necessary for a man like Liszt to sponsor a work of Wagner's—Liszt, courted by kings, greatest of pianists, universally acknowledged, yet subject to endless criticism; Wagner, a political exile and comparatively unknown. Thanks to Liszt's friendly support, *Lohengrin* was produced at Weimar, and with more success than Wagner might have expected. The opera grew in popularity, and was performed throughout Germany, so that in the course of time, Wagner, still an exile, was able to say with some ironic truth that he was the only German who had not heard *Lohengrin*. Not until 1861, when, through the intervention of the Princess Metternich, he was permitted to return to Germany, was the composer enabled to hear his own opera, thirteen years after completing it.

To us the beauty of the score is familiar enough, but in the day of its origin it must have seemed like a strange language—this music which shows Wagner making another step in advance of *Tannhäuser* in the development of his style even as in *Tannhäuser* he had progressed beyond *The Flying Dutchman*. Here Wagner also reveals his increasing ability as a dramatist, for he made of the old legend with which he dealt a much more dramatic and human story than one would have expected. The character, Lohengrin, is a symbol of the man who, in Wagner's own words, seeks "the woman who would not call for explanations or defense, but who should love him with an unconditioned love."

CHARACTERS

HENRY THE FOWLER, *King of Germany*	Bass	FREDERICK OF TELRAMUND, *Count of Brabant*	Baritone
LOHENGRIN, *a Knight of the Grail*	Tenor	ORTRUD, *his wife*	Contralto
ELSA OF BRABANT	Soprano	THE KING'S HERALD	Bass
		DUKE GODFREY	Mime

SAXON, THURINGIAN, AND BRABANTIAN COUNTS AND NOBLES, LADIES OF HONOR, PAGES, ATTENDANTS

The action takes place at Antwerp during the first half of the tenth century

The Prelude, an epitome of the entire opera and one of Wagner's great inspirations, has for its one and only theme the "Grail," the sacred vessel of the Last Supper. The "story" of the Prelude, briefly told, is this: In the wonderful blue of the sky, a vision appears: angels bearing the Grail. Gradually coming earthward, its effulgent glory is shed on the worshiper who kneels transported in ecstasy. The celestial vision then recedes and disappears into the blue of the sky. This is wonderfully expressed in the Prelude with its gradual crescendo, magnificent climax, and ethereal close.

ACT I

SCENE: *The Banks of the Scheldt River, Near Antwerp.* Seated upon a throne beneath the Oak of Justice is Henry the Fowler, King of Germany. On one side of him are gathered the knights and nobles of Saxony and Thuringia; opposite them are the counts and nobles of Brabant, headed by Frederick of Telramund; beside him, his wife, Ortrud. The King has come to gather an army together, but he finds the people of Brabant torn in dis-

Morton & Co.

ACT I—SAN FRANCISCO OPERA PRODUCTION

sension. The trouble is due to the disappearance of young Duke Godfrey of Brabant, who with his sister, Elsa, lived under the care of Telramund. Telramund advances to make the charge that Elsa herself has killed the boy in the hope that she would succeed to the estate left by the elder duke. So certain is he of Elsa's guilt, says he, that he has married Ortrud instead. Telramund is indeed a knight of proved courage and loyalty, for in a fight against the Danes, he saved the life of the King. Yet Henry the Fowler is loath to believe the monstrous charge of fratricide against the girl, and commands that she shall be brought before him. Elsa, accompanied by her women attendants, approaches, a mystic look in her deep blue eyes. Replying to Telramund's charge, the King decrees that justice shall be done through ordeal by battle. Elsa is asked to name her champion. She at first declines and, when urged, replies by telling of a wonderful, mysterious vision she had, in which a knight in shining armor came to her protection. The soft, ethereal music of the Grail accompanies her words, its shimmering colors and harmonies bringing a vivid impression of her dream. Elsa exclaims in her ecstasy that this glorious knight shall be her champion.

Four trumpeters blow a summons to the four points of the compass, and the Herald calls for a champion to step forward to defend Elsa. There is no answer, but Elsa confidently declares that her champion abides in a remote place. She asks the Herald to repeat the call. In the meantime, Ortrud looks upon her with an evil gleam in her eyes. The King, however, is touched by the young girl's trust. Whereupon the Herald repeats the summons, and after a few anxious moments for Elsa, who falls to her knees in prayer, there is a commotion among the nobles nearest the river edge. Excitement seizes them; they walk up and down, peering into the distance, and presently they shout that a miracle is taking place. There is a swan drawing a boat, in the prow of which is a stalwart warrior. The radiant theme of the Deliverer, which was first heard in "Elsa's Dream," sounds in the orchestra. The people now become more and more agitated, and almost all crowd the riverbank to watch the approach of this strange knight in shining armor, as his boat is drawn shoreward by a swan.

As his strange conveyance nears the bank, the knight steps on land. He takes leave of his swan, ending his song with the words, *"Leb' wohl, leb' wohl, mein lieber Schwan"* ("Farewell, farewell, my beloved swan"). A mood of awe settles over the assemblage, who sing of the wonder of the event they have just witnessed.

The knight, having made obeisance to the King, advances to Elsa and, his gaze resting upon her radiant beauty, tells her that he has come at her summons, and asks if she will accept him as her betrothed, and Elsa, in an emotional transport, readily does.

Continuing, he declares in the utmost solemnity that if he should succeed as her champion and become her husband there is one promise she must make: she must never ask whence he came, his rank, or his name.

She promises, demurely. Again he repeats his charge; Elsa wholeheartedly accepts.

King Henry prays that the result of the combat may be heaven's own judgment. The prayer is repeated by the King and the four other principals, and, as the chorus joins them, there is a great and exciting crescendo.

The nobles warn Telramund that he may not hope to worst such a heaven-sent champion; but Telramund, urged on by his wife, will not assent. A field of battle is measured off by six nobles who solemnly stride forward and plant their spears to form a complete circle. The King beats three times with his sword upon his shield, and the fight begins. The white knight succeeds in striking Telramund to earth, but mercifully spares his life. Her innocence proved, Elsa plights her troth to the stranger amid the cheering of the crowd, while Telramund, unobserved and in disgrace, drags himself to the feet of Ortrud, who is still uncowed.

ACT II

SCENE: *In the Fortress of Antwerp.* It is night: the moon precipitates gloomy shadows off the battlements of the great castle that rises in the background. On the steps of the cathedral, at the right of the courtyard, Telramund and Ortrud, clad in the habiliments of disgrace, crouch dejectedly. Telramund irritably blames his wife for having deceived him. Skillfully she replies that this strange knight has won by magic; if he could be compelled to divulge his name and state, his power would cease. Elsa alone has the right to compel him to reveal this secret. Possessed of it, Telramund can freely fight him again, for the first loss of blood will weaken this stranger

248

Morton & Co.

ACT II—SAN FRANCISCO OPERA PRODUCTION

and reduce him to nothing. Through her magical practices she has divined all this. The last of her race, Ortrud clings to the old religion of the ancient gods, Wotan and Freia, whose wrath she now calls down upon Elsa and her champion. Telramund has listened breathlessly.

Elsa comes to her window at the left of the courtyard and confides her happiness to the nocturnal breezes, in the expressive aria, *"Euch Lüften, die mein Klagen"* ("Ye wandering breezes"). Ortrud bids Telramund be gone, then imploringly calls Elsa's name. The girl is startled at hearing her name through the darkness; Ortrud feigns repentance, and begs for protection, both of which, in her new-found happiness, Elsa grants. At the same time Ortrud succeeds in implanting the seeds of doubt in the girl's heart, hinting at mystery and magic, things easily believed under the circumstances. But outwardly Elsa rejects all suspicion and takes Ortrud with her into the palace.

Trumpets answering one another from the turrets of the castle announce the dawn of Elsa's wedding day. With the growing light, the courtyard begins to bustle with preparations. Servitors pass hurriedly, then come knights glittering in their armor, and nobles arrayed in festive attire, a blazing pageant in the sunlight. A herald announces that Telramund has been banished, and that the mysterious champion, having refused the dukedom, has been proclaimed leader of the country's forces.

The orchestra begins a soft, graceful melody while a long procession of women, dressed in the court robes of the period, come gradually from the palace and, slowly crossing the courtyard, group themselves around the doorway of the cathedral.

As Elsa approaches the cathedral, all joyfully shout, "Hail! Elsa of Brabant!" and voices and orchestra swell in a climax of radiant beauty.

Just as Elsa sets foot on the church steps, Ortrud springs before her—a very different Ortrud from the suppliant of a few hours previous. She now

demands priority over the bride-elect of a nameless knight. Her stormy outburst causes considerable excitement; soon the King and Elsa's champion
appear. Ortrud is silenced; the knight supports his trembling bride, and the
procession is resumed. Suddenly from behind a buttress where he has been
lurking, Telramund steps out before them, and wildly proclaims that this
unknown knight is a sorcerer; the swan-drawn boat is evidence enough, and
he demands his name. But the King will not listen, and the banished pair are
driven away in disgrace. Elsa, her wedding processional twice interrupted,
is filled with fear and grief, yet she affirms her trust in her defender. The
procession is again resumed and the music grows to a splendid climax as it
enters the cathedral.

Before the curtain rises on Act III there is an orchestral prelude which,
like that to the opera itself, is a great favorite of concert audiences. In this
piece Wagner sets the festive mood for the wedding, the joy of the lovers,
and the purity of Elsa, and he also reintroduces the ominous theme of Warning, which has already been heard in the previous scenes. The Prelude gradually diminishes in sound and flows into the strains of the equally famous
"Bridal Chorus." The ecstatic burst of strings, woodwinds, and brass, the
crash of cymbals, the masculine strength of the theme for the trombones, the
feminine grace of the middle portion, are only too well known. Rarely has
a wedding festival been more happily, riotously expressed in music!

ACT III

SCENE 1: *The Bridal Chamber*. As the music grows softer, the curtain rises
upon the bridal chamber, and the bridal procession enters. The ladies are
leading Elsa, the King and the nobles conducting the bridegroom. They sing
the familiar "Bridal Chorus."

The procession encircles the chamber. Then, after saluting the bridal
pair, the guests depart, their song gradually dying away in the distance.

Now it is that Elsa first shows the doubt in her heart.

The stranger knight gently reproves her. She scarcely hears, for the
poison instilled into her mind is at work. She grows more and more insistent,
her own curiosity strengthened by her lover's kind protests. She fears that
he will be lost to her, that he will return to the unknown land whence he has
come—even now she thinks she sees the swan returning for him. In a sudden
frenzy she demands to know his name. At this very moment Telramund and
four henchmen steal into the chamber, swords drawn. Elsa quickly hands her
husband his sword, and with the weapon he strikes Telramund dead. His
followers cringingly sink down.

He gently picks up Elsa, who has fallen senseless, and places her on the
couch. He bids Telramund's men to take up his body and bring it to the

Lohengrin

Byron   ACT II—THE KING DENOUNCING TELRAMUND

King. He then strikes a bell, summoning two lady attendants, and he instructs them to dress Elsa in her choicest attire for her appearance before the King. There, he says, he will reveal to her who he is, the rank he bears.

SCENE 2: *The Banks of the Scheldt River, Near Antwerp.* At the Oak of Justice, the King and the nobles await the knight and, when he appears, the nobles hail him as their leader. Their rejoicing gives way to amazement as they see the body of Telramund being borne along, and Elsa approaching, her face pale as death. The knight explains the slaying of Telramund; now he is compelled to answer the question Elsa has asked. From the orchestra are heard the ethereal harmonies of the Grail, and the knight begins his narrative.

He says that he is one of the knights of the Grail at the distant place Monsalvat; that once each year a dove is sent down from heaven to renew the wondrous powers of the Grail. All who see It are magically cleansed of earthly sin, the knights guardians are equipped with invincible might, before which all evil influences lose their powers. Yet the knights must remain unknown for this might to be with them, because if they are recognized, as they roam about righting the wrongs of the world, they must return. Further, he reveals that he is the son of Parsifal, King of the Grail, and that his name is Lohengrin.

The people, in a chorus of remarkable beauty, express their awe at his wonderful narrative. The swan is seen approaching, and Elsa gives way to her grief. Lohengrin bids her farewell most tenderly, and leaves with her his horn, his sword, and his ring—for her brother, should he ever return.

As Lohengrin steps aboard his boat, Ortrud suddenly appears from among the crowd and with a cry of triumph exclaims that her magic is superior, for it was she who changed Elsa's brother into the swan that is now to

251

Lohengrin

draw Lohengrin away. Thus have Ortrud's gods rewarded Elsa's faithlessness! But she has spoken too soon. Lohengrin kneels for a moment in prayer while all eyes are instinctively turned upon him. The white dove of the Holy Grail flutters down from above, the swan sinks, and in its place, Lohengrin raises from the water a boy in shining raiment and lifts him to land. "Behold the ruler of Brabant!" cries he. The boy rushes into Elsa's arms, while the dove mysteriously draws the boat on its course to Monsalvat. Lohengrin is seen, ere he disappears in the distance, his head bent sorrowfully, leaning upon his shield. "My husband! My husband!" cries Elsa, and sinks back lifeless in her brother's arms.

THE RCA-VICTOR RECORDS
(Sung in German)

PRELUDE: *Arturo Toscanini and the NBC Symphony Orchestra* 11-9287, 12″
(In Album M-1074)
11-8807, 12″
Arturo Toscanini and the New York Philharmonic-Symphony Orchestra
14006, 12″
(In Album M-308)
Leopold Stokowski and the Philadelphia Orchestra 6791, 12″

ACT I
ELSA'S TRAUM (Elsa's Dream): *Kirsten Flagstad, Soprano, with Orch.* 14181, 12″

ACT II
EUCH LÜFTEN, DIE MEIN KLAGEN (Ye Wandering Breezes): *Kirsten Flagstad, Soprano; the Philadelphia Orchestra, Eugene Ormandy, Cond.* 1901, 10″

ACT III
PRELUDE (Introduction): *Arturo Toscanini and the New York Philharmonic-Symphony Orchestra* 14007, 12″
(In Album M-308)
11-9233, 12″
(In Album M-1064)

Franz Hanfstaengl
CLOSE OF ACT I

HELEN TRAUBEL AS ELSA

252

Mishkin

LAWRENCE TIBBETT AS TELRAMUND   LAURITZ MELCHIOR AS LOHENGRIN

Leopold Stokowski and the Philadelphia Orchestra 17568, 12"
(In Album M-731)
Boston "Pops" Orchestra, Arthur Fiedler, Cond. 10-1091, 10"
(In Album M-968)

BRAUTCHOR (Bridal Chorus): *RCA-Victor Choral and Orch., Robert Shaw, Cond.* 11-9294, 12"

Metropolitan Opera Chorus and Orch. 11249, 12"

Mark Andrews, Organ 20036, 10"

BRIDAL CHAMBER SCENE (Love Duet); DAS SÜSSE LIED VERHALLT (The Sweet Song Dies Away): *Kirsten Flagstad, Soprano; Lauritz Melchior, Tenor; Victor Symphony Orchestra, Edwin McArthur, Cond.*

DM-897 (11-8161 & 11-8162), 2-12"
M-897 (11-8159 & 11-8160)

IN FERNEM LAND (In Distant Lands): *James Melton, Tenor, with Orch.* 11-8931, 12"
(In Album M-1013)

Lauritz Melchior, Tenor; the Philadelphia Orchestra, Eugene Ormandy, Cond. 17726, 12"
(In Album M-749)

Richard Crooks, Tenor, with Orch. 7105, 12"

LOHENGRIN'S ABSCHIED (Lohengrin's Farewell): *Lauritz Melchior, Tenor; the Philadelphia Orchestra, Eugene Ormandy, Cond.* 15213, 12"
(In Album M-516)

253

ACT II, SCENE 1—STREET SCENE

Louise

"MUSICAL ROMANCE" in four acts. Music and libretto by Gustave Charpentier. First performance at the Paris Opéra-Comique, February 2, 1900. American *première* at Oscar Hammerstein's Manhattan Opera House, New York, January 3, 1908, with Mary Garden making her American debut in the title role. First Metropolitan performance, January 15, 1921, with Geraldine Farrar in the name part.

Louise brought its indigent, socialist-minded composer fame and money. Although it stirred up a sharp controversy because of its style and content, the opera won an emphatic success with the Parisian public, in the long run becoming the most popular French opera since Bizet's *Carmen.* Several factors combined to make a spectacular novelty of this so-called "proletarian opera." First, there was Charpentier's musical language, protean and many-faceted in its vivid evocation of a giant metropolis in the varied moods of its teeming life. This was music pulsating with communal life, music through which wove brief, evanescent themes in a fascinating web of impressions. And in emotional range, from gay vivacity and hearty abandon to tense drama, this music was French to the core. Then, the setting of *Louise* was something of a jolt to many reared operatically on more remote locales. Here was contemporary realism with a vengeance— the drab family life of Parisian tenement-house dwellers into which the devil-may-care freedom of a struggling young poet brought a disturbing note. The mansard atmosphere of working-class drudgery was a marked change from the fabled tapestries of standard opera. But the people soon came to feel the great human throb of *Louise.* The pulse of a wondrous city beat in its texture. This was Paris enshrined in warm, vibrant tone, the Paris of bright, cheery street life, the Paris of soft, sensuous nights, the Paris of Montmartre. Truly the protagonist of this opera was not the girl Louise, but the city Paris. Yet Louise is its incarnation of conflicting feelings, the symbol, perhaps, of the new freedom, the break with convention and outmoded code. Louise's final chant of liberation is paralleled in the masterly symphonic hymn expressing the city's awakening to fresh life.

For Mary Garden Friday the thirteenth of April, 1900, was indeed a lucky day. She was in Paris, studying. As an understudy at the Opéra-Comique she had learned and mastered the role of Louise. She was at the opera house on that fateful Friday when Marthe Rioton, who had created the part, fell suddenly ill and was unable to continue after the second act. This was Miss Garden's great chance. She was promptly summoned by the management. Her name was announced to a public that had never heard of her and was probably none too happy over the abrupt substitution. The fair unknown sang the last two acts and the Parisians were at her feet. In the years that followed Mary Garden sang Louise over two hundred times at the Paris Opéra-Comique. Her interpretation of the working-class heroine was regarded as one of the most absorbing portraits in the soprano wing of the opera gallery.

CHARACTERS

LOUISE	*Soprano*	IRMA	*Soprano*
HER MOTHER	*Contralto*	AN ERRAND GIRL	*Mezzo-soprano*
HER FATHER	*Baritone*	THE KING OF THE FOOLS	*Tenor*
JULIEN	*Tenor*		

PEDDLERS, HOUSEKEEPERS, WORKING PEOPLE, GRISETTES, STREET BOYS, BOHEMIANS

The action takes place in Paris toward the end of the nineteenth century

ACT I

SCENE: *The Attic Flat of Louise's Family in a Paris Tenement House.* Julien, a young, easygoing artist, who lives across the way, is secretly conversing with Louise. Her parents frown on his attentions because of his carefree Bohemian ways, hoping for someone steadier for their daughter. It develops that Louise's parents are so bitter about Julien that they have refused to answer a letter of his. Louise now promises that should this happen again, she will give in and elope with him. Julien has written a second letter. Louise is now eager to know when Julien, whom she has known intimately for some weeks only, first knew he was in love with her. He explains in a tender passage beginning *"Depuis longtemps j'habitais cette chambre"* ("I occupied this room for some time"). He had lived in a room in the house next door, never realizing that a beautiful girl lived so close to him. Then he had met Louise, and a great hope and joy awoke in him; new songs of love had come to his lips. . . . The two are so occupied with one another that they hear and see nothing else. They are unaware that Louise's mother is standing there, listening. The startled lovers separate, and the mother grasps Louise by the arm, violently upbraiding her. Sarcastically, she quotes some of Julien's impassioned words and calls him an impudent ne'er-do-well. Leaping to her lover's defense, Louise retorts that he is none of these things; that, moreover, she is old enough to make up her own mind.

The quarreling is interrupted by the entrance of Louise's father, who is ready for food and rest after a hard day's work. But the bickering is renewed the moment the father opens Julien's second letter. The young neighbor is again asking to marry Louise, and the father now seems sympathetic. Extremely fond of Louise, he is prepared to yield to her wishes, but first they must look into the young man's character. The mother, however, puts her foot down: she will not have Julien as a son-in-law! He is a bad lot. The father, to end the matter, asks Louise to promise she will not see him again, and Louise, with an affectionate hug, gives him her word. Meanwhile preparations for supper are being made, with Louise and her mother setting the table and bringing the food. The father tenderly asks Louise to read from the evening paper to him. When by chance she begins reading an article about Paris in the spring and the gay festivities in store, the irony of it, in her present plight, brings a sob from the unhappy girl.

ACT II

SCENE 1: *A Street at the Foot of the Hill of Montmartre.* A light mist lies over the rooftops of Paris, which is gradually coming to life. We begin to hear its first signs of awakening in the orchestra, slowly evoking the coming of dawn and the return of bustling life. As the shadows of night disappear with the last few stragglers of the streets, men and women cross the scene on their way to work. Myriad sounds and street cries enliven the morning picture of a city going about its business. Louise and her mother appear. As they reach the workshop, the girl takes leave of her mother. Julien, who has been strolling about with his Bohemian friends, waits for the mother to depart and then brings Louise out of the shop. As Julien's written request to the parents for Louise's hand has again been turned down, he now reminds her of her promise. They must run away together! Louise listens avidly to the call of love and youth and spring, and just as she is about to yield, a stern sense of duty holds her back and she asks Julien to be patient. Perhaps someday. . . . Louise rushes back into the shop, leaving Julien to nurse his grief amid the street cries of Paris.

Wide World Studio
ACT II, SCENE 2—THE DRESSMAKERS—METROPOLITAN OPERA PRODUCTION

Wide World Studio
ACT III—OVERLOOKING PARIS—METROPOLITAN OPERA PRODUCTION

SCENE 2: *A Dressmaker's Workroom* (This scene is often omitted in American performances). At their sewing machines, a group of girls are singing and joking—all but Louise, who is buried in thought. Her companions begin speculating out loud on the reason for her serious mood. Irma suggesting that she is in love. This Louise denies angrily. From the courtyard below now come the soft strains of a serenade as Julien returns with his gay comrades. The girls shriek with delight and begin flirting with the serenader. Then, as the popular love song turns to an impassioned reproach of woman's faithlessness, the girls become bored, mock him, and turn their attention to a passing band. Louise, unable to pretend any longer, rushes from the shop to join Julien. The other sewing girls look out the window and laugh as they observe the couple together.

ACT III

SCENE: *A Garden and House on the Side of the Hill of Montmartre.* The shadows of night are gathering. In the garden of their little house Louise and Julien are together, wrapped in their love. Beyond the garden the city is spread out in a great panorama, and in the distance lights are beginning to glimmer. The lovers have defied the parents' veto and are living together on the slope of Montmartre. Rapturously now Louise recalls the day she first gave herself to Julien—"*Depuis le jour où je me suis donnée.*" The memory of it still leaves her trembling, Louise sings in a passionate aria, for everything about them seems to smile on their love. "In the garden of my heart a new joy sings!" Louise exclaims. While more and more lights of the city begin to pierce the darkness, the lovers join in an ecstatic duet, and through their combined song the throbbing life of the city seems to chant. Scarcely have they re-entered their villa, when a gay troop of Bohemian revelers arrives on the scene. They hang lanterns about the garden and call out the lovers. In an elaborate ceremony Louise is crowned Queen of Montmartre. After the King of the Fools delivers a mock heroic talk, all bow respectfully before the new queen, and the crowd resumes its merrymaking with song and dance. The festivities come to an abrupt halt as Louise's mother enters, her appearance being a signal for the crowd to disperse. With mounting grief, Louise hears the bad news: her father is ill, dying from sorrow over his daughter's elopement with Julien. Bitterly her mother assures her that if she wants him to live, she must come back at once. Louise, realizing how strong her love for her father is, consents to go. Julien permits Louise to depart on the mother's promise that she will be free to come back to him.

ACT IV

SCENE: *The Attic Flat of Louise's Family (same as Act I)*. Again with her parents, Louise is beginning to sulk over the restraints of home life. Though still weak, her father is well enough now to return to work. While Louise is in her room and the mother in the kitchen, the father begins to complain of the worker's lot, how it is made doubly hard by ungrateful children. Louise suddenly flares up over the mother's broken promise to allow her to return to Julien. The father, in a conciliatory mood, draws her onto his knees and sings a tender little lullaby to her, as if she were a slumbering infant. A haunting melody passes through the orchestra as the father recalls quieter and happier days in their home life. When Louise replies there would be no quarrel if the parents did not stand in the way of her happiness, the father reminds her of all they have done for her. To this Louise retorts that she will not be cooped up, that she is starving for freedom. One word leads to another, and soon a heated quarrel develops. Excited to a pitch of delirium, Louise shouts out defiantly that she wants nothing but her Julien and the free, unfettered life of Paris. In a rage, the father opens the door and orders her out of the house. As Louise dashes out, the father runs to the door and shouts remorsefully after her: "Louise! Louise!" Then, in a fit of uncontrollable fury at the city that has lured his daughter away, he cries out, shaking his fist, "Paris! Paris!"

Louise

THE RCA-VICTOR RECORDS
(Sung in Frênch)

ACT III

DEPUIS LE JOUR (Ever Since the Day):
Dorothy Maynor, Soprano; the Philadelphia Orchestra, Eugene Ormandy, Cond.   17698, 12″

Grace Moore, Soprano, with Orch.   17189, 12″

Jeanette MacDonald, Soprano, with Orch.   15850, 12″

Mary Garden, Soprano, with Orch.   6623, 12″

Helen Jepson, Soprano, with Orch.   14204, 12″
(In Album M-329)

ACT IV

BERCEUSE (Lullaby): Marcel Journet, Bass, with Orch.   6785, 12″

MARY GARDEN AS LOUISE

LUCREZIA BORI AS LOUISE

259

Morton & Co. ACT II—SAN FRANCISCO OPERA PRODUCTION

The Love of Three Kings

(L'AMORE DEI TRE RE)

OPERA IN three acts. Music by Italo Montemezzi. Libretto by Sem Benelli, taken from his tragedy of the same title. First performance at Teatro alla Scala, Milan, April 10, 1913. Initial American performance at the Metropolitan Opera House, January 2, 1914, with Lucrezia Bori, Edoardo Ferrari-Fontana, Pasquale Amato, and Adamo Didur, Arturo Toscanini conducting.

A work of dramatic impact and searing passion, *The Love of Three Kings* boasts not only an excellent score, but also a first-class libretto. It is not a spectacle work, since there is little in it of such quality. It is, in fact, a close-up of tragedy which grips the main characters. Through them it is expressed.

CHARACTERS

ARCHIBALDO, *King of Altura*	*Bass*	A BOY CHILD	
MANFREDO, *his son*	*Baritone*	A VOICE BEHIND THE SCENES	*Tenor*
AVITO, *a former prince of Altura*	*Tenor*	A HANDMAIDEN	*Soprano*
FLAMINIO, *a castle guard*	*Tenor*	A YOUNG GIRL	*Soprano*
FIORA, *Manfredo's wife*	*Soprano*	AN OLD WOMAN	*Mezzo-soprano*
A YOUTH	*Tenor*	MEN, WOMEN, YOUTHS OF ALTURA	

The action takes place in the Middle Ages in a remote castle in Italy, forty years after a barbarian invasion led by Archibaldo

ACT I

SCENE: *A Hall of Archibaldo's Castle.* The scene shows an immense hall in a somber medieval castle at the hushed hour that precedes dawn. Through the curves of arches one can look across a terrace out into the night penetrated

260

only by the reddish light of a signal lantern. The aged and blind Archibaldo, restless and unable to sleep, is led into the hall by the servant, Flaminio. He has been stirred by recollections of the time forty years earlier when he led his soldiers into Italy, subdued the people, and became ruler of Altura. Flaminio, one of the conquered natives, recalls that it was for the sake of peace that Fiora, the intended bride of the local prince, Avito, was given to the conquerors to marry Archibaldo's son, Manfredo. The old man is expecting the return of his son, now away at war, and it is for him that the signal light burns. As dawn is approaching, Archibaldo has Flaminio extinguish the light; then both return to the blind man's apartment.

From another room now comes forth Avito, the former Prince of Altura, stealthily looking about to see if anyone is in the hall. He is followed by Fiora, who would have him linger yet longer. Avito is fearful lest the door to the aged Archibaldo's room be open, but Fiora assures him it is tightly closed. She says that there is great peace in her soul; Avito exclaims that he knows no peace when parted from her lips. Entirely overcome by the power of their mutual infatuation, the two embrace passionately, heedless of the growing daylight. Suddenly, perceiving that the signal lantern has been extinguished and thereby knowing that someone has already been there at this early hour, Avito flees in terror. Archibaldo has entered just at this moment, and though Fiora would escape silently, he is, with a blind man's sure instinct, aware of her presence and her excited condition. He orders her to stay, and fain would learn who was with her. She insists that she has been alone, and then with shockingly deceitful naïveté, adds that she came out on the terrace because she could not sleep for thinking of her husband. Archibaldo, justly horrified by her duplicity, orders her to her room.

Manfredo's return is announced by the sound of trumpets outside of the castle, and in a few moments he is warmly welcomed by his father. Manfredo has been looking forward to this return with all the fervor of a young husband. Fiora enters and greets him with a cruel coldness that the noble Manfredo neither realizes nor comprehends. As they leave, Archibaldo exclaims to himself, "O God, since Thou hast taken away mine eyes, let me indeed be blind!"

ACT II

SCENE: *A Terrace Atop the Castle Walls.* The afternoon sky is covered with fleeting clouds. Below, trumpets sound a retreat. Manfredo, about to leave again for the wars, is bidding Fiora a most affectionate farewell, and begs some little token of her that he may keep near him while away. Failing in this, he pleadingly asks that she remain on the summit of the castle wall a little while and wave her scarf in greeting to him. Fervently he adds that, as he is riding away with his soldiers and looks back, it will seem to him that

Wide World Studio   ACT II—METROPOLITAN OPERA PRODUCTION

she is drying the tears upon his heart. Fiora, moved with sincere pity, promises that it shall be done.

No sooner has Manfredo left her, and Fiora gone to the summit of the battlement to watch his departure, than Avito, disguised as Flaminio, stealthily approaches. Fiora bids him leave her forever, though he begs for her compassion. They are interrupted for a moment by the arrival of a servant who brings Fiora a casket containing a scarf from Manfredo. This she very slowly removes from the casket. Then falteringly, she reascends the stairs to the parapet and endeavors to wave the scarf. After three attempts, her arm drops wearily to her side. Avito comes from his hiding place, saying he is going, never to return, but he longs to see her for this last farewell, and begs a parting kiss. Fiora tries to ward off his advances and feebly attempts to resume waving the scarf. Yielding, she says that he may kiss the fringe of her garment, which she has herself embroidered. Avito runs to her hastily, seizes her dress, and feverishly kisses it. Fiora would again wave the scarf, but her arms droop helplessly; she is overcome by the thought of the contrast between her real desire and her husband's ideal, but powerless before Avito. she gradually yields herself to him. They kiss and, lost in the ecstasy of love, they remain in a close embrace, oblivious to all around them. They do not even hear the approach of Flaminio and Archibaldo, who calls, "Fiora." The lovers suddenly awaken from their trance. Avito rushes with drawn dagger at the blind man. He is restrained by the servant and, at a sign from Fiora, escapes silently. Manfredo is heard returning in the distance, and Archibaldo peremptorily orders Flaminio to go forth and meet him, thus giving himself the opportunity to be alone with Fiora. He denounces the faithless woman, demanding to know the name of her lover. First denying, then acknowledging her guilt, she refuses to name the man who has just left her. Overpowered by his rage, Archibaldo seizes her as she lies on a bench, and, half conscious of his actions, he chokes her until she is still. Manfredo has returned, fearing that Fiora has fallen from the parapet, since he had not seen her waving the scarf after the first few attempts. He is appalled when his father proclaims her guilt and acknowledges himself the murderer.

ACT III

SCENE: *The Crypt of the Castle.* In the somber light of the crypt in the chapel of the castle, the body of Fiora is seen reclining, clothed in long white garments. From the chapel itself are heard the voices of the choir, singing a dirge. In the crypt are a group of mourners, old men, women, and youths, standing at a respectful distance from the corpse and lamenting the loss of their beloved princess. Thinking how Fiora has been cruelly murdered, the mourners grow angry and call for vengeance, but under the spell of the solemnity of the place and the impressive chanting in the chapel, their wrath subsides and, singing an eternal farewell, they depart. As they are going they notice the arrival of the Prince of Altura, Avito, who likewise has come to bid Fiora adieu. The mourners gone, he speaks to Fiora as though she were yet alive; then, with a sudden realization of her eternal silence, he weeps in agony. Perhaps a breath of her dear soul yet remains in her body, he thinks; and desperately he kisses her now icy lips. His body is shaken by a strange sensation; he believes himself dying and, even in the sudden death

Morton & Co.

ACT III—SAN FRANCISCO OPERA PRODUCTION

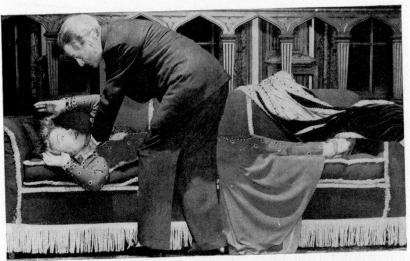

The Newspaper PM
GRACE MOORE REHEARSING *THE LOVE OF THREE KINGS* WITH THE COMPOSER,
ITALO MONTEMEZZI

pangs, rejoices. As he staggers away, Manfredo enters, recognizes him, and reveals the fact that in order to trap Fiora's lover, a powerful poison was placed on her lips—a desecration of which Archibaldo alone was capable. Manfredo is not happy in the death of his rival, he only sorrows that Fiora should have had so great a love for another than himself; and, as Avito breathes his last, supports him gently as he sinks lifeless to the ground. Then, turning to Fiora, he throws himself over her, kisses her also on the lips, and remains there quivering while the deadly poison creeps through his veins. Nor has the poison quite finished its work when Archibaldo enters, groping his way. He approaches the bier and, thinking he has caught the guilty man, shouts triumphantly; then, hearing the voice of his own son, dying, the old ruler cries out in the utmost agony and despair.

Moffett
MARY GARDEN AS FIORA

The Love of Three Oranges
(L'AMOUR DES TROIS ORANGES)

OPERA IN four acts, with a prologue. Music by Serge Prokofiev. Libretto by the composer, after Carlo Gozzi's *Fiaba dell' amore delle tre melarancie* (*The Tale of the Love of the Three Oranges*). First performance, December 30, 1921, at the Chicago Auditorium, by the Chicago Opera Company, in French, with the composer conducting, and Nina Koshetz making her American debut as the Fata Morgana. New York *première*, by the Chicago Opera Company, February 14, 1922, at the Manhattan Opera House, the composer again conducting.

Gozzi, the eighteenth-century dramatist and storyteller, had a genius for giving fresh form to old tales and legends and for devising new ones. The tales were called *fiabe*, or fables. Later dramatists found them a fertile source of suggestions for plot, and opera composers have been no less indebted to this gifted teller of tales. Puccini's *Turandot* is only one of at least six operas founded on Gozzi's masterly little *fiaba* of legendary China. The vein of satire running through Gozzi's *fiabe* has also exerted a strong appeal on subsequent writers and composers. It is not surprising that Prokofiev, no mean satirist himself, found inspiration for an opera in one of these delightful *fiabe*. Typical in this "burlesque opera" is Prokofiev's penchant for witty, sardonic writing. Moreover, in its ingenious handling of childlike fantasy and enchantment the opera belongs with Prokofiev's *Peter and the Wolf*. This cleverly evoked world of satiric sorcery is perhaps far removed from Prokofiev's main areas of artistic interest, which are Russian history and the fresh exploitation of symphonic form. The pungent note of modernism is readily heard in this music, though, compared with the more dissonant writing of Prokofiev's piano and violin concertos, it is a kind of modified modernism, diverting in its sophisticated discourse on the child's world of fairyland wonder.

CHARACTERS

THE KING OF CLUBS, *ruler of an imaginary kingdom, whose costume is that of the playing card*   Bass

THE PRINCE, *his son*   Tenor

THE PRINCESS CLARISSE, *the King's niece*   Contralto

LEANDER, *the King's prime minister, dressed as the King of Spades*   Baritone

TRUFFALDINO, *a jester*   Tenor

PANTALON, *a courtier in the confidence of the King*   Baritone

THE MAGICIAN TCHELIO, *who protects the King*   Bass

FATA MORGANA, *a sorceress who protects Leander*   Soprano

LINETTE   *princesses con-*   Contralto
NICOLETTE   *cealed in the*   Mezzo-soprano
NINETTE   *three oranges*   Soprano

THE COOK (*woman*)   Hoarse Bass (Basse enroué)

FARFARELLO, *a demon*   Bass

SMERALDINE, *a Negress*   Mezzo-soprano

MASTER OF CEREMONIES   Tenor

THE HERALD   Bass

THE TRUMPET   Bass Trombone

JOYS, GLOOMS, EMPTYHEADS, JESTERS, DEMONS, DOCTORS, COURTIERS, MONSTERS, DRUNKARDS, GLUTTONS, GUARDS, SERVANTS, SOLDIERS

The action takes place in an imaginary kingdom in the mythical long ago

PROLOGUE

SCENE: *Stage, with Lowered Curtain and Grand Proscenium, on Each Side of Which Are Little Balconies and Balustrades.* An artistic discussion is on among four sets of personages on what kind of play should be enacted on the present occasion. The Glooms, clad in appropriately somber robes, argue for tragedy. The Joys, in costumes befitting their temperament, hold out for romantic comedy. The Emptyheads disagree with both and call for frank farce. At last, the Jesters (also called the Cynics) enter, and succeed in silencing the squabbling groups. Presently a Herald enters to announce that the King of Clubs is grieving because his son never smiles. The various personages now take refuge in balconies at the sides of the stage, and from there make comments on the play that is enacted. But for their lack of poise and dignity, they would remind one of the chorus in Greek drama.

ACT I

SCENE: *The King's Palace.* The King of Clubs, in despair over his son's hopeless dejection, has summoned physicians to diagnose the ailment. After elaborate consultation, the doctors inform the King that to be cured the Prince must learn to laugh. The Prince, alas, like most hypochondriacs, has no sense of humor. The King resolves to try the prescribed remedy. Truffaldino, one of the comic figures, is now assigned the task of preparing a gay festival and masquerade to bring cheer into the Prince's smileless life. All signify approval of the plan except the Prime Minister Leander, who is plotting with the King's niece Clarisse to seize the throne after slaying the Prince. In a sudden evocation of fire and smoke, the wicked witch, Fata Morgana, appears, followed by a swarm of little devils. As a fiendish game of cards ensues between the witch, who is aiding Leander's plot, and Tchelio, the court magician, attendant demons burst into a wild dance. This is graphically depicted in the deftly contrived music of an eerie waltz-scherzo. The Fata Morgana wins and, with a peal of diabolical laughter, vanishes. The jester vainly tries to make the lugubrious Prince laugh, and as festival music comes from afar, the two go off in that direction, whereupon the orchestra plays the brilliant and bizarre "March," built around a swaying theme of irresistible charm.

ACT II

SCENE: *The Main Courtroom of the Royal Palace.* In the grand court of the palace, merrymakers are busy trying to make the Prince laugh, but their efforts are unavailing for two reasons: the Prince's nature is adamant to gaiety and the evil Fata Morgana is among them, spoiling the fun. Recognizing her, guards seize the sorceress and attempt to eject her. In the struggle that ensues she turns an awkward somersault, a sight so ridiculous that even the Prince is forced to laugh out loud. All rejoice, for the Prince, at long last, is cured! In revenge, the Fata Morgana now pronounces a dire curse on the recovered Prince: he shall again be miserable until he has won the "love of the three oranges."

ACT III

SCENE. *A Desert*. In the desert the magician Tchelio meets the Prince and pronounces an incantation against the cook who guards the three oranges in the near-by castle. As the Prince and his companion, the jester Truffaldino, head for the castle, the orchestra plays a scherzo, fascinating in its ingeniously woven web of fantasy. Arriving at the castle, the Prince and Truffaldino obtain the coveted oranges after overcoming many hazards. Fatigued, the Prince now goes to sleep. A few moments later Truffaldino is seized by thirst and, as he cuts open one of the oranges, a beautiful Princess steps out, begging for water. Since it is decreed that the oranges must be opened at the water's edge, the helpless Princess promptly dies of thirst. Startled, Truffaldino at length works up courage enough to open a second orange, and, lo! another Princess steps out, only to meet the same fate. Truffaldino rushes out. The spectators in the balconies at the sides of the stage argue excitedly over the fate of the Princess in the third orange. When the Prince awakens, he takes the third orange and cautiously proceeds to open it. The Princess Ninette emerges this time, begs for water, and is about to succumb to a deadly thirst, when the Jesters rush to her rescue with a bucket of water.

ACT IV

SCENE: *The Throne Room of the Royal Palace*. The Prince and the Princess Ninette are forced to endure many more trials through the evil power of the Fata Morgana. At one juncture the Princess is even changed into a mouse. The couple finally overcome all the hardships the witch has devised, and in the end are happily married. Thus foiled in her wicked sorcery, the Fata Morgana is captured and led away, leaving traitorous Leander and Clarisse to face the King's ire without the aid of her magic powers.

THE RCA-VICTOR RECORDS

PRINCE AND PRINCESS; MARCH AND "SCÈNE INFERNALE": *Leopold Stokowski conducting the NBC Symphony Orchestra* 18497, 12"

MARCH AND SCHERZO: *Boston Symphony Orchestra, Serge Koussevitzky, Cond.* 14950, 12" (In Album M-459) 7197, 12"

R. Strohmeyer   ACT II, SCENE 2—SAN FRANCISCO OPERA PRODUCTION

Lucia di Lammermoor

OPERA IN three acts. Music by Gaetano Donizetti. Text by Salvatore Cammarano, after Sir Walter Scott's novel, *The Bride of Lammermoor*. First performance at the San Carlo Theater, Naples, September 26, 1835. Initial United States production, in French, at the Théâtre d'Orléans, New Orleans, December 28, 1841. First New York performance, Niblo's Garden, in Italian, September 15, 1843. Also given at the Park Theater, in English, November 17, 1845. The opera obtained its first hearing at the Metropolitan Opera House on October 24, 1883, it being the debut of Marcella Sembrich. This was the second work to be produced at the Metropolitan, whose inaugural took place two evenings before, with *Faust*. Among the celebrated interpreters of the role of Lucia have been Fanny Persiani, who created it, Jenny Lind, Adelina Patti, Emma Albani, Christine Nilsson, Luisa Tetrazzini, María Barrientos, Amelita Galli-Curci, Toti dal Monte, and Lily Pons. The Edgardos have had such noted impersonators as Italo Campanini, Tamagno, Caruso, Bonci, Martinelli, Schipa, Gigli, Lauri-Volpi, Jussi Bjoerling, Ferruccio Tagliavini, and Jan Peerce.

This work, when first produced, won for its composer the appointment to the position of professor of counterpoint at the Real Collegio di Musica (Royal College of Music), Naples; moreover, it gained for him an abiding place in popular affection. It is the habit of some modernists to scoff at this, Donizetti's masterpiece; it is performed too often and regarded merely as a vehicle for showing off some popular prima donna. In reality its melodies are fresh and, though simple, possess genuine beauty; even in the ornate passages they are basically expressive of the situation in which they are placed in the drama. The ensemble numbers, including the world-renowned Sextet, rank among the finest in Italian opera.

CHARACTERS

LORD ENRICO (HENRY) ASHTON,   LUCIA (LUCY), *his sister*   *Soprano*
  of Lammermoor   *Baritone*

RAIMONDO (RAYMOND) BIDE-THE-
BENT, *chaplain at Lammermoor* Bass

EDGARDO (EDGAR), *master of*
Ravenswood Tenor

LORD ARTURO (ARTHUR) BUCKLAW,
Lucia's prospective husband Tenor

ALISA (ALICE), *companion to*
Lucia Soprano or Mezzo-soprano

NORMANDO (NORMAN), *follower*
of Lord Ashton Tenor

FOLLOWERS OF ASHTON, INHABITANTS OF LAMMERMOOR, ETC.

The action takes place in Scotland near the close of the seventeenth century

ACT I

SCENE 1: *A Wood Near Lammermoor.* In the somber gardens of Lammermoor Castle, the guards and their leader, Norman, are discussing a stranger who has been seen prowling around the place, perhaps on secret mischief. The guards leave hurriedly to search for him, but Norman remains behind to suggest to Lord Henry Ashton, who now enters, that the intruder may very likely be none other than Edgar of Ravenswood. Lord Henry is Edgar's mortal enemy and has recently acquired through treachery the Ravenswood estates. The talkative Norman further narrates, in the hearing of the kindly disposed Bide-the-Bent, that one day Lord Henry's sister, Lucy, was saved from the attack of an angry bull by some unknown person. She has fallen in love with him and secretly meets him every day. Lord Ashton's anger grows even more intense when the guards report that they saw the intruder and were able to recognize him as the hated Edgar. Ashton vows speedy vengeance.

SCENE 2: *A Park Near the Castle.* Lucy, accompanied by her maid, Alice, awaits Edgar at their daily trysting place. She looks with dread at a fountain near by and tells Alice the legend about one of the Ravenswoods who stabbed his sweetheart beside it. To a wistful, pathetic melody she vows that she has seen in the dark waters an apparition of the murdered woman, in the aria *"Regnava nel silenzio"* ("The night reigned in silence").

Edgar arrives, a gloomy figure with black-plumed cavalier hat and cloak of sable. This, he tells her, must be their last meeting, for he has been ordered to France. But he proposes first to go to Henry and endeavor to end the mortal feud which exists between the two families. Lucy, knowing her brother only too well, declares that it would be useless, and entreats Edgar to keep their love secret lest they will be forever parted. The information causes Edgar again to renew his vow of vengeance. Then they begin their lovely duet of parting, *"Verranno a te sull' aure"* ("My ardent sighs will come to you"). Both impassionedly unite again, repeating their vow of devotion.

ACT II

SCENE 1: *An Anteroom in Lammermoor Castle.* Edgar was mistaken in his

ACT II, SCENE 2—THE SEXTET

supposition that Lord Ashton's conduct is entirely a matter of hatred. In reality Ashton is in desperate straits and his only chance to improve his fortune is to have Lucy marry Lord Arthur Bucklaw. He intercepts all of Lucy's and Edgar's letters, and now he has forged in Ravenswood's handwriting a letter which seems to prove beyond doubt that Lucy is betrayed, her lover having deserted her for another. Ashton heaps upon her his scorn for having dared love his enemy and asserts that he will be disgraced and ruined unless she consents to marry Lord Arthur Bucklaw, as he has arranged. The unfortunate girl, stricken nearly dumb with grief, finally consents to the sacrifice.

SCENE 2: *The Great Hall of the Castle.* In the great armorial hall of the castle, knights and ladies are assembled to witness the wedding, and sing a gay chorus of welcome; but the pale, agitated appearance of the bride gives the lie to their joyful song. Ashton tries to explain away her condition by saying that she still mourns her mother. Wan and almost fainting, she is escorted to the table where a notary is preparing the marriage papers; then with trembling hands she signs the document that makes her Lady Arthur Bucklaw.

No sooner has she set down the pen than a stranger enters the room. All eyes are turned upon him in fear and amazement. Edgar of Ravenswood, sword in hand, pistol in belt, stalks boldly toward the table. At this most

270

White

THE HALL IN LAMMERMOOR CASTLE—METROPOLITAN OPERA SETTING

dramatic moment begins the famous Sextet, *"Chi mi frena?"* (What re-strains me?") Its flowing melody, majestic rhythm, gorgeous harmonies, and soaring climax are known to all; but only those who know the action of the opera can fully realize how magnificently it expresses in sound the con-flicting emotions of this scene. It begins with Edgar and Henry; Edgar won-ders why he has not rushed ahead to claim his vengeance and, on beholding the despairing Lucy, realizes that he still loves her. Henry fears for his own future and the effect that this excitement may have on his sister. The voices of Lucy and Bide-the-Bent enter, Lucy expressing her despair that death has not come to save her from this grief and shame, Bide-the-Bent kindly praying that heaven will aid and protect her. Now the voices of Alice and the attend-ant knights and ladies unite in this prayer, but above the outpouring of all these conflicting feelings rise the tones of Lucy's lament, forming a climax of stirring effect.

The eternal enemies, Edgar and Ashton, rush at one another with drawn swords, but Bide-the-Bent restrains them, bidding them both, in heaven's name, to sheathe their weapons. Coldly asking Edgar the reason for his un-welcome visit, Ashton shows him the marriage contract. Unable to believe his eyes, Ravenswood turns to Lucy for confirmation; forlorn and in misery she tremblingly nods assent. Edgar, in furious rage, calls down the curse of heaven on Lucy and all her hated family and rushes away.

ACT III

SCENE 1: *The Tower of Ravenswood Castle.* Ashton comes to the gloomy Ravenswood Castle and there challenges Edgar to a duel to take place at dawn. Amid the terrors of a terrific storm they unite in an agitated duet, praying that the vengeance-bringing morn may soon arrive.

SCENE 2: *The Hall at Lammermoor Castle.* Meanwhile, at the castle, the wedding guests are still feasting and making merry. Suddenly the laughter ceases and the song dies upon their lips as Raymond enters, horror-stricken, and cries out that Lucy has gone mad and slain her husband. An instant later Lucy herself appears, pale and lovely, robed in white, her hair loose upon her shoulders. In her eyes gleams an unnatural light and her face bears the tender, questioning expression of one who strives to recall a dream. Her brain unable to endure a suffering too intense, Lucy is mad, indeed; but she is happy in her madness, for she believes herself with her lover. Singing a melody of great sweetness, she imagines that she and Edgar are being married. And here is the famous "Mad Scene," which is anything but a coloratura holiday.

Heard outside of the opera, this number seems hardly more than an unusually brilliant, florid aria. But in its proper setting, caroled out by the demented Lucy amid the startled retainers, it takes on an ironic character quite its own. The scales seem what they are, the audible wanderings of a mind distraught. The flute joins her in these difficult cadenzas, forming an ensemble effect of great brilliance and loveliness. After a brief interruption by Ashton, she resumes her song. Still imagining that Edgar is with her, she kneels and begs him not to leave; then requests, *"Spargi d'amaro pianto"* ("Shed no bitter tears").

She sings this to a whimsical melody, half sad, half gay. Then growing more and more agitated at the thought that she will await her beloved in heaven, her voice rises ever higher, until at the end she falls swooning into Alice's arms.

SCENE 3: *The Tombs of the Ravenswoods.* As the night wears on, the lights still winking gaily from the castle at Lammermoor convey to the silent watcher who stands amid the graves of the Ravenswoods no knowledge of these tragic events. In somber meditation, he soliloquizes, *"Tombe degli avi miei, l'ultimo avanzo d'una stirpe infelice. Deh! Raccogliete voi!"* ("Tombs of my ancestors, the last am I of a doomed race. Gather me unto you!") Then, his thoughts instinctively turning to Lucy, Edgar decries Lucy's apparent treachery. Yet even as in self-pity he heaps reproaches upon the absent Lucy, he notes a train of mourners coming from the castle. He inquires of whom they lament. And they tell him of Lucy's madness and of her love for him. She lies, they say, in the castle at the point of death. And as they speak, the sound of a tolling bell announces her death.

De Bellis

LILY PONS AS LUCIA

The reality of the tragedy dawning upon him, he vows that he has decided his own fate; he, too, will die, hoping to join Lucy in heaven. And he expresses these sentiments in the aria *"Tu che a Dio spiegasti l'ali"* ("Thou hast spread thy wings"). The others, including Raymond, try to desist him from his suicidal purpose, but he plunges his dagger into his heart, and, as the chorus prays for his pardon, expires.

273

Lucia di Lammermoor

From the Painting by Millais

THE PARTING OF
LUCIA AND EDGAR

Victor George

AMELITA GALLI-CURCI AS LUCIA

THE RCA-VICTOR RECORDS
(Sung in Italian)

ACT II

SEXTET—CHI MI FRENA? (What Restrains
Me?): *Amelita Galli-Curci, Soprano;
Louise Homer, Contralto; Giuseppe
de Luca, Baritone; Ezio Pinza, Bass;
Beniamino Gigli, Tenor; Angelo
Bada, Tenor; with Orch.* 10012, 12″

*Amelita Galli-Curci, Soprano; Minnie
Egener, Contralto; Enrico Caruso,
Tenor; Giuseppe de Luca, Baritone;
Marcel Journet, Bass; Angelo Bada,
Tenor* 10000, 12″
(Acoustical Recording)

*Luisa Tetrazzini, Soprano; Irene Jacobi,
Contralto; Enrico Caruso, Tenor;
Pasquale Amato, Baritone; Marcel
Journet, Bass; Angelo Bada, Tenor*
16-5000, 12″
(Acoustical Recording) (In Album M-953)

SCENA DELLA PAZZIA (Mad Scene): *Miliza
Korjus; Chorus and Orch.*
13808, 12″ (In Album M-871)

Lily Pons, Soprano, with Orch.
7369, 12″

Nellie Melba, Soprano, with Orch.
18143, 12″
(In Album M-816)
(Acoustical Recording)

ACT III

TOMB SCENE (Complete): *Jan Peerce,
Tenor; Arthur Kent, Baritone; Chorus
and Orch.*
DM-845 (18308 & 18309), 2-12″
M-845 (18306 & 18307)

GIUSTO CIELO! RISPONDETE (Why Lament
Ye!)

TU CHE A DIO SPIEGASTI L'ALI (Thou Hast
Spread Thy Wings): *Beniamino
Gigli, Tenor; Ezio Pinza, Bass; Metropolitan Opera Chorus; with Orch.*
8096, 12″

274

ACT I—VENICE PRODUCTION

Lucrezia Borgia

OPERA IN a prologue and two acts. Music by Gaetano Donizetti. Text by Felice Romani, after Victor Hugo's play, *Lucrèce Borgia*. First performance, Teatro alla Scala, Milan, December 26, 1833. United States *première*, New Orleans, April 27, 1844. First New York performance, Palmo's Opera House, November 25, 1844. Later given at the German Stadt Theater, New York, March 18, 1856, in German. Presented in English, Academy of Music, New York, October 13, 1871. First and only performance at the Metropolitan Opera House, December 4, 1904, with Maria de Macchi, Edyth Walker, Enrico Caruso, and Antonio Scotti.

Owing to difficulties with censorship bureaus, sensitiveness in high places, and the like, this opera was produced in a variety of versions and revisions, not to say titles, in many theaters of Italy and France. For example, in Florence, November 12, 1838, it was given under the title of *Eustorgia da Romano*; in Trieste, autumn of 1838, as *Alfonso, Duca di Ferrara*; in Ferrara, April 14, 1841, as *Giovanna I di Napoli*; in Rome, December 26, 1841, as *Elisa da Fosco*. Moreover, Victor Hugo objected strenuously to the opera's being given in the original version, finally succeeding in getting it altered and produced in Paris under the title *La Rinnegata*, a version also given in Italy several times. The story was again revised and the music adapted to a French libretto by E. Monnier, bearing the title *Nizza de Grenade*, for a production in Versailles, 1842. Elsewhere *Lucrezia Borgia* has always been performed in its original version.

Of the music of *Lucrezia Borgia* the prologue, the first-act trio sung by Lucrezia, Gennaro, and the Duke, and the drinking song of Orsini are the high lights.

CHARACTERS

DON ALFONSO, *Duke of Ferrara*	Baritone	ORSINI	*young Venetian*	Contralto
LUCREZIA BORGIA, *his wife*	Soprano	PETRUCCI	*noblemen in*	Bass
GENNARO, *her illegitimate son*	Tenor	LIVERETTO	*attendance on the*	Tenor
RUSTICHELLO, *servant to the Duke*	Tenor	VITELOZZI	*ambassador to*	Bass
GUBETTA, *servant to the Duchess*	Bass	GAZELLA	*Ferrara*	Tenor

275

Lucrezia Borgia

The action takes place in Venice and Ferrara during the sixteenth century

PROLOGUE

Lucrezia Borgia is in Venice, where she is desirous of meeting Gennaro (her illegitimate son), from whom she has long been separated. The boy has no idea who the masked lady is, but in a confiding mood tells her of his life and the devotion he bears the unknown mother. Some friends of his enter, among them Orsini (sung by a contralto), who tears the mask from the lady's face and exposes her as the fearsome poisoner, Lucrezia Borgia. As they all recoil from her, including Gennaro, Lucrezia falls into a swoon.

ACT I

The scene changes to Ferrara, where the Duke, unaware of the relationship between Lucrezia and Gennaro, mistakes him for her lover and plots to poison him. Lucrezia's skill with lethal chemicals, however, embraces also a knowledge of their antidotes, and with one of these she saves Gennaro from the death prepared for him by the Duke. Further, she exhorts him to leave Ferrara immediately.

ACT II

Orsini prevails upon Gennaro to stay in Ferrara until after the supper which is to be given by one of the nobility, and this he does. In the midst of festivities Lucrezia, eager to avenge herself on the Venetians who had reviled her, appears and announces to all present that she has paid them for their kindness with one of her own—poison—and that coffins now await their earthly remains. Espying Gennaro, however, she pleads with him to take an antidote. She tells him, in desperation, that she is his mother. But he proudly refuses her, preferring, as he says, to die with his loyal friends. He falls dead, and Lucrezia, horrified, throws herself on his lifeless body.

THE RCA-VICTOR RECORDS
(Sung in Italian unless otherwise noted)

ACT III	with Orch.	1367, 10″
Brindisi—Il segreto per essere felice (Drinking Song—It Is Better to Laugh): *Sigrid Onegin, Contralto,*	Ernestine Schumann-Heink, Contralto, with Orch. In German (Acoustical Recording)	15-1012, 12″

ACT II—LA SCALA PRODUCTION, MILAN

Macbeth

OPERA IN four acts. Music by Giuseppe Verdi. Book, after Shakespeare, with verses by
Francesco Piave, in collaboration with Andrea Maffei. First produced at the Teatro
della Pergola, Florence, March 14, 1847. A new version, involving considerable revision, was produced at the Théâtre-Lyrique, Paris, on April 21, 1865, the French text
being the work of Nuitter and Beaumont. The American *première* of *Macbeth*, in the
original version, occurred at Niblo's Garden, New York, on April 24, 1850. Ninety-one
years later, on October 24, 1941, the New Opera Company produced the revised version
for the first time in America at the Forty-fourth Street Theater, New York. Fritz Busch
conducted, and the cast was headed by Jess Walters as Macbeth and Florence Kirk as
Lady Macbeth.

Verdi was only thirty-four when he wrote the first of his three Shakespearean
operas. The other two, *Otello* and *Falstaff*, belong to the very last phase of his career,
the period of perhaps his greatest dramatic and expressive power. Yet in *Macbeth* this
power is already foreshadowed in the broad sweep of style and the marked flair for
compelling dramatic emphasis. A great devotee of Shakespeare's works, Verdi resolved
to be as faithful as possible to the original play, even supplying Piave with his own
prose version, besides strict instructions about the sequence of scenes and details of
characterization. Still, certain sharp differences may be noted by anyone familiar with
both the play and the opera—differences stemming in part from the special romantic
approach of the period to Shakespeare. Macduff and Malcolm are reduced to vague
semblances of the Shakespearean originals, and because of the need to tighten the
earlier scenes, the nobler side of Macbeth is almost lost in the unrelieved portrait of
villainy. Actually, it is Lady Macbeth who looms as the dominant figure of the opera,
and to her Verdi allotted the best pages of his score. Among the most absorbing moments of the opera are her aria, *"La luce langue"* ("The light fails"), in which she
voices a conflict of fear and exultation; her ironic toast to the slain Banquo; and the
stupendous *scena* of the sleepwalking episode, in which a Verdi biographer averred that
"the composer rises to the level of the poet and gives the full equivalent in music of
the spoken word."

The action takes place in medieval Scotland

277

The opera opens on "a blasted heath," where a chorus of witches hails Macbeth prophetically as thane of Cawdor and King of Scotland. Banquo, who accompanies Macbeth, is greeted in similar prophetic vein as the father of kings. Word soon arrives from King Duncan that the incumbent thane of Cawdor has been found guilty of treason and been executed. Moreover, Macbeth has been named his successor, thus fulfilling the first of the witches' predictions. In the next scene Lady Macbeth is shown reading a letter from her husband in which he alludes to the witches' strange prophecy. When Macbeth returns, his wife confronts him with a plan to bring about the fulfillment of the other half of the prophecy. Together they will slay King Duncan, who is a guest at the castle. At midnight, while the King is asleep, the murder is carried out. After the deed, at the height of Macbeth's frenzied terror, a knocking is heard. Macduff enters, followed by Banquo, and both give the alarm when they find the King slain.

The second act begins with the assassination of Banquo and the miraculous flight of his son. Toward the end occurs the banquet scene in which Macbeth, having assumed power, is faced by Banquo's ghost and steadied by his more cold-blooded wife.

In the third act we are back among the witches, who now pronounce an invocation to Hecate and enact a grisly pantomime for Macbeth. As they swirl about a boiling caldron, they conjure up prophetic visions for the haunted regicide. One in particular alarms Macbeth, that of a child wearing a crown. Finally, the awesome chant is heard that Macbeth will only be overthrown when "Great Birnam wood to high Dunsinane hill Shall come against him." Lady Macbeth is furious when Macbeth tells her of the weird vision of the crowned child. The memory of the witches' prophecy about Banquo's son returns to taunt them. Together they vow to remove all remaining obstacles from their path of power.

In the first scene of the last act we are near the fateful Birnam wood. In a magnificent chorus Scottish exiles bemoan their country's plight under the usurper's bloody tyranny. From Macduff we learn that his wife and child have been slain in Macbeth's reign of terror. To conceal the strength of his forces, Duncan's son Malcolm urges each soldier to cut down a branch and carry it before him.

For the next scene at the castle Verdi reserved some of his most overpowering music. This is the famous scene of Lady Macbeth's sleepwalking, during which she makes gruesome efforts to wipe out the invisible stains of murder. Later Macbeth is heard in a somber soliloquy when he hears of his wife's sudden death. Then, in the battle in the plain before the castle he is killed by Macduff. A jubilant chorus of the exiled patriots ends the opera.

Cambridge - 1940's - Delightful -

ACT I—JAMES MELTON AS LT. PINKERTON AND LICIA ALBANESE AS MADAME BUTTERFLY

Madama Butterfly

OPERA IN three acts (originally two). Music by Giacomo Puccini. Libretto by Illica and Giacosa, based on the play by David Belasco, in turn founded on John Luther Long's short story, "Madame Butterfly." First performance, La Scala, Milan, February 17, 1904. American *première*, in English, Washington, D. C., October 15, 1906. First performance at the Metropolitan Opera House, in Italian, February 11, 1907, with Geraldine Farrar in the title role and Enrico Caruso as Lieutenant Pinkerton.

It was Frank Neilson, stage manager of Covent Garden, who induced Puccini to see Belasco's play at the Duke of York's Theatre in London. Though he knew no English, Puccini immediately grasped its operatic possibilities. Later he confessed he fell in love on the spot with the pathetic little geisha girl. The years 1902 and 1903 were occupied with writing the new opera. Intent on achieving authentic atmosphere, Puccini went so far as to consult the wife of the Japanese Ambassador on many details. Friends of hers even supplied him with actual Japanese tunes, and Victor records of native music made in Japan were also made available to Puccini. When the opera was finished, Puccini was convinced he had written his masterpiece. The Milanese public and press failed to agree with him, however. In fact, the world *première* of *Madama Butterfly* brought Puccini his most humiliating experience in the theater, for the occasion was a resounding fiasco. This, despite the fact that Rosina Storchio (later to become celebrated in the role) sang Cio-Cio-San, Giovanni Zenatello was the Pinkerton, and Cleofonte Campanini conducted. With the very entrance of Cio-Cio-San the crowd showed its opposition. After the first act, Puccini, limping from injuries suffered in a motor crash, appeared on the stage, only to be greeted by a volley of catcalls. For the rest of the performance he remained fuming in the wings. As the jeers of the crowd reached him, he would mutter: "Louder, louder, you beasts! Shriek at me! Yell your lungs out! You shall see who is right! This is the best opera I have ever written!" After the riotous performance Puccini, pale and shaken, expressed his thanks to Campanini and the singers, and returned home with the mistreated score under his arm.

The failure of that *première* has been variously explained. Some insist an anti-Puccini cabal was at work. Others blame the fiasco on the absence of any real solo for tenor in the first version. The long second act (again in the original version) has been

279

given as another cause. In any case, Puccini was right in his angry prophecy, in the opinion of many critics. Time has borne him out. *Madama Butterfly* became a world favorite, its main aria, Cio-Cio-San's *"Un bel di,"* almost reaching the status of a "hit" song. However, Puccini did make some revisions. He broke up the second act into two parts, separating them by an intermezzo. Moreover, the tenor role was augmented by an arioso. Three months after the disastrous *première* at Milan, *Madama Butterfly* proved a spectacular success at the opera house of Brescia. That performance marked the beginning of its conquest of the world. Puccini's revenge on the Milanese hooters had come sooner than expected.

CHARACTERS

CIO-CIO-SAN (MADAMA BUTTERFLY)	Soprano	SHARPLESS, *United States Consul at Nagasaki*	Baritone
SUZUKI, *Cio-Cio-San's servant*	Mezzo-soprano	GORO, *a marriage broker*	Tenor
B. F. PINKERTON, *Lieutenant in the United States Navy*	Tenor	PRINCE YAMADORI, *suitor for Cio-Cio-San*	Baritone
KATE PINKERTON, *his American wife*	Mezzo-soprano	THE BONZE, *Cio-Cio-San's uncle*	Bass

CIO-CIO-SAN'S RELATIONS AND FRIENDS; SERVANTS

The action takes place in the early 1900's at Nagasaki, Japan

ACT I

SCENE: *Exterior of Pinkerton's House at Nagasaki.* It is all vastly amusing. This matchbox of a house and its sliding panels, or *shoji,* in place of walls, neat and ingenious devices—and ridiculously inexpensive! Pinkerton, Lieutenant in the United States Navy, is charmed and amused as the self-important matrimonial agent, Goro, shows him over the little house he is to make his home during a not-too-prolonged stay in Japan. Presently Sharpless, United States Consul, turns up. Pinkerton tells him delightedly about the beautiful Japanese girl by whom he has been captivated, and whom he is to marry Japanese fashion for nine hundred and ninety-nine years, but with the privilege of annulling the marriage any month. The Consul has a dim suspicion that the experiment may turn out more seriously than his friend anticipates, but Pinkerton will not listen to hints of tragedy. "Whisky?" proposes the naval Lieutenant. Having filled their glasses, the men drink to the toast, "America forever!" and then to the folks at home and to the time when Pinkerton will have a "real" wedding back in "God's country."

The two men stand looking out over the glorious scenery, so different from the homeland that to an American it is a make-believe world. From the foot of the hill girlish voices are heard, gradually drawing nearer. The music pulsates glowingly while the girls chatter about the beauty of the day and the flowers. Among them is Cio-Cio-San, "Madame Butterfly," and to Pinkerton this little creature in her kimono is a butterfly indeed. Her voice soars above the others while she sings of the ecstasy of her love.

As the music reaches its climax the girls appear on the terrace and pros-

LICIA ALBANESE AS BUTTERFLY

trate themselves before the "augustness" of Pinkerton. Sharpless enters into a conversation with Butterfly and learns that what he feared is true—the girl is seriously in love with Pinkerton. He also learns that since the death of her father she has had to support herself and mother by becoming a geisha.

The bride's relatives, great numbers of them, now arrive. While the guests are all busied with the refreshments, Pinkerton amusedly watches Butterfly, who draws from her capacious sleeves her possessions—such trifles as handkerchiefs, a jar of carmine, a fan, and, with great solemnity, a long sheath. The officious Goro whispers an explanation to Pinkerton: the dagger was sent to her father by the Mikado, and he was obedient, Goro adds grimly. Thus is Pinkerton reminded that he is in the land given to seppuku, or hara-kiri, a condemned gentleman's privilege to die by his own hand. Butterfly also shows her *ottoke*, images of her forefathers; but she confides to Pinkerton that she has been to the mission and adopted his religion, innocently add-

281

ing that she will try to be frugal, for she knows that he has paid for her the whole sum of a hundred yen. She declares that for his sake she is willing to forget race, kindred, and ancestors; and to prove this last, she throws away their images.

Goro commands silence, and the quaint ceremony of signing the marriage contract takes place. The gaiety of congratulations is suddenly interrupted, for Cio-Cio-San's uncle rushes in, violently enraged. Being a bonze, or Japanese priest, he has learned that Butterfly has forsaken the faith of her ancestors upon marrying this foreigner. Therefore, he curses her with threats of eternal punishment; and all her relatives likewise denounce her, for in deserting her gods she has likewise deserted her people. All rush away in horror, leaving Butterfly weeping bitterly. Pinkerton consoles her, and in the thought of his love she is again happy. Night falls over the scene, and they sing of their happiness together.

ACT II

SCENE: *The Interior of Butterfly's House.* Beyond the room one can see the garden with cherries in bloom, bright in the spring sunshine; but the wall panels being only partly open, the room remains in semidarkness. Before an image of Buddha kneels Suzuki. Occasionally she rings a handbell while she prays that Butterfly's weeping may be ended. Butterfly, who is standing motionless near a screen, tells her that the gods of Japan are lazy—her husband's God will answer her more quickly. Although the money that Pinkerton left is almost gone, Butterfly is still so firm in her belief that her husband will return that she commands the doubting Suzuki to say that he will. Suzuki complies in spite of her tears.

Greatly touched by this, Butterfly, to reassure herself as well as Suzuki, affirms her belief, in an impassioned aria, that some fine day (*"Un bel di"*) a great ship will appear far in the horizon . . . the boom of cannon will announce its arrival in the harbor . . . they will see him coming from a distance . . . climbing the hill. Butterfly will hide for a moment just to tease him . . . he will call for her by the old names of endearment . . . so let fears be banished, Butterfly declares, utterly carried away by the joy of her anticipation, for he will return. She knows it!

At the moment she has finished this declaration of her trust, Sharpless appears. Goro, who has conducted him here, waits outside. "Madame Butterfly," he calls. "Madame B. F. Pinkerton, beg pardon!" the wife corrects. Then turning and recognizing her visitor, she greets him cheerfully. He has a letter from Pinkerton, he tells her. She is the happiest of women, she replies; and then without waiting for Sharpless to read she asks him when the robins build their nests in America . . . for, she continues, Pinkerton had said that he would come back in the happy season when the robins return . . .

ACT III—LICIA ALBANESE SINGING BUTTERFLY'S FAREWELL TO LITTLE "TROUBLE"

now, for the third time, the robins are building their nests. Sharpless, in his embarrassment, is forced to reply that he never studied ornithology. Goro laughs outright at this.

The marriage broker now presents Yamadori, a wealthy suitor, who, though he has had many consorts and divorced them all, says that he is madly in love with Butterfly and is prepared to swear eternal faithfulness to her. She repulses him and his proffered wealth, for she is married to an American, and in his country people remain faithful! Broker and suitor disposed of, Sharpless attempts to resume reading the letter; everything he reads is interpreted by Butterfly as some happy assurance that her husband will soon return. The Consul has not the heart to go on. He asks Butterfly what she would do if Pinkerton were never to come back to her. As if struck by a deathblow, Butterfly gravely replies that she might again become a geisha or she might kill herself. Horrified, Sharpless advises her to marry Yamadori. This greatly insults Butterfly. Ordering Suzuki to bring in "Trouble," the name she has bestowed on her little son, she points to the child in agitated pride, and exclaims, "And this? Can such as this be forgotten?" She asks Sharpless to write to her husband and tell him what a beautiful son he has. Thus does the Consul learn to his surprise that, unknown to Pinkerton, there is a child. In true motherly joy, her attention concentrated entirely on little "Trouble," Butterfly bids her child not to believe the bad man when he says that Father will not return but will leave them to wander through the streets for a living.

Sharpless leaves, fearful for the future. Soon after he has gone a cannon shot is heard booming from over the harbor, announcing the arrival of

283

an American warship. With the help of a telescope Butterfly spells out its name—*Abraham Lincoln*. Pinkerton's ship!

So, then, the agony of waiting is over! He has come with the robins— her lover, her husband, her adored one! In a moment the two women are feverishly rushing to the garden to gather cherry blossoms to deck the house. They sing the joyous "Duet of the Flowers" throbbing with the excitement and exultation of the rejoicing Butterfly, who then hastens to put on the wedding dress she wore on that day long ago, so that she may greet her lover as he first knew her. Little "Trouble," too, is arrayed in his finest.

Night has been falling; the servant closes the *shoji* and brings in several Japanese lanterns, which cast a dim glow over the darkened room. But they must await Pinkerton's return. They must be ready to welcome him. In her anxious, joyful expectancy Butterfly has pierced three little holes through the wall so that they may watch for him. "Trouble" sits before one, supported by cushions; at another kneels Suzuki; close up against a third stands Butterfly, rigid and motionless, watching, waiting. A wonderful melody, first heard during the reading of the letter, floats across the scene, softly hummed from a distance. "Trouble" soon nods, then falls asleep. Next Suzuki dozes off. Now Butterfly keeps her vigil alone.

ACT III

SCENE: *Same as Act II*. The gray light of dawn begins to enter the room. Butterfly still stands, motionless, watching; Suzuki and "Trouble" are sound asleep. The lanterns become even dimmer as the day grows brighter. Like the morning sunlight, the music now sparkles with vagrant Japanese melodies. Suzuki having awakened and begged her to lie down to rest awhile, Butterfly takes little "Trouble" and goes with him into an inner room. No sooner has she gone than Sharpless and Pinkerton arrive. Suzuki is overjoyed at seeing them, but they motion her to keep silent. She points out how Butterfly has decorated the house and tells how she waited all night. The servant, on opening the *shoji*, exclaims in surprise as she catches sight of a strange woman in the garden. Fearfully she asks who it is. When Sharpless explains that it is Pinkerton's wife, Suzuki cries out in grief.

Sharpless asks Suzuki to prepare Butterfly for this bitter revelation, adding that the American woman has come to adopt the child. Pinkerton, overwhelmed with remorse, leaves the house after asking Sharpless to console Butterfly the best he can. A moment later Butterfly rushes in, joyfully expecting to find Pinkerton. Instead she sees Sharpless, a foreign woman, and Suzuki in tears. Slowly she begins to suspect the dreadful truth. She asks if *he* is alive, her voice hushed with expectant fear. Only Suzuki's broken "yes" is needed, and Butterfly now knows that she has been deserted. Mrs. Pinkerton expresses her helpless sympathy and asks to take the child. Butterfly, having listened in pathetic dignity, replies that only to Pinkerton will she yield her son. She will be ready in half an hour. Sharpless and Mrs. Pinkerton take their leave; Butterfly orders Suzuki to go into another room with the child.

Then she takes from its sheath the dagger with which her father had carried out the custom of his people, and reads the inscription written upon its blade: "To die with honor when one can no longer live with honor." She raises the knife to her throat. At that instant, the door opens and little "Trouble" runs to her with outstretched arms. Butterfly drops the knife, impetuously seizes the child and covers him with kisses. Having bade him a heart-rending farewell, she gives her son a doll and an American flag, urges him to play with them, then gently bandages his eyes. Again she takes the dagger and goes behind the screen. A moment later the blade is heard falling to the floor. Butterfly staggers forward, groping her way to her child, takes his hand, and smiles feebly as she embraces him, and dies.

Pinkerton is heard calling her name. A moment later he rushes into the room, followed by Sharpless. He kneels beside Butterfly, sobbing with grief and shame. Sharpless takes the child and turns away.

The orchestra thunders out a solemn Japanese melody. Over and above the very last note of that melody there sounds a poignant, questioning chord, as though this tragedy were not yet, nor ever would be, ended.

THE RCA-VICTOR RECORDS
(Sung in Italian unless otherwise noted)

COMPLETE RECORDING: *Toti dal Monte, Soprano; Beniamino Gigli, Tenor; Mario Basiola, Baritone; Adelio Zagonara, Tenor; Vittoria Palombini, Mezzo-soprano; Maria Huder, Soprano; Gion Conti, Baritone; Ernesto Dominici, Bass; with Chorus and Orchestra of the Royal Opera, Rome; Oliviero de Fabritiis, Cond.*
DMC-111 (DM-700) (Vol. 1)

(17389-17394), 6-12"
(DM-701) (Vol. 2)
(17395-17404), 10-12"
MC-111 (M-700) (Vol. 1)
(17357-17362)
(M-701) (Vol. 2)
(17363-17372)

HIGHLIGHTS: *Licia Albanese, Soprano; James Melton, Tenor; Lucielle Browning, Mezzo-soprano; with RCA-Victor Orchestra; Frieder Weissmann, Cond.*
DM-1068 (11-9257-11-9259), 3-12"
M-1068 (11-9254-11-9256)

ACT I

DUETTO D'AMORE (Love Duet): *Dusolina Giannini, Soprano; Marcel Wittrisch, Tenor; with Orch. In German*

8921, 12"

ACT II

UN BEL DI VEDREMO (Someday He'll Come): *Jeanette MacDonald, Soprano, with Orch.* 11-9599, 12"

Lucrezia Bori, Soprano, with Orch.
6790, 12"

Geraldine Farrar, Soprano, with Orch.
18141, 12"
(In Album M-816)
(Acoustical Recording)

Emmy Destinn, Soprano, with Orch.
15-1014, 12"
(Acoustical Recording)

Cambridge 1942 - (Not for beginning opera fans.)

SCENE FROM CHICAGO CIVIC OPERA PRODUCTION

The Magic Flute
(DIE ZAUBERFLÖTE)

OPERA IN two acts. Music by Wolfgang Amadeus Mozart. Libretto by Emanuel Schikaneder, based on a tale by Wieland, "Lulu, or The Magic Flute." First performance, Theater auf der Wieden, Vienna, September 30, 1791, with Mozart conducting. Paris *première*, as *Les Mystères d'Isis*, August 20, 1801. American *première*, in English, Park Theater, New York, April 17, 1833. First performance at the Metropolitan Opera House, March 30, 1900, with a cast headed by Marcella Sembrich, Emma Eames, Milka Ternina, and Pol Plançon.

Schikaneder, who provided Mozart with the libretto of this immortal operatic allegory, has been called everything from arrant scalawag to wayward genius. So with his libretto. Sober critics have dismissed it as a fabric of absurdities. Others, equally sober, have found it a consistent tissue of allegorical symbols, the work of a master of subtle suggestion and satire. If the latter position is correct, *The Magic Flute* is a wondrous representation of Freemasonry, of which both Mozart and his erratic collaborator were enrolled members.

A seeming wonder book of sorcery and fantasy thus becomes the illustrated manifesto of a social and political creed, perhaps even a shrewdly veiled assault on all forms of autocratic rule, including that of the Hapsburgs. With this interpretation, the "Mysteries of Isis" are nothing more than the mysteries of Freemasonry. Maria Theresa, who actually used violence in breaking up Masonic gatherings, presumably appears as the Queen of the Night. In Tamino scholars have discerned the Emperor Joseph II, who often acted in defense of the secret order. And the Austrian people themselves supposedly have a spokeswoman in Pamina. Again assuming the presence of Masonic ritual, *The Magic Flute* reveals three levels of meaning. The fantastic tale itself, with its fairyland aura of wonder and witchcraft, is one. The Masonic symbolism is another. And the third is the moral allegory involved: the struggle of humanity through adversity, self-sacrifice, and love to achieve true wisdom and nobility.

And what kind of music did the divine Mozart give to this fairy extravaganza with a double allegory? A godlike magic breathes through this score, said Wagner. The quintessence of art, he called it. The young of all ages are drawn by this miraculous blend of mystery, romance, and comedy. *The Magic Flute* is perhaps the most original flight of Mozart's creative fancy. It owes next to nothing to his predecessors of opera and symphony. Ravishing melodies abound in every scene. *The Magic Flute* is indeed magic.

CHARACTERS

SARASTRO, *High Priest of Isis*	*Bass*	FIRST LADY	*attendants of the Queen of the Night*	*Soprano*
TAMINO, *an Egyptian prince*	*Tenor*	SECOND LADY		*Mezzo-soprano*
PAPAGENO, *a birdcatcher*	*Baritone*			
THE QUEEN OF THE NIGHT	*Soprano*	THIRD LADY		*Contralto*
PAMINA, *her daughter*	*Soprano*			
MONOSTATOS, *a Moor, chief of the slaves of the temple*	*Tenor*	FIRST BOY	*belonging to the Temple and fulfilling the designs of Sarastro*	*Soprano*
		SECOND BOY		*Mezzo-soprano*
PAPAGENA	*Soprano*			
		THIRD BOY		*Contralto*

PRIESTS AND PRIESTESSES OF THE TEMPLE OF ISIS; MALE AND FEMALE SLAVES, WARRIORS OF THE TEMPLE; ATTENDANTS, ETC.

The action takes place in the Temple of Isis at Memphis and its vicinity about the time of Ramses I

A contrapuntal skill of phenomenal range is evident throughout the score, from the masterly fugue of the Overture, in which the clarinets first announce the fascinating main theme, to the massive chorus at the very end. The Overture, in E flat major, 4-4, opens with three massive chords for full orchestra. These later break into the brilliant allegro of the fugue section. A mysterious Masonic significance is supposed to attach to these solemn chords, which form the only part of the Overture to appear in the opera itself.

ACT I

SCENE 1: *A Lonely Landscape.* Rugged cliffs loom on all sides. To the left, in the foreground, is a cave. In the background the Temple of the Queen of the Night is visible. Alone and unarmed, Tamino, an Egyptian prince separated from his traveling companions, is being pursued by a serpent. Overcome by fright and fatigue, he collapses at the entrance to the cave. Three veiled ladies, attendants of the Queen of the Night, fly from the Temple, armed with silver javelins, and with the cry, "Die, monster!" they pierce the serpent with their weapons. The three ladies gaze admiringly on the unconscious youth, then hurry off to tell the Queen of the occurrence.

At the sound of a flute, Tamino revives, sees the dead serpent, and hides himself. Papageno, a roguish birdcatcher and would-be ladies' man, enters. Prepared to strike a bargain with the Queen's attendants, he places his bird cage on the ground and announces his presence by blowing on his pipes. The roguishness of the man may be gathered from his merry song, *"Der Vogel-*

jänger bin ich ja" ("The birdcatcher am I"). Though birdcatching is his occupation, he would much rather be catching pretty girls, confesses Papageno the fowler. Tamino steps from his hiding place and, assuming that Papageno killed the serpent, thanks him for saving his life. As Papageno showily accepts the honor, the three veiled ladies, who have overheard the falsehood, step forward and rebuke him. One of them places a padlock on his lips, reducing his vocabulary to "hm, hm, hm." The three ladies turn to Prince Tamino, one of them offering him a picture of the Queen's beautiful daughter. In a suavely tender song—*"Dies Bildnis ist bezaubernd schön"* ("This picture is bewitchingly lovely")—Tamino rhapsodizes on the girl's beauty, ending with a vow to make her his forever.

On that pledge there is a loud clap of thunder, and as the scene darkens, the mountains open and show the star-bedecked throne of the Queen of the Night. In anxious tones the Queen informs Tamino of her daughter's plight, and the purpose of the picture now becomes clear. The lovely Pamina has been abducted by a scoundrel, and the Queen can still hear her helpless screams. Tamino is to recover the girl and avenge the Queen, for which he will be rewarded with Pamina's hand. There is another thunderclap as the Queen withdraws, leaving Tamino deeply moved by her plea. From the three ladies, Tamino learns that the abductor was none other than Sarastro, high priest of Isis. His interest excited by Pamina's beauty and the mother's words, Tamino promptly agrees to undertake the rescue. A magic flute is given Tamino, one capable of protecting its bearer in all dangers. Papageno is instructed to accompany him on his adventure. Before the two men leave, the ladies remove the padlock from the birdcatcher's lips, with a warning about future lying. Papageno is now given a casket containing chimes whose magic power will offer them further protection. The ladies take leave of Tamino and Papageno, who set out on their mission, guided by three boys.

SCENE 2: *A Room in Sarastro's Palace.* Pamina is being guarded by Monostatos, a Moor, who has been using his position to force his attentions on her. Papageno breaks into the room while the Moor is absorbed in watching the captive princess. True to form, the birdcatcher is entranced by the girl's beauty. The Moor, turning around, starts up in fright, and for his part Papageno is just as frightened by the Moor's appearance. Each takes the other for the devil, and they scurry off in opposite directions. Remembering Tamino's instructions, Papageno finally overcomes his fear and returns to Pamina's chamber. Once back, he tells her the purpose of his visit and proceeds to compare her, itemizing all details, with the portrait that he wears on a ribbon around his neck. He urges Pamina to place her trust in him. When Pamina learns that Papageno has neither wife nor sweetheart, she counsels him to have patience, and the pair join in a duet of infinite grace and rip-

SCENE FROM TEATRO COMUNALE PRODUCTION, FLORENCE

pling gaiety on the theme that "men who are in love cannot fail to be good-hearted"—*"Bei Männern, welche Liebe fühlen, fehlt auch ein gutes Herze nicht."* The melody of this duet is from an old German folk song. After some hesitation, Pamina leaves the castle in Papageno's company.

SCENE 3: *A Grove and Entrance to the Temples.* Led by three boys carrying silver palm branches, Tamino has reached Sarastro's castle and is now in a secret grove in the middle of which stand three temples. At two of the entrances Tamino is denied admittance. At the third a priest of Isis appears, and for the first time Tamino hears of the true character of Sarastro. He is a man of lofty ideals, governing with virtue and truth. Still incredulous, Tamino sneeringly reminds the priest of Pamina's abduction. The priest refuses to explain, mysteriously promising an answer to the riddle when "the hand of friendship" will lead Tamino into "the sanctuary of eternal union." The priest disappears through the same portal from which he emerged.

Alone, Tamino is a prey to conflicting thoughts. Love for the Pamina of the portrait and pity for the Queen still dominate his heart, but a yearning for true wisdom and a desire to know the real nature of Sarastro have gripped him, too. A mysterious voice assures him that Pamina still lives and that soon—or never—his eyes will find the light. As Tamino puts the magic flute to his lips and plays, its effect is truly magical! The Panpipes of Papageno immediately answer, and Tamino rushes off to find his lost companion. Misled by echoes, he takes the wrong direction. He has scarcely left when Pamina and Papageno appear before the castle. Papageno silences the terrified girl when she thoughtlessly calls aloud for Tamino. Papageno tries his

Panpipes, and promptly comes the response of the magic flute. But Pamina's outcry has brought Monostatos and a troop of slaves upon them. When all hope seems lost, Papageno remembers the casket of chimes. As the cover flies open and the magic bells begin to play, a spell is cast over the slaves, whose enchanted limbs move only in time with the music.

Pamina and Papageno again set out to find Tamino, but it is too late! A brilliant flourish of trumpets and drums is heard, and to the cry, "Long live Sarastro!" the high priest of Isis makes a majestic entrance, followed by a host of celebrants. Throwing herself at Sarastro's feet, Pamina admits her guilt for trying to escape, but accuses the Moor of evil designs upon her. Sarastro urges her to rise and tells her that he knows what is in her heart, but warns her that only evil can come from her mother. At that moment Monostatos and his slaves bring in the captured prince. As they catch sight of one another, Tamino and Pamina rush into each other's arms. Sarastro orders Monostatos whipped; then, turning to two of his priests, he instructs them to bring veils for Pamina and Tamino. The lovers are then conducted into the temple of probation, to be purified by the secret rites.

ACT II

SCENE 1: *A Palm Grove.* In the Temple of Wisdom the priests of Isis have assembled to consider whether Tamino is ready to be initiated into the final mysteries. Sarastro pleads warmly for the youth and reveals that the gods have ordained his marriage to Pamina. All signify their approval by blowing into their horns. Sarastro now leads the priestly gathering in a solemn invocation to the gods, *"O Isis und Osiris!"* begging them to grant the worthy couple strength and courage for their impending trials. Sarastro and the priests then depart in a solemn procession.

SCENE 2: *Courtyard of the Temple.* Tamino and Papageno are led out by priests, who warn them that they are to be subjected to severe tests of faith and fortitude. Tamino will see Pamina, but he must not speak to her, for the probation will have begun. Papageno is undecided, but his hesitation vanishes when a priest announces that Sarastro has reserved a beautiful bride—appropriately named Papagena—for him. But he, too, is not to speak to her till the appointed time. Before they leave, the priests caution the companions against the wiles of women. Silence must be maintained at all costs! It now grows dark. Suddenly three torches, borne by the three veiled ladies of the Queen of the Night, flash in the dark, and Tamino's trial begins. Expressing horror at finding the prince and his companion in this den of evil, the ladies implore him to flee before it is too late. They warn them that their death is already ordained and remind Tamino of his vow to help the Queen, who has herself stolen into Sarastro's temple in search of her kidnaped daughter. Tamino listens unmoved, then rebukes Papageno for speaking out and breaking his oath of silence. The three ladies flee in terror as a burst of thunder is heard and priests rush in, wrathfully condemning the intruders to perdition for defiling the sacred threshold.

SCENE 3: *A Garden.* Moonlight falls upon Pamina, who lies sleeping on a bench overhung with roses. Monostatos steals in cautiously and, ravished by the sight of Pamina, attempts to steal a kiss. As he approaches the sleeping girl, the Queen of the Night appears and cries out, "Back!" In imperious tones she bursts into a magnificent soliloquy, *"Der Hölle Rache kocht in meinem Herzen"* ("The vengeance of hell seethes in my heart"), the delivery of which demands great dramatic power and supreme vocal technique in handling the brilliant flurry of staccati in the high soprano register. The Queen addresses the sleeping girl in dire tones. Avenge your mother, she cries, or be forever disowned as her daughter! Pamina awakens, and with a cry of "Mother! Mother!" falls into the Queen's arms. Pamina recoils, however, when the Queen hands her a dagger. "You must kill Sarastro and bring me back the mighty zodiac!" demands the Queen. Before Pamina can protest, there is a roar of thunder and the Queen disappears. Monostatos again approaches the anxious girl, promising a way out for mother and daughter if she will yield to him. Pamina draws back horrified, and as the Moor comes nearer Sarastro appears and steps between them. Angrily, the high priest orders Monostatos out. As Pamina pleads for her mother's safety, Sarastro in a noble and moving cavatina—*"In diesen heil'gen Hallen"* ("Within these sacred halls")—assures her that in this holy place vengeance is a stranger and enemies are forgiven.

ACT I, SCENE 3—METROPOLITAN OPERA PRODUCTION

SCENE 4: *A Hall in the Temple of Probation.* Though Sarastro is satisfied with their behavior thus far, the ordeal has only begun for Tamino and Papageno. Led in once more by the priests, the companions are again warned about keeping their lips sealed. But Papageno, unable to restrain himself, begins chattering away with an Old Woman who brings him a drink of water. A menacing roar of thunder speedily frightens her away and reminds Papageno of his vow. Presently the three youths reappear, bringing with them the flute, the bells, and a table covered with food. Papageno applies himself diligently to a repast as Tamino plays on his flute. Drawn by the magic tones, Pamina appears and greets Tamino rapturously, only to be met by a stony silence. Certain now that Tamino no longer loves her, the girl expresses her sadness in a touching aria, *"Ach, ich fühl's, es ist verschwunden, ewig hin mein ganzes Glück!"* ("Ah, I feel it, love's happiness has vanished forever!")—an aria calling for infinite grace of phrasing and delicacy of style. Hoping now only for death, Pamina leaves, with Tamino gazing sorrowfully after her. At that point the priestly trumpets ring out again, and Tamino wrenches Papageno away from his feasting, reminding him of the tests still to come.

SCENE 5: *A Place Near the Pyramids.* Still obliged to keep silent, Tamino is brought in, veiled by the priests, to be subjected to further trials of faith and endurance. Pamina, also wearing a veil, follows him, and is soon informed that Tamino is waiting to bid her good-by. Hopefully Pamina rushes to him, only to be motioned away in apparent coldness. Again Pamina reproaches him on his apathy, declaring that her love is stronger than his. Sarastro assures them both of a happy outcome to the trial if they will only be patient, and as he accompanies Tamino, two priests lead the despairing Pamina away. As they all depart, Papageno enters, thirsty and bewildered. Angrily, he cries out to the Speaker that he would renounce all hope of heavenly bliss for one glass of wine. A huge wine goblet appears, and as Papageno drinks and grows gay, he plays his magic chimes and chants merrily of the tender little wife he would like to have. Suddenly his wish comes true. In comes the Old Woman again, announcing herself as the coveted bride and swearing eternal constancy to him. Papageno is warned that to spurn her will mean an everlasting diet of bread and water for him. With the whispered reservation of remaining true to her "as long as I see no fairer one," Papageno accepts, and the Old Woman is suddenly transformed into a young beauty. With a cry of "Papagena!" the birdcatcher tries to embrace her, but the Speaker intervenes, and, taking the young woman by the hand, drags her off with the words: "He is not yet worthy of you!"

SCENE 6: *A Garden With a Lake in the Background.* The three youths meet Pamina, who is delirious in her grief. Her mother's command to murder

Samuel H. Gottscho   SCENE FROM JUILLIARD SCHOOL OF MUSIC PRODUCTION

Sarastro and Tamino's apparent coldness are too much for her. Her mind is beginning to snap, and Pamina raises the dagger to kill herself, when the three youths stop her, warning her gravely that suicide is punished by God. They assure her that Tamino loves her dearly and would be driven insane were he to witness this rash act of hers. Pamina rejoices over this assurance and asks to be led to Tamino.

SCENE 7: *A Wild Mountain Spot.* A huge iron gate stands between two eaves on a mountainside. On one side is a roaring stream, on the other a brightly glowing fire. It is twilight. Tamino appears with two priests. From outside comes the sound of Pamina's voice. The priests tell Tamino that he who overcomes dangers in pursuing his ideals will conquer death and become god-like. Tamino attests his fearlessness, and as a reward the priests bring out Pamina. The lovers embrace ardently. Tamino points to the deadly caverns through which they must venture as a final test. Pamina, certain that love will smooth the way, takes him by the hand and urges him to play the magic flute for protection—the flute that she now reveals was fashioned by her father from a thousand-year-old oak. The lovers emerge from probation of fire unscathed. Once more with the help of the flute's protective tones, they brave the cavern of water. As they reappear, again unharmed, the gathered priests hail them in an exultant chorus on their consecration to Isis. Pamina and Tamino now wend their way to the temple.

SCENE 8: *A Small Garden.* Despairing over his unrequited love for Papagena, Papageno resolves to kill himself by hanging. As he sallies out dramatically with a rope, a near-by tree beckons conveniently. Just then the three youths hurry in, chiding Papageno on his rashness and asking him why he does not use his magic chimes to help him out of his misery. Papageno jumps at the suggestion, and now the bells peal cheerily as he wishes out loud for the little maiden. The three youths vanish, and presto! they are back with Papagena. The two greet each other ecstatically and chatter gaily about the lovely little Papagenos and Papagenas that will be theirs once they are wed. They leave arm in arm.

SCENE 9: *Rugged Cliffs.* It is night. Monostatos, the Queen of the Night, and the three ladies steal silently toward Sarastro's temple, all bearing torches. These creatures of evil are making one final effort to destroy Sarastro's power. For his connivance Monostatos has been promised Pamina as bride. Thunder and the roar of rushing water reach the ears of the conspirators. There is a flash of lightning as the earth opens and wraps the villainous crew in eternal night.

SCENE 10: *The Temple of the Sun.* Sarastro is presiding over a solemn conclave of priests and priestesses. As the three youths stand by with flowers in their hands, Tamino and Pamina appear before him in priestly robes. In a majestic address, Sarastro pronounces the couple consecrated in the worship of Isis. The sun's rays have banished night and the forces of darkness. And now the celebrants raise their voices in homage to Isis and Osiris, chanting, "The strong have conquered, and may beauty and wisdom be their eternal reward!"

THE RCA-VICTOR RECORDS
(Sung in German unless otherwise noted)

COMPLETE RECORDING: *Wilhelm Strienz, Bass; Helge Roswaenge, Soprano; Erna Berger, Soprano; Tiana Lemnitz, Soprano; Gerhard Hüsch, Baritone; Irma Beilke, Soprano; Heinrich Tessmer, Tenor; Walther Grossmann, Bass; Ernst Fabry, Baritone; Hilde Scheppan, Soprano; Elfriede Marherr, Soprano; Rut Berglund, Alto; Carla Spletter, Soprano; Berlin Philharmonic Orchestra; with Chorus; Sir Thomas Beecham, Cond.*
DMC-110 (DM-541) (Vol. 1)
(12653-12661), 9-12″
(DM-542) (Vol. 2)
(12662-12671), 10-12″
MC-110 (M-541) (Vol. 1)
(12551-12559)
(M-542) (Vol. 2)
(12560-12569)

OVERTURE: *Arturo Toscanini and the BBC Symphony Orchestra* 15190, 12″

ACT I

BILDNIS ARIE (Portrait Aria) (O Image Angel—Like and Fair!): *James Melton, Tenor, with Orch. In English*
11-8929, 12″
(In Album M-1013)

BEI MÄNNERN (Manly Heart): *Margherita Perras, Soprano; Gerhard Hüsch, Baritone; with Orch.* 4374, 10″

ACT II

INVOCATION—O ISIS UND OSIRIS (Possenti Numi) (Great Isis!): *Alexander Kipnis, Bass, with Chorus and Orch.*
1738, 10″

PAPAGENA AND PAPAGENO

Pol Plançon, Bass, with Piano. In Italian
15-1007, 12″
(Acoustical Recording)

DER HÖLLE RACHE KOCHT IN MEINEM HERZEN (Aria of the Queen of the Night) : *Miliza Korjus, Soprano, with Orch.* 11921, 12″

IN DIESEN HEIL'GEN HALLEN (Within These Sacred Halls) : *Alexander Kipnis, Bass, with Orch.* 8684, 12″

ACH, ICH FÜHL'S (Ah! Je le sais) (Ah, I Feel Grief and Sadness) : *Eleanor Steber, Soprano, with Orch. In English* 11-9114, 12″

Dorothy Maynor, Soprano; Boston Symphony Orchestra, Serge Koussevitzky, Cond. 15826, 12″

Lily Pons, Soprano, with Orch. In French 8733, 12″

295

JARMILA NOVOTNA AS MANON

Manon

OPERA IN five acts, music by Jules Massenet. Libretto by Henri Meilhac and Philippe Gille, after the novel *L'Histoire de Manon Lescaut* by the Abbé Prévost. First produced at the Opéra-Comique, Paris, January 19, 1884. First American performance, at the Academy of Music, New York, December 23, 1885, in Italian. Initial performance at the Metropolitan, in French, January 16, 1895, with a cast comprising Sybil Sanderson, who made her American debut, Jean de Reszke, Mario Ancona, and Pol Plançon. The following year the Metropolitan offered a cast starring Nellie Melba and Victor Maurel. In subsequent showings in the same theater Geraldine Farrar assumed the role of Manon, Enrico Caruso that of des Grieux, and Léon Rothier that of the Count des Grieux, with

Arturo Toscanini conducting. From the year 1909 on, the Metropolitan production of the opera omitted the Cours-la-Reine scene, which was restored in the revival of the season 1919–20, while omitting the scene in the Hôtel de Transylvanie. Still later the Cours-la-Reine scene was again cut out and the other put back. After an absence of six years from the repertoire (it had last been put on April 14, 1923), *Manon* was revived at the Metropolitan (April 3, 1929), Lucrezia Bori, Beniamino Gigli, Giuseppe de Luca, and Rothier as the principals; Louis Hasselmans conducting.

The Prévost romance has had several operatic settings besides Massenet's, including one each by Auber and Puccini, while Halévy made it the subject of a ballet. The libretto for the present setting is rather fragmentary, although the delicately molded score does everything to disguise such shortcomings. Massenet, it is said, composed the music during the summer of 1882, at The Hague, while residing in the very quarters formerly occupied by the Abbé Prévost.

CHARACTERS

CHEVALIER DES GRIEUX	*Tenor*	GUILLOT DE MORFONTAINE, *a roué,*	
COUNT DES GRIEUX, *his father*	*Bass*	*Minister of France*	*Bass*
LESCAUT, *Manon's cousin, one of*		DE BRÉTIGNY, *a nobleman*	*Baritone*
the Royal Guards	*Baritone*	MANON, *an adventuress*	*Soprano*

ACTRESSES, STUDENTS, GUARDS, TRAVELERS, ETC.

The action takes place in Amiens, Paris, and Le Havre, about the year 1721

ACT I

SCENE: *The Courtyard of the Inn at Amiens.* Among the variegated crowd gathered at the courtyard of an inn at Amiens to meet the arrival of the coach is Lescaut, member of the Royal Guard and soldier of fortune. He has come to meet his cousin, Manon, and is to escort her to a convent. He is pleasurably surprised to find her as beautiful as she is unsophisticated. He accepts her proffered lips in cousinly greeting, then hastens within to engage rooms.

No sooner has he gone than the old roué, Guillot de Morfontaine, trots out into the courtyard and begins to pay marked attention to the girl, who is thereby amused and a trifle flattered. There are some among the crowd who make game of the old libertine, who, however, is soon called back to the inn by his traveling companion, de Brétigny. Among those haunting the courtyard are three girls of doubtful character, whose fine apparel is not lost on Manon. She thinks, between sighs and tears, of her own sad lot and her approaching gray life in a convent. Her musings are interrupted, for the handsome Chevalier des Grieux, son of the Count des Grieux, has entered, and, struck by Manon's beauty, addresses her. They become quickly acquainted and, almost before they know it, fall in love.

A carriage previously placed at the disposal of the girl by the infatuated Guillot unexpectedly draws near; intoxicated with her new-found love, she suggests impulsively that they fly together to Paris. Des Grieux joyfully agrees, and they sing rapturously of the life they will live together there. Suddenly Manon hears the voice of her cousin, Lescaut; the lovers leap into the carriage and disappear.

Lescaut comes out wrathfully; there has been gambling in the inn and he has lost his money, and now he learns that he has also lost his cousin. Guillot appears, anticipating another tête-à-tête with Manon; instead he is accused by Lescaut of having abducted the girl. A crowd assembles, watching the growing argument, which is calmed by the observing innkeeper, who says that Manon departed with a young man. In the distance they hear the departing coach.

ACT II

SCENE: *The Chevalier des Grieux's Apartment in Paris*. Manon and des Grieux are together in his apartment in Paris. Des Grieux is writing to his father and trembles for fear the old man may read in anger what he writes from the heart. "Afraid?" says Manon, who stands looking over his shoulder. "Then we'll read together." She takes the letter and begins to read: "She is called Manon, so young and fair . . ." Some little glint of the girl's weakness is visible in her response to his glowing phrase, "In her eyes shines the tender light of love." "Is this true?" asks Manon. Des Grieux will soon ask himself the same question, but now he continues reading his poetic rhapsody. He is certain that his father will give his consent, and they embrace tenderly. As he passes to go out, he notices a bouquet of flowers mysteriously left for Manon. She returns only an evasive answer to his questions. As the perturbed des Grieux opens the door to leave, Lescaut and de Brétigny enter. Lescaut demands satisfaction for the abduction of his cousin. Des Grieux takes him aside, and shows him the letter to his father as proof of his honorable intentions. De Brétigny, left with Manon, makes the best of his time; he says that des Grieux is to be carried away by his own father that very night and urges her to fly with him. Knowing that de Brétigny can give her the pretty things for which her heart longs, Manon hesitates—and is lost. Lescaut, now seemingly appeased, departs with de Brétigny, and des Grieux goes out to mail his letter. Left alone, Manon struggles with herself and sings a charming farewell to the little table at which des Grieux and she have been so happy, "*Adieu, notre petite table*" ("Farewell, our little table").

When he returns he finds her in tears which she cannot quite conceal. Seeking to comfort her, he tells her of his dream, singing a sweet, rapturous melody, while the orchestra supplies a softly murmuring accompaniment. He describes the little home he plans to share with her, in the aria "*En fermant les yeux*" ("As I close my eyes"), better known, perhaps, as "The Dream."

A knock on the door halts the dream; Manon starts guiltily. She tries to prevent him from opening the door, knowing that he is to be abducted, but he insists—is captured and borne off. Now Manon is in despair.

Bruno

LICIA ALBANESE AS MANON

RICHARD CROOKS AS DES GRIEUX AND
LUCREZIA BORI AS MANON

ACT III

SCENE 1: *Cours-la-Reine, Paris.* Manon and de Brétigny mingle with the merrymakers that crowd the streets of Paris on a festival day, the music depicting the holiday spirit in the spirited Gavotte, which all sing.

Count des Grieux, an old acquaintance of Brétigny's, chances by and informs them that his son is at Saint-Sulpice, about to enter the priesthood. This revives all Manon's love, and forsaking de Brétigny, she hurries to Saint-Sulpice.

SCENE 2: *A Parlor in the Seminary of Saint-Sulpice.* The Count arrives there before her, and attempts in vain to persuade his son to abandon this rash resolve. Left alone, des Grieux sings a fervent song of renunciation, declaring that he will now seek the peace of mind which only heaven can give, *"Ah! fuyez, douce image"* (Ah! Depart, fair vision").

When he has gone his way, Manon arrives. Manon prays, and by the time des Grieux comes to the anteroom to meet her, she is in a fine mood of repentance and even more fascinating than usual. Des Grieux yields to her entreaties, and, forsaking the seclusion of the priesthood, goes with her into the world.

ACT IV

SCENE: *A Fashionable Gambling Room in Paris.* Des Grieux and Manon come to a fashionable gambling house in Paris. After much persuasion, the Chevalier, hoping to win riches for Manon, consents to play. He has remarkable luck and, after continuous winning from Guillot, is falsely accused of cheating. A brawl results, and des Grieux and Manon are both on the point of being arrested by the police when the Count appears and protects his son. Manon, however, as an "abandoned woman," is captured and exiled.

ACT V

SCENE: *A Lonely Spot on the Road to Le Havre.* Lescaut and des Grieux are hiding by the road to Le Havre, along which Manon will pass on her way to exile. Des Grieux bribes a soldier and is thus able to talk to Manon. He begs her to try to escape with him, but she is too weak from fatigue. After entreating him to forgive her for her unworthiness, she dies in his arms.

THE RCA-VICTOR RECORDS
(Sung in French unless otherwise noted)

ACT II

ADIEU, NOTRE PETITE TABLE (Farewell, Our Little Table) : *Grace Moore, Soprano, with Orch.* 11-8259, 12" (In Album M-918)

Lucrezia Bori, Soprano, with Orch. 14616, 12" (In Album M-405)

Licia Albanese, Soprano; RCA-Victor Orchestra, Jean Paul Morel, Cond. 12-0525, 12"

LA RÊVE (Il Sogno) (The Dream) : *Richard Crooks, Tenor, with Orch.* 8421, 12" 14203, 12" (In Album M-329)

Jussi Bjoerling, Tenor, with Orch. 12635, 12"

James Melton, Tenor, with Orch. 11-8930, 12" (In Album M-1013)

Tito Schipa, Tenor, with Orch. In Italian 1183, 10"

ACT III

GAVOTTE—OBÉISSONS QUAND LEUR VOIX APPELLE (List to the Voice of Youth) : *Grace Moore, Soprano, with Orch.* 11-8259, 12" (In Album M-918)

Lucrezia Bori, Soprano, with Orch. 1846, 10" (In Album M-405)

AH! FUYEZ, DOUCE IMAGE (Depart, Fair Vision) : *Enrico Caruso, Tenor, with Orch.* 15-1004, 12" (Acoustical Recording)

James Melton, Tenor, with Orch. 11-8930, 12" (In Album M-1013)

Richard Crooks, Tenor, with Orch. 15543, 12" (In Album M-585)

Jussi Bjoerling, Tenor, with Orch., Nils Grevillius, Cond. 12-0527, 12"

Carlo Edwards
RICHARD CROOKS AS DES GRIEUX

From an Old Print   THE BURIAL OF MANON LESCAUT

Manon Lescaut

OPERA IN four acts. Music by Giacomo Puccini. Libretto by a group of writers, including Domenico Oliva, Marco Praga, Giuseppe Giacosa, Luigi Illica, and Giulio Ricordi, after the romance by the Abbé Prévost. First performance at the Teatro Regio, Turin, February 1, 1893. First United States performance, Grand Opera House, Philadelphia, August 29, 1894. Initial showing in New York at Wallack's Theater, May 27, 1898. Metropolitan *première*, January 18, 1907, with Lina Cavalieri as Manon and Enrico Caruso as des Grieux. Puccini's opera served to introduce two artists new to the Metropolitan, Lucrezia Bori, who made her debut as Manon, and Giorgio Polacco, who conducted, on November 11, 1912, Caruso again appearing as des Grieux.

Manon Lescaut is the earliest of Puccini's operas to hold a permanent place in the repertoire in this country. In *Manon Lescaut*, Puccini gives promise of the genius for effective operatic composition that was to flower three years later in *La Bohème*, and eventually to win him the rank of the foremost of modern Italian opera composers. In writing *Manon Lescaut*, Puccini also displayed a certain boldness of spirit, for only a few years previously Massenet had written his own successful setting of Prévost's novel, while Puccini was himself still a young and relatively unknown composer. It seems inevitable to compare the two works: Puccini's presents four relatively detached scenes that follow the novel rather closely; Massenet's departs somewhat from the novel in order to present a more unified drama, yet neither may be considered as having a better-than-average libretto. Puccini's opera makes no attempt to be anything other than Italian opera; Massenet's is thoroughly French in character; both remain favorites.

CHARACTERS

MANON LESCAUT, *a young girl*   Soprano

LESCAUT, *her brother, a sergeant of the King's Guards*   Baritone

CHEVALIER DES GRIEUX   Tenor

GÉRONTE DE RAVOIR, *Treasurer General*   Bass

EDMOND, *a student, friend of des Grieux*   Tenor

301

ACT I—THE INN AT AMIENS—METROPOLITAN OPERA PRODUCTION

AN INNKEEPER, A DANCING MASTER, A SERGEANT, A CAPTAIN, SINGERS, STUDENTS, CITIZENS,
COURTESANS, SAILORS

*The action takes place in Amiens, Paris, Le Havre, and Louisiana during the early part
of the eighteenth century*

ACT I

SCENE: *In a Square of Amiens.* Students are singing and whiling away the
time in front of an inn at Amiens. Des Grieux, dressed as a student, pensive
and lonesome, enters but does not join heartily in their revels. Manon,
with her rather irresponsible brother, Lescaut, and a chance acquaintance,
Géronte, alight from a coach; and while the men are busied with arrangements at the inn, des Grieux speaks to her. She is, she tells him, on her way
to a convent, rather against her will; just then her brother calls her from the
inn. She assures des Grieux she will return later. Left alone, des Grieux meditates on the beauty of the woman he has just seen, singing an air in which he
declares that he has never before seen such a wonderful beauty,*"Donna non
vidi"* ("Maiden so fair").

Géronte, an old libertine, secretly orders a swift horse and carriage with
which he intends to abduct Manon, but Edmond, a student friend of des
Grieux, overhears the plot. Warned by Edmond, the young people elope and
leave the irate Géronte to be consoled by Lescaut's suggestion that they will
be found in Paris. It will be easy, he says, to lure a woman from a poor
student.

White

ACT III—THE HARBOR OF LE HAVRE

ACT II

SCENE: *De Ravoir's Apartment in Paris.* The opening of the second act reveals that Lescaut's prophecy has come true, for Manon, tiring of the humble life with des Grieux, is established in Géronte's luxurious apartment. But now, we discover, she is also tiring of that, for she asks Lescaut about des Grieux. When told that he has been gambling heavily, in order to obtain enough money to win her back, she gazes at the rich hangings, the wealth about her, and sighs longingly for des Grieux and his simple little cottage. A group of musicians, sent by Géronte, come to sing for her entertainment; they are followed by the old gallant himself and a crowd of his cronies. Manon delights them all by dancing a minuet under the guidance of the dancing master. Then all but Manon leave for some brilliant party or other, she to follow presently. Suddenly des Grieux appears. He reproaches her for her faithlessness, singing, *"Ah! Manon, mi tradisce"* ("Ah! Manon betrays me"), but overcome by her nearness and earnest pleading, he soon joins her in a passionate duet of love.

They are found thus by Géronte, who returns to discover the cause of Manon's delay. He conceals his anger under the cold, polished manner of the man of the world, pretends to be forgiving, and leaves them with what seems to them to be an ironic indifference, although he does utter a threat or two. Alarmed, des Grieux urges her to come away with him, but, characteristically, she hesitates to give up all this splendor. However, she asks des Grieux's forgiveness for her apparent lack of enthusiasm, and just then Lescaut rushes in with the news that Géronte has turned her in to the police; the lovers must save themselves quickly. Again her love of pretty things is her undoing, for she stops to gather up her valuables, or as many as she can pick up under pressure, and secretes them in her cloak. She hides in an alcove, panic-stricken, and when Géronte and guards appear, they demand her surrender. Manon comes forth, and in her fear lets slip the cloak, the jewels falling to the floor. Géronte, at this, laughs sarcastically, and Manon is led away alone, charged with being an abandoned woman.

An intermezzo is played here, expressing Manon's grief and des Grieux's despair.

ACT III

SCENE: *In a Square of Le Havre Near the Harbor.* Banished from France as an abandoned woman, Manon is to embark for the French province of Louisiana. Des Grieux and Lescaut bribe the guard, and are prevented from rescuing her only by the sudden arrival of the ship's captain. Des Grieux would follow when Manon is led away with a crowd of women who are also to be deported, but is restrained by the guard. In desperation he pleads with the captain, singing an intensely fervent aria. The captain is sympathetic and finally consents to smuggle him aboard.

ACT IV

SCENE: *A Vast Plain Near New Orleans.* The country is barren and uneven, and the approaching night is made gloomier by low overhanging clouds. Manon and des Grieux have fled to this desolate spot. They wander about, vainly seeking shelter, until Manon is exhausted, then des Grieux continues the search alone. When he returns Manon sinks, dying, into his arms.

THE RCA-VICTOR RECORDS
(Sung in Italian)

ACT I

DONNA NON VIDI MAI (Maiden So Fair):
  Alessandro Ziliani, Tenor, with Orch.
  1735, 10"

ACT II

IN QUELLE TRINE MORBIDE (In Those Silken Curtains): *Dorothy Kirsten, Soprano, with Orch.* 11-9792, 12"

Mishkin
ENRICO CARUSO AS DES GRIEUX

DOROTHY KIRSTEN AS MANON

ACT II—ELISABETH RETHBERG AS THE COUNTESS, JOHN BROWNLEE AS THE COUNT,
AND EZIO PINZA AS FIGARO

The Marriage of Figaro
(LE NOZZE DI FIGARO—FIGAROS HOCHZEIT)

OPERA BUFFA in two acts. Music by Wolfgang Amadeus Mozart. Book by Lorenzo da Ponte, after Beaumarchais' comedy, *Le Mariage de Figaro*, the second in a trilogy which opens with *The Barber of Seville*, subject of Rossini's famous operatic comedy, and closes with *The Culpable Mother*. Mozart's work was first performed at the Burgtheater, Vienna, May 1, 1786, the composer conducting. There is some dispute as to the first performance of the opera in America, since it is said to have been given in New York, under the title *The Follies of a Day*, as early as 1799, although a performance at the Park Theater, New York, in English, presented on May 10, 1824, was advertised as the "first time in America." Be this as it may, *The Marriage of Figaro* was quite popular in English versions produced during the early part of the nineteenth century. It was given in Italian at the Academy of Music, New York, on November 23, 1858, and in German at the German Opera House, also New York, on December 18, 1862. The Metropolitan *première* took place in Italian on January 31, 1894, with Lillian Nordica as Susanna, Emma Eames as Countess Almaviva, Sigrid Arnoldson as Cherubino, Mario Ancona as Figaro, and Édouard de Reszke as Almaviva. Emilio Bevignani conducted.

Other productions at the Metropolitan have offered casts with Marcella Sembrich and Frieda Hempel as Susanna, Johanna Gadski and Margarete Matzenauer as the Countess; Zélie de Lussan, Marie Engel, Suzanne Adams, Bella Alten, and Geraldine Farrar as Cherubino; Victor Maurel, Giuseppe Campanari, Adamo Didur, and Giuseppe de Luca as Figaro; Antonio Scotti and Didur as the Count; Gustav Mahler and Artur Bodanzky conducting.

The Marriage of Figaro

In recent years the Susanna has been impersonated at the Metropolitan by Bidu Sayao and Licia Albanese; the Countess by Lotte Lehmann; Cherubino by Jarmila Novotna and Risë Stevens; Figaro by Ezio Pinza; the Count by John Brownlee, and Bartolo by Salvatore Baccaloni, mostly under the conductorship of Fritz Busch.

The Marriage of Figaro remains one of the greatest masterpieces of comedy in music. Mozart's melodies, with all their charm, perfection of form, utter spontaneity, and apparent naïveté, are enormously faithful to character and situation. Moreover, they sparkle with all the wit and gaiety of Beaumarchais' humorous work. Nor, for that matter, can anything but praise be said for the shrewdly contrived libretto of da Ponte, who here, as in *Don Giovanni*, is at the top of his art.

Although Beaumarchais' comedy teems with social and political implications— Figaro's witty and highhanded attitude toward his aristocratic master, Almaviva, being in those days a sign of things to come—there is really little of it in the opera.

CHARACTERS

COUNT ALMAVIVA, *Grand Corregidor of Andalusia*	*Baritone*	DON CURZIO, *counselor-at-law*	*Tenor*
FIGARO, *his valet and major-domo of the château*	*Baritone*	CHERUBINO, *head page to the Count*	*Soprano*
DR. BARTOLO, *a physician of Seville*	*Bass*	COUNTESS ALMAVIVA	*Soprano*
DON BASILIO, *music master to the Countess*	*Tenor*	SUSANNA, *head waiting woman to the Countess, betrothed to Figaro*	*Soprano*
ANTONIO, *gardener of the château and Susanna's uncle*	*Bass*	MARCELLINA	*Contralto*
		BARBARINA, *Antonio's daughter*	*Soprano*

SERVANTS, OFFICERS OF THE COURT, AND PEASANTS

The action takes place at Count Almaviva's château in the country near Seville

The Overture to *The Marriage of Figaro* is a bubbling, delightful piece of music more or less in sonata form, full of good humor and activity. Its themes are its own, not appearing anywhere else in the opera, yet they are entirely in the spirit of the whole work. There is no free fantasia, although the coda is longer than ordinary. This overture is a very popular one in the concert hall.

Mozart and da Ponte wrote their opera in two acts, each having two scenes. Most often, however, it has been performed as a work in four acts, one for each scene.

ACT I

SCENE: *The Room Assigned to Figaro and Susanna.* Figaro, in high spirits, is preparing the room assigned to him and his bride-to-be, Susanna. He remarks how convenient it will be for him to wait on his master, the Count, and yet equally convenient for Susanna to attend her mistress, the Countess. Susanna suddenly dampens his ardor by remarking that the Count has had a more subtle reason in giving them a room so near his own. She calls Figaro a "goose" for not observing this or realizing that the Count was moved by anything other than generosity in paying her dowry. Figaro intends to investigate these matters, feeling quite capable of handling his employer. He makes this attitude known in the aria *"Se vuol ballare, signor contino"* ("If you

306

ACT III—MUNICH OPERA PRODUCTION

wish to dance, my little Count"). So soon has the gallant young Count Almaviva grown faithless to his wife, the formerly beloved Rosina! Still further
troubles are to beset the erstwhile Barber of Seville, for old Dr. Bartolo,
whom he outwitted in former days, still bears a grudge against him. Bartolo
discovers that in a weak moment Figaro promised to marry the aged Marcellina, and that the old dame would compel him to fulfill the contract.
Susanna fortunately overhears the plotting of this unseemly couple. After
a short encounter Susanna and Marcellina make for the center door, where,
in an amusing duet, exaggerated compliments give way to abuse. When they
have gone, the adolescent Cherubino enters, who is at the tender age susceptible to anything feminine, and has fallen deeply in love, if you please, with
no less a personage than the Countess herself. He describes his feeling in a
remarkable aria, *"Non so più cosa son"* ("I know not what I am doing").

Suddenly the Count is heard approaching, and Cherubino hastily conceals himself behind a large armchair. The Count has come to complain
against Cherubino, whom he suspects of paying attention to the Countess.
But even as he speaks, a knock is heard. The Count hastily hides behind the
same chair as the page, who, cleverly darting around out of the Count's way,
sinks into the depths of the chair. Susanna quickly covers him with a dress
that happens to lie at hand. The busybody Basilio enters and taunts Susanna
for flirting with the Count, then twits her about Cherubino. As soon, however, as Basilio mentions Cherubino's name in connection with that of the
Countess, Almaviva, unable to stand it longer, jumps from his hiding place

307

and demands an explanation. He goes on to tell how a short while ago he discovered the boy concealed under a table, flirting with Barbarina. In order to demonstrate how he found the youth when he lifted up the tablecloth, the Count goes over to the armchair and pulls away the dress. And lo! there again is Cherubino! The Count is beside himself with rage; then a sudden inspiration comes to him. There is a commission vacant in his regiment; Cherubino shall have it. He must go at once. Figaro, who has returned, laughingly tells the page that now instead of tender love-making he will have weary marching, and he apprises him of all this in the tripping, mock-military aria, *"Non più andrai"* ("No longer will you flutter").

ACT II

SCENE: *The Countess' Apartment.* When the curtain rises, we find the Countess alone. She is meditating upon her happy past and unhappy present. Still deeply in love with her husband, she slowly realizes that she is not the only woman in his life. She then gives vent to her feelings in a touching and expressive song in which she prays that her husband's affection may be restored to her, or else to let her find escape from her grief in death. This is the aria *"Porgi amor"* ("Love, thou holy purest impulse").

Susanna then enters, and the two ladies despair because of the Count's wayward affections, although Susanna tries to hearten her mistress. The resourceful Figaro, entering, reveals a plan, already put into effect, for reawakening the Count's interest in his wife—make him jealous by letting him discover a note arranging a rendezvous between the Countess and a lover. They decide to send Susanna in the Countess' place, and Cherubino, dressed as Susanna, to meet the Count. Thus it is hoped that through ridicule the Count will be persuaded to remain faithful to his Countess.

Cherubino comes, delighted at the thought of seeing the Countess before his departure. He sings *"Voi che sapete"* ("What is this feeling?"), one of the most famous arias in the opera, a wonderful delineation of the love emotion characteristic of early youth.

Continuing with their plot, the women proceed to dress him in the maid's garments. Susanna sings a fascinatingly humorous aria in which she coquettishly bids him kneel before her and tells him first to turn one way and then another while she adapts the feminine apparel to his person, *"Venite, inginocchiatevi"* ("Come, kneel down").

The Countess happens to notice Cherubino's officer's commission, and observes that the seal to it has been forgotten. Suddenly her husband is heard angrily knocking outside. Cherubino scurries into hiding in a closet. The Count enters just in time to hear him upset a chair in his blind haste, and, observing his wife's confusion, he demands admission to the closet. Susanna, concealed in an alcove, hears the Countess refuse on the ground

From the Painting by Becker THE MARRIAGE OF FIGARO AND SUSANNA

that her maid is in the closet, dressing. The suspicious Count, however, goes out for a crowbar to break down the door and insists on taking the Countess with him. As soon as they have gone Cherubino emerges and escapes through the window; Susanna quickly hides in the cabinet in his place. When the Count returns, prepared to batter away, the Countess finally confesses that Cherubino is there. Then follows a dramatic duet which depicts the Count's heated anger and the anxious pleading of the Countess. Thus she is quite as startled as her husband when Susanna suddenly appears! The Count then becomes penitent and asks his wife's forgiveness. Figaro then enters to accompany Susanna to the wedding. Shortly after, as luck would have it, Antonio, the gardener, enters in an inebriated state. He is carrying a couple of shattered flowerpots and demands an audience with his master. He wants to lodge a complaint against someone who had jumped out of the window of the Countess' room and escaped through the garden. Figaro with great difficulty silences the Count's newly aroused suspicions, by announcing himself the culprit. The gardener spoils this by producing a paper that was dropped by the fugitive; the Count says that he will believe Figaro's story if he is able to tell what this paper contains. Through a quick whisper from the Countess passed along by Susanna, Figaro learns it is Cherubino's commission. This would make things look rather bad for the Countess, but the quick-witted Figaro, again prompted by the women, declares that he had the commission in his pocket in order to have it looked after, for it lacked a seal. The day is saved, but Figaro now has a worse problem to face. Marcellina enters with her lawyer and demands that Figaro shall keep his promise to marry her. The Count, rather eager to settle accounts with the valet, says that he will look into this!

Wide World Studio   DRAWING FOR ACT IV BY JONEL JORGULESCO

ACT III

SCENE: *A Hall in Almaviva's Château.* Count Almaviva plans to force
Susanna to accept his attentions by threatening to make Figaro wed the aged
Marcellina; and Susanna, wishing to further the plans of her mistress, seems
to surrender. As he goes away, rejoicing in his triumph, the Count overhears
Susanna exclaim to Figaro, "Our cause is victorious." Growing suspicious,
the Count resolves to punish Figaro at once and deal with Susanna later.

Accordingly, Marcellina, her lawyer, the Count, and Bartolo arrive to inform Figaro that he must marry as he has promised, or pay damages. Figaro
thinks he may be rich enough to pay the damages, for he has just discovered
clues that suggest that he may be of noble birth. While he is explaining, Marcellina suddenly asks if he has a spatula mark upon his right arm. He has.
By this she knows him to be her long-lost son; the Count's plans are spoiled!
Mother and son embrace and are so discovered by Susanna, who is much distressed until matters are explained. At last Susanna and Figaro are free to
go ahead with preparations for their wedding. The Countess then arrives.
She is deeply concerned as to how her husband will take the deception that
is to be practiced on him in the garden. She is still deeply in love with him
and deplores the fact that she must seek the help of her servants to win back
his affection. In an aria of tenderness and beauty, she regrets her lost days of
happiness, *"Dove sono"* ("They are over").

Continuing with the plot, Susanna meets with the Countess and at her
dictation writes a letter to the Count fixing exactly the time and place of their
rendezvous. The letter is sealed with a pin which the Count is to return as a

sign that he will keep the appointment. Rather than send Cherubino, the Countess herself has decided to go, disguised as Susanna.

The wedding of Susanna and Figaro forthwith takes place. Cherubino, in female attire, Barbarina, and a group of peasant girls present a bunch of flowers to the Countess, as the festivities commence. Susanna contrives, even during the ceremony, to slip the letter to the Count, who pricks his finger on the pin. Figaro observes this without, however, suspecting anything.

ACT IV

SCENE: *The Garden of the Château.* Barbarina, the gardener's daughter, is looking for a pin she has lost, the pin with which Susanna had sealed her letter to the Count, and which Barbarina had been entrusted to return. Figaro learns of this from the unsuspecting child, and hastily decides that Susanna actually is faithless and intends to yield to the Count that very evening.

It is night in the park of the château, just such a night as is made for love and intrigue. Figaro has come to the rendezvous intending to spy on the supposed infidelity of his bride; he conceals himself just as the Countess and Susanna enter. The mistress hides, too, and the maid, awaiting the Count, and knowing that her husband is listening, sings a wonderfully beautiful soliloquy addressed to her supposed lover, *"Deh vieni, non tardar"* ("Come, do not delay"). She does this with the quaintly humorous idea of harassing her husband.

Cherubino, having an appointment with Barbarina, suddenly appears on the scene, and seeing the Countess, whom he believes to be Susanna, attempts to kiss her. The Count arrives, just in time to see this, and, stepping between them, unexpectedly receives the kiss himself. As Cherubino draws back, Figaro advances into his place. The Count then gives a box on the ear

ACT II—METROPOLITAN OPERA PRODUCTION

to Figaro, whom he takes for Cherubino. The page then takes flight. The Count then proceeds to make ardent love to his wife, whom he believes to be Susanna, so cleverly does she imitate her maid's voice and manners.

Figaro, wild with fury at this spectacle, unexpectedly meets Susanna, who similarly is impersonating the Countess. He accordingly tries to awaken the jealousy of the supposed Countess by telling her of her husband's conduct. Susanna, however, reveals herself; and the Count, seeing Figaro apparently embracing the Countess, promptly forgets the supposed Susanna and, violently seizing Figaro, calls for help. Explanations follow, and the Count, perceiving himself outwitted, begs his wife's forgiveness.

THE RCA-VICTOR RECORDS
(Sung in Italian)

COMPLETE RECORDING: *Audrey Mildmay, Soprano; Aulikki Rautawaara, Soprano; Luise Helletsgruber, Soprano; Constance Willis, Soprano; Winifred Radford, Soprano; Willi Domgraf-Fassbaender, Baritone; Roy Henderson, Baritone; Norman Allin, Bass; Italo Tajo, Bass; Heddle Nash, Tenor; Fergus Dunlop, Bass; Morgan Jones, Tenor; with Chorus and Orchestra of the Glyndebourne Festival Company, Fritz Busch, Cond.* (Recorded in the Glyndebourne Opera House, Glyndebourne, England)

DMC-105 (DM-313, 314, 315)
    (Vol. 1—16899-16904), 6-12
    (Vol. 2—16905-16910), 6-12"
    (Vol. 3—16911-16915), 5-12"
MC-105 (M-313, 314, 315)
    (Vol. 1—14042-14047)
    (Vol. 2—14054-14059)
    (Vol. 3—14066-14070)

OVERTURE: *Minneapolis Symphony Orchestra, Eugene Ormandy, Cond.*
14325, 12"

Pierre Luboshutz and Genia Nemenoff (Duo-Pianists) 11-8455, 12"

ACT I

SE A CASO MADAMA (If Madame Should Call You): *Elisabeth Rethberg, Soprano; Ezio Pinza, Bass; with Orch.*
2154, 10" (In Album M-783)

NON SO PIÙ COSA SON (I Know Not What I Am): *Eleanor Steber, Soprano, with Orch.* 11-9772, 12"
(In Album M-1157)

NON PIÙ ANDRAI (No Longer Will You Flutter): *Ezio Pinza, Bass, with Orch.*
18015, 12" (In Album M-783)

ACT II

PORGI AMOR (Love, Thou Holy Purest Impulse): *Eleanor Steber, Soprano, with Orch.* 11-8850, 12"
Elisabeth Rethberg, Soprano, with Orch. 2155, 10" (In Album M-783)

VOI CHE SAPETE (What Is This Feeling?): *Luisa Tetrazzini, Soprano, with Orch.* 15-1001, 12" (Acoustical Recording)
Eleanor Steber, Soprano; RCA-Victor Orchestra, Jean Paul Morel, Cond.
12-0526, 12"

ACT III

CRUDEL! PERCHÈ FINORA (Cruel One! Why Have You): *Elisabeth Rethberg, Soprano; Ezio Pinza, Bass; with Orch.* 2155, 10"
(In Album M-783)

DOVE SONO (They Are Over): *Eleanor Steber, Soprano, with Orch.* 11-8850, 12"
Elisabeth Rethberg, Soprano, with Orch. 18015, 12" (In Album M-783)

ACT IV

DEH VIENI, NON TARDAR (O Come, Do Not Delay): *Lucrezia Bori, Soprano, with Orch.* 14614, 12"
(In Album M-405)
Eleanor Steber, Soprano, with Orch. 11-9772, 12" (In Album M-1157)

Byron

ACT I, SCENE 2—THE FAIR

Martha

OPERA IN four acts. Music by Friedrich von Flotow. Libretto by W. Friedrich, adapted from the original French libretto by Vernoy de Saint-Georges. First performance at the Kärntnertor-Theater, Vienna, November 25, 1847. American *première*, in English, at Niblo's Garden, New York, November 1, 1852. First performance in America in Italian at the New York Academy of Music, January 7, 1859. Among great Lady Harriets have been Adelina Patti, Marcella Sembrich, Frieda Hempel, and Frances Alda. It was during the Metropolitan performance of February 10, 1897, that the French basso, Armand Castelmary, suffered a heart attack and died on stage in the arms of the Polish tenor, Jean de Reszke, the Lionel of the cast.

The libretto of *Martha* has an interesting linguistic history. It began in French. J. H. Vernoy de Saint-Georges, who had earlier collaborated on the text of Donizetti's *La Fille du régiment*, was commissioned by the director of the Paris Opéra to write a sketch for a ballet. It happened that the French gentleman had two aristocratic lady friends who had been mistaken for servant girls at a carnival. They related their experience to Vernoy de Saint-Georges, who immediately saw a ballet in the episode. Flotow, one of three composers engaged to compose the music for it, liked the ballet story so much he asked Vernoy de Saint-Georges to turn it into an opera libretto. This the obliging Frenchman did, writing it, of course, in his native French. Flotow then had the libretto freely translated into his native language, German, by W. Friedrich. Later an Italian translation was made, and after that one in English, both excellent. Soon the opera *Martha* became so familiar to English operagoers that they came to think of it as an English opera. This was understandable because the locale is the English countryside. Besides, the beautiful Irish folk tune, "The Last Rose of Summer," with Thomas Moore's words, was inserted into the opera by Flotow. On the other hand, the Italians found the no less celebrated aria, "*M'appari*," so Italian in language and style that many assumed both the original language and the composer were Italian. Donizetti would have proudly signed his name to that luscious melody. There was further confusion, however. Each country changed both the setting and the century of the story. In the original version, the time is the eighteenth century, the place England. The French altered it to the nineteenth century, and the Italians threw it back to the fifteenth. In whatever language or setting, *Martha* was a huge success, thanks to its gracious blend of romance and tunefulness, the brisk ensembles, the colorful fair scene, and of course the two supreme moments of Lionel's aria and Martha's delivery of "The Last Rose of Summer."

CHARACTERS

LADY HARRIET DURHAM, *Maid of Honor to Queen Anne*	*Soprano*	LIONEL, *his foster brother, afterwards Earl of Derby*	*Tenor*
NANCY, *her maid and friend*	*Mezzo-soprano*	THE SHERIFF OF RICHMOND	*Bass*
SIR TRISTAN MICKLEFORD, *Lady Harriet's cousin*	*Bass*	THREE SERVANTS OF LADY HARRIET	*Tenor and two Basses*
PLUNKETT, *a wealthy farmer*	*Bass*	THREE MAIDSERVANTS	*Soprano and Mezzo-sopranos*

CHORUS OF LADIES, SERVANTS, FARMERS, HUNTERS AND HUNTRESSES, PAGES, ETC.

The action takes place in England during the reign of Queen Anne

To make the opera complete as an enjoyable unit there is a charming and melodious Overture, which pictures the shifting moods of comedy, romance, and dramatic conflict arising in this so-called *opera semi-seria*. From the finale of Act III comes the melody of the lovely horn solo that follows the brief and somber opening of the Overture. This is worked up to a resounding climax, and a bright and restless little theme enters, developed into a passage of frank gaiety. A rustic tune follows, accompanied by a jangling tambourine, picturing the servant girls at the fair. The two main themes are then reviewed, varied, and combined, and the coda sets in for a merry drive to the brilliant end.

ACT I

SCENE 1: *Lady Harriet's Boudoir.* Beautiful young Lady Harriet, Maid of Honor to Queen Anne, has grown weary of the monotonous ritual of court life. Admirers, social position, and court festivities have begun to bore her, and the brilliant pageant of fashion, jewels, and flowers has become an empty show. Her faithful maid, Nancy, enters. Finding her mistress weeping, she tries to comfort her, reminding her of her enviable position, but Lady Harriet replies that it has only brought her boredom. Nancy now boldly ventures that it is love that is missing in her life. Harriet's cousin, Sir Tristan Mickleford, is announced. He is an absurd old coxcomb who prides himself on a vast knowledge of women. To amuse Lady Harriet he proposes a whole new set of elegant diversions, but the proposal only brings gales of laughter. The song of servant maids on their way to Richmond Fair comes through the open window, giving Lady Harriet a sudden inspiration. The three of them will join the merrymakers! Nancy and Sir Tristan object stoutly, but Lady Harriet orders them along. Peasant costumes worn at a recent court ball are procured for the adventure. Sir Tristan, accordingly, is transformed into a farmer named "John"; Nancy becomes the servant girl "Julia"; and Lady Harriet is disguised as her friend, "Martha." Hence the title and the opera.

SCENE 2: *The Fair at Richmond*. The fair is in full swing. In the fashion of the time, servant girls have come here to seek employment with wealthy farmers, and they may be heard bargaining sharply with prospective masters. Two young farmers, Lionel and Plunkett, mingle with the motley crowd. From their conversation we learn that Lionel is Plunkett's adopted brother; also, that Lionel's father, a mysterious stranger in the neighborhood, had given Plunkett a ring on his deathbed. Should his son ever find himself in trouble, he had instructed, the ring should be presented to Queen Anne. So far no occasion has arisen to test the ring's power. When the three masqueraders appear, Lionel and Plunkett are immediately attracted by the beauty of the two "servant girls" and offer to hire both of them. In the spirit of the prank the girls accept, Sir Tristan remonstrating in vain. "Julia" and "Martha" take the money proffered them and by so doing unwittingly bind themselves legally to their new masters for one year. Sir Tristan tries to drag the girls off, but the crowd drives him away with jeers. The terrified impostors are now led away by the two farmers.

ACT II

SCENE: *A Farmhouse*. As the curtain rises, Lionel and Plunkett enter, dragging with them their reluctant new hired help. The ladies soon recover their breath and, realizing they are not in any serious danger, resolve to plague their new employers. When the two young farmers show the girls the room that is to be theirs, the girls promptly announce they are tired and will shut themselves in indefinitely. Taken aback, the farmers remind them they have been paid to work. But when they order supper, their command again falls on deaf ears. Lionel, the more gallant of the farmers, requests the girls to show their skill at spinning. Blandly they plead ignorance, and Lionel and Plunkett are obliged to sit down and show them. At this point the orchestra begins a merry little tune that moves at breakneck speed to the end of the ensemble. Rapid scales and darting staccato passages illustrate the hustle and bustle involved in the act of setting up the spinning wheels and fetching chairs. The men sing *brr-brr* in imitation of the humming wheels, as the girls raise their cheerful voices in a bright outcry of wonder over the strange spectacle of men spinning.

The lesson ends abruptly as "Julia" upsets Plunkett's spinning wheel and runs out of the room, with Plunkett, obviously infatuated, dashing after her. The scene is set for Lionel's avowal to "Martha." Though she laughs at him, his good looks and manly bearing have impressed her. When Lionel assures her he will be a kind and gentle master, "Martha" smilingly replies she will not make a good servant, for she can do nothing but laugh and joke. Lionel professes not to care, since his only concern is that she should be happy. Then he asks "Martha" to sing for him, and in his elation he snatches a rose from her. This gives "Martha" a cue, and she sings "The Last Rose of Summer," the old Irish melody, "The Groves of Blarney," to which the poet Moore adapted his verses. Captivated by her singing, Lionel falls to his knees and protests his love, assuring her that rank means nothing to him, that, in any case, his love will elevate her to his position. "Martha" bursts out laughing at the thought of Lady Harriet rising to a farmer's rank. Lionel is crushed by this unexpected reaction, and only the noisy return of "Julia" and Plunkett relieves the strained situation. The orchestra now sounds a saucy little melody as the charming "Good Night Quartet" begins. Holding her tightly, Plunkett exclaims to "Julia": "Don't you try this game again, young lady!" Then turning to Lionel he asks: "Where do you suppose this little vixen was? In the kitchen, breaking glasses and the dishes and spilling the wine. At last I've caught her!" The two struggle half seriously, and Plunkett is impressed by the girl's strength and spirit. The clock suddenly strikes, and all exclaim "Midnight!" in surprise. Lionel sings a pretty melody, bidding the others good night and pleasant dreams. "Julia" sarcastically echoes his words, "Good night!" Then, as the young men take their leave, all four unite in a final ensemble of great loveliness. There is a pause, and the girls peep out from their room. Seeing no one, they slip out quietly and hold an excited consultation. The game has gone too far! How can they escape? What would the Queen say if she heard of it? The "servant girls" shudder at the very thought. There is a furtive tap at the window. It is Sir Tristan come to rescue them. Overjoyed, the girls make their escape through the window and leap into the waiting carriage.

ACT III

SCENE: *A Hunting Park in Richmond Forest.* Despondent over the loss of their fascinating servants, Lionel and Plunkett seek distraction. They have come to watch the Queen and her train at the hunt. Plunkett is at an inn with a crowd of farmer friends. In spirited style he launches into a gay apostrophe to that revered tavern staple, porter. To this famous old English beverage Plunkett grandly ascribes the vigor and valor of every Briton. As the farmers disperse, leaving Lionel alone—alone with his gloomy thoughts—he meditates on his hopeless love, and a beautiful song rises to his lips, *"M'appari"* ("Like a Dream"), a song telling how "Martha" comes to him like a vision, soothing his pain and banishing his sorrow. And abruptly the vision vanishes, leaving him joyless again. This number justly retains its place among the enduring favorites of the tenor repertory. As if to bear out the song, "Martha" suddenly appears to Lionel, garbed now in the splendid raiment of a lady of the court. Puzzled and ravished by the sight of her, Lionel at once declares his love. Lady Harriet, against the promptings of her own heart, pretends he is a stranger to her. Desperate, Lionel reminds her that she still owes him a year's service. Lady Harriet now calls the hunters, crying that this man must be mad. "May God forgive you!" Lionel exclaims as he is placed under arrest. Before being led away, he gives Plunkett the ring with instructions to present it to the Queen, whose approach is announced.

ACT IV

SCENE 1: *Plunkett's Farmhouse* (same as Act II). Lionel's true identity and the innocence of his banished father have now been established. Lady Harriet herself has presented the ring to the Queen, and she comes to inform him that the title and property of the Earl of Derby are now his. She comes, too, to confess her love for him, but Lionel, his reason almost gone, waves all aside—title, wealth, and Lady Harriet. In hopes of restoring his mind, she again sings "The Last Rose of Summer"—to no avail. She pleads for forgiveness, but Lionel, still obsessed by the cruelty of her rebuff, reviles her wildly, and rushes from the room, leaving Lady Harriet in tears. The reunion of Nancy and Plunkett, however, has ripened into a real romance, and their one thought now is to bring their unhappy friends together. They agree heartily to a plan devised by Lady Harriet.

SCENE 2: *A Representation of the Richmond Fair.* A crowd of merrymakers is milling about on Lady Harriet's private grounds. A reproduction of the fair scene of Act II, complete with booths and farmers and "servant girls," has been arranged as part of the plan to reunite the lovers. Harriet, Nancy, and Plunkett are dressed in the costumes they wore at their first meeting, and farmers are again bargaining with the hired help. Into this bustling scene Plunkett gently leads his ailing friend. The remembered sights and sounds begin to work on Lionel's clouded mind, and when, suddenly, he sees Harriet, clad once more as a servant, the last mist lifts. Lionel embraces her tenderly, and as the two couples pledge their troth, they blend their voices in a final delivery of "The Last Rose of Summer," altering the words this time to "The spring has returned, fresh roses now bloom."

BENIAMINO GIGLI AS LIONEL

Martha

Bruno　　　　　　　　　LICIA ALBANESE AS MARTHA

THE RCA-VICTOR RECORDS
(Sung in Italian unless otherwise noted)

OVERTURE: *Victor Symphony Orchestra, Rosario Bourdon, Cond.*　35916, 12"

ACT II

QUI SOLA, VERGIN ROSA (The Last Rose of Summer): *Lily Pons, Soprano, with Orch. In English*　17231, 12"
(In Album M-702)

QUARTETTO NOTTURNO (Good-night Quartet): *Enrico Caruso, Tenor; Marcel Journet, Bass; Frances Alda, Soprano; Josephine Jacoby, Mezzo-soprano; with Orch.*　16-5002, 12"
(In Album M-953)
(Acoustical Recording)

ACT III

M'APPARI TUTT' AMOR (Like a Dream):

Enrico Caruso, Tenor, with Orch.　7720, 12"

Beniamino Gigli, Tenor, with Orch.　7109, 12"

Tito Schipa, Tenor, with Orch.　6570, 12"

Jussi Bjoerling, Tenor, with Orch.　13790, 12"

James Melton, Tenor, with Orch.　10-1329, 10"

ACT IV

IL MIO LIONELLO (My Unhappy Lionel): *Mattia Battistini, Baritone, with Orch.*　15-1010, 12"
(Acoustical Recording)

318

FINAL SCENE—METROPOLITAN OPERA PRODUCTION

The Masked Ball
(UN BALLO IN MASCHERA)

OPERA IN three acts. Music by Giuseppe Verdi. Book by Antonio Somma, after Scribe's libretto for Auber's *Gustave III, ou Le Bal masqué*. First produced at the Apollo Theater, Rome, February 17, 1859. American *première*, Academy of Music, New York, February 11, 1861, in Italian. Initial performance at the Metropolitan Opera House, December 11, 1889, in German, with Lilli Lehmann as Amelia. First time in Italian at the Metropolitan, February 23, 1903, with Johanna Gadski as Amelia, Fritzi Scheff as Oscar, Louise Homer as Ulrica, Emilio de Marchi as Riccardo, Giuseppe Campanari as Renato, Édouard de Reszke as Sam, and Marcel Journet as Tom. Subsequent performances at the Metropolitan have boasted, as on February 6, 1905, casts with such artists as Emma Eames, Bella Alten, Mme. Homer, Enrico Caruso, Antonio Scotti, Pol Plançon, and Journet; and, further, as on November 22, 1913, Emmy Destinn, Frieda Hempel, Margarete Matzenauer, Caruso, Pasquale Amato, Andrés de Segurola, and Léon Rothier.

The story has some historical foundation in that Gustavus III, of Sweden, was assassinated during a masked ball at Stockholm. As luck would have it, while negotiations for the production of Verdi's opera were in progress, an Italian revolutionist made an attempt on the life of Napoleon III. Naturally, the authorities demanded changes in the opera. The composer refused to adapt his music to a butchered libretto and refused to allow its production. As a result great excitement prevailed in Naples. Crowds of people paraded, shouting "Viva Verdi!" using the popular composer's name as a slight disguise of the fact that they were favoring a united Italy under Victor Emmanuel, thus: Vittorio Emmanuele Rè d'Italia (Victor Emmanuel, King of Italy). An odd acrostic, the letters of a composer's name! As a way out of the difficulty, the censor at Rome suggested that the title be changed and the scene transferred to Boston. The assassination of a governor in provincial Boston would not disturb the authorities. A colonial governor singing on the Italian operatic stage is not an unamusing thing for American audiences to contemplate, and Europe having more or less recovered from its sensitiveness about royal assassinations, the scene of the opera when given there is now frequently placed in Naples.

For the Metropolitan revival of the season 1940–41—and ever since—the action was placed in its original locale of Sweden in the reign of Gustavus III. The names of the characters, however, were not changed. In the cast were Zinka Milanov, Jussi Bjoerling, and Alexander Sved.

CHARACTERS

RICCARDO *(Gustavus III, King of Sweden)* — Tenor
RENATO, *his friend and secretary* — Baritone
AMELIA, *Renato's wife* — Soprano
ULRICA, *a fortuneteller* — Contralto
OSCAR, *a page* — Soprano
SILVANO, *a sailor* — Baritone
SAM } *conspirators* — Bass
TOM } — Bass

A JUDGE, GUARDS, CONSPIRATORS, DANCERS, ETC.

ACT I

SCENE 1: *Gustavus III's Palace.* Among the assembly gathered at the house of Riccardo are two of his enemies, Sam and Tom. Many of the others are friendly toward the King, however, and, when he enters, sing his praises. He greets them with assurances of his interest in their welfare. Then his page, Oscar, presents him with a list of the guests invited to the ball. Riccardo reads the list until he comes to one name that makes him start with delight; he exclaims, "Amelia!" Meanwhile, Oscar and the people unite in singing the praises of their King. And the conspirators, headed by Sam and Tom, agree that the hour is not propitious for the success of their plans. These varied comments are expressed in a highly melodious quartet and chorus.

A fortuneteller, Ulrica, is brought in and accused of being a witch. Riccardo laughs at the accusation and dismisses the woman. He calls his courtiers around him and suggests that for a lark they go disguised to the hut of the sorceress and consult her. All agree, his enemies seeing a chance to further their plan.

SCENE 2: *Ulrica's Hut.* The King, dressed as a sailor, arrives at the witch's cottage with his companions. While they are conversing a knock is heard. At Ulrica's request all leave the hut—all save Riccardo, who conceals himself in a corner. A veiled woman enters. It is none other than Amelia, whom he loves. She returns his affection, although she is the wife of Renato, the King's secretary and most trusted friend. She desires to remain a loyal wife and asks the sorceress to give her peace of mind by banishing a love which she cannot control. Ulrica tells her of an herb from which can be brewed a magic potion; to be effective it must be gathered only at night near a gallows.

Amelia departs, the people re-enter, and Riccardo, in his sailor's disguise, asks to be told his fortune. The request takes the form of a barcarolle—a favorite type of sea song.

Ulrica rebukes him and, examining his palm, tells him he is soon to die by the sword of that friend who will next shake his hand. Oscar and the courtiers exclaim in horror at her pronouncement, which launches the famous Quintet, *"E scherzo"* ("Your prophecy absurd"). Ulrica insists that such is the decree of relentless fate. Sam and Tom are fearful lest their plot be discovered, although Riccardo sings jestingly.

Renato enters, anxious for Riccardo's safety, for he has learned of the conspiracy. Happy at finding him, he greets him with a vigorous shake of the hand. Riccardo tells the witch she is a poor fortuneteller, for this is the best friend he ever had, and throws her a fat purse. For his bravery and gallantry he wins the applause of the people.

ACT II

SCENE: *A Lonely Field Near a Gallows.* Amelia goes by night to seek the magic herb at the foot of the gallows. She sings a dramatic aria, praying heaven to release her from her hopeless love. A clock striking midnight, she fancies that she sees a phantom rising before her.

The vision resolves itself into Riccardo, who now approaches. Although she confesses her love, she begs him to leave. Renato suddenly appears; he has come to warn the King that his life is in danger and urges him to flee down a side path. Renato consents, at Riccardo's request, to escort this veiled lady back to the city without speaking or otherwise trying to learn her identity. This Renato is prevented from doing by the arrival of the conspirators, who, enraged at the escape of the King, would know the identity of the lady. Renato threatens them, whereupon she herself lifts the veil and he recognizes his wife. Filled with rage, he arranges a secret meeting with the conspirators.

ACT III

SCENE 1: *The Study of Renato's House.* At home with Amelia, Renato assails her with the most bitter fury and is at the point of killing her. She swears she is innocent and begs for a moment's respite to bid farewell to their child. This request he grants. Then, left alone, he repents of his desperate intention, reserving his wrath and vengeance, now, for Riccardo, whose portrait is on the wall, and he remarks on this in the aria *"Eri tu"* ("Was it thou?").

The conspirators enter, and Renato joins them in their plot to murder the King. Lots are drawn, and Renato is the one fated to do the deed.

SCENE 2: *Riccardo's Apartment in the Palace.* Convinced that he and Amelia must be separated, Riccardo is in process of signing an order sending Renato and his family abroad, although he is desolate at the thought of never again seeing Amelia.

SCENE 3: *The Ballroom in the Palace.* Amid the brilliant merrymaking at the masked ball, Renato cleverly finds out Riccardo's disguise from the King's page. Riccardo has come to the ball in spite of Amelia's warnings, and though she again warns him, he refuses to leave—he is no coward. He tells Amelia of his plan for the future; he will never see her again. Just as he is saying "Farewell," Renato rushes in and stabs him in the back. Riccardo forgives him, and assures him that Amelia is guiltless; then with his dying breath he begs that no one attempt to avenge his death.

THE RCA-VICTOR RECORDS
(Sung in Italian unless otherwise noted)

ACT I

QUINTETTO—È SCHERZO, ED È FOLLIA (Your Prophecy Absurd): *Enrico Caruso, Tenor; Frieda Hempel, Soprano; Léon Rothier, Bass; Andrés de Segurola, Bass; Maria Duchêne, Soprano; Metropolitan Opera Chorus; with Orch.* 16-5000, 12″
(In Album M-953)
(Acoustical Recording)

ACT II

MA DALL' ARIDO STELO DIVULSA (Yonder Plant Enchanted): *Celestina Boninsegna, Soprano, with Orch.* 15-1006, 12″
(Acoustical Recording)

ACT V

ERI TU, CHE MACCHIAVI (Was It Thou?): *Leonard Warren, Baritone, with Orch.* 11-9292, 12″

Lawrence Tibbett, Baritone, with Orch. 7353, 12″
11-8861, 12″
(In Album M-1015)
15819, 12″
(In Album M-633)

Mario Ancona, Baritone, with Orch. 15-1002, 12″
(Acoustical Recording)

ROMANZA—MA SE M'È FORZA PERDERTI (Forever to Lose Thee): *Jan Peerce, Tenor, with Orch.* 11-9295, 12″

New York Times　　　　　FRIEDRICH SCHORR AS HANS SACHS

Die Meistersinger

OPERA IN three acts. Music and libretto by Richard Wagner. First performance, in the original German, at the Hof-und-National-Theater, Munich, June 21, 1868. American *première*, at the Metropolitan Opera House, January 4, 1886. An Italian version followed on March 2, 1892, continuing for many years. Though completed in 1867, *Die Meister-singer* was first sketched out by Wagner in 1845 as a companion piece to *Tannhäuser*. Twenty-two stormy years intervened before the completion of a masterpiece which the celebrated Polish pianist, Ignace Paderewski, once hailed as "the greatest work of genius ever achieved by any artist in any field of human activity." It was with perhaps a sense of mingled relief and regret that Wagner finally scrawled on the bottom of the last score sheet: "The completion of *Die Meistersinger*, Triebschen, Thursday, October 24, 1867, 8 o'clock in the evening."

Though they all bear the unmistakable stamp of his style, Wagner's great music dramas differ markedly from one another. The music of each is so appropriate to the action that the two become an inseparable unit in our minds. Thus, we have the passionately throbbing *Tristan und Isolde*, the fervidly mystical *Parsifal*, and the mellow and humorous *Die Meistersinger*. This blend of humor and humanity in his great comedy quickly appealed to Wagner's growing public, and to this day the great comedy remains one of his most popular works.

The vast contrapuntal power of the music is never there for its own sake, but as a kind of inevitable flowering of the very theme of the opera, of the poetic idea embedded in the conflict of schools. This poetic, or aesthetic, idea is represented in the struggle between the liberal-minded Walther, rebelling against the doctrinaire tenets of the guilds, and Beckmesser, the scoundrelly pedant, opposed, like all hidebound custodians of the older ways, to any progress in the arts. As everyone knows, in this Beckmesser the composer pilloried forever Eduard Hanslick, the dreaded critical oracle of Vienna who had become the archenemy of Wagnerism. In the fair-minded Hans Sachs, Wagner represented enlightened public opinion, respectful of the great masters, yet willing to grant all innovators the right to be heard and, if genuine, to be accepted. The historic Sachs was, of course, somewhat different from Wagner's cobbler-poet. In a deeper sense, it is the aging Sachs' hopeless and self-denying love for the young and beautiful Eva that explains why *Die Meistersinger* is often called a "tragicomedy."

Instead of legendary sources, Wagner this time depends to a large extent upon actual history for the basis of his comedy. He conceived the work at first as a sort of humorous variation on the contest theme of *Tannhäuser*. In that opera Wagner had treated of the medieval minnesingers, nobles who sang of exalted love—the German counterparts of the French *trouvères*, or troubadours. Like the chivalry of which they were an expression, the minnesingers disappeared with the coming of the Renaissance. In their place there arose, among the middle-class trade guilds, bands of singers who, patterning themselves after the minnesingers, took the name "mastersingers" (*Meistersinger*). To become an enrolled member of one of these groups of "mastersingers," the ambitious youth, while learning his trade, was obliged to study the arts of singing and poetry, too. After passing various examinations, he then worked his way up through the several degrees of "Scholar," "Schoolman," "Singer," "Poet," and finally "Master." The purpose of the guild was to foster a love of the noblest ideals in art. However, in the course of time, the Mastersingers' Guild inevitably adopted a fixed dogmatic outlook. Excessive value was now given to pedantic and traditional rules. Most famous of the mastersingers was Hans Sachs, cobbler, poet, and dramatist, who lived at Nuremberg (1494–1576) and helped combat the pedantry of his colleagues.

Wagner made a thorough historical research before he penned this vivid picture of life in Nuremberg, crowded with its wealth of amusing and picturesque details. Two of the musical motives employed, "The Banner" and "The Art Brotherhood," were gleaned from some "Prize Master Tones" included in an old book by J. C. Wagenseil, printed at Nuremberg in 1697. Yet Wagner does not thrust this history upon us, but allows it to form a diverting and realistic background for the human and romantic story he has to tell.

CHARACTERS

HANS SACHS, *cobbler*	*Bass or Baritone*	MAGDALENA, *Eva's nurse*	*Soprano*
POGNER, *goldsmith*	*Bass*	VOGELGESANG, *furrier;* NACHTIGALL,	
BECKMESSER, *town clerk*	*Bass*	*buckle-maker;* KOTHNER, *baker;*	
WALTHER VON STOLZING, *a young*		ZORN, *pewterer;* EISLINGER, *grocer;*	
Franconian knight	*Tenor*	MOSER, *tailor;* ORTEL, *soap boiler;*	
DAVID, *apprentice to Hans Sachs*	*Tenor*	SCHWARZ, *stocking weaver;* FOLZ,	
EVA, *Pogner's daughter*	*Soprano*	*coppersmith*	

BURGHERS OF ALL GUILDS, JOURNEYMEN, APPRENTICES, GIRLS, AND PEOPLE

Die Meistersinger

ACT II—SALZBURG FESTIVAL PRODUCTION

The action takes place in Nuremberg in the middle of the sixteenth century

The Prelude (or *Vorspiel*) begins at once with the theme of the master-singers, assertive, pompous, even stolid, but nevertheless of a striking vigor and beauty.

After these characteristics of the mastersingers have been emphasized by repetition, the placid, springlike motive of "Waking Love" is heard in the woodwinds. This soon gives way to the proud "Banner" of the mastersingers, emblem-theme of the self-complacent pride of that group of tradesmen-musicians. Closely joined with it is the suave theme of the "Art Brother-hood," the melody with which the citizens of Nuremberg hymn their praise of all that is finest in their native art. This is developed to a magnificent climax; then follows a motive expressive of Walther's love, the motive of "Longing." This leads directly into the beautifully lyric theme that will finally blossom in its fullest glory during the "Prize Song," the theme of "Love Confessed." This, in turn, grows directly into the more impassioned motive of "Love's Ardor." These melodies are then combined, and, "Love's Ardor" seemingly in the ascendancy, developed into a climax. This climax is suddenly broken off, and we hear the pompous theme of the mastersingers, parodied in a perkish manner by the woodwind. Into this the motives of "Love's Ardor," "The Art Brotherhood," and "Longing" make various at-tempts to enter. In the bass is heard the derisive theme of "Ridicule." "Love's Ardor" again triumphant, there is now a dazzling climax during which the motive of the "Mastersingers" sounds forth in the bass like a call to arms. As this tumult subsides we hear in broad, magnificent phrases the theme of

"Love Confessed," sung by the violins, while far below is played the motive of the "Mastersingers." At the same time, woodwind instruments in the middle voices chatter along with the "Banner"—one of the most remarkable feats of thematic interweaving ever achieved; yet there were once musicians who said that Wagner knew no counterpoint! These various motives are then heard separately, in ever-growing sonority and richness, until the brilliant close of the Prelude.

ACT I

SCENE: *The Church of St. Catherine in Nuremberg.* With the very last chord of the Prelude, the curtain rises and we behold the interior of the Church of St. Catherine in Nuremberg. The people gathered there are singing a fine, stately chorale to Saint John, for this is the eve of that saint's day.

Only a few of the last rows of pews are visible. One of them is occupied by Eva and her nurse, Magdalena. At one side, leaning against a pillar, is Walther von Stolzing. According to a custom of the period, long pauses occur at the end of each line of the chorale that is being sung. During these pauses Walther and Eva exchange glances. The knight is plainly enamored of the girl, and she, though shy and modest, betrays considerable interest in him. Their mutual awareness is romantically expressed by the orchestra during these pauses.

When the chorale is ended and the congregation leaves, Walther, a total stranger in Nuremberg, for the first time learns that Eva's father has made a singular arrangement: he intends to give his daughter as bride to the winner of the song contest to be held on the morrow. Only masters of the guild may compete, however.

Walther promptly decides to become a master and win the contest—and Eva. Yet he has not the slightest idea of the conditions and requirements of the contest. Magdalena is now called on to assist. She in turn calls upon her suitor David, a young apprentice, to instruct Walther in the rules observed by the Mastersingers' Guild. As there is to be a test immediately, David begins his instruction at once, while his brother apprentices arrange the chairs and furniture for the guild meeting. But David, an apprentice cobbler as well as musician, so garbles the rules of art and the rules of his trade that Walther is left helpless and confused. Soon the mastersingers arrive to stately march rhythms, and the guild roll is called. Pogner addresses them, saying that he offers his daughter, Eva, in marriage to the winner of the coming contest, provided, of course, that he meets with her approval as well. Walther now asks to be given a trial for admission to the Mastersingers' Guild. The masters, though surprised at his boldness, give their consent.

ACT II—THE RIOT—ROME OPERA PRODUCTION

As their duly appointed "Marker," Beckmesser takes his place in the enclosed stand erected for him. Besides being a formidable stickler for rules, he is also eager to wed Eva. The result can well be imagined. Walther's freely improvised song, *"Fanget an"* ("Now begin"), is punctuated by the sound of the scratching of the pencil on a slate as the Marker notes down the "errors." At the end of the first verse the masters refuse to hear any more. Hans Sachs alone is in favor of having the youth continue.

A master of genuine merit, Sachs has detected in the song a touch of true inspiration. He admits that the "rules" of the guild have been disregarded, but suggests that other rules may govern in this instance. He is shouted down, however, and the indignant young knight is dismissed amid the jeers of the apprentices. The trial has ended in confusion, and Sachs turns away in a mood of semihumorous despair.

ACT II

SCENE: *A Street in Nuremberg (the houses of Pogner and Hans Sachs are seen separated from each other by a narrow alley, but both facing the same broader street, which is shown sectionally across the stage).* As night falls over the town the apprentices are busily putting up the shutters on the quaint old Nuremberg houses. Meanwhile they sing in joyful anticipation of the midsummer festival. They are disposed to ridicule David, who has suffered Magdalena's ire as a result of Walther's failure. Sachs drives them away, chasing David off to bed, but first he has his workman's bench so placed that he can work at his cobbling and at the same time watch the street. But soon he finds he cannot work, for the beauty of the summer's evening and recollections of Walther's song have obsessed him. The orchestra murmurs, like a merest breeze stirring in the summer night, and Sachs, putting aside his work, dreamily notes the scent of elder blossoms in the air (*"Was duftet doch der Flieder"*), and reverts to the strangely fascinating song of Walther, the song defying all rule and measure (*"Kein' Regel wollte da passen"*). Eva appears. Despairing of her chances to have Walther for a husband, she coyly hints that Sachs himself might be a welcome suitor. The captivating duet begins with her words, *"Gut'n Abend, Meister!"* ("Good evening, Master!") She has known and loved this kind man from childhood and is aware of his sterling qualities. Indeed, Sachs, a middle-aged widower, has had dreams of winning Eva for himself. But now he realizes that her true love is for Walther, and accepts this with manly resignation. He merely shakes his head over the turn of events as Eva leaves him and he resumes work. Soon Sachs observes Walther and Eva across the street, talking together. The lovers have decided to elope. Sachs "accidentally" places his lamp where the light will fall upon them, and they are deterred for fear of being seen. While they debate their plan, however, a stranger approaches, and they quickly draw back into the shadows. The stranger is Beckmesser. The pompous scalawag has come to serenade his mistress with the song he hopes to sing on the morrow. Sachs, hearing him tinkle on his lute, breaks in with a lusty song of his own, *"Jerum! Jerum!"* ("Cobbler's Song"), and Beckmesser is greatly discomfited.

He pretends that he has come to inquire about a pair of shoes, and Sachs replies civilly that he is working on them. In the meantime Magdalena, in Eva's stead, has appeared at the window, and Beckmesser, thinking her to be the lady of his dreams, grows more ardent in his serenading. Then he pretends that he wants Hans Sachs to appraise the song. Sachs agrees to act as "Marker," hammering on the shoe at every mistake. In this way, accompanied by a sharp obbligato, Beckmesser proceeds. In his agitation, however, his song runs wild, and Sachs' hammer blows become loud and frequent. The thumping waxes more and more vehement as the mistakes of the now irate Beckmesser increase. The disturbance naturally arouses the neighbors, who begin peering through the windows. Even David is awakened, and seeing the Town Clerk apparently serenading Magdalena, who is still at the window, he curses furiously and, jumping quickly from his room, proceeds to give the astonished Beckmesser a sound beating. Magdalena screams aloud at seeing her David fighting in the street, and the towns-

Morton & Co.

ACT III, SCENE 2—SAN FRANCISCO OPERA PRODUCTION

people, still in their picturesque nightgowns, hurry down to the scene. Observing two of their members fighting, the guildsmen join in eagerly, and soon the street is in an uproar.

Walther and Eva, who have been in hiding, decide that this is a good opportunity to elope. But the observant Sachs seizes the pair by the arm and pushes Eva in the door of Pogner's house. Then with a well-placed kick he sends David scurrying into his own house, and follows him, drawing Walther after him. Meanwhile, the good women of the town, distressed at the behavior of their husbands and sweethearts, suddenly pour water upon the brawlers from the windows above. All quickly scatter to the safety of their homes. At that moment the night watchman is heard sounding his horn in the distance. When he reaches the scene of the disturbance, all is miraculously quiet again. He announces the hour, singing an antique ditty in a quavering voice. His horn is again heard in the distance as he wanders off, staff and lantern in hand, through the slumbering streets.

ACT III

The third act is preceded by a prelude of remarkably evocative beauty. It is built principally on the theme of Sachs' monologue, in which, during a moment of despair, he declares that all things human are but vanity, and on the vigorous chorale with which the people greet him in the closing scene of the opera.

SCENE 1: *Interior of Sachs' Workshop.* The early-morning sun streams through the window at which Sachs sits. Engrossed in reading a large folio, he fails to notice David entering with a basket of good things to eat. David has patched it up with Magdalena and is thus in a happy frame of mind. But he is still fearful that his rowdy behavior in the previous night's disturbance will bring a thrashing from his master. Falteringly, he now begins to explain, declaring that the night before was just a *Polterabend*—a night of merry-making on the festival of Saint John. Sachs appears to pay little heed; then suddenly he asks the amazed youth to sing the song of the day—a carol of Saint John. This tells the story of the child of a woman of Nuremberg christened in the river Jordan by Johannes, the saint, after whom Sachs was named; though on his return to Nuremberg the name "Johannes" was abbreviated to "Hans." David, struck with a sudden thought, exclaims joyfully: "Hans! Hans! Why, then, it's your name day too, Master!" In childish glee, he offers Sachs the flowers and cakes that Magdalena has just regaled him with. Sachs declines them graciously. Though still preoccupied, he understands the apprentice's hopes and desires and dismisses him with a pleasant word. The kindly cobbler then sits in meditation—a meditation which becomes vocal in the stirring lines beginning with the words *"Wahn! Wahn! Überall Wahn!"* ("Mad! Mad! The whole world is mad!").

Having just awakened, Walther now enters from an adjoining room and joins Sachs in a superb duet. He is bursting with a wonderful dream he has had in which a marvelous poem and melody found their way into his heart. Sachs desires to hear it, and we now hear the first lovely stanzas of the *"Preislied"* ("Prize Song").

The older master is struck with amazement by its beauty and inspiration, and tactfully he instructs the young poet-composer in the technical devices necessary to make the song acceptable to the judges.

After the two men have written down the poem, they leave the room. Presently Beckmesser enters and, snooping about, notices the song. Believing it to be by Hans Sachs himself, he pockets it for his own use, after the manner of plagiarists the world over. When Sachs returns, the Town Clerk scolds him for planning to enter the contest. Sachs denies this. Beckmesser accordingly produces the manuscript, and Sachs, grasping the situation, does not undeceive him. Divining Beckmesser's intentions, and knowing the Town Clerk incapable of making good use of the poem, Sachs gives it to him, promising not to divulge its true authorship. Greatly delighted, Beckmesser leaves.

Eva enters now, clad in festival robes. Her shoe pinches, she says, and Sachs, knowing well what is in her heart, pretends to busy himself adjusting the offending footwear. Walther enters, also festively garbed in a knightly costume. On seeing his adored one, he stands as in a trance and softly sings the last stanza of his song. Overwhelmed with emotion, Eva sinks weeping

Morton & Co. ACT III, SCENE 1—SAN FRANCISCO OPERA PRODUCTION

into Sachs' arms. Deeply moved himself, Sachs gives her into Walther's care and then bursts into a stanza of his brusque cobbler's song to steady himself. Eva vows her gratitude and love to her old friend, but Sachs sagaciously replies that he would avoid the fate of King Mark. At this the orchestra knowingly quotes a phrase from *Tristan und Isolde*. David and Magdalena now appear, also in gala attire. Sachs invites them all to a christening. But first he seeks to name Walther's song. Since a qualified witness is needed, and a mere apprentice will not do, the kindly cobbler gives David his freedom, making him a full journeyman cobbler with the customary box on the ear. David is overjoyed, for now he will be able to marry Magdalena. These five characters now give voice to their mingled emotions of happiness, love, and, for Sachs, a mellow nostalgia, in an indescribably lovely quintet, *"Selig wie die Sonne"* ("Brightly as the sun"). Then they leave together for the contest, David carefully closing the door after them.

SCENE 2: *A Field on the Shores of the River Pegnitz.* In an open meadow on the banks of the river, the people of Nuremberg have assembled for the song contest. The various trade guilds arrive in procession—tailors . . . shoemakers . . . bakers. The band of youthful apprentices is there also, and soon a gaily decorated boat overflowing with smartly dressed girls arrives. The apprentices hurry to help them ashore, then at once begin dancing with them, the orchestra accompanying them with a delightfully rustic, waltzlike tune. David seizes a pretty girl and starts to dance with her. The other apprentices frighten him by saying his Lena is watching (*"Aha! da streicht die Lene!"*).

Finally the mastersingers arrive in great pomp, their banner with the picture of their patron, King David, fluttering at the head of the procession.

331

At the sight of Sachs, the crowd rises briskly and breaks into an exultant chorale, the words of which were taken from an actual poem by the historical Hans Sachs, *"Wach' auf! es nahet gen den Tag"* ("Awake! the dawn of the day draws near"). Sachs, deeply moved, thanks them for their kindness, and announces the terms of the contest in an impressive address beginning, *"Euch macht ihr's leicht"* ("Words light to you").

As the oldest of the contestants, Beckmesser is selected to begin. Still smarting from his beating of the previous night, grievously flustered, and with his stolen song only half learned, he now attempts to adapt the poem to his own serenade melody. The result is a hopeless jumble which at first excites the wonder, then the derision of the audience. Enraged, Beckmesser declares that the song is not his, but the work of Hans Sachs. The masters, believing this a spiteful fabrication, call upon Sachs for an explanation. Eloquently he insists that the song would be good if properly sung, and persuades the crowd and the judges to let it be interpreted by the author, Walther von Stolzing. The crowd listens in wondering silence as the young knight begins his rapturous song, *"Morgenlich leuchtend in rosigem Schein"* ("Morning was gleaming with roseate light"). This tells of the vision of a lovely garden in which the singer found the most beautiful of all maidens, Eva. Around the melodic beauty and expressiveness of the song a glowing orchestral accompaniment seems to entwine itself tenderly.

The people listen with growing excitement, and at the close of the song the masters rise and acclaim Walther as victor. Eva confers on her lover a wreath of laurel and myrtle, then leads him to her father, before whom they both kneel. Pogner extends his hands over them in benediction and presents the emblem of the Masters' Guild to the young knight. But Walther, remembering his reception of the day before, and conscious also of his noble birth, refuses the honor. In consternation, all turn to Sachs for guidance. The cobbler-poet goes to Walther, takes him impressively by the hand, and, while the orchestra brings into review many of the motives first heard in the Prelude, urges him not to despise the old masters, *"Verachtet mir die Meister nicht."* Then, turning to the crowd, he warns that disunity among the Germans would be the death of holy German art (*"die heil'ge deutsche Kunst"*).

Thoroughly won over, Walther is now willing to accept the mastersingers' emblem. Sachs embraces the couple, who then remain standing beside him, Walther at one hand, Eva at the other. Before this group Pogner kneels as if in homage. Thus the cobbler-musician and the two lovers become symbols of Art and Life, enshrined in the incomparable splendor of the song of the people, who now repeat the final words of their beloved cobbler-poet, and shout exultantly, "Hail Sachs! Hans Sachs! Hail Nuremberg's darling Sachs!"

JOEL BERGLUND AS HANS SACHS

THE RCA-VICTOR RECORDS
(Sung in German)

OVERTURE: *Arturo Toscanini and the NBC Symphony Orchestra* 11-9385, 12"
Leopold Stokowski and the Philadelphia Orchestra
DM-731 (18464 & 18465), 2-12"
M-731 (17567 & 17568)

ACT I

DAS SCHÖNE FEST, JOHANNISTAG (The Feast of Saint John): *Alexander Kipnis, Bass, with Orch.* 7894, 12"
AM STILLEN HERD (By Silent Hearth): *Lauritz Melchior, Tenor; the Philadelphia Orchestra, Eugene Ormandy, Cond.* 17728, 12" (In Album M-749)
Set Svanholm, Tenor, with Orch. 11-9791, 12"

ACT II

WAS DUFTET DOCH DER FLIEDER (How Sweet the Elder's Scent) ; KEIN' REGEL WOLLTE DA PASSEN (I Found No Rule That Would Fit It) : *Friedrich Schorr, Baritone, with Orch.* 7425, 12"

GUT'N ABEND, MEISTER! (Good Evening, Master) ; ICH SEH'! 'SWAR NUR (I See How It Was) : *Göta Ljungberg, Soprano; Friedrich Schorr, Baritone; with Orch.* 7680, 12"

SCHUSTERLIED (Cobbler's Song) : *Friedrich Schorr, Baritone, with Orch.* 7426, 12"

ACT III

COMPLETE RECORDING: *Torsten Ralf, Tenor; Hans Hermann Nissen, Baritone; Margarete Teschemacher, Soprano; Eugen Füchs, Bass; Sven Nilsson, Bass; Martin Kremer, Tenor; Lene Jung, Contralto; Chorus of the Dresden State Opera; Saxon State Orchestra, Karl Böhm, Cond.*
DMC-108 (DM-537) (Vol. 1)
(16077-16086), 10-12"
(DM-538) (Vol. 2)
(16087-16091), 5-12"
MC-108 (M-537) (Vol. 1)
(15683-15692)
(M-538) (Vol. 2)
(15693-15697)

VORSPIEL (Prelude): *Leopold Stokowski and the Philadelphia Orchestra*
1584, 10"

WAHN! WAHN! ÜBERALL WAHN! (Mad! Mad! The Whole World Is Mad!);
EIN KOBOLD (An Impish Spell): *Friedrich Schorr, Baritone, with Orch.*
7319, 12"

GRÜSS' GOTT, MEIN JUNKER! (Greetings, Sir Knight)
MEIN FREUND, IN HOLDER JUGENDZEIT (My Friend, in My Bygone Youth): *Friedrich Schorr, Baritone; Rudolf Laubenthal, Tenor; with Orch.* 7427, 12"

ABENDLICH GLÜHEND (The Light of Evening): *Lauritz Melchior, Tenor; Friedrich Schorr, Baritone; with Orch.* 7681, 12"

FOOTSTOOL DUET — SIEH' EV'CHEN? (Where Was Eva?); HAT MAN MIT DEM SCHUHWERK (A Shoemaker's Life): *Elisabeth Rethberg, Soprano; Friedrich Schorr, Baritone; with Orch.* 8195, 12"

AHA! DA STREICHT DIE LENE! (There's Magdalena!): *Friedrich Schorr, Baritone, with Orch.* 7681, 12"

QUINTET—SELIG, WIE DIE SONNE (Brightly as the Sun): *Elisabeth Schumann, Soprano; Lauritz Melchior, Tenor; Friedrich Schorr, Baritone; Ben Williams, Tenor; Gladys Parr, Contralto; with Orch.* 7682, 12"

TANZ DER LEHRBUBEN (Dance of the Apprentices);
AUFZUG DER MEISTERSINGER (Procession of the Mastersingers): *The Philadelphia Orchestra, Eugene Ormandy, Cond.* 1807, 10"

EUCH MACHT IHR'S LEICHT (Words Light to You): *Friedrich Schorr, Baritone, with Orch.* 7862, 12"

PREISLIED (Prize Song): *James Melton, Tenor, with Orch.* 11-8931, 12"
(In Album M-1013)

Set Svanholm, Tenor, with Orch.
11-9791, 12"

Lauritz Melchior, Tenor, with Orch.
17728, 12"
(In Album M-749)

Richard Crooks, Tenor, with Orch.
7105, 12"

Raya Garbousova, Cellist, with Piano
11-8870, 12"
(In Album M-1017)

Pablo Casals, Cellist, with Piano
6620, 12"

ANSPRACHE DES HANS SACHS (Sachs' Eulogy);
VERACHTET MIR DIE MEISTER NICHT (Disparage Not the Masters' Ways);
WAS DEUTSCH UND ECHT (Our Native Art Will Fade): *Friedrich Schorr, Baritone; Berlin State Opera Chorus and Orch.* 9285, 12"

ACT I—SEXTET—METROPOLITAN OPERA PRODUCTION

Mignon

OPÉRA-COMIQUE in three acts. Music by Ambroise Thomas. Libretto by Michel Carré and Jules Barbier, based on episodes in Goethe's novel, *Wilhelm Meister*. First performance, Opéra-Comique, Paris, November 17, 1866. American *première*, in Italian, New York Academy of Music, November 22, 1871. First Metropolitan performance, in Italian, October 31, 1883. After Célestine Galli-Marié, a mezzo-soprano, created the role of Mignon, Thomas revived it for the high soprano voice of Christine Nilsson, adding the charming *"Styrienne."* We owe the rondo-gavotte, based on a motive from the orchestral interlude between Acts I and II, to Zelia Trebelli, for whom Thomas wrote it when she sang the part of Frederick in the London *première* of *Mignon* at Drury Lane on July 5, 1870. Nilsson was the Mignon of both the American and Metropolitan *premières*. Geraldine Farrar headed the cast of the Metropolitan revival, in Italian, of March 6, 1908, when Alessandro Bonci sang Wilhelm Meister. A subsequent revival on March 10, 1927, featuring Lucrezia Bori (Mignon), Marion Talley (Philine), and Beniamino Gigli (Wilhelm Meister) was in the original French. Gladys Swarthout and Risë Stevens have brought Mignon back into the mezzo-soprano wing of the Metropolitan.

Thomas was fifty-five and a composer of modest reputation when *Mignon* brought him fame and money. Largely because of *Mignon* and the subsequent opera, *Hamlet*, the grand cross of the Legion of Honor was conferred upon him in 1894, when he was eighty-three years old. A man of vast learning, he was appointed director of the Paris Conservatory in 1871, remaining in that post till his death on February 12, 1896. Thomas' instinct for the theater shows clearly in both *Mignon* and *Hamlet*. A flair for fluent, romantic melody marks his music, and his facile skill as orchestrator is evident in the ever-popular Overture to *Mignon*. Grace and elegance go hand in hand in Thomas' music, and in lyric expression he is related to Gounod. Of course, the plot of *Mignon* differs radically from the original story in Goethe's weighty philosophical novel. Little of the tragic poetry and cynicism of the novel survives in the libretto, and the central situation is saved by the familiar theatrical device of mistaken identity. Yet with all the liberties taken, the opera has its own dramatic and romantic appeal. Its three great

Mignon

numbers—the Overture, Mignon's nostalgic air, *"Connais-tu le pays?"* (Goethe's famous lyric, *"Kennst du das Land"*), and Philine's brilliant polonaise, *"Je suis Titania"*—are in everyone's book of musical favorites.

CHARACTERS

MIGNON, *a young girl stolen by gypsies*	*Mezzo-soprano*	WILHELM MEISTER, *a student on his travels*	*Tenor*
PHILINE, *an actress*	*Soprano*	LAERTES, *an actor*	*Tenor*
FREDERICK, *a young nobleman*	*Buffo tenor or Contralto*	LOTHARIO, *an Italian nobleman*	*Basso cantante*
		GIARNO, *a gypsy*	*Bass*

TOWNSFOLK, PEASANTS, GYPSIES, ACTORS, AND ACTRESSES

The action takes place in Germany (Acts I and II) and Italy (Act III) in the late eighteenth century

The Overture to *Mignon* is typically French in its lilting grace and delicacy. Woven into an adroitly balanced fabric are the principal themes of the opera. The tranquil mood of the opening, with its harp cadenza, reminds us of the kindly minstrel, Lothario. Next, the horn evokes a mood of romantic nostalgia in the melody of Mignon's *"Connais-tu le pays?"* Violins take up the strain, letting it die away in a mood of calm mystery. Philine's rippling polonaise, *"Je suis Titania,"* then brings in a contrasting note of vivacious coquetry, and the Overture ends on a bright note of gaiety.

ACT I

SCENE: *Courtyard of a German Inn.* Mignon, daughter of noble parents, has been stolen from her home by gypsies. Shortly after, her mother dies of grief, and her father, Lothario, driven nearly mad by the loss, wanders abroad as a minstrel in search of his child.

As the opera opens, Lothario has found his way to the courtyard of a German inn where a crowd of people are having a gay time drinking and feasting. Broken with age, Lothario has lost his memory. Yet, though even his name and home are forgotten, he is still blindly seeking the lost daughter whom he vaguely believes to be alive.

Into the courtyard troops a band of gypsies. Giarno, their mercenary leader, orders Mignon to dance for the crowd, but Mignon, grown tired of her master's insolent commands, refuses to go through her performance. When Giarno threatens to beat her, Lothario, stirred with a sudden sympathy for this young girl, runs to protect her. As the feeble old man is powerless before the gypsy, a young student, Wilhelm, who is looking on, rushes to the rescue. With his pistol drawn he forces Giarno to release the girl, and in gratitude Mignon divides a bouquet between her rescuers. Wilhelm receives the applause of a troupe of traveling actors, among whom is Philine. This

ACT I—METROPOLITAN OPERA PRODUCTION

beautiful young actress of designing temperament attracts Wilhelm's attention, much to the jealousy of Frederick, a young nobleman.

Curious about the girl he has rescued, Wilhelm questions her regarding her childhood. But Mignon remembers nothing except that she was captured as a child by gypsies in some distant country, which she now describes in the nostalgic aria, *"Connais-tu le pays?"* ("Knowest thou the land?"). One of the best-loved melodies in the whole range of opera, this song expresses the passionate longing of the orphan for the home of her infancy, and reaches a fervent climax in the hope that she could die there. Moved to pity, Wilhelm arranges to buy the girl's freedom from her master. Mignon, infatuated with her rescuer, wishes to follow him on his travels, but Wilhelm, rather embarrassed, suggests that she remain in the village with some kind-hearted people. Mignon is saddened by this, but agrees to accompany the aged Lothario, who, moved by some strange impulse, has come back to bid her good-by. Wilhelm at length yields to the girl's entreaties and allows her to accompany him disguised as a servant. Philine, meanwhile, receives an invitation to visit the castle of Baron Rosenberg for a party in honor of Prince Tieffenbach. She is to bring along the troupe of actors and any guests she may care to. She promptly invites Wilhelm, who has caught her fancy. He accepts her invitation eagerly and goes along as poet of the company.

ACT II

The second act is preceded by the very popular Intermezzo, a dainty gavotte, gay and graceful in its eighteenth-century elegance.

SCENE 1: *A Boudoir in the Castle*. Philine sits at her mirror, studying her charms and applying cosmetics. She is thinking of Wilhelm, for she is much infatuated with this handsome, romantic student. Soon he enters, accompanied by Mignon, who is greeted by the actress with civil yet subtly cattish remarks. The poor girl does not resent this, however, and, curling up in a great chair by the fire, apparently goes to sleep. Yet she observes, under half-closed lids, that Wilhelm is paying court to the actress, to whom he has given the bouquet of blooms presented to him by Mignon herself. Presently Philine and Wilhelm leave, and Mignon, longing to emulate the actress, goes to the adjoining room and tries on one of Philine's many gowns. Frederick leaps in through the window. "I'm here!" he exclaims. "I've broken all the rules of etiquette, but I'm here!" Then he begins to sing the charming gavotte, telling of his rapture at being in his beloved Philine's room, *"Me voici dans son boudoir"* ("Here am I in her boudoir").

Wilhelm unexpectedly enters, in search of Mignon. Jealous accusations about Philine are exchanged by the young men, and in the heat of the quarrel they draw swords. But as Mignon rushes between them, Frederick recognizes Philine's gown and goes away laughing. Wilhelm, realizing the difficult situations that may arise from having the girl constantly about, has now come to tell Mignon that they must part. The girl begins to cry, saying that it is Philine who has persuaded him to drive her away, but he calms her fears in a tender farewell, promising never to forget her.

Philine, re-entering, utters some sarcastic remarks about Mignon's borrowed raiment, words that bring a flush of anger to the girl's cheeks. Rushing from the room, Mignon dons her old gypsy costume and returns in time to see Wilhelm leading the actress away on his arm. "That woman! I detest her!" cries the gypsy girl in despair.

SCENE 2: *The Gardens of the Castle.* Thinking her love for Wilhelm hopeless, Mignon is about to drown herself when she hears the strains of a harp. It is the minstrel Lothario. He now enters and listens sympathetically to the girl's tale of sorrow and her desire for vengeance. The half-crazed old man starts curiously when she expresses the hope that heaven's lightning will strike and burn down the castle, and he goes away muttering her words to himself. The performance in the theater having ended, the players and guests come out into the garden. Philine, who is still in her costume of the Fairy Queen in *A Midsummer Night's Dream*, has had a brilliant success. Glowing with triumph, she sings "I am Titania," the rhythm of which is that of a polonaise. Dashing and showy, this fascinating number ranks high among the coloratura favorites. *"Je suis Titania la blonde, Titania, fille de l'air!"* ecstatically sings Philine—"I am the blond Titania, daughter of the air!" Lothario returns and whispers to Mignon that she need not grieve—her vengeance is now complete, for he has set fire to the castle. Noticing Mignon, Philine is suddenly seized by a cruelly jealous thought. She orders the girl to bring from the castle a bouquet she has forgotten. Since Philine knows that the flowers were given by Mignon to Wilhelm there is malice enough in her request; yet Mignon goes gladly. Immediately, word comes that the castle is on fire, and Wilhelm, realizing that Mignon is in danger, rushes off to her rescue. Soon he returns with the unconscious girl in his arms. Mignon is still clasping the withered flowers, and Wilhelm now exclaims that he saved her against her will.

ACT III

SCENE: *Count Lothario's Castle in Italy*. Wilhelm has brought Mignon and Lothario to an old castle in Italy, one that he is half inclined to purchase. Mignon is recovering from a dangerous illness, and Wilhelm comes to take Lothario's place outside her sickroom. Satisfied that he has quieted the restless girl, Lothario sings a suave lullaby, *"De son coeur j'ai calmé la fièvre"* ("I have calmed the fever of her heart"). Wilhelm now meditates on her guileless heart and loyalty, and as the realization dawns on him that he loves her, he sings a romance—a melody of the utmost simplicity, naïve as Mignon herself, *"Elle ne croyait pas dans sa candeur naïve"* ("She did not believe in her utter frankness"). The song rises to a passionate climax as the young man exclaims: "Gentle spring! give her one soft, caressing kiss! O my heart, give her one fond sigh of love!"

Mignon comes with feeble steps to the balcony. As she looks out on the landscape, strange memories begin to stir within her. Seeing Wilhelm, she becomes greatly agitated, fearing that Philine may be with him. He soothes her with the assurance that he loves her alone, but she insists that only Lothario is faithful. Meanwhile a strange thing has happened. Once more in familiar surroundings, Lothario has recovered his reason and memory. He has remembered finally that he is Count Lothario and that the castle is his! But a great sadness comes over him as he recalls the disappearance of his daughter, Sperata. At the sound of that name, echoes sound in Mignon's reawakened memories. When Lothario shows her the jewels and prayer book of his lost child, she recognizes them, and, unconsciously, she now begins to sing the prayers of her early childhood. Thus father and daughter are reunited, and Wilhelm being admitted to the family circle, their happiness is complete.

THE RCA-VICTOR RECORDS
(Sung in French unless otherwise noted)

OVERTURE: *Arturo Toscanini and the NBC Symphony Orchestra*   11-8545, 12"

Boston "Pops" Orchestra, Arthur Fiedler, Cond.   12038, 12"

ACT I

CONNAIS-TU LE PAYS? (Knowest Thou the Land?): *Gladys Swarthout, Mezzosoprano, with Orch.*   11-8281, 12"
(In Album M-925)

Lucrezia Bori, Soprano, with Orch.   1361, 10"

ACT II

ENTR'ACTE (Gavotte): *Leopold Stokowski and the Philadelphia Orchestra*   7456, 12"
(In Album M-116)

Florentine Quartet   20443, 10"

Hans Printz
MIGNON AND LOTHARIO

GLADYS SWARTHOUT AS MIGNON

GAVOTTE—ME VOICI DANS SON BOUDOIR (Here Am I in Her Boudoir): *Lucrezia Bori, Soprano, with Orch.*   1361, 10"

Nan Merriman, Mezzo-soprano, with Orch.   12-0067, 12"

ADDIO, MIGNON: *Giuseppe di Stefano, Tenor, with Orch., Alberto Erede, Cond.*   12-0529, 12"

POLONAISE—JE SUIS TITANIA (Io son Titania) (I'm Fair Titania): *Patrice Munsel, Soprano, with Orch.*   11-8886, 12"

Lily Pons, Soprano, with Orch.   17232, 12"
(In Album M-702)

Amelita Galli-Curci, Soprano, with Orch. In Italian   7110, 12"

ACT III

AH, NON CREDERE (Ah, Little Thought the Maid): *Giuseppe di Stefano, Tenor, with Orch., Alberto Erede, Cond.*   12-0529, 12"

ACT II—"MY OBJECT ALL SUBLIME"—D'OYLY CARTE OPERA PRODUCTION

The Mikado

(OR, THE TOWN OF TITIPU)

COMIC OPERA in two acts. Music by Arthur Sullivan. Libretto by W. S. Gilbert. First produced at the Savoy Theater, London, March 14, 1885. Generally regarded as the masterpiece of Gilbert and Sullivan's collaboration, *The Mikado* was partly the result of an ultimatum. Sullivan had grown tired of plots about Fairy Queens and magic potions and now demanded that his librettist supply him with a real story for a change, a story, moreover, giving him greater leeway as composer. Some sharp exchanges resulted between the gifted friends, and after a period of strain, ended only by the intervention of Richard D'Oyly Carte—that shrewd and tireless impresario—Gilbert submitted the new book. Sullivan was enchanted, and there presently followed that delicious blend of musical and verbal drollery which remains for the English-speaking world perhaps the most popular work of the whole comic-opera repertory. Gilbert, it is said, was struck with the idea of an Oriental extravaganza when he saw an old Japanese sword accidentally fall from a wall in his studio.

So successful was *The Mikado* in London that an American producer named John C. Duff, eager to make a quick haul, staged a pirated production at New York's Union Square Theater on August 8, 1885, using an orchestral version made from a piano score. The unauthorized production did not get very far. D'Oyly Carte no sooner heard of the project than he secretly shipped a company over and mounted a sumptuous rival production at the Fifth Avenue Theater. The pirated *Mikado* was soon forced to yield to superior competition, and John C. Duff took his purloined version out of town. In England *The Mikado* brought some imperial dissent to the vast chorus of praise and delight that greeted it. Queen Victoria dismissed the plot as "rather silly," and the Japanese Ambassador attempted to halt the production, charging that his country and Emperor were grossly ridiculed by the operetta. But no one need take offense, really, at this topsy-turvy spectacle of human folly amiably mantled in droll mockery and ridicule. The delicious music alone would refute any charge of grave misconduct against *The Mikado*.

CHARACTERS

THE MIKADO OF JAPAN	Bass	PISH-TUSH, *a noble lord*	*Baritone*
NANKI-POO, *his son, disguised*		YUM-YUM ⎤	*Soprano*
as a minstrel	*Tenor*	PITTI-SING ⎬ *wards of Ko-Ko*	*Contralto*
KO-KO, *Lord High Executioner*		PEEP-BO ⎦	*Contralto*
of Titipu	*Baritone*	KATISHA, *an elderly lady, in*	
POOH-BAH, *Lord High Every-*		*love with Nanki-Poo*	*Contralto*
thing Else	*Baritone*		

SCHOOLGIRLS, NOBLES, GUARDS, AND COOLIES; CHORUS OF LADIES AND GENTLEMEN

ACT I

SCENE: *Ko-Ko's Palace at Titipu.* After a captivating overture in which some of the choicest melodies from the opera are first heard, the curtain rises on the courtyard of Ko-Ko's palace at Titipu. Japanese nobles gathered there sing a lively chorus revealing their identity:

> *If you want to know who we are,*
> *We are gentlemen of Japan . . .*

Nanki-Poo enters excitedly, carrying a native guitar and a bundle of ballads. He asks to be directed to the maiden Yum-Yum, the ward of Ko-Ko. In turn the nobles ask his name and occupation. He replies with the song, "A Wand'ring Minstrel I." He offers them his wares, that is, his songs—sentimental, patriotic, or nautical. Pish-Tush asks his business with Yum-Yum. Nanki-Poo replies that a year ago he saw Yum-Yum and immediately fell in love with her, but at that time she was betrothed to her guardian, Ko-Ko. Now, having heard that Ko-Ko is condemned to death for flirting, he has come to see Yum-Yum. Pish-Tush replies that Ko-Ko has been pardoned and made Lord High Executioner in a set of remarkable circumstances, which he now relates in the song, "Our Great Mikado." As he finishes, the Lord High Everything Else, Pooh-Bah, enters. Singing the song, "Young Man, Despair," Pooh-Bah tells him to give up hope, for Yum-Yum is to marry Ko-Ko this very day.

Nanki-Poo's lament is cut short by the arrival of Ko-Ko himself, who enters in state, with his attendants singing the rousing chorus, "Behold the Lord High Executioner!" Thanking them for their reception, he responds with the amusing song, "I've got a little list . . . of society offenders who might well be underground"—possibilities for his own professional employment! Soon there enters a procession of Yum-Yum's schoolmates, singing their girlish chorus, "Comes a train of little ladies from scholastic trammels free." And now Yum-Yum herself appears, with her two sisters, Peep-Bo and Pitti-Sing, "Three little maids from school." The girls happen to offend the haughty Pooh-Bah, so they are obliged to beg his pardon, singing, "So please

342

Stage Photo Co.
"MERCY! EVEN FOR POOH-BAH!"—D'OYLY CARTE OPERA PRODUCTION

you, sir, we much regret if we have failed in etiquette." Then all depart, save Nanki-Poo and Yum-Yum. The young man at once declares his love and reveals to Yum-Yum that he is none other than the son of the Mikado. He has assumed this disguise in order to avoid marrying an elderly lady of the court, Katisha, who has claimed him. The couple sing their duet, "Were you not to Ko-Ko plighted," suggesting that if Yum-Yum were not engaged to Ko-Ko they would fondly kiss one another, and audibly demonstrate how it would be done. Then each goes away sorrowfully.

Pooh-Bah and Pish-Tush enter with a letter for Ko-Ko from the Mikado. Struck by the fact that no one has been beheaded in Titipu for a year, the Mikado threatens to abolish the office of Lord High Executioner unless somebody is executed within a month. In the trio that follows, "I am so proud," each of the men declines the honor of decapitation—Ko-Ko because of his duty to Titipu; Pooh-Bah because he must mortify his family pride, and Pish-Tush, who really doesn't greatly care. Nanki-Poo enters opportunely, carrying a rope with which he intends to hang himself in despair over his loss of Yum-Yum. Ko-Ko suggests that Nanki-Poo allow himself to be executed instead. After some argument Nanki-Poo consents, on condition that he be permitted to marry Yum-Yum at once—the execution to be a month later. Ko-Ko reluctantly agrees. The nobles and ladies enter to learn the decision. Ko-Ko announces that Yum-Yum is to marry Nanki-Poo, and all rejoice, merrily singing, "The threatened cloud has passed away."

Suddenly the dreaded Katisha appears, declaring melodramatically, "Your revels cease." She balefully claims Nanki-Poo as her own, but Pitti-

Sing mockingly replies that they are not concerned with her connubial views—

> *For he's going to marry Yum-Yum!*
> *Your anger pray bury,*
> *For all will be merry,*
> *I think you had better succumb!*

The wicked and tottering Katisha then turns to Nanki-Poo, declaring: "Oh, faithless one . . . I'll tear the mask from your disguising!" But as soon as she begins her denunciation, "He is the son of your . . ." Nanki-Poo, Yum-Yum, and chorus interrupt, singing Japanese words loudly and drowning out her voice. Thus foiled, Katisha furiously vows vengeance, while all the others gaily sing, "For joy reigns everywhere around!"

ACT II

SCENE: *Ko-Ko's Garden.* Yum-Yum is attended by her maidens, who, while preparing her for the wedding, sing the graceful chorus, "Braid the raven hair." Pitti-Sing interpolates a short solo, "Sit with downcast eye . . . Try if you can cry." Yum-Yum, gazing into the mirror, is thrilled by her own loveliness and expresses her appreciation of it in the song:

> *The sun whose rays*
> *Are all ablaze*
> *With ever-living glory,*
> *Does not deny*
> *His majesty,*
> *He scorns to tell a story!*

Reminded that her married happiness is to be "cut short," Yum-Yum bursts into tears. Nanki-Poo enters and tries to console her. With a forced, melancholy laugh, Yum-Yum, Pitti-Sing, Nanki-Poo, and Pish-Tush attempt a cheerful quartet, "Brightly dawns our wedding day," but each time their "Sing a merry madrigal—Fal-la!" ends in sorrow. Their unhappiness is further increased when Ko-Ko enters with the shocking news that a law has just been discovered which decrees that when a married man is beheaded, his wife is to be buried alive. So far, the law has never been put into force, since the only crime punishable with decapitation is flirting, and, of course, married men never flirt. Yum-Yum complains that being buried alive is such a stuffy death: yet if Nanki-Poo releases her she will have to marry Ko-Ko. Completely bewildered, they break into the incomparable trio, "Here's a how-de-do!"

A moment later the stately Japanese melody played at the opening of the overture is heard, and a procession enters, singing Japanese words, "Miya sama," announcing the arrival of the Mikado, who now enters, accompanied

ACT I—LESLIE RANDS AS PISH-TUSH, MARTYN GREEN AS KO-KO,
AND SYDNEY GRANVILLE AS POOH-BAH

by Katisha, "His daughter-in-law elect." The Mikado introduces himself
with the song, "A more humane Mikado never did in Japan exist," boasting
the celebrated Gilbertian refrain:

> *My object all sublime*
> *I shall achieve in time—*
> *To let the punishment fit the crime.*

Pooh-Bah now comes forward to assure the Mikado that his wishes have
been respected: the execution has just taken place. Ko-Ko, Pitti-Sing, and
Pooh-Bah describe it graphically in their song, "The criminal cried." Although the Mikado is gratified at the news, this was not the purpose of his
coming. He is really seeking his son, who is reputed to be in Titipu, disguised
under the name of Nanki-Poo. At this moment Katisha, who is reading the
death certificate, finds the name there—Nanki-Poo beheaded! Ko-Ko, Pooh-
Bah, and Pitti-Sing pretend to be dismayed at the thought that they have
executed the Heir Apparent. The Mikado reminds them that they will have to
be punished for this. Not that he is in the least angry, but the laws decree that
for "compassing the death of the Heir Apparent," they shall be punished by
boiling in oil, or by some similar protracted torture. Such is the injustice of
fate—of which they now sing in the glee, "See how the Fates their gifts allot."

The Mikado and Katisha go away, and while the trio remain bemoaning
their ill-luck, Nanki-Poo and Yum-Yum appear, ready to start on their
honeymoon. The unlucky trio attempt to persuade Nanki-Poo to "come back

to life," but the Prince, wishing to be free of Katisha, refuses unless Ko-Ko will himself marry her. For then, he says, life will be as welcome as "the flowers that bloom in the spring." Ko-Ko replies with the delicious lines:

> *The flowers that bloom in the spring,*
> *Tra la,*
> *Have nothing to do with the case.*
> *I've got to take under my wing, Tra la,*
> *A most unattractive old thing, Tra la,*
> *With a caricature of a face* . . .

All go out, and Katisha enters, singing, "Alone, and yet alive!"

To her now comes Ko-Ko, declaring a passionate love for her. When she sternly refuses him, he sings the pathetic ballad of a bird's unhappy affection, "Willow, titwillow." Katisha is so moved by his song and his threatened death from a broken heart that she yields. She even asks if he does not mind that she is in the least wee bit bloodthirsty, but Ko-Ko finds beauty even in bloodthirstiness, and the two sing their duet, "There is beauty in the bellow of the blast," then go away together joyfully. The Mikado now enters, ready to behold the execution of the three culprits.

A moment later they rush in, but Katisha is with them, imploring mercy, for she has married Ko-Ko. The Mikado hesitates, since the law must be enforced. The situation is saved by the appearance of Nanki-Poo, whose non-execution is marvelously explained, all then taking their turns in the exhilarating finale, "For he's gone and married Yum-Yum!"

THE RCA-VICTOR RECORDS

(Sung in English)

COMPLETE RECORDING: *D'Oyly Carte Company; Isidore Godfrey, Cond.; under the personal direction of Rupert D'Oyly Carte. (The cast includes: Darrell Fancourt; Derek Oldham; Martyn Green; Sydney Granville; Leslie Rands; Radley Flynn; Brenda Bennett; Marjorie Eyre; Elizabeth Nickell-Lean; Josephine Curtis.)*
DC-26 (12956-12966), 11-12″
C-26 (11961-11971)
GEMS: *Light Opera Company with Orch.*
36148, 12″

ACT I

A WAND'RING MINSTREL;
THE MOON AND I: *Kenny Baker, Tenor, with Orch.* 26252, 10″

MARTYN GREEN AS KO-KO

GLADYS SWARTHOUT AS ADALGISA

Norma

OPERA IN four (originally two) acts. Music by Vincenzo Bellini. Libretto by Felice Romani, based on a tragedy by L. A. Soumet. First appearance, Teatro alla Scala, Milan, December 26, 1831. Produced in New York in an English version, Park Theater, February 25, 1841. Also in New York, given in Italian at Niblo's Garden, September 20, 1843. The United States *première* of *Norma* took place in Philadelphia, January 11, 1841, when it was given (in English) simultaneously in two different theaters. Revived at the Metropolitan, November 16, 1927, with Rosa Ponselle in the name part, Giacomo Lauri-Volpi as Pollione, Marion Telva as Adalgisa, and Ezio Pinza as Oroveso. Subsequent casts at the Metropolitan have offered Gina Cigna and Zinka Milanov as Norma, Gladys Swarthout and Bruna Castagna as Adalgisa, Giovanni Martinelli as Pollione, and Pinza again as Oroveso.

Bellini's *Norma* appeared in the same year *La Sonnambula* had won exceptional favor, and it was no less successful. The technique of the work is that of the older Italian opera school, in which airs and ensemble numbers, based on the simplest harmonic and melodic architecture, are plentiful. This does not mean, however, that emotional quality is absent, or even meager; and such numbers as *"Casta diva"* and the great duet, *"Mira, o Norma,"* are remarkable for sincerity of emotional expression, notwithstanding their clear simplicity of style, and recent revivals of the opera have proved that they still are effective. Those who weary of declamatory modern opera, in which the music is constantly changing in agreement with the most swift and subtle moods

347

that emotion throws upon the stage, at the expense of clearly defined melody, will have no quarrel with the simplicity of *Norma*. Certainly the role of Norma ranks as one of the very greatest and most difficult of soprano roles and has been a favorite with many generations of singers. Among the great sopranos who have sung the role are Jenny Lind, Grisi, and Lilli Lehmann; and in our own day Rosa Ponselle achieved one of her greatest successes in the part of the Druidical priestess.

CHARACTERS

POLLIONE, *Roman proconsul in Gaul*	*Tenor*	NORMA, *high priestess of the Druid temple of Esus*	*Soprano*
FLAVIO, *a centurion*	*Tenor*	ADALGISA, *a virgin of the temple of Esus*	*Mezzo-soprano*
OROVESO, *the Archdruid, Norma's father*	*Bass*	CLOTILDA, *confidante of Norma*	*Soprano*

PRIESTS AND OFFICERS OF THE TEMPLE, GALLIC WARRIORS, PRIESTESSES AND VIRGINS OF THE TEMPLE, AND THE TWO CHILDREN OF NORMA AND POLLIONE

The action takes place in Gaul during the Roman occupation, about 50 B.C.

The Overture introduces us to the prevailing moods of the opera. After a few introductory measures of a martial nature, the first theme is heard. This is soon followed by a melody of the opening chorus of Druid soldiers. These subjects are developed into a flowing overture whose purpose is not to present a musical synopsis of the plot, but to set the stage, so to speak, for its unfolding.

ACT I

SCENE: *Night in the Sacred Druid Forest*. In the dark forest, Oroveso, the Archdruid, and the Druidical soldiers and priests await the rising of the moon, at which mystic hour Norma is to perform the sacred rite of cutting the prophetic bough of mistletoe. They sing a sturdy chorus, swearing vengeance upon their Roman oppressors.

The Druids having gone away, Pollione, the Roman proconsul, and his lieutenant, Flavio, approach. From their conversation we learn that Norma, the daughter of Oroveso and Druidical high priestess, has fallen in love with Pollione, and violating her vows of chastity has borne him two sons. Now, however, Pollione is secretly in love with Adalgisa, one of the virgins of the temple; and that he is conscience-stricken he reveals in his cavatina, *"Meco all' altar di Venere."*

The narrative suddenly interrupted by the sounds of footsteps of approaching Druids, the two Romans conceal themselves. Norma appears before her people and, fearing for the life of her lover, addresses them, saying in a recitative that the time is not yet ripe to rise against their oppressors; then in the famous aria, *"Casta diva"* ("Queen of heaven"), she prays for peace, and in an aside, *"Ah! bello, a me ritorna"* ("Return to me"), gives voice to her love, while the Druids hymn the day of their vengeance.

Adalgisa, meanwhile, meeting Pollione in the forest, consents to elope

From an Old Print   NORMA AND POLLIONE

with him, after the persuasions implicit in his aria *"Va, crudele"* ("Go, cruel one"), and they plan to seek safety and happiness in Rome.

ACT II

SCENE: *Norma's Secret Dwelling in the Forest.* Norma and her faithful confidante, Clotilda, discuss the high priestess' difficulties, and Norma tells her that she both loves and hates her children. They hear footsteps, and Clotilda spirits the children away, as Adalgisa enters. The latter falls upon her knees before Norma, confessing her shameful devotion, and under prompting points to the man involved, Pollione, who has just come in. Whereupon Norma, revealing him as her own lover, heaps imprecations on the head of the proconsul, in which she is joined by Adalgisa, all three thus singing the powerful trio, *"Oh! di qual sei tu"* ("Oh, whose are you?"). The clanging of the sacred shield is heard, and Norma hastens to her religious duties.

ACT III

SCENE: *Interior of Norma's Dwelling.* Nearly crazed with anger, Norma thinks of killing her husband and her children and letting herself be burned on the funeral pyre. Only thus can she atone for her secret relationship, since death is the punishment for any priestess who dares violate her vows of chastity. She advances, in a very dramatic *scena,* with uplifted dagger toward the sleeping children, but the sight of the innocent victims overcomes her. Then she summons Adalgisa, and, urging her to go with Pollione, begs her to care for the children, who, following her death, will be motherless. Moved by her generosity, Adalgisa entreats Norma not to do this, and the two priestesses unite in singing the celebrated duet, *"Mira, o Norma"* ("Hear me, Norma").

ACT IV

SCENE: *A Wooded Region Near the Temple.* The Gallic warriors, summoned by Norma, convene in the sacred forest. Apprised by Clotilda that Pollione will not do as she bids, Norma now would proclaim war and destruction on the Romans, and she looses her anger in *"Guerra, guerra!"* ("War! war!"), the passion of her outburst being echoed by the massed Druids. When Pollione is discovered in the midst of the soldiers, he is seized and brought before the high priestess for judgment. He is given the choice of death or immediate departure—without Adalgisa—from Gaul.

Norma, rising to emotional heights, sings, *"In mia mano alfin tu sei"* ("At last, you are in my hands"). But the mingled feelings of pity, duty, and love are too much for her, and she would pardon him, but Pollione rejects this generosity contemptuously, saying that he will not give up Adalgisa. Therefore, Norma confesses her guilt to the astonished people and claims purification by death on the funeral pyre. Now Pollione, overwhelmingly affected by her devotion, asks only that he may die with her. After confiding her children to her father's care, Norma is covered with a black veil. She takes the hand of her lover in her own, and together they walk toward the flames of expiation.

THE RCA-VICTOR RECORDS

(Sung in Italian)

ACT I

CAVATINA—CASTA DIVA CHE INARGENTI (Queen of Heaven): *Zinka Milanov, Soprano, with Chorus and Orch.* 11-9293, 12"

Rosa Ponselle, Soprano; Metropolitan Opera Chorus and Orch. 8125, 12"

ACT II

AH! DEL TEBRO (Haughty Roman): *Ezio Pinza, Bass; Metropolitan Opera Chorus and Orch.* 1753, 10"

ACT III

MIRA, O NORMA! (Hear Me, Norma!): *Zinka Milanov, Soprano; Margaret Harshaw, Contralto; with Orch.* 11-8924, 12"

Rosa Ponselle, Soprano; Marion Telva, Mezzo-soprano; with Orch. 8110, 12"

Bruckner

FINAL SCENE

Oberon
(OR, THE ELF KING'S OATH)

OPERA IN three acts. Music by Carl Maria von Weber. Libretto by James Robinson Planché, after the old French romance, *Huon de Bordeaux,* as adapted by the German poet Wieland and translated into English by Sotheby. First performance, Covent Garden, London, April 12, 1826. Produced in America at the Park Theater, New York, October 9, 1828. Revived in English at the Metropolitan Opera House on December 28, 1918, with recitatives prepared by Artur Bodanzky, who also edited the score.

Weber's *Der Freischütz* immediately became so popular that he was soon commissioned to write an opera for Covent Garden, London. After many difficulties with librettist and singers, the opera was ready. Weber was in an advanced stage of consumption, however, and by the time of the first performance he was almost too exhausted to conduct. Nevertheless, the opera was a great success; but within three months the composer died.

In this work Weber's extraordinary gift in writing music of romantic fantasy is shown at its best.

CHARACTERS

OBERON, *King of the Fairies*	*Tenor*	SHERASMIN, *his squire*	*Baritone*
TITANIA, *his Queen*	*(acting part)*	BABEKAN, *a Persian prince*	*Baritone*
PUCK, *his attendant sprite*	*Contralto*	MESROUR, *chief of the harem*	
DROLL	*Contralto*	*guards*	*(acting part)*
HARUN-AL-RASHID, *Caliph of*		ALMANZOR, *Emir of Tunis*	*Baritone*
Bagdad	*Bass*	ROSCHANA, *his wife*	*Contralto*
REZIA, *his daughter*	*Soprano*	ABDALLAH, *a corsair*	*Baritone*
FATIMA, *her attendant*	*Mezzo-soprano*	CHARLEMAGNE	*Bass*
SIR HUON DE BORDEAUX, *Duke*			
of Guienne	*Tenor*		

ELVES, NYMPHS, SYLPHS, GENII, MERMAIDS; SPIRITS OF THE AIR, EARTH, WATER, AND FIRE; MERMEN; RETINUE OF THE CALIPH, LADIES ATTENDANT ON REZIA, BLACK AND WHITE SERVANTS OF THE HAREM, SLAVES, DANCERS OF BOTH SEXES, A JANISSARY BAND, WATCHMEN, MOORISH BOYS, CORSAIRS, RETINUE OF CHARLEMAGNE, PAGES, NOBLES, PRIESTS, CHOIRBOYS, HALBERDIERS, ETC.

The action is laid in France, Bagdad, and Tunis at the beginning of the ninth century

351

The Overture to *Oberon* takes us from the very start to that elfin land of Oberon and his sprites. The delicate, golden tones of Oberon's fairy horn summon the Elf King's subjects, who come tripping to the fluttering passages of the woodwind. The brilliant march of Charlemagne follows, and as a closing theme the violins sing the ecstatic melody of Rezia's great aria.

Queen Titania, having quarreled with her husband Oberon, the King of the Fairies, says that she will not speak to him until he shows her two lovers who, despite all obstacles, remain faithful to one another. Oberon is helped by his "tricksy spirit," Puck, who discovers a likely mortal in the person of Sir Huon of Bordeaux, a knight of the court of Charlemagne. This knight is in disgrace, and for penance must travel to Bagdad to slay the person he finds sitting at the left hand of the Caliph, Harun-al-Rashid. Having been permitted by Oberon to see in a vision Rezia, Harun's beautiful daughter, Huon at once falls in love with her. Oberon also gives Huon a magic horn with which to summon aid should he ever be in great danger.

Huon reaches Bagdad, conquers in battle all who oppose him, wins the hand of the fair Rezia, and sails away with her toward the sunset—and home.

Oberon has now to test the lovers' faithfulness. He causes a terrific storm to come up, and in the midst of it, the ship becomes stranded on a desert isle inhabited by pirates. Rezia swoons, and Huon at her side prays to the Ruler of this awful hour, beseeching him to protect Rezia. After Rezia revives, Huon departs in search of aid for the shipwrecked pair. Rezia, then alone, comes to her senses and, in a recitative and aria of great sweep and power, gives vent to her feelings about the mighty force and destructive wrath of the ocean, "Ocean, thou mighty monster."

Before the return of Huon, Rezia is abducted by pirates. In his attempt to save his beloved Rezia, Huon, after a fight with one of the pirates, is struck down, senseless. The pirates capture them and sell Rezia as a slave to the Emir of Tunis. Rezia repulses the Emir in his advances, and Huon, entering, saves her from the brute's embrace. When the band of slaves would close in on the lovers, Sherasmin, who has suddenly appeared, rushes to Huon's side and winds the horn. Instantly all stand perfectly still, as if petrified. The Elf King and his Queen appear, both happily reconciled now, and thank Huon and Rezia for their constancy. The lovers are transplanted back to Charlemagne's court, where honors and happiness await them.

THE RCA-VICTOR RECORDS
(Sung in German)

OVERTURE: *The Boston "Pops" Orchestra,
Arthur Fiedler, Cond.*   12043, 12"

*Boston Symphony Orchestra, Serge
Koussevitzky, Cond.*   11-9951, 12"

ACT II

OZEAN, DU UNGEHEUER! (Ocean, Thou Mighty Monster!): *Kirsten Flagstad,
Soprano; the Philadelphia Orchestra,
Eugene Ormandy, Cond.*   15244, 12"

Lande

ELYSIUM

Orfeo ed Euridice

(ORPHEUS AND EURYDICE)

OPERA IN four acts. Music by Christoph Willibald von Gluck. Book, in Italian, by Raniero de' Calzabigi. First produced at the Burgtheater, Vienna, October 5, 1762. American *première* at the Winter Garden, New York, May 25, 1863, in an English translation by Fanny Malone Raymond. First performance at the Metropolitan Opera House, in German, in 1885, with Leopold Damrosch conducting. In the original Italian version the Metropolitan staged it for the first time in America on December 30, 1891, with a cast headed by Giulia Ravogli (Orpheus) and Sofia Ravogli (Eurydice). A magnificent revival of the opera was that of Arturo Toscanini on December 23, 1909, when Louise Homer, Johanna Gadski, and Alma Gluck were in the cast. Performances recurred till 1913. Gluck's masterpiece was then shelved by the Metropolitan for twenty-two years, returning during the spring season of 1936. For that production a double cast was used, members of the American Ballet Ensemble miming the action on the stage, while the singers held forth from the orchestra pit. On November 26, 1939, Kerstin Thorborg won great acclaim with her performance of the title role.

Like many other operas, *Orfeo ed Euridice* was subjected to the trials of versions and revisions before achieving a single final status. Gluck rewrote the opera for the Paris production of August 2, 1774, using a French text by Pierre Louis Moline. Much music was added, and the part of Orpheus, originally for contralto, like so many other male roles in the operas of the time, was rewritten for tenor. The Viennese version, however, regained its primacy with the performance of November 19, 1859, at the Théâtre-Lyrique, Paris. Partly responsible for this was the sensational portrayal of the main role by the noted contralto, Pauline Viardot.

In the power and pathos of its direct style, *Orfeo* was something of a revolution in opera composition. Preceding *Alceste* and its aesthetic manifesto (see p. 19), it already pronounced the challenge of truth of expression against artifice and display. There is nobility of speech here, the classic, serene beauty that one associates with Grecian art. *Orfeo* is the oldest of the repertory operas, yet in some ways the youngest, for an imperishable youth is on this music, especially the music of Orpheus' poignant outcry, *"Che farò senza Euridice?"* and the "Dance of the Happy Shades," with its ethereal flute reverie. It is said that Marie Antoinette, something of a Lady Bountiful to Gluck in Paris, promptly granted him a pension of six thousand francs after the performance of *Orfeo* at the Académie Royale de Musique. For that single gesture of appreciation much could have been forgiven the tragic queen in the harsh years of revolution ahead. In ending happily, Gluck's *Orfeo* differs not only from the standard legend, but from the *Orfeo* of his great predecessor, Monteverdi. The Italian composer makes the loss of Eurydice irrevocable after Orpheus yields to her pleas and turns around to look at her.

CHARACTERS

ORPHEUS, *legendary Greek singer and musician*		AMOR *(Love)*	*Soprano*
	Contralto	HAPPY SHADE	*Soprano*
EURYDICE, *his wife*	*Soprano*		

HAPPY SHADES, FURIES, SHEPHERDS, SHEPHERDESSES, HEROES, AND HEROINES

The action takes place in legendary Greece

ACT I

SCENE: *The Tomb of Eurydice.* Orpheus mourns his lost Eurydice at her tomb, while shepherds and shepherdesses bring flowers and join in a touching lament. Orpheus is inconsolable in his grief, Orpheus the unrivaled musician of antiquity, at whose divine music, legend tells us, trees uprooted themselves and rocks became loosened from their ledges in order to follow the wonderful sounds. For this Orpheus was the son of Apollo, god of music, and Calliope, muse of epic poetry. Amor, the god of love, is so touched by the anguish of Orpheus that he tells him he may descend to the nether world, the dark realm of Pluto, there to seek the shade of Eurydice. One condition, however, is made: if Orpheus would have Eurydice return to earth with him, he must not turn to look at her until he has recrossed the river Styx.

ACT II

SCENE: *Tartarus.* In the awesome depths of Tartarus the frightening bark of Cerberus is heard, and Furies join in a grotesque dance. Although they try to frighten him away, these dark spirits are finally moved to pity with the song of Orpheus' grief, and they allow him to continue his quest.

ACT III

SCENE: *The Happy Valley.* In the happy Elysian fields beneath cheerful skies, the Spirits of the Blessed dance to the song of birds and the murmur of brooks. Gluck's music is marvelously descriptive of the chaste beauty and the tranquil felicity of these happy spirits. A flute solo of ravishing sweetness

Wide World Studio

FINALE—METROPOLITAN OPERA PRODUCTION

accentuates the mood of classical antiquity. Here Orpheus finds his beloved, clasps her joyfully to his breast, begs her to follow him, but never looks upon her face.

ACT IV

SCENE: *A Forest*. As they mount higher and higher Eurydice becomes increasingly downcast because Orpheus seems no longer to love her. Not once have their eyes met. She would rather remain below than return to earth without his love. Orpheus is bound by the agreement not to reveal the cause of his strange behavior. When they are almost in sight of the land of the living, she cries out with such heart-rending pathos that, in a moment of forgetfulness, Orpheus looks back, only to see her sink lifeless to the ground. Now his sorrow is even more profound than before. Utterly disconsolate, he expresses his grief in a melody of sublime pathos, *"Che farò senza Euridice?"* ("I have lost my Eurydice"). Amor, who has been watching Orpheus, is so deeply moved by this impassioned outcry that he restores Eurydice to life and permits the rejoicing lovers to proceed to the world above.

THE RCA-VICTOR RECORDS

(Sung in French unless otherwise noted)

ACT III

CHE FARÒ SENZA EURIDICE (J'ai perdu mon Eurydice) (I Have Lost My Eurydice): *Nan Merriman, Mezzo-soprano, with Orch. In Italian*   12-0067, 12"

Wide World Studio
ACT II—IAGO AND CASSIO—METROPOLITAN OPERA PRODUCTION

Otello
(OTHELLO)

OPERA IN four acts. Music by Giuseppe Verdi. Libretto by Arrigo Boïto, after Shakespeare. First performance, Teatro alla Scala, Milan, February 5, 1887. United States *première*, Academy of Music, New York, April 16, 1888, with Marconi in the title role, Antonio Galassi as Iago, Eva Tetrazzini as Desdemona, and Sofia Scalchi as Emilia, Cleofonte Campanini conducting. Francesco Tamagno made his American debut in the part of Otello on March 24, 1890, during a spring season of opera at the Metropolitan Opera House. The official first performance at the Metropolitan took place January 11, 1892, with Jean de Reszke, Camera, Albani, and Scalchi. The first all-star cast at the Metropolitan was that of the performance given on December 3, 1894, with Tamagno, Victor Maurel, Emma Eames, and Eugenia Mantelli as principals, and Luigi Mancinelli conducting. On November 24, 1902, *Otello* inaugurated the Metropolitan season with the following principals: Albert Alvarez, Antonio Scotti, Eames, and Louise Homer. Oscar Hammerstein's revival of the opera at the Manhattan Opera House, December 25, 1908, offered in the cast Giovanni Zenatello, Mario Sammarco, and Nellie Melba. Cleofonte Campanini conducted.

Under the Gatti-Casazza regime Arturo Toscanini revived *Otello* on November 17, 1909, with a cast consisting of Leo Slezak, the Bohemian tenor making his American debut as the Moor, Antonio Scotti, Frances Alda, and Florence Wickham, an American contralto in her debut as Emilia. After Slezak's time no other performances of the opera were given until March 19, 1935, when Lauritz Melchior, together with Elisabeth Rethberg, appeared in the work's last act, during a special gala evening. Since then the role of the Moor has been sung at the Metropolitan by Giovanni Martinelli, Torsten Ralf, and Ramon Vinay; Desdemona, Rethberg, Helen Jepson, Stella Roman, and Daniza Ilitsch; Iago, Lawrence Tibbett and Leonard Warren.

Sixteen years after *Aida* had seemed to be the crowning glory of Verdi's long

356

musical career, the great composer astonished the musical world with *Otello*. At the age of seventy-four he showed, past all doubt, that the fierce creative spirit which burned within him was not only alive, but still glowing brightly. In that sixteen-year interval Verdi had kept close touch with the development of music. *Otello*, therefore, is essentially modern in spirit and technique. The characterization is marvelous; there are no set airs or ensembles, the scenes fusing into each other without a break. Its power and almost youthful energy, set upon a lifetime of practical musical and dramatic experience, give the work a unique place in music. Verdi, greatly daring, successfully achieved what few have attempted; he measured skill with Shakespeare himself.

Arrigo Boïto's libretto, a masterpiece of literary and dramatic power, is, with the possible exception of his libretto for Verdi's *Falstaff*, the greatest of his career.

CHARACTERS

OTELLO, *a Moor, general in*		MONTANO, *predecessor of Otello*	
the Venetian army	*Tenor*	*as Governor of Cyprus*	*Bass*
IAGO, *his aide*	*Baritone*	A HERALD	*Bass*
CASSIO, *lieutenant to Otello*	*Tenor*	DESDEMONA, *Otello's wife*	*Soprano*
RODERIGO, *a Venetian gentleman*	*Tenor*	EMILIA, *Iago's wife*	*Mezzo-soprano*
LODOVICO, *Ambassador of the*			
Venetian Republic	*Bass*		

SOLDIERS AND SAILORS OF THE VENETIAN REPUBLIC; VENETIAN LADIES AND GENTLEMEN; CYPRIOT MEN, WOMEN, AND CHILDREN; HERALDS; GREEK, DALMATIAN, AND ALBANIAN SOLDIERS; AN INNKEEPER, AND FOUR SERVANTS

The action takes place at a seaport of Cyprus toward the end of the fifteenth century

ACT I

SCENE: *Exterior of Otello's Castle (with a view of the harbor and the sea; in the foreground a tavern).* A storm rages and the angry sea is visible in the background. A group of Venetian citizens and soldiers watch the vessel bearing the victorious Otello as it struggles with the storm. His vessel arrives safely, and amid great rejoicing the Moor announces a complete victory over the Turkish fleet, in the difficult music of *"Esultate!"* ("Exult!").

When he has entered the castle, the soldiers begin drinking in celebration of the victory. Among them is Iago, who is secretly smarting with a desire for revenge since his comrade in arms, Cassio, has been promoted to a higher rank than himself by Otello. Iago is, moreover, greatly incensed that this Moor should have risen to be a general in the Venetian army, and now honored by being made Governor of Cyprus. He finds a willing ally in Roderigo, who loves Desdemona, and still desires her, even though she has married Otello. Iago, therefore, induces Roderigo to help in plying Cassio with wine.

Cassio at first refuses to drink, knowing his own particular weakness; but when Iago toasts Desdemona, he is obliged to respond. He is soon hopelessly befuddled, grows hilarious, finally quarrelsome. Iago now cunningly manages to have him pick a quarrel with Montano, Otello's predecessor in the government of Cyprus. Swords are drawn, Montano is wounded, and Iago fans the disturbance into a small riot.

This is put down by the appearance of Otello, who is enraged that his own soldiers should thus be fighting among themselves, and deprives Cassio of his command. Iago's crafty planning has already begun its work!

The crowd departs, leaving Otello alone with his wife, the gentle Desdemona. They sing a version in duet form of the lines in Shakespeare's play where Otello describes how Desdemona, hearing him tell of his hardships and dangers in battle, came to love him, *"Già nella notte densa"* ("Dark is the night").

As Otello kisses her, the orchestra plays an impassioned phrase that will be repeated with telling effect at the end of the opera. Husband and wife now re-enter the castle. The peace of a starlight night envelops the scene.

ACT II

SCENE: *A Hall on the Ground Floor of the Castle (with a view of the garden).* Iago plays still more subtly upon the unsuspecting Cassio; he begs him to ask Desdemona to intercede for him with Otello. Cassio goes in search of her, and, well satisfied with his work, Iago gazes after him, soliloquizing on his own philosophy of life. Like a true believer, he begins by saying that he believes in one God, but a cruel god, who has fashioned mankind in his own vile image; that life is made but to feed death, and heaven's only a lie. Verdi has matched this grim confession of faith with a remarkable musical portrayal of Iago's heartless cynicism, in the *"Credo,"* which, incidentally, was a textual invention of Boïto's, since it has no counterpart in Shakespeare's work.

As soon as Iago sees Cassio in conversation with Desdemona, he hurriedly calls Otello and sows in the heart of the Moor the first seed of jealousy, bidding him watch his wife carefully. Otello, much troubled, finds Desdemona and questions her. As she at once begins to plead Cassio's cause, his suspicions are more fully awakened; and when she seeks to wipe his perspiring brow with a handkerchief that was his own first gift, he tears it from her and throws it to the floor. It is picked up by Emilia, Desdemona's maid and Iago's wife. While Otello roughly berates his alarmed Desdemona, Iago forces Emilia to give him the kerchief.

Left alone with Iago, Otello gives expression to his grief, singing a fervent and heartbroken air in which he bids farewell to peace of mind, ambition, and the glory of conquest, *"Ora e per sempre addio, sante memorie"* ("And now, forever farewell").

Now Iago, the Iago that Otello knows only as "honest Iago," pours fuel on the flame of jealousy by avowing that he has seen Desdemona's handker-

Otello

Wide World Studio
ACT III—GIOVANNI MARTINELLI AS OTELLO, LAWRENCE TIBBETT AS IAGO, AND A
MESSENGER—METROPOLITAN OPERA PRODUCTION

chief in Cassio's room. He also declares that he has heard the sleeping Cassio speak of her in his dreams.

Otello becomes frantic with rage. Iago offers to help him to vengeance. Uniting in a most impressive duet they call on all the heavenly bodies to witness this solemn oath in which they swear never to relent or pause until the guilty shall have been punished, *"Sì, pel ciel"* ("By heaven and earth").

ACT III

SCENE: *The Great Hall of the Castle.* Otello seeks Desdemona, and contrives an excuse to borrow her handkerchief. She offers it, but he says this is not the one, for he would have that which he had given her. Though inwardly trembling at its loss, she says it is in her room; she will go fetch it. But Otello at once denounces her and sends her rudely away, and his wife is astonished and grief-stricken at this strange, sudden jealousy. He remains looking after her in the deepest dejection and sings a sorrowful soliloquy, declaring that nothing that fate might have done to mar his fame or fortune would have been so terrible a blow as this, *"Dio mi potevi scagliar"* ("Lord, you could have saved me from this").

Cassio enters, and Iago, bidding Otello watch and listen from behind a pillar, goes to the demoted young officer, and with fiendish ingenuity induces him to talk of his affairs with a woman of the town, Bianca. But Otello does not hear the name, in fact is only able to grasp a part of this half-whispered, rather lewd conversation. Cassio produces the fatal handkerchief, telling Iago that he had found it in his room; he wonders who placed it there. Otello sees the handkerchief; he sees Cassio laughing; and though he does not hear

359

Morton & Co. ACT IV—SAN FRANCISCO OPERA PRODUCTION

all that is said, this is indeed proof enough of Desdemona's guilt. By the time Cassio has left, Otello is insane with jealousy and rage; he asks Iago to procure him poison wherewith to kill Desdemona. Iago craftily evades being involved by suggesting that she had better be strangled in the bed she has dishonored; but he will "take care" of Cassio himself. Otello agrees.

The Venetian ambassador, Lodovico, arrives in state, to inform Otello that he has been recalled to Venice, while Cassio is to be Governor of Cyprus in his stead. Desdemona, who has also entered, weeps for pity at seeing her lord's distress. Her every remark brings a rebuke from Otello, who believes that she weeps because of the approaching separation from Cassio. He announces his departure on the morrow, then, unable longer to contain his smoldering anger, publicly insults Desdemona and flings her to the ground. Overcome with his own feverish emotion he falls to earth in a swoon. Meanwhile, the public outside, hearing that new honors have fallen to their hero, shout, "Hail, Otello! Hail to the Lion of Venice!" But Iago points with horrible triumph to the prostrate Moor, and cries, "Behold the Lion!"

ACT IV

SCENE: *Desdemona's Bedroom.* Desdemona is preparing to retire, assisted by Emilia. She tells Emilia of an old song she used to hear in her childhood, a song that keeps coming back to her mind this evening. The words tell of a girl who, like herself, loved too well, and she sings this pathetic little song for Emilia, *"Salce, salce"* ("Willow, willow"), which is known in English as the "Willow Song."

When Emilia has bid her good night and gone, Desdemona kneels before the image of the Madonna, which stands over a faldstool. Here Desdemona sings her prayer, the noble "*Ave Maria*," at first in a whispered monotone, then soaring aloft in a melody which is probably the loveliest in the entire opera. The song ends with the quiet and peace of the "Amen."

Scarcely has she finished when the sinister figure of Otello is seen appearing through a secret door. He makes his way to her bed, contemplates her for a time. Then he kisses her, while the orchestra plays the passionate theme that ended the love duet in the first act. Otello asks her if she has said her prayers, for, he explains, he would not kill her soul. Again he accuses her of being a paramour of Cassio's. Denials are useless. He repeats charge after charge, his jealous rage mounting, and the horrified Desdemona cries for help, as he takes her by the throat. Emilia knocks frenziedly on the door, and when Otello finally admits her into the room, she is stunned by the tragedy facing her and shrieks for aid. In answer others rush into the bedroom, and Otello says that he has killed his wife because of her faithlessness. Emilia explains about the handkerchief, and Montano tells Otello that Roderigo, dying, has exposed Iago's wiles. That villain makes a hurried exit, and Otello sings a lamentation, as he gazes at the lifeless form of Desdemona. He unsheathes his dagger and stabs himself and, drawing himself close to her with his remaining strength, kisses her, as the orchestra takes up again the "Kiss" motive.

Mishkin

ANTONIO SCOTTI AS IAGO

Crimella

GIOVANNI MARTINELLI AS OTELLO

THE RCA-VICTOR RECORDS
(Sung in Italian unless otherwise noted)

COMPLETE RECORDING: *Nicola Fusati, Tenor; Apollo Granforte, Baritone; Maria Carbone, Soprano; Piero Girardi, Tenor; Nello Palai, Tenor; Corrado Zambelli, Bass; Enrico Spada, Bass; Tamara Beltacci, Soprano; Chorus and Orchestra of La Scala, Milan; Carlo Sabajno, Cond.*
DMC-115 (DM-152) (Vol. 1)
(13314-13321), 8-12″
(DM-152) (Vol. 2)
(13322-13329), 8-12″
MC-115 (M-152) (Vol. 1)
(11363-11370)
(M-152) (Vol. 2)
(11371-11378)

ABRIDGED RECORDING: *Giovanni Martinelli, Tenor; Lawrence Tibbett, Baritone; Helen Jepson, Soprano; Herman Dreeben, Tenor; Nicholas Massue, Tenor; Metropolitan Opera Chorus and Orchestra; Wilfred Pelletier, Cond.*
DM-620 (15989-15994), 5-12″
M-620 (15801-15806)

ACT I

URAGANO ED ESULTATE! (Storm and Entrance of Otello): *Renato Zanelli, Tenor; Roggio, Baritone; Nello Palai, Tenor; Guglielmo Masini, Bass; La Scala Chorus and Orch.* 7366, 12″

LOVE DUET—GIÀ NELLA NOTTE DENSA (Nun in der nächt'gen Stille) (Dark Is the Night): *Tiana Lemnitz, Soprano; Torsten Ralf, Tenor; Berlin State Opera Orchestra. In German*
18363, 12″
(In Album M-860)

ACT II

CREDO IN UN DIO CRUDEL (I Believe in a Cruel God): *Leonard Warren, Baritone, with Orch.* 11-9292, 12″
John Charles Thomas, Baritone, with Orch. 17639, 12″
Titta Ruffo, Baritone, with Orch.
8045, 12″
(Acoustical Recording)

ORA E PER SEMPRE ADDIO (And Now, Forever Farewell): *Renato Zanelli, Tenor, with Orch.* 7366, 12″

SÌ, PEL CIEL MARMOREO GIURO! (We Swear by Heaven and Earth!): *Enrico Caruso, Tenor; Titta Ruffo, Baritone; with Orch.* 8045, 12″
(Acoustical Recording)

ACT IV

CANZONE DEL SALCE (Weidenlied) (Willow Song): *Tiana Lemnitz, Soprano, with Orch. In German* 18364, 12″
(In Album M-860)
Licia Albanese, Soprano, with Orch.
11-9957, 12″
Frances Alda, Soprano, with Orch.
15-1000, 12″
(Acoustical Recording)

AVE MARIA (Hail! Mary): *Tiana Lemnitz, Soprano, with Orch. In German*
18364, 12″
(In Album M-860)
Licia Albanese, Soprano, with Orch.
11-9957, 12″
Frances Alda, Soprano, with Orch.
15-1000, 12″
(Acoustical Recording)

F.O. Cog. Shrine - L.A. Oct. 52   - Jan Peerce. Wonderful Opera.
~18.4 ~ L.A. Op Co ~ Wonderful 4.

ACT I—GIOVANNI MARTINELLI AS CANIO—METROPOLITAN OPERA PRODUCTION

Pagliacci

(STROLLING CLOWNS)

OPERA IN two acts. Music by Ruggiero Leoncavallo, who also wrote the libretto. First performance, Teatro dal Verme, Milan, May 21, 1892. First American performance, Grand Opera House, New York, June 15, 1893. On December 11, of the same year, *Pagliacci* obtained its Metropolitan *première*, with Nellie Melba as Nedda, Fernando de Lucia as Canio, and Mario Ancona as Tonio. Since then *Pagliacci*—until a few seasons ago—was a mainstay of the Metropolitan's repertoire, and the first-line artists who appeared in the gory lyric tragedy number in the dozens, chief of whom, of course, were Enrico Caruso, an incomparable Canio, and Titta Ruffo, a celebrated Tonio.

Pagliacci was composed, one might say, in a fit of temper. Leoncavallo, who had received his musical training at the Conservatory of Naples, had, as a young musician, a hard struggle in the world. An early opera failed to be produced because the impresario ran away with the funds and left the composer nearly penniless. He managed to exist by teaching and playing the piano at café-concerts. In this latter capacity he toured the whole of Europe. During these travels he outlined a vast trilogy which was to do for Italian music what Wagner's *Ring* did for German. On his return to Italy the outline was accepted by a publisher, and Leoncavallo completed the score of the first of the three dramas in a year. No production followed, however, and the composer waited three years. Enraged at this treatment, he made overtures to a rival publisher who had conducted the competition resulting in Mascagni's sensationally successful *Cavalleria rusticana.* Favorably received, he set to work on a short opera in a similar realistic vein. Leoncavallo wrote his libretto, drawing on his own experience for inspiration, and impetuously completed the entire work, libretto and music, in four months. It had a successful production, comparable with that of *Cavalleria* itself. This paved the way for the trilogy, but as the first of these operas failed, Leoncavallo never completed the others. Of his subsequent works, only *La Bohème* and *Zaza* have achieved any measure of success, and even these lack the fire of his earlier work.

At one time a suit was brought against the composer for having plagiarized, for *Pagliacci*, the plot of another author. Leoncavallo thereupon stated that an incident similar to the plot of the opera occurred when he was a child—a case of an actor killing his wife. Leoncavallo's father was the judge before whom the guilty man was tried. The occurrence so impressed itself upon the youthful mind of the composer-to-be that in later life he turned to it as a basis for his opera. This explanation was accepted and the suit withdrawn.

At any rate, *Pagliacci* continues to remain one of the most popular operas on the modern operatic stage; a distinction shared with it only by *Cavalleria rusticana* of all the early realist, so-called *verismo*, operas. They hold this position not without cause, for both are tellingly dramatic as plays, yet contain many attractions in the power and vividness of the music.

Dramatically *Pagliacci* has several features of novel interest on the operatic stage. The composer adopted an old theatrical custom, dating back to Greek drama and used at times by Shakespeare, that of having one of the actors appear before the beginning of the action proper and deliver a more or less formal speech concerning the play that is to follow. Leoncavallo's treatment of this is most original, even though from the point of view of musical form it bears a certain resemblance to the prelude to *Cavalleria* in which a vocal portion, sung backstage, however, is heard in the midst of an instrumental introduction.

Likewise the idea of "play within a play," that gives to *Pagliacci* its unusual ironic quality, is of considerable antiquity, *Hamlet* being its most famous prototype in this respect. The play that occurs in *Pagliacci* is one of the Commedia dell' Arte type that has been acted for centuries by troupes of strolling players in Italy. In that antique and rather crude farce, Pagliaccio discovers his wife, Columbine, with Harlequin, her lover. Harlequin chases the irate husband around the room and finally kicks him out of his own house. This, in the old play, is the climax of the laugh-producing scenes.

The word *pagliaccio* is sometimes translated "Punchinello," sometimes "clown," meaning not clown in the sense of a circus performer, but the buffoon who received all the "hard knocks" in old Italian comedy; the plural, *pagliacci*, refers to the whole group of actors playing such a comedy. Moreover, the final exclamation, *"La commedia e finita!"* (The comedy is ended!"), is said to have been almost the last speech of the dying Beethoven. The tragedy becomes all the more poignant since it strikes Canio, who is compelled to make others laugh even though his heart breaks; an old but ever effective dramatic device.

The part of Canio, the Pagliaccio, a favorite of many of the great tenors, was a role in which the late Enrico Caruso was especially famous; his singing of the aria *"Vesti la giubba"* was considered to be one of his very greatest achievements.

CHARACTERS

CANIO, *master of the troupe of street players ("Punchinello")* Tenor	TONIO, *a clown ("Taddeo")*	Baritone
	SILVIO, *a villager*	Baritone
NEDDA, *his wife ("Columbine")* Soprano	BEPPE, *a clown ("Harlequin")*	Tenor

VILLAGERS AND PEASANTS

The action takes place in the village of Montalto, in Calabria, on the Feast of the Assumption

PROLOGUE

The Prologue opens with a brief orchestral introduction that in itself presages the drama to follow. It depicts the players themselves, as a group, in the bustle and verve of the music, then refers to Canio with a somber strain

Pagliacci

Le Théâtre

ACT II—THE COMEDY IS ENDED

suggestive of his unhappiness and jealousy, to Nedda by way of a sinuous theme indicative of her guilty love for Silvio, and ends with the first idea of the troupe itself.

Tonio, coming through the curtain on an abrupt dissonance, asks the audience's permission with the words *"Si può?"* ("A word?"). Thereafter he launches into a lengthy explanation of the work. These players, he says, are men and women, and the author, borrowing the idea of a prologue from the "glory of old," would not repeat to his hearers that the sighs and tears of the actors are false or that they have no hearts. On the contrary, he would show them to be players in a fragment from life. So he has written the story for men, and the story is true.

With his last words the music grows to a tumultuous climax, as the orchestra peals out the *pagliacci* theme. Tonio knocks on the curtain, saying, "Come, let's begin."

ACT I

SCENE: *The Entrance to a Little Italian Village, at the Junction of Two Roads.* A rude stage has been erected; before it Tonio stands on guard. A trumpet is heard, crude and out of tune, and the booming of a bass drum. It is a holiday, the Feast of the Assumption, and gaily dressed villagers hurry to the spot, in no mood for work. Excited with the anticipation of a good time, they exclaim, "They're here, the *pagliacci!* Welcome!"

Down the road comes a characteristic procession: Beppe, dressed as Harlequin, leading a donkey, which in turn draws a brightly painted cart; in the cart lies Nedda; back of it walks Canio, in the costume of Pagliaccio, with trumpet and drumsticks. The troupe halts before the little theater, and Canio silences the noisy welcome by hammering the bass drum. With mock solemnity he announces their performance, then adds, *"Venite onorateci, signor' e signori"* ("So come then, and honor us, ladies and gentlemen").

365

He turns to help his wife down from the cart, but Tonio, the misshapen clown, is there before him, much to the amusement of the crowd. Canio pays him for this with a hearty box on the ear. Tonio slinks off back of the stage, muttering to himself, while the villagers rock with laughter.

One of the men suggests they go for a drink. Canio calls to Tonio to come along, but the clown answers that he must stay to rub down the donkey. A villager jestingly hints that Tonio might prefer staying behind with Nedda.

At once on the alert, Canio exclaims, "Eh! What!—You think so?" Then, with a wry smile, he continues, *"Un tal gioco"* ("Such a game is better not played").

Nedda understands very well the cause of her husband's black looks, yet exclaims to herself, "What does he mean?" The villagers are somewhat puzzled and ask if he is serious. He rouses himself with an effort and says lightly, "Not I—I love my wife most dearly," and thereupon he kisses her on the forehead.

A troupe of bagpipe players passes, suggested in the orchestra by the oboe, and church bells are heard ringing in the village; toward it the people now turn, slowly, in couples. As they go they sing the famous "Chorus of the Bells," a charming melody with something of the spirit of Italian folk song.

The voices fade away in the distance, and Nedda is left alone to muse over the jealous fire she saw in Canio's eyes. "If he were to catch me!" she shudders. The bright summer sunlight soon drives away these ominous thoughts and, looking up to the sky, she sings the *ballatella, "Che volo d'augelli"* ("Birds without number").

The orchestra supplies a shimmering, twittering background while she sings a carefree, florid melody that waltzes along to the most luminous heights of the soprano voice. Nedda has forgotten her tawdry world, as she thinks of the freedom of the birds.

Her musing is interrupted by the unwelcome reappearance of Tonio. He tells her that he could not resist her singing; she laughs at him, saying he talks like a poet. He knows that he is ugly and deformed, yet he cannot help loving her, desiring her, violently. Nedda orders him to go or she will call Canio. "Not before I have kissed you!" he cries, rushing at her. She darts away, picks up a whip, and strikes him across the face, shouting, "You cur!" Tonio screams with pain, then cries, "By the Blessed Virgin of the Assumption I swear you'll pay me for this!"

No sooner has Tonio gone than a more welcome lover approaches. He vaults lightly over the wall and greets Nedda with a laugh. It is Silvio, one of the villagers, whom she has met on previous visits and found much to her liking. She is alarmed at the sight of him during broad daylight, but he reassures her, for he has left Canio with Beppe at the tavern, where they are drinking and are likely to remain.

Nedda tells Silvio of the clown's threats, bidding him be cautious; but the young villager laughs at her fears, and consoles her by pleading his own love with great earnestness. He begs her to run away with him to some place where they can be happy. Nedda is greatly fascinated, yet remains fearful; she is so charming when she implores him not to tempt her that he only grows more impetuous in his love-making. He reproaches her for her coldness, until at last, throwing discretion to the winds, she yields herself to the bliss of the moment and consents to go. They are so lost in the ecstasy of their passion that they do not observe Canio, who, warned by the overobservant clown, approaches just in time to hear Nedda's parting exclamation, "Till tonight, then! and forever I'll be yours!" Canio is unable to restrain a subdued "Ah!" Silvio disappears over the wall, and Canio, who has not seen his face, runs to follow him. Nedda bars the way. Canio thrusts her aside in fierce anger and leaps over the wall in pursuit. He is too late, for Silvio knows a path hidden by the brush, and Canio fails to discover it. Tonio, who is looking on, laughs in glee, and to Nedda's scornful "Bravo! Well done, Tonio!" replies that he will do better next time. Canio returns out of breath, exhausted, trembling with anger.

The outraged husband commands his wife to pronounce the name of her lover, but she proudly refuses. Wild with jealousy he rushes at her with drawn dagger. Beppe, who has returned unobserved, runs forward and holds him back. People are coming from church, he says, it will soon be time for their performance; they must hurry and dress for it. Nedda, glad for an excuse, disappears into the tentlike stage; Beppe and Tonio go on about their work.

With bowed head, worn out by passion and jealousy, Canio remains alone to consider his fate. Heavy chords are played by the orchestra as he meditates, *"Recitar! mentre preso dal delirio"* ("To perform, while in this frenzy").

He continues, singing the famous arioso of heart-rending pathos, *"Vesti la giubba,"* freely rendered in English as "On with the play."

He moves slowly toward the theater, sobbing. Reaching the curtain that opens on the little stage, he pushes it roughly, as if not wanting to enter; then, seized by a new fit of sobbing, he again buries his face in his hands. Finally he takes several steps toward the curtain from which he had recoiled in fury, enters, and disappears.

ACT II

SCENE: *The Same.* It is the hour appointed for the performance. Tonio is beating the drum to summon the villagers—it would seem rather to drown out their animated chatter as they rapidly congregate. Silvio also arrives, to feast his eyes on Nedda, greeting his friends among the spectators as he takes

his seat. All are excited. Some exclaim as they enter, "Let's try to put ourselves well up in front there!" Others, true villagers impatient for the show,
ask, "What are you waiting for? Why this delaying? Everyone's here!"
Then as the play begins, all shout, "Keep quiet! Be still!"

The curtains of the theater are drawn aside, revealing this scene,
roughly painted: a small room with two side doors and a window at the back.
A plain table and two ordinary chairs are at the right. Nedda is there alone,
dressed in the costume of Columbine. She seems to be nervously awaiting
someone, although she informs her audience that her husband will not be
home till late this evening. From outside comes the sound of a guitar, and
Columbine rushes toward the window with a little cry of joy. The voice of
Harlequin (Beppe) is heard without, singing a serenade; the Italianate
melody is at once dainty and sentimental; the words, a bit extravagant, are
perfectly in keeping with the character and the occasion,*"O Colombina"*
("O Columbine").

Before Harlequin can enter, however, Taddeo arrives (this clownish
role is justly assigned to Tonio), bearing a basket. He sings a pompous greeting, which brings a roar from the assembled villagers. He forthwith begins to
make love to Columbine. Her reply is a demand for the chicken he had been
sent to fetch; Taddeo kneels before her, holding up the fowl in grotesque
devotion. His buffoonery is cut short by Harlequin, who enters and leads him
out by the ear—to the delight of the village audience.

With Taddeo banished, the lovers can make merry. Harlequin gives his
Columbine a little vial, telling her to give it to Pagliaccio.

Columbine assents. Suddenly Taddeo reappears, bawling out in mock
alarm, "Be careful! Pagliaccio is here!"

The "lovers" simulate the greatest alarm, while the spectators applaud
lustily. Harlequin leaps from the window just as Pagliaccio enters. At that
moment Columbine calls to Harlequin the very words previously spoken by
the villager Silvio, "Till tonight, then! and forever I'll be yours!"

This is almost too much for Canio, who forgets for a moment his part of
Pagliaccio. Then, recalling that he is supposed to be acting, he continues
with his lines, "Who has been here with you? Tell me his name?" She insists
that it was only Taddeo, the clown, who, having rushed into hiding, now calls
from the closet, "Believe her, sir, she is faithful! Ah, they could never lie,
those lips." There is more laughter from the spectators.

Again Canio forgets his part; he demands, "Woman, it's your lover's
name I want!" Nedda, still boldly playing Columbine, replies jokingly,
"Pagliaccio! Pagliaccio!" This reminder of his part only angers the jealous
actor; throwing aside his role, he answers, to music of unusual ominous
force, *"No, Pagliaccio non son"* ("No! Punchinello no more!"). And in a
long speech he tells her that he is a man seeking vengeance.

Culver Service

ENRICO CARUSO AS CANIO

Overwhelmed, he sinks on the chair by the table. The spectators murmur at the intense realism of the acting; Silvio exclaims to himself, "This is too genuine!"

The audience, not knowing that this has no part in the play, cries, "Bravo!" Pale, but courageous, Nedda continues the role of Columbine; to a frivolous gavotte tune she remarks that the man who was with her was only the harmless Harlequin. The villagers start to laugh, but stop short on seeing the expression on Canio's face. They begin to realize that this is no mere play-acting. The faithful Beppe approaches in the background; he would interfere, but Tonio craftily holds him back. Canio, crazed with anger and jealousy, again demands her lover's name; again Nedda refuses, boldly declaring, "I will not speak! No, not even if you kill me!" In their excitement, the villagers have risen to their feet, overturning benches; some of the women run away. Silvio draws his dagger, but the men near him, not understanding his excitement, hold him back. Nedda tries to escape toward the spectators, but Canio is too quick. With lightning speed he seizes her. There is a sudden flash, and he plunges his dagger into her heart, crying, "To you! To you!" She shrieks,

Pagliacci

then falls with a choking sound. Making a last faint effort, she calls, "Help me, Silvio!" The young villager breaks away from the men holding him and runs to his beloved. Muttering, "Ah, it's you!" Canio springs forward and strikes the dagger into him. Then, as if stupefied, he lets the knife fall and, addressing his audience for the last time, says with most bitter irony, *"La commedia è finita!"* ("The comedy is ended!").

THE RCA-VICTOR RECORDS
(Sung in Italian)

COMPLETE RECORDING: *Beniamino Gigli, Tenor; Iva Pacetti, Soprano; Mario Basiola, Baritone; Giuseppe Nessi, Tenor; Leone Paci, Baritone; with Chorus and Orchestra of La Scala, Milan; Franco Ghione, Cond.*
DM-249 (17035-17043), 9-12"
M-249 (8524-8532)

PROLOGO—SI PUÒ! (Prologue—A Word!):
Leonard Warren, Baritone, with Orch.
11-9288, 12"
(In Album M-1074)
11-9790, 12"

Lawrence Tibbett, Baritone, with Orch.
6587, 12"

ACT I

BALLATELLA—CHE VOLO D'AUGELLI! (Ballad—Ye Birds Without Number!):
Licia Albanese, Soprano, with Orch.
11-9848, 12"

VESTI LA GIUBBA (On with the Play):
Jussi Bjoerling, Tenor, with Orch.
11-9387, 12"

Enrico Caruso, Tenor, with Orch.
7720, 12"
6001, 12"
(Acoustical Recording)
Giovanni Martinelli, Tenor, with Orch.
6754, 12"

Jan Peerce, Tenor; RCA-Victor Orchestra, Erich Leinsdorf, Cond.
MO-1250 (12-0497-B)
VO-22 (18-0175-B)

ACT II

SERENATA D'ARLECCHINO (Harlequin's Serenade): *James Melton, Tenor, with Orch.*
18365, 12"

Tito Schipa, Tenor, with Orch.
1183, 10"

No, PAGLIACCIO NON SON! (No! Punchinello No More!): *Enrico Caruso, Tenor, with Orch.*
6001, 12"
(Acoustical Recording)

Giovanni Martinelli, Tenor; Metropolitan Opera Chorus and Orch.
6754, 12"

JOHN CHARLES THOMAS AS TONIO

370

Pach Bros. PARSIFAL, KUNDRY, AND GURNEMANZ ENTERING THE CASTLE

Parsifal

CONSECRATIONAL FESTIVAL drama in three acts. Words and music by Richard Wagner. First produced at Bayreuth, July 26, 1882. First regular performance elsewhere, December 24, 1903, at the Metropolitan Opera House, New York. Because of its sacred character, the composer expressed a wish that this work should not be performed as a part of the everyday repertoire of opera houses; he hoped that it would ever remain as a "Stage-consecrating Festival Drama," played only at his own theater at Bayreuth. Accordingly *Parsifal* was not produced elsewhere until 1903, except in concert form. Then, in spite of the legal protest of Wagner's widow, the Metropolitan Opera Company was enabled to give *Parsifal* its first performance outside of Bayreuth, some technicality in connection with the copyright having been discovered. In Europe, however, *Parsifal* was not performed outside of the composer's theater until after the expiration of the copyright in 1913 with the exception of a performance at Amsterdam in 1905.

Parsifal has always held a unique position in the world of opera, partly because of the religious nature of the story, partly because of its being the last of the composer's works, and partly because of the singular beauty of the music. Certainly no other work for the musical stage has been the cause of so long continued a controversy, and in the case of no other work is a just appraisal so difficult—difficult because of sentimental reasons associated with the composer's last work, difficult because of its religious nature. On the one hand, it makes a very pretty theory to say, here is Wagner's final opus, here the master hand reached the culmination of its skill and achieved its ultimate perfection: on the other hand, it makes an equally pretty theory to say that here at last are signs of weakening, the waning powers of old age, even in Wagner. Before one attempts a final appraisal, however, *Parsifal* should be considered in the light of Wagner's peculiar genius, remembering his uncanny and unequaled ability to enter into and be absorbed by the dramas upon which he was working; how for him the drama was thought of in terms of music, and the music took its form, even down to the minutest details of modulation and orchestration, from the drama; and yet, how each music drama has a specific

371

character of its own growing from the very idea back of its action. All this is just as true of *Parsifal* as of the other music dramas; music and drama are perfectly welded together, yet all is keyed to the glowing mysticism of the Grail legend. Thus it may well be that those who are sympathetic toward religious mysticism will find in *Parsifal* a masterwork, those who are not will remain unconvinced. Certain it is that this is no mere "opera" for everyday entertainment; Wagner did not so conceive it, and, in fact, added to *Parsifal* the subtitle, "Stage-consecrating Festival Drama." If the youthful exuberance of *Siegfried* is not in evidence it may be because such overflowing life would be out of place here, rather than because Wagner was no longer possessed of such vitality. Yet the converse, as Mr. Ernest Newman has pointed out, may be true, that when Wagner wrote *Siegfried* he was not yet ready for *Parsifal.* Certain it is that for some twenty years the *Parsifal* theme, as narrated in the poem of Wolfram von Eschenbach, had been germinating in Wagner's mind before it was sketched in 1865, when the *Ring* was well on the road to completion. Evidently during all this time, the composer had been more inclined toward other subjects—perhaps subconsciously felt himself still unripe for the *Parsifal* theme. The text was not completed until 1877 and the music not all written and orchestrated until 1882. Whatever the ultimate verdict of the worth of *Parsifal* may be, opinion is now nearly unanimous that portions of the work rank with the most sublime and beautiful music ever written, notably the remarkable Prelude, the lovely "Good Friday Spell," and the majestic music of the scenes in the Hall of the Grail.

CHARACTERS

TITUREL, *founder and retired King of the Knights of the Grail*	*Bass*	PARSIFAL, *a "guileless fool"*	*Tenor*
AMFORTAS, *his son and present ruler*	*Baritone*	KUNDRY, *an enigmatic character, serving both the Brotherhood of the Grail and their enemy, Klingsor*	*Contralto*
GURNEMANZ, *a veteran Knight of the Grail*	*Bass*	KLINGSOR, *a magician*	*Baritone*

KNIGHTS OF THE GRAIL, KLINGSOR'S FLOWER MAIDENS, ESQUIRES, AND BOYS

The action takes place during the Middle Ages in Spain, at Monsalvat, near and in the Castle of the Grail and in Klingsor's enchanted garden and castle

The Prelude is conceived with a simplicity and dignity of form worthy of the lofty subject of the drama. Without any preliminaries, without any accompaniment, the motive of "The Last Supper" rises, calm and reverent, yet most poignant in its tone color. It is repeated with an accompaniment that induces an aspect of awesome mystery. Then is heard the tranquil motive of "The Grail." Its mood of subdued veneration is soon effaced by the motive of "Faith," which is pealed out in the most solemn majesty by the orchestral brasses. These themes are at once repeated in the loveliest of the softer orchestral voices. The theme of "The Last Supper" returns, surrounded by mysterious, ominous harmonies, and against tremulous tones low in the bass. From a fragment of it is fashioned the motive of "The Spear"—the Spear that pierced the side of the Saviour at the Crucifixion, growing into the most heart-rending, questioning lamentation—the cry of anguish of the suffering Amfortas. This resolves itself into the motive of "The Last Supper" soaring upward and dying softly away, like an unanswered question—for the thought back of the entire Prelude is, as Wagner expressed it: "Love—Faith

—Hope?" The answer to the question is in the drama that follows.When played as a separate concert piece, the motive of "The Grail" is added as a final cadence, bringing the Prelude to a close in the most sublime, radiant tranquillity.

ACT I

SCENE 1: *A Forest Near the Castle of the Holy Grail at Monsalvat.* As dawn lights up the woods of Monsalvat, and the waking call rings out from the Castle of the Grail, Gurnemanz and his esquires awaken and kneel to offer up their morning prayer. Having so done, they would prepare for their King, who will soon approach for his morning bath in the lake, but now a weird interruption occurs: a woman hurriedly approaches—Kundry, unkempt in her apparel and fierce and dark of mien, a strange, enigmatic character who is as industrious in the service of the knights as she is in that of their archenemy, Klingsor. Upon Gurnemanz she urges a vial which she has brought, and bids him give it to the King of the Grail. Perhaps it will heal the grievous wound which afflicts him. Then, utterly exhausted, she throws herself on the ground to rest just as the litter is brought in carrying Amfortas, who is the King of the Knights of the Grail. In his suffering he despairs of a cure, for balms and ointments have been tried from every land, and all have failed. Gurnemanz offers him the vial which Kundry brought. He turns to thank her, but she only bids him begone to his bath.

Kundry's strange behavior has not increased the esquires' confidence in her, and as soon as Amfortas has been taken away they accuse her of being the source of all their misfortunes. Gurnemanz rebukes them, however, recalling the help which she has frequently brought; their misfortunes happen when she is absent. Falling into a mood of reminiscence, he tells them the history of the Grail: The two treasures of Monsalvat are the Cup from which Our Lord drank at the Last Supper, and the Spear which pierced His side. In a vision these were given to Titurel, the father of Amfortas. He it was who built the sanctuary of Monsalvat and gathered together the band of knights for the defense of these sacred relics. Among those who wished to become a knight of the Grail was Klingsor, who was excluded by the very blackness of the passions which filled his heart. Unable to become a true guardian of the Grail, he resolved to obtain the sacred vessel by means of magic, and through sorcery he created a garden of enchanting women to lure the knights to their undoing. In time Titurel grew old and bestowed his kingdom upon his son. But Amfortas, straying too near Klingsor's realm, allowed himself to be enticed away by a woman of wonderful beauty; the magician obtained the sacred Spear and with it attacked Amfortas, who, grievously wounded, escaped only through the timely intervention of Kundry. None have since been able to win back the Spear from Klingsor, who, with the aid of that weapon, will soon have gained the Grail itself. There is a single hope that the Spear may be restored and Amfortas find healing for his wound: once when in the agony of his suffering the King knelt before the shrine in prayer, a heavenly vision spoke to him, saying that a chosen one, a guileless fool, would be the deliverer.

The mystical harmonies of the theme of "The Promise" are suddenly interruped by an outcry from the shore of the lake. A wounded swan falls dying to the ground, an arrow in its breast. Since all wild life is sacred at Monsalvat, the guilty one is quickly apprehended. The author of this outrage is a youth who is quite unconscious of having done any wrong; but Gurnemanz' reproof soon humbles his pride in his archery, his eyes fill with tears, and he throws away his arrows and breaks his bow. When questioned he betrays the astonishing fact that he knows neither his own name nor that of his father. His mother he left only recently and, wandering about aimlessly, has come to this sacred domain. Kundry listens to his narrative with marked interest, displays some knowledge of his history, and startles the youth by informing him that since he left his home, his mother has died. In a sudden fury he springs at her; then, overcome by grief, he seems about to faint, and Kundry revives him with water. Then, while the weird theme of "Enchantment" is heard in the orchestra, she sinks down, unable to withstand the trancelike sleep which overcomes her. Gurnemanz, thinking that this boy may be the Promised One, turns to conduct him to the Castle of the Grail. As they walk, the scene moves, to the accompaniment of the stupendous Transformation music, and the shifting panorama ends when they enter the great hall of the Grail. (At many performances this moving background is omitted and the curtain merely lowered while the scenes are being changed.)

SCENE 2: *The Great Hall of the Holy Grail.* The music assumes a stately and solemn character as the aged knight and the boy enter the sanctuary. The hall is at first empty, but is gradually filled with knights who enter in a dignified procession and take their places at the tables which are ranged around an altar beneath the great central dome. It is the hour of the sacred rite, and while the song of the liturgy echoes throughout the hall, Amfortas is carried in and assisted to a couch at the altar. From a near-by recess, the voice of Titurel is heard speaking as though from a tomb. He bids his son uncover the Grail. But Amfortas cries out in agonized protest, for this sight which brings joy and peace to others only increases his suffering, and, sending the blood coursing wildly through his veins, causes the wound to break out afresh. He sinks down exhausted, but presently yields to the command of his father. The shrine is uncovered, disclosing a crystal Cup, and the hall is permeated by a mysterious darkness. Soon an increasingly dazzling light falls from above, and as the Grail becomes radiant with a soft glow, Amfortas lifts the sacred

German Railroads Information Office

ACT III—THE TEMPLE OF THE GRAIL

vessel and slowly moving it from side to side consecrates the bread and wine. The heavenly light gradually vanishes, the Grail is again enclosed in its shrine, and daylight returns. The knights and esquires sing a reverent hymn while the consecrated elements are distributed; but the exaltation which filled Amfortas during the ceremony passes, his wound breaks out afresh, and falling back weakly, he is carried from the hall. The knights follow, and only Gurnemanz and his companion remain. The youth has stood watching the ceremony, silent and motionless, nor does he reply when the veteran knight questions him concerning what he has seen. Irritated at his apparent stupidity, Gurnemanz opens a side door and irately turns him out.

ACT II

SCENE 1: *The Inner Keep of a Tower Atop Klingsor's Castle.* The Prelude to the second act, with its sinuously winding theme of "Enchantment" and the wild crying of "Kundry," transports us to an entirely different world. At the rise of the curtain we discern vaguely the keep of Klingsor's castle so shrouded in gloom that the strange instruments of necromancy scattered about can hardly be seen. Klingsor himself is nearly invisible in the mysterious blue smoke that comes from the magic flame at which he stands, invoking some unearthly power. He summons Kundry, who rises from the shadows still in her trancelike slumber and awakens with a terrible cry. Klingsor mocks her for her devotion to the knights of the Grail whenever he releases her from his spell; yet, he says, she was a priceless aid to him in overpowering Amfortas. She struggles against these remorse-bringing memories and curses the very thought of them. Yet Klingsor proudly tells her that a more splendid victory shall be hers today. There is but one obstacle between him and the attainment of his ambition and that is the stainless youth who even now is approaching. Let her successfully tempt him as she did Amfortas and the battle will be won. Crying out in the wildest agony, Kundry refuses to obey, but Klingsor's magic is the stronger, and at last she disappears to carry out his will. From the parapet of the tower, Klingsor watches the enemy scale the ramparts and overcome the castle's defenders.

SCENE 2: *Klingsor's Magic Garden.* Suddenly, the tower and magician sink into the earth, and instead there rises from the ground an enchanted garden filled with flowers of weird, exotic beauty. On the wall surrounding the garden stands the strange, little-knowing youth whom we saw ejected from Monsalvat. As he gazes about bewilderedly, there come from all sides the beautiful denizens of the place, Klingsor's flower maidens, clad in their flowing, diaphanous garments. They are in alarm, for they have discovered that some of their lovers have been slain by an unknown foe. Seeing the stranger, they accuse him. He innocently claims the victory, saying that had he not conquered he never could have entered their lovely domain. They soon accept him as a friend; they dance about him, touching his cheeks with their soft hands. But one more lovely than they approaches. Beholding Kundry, they depart, laughing at the youth for his naïve response to their allurements —he has grown angry and turns to flee. "Tarry, Parsifal," Kundry calls, and the astonished youth remains. He remembers that once in the dim past his mother called him by that name. Kundry draws nearer through the luxuriant foliage. She tells the wondering youth that it was she who first gave him the name of Parsifal, an inversion of the Arabian *Fal parsi*—"guileless fool." She tells him of his father, the knight Gamuret, and of how he was slain in battle before the birth of his son; how Herzeleide (Heart's Sorrow), Parsifal's mother, reared him in the forest, far from the ways of men; and how, her son having departed, she pined away and died. Parsifal is naturally greatly affected and bows in grief. Kundry takes him in her arms caressingly, and while he is still shaken with emotion tells him that she comes to him as his mother's last gift. She bends over him and presses a long kiss upon his lips. Kundry's carefully thought-out plan seems to have succeeded, but only for a moment. Suddenly Parsifal starts up, crying out, *"Amfortas, die Wunde"* ("Amfortas, the wound"). He beholds as in a vision the scene in the hall of the Grail and understands for the first time its significance. Kundry's endeavors to lead his mind back to thoughts of passion only reveal to him more clearly the nature of Amfortas' temptation, and he pushes her angrily away. Now she appeals to his pity by telling him of the curse under which she lives. Ages ago she saw Him staggering under His Cross and laughed. His look fell upon her and since that hour she has wandered over the earth, vainly seeking to see Him again. Now she has found Parsifal, her deliverer; if he will but embrace her, salvation shall be hers. Parsifal rebukes her, saying that she can win deliverance by leading him to Amfortas. Turning upon him with the

Mishkin

OLIVE FREMSTAD AS KUNDRY

full hatred of thwarted desire, Kundry curses him—may he never find his homeward road. She calls Klingsor to come to her aid, and the sorcerer immediately appears on the ramparts of his castle. He flings the sacred Spear at the youth. And now a miracle happens. The Spear, changed from its course, hovers over Parsifal. He seizes it and makes with it the sign of the Cross. As with an earthquake the castle falls into ruins, the garden withers to a desert, and Kundry sinks down with a cry. In turning to depart, Parsifal exclaims to her significantly that she knows where they will meet again.

ACT III

SCENE 1: *A Hermit's Hut in the Grail's Domain.* The Prelude to the third act at once plunges us into the gloom and desolation that have now fallen over the knights of the Grail. The themes of "Kundry," "The Spear," "The Grail," "The Promise," and "Enchantment" all enter, but in a somber broken form. At the rise of the curtain we are shown the rude hut where Gurnemanz now makes his solitary abode. The early light of a spring morning is breathing through the leaves of the forest as the faithful knight, now bent and hoary with age, issues from his dwelling. A strange moaning from a woodland thicket near by has aroused him; he approaches and discovers Kundry, unconscious, yet crying out as though troubled by some frightful dream. Tending her carefully, he restores her to consciousness. She is less savage but even more wan in her appearance than when we last saw her serving the knights of the Grail at Monsalvat. She at once resumes her humble duties and in bringing a pitcher of water from the spring observes a new arrival at the domain of the Grail. It is a knight in black armor, with visor closed; Parsifal, weary from long searching, has at last found Monsalvat. Gurnemanz asks him to remove his armor, for this is holy ground and should not be profaned, least of all on this, the most holy of days, Good Friday. Parsifal complies and, striking the Spear which he carries into the ground, kneels before it in fervent prayer. Gurnemanz and Kundry, now recognizing Parsifal, are filled with mingled emotions. Parsifal, rising from his meditations, tells Gurnemanz of his joy at seeing him, of the many hardships that beset his path, of the wounds and suffering which he endured during the long search for Monsalvat, hardships all brought about because of a curse which had been placed on him. Gurnemanz is profoundly stirred on beholding again the sacred Spear. He tells Parsifal of the sad estate of the knighthood: Amfortas, driven by his intense sufferings of body and soul, longs only for death and refuses to fulfill his holy office; deprived of the heavenly sustenance of the Grail, the knights are powerless. No longer, he continues, do they journey forth in holy warfare; Titurel, deprived of the vision of the Grail, has died. Parsifal cries out in grief, accusing himself of being the cause of all these misfortunes, and sinks back, fainting. Kundry brings water, but Gurnemanz reproves her gently, saying that the sacred spring itself would be better. To it they now lead Parsifal. On reviving he asks to be conducted to Amfortas. Gurnemanz assures him that this shall be done, for this very day the obsequies of Titurel are to be celebrated, and Amfortas will again unveil the Grail. Now Kundry, eager and humble, bathes his feet, and Gurnemanz, taking water from the spring, baptizes him, pronouncing the solemn words of invocation. Kundry takes a golden vial from her bosom and, pouring a part of its contents over Parsifal's feet, dries them with her hair, hastily unbound. Parsifal, who has been observing these ministrations in deep emotion, takes the vial from Kundry and, giving it to Gurnemanz, bids the knight anoint his head; thus it is that Gurnemanz consecrates Parsifal as King of the Grail, while in the orchestra the theme of "Parsifal" is proclaimed with great majesty.

As a first act of compassion, the new King baptizes Kundry, who falls weeping to the ground. Now the soft weaving of the theme of the "Good Friday" music rises in the orchestra, and Parsifal, looking out over the woods and meadows, remarks beatifically on the beauty of the fields and meadows on this day. Gurnemanz explains, saying, "That is Good Friday's spell, my lord!" and Parsifal speaks of the sadness of that day.

Gurnemanz explains that it is not so, that this beauty of the woods and fields is caused by the spell of Good Friday, and that the flowers and trees, watered by the tears of repentant sinners, express by their luxuriance the redemption of man.

Kundry has slowly raised her head again, and gazes at Parsifal with moist, beseeching eyes. A distant tolling of bells being heard, Gurnemanz says that it is midday and that the long-awaited hour has come.

Gurnemanz has brought out a coat of mail and mantle of the knights, which he and Kundry put on Parsifal. As they go their way, the landscape gradually changes until finally they disappear in the rocky entrance to the castle. Processions of knights are seen in the long arched passageways; the tolling of bells constantly increases.

SCENE 2: *The Great Hall of the Grail.* At last the great hall becomes visible, but the tables are no longer there, and the place is dimly lighted. There enter two processions of knights, singing to one another antiphonally.

The bier of Titurel is placed at one side, and Amfortas is helped to his throne back of the altar. He exclaims weakly at his misfortune, then breaks into an agonizing prayer. But the knights, pressing nearer to Amfortas, insist that he uncover the Grail. Amfortas, in a paroxysm of despair, cries that he will never again do so. He tears open his robe and shows them the wound, asking them, as he does so, to kill him and end his suffering. All shrink back in awe, and Amfortas stands alone in fearful ecstasy.

Parsifal, accompanied by Gurnemanz and Kundry, has entered unperceived, and now advancing stretches out the Spear, touching Amfortas' side with the point. Amfortas' countenance shines with holy rapture, and trembling with emotion, he is supported by Gurnemanz. Parsifal says, "Be whole, unsullied, and absolved." And he proclaims himself King in Amfortas' place. All gaze with intense rapture on the Spear, which Parsifal holds aloft.

He ascends the altar steps and, taking the Grail from the shrine already opened by the esquires, sinks before it in silent prayer. The sacred Cup begins to glow with a soft light, and while the lower portion of the hall becomes plunged in darkness, the dome is filled with a heavenly radiance. As the splendor increases, the voices of the kneeling knights, esquires, and boys join in a wonderful cadence, rising through marvelously changing harmonies and dying away in the distance.

A ray of dazzling light falls from above, and in it a white dove descends, hovering over Parsifal. Kundry, looking up at him, slowly falls to the ground; she is dead. Gurnemanz and Amfortas bow in homage before him. Parsifal waves the Grail over the brotherhood, blessing them, and while the orchestra plays in a final seraphic form the themes of "Faith," "The Grail," and "The Last Supper," the curtain falls.

Parsifal

THE RCA-VICTOR RECORDS
(Sung in German)

PRELUDE AND GOOD FRIDAY SPELL (Orchestral Version): *Boston Symphony Orchestra, Serge Koussevitzky, Cond.*
DM-1198 (12-0149-12-0151), 3-12"
M-1198 (12-0146-12-0148)

Leopold Stokowski and the Philadelphia Orchestra:
DM-421 (16464-16467), 4-12"
M-421 (14728-14731)

ACT II

HERZELEIDE SCENE (Heart's Sorrow): *Kirsten Flagstad, Soprano; Lauritz Melchior, Tenor; Gordon Dillworth, Baritone; Victor Symphony Orchestra, Edwin McArthur, Cond.*
DM-755 (17782-17785), 4-12"
M-755 (17774-17777)

ICH SAH' DAS KIND (I Saw the Child): *Kerstin Thorborg, Mezzo-soprano, with Orch.* 17223, 12"
(In Album M-707)

AMFORTAS! DIE WUNDE! (Amfortas! the Wound!): *Lauritz Melchior, Tenor; the Philadelphia Orchestra, Eugene Ormandy, Cond.* 15212, 12"
(In Album M-516)

ACT III

SYMPHONIC SYNTHESIS: *Leopold Stokowski and the Philadelphia Orchestra*
8617 & 8618, 2-12"

NEARLY COMPLETE RECORDING: *Gotthelf Pistor, Tenor; Ludwig Hoffmann, Bass; Cornelius Brongeest, Baritone; Berlin State Opera Chorus and Orchestra; Karl Muck, Cond.*
DM-67 (17238-17245), 8-12"
M-67 (7160-7167)

NUR EINE WAFFE TAUGT (Only One Weapon Serves): *Lauritz Melchior, Tenor; the Philadelphia Orchestra, Eugene Ormandy, Cond.* 15213, 12"
(In Album M-516)

Talbot

CHARLES DORNING AS ARCHIBALD GROSVENOR AND MARGARET MITCHELL AS PATIENCE

Patience

(OR, BUNTHORNE'S BRIDE)

COMIC OPERA in two acts. Music by Arthur Sullivan. Libretto by W. S. Gilbert. First produced at the Opéra-Comique, London, April 23, 1881, as "an entirely new and original aesthetic opera in two acts." *Patience* was designed as a burlesque of two rival schools of poetry then flourishing in England, one headed by Oscar Wilde, the other by Algernon Charles Swinburne. Spokesman of the "fleshly" school, Wilde was an easy mark for Gilbert's caricature because of his spectacular way of dressing and his no less spectacular pronouncements on life and art. Few failed to recognize in Bunthorne the flamboyant young writer so maliciously lampooned in the columns and cartoons of the magazine *Punch*. Swinburne, as standard-bearer of the Pre-Raphaelite camp and the poet of "aesthetics" and "culture," was no less the predestined model for Bunthorne's rival poet, Grosvenor. Unfortunately, much of the satire of *Patience* has evaporated with the years. Many of its lines have lost point, and its story is conspicuously outdated. But the music has imparted an imperishable quality to *Patience*. The "original aesthetic opera" is also fondly remembered by all true Savoyards as the work that opened the new house that D'Oyly Carte built for the exclusive production of works by Gilbert and Sullivan. This was the Savoy Theatre, and it was on October 10, 1881, that the collaborators entered their magnificent new home with a performance of *Patience*.

CHARACTERS

COLONEL CALVERLEY	*officers of*	THE LADY ANGELA		Soprano
MAJOR MURGATROYD	*Dragoon*	THE LADY SAPHIR	*rapturous*	Soprano
LIEUT. THE DUKE OF DUNSTABLE	*Guards*	THE LADY ELLA	*maidens*	Soprano
REGINALD BUNTHORNE, *a fleshly*		THE LADY JANE		Contralto
poet	*Baritone*			
ARCHIBALD GROSVENOR, *an idyllic*		PATIENCE, *a dairy maid*		Soprano
poet	*Tenor*			

CHORUS OF RAPTUROUS MAIDENS AND OFFICERS OF DRAGOON GUARDS

381

ACT I

SCENE: *Exterior of Castle Bunthorne*. Enthralled by the glowing talk of Bunthorne, poet of the "fleshly" school, twenty "lovesick maidens" are sighing and singing their despair to the erratic bard. Insensible to their charms, Bunthorne elaborately explains the mysteries of love. Only proper medical treatment, he asserts, can cure the ailment. We now learn from Lady Jane the reason why Bunthorne is indifferent: he is himself hopelessly in love with Patience, a simple dairy maid. Patience, who knows nothing of Bunthorne's love, comes upon the scene and proceeds to ridicule the girls for their silly brooding. Let them return to the Dragoon Guards who have just arrived in the village, she urges. But the "lovesick maidens" are too far gone in their adoration of Bunthorne to be interested in more prosaic suitors. The Dragoons arrive, led by a blustering colonel, only to leave in a huff when the girls, spellbound by Bunthorne's latest poem, completely ignore them.

Bunthorne now finds himself alone, and we soon learn why Patience attracts him. He is a sham, he confesses, but with this village maid he can be himself, natural and without pretense. When Patience reappears, Bunthorne begins to make ardent love to her, but the girl, who has loved no one but an aunt, is utterly bewildered by Bunthorne's language. Later, when Lady Angela, one of Bunthorne's lovesick victims, assures her of the ennobling powers of love, Patience resolves to find herself a sweetheart that very day.

There now enters Archibald Grosvenor, a poet of the "idyllic" school and a childhood friend of Patience's. The two promptly fall in love, but Patience is suddenly troubled by the thought that since love, which is "utter unselfishness," must involve some sacrifice, she cannot marry anyone as perfect as Grosvenor. Meanwhile, Bunthorne has decided to put himself up to be raffled, and just as the lot is about to be drawn, Patience, still clinging to her ideal of "utter unselfishness," announces she will marry him because "she detests him so." Heartbroken, the twenty "lovesick maidens" decide to return to the spurned Dragoons. However, the moment they see Grosvenor, they speedily transfer their affections to him, the reason being that "he is aesthetic!" Bunthorne is stung with jealousy, and the Dragoons are in a rage over this fresh humiliation.

ACT II

SCENE: *A Rural Glade*. The unattractive Jane is heard bewailing the lot of maidens who have been in that state too long. The thought of Bunthorne brings a sigh, for she too has succumbed to his rapturous talk. In following Grosvenor the others have proved faithless to their idol, but she, Jane, will remain loyal to the end. Presently Grosvenor appears, trailed by the retinue of sighing maidens. Bored with all this worshipful attention, he pleads for the "usual half-holiday on Saturday." As they leave him, Patience enters and adds to his sorrows by reminding him that she loves him but is compelled on principle to marry Bunthorne.

The "fleshly" and "idyllic" poets now meet. In a jealous rage, Bunthorne threatens to lay a curse upon his rival unless he makes himself less attractive to the ladies. Grosvenor, he declares, must consent to cut his hair and become thoroughly commonplace. Though outwardly appalled at the prospect of becoming prosaic, Grosvenor is secretly relieved and agrees to transform himself into an "everyday young man." But now that Bunthorne is happy, Patience, again in "utter unselfishness," is forced to break her engagement. When Grosvenor returns, clad now in a plain tweed suit, she announces that since he is a commonplace young man she can marry him. Bunthorne is further abashed when he discovers that the twenty maidens have returned to their soldier lovers; that, in fact, they are no longer lovesick. He now decides to console himself with the matronly Lady Jane. But, alas, he is again rebuffed, for the Duke of Dunstable, having resolved to marry a plain woman, has already courted and won her. Plainness has triumphed over poetry, and Bunthorne, only a few days before the most pursued of lovers, is left without a bride.

THE RCA-VICTOR RECORDS
(Sung in English)

COMPLETE RECORDING: *D'Oyly Carte Company; Dr. Malcolm Sargent, Cond.; under the personal direction of Rupert D'Oyly Carte. (Cast includes: Nellie Briercliffe, Rita Mackay, Bertha Lewis, Winifred Lawson, Marjorie Eyre, Darrell Fancourt, George Baker, Leslie Rands, Derek Oldham, Martyn Green.)*

DC-14 (12936-12945), 10-12"

C-14 (11070-11079)

White ACT II—ZURGA PRONOUNCES JUDGMENT UPON LEILA AND NADIR

Les Pêcheurs de Perles
(THE PEARL FISHERS)

OPERA IN three acts. Music by Georges Bizet. Libretto by Michel Carré and Eugène Cormon. First performance at the Théâtre-Lyrique, Paris, September 30, 1863. United States *première* at the Grand Opera House, Philadelphia, August 25, 1893. A version omitting the third act was staged at the Metropolitan Opera House on January 11, 1896. The cast was headed by Calvé, Cremonini, Ancona, and Édouard de Reszke. New York waited twenty more years for the complete opera. It then opened the season on November 13, 1916, with a cast headed by Enrico Caruso, Frieda Hempel, Giuseppe de Luca, and Léon Rothier.

Preceding *Carmen* by twelve years, *Les Pêcheurs de Perles* lacks the dramatic power and emotional intensity of Bizet's masterpiece. Though less impassioned in speech than the maturer work, it boasts lovely melodies of a slightly Oriental tinge and an appealing mood of exotic fantasy. The beautiful prelude shows Bizet's superb grasp of orchestral color and already hints at the power to come in the firm symphonic web of *Carmen*.

CHARACTERS

LEILA, *a priestess*	*Soprano*	ZURGA, *a chief*	*Baritone*
NADIR, *a pearl fisher*.	*Tenor*	NOURABAD, *high priest*	*Bass*

PRIESTS, PRIESTESSES, PEARL FISHERS, WOMEN, ETC.

Les Pêcheurs de Perles

The action takes place in legendary Ceylon

ACT I

SCENE: *The Coast of Ceylon.* Zurga, the newly elected leader of the little
world of Cingalese fishermen, has scarcely been inaugurated when Nadir, a
long-lost friend of his youth, appears. After greeting one another with affection, they recall the time when they were foolish enough to quarrel over a
beautiful priestess in the temple of Brahma, Leila. In the duet, *"Au fond du
temple"* (*"Del tempio al limitar"*)—"In the depths of the temple"—they
sing of the moment when they first saw her. Both had fallen in love with her
as she was revealed to them for an instant in the dim, incense-clouded temple.
Believing themselves cured of the old infatuation, they swear eternal friendship.

A veiled priestess approaches on her way to the temple to pray for the
success of the fishermen. Every year she comes thus, mysteriously, and none
has dared gaze upon her face, for she is held to be sacred to Brahma. At
Zurga's behest, the priestess is about to take the oath of chastity when she
recognizes Nadir and is startled. She is reminded by the high priest, Nourabad, that she may revoke her vow, but this she refuses to do and enters the
temple. The people disperse, leaving Nadir alone. Agitated by the discovery
that he still loves Leila, he sings an air, pathetic yet beautiful, in which he
describes the lovely girl as he once heard her singing among the palms on a
starlit tropical night. Around this haunting melody, with its faintly Oriental
color, orchestral strings weave a fascinating atmosphere. Nadir is about to
go to warn Zurga of all this, but overcome with weariness, he falls asleep on
the temple steps. There Leila finds him. While appearing to pray to Brahma,
she subtly reveals her love for Nadir. Completely under the sway of his former passion, Nadir forgets Zurga and, under cover of darkness, hastens to
his love.

ACT II

SCENE: *A Ruined Temple.* Leila, about to begin her lonely watch, is reminded by Nourabad of the punishment that is certain to overtake her should
she violate her solemn oath. She replies that she is in no danger, for once as
a child she swore to protect a fugitive who had implored her aid, and even
though his enemies threatened to kill her, she had kept her vow. The man was
enabled to escape, and in gratitude he had given her a golden chain as a
remembrance. Yet Leila now cowers in fear as the priest again threatens her
with the doom certain to be hers if she prove unfaithful. But her fears vanish
with the arrival of Nadir, and soon the two are completely lost in the ecstasy
of their love. They are surprised by Nourabad, who alarms the people. But

385

when fishermen advance with drawn swords, demanding death for the couple, Zurga, mindful of his pledge of friendship to Nadir, intervenes. Nourabad draws aside the veil from the girl's face, and, lo! it is none other than Leila, the very woman Nadir has sworn with Zurga to forget! Enraged at his friend's treachery, the chieftain condemns the guilty pair to death.

ACT III

SCENE 1: *The Camp of Zurga.* Leila pleads with Zurga for the life of her lover, but Zurga only reveals his own jealousy. Too proud to sue for her own life, the condemned priestess excites the chieftain's wrath with her scorn. Presently Nourabad enters to announce the execution, and to him Leila gives the golden chain of the fugitive, with the plea that he send it to her mother.

SCENE 2: *The Place of Execution.* Just as the lovers are about to mount the funeral pyre, a distant glow, at first thought to be dawn, is seen. Zurga rushes in, crying out that the camp is on fire. When the people have scattered to save their children and possessions, Zurga explains to the couple that he has set fire to the camp in order to save them, for he has recognized Leila's golden chain. It was he who gave it to her years before when she had saved his life. Thus the lovers are permitted to escape. When the people return, Nourabad denounces Zurga, for he has again been eavesdropping. Zurga is now condemned to mount the funeral pyre, and as the flames roar about him, a fiery glow reveals that the forest itself is ablaze. Surrounded and overcome by this sea of flames, the people fall prostrate before the wrath of Brahma.

THE RCA-VICTOR RECORDS
(Sung in Italian)

ACT I

DEL TEMPIO AL LIMITAR (In the Depths of the Temple): *Beniamino Gigli, Tenor; Giuseppe de Luca, Baritone; with Orch.* 8084, 12″

MI PAR D'UDIR ANCORA (I Hear as in a Dream): *Enrico Caruso, Tenor, with Orch.* 7770, 12″
Richard Crooks, Tenor, with Orch. 15544, 12″ (In Album M-585)

ACT II

CAVATINA—SICCOME UN DÌ CADUTO IL SOLE (A Fugitive One Day): *Toti dal Monte, Soprano; La Scala Orch.* 7721, 12″

BRAHMA, GRAN DIO! (Brahma, Great Deity!): *Toti dal Monte, Soprano; La Scala Chorus and Orch.* 7721, 12″

MAGGIE TEYTE AS MÉLISANDE

Pelléas et Mélisande

OPERA—OR an "impressionistic tone picture"—in five acts; music by Claude Debussy; poem by Maurice Maeterlinck. First produced, April 30, 1902, at the Opéra-Comique, Paris, with Mary Garden and Jean Périer in the title roles. First performance in the United States, at the Manhattan Opera House, New York, February 19, 1908, with mostly the original cast.

Maeterlinck's drama, *Pelléas et Mélisande*, has for the basis of its plot such a simple form of the eternal triangle that a mere recital of it fails to convey any of the play's great poetic charm and beauty. In fact, stripping the plot of the subtle symbolism of the lines is like trying to present the wonderful impressionistic colors of a Monet painting in a black-and-white copy.

For this very subdued and appealing drama, Debussy supplied music of great delicacy and subtly suggestive power. Often the orchestra furnishes a decorative background while the voices sing in a recitative style that closely follows the natural inflections of the speaking voice. At times of climax, the music rises to greater prominence and attains remarkable beauty and emotional force, though still serving to underline the poetic sentiment of the text.

The collaboration of Debussy and Maeterlinck did not come to the greatest cordiality imaginable, for the poet objected, first of all, to Debussy's having altered the text for musical purposes, omitting sizable parts of it, here and there. Then—and probably the important point—Maeterlinck had taken it more or less for granted that his wife, Georgette Leblanc, would be entrusted with the name part. Ten years before that Maeterlinck had given Debussy carte blanche with the play, instructing him to do as he pleased with it. Now, when the opera was completed, the troubles began.

Maeterlinck, in the bitterness of his disappointment over the choice of another artist for the leading role, found everything wrong with Debussy's work. He wrote a letter to the publisher of the Paris *Figaro*, in which he excoriated the opera and everything connected with it. He said, among other things, "The *Pelléas* in question has become foreign, almost inimical to me; and, deprived as I am of any control over my own work, I am reduced to hoping that its failure [the opera's] will be immediate and resounding." However, Debussy's opera was anything but a failure, although there were those at the *première* who threw a few epithets at its "stammering phantoms," at its music for being a "succession of sound wraiths." And after the work's first American performance, one critic discovered that Debussy's tonal combinations "sting and blister and pain and outrage the ear."

All such feeling about a truly great work, however, had disappeared completely when it was given its first performance at the Metropolitan, March 21, 1925, with Lucrezia Bori, Kathleen Howard, Edward Johnson, Clarence Whitehill, and Léon Rothier as the chief artists. The delicacy of the text had found its mate in Debussy's treatment of it. The "spoken" song of the opera, the subtlety of the musical suggestion, and the fluid, captivating score had, by that time, become matters of common knowledge and appreciation.

CHARACTERS

ARKËL, *King of Allemonde, a fictitious domain*	Bass	MÉLISANDE, *a mysterious young princess*	Soprano
GENEVIÈVE, *wife of his son*	Soprano	YNIOLD, *young son of Golaud through a former marriage*	Soprano
GOLAUD, *her elder son*	Baritone		
PELLÉAS, *his half brother*	Tenor		

A PHYSICIAN, SERVANTS, BLIND BEGGARS, ETC.

The action takes place in legendary times

ACT I

SCENE 1: *A forest.* Golaud has lost his way in the depths of the forest and, while wandering aimlessly about, finds a beautiful young woman weeping at the edge of a spring. Her answers to his questions are so vague and mysterious that he cannot learn whence she came, how she happens to be there, or why. She has dropped a golden crown in the spring, but will not permit him to recover it for her; nor will she allow him to come near her. She does,

New York Times
LUCREZIA BORI AS MÉLISANDE

New York Times
EDWARD JOHNSON AS PELLÉAS

finally, tell him her name, Mélisande. Then, as it is growing dark and Golaud insists that they seek shelter, she follows him nervously at a distance.

SCENE 2: *A Hall in Arkël's Castle.* The change of scene is accompanied by a beautiful orchestral interlude in which is heard prominently a theme associated with the unhappy fate of the lovers. Six months are supposed to have elapsed, and the curtain rises disclosing the room in the somber castle of Arkël, King of Allemonde. Geneviève is reading to the King a letter that Pelléas has just received from his brother, Golaud, telling of his marriage to Mélisande. Golaud fears that Arkël will not forgive him for having thus married without his consent when a union of political importance had been planned for him. Pelléas enters to ask the King's permission to go to visit a dying friend. But the father of Pelléas, who is in the castle, also is ill, and Arkël, reminding him of this, bids him place a signal light for Golaud and remain at the castle until his half brother's return.

SCENE 3: *A Terrace in Front of the Castle.* Again a beautiful interlude accompanies the change of scene. Mélisande, Geneviève, and Pelléas, having come out of the gloomy castle to watch the ocean at sunset, see a ship that bravely embarks in spite of the threatening storm. Night approaches suddenly, and Geneviève, hurrying off to take care of her little grandson, Yniold, asks Pelléas to conduct Mélisande back to the castle. To Pelléas' seemingly casual remark that on the morrow he must leave, Mélisande responds with the childlike cry, "Why must you go?"

ACT II

SCENE 1: *A Fountain in the Park*. To escape the stifling summer noon's heat at the castle, Pelléas and Mélisande have come to an ancient, deserted fountain in one of the most remote and silent parts of the woods. After asking, "Do you know where I have brought you?" Pelléas tells her of this fountain. It is reputed to have had miraculous powers. Once it is said to have restored sight to the blind; but now even the old King is nearly sightless, and not a soul comes to the place. Mélisande's childlike question, "Does it open the eyes of the blind no more?" is symbolic, since that very well is where the young people's eyes are opened to their love. She is fascinated by the water; she tries to reach it as she sits on the edge of the well, but only her long, loose-flowing hair is able to penetrate beneath its surface. Pelléas recalls it was beside a spring that Golaud found Mélisande. Now Mélisande begins to play with a ring—a ring that Golaud has given her. She throws it up in the air, high up so as to see it sparkle in the few rays of sunlight that manage to penetrate through the dense foliage. Pelléas begs her to be careful; suddenly the ring slips through her fingers into the dark waters of the well. They think they can see it glisten as it sinks. It never will be recovered, for the well is immeasurably deep. Moreover, they cannot stop longer now, for Pelléas heard twelve o'clock being struck just as the ring disappeared, and they will be sought at the castle.

SCENE 2: *Golaud's Chamber in the Castle*. The change of scene is accompanied by an orchestral interlude in which the bright, flowing music of the fountain sinks down and vanishes beneath the stern tread of a motive which can be called that of "Fate."

Golaud is lying on his bed in a room in the castle; Mélisande is at the bedside. All is going well now, he remarks, while telling her how he came to be injured. He cannot understand how it was that just as he finished counting the twelve strokes of noon, the horse on which he was riding at the hunt ran wildly away, for no apparent reason. His injuries were not serious, however, and he tenderly bids Mélisande go to sleep for the night. Suddenly she bursts into tears; and to Golaud's anxious questions she only replies that she is not happy there—it is no one's fault, not the King's, not Golaud's mother, Pelléas, no—it is not Pelléas', it is the darkness of the place: one never sees the blue sky. Golaud tries to console her. Tenderly he takes her hands, and then he notices that the ring he gave her is missing. Instantly he is alarmed. To his insistent questions she replies with childish and evasive answers, finally saying that she dropped the ring in a grotto by the sea. Golaud orders her to go at once to find it, even in the darkness of night. Pelléas, he says, will conduct her safely.

BIDU SAYAO AS MÉLISANDE MARTIAL SINGHER AS PELLÉAS

SCENE 3: *A Grotto by the Sea.* During the orchestral interlude, the gentle theme associated with Mélisande is heard in poignant, sorrowful form and the rippling music of the fountain enters briefly. Then all is broken by an eerie formlessness, and the curtain rises on a dark cavern by the sea.

Pelléas and Mélisande come groping their way like children through the dense obscurity. He leads Mélisande into the grotto so that in case Golaud asks she will be able to describe the place. The roar of the sea echoing through the grotto makes it seem even more dismal and terrifying. The moon throws a sudden flood of light into the cavern and reveals a group of paupers who have sought shelter there, for now a famine is raging in the land. Mélisande is so greatly frightened that Pelléas has to hurry back to the castle with her.

ACT III

SCENE 1: *A Turret of the Castle.* Mélisande is at a window, up in one of the towers of the castle. While she combs her unbound hair, arranging it for the night, she sings some ancient song that quaintly lists a number of saints. Pelléas comes up the watchman's path around the tower. He halts beneath the window, for tomorrow he must leave. Again in her childish way she tells him he must not leave—she will not let him take her hand to kiss it in farewell if he goes. Pelléas promises to delay his departure; she leans far out of the window so that he can reach her hand. In so doing her long, magnificent hair comes streaming down over Pelléas, overwhelming him with delicious excitement at the touch of her glorious tresses. In his ecstasy he exclaims that he will hold her thus forever. Some frightened doves fly out of the tower and hover around them in the darkness. Golaud comes silently around the path. He is agitated at finding Pelléas and Mélisande thus and, laughing nervously, scolds them for playing like children in the night—both children.

SCENE 2: *The Vaults Beneath the Castle.* The "Fate" motive is heard. It grows suddenly to a climax, at which the expressive "Mélisande" theme enters. This in turn subsides, and the interlude closes with the ominous theme of "Vengeance."

Golaud has led Pelléas down into the subterranean vaults beneath the castle to see the stagnant pool that lies there. He bids Pelléas let him hold his arm, and then lean out over the chasm. Does he smell the deathlike stench that rises? Pelléas is alarmed at the way Golaud's hand holding aloft the lantern trembles; the two hurry out in silence.

SCENE 3: *A Terrace at the Entrance of the Vaults.* The brothers come out from the vaults; Pelléas is happy again to breathe the pure air from the sea. Golaud cautions Pelléas about continuing such childish play with Mélisande as took place the night before. She may become a mother soon and must be spared any shock. Almost threateningly he warns Pelléas to avoid Mélisande as much as possible—though not too markedly, he adds.

SCENE 4: *A Turret of the Castle.* Golaud brings Yniold, his little son by a former wife, out before the castle, and by repeated questioning tries to learn more of the state of affairs between Pelléas and Mélisande. But the child's answers are so vague that they only tantalize Golaud's suspicions. A light appears in Mélisande's window, and Golaud holds Yniold up high so he can look in the room. Yes, Pelléas is there with Mélisande, but they do not speak. No, they do not come near one another, and they do not close their eyes. Then the child becomes frightened and is about to cry aloud, so the unhappy Golaud has to go, his fears only partly confirmed.

ACT IV

SCENE 1: *A Corridor in the Castle.* Pelléas meets Mélisande along a corridor in the castle, and certain that he will leave on the morrow, he begs and obtains a rendezvous with Mélisande—midnight at the well of the blind. The two go their separate ways: Mélisande returns, after a moment, with Arkël. The old King is filled with sympathy and kindness for her; he hopes that now since Pelléas' father has recovered, the castle will seem less gloomy and that she will be happier. Half soliloquizing, he says he believes that a young, fair, and joyful being will create an atmosphere of joy around itself. In the utmost tenderness, as if speaking to a grandchild, he asks to kiss her. The aged, he says, need to be reminded of youth in order to drive away for a time the menaces of death. Golaud enters, searching for his sword. Blood is noticeable on his brow. "I have been through a hedge of thorns," he says, and, again, the symbolic meaning of his words is not to be missed. He rebukes Mélisande for her nervousness; he cannot endure the gaze of her great open eyes. Arkël says he sees in them only a great innocence. This releases the flood of Golaud's pent-up fury. In cruelest irony he cries that God himself might take a lesson in innocence from her eyes—one would say that the angels were continually baptizing themselves in that innocence. He seizes Mélisande by her long hair and drags her savagely to and fro across the floor. Arkël restores quiet; if he were God, he says, he would have pity on the hearts of men!

SCENE 2: *A Fountain in the Park.* An interlude of great expressiveness accompanies the change of scene: the "Fate" motive, played with passionate intensity. Then appears the theme of Mélisande for a moment as the music subsides. Another tense climax, and finally gloom and foreboding.

In the uncanny silence and obscurity of midnight the desolate fountain of the blind seems doubly mysterious and supernatural. There Pelléas now awaits Mélisande. He reflects how he has played with the forces of destiny; perhaps it would be better if he never again saw her. Yet it seems that a century has passed since last they met. Soon he forgets his fears under the thrill of his excitement at her approach. Mélisande recalls that they came here once long ago. Tenderly she asks why he must leave. He hesitates, saying, "It is because . . ." then he kisses her suddenly, "I love you." Mélisande answers quietly, "I also love you." Pelléas is overwhelmed by the simple fact of her declaration. They hear the castle gates being closed for the night; but they assure themselves that they are not afraid. They rejoice that they are together. Mélisande believes that she hears Golaud behind them among the trees; Pelléas scoffs, saying that it is only the wind in the leaves; an instant later they are sure that it is he crouching in the darkness. They would conceal themselves among the shadows; but they realize Golaud has seen all; he carries his sword, Pelléas has not his. Filled with a sudden desperate abandon, they embrace wildly—it seems that the stars of the whole heavens are falling upon them. Golaud rushes out, stabs Pelléas, and pursues the fleeing Mélisande.

ACT V

SCENE: *Mélisande's Chamber.* Mélisande is lying on a bed. Arkël, Golaud, and a physician are watching. The physician says that it is not of the very trifling wound Golaud gave her that she is dying—perhaps, indeed, she may recover. The others having left him alone with Mélisande in response to his earnest entreaties, Golaud begs her forgiveness. Anxiously he asks her if she will answer just one question and tell the exact truth. Then, on her assent, he asks excitedly, "Did you love Pelléas?" With the utmost naïveté she replies, "Yes, indeed, I loved him. Is he here?" Golaud believes she does not understand. Again she replies that their love was not guilty; the childlike simplicity of her manner racks the soul of Golaud. Impassionedly he demands to know the truth; Arkël and the physician re-enter, and the despairing Golaud remains as one blind. Though the air is cold, Mélisande wishes the window left open so that she may watch the setting sun. She scarcely seems to realize that she has become the mother of a little girl. When Arkël gently shows the child to her she quietly remarks, "She is very tiny, she is going to weep also." The servants of the castle gradually enter the room and take their places along the wall, where they remain waiting, silently. This is symbolic of the fact that death is near. They have not been sent for, why do they come? Golaud wonders. They make no reply to Golaud's excited questions. Mélisande stretches forth her arms—it is the struggle of the mother. Suddenly the servants drop to their knees. "What is it?" asks Arkël. The physician goes over to Mélisande, then replies, "They are right." Arkël speaks to the sobbing Golaud, "Come, now she needs silence. She was such a quiet, timid creature, a mysterious being, as is everyone. Come, we must not leave her child in this room; it must live on now and take her place. It's the turn of the poor little one...."

THE RCA-VICTOR RECORDS
(Sung in French)

VOCAL AND ORCHESTRAL SELECTIONS: *Yvonne Brothier, Soprano; Charles Panzéra, Baritone; Willy Tubiana, Bass; Vanni-Marcoux, Baritone; Or-* *chestra of the Opéra-Comique, Paris, Piero Coppola, Cond.* M-68 (1444, 4174-4176, 9636-9639), 4-10" 4-12"

J. Quentin Jaxon

PELLÉAS AND MÉLISANDE

Peter Ibbetson

OPERA IN three acts. Music by Deems Taylor. Libretto by the composer and Constance Collier, based on the novel by George du Maurier. Commissioned by the Metropolitan Opera Company, through its general manager, Giulio Gatti-Casazza. First performance, Metropolitan Opera House, New York, February 7, 1931, with a cast comprising Edward Johnson as Peter Ibbetson, Lawrence Tibbett as Colonel Ibbetson, Léon Rothier as Major Duquesnois, Lucrezia Bori as Mary, Duchess of Towers, and Marion Telva as Mrs. Deane. The conductor was Tullio Serafin. *Peter Ibbetson*, although not in the recent repertoire of the Metropolitan, was quite popular for three seasons. In fact, it inaugurated the season 1933–34, the only opera by an American composer to be so honored. It has also obtained performances elsewhere in the United States.

Peter Ibbetson is the second opera by Deems Taylor to have been produced at the Metropolitan, the other being *The King's Henchman*, which preceded it by four years. The score of *Ibbetson* is notable for its effective employment of French folk songs in the dream sequences and for the often telling contrasts between dramatic and lyrical expression, as well as for the theater-wise creating of mood in the dream episodes.

CHARACTERS

PETER IBBETSON, *a young architect*	*Tenor*	CHARLIE PLUNKETT	*friends*	*Tenor*
COLONEL IBBETSON, *his uncle*	*Baritone*	MADGE PLUNKETT	*of*	*Mezzo-soprano*
MARY, DUCHESS OF TOWERS	*Soprano*	GUY MAINWARING	*Mrs.*	*Tenor*
MRS. DEANE, *a wealthy young*		DIANA VIVASH	*Deane*	*Mezzo-soprano*
widow	*Mezzo-soprano*	VICTORINE, *a waitress*		*Soprano*
MRS. GLYN, *her mother*	*Contralto*	A SISTER OF CHARITY		*Mezzo-soprano*
ACHILLE GREGOUX, *an innkeeper*	*Tenor*	MANSERVANT		*Baritone*
MAJOR DUQUESNOIS, *a Napoleonic*		THE PRISON GOVERNOR		*Baritone*
veteran	*Bass*	A TURNKEY		*Baritone*
THE PRISON CHAPLAIN	*Bass*	A FOOTMAN		*Tenor*

THE PEOPLE OF THE DREAM

PASQUIER DE LA MARIÈRE,		MRS. SERASKIER, *mother of Mimsey*	
Peter's father	*Baritone*	(*Duchess of Towers*)	*Soprano*
MARIE PASQUIER, *his mother*	*Soprano*		

MIMSEY SERASKIER   GOGO PASQUIER

GUESTS, THE WARDEN, THE PRISON DOCTOR, ETC.

The action takes place in London and Paris, between 1855 and 1857

ACT I

SCENE: *Drawing Room of an English Country House, 1855.* Peter Ibbetson, a guest at a reception given by Mrs. Deane, angers his uncle, Colonel Ibbetson, who is the cousin of Peter's mother, by innocently exposing him as a plagiarist. The hostess, inclined to side with Peter, talks with him and learns about his boyhood life in the Passy quarter of Paris and of Mimsey, his sweetheart, and during his reminiscences echoes of those days are brought back through the singing of French folk songs in the background. When this sequence ends, Mary, Duchess of Towers, arrives at the reception, and although she and Peter exchange interested glances, neither remembers the other as a principal in the story Peter has just been telling.

ACT II

SCENE 1: *The Salon of the Inn La Tête Noire at Passy-Paris, 1857*. At the Tête Noire Peter meets his old friend, Major Duquesnois, a veteran of the Napoleonic wars, now senile. The Major remembers the people of Peter's childhood but he does not recognize Peter as the young Gogo of long ago.

SCENE 2: *The Dream: Garden of Parva Sed Apta, Passy, 1840*. The meeting serves to revive Peter's childhood memories, and in an ensuing dream a scene is re-enacted, during which Colonel Ibbetson is guilty of a vile innuendo about Peter's mother.

SCENE 3: *La Tête Noire, 1857*. When Peter awakens, he discovers that Mary, seeking shelter from a sudden rain, has come to the inn. This time they remember each other and, besides, learn that both had had the same dream. However, strongly though they are drawn to one another, Mary says seriously that she is not free and that they must never meet again.

ACT III

SCENE 1: *Colonel Ibbetson's Rooms in London, 1857*. A quarrel takes place between Peter and his uncle, when the Colonel refers insultingly to Peter's mother. During their scene Peter strikes the Colonel a fatal blow.

SCENE 2: *The Chaplain's Room in Newgate Prison, 1857*. Peter has been found guilty of the murder of his uncle and has been condemned to be hanged. All through his trial and the subsequent weeks Peter has kept secret the reason for the killing, and despite the appeals of the chaplain he will not even now, on his last day, break his silence. In the midst of preparations for his execution Mrs. Deane arrives with the exciting news that, through Mary's intercession, his sentence has been commuted to life imprisonment. But Peter says dramatically that he prefers actual death to a lifetime of living death. However, Mrs. Deane reassures him, disclosing that Mary wishes him to "sleep and dream true."

SCENE 3: *The Dream: The Mare d'Auteuil, Paris, 1840*. In the dream sequence that follows, Peter is transported to the banks of the Mare d'Auteuil, where he and Mimsey played as young children. He sees there his loved ones, his father and mother, Major Duquesnois, Mimsey's mother, and himself and Mimsey, both as children, of course. Though he tries valiantly to enter into the life of the scene, to speak with these dear ones again, he cannot. And finally Mary, the grown-up Mimsey, appears. She calms him, telling him that always she will be there in his dreams, that they will roam the world together so, that their true life has just begun.

SCENE 4: *A Cell in Newgate Prison, 1887.* Thirty years later Peter is dying in his cell at Newgate Prison. He is visited by an elderly woman, Mrs. Deane, who brings news that Mary has died, news which he already knows, because the previous night she did not appear to him in his dream. In a few moments Peter falls back on his cot and in a reverie sees Mary, who has now come to take him with her. Mrs. Deane's fears about Peter are confirmed, and together with the turnkey she goes for the doctor. They all know, when they return, that it is too late. Peter, still in his dream, is at the Mare d'Auteuil. Mary extends her arms to him, and from the cot arises the young Peter Ibbetson, as he appeared in the first act of the opera. He joins Mary in an embrace, while the others are grouped about the deathbed in solemn attitudes, and the chorus, offstage, exhorts the wanderer to "Arise, and greet the day!"

Culver Service   LAWRENCE TIBBETT AS COLONEL IBBETSON

Campbell's Press Studio
MARJORIE EYRE AS HEBE AND MARTYN GREEN AS SIR JOSEPH PORTER, K.C.B.

H. M. S. Pinafore

(OR, THE LASS THAT LOVED A SAILOR)

COMIC OPERA in two acts. Music by Sir Arthur Sullivan. Libretto by W. S. Gilbert. First performance, Opéra-Comique, London, May 25, 1878. *H.M.S. Pinafore* proved to be Gilbert and Sullivan's first world success, obtaining performances, within two years of its *première*, at New York, Calcutta, Cape Town, and Sydney.

The Sorcerer had no sooner been produced than Gilbert set to work on the libretto for his next opus. Actually it was in December, 1878, that he was able to send his partner Sullivan a libretto, accompanied by an assured note which read, "I have very little doubt whatever but that you will be pleased with it." As for Sullivan, his muse worked just as rapidly, for he began composing the music almost on receipt of the libretto.

Three days after *The Sorcerer* closed its run, at the Opéra-Comique, *H.M.S. Pinafore* made its bow before the London public.

The work, however, was not, as the two previous collaborations, an instantaneous success, owing to a variety of circumstances, such as the hot weather suffered in the month of June and the disappearance, therefore, of ticket buyers.

In August, Sullivan accepted the post of conductor for a series of concerts known under the name of "Classical Nights." These were part of the prom concerts given at Covent Garden. One evening, among the numbers played, was a medley of airs from Sullivan's own score to *H.M.S. Pinafore*, and the audience took to it enthusiastically. Soon the operetta itself profited by the many new visitors.

CHARACTERS

RT. HON. SIR JOSEPH PORTER, K.C.B.,
   First Lord of the Admiralty Baritone
CAPTAIN CORCORAN, *Commanding*
   H.M.S. Pinafore   Baritone

RALPH RACKSTRAW, *able seaman*   *Tenor*

DICK DEADEYE, *able seaman*   *Bass*

TOM TUCKER, *midshipmite*   *Tenor*

398

H. M. S. Pinafore

BILL BOBSTAY, *boatswain's mate*	*Baritone*	HEBE, *Sir Joseph's first*	
BOB BECKET, *carpenter's mate*	*Baritone*	*cousin*	*Mezzo-soprano*
JOSEPHINE, *the Captain's*		LITTLE BUTTERCUP, *a bumboat*	
daughter	*Soprano*	*woman*	*Contralto*

FIRST LORD'S SISTERS, HIS COUSINS AND AUNTS, SAILORS, MARINES

The action takes place on the quarterdeck of H.M.S. Pinafore, *off Portsmouth, 1878*

ACT I

SCENE: *The Deck of* H.M.S. Pinafore. *H.M.S. Pinafore* is anchored in the harbor at Portsmouth. The sailors are busy scrubbing the decks for the expected arrival of Sir Joseph Porter, K.C.B., and they sing "We Sail the Ocean Blue." Little Buttercup, a bumboat woman who is by no means as small as her name would imply, comes aboard with a stock of "snuff and tobaccy and excellent jacky," not to mention "excellent peppermint drops," and she plunges into a self-informative waltz ditty, "I'm Called Little Buttercup." It transpires that a handsome young sailor, Ralph Rackstraw, is in love with the Captain's daughter, Josephine, and he proceeds to tell about that in his song, "A Maiden Fair to See." She, however, is to be betrothed to Sir Joseph Porter, who duly arrives, attended by "his sisters and his cousins and his aunts," and makes his importance felt in "I Am the Monarch of the Sea," and later in "When I Was a Lad." In the meantime, Ralph plans to elope with Josephine, who at first shies away from him, singing "Refrain, Audacious Tar." The plot is overheard by Dick Deadeye, the lugubrious boatswain.

ACT II

SCENE: *The Deck of* H.M.S. Pinafore *at Night.* Captain Corcoran, alone on the poop deck, sings to the moon. Little Buttercup on the quarterdeck watches him. When he comes down to the quarterdeck, she reveals her affection. He tells her that because of his rank he can only be her friend; but she hints darkly that a change is in store for him, saying that "things are seldom what they seem." Sir Joseph returns, complaining that Josephine does not favor his suit, and the Captain comforts him by averring that she is awed by his lofty station and suggests that he plead his cause on the ground that love levels all ranks. Still Josephine does not respond, for her heart is set upon Ralph. Dick Deadeye reveals the elopement plan, and he and the Captain lie in wait for the crew, "carefully on tiptoe stealing." The elopers are captured, and the Captain is so exasperated that he actually swears, using a "big, big D," which is overheard by Sir Joseph Porter. For this serious breach of morals, a horrible example of depravity before the whole crew, the Captain is ordered to his cabin. Affairs are interrupted by Little Buttercup, who discloses a secret, telling how the Captain and Ralph

399

had been accidentally exchanged while they were both babies. Whereupon Sir Joseph, with true Gilbertian logic, sends for Ralph and makes him Captain, and at the same time reduces Corcoran to Ralph's former humble grade of "able seaman." Now, since it is out of the question for one of Sir Joseph's exalted station to marry the daughter of a mere seaman, his Lordship nobly consents to the marriage of Ralph and Josephine. The erstwhile Captain consoles himself with Little Buttercup.

THE RCA-VICTOR RECORDS
(Sung in English)

COMPLETE RECORDING: *D'Oyly Carte Company; Dr. Malcolm Sargent, Cond.; under the personal supervision of Rupert D'Oyly Carte. (The cast includes: Bertha Lewis, Nellie Briercliffe, Elsie Griffin, Charles Goulding, George Baker, Henry Lytton, Sydney Granville, Stuart Robertson, Darrell Fancourt.)* DC-13 (12927-12935), 9-12″
C-13 (9937-9945)

ABRIDGED RECORDING: *Victor Light Opera Company, Emil Coté, Cond.*
P-120 (27833-27836), 4-10″

GEMS: *Victor Light Opera Company with Orch.* 35386, 12″
(Acoustical Recording)

WHEN I WAS A LAD: *John Charles Thomas, Baritone* 18223, 12″

MARTYN GREEN AS SIR JOSEPH PORTER, K.C.B.

Campbell's Press Studio
LESLIE RANDS AS CAPTAIN CORCORAN AND
DARRELL FANCOURT AS DICK DEADEYE

DARRELL FANCOURT
AS DICK DEADEYE

Pique-Dame

(THE QUEEN OF SPADES)

TRAGIC OPERA in three acts. Music by Peter Ilyich Tchaikovsky. Libretto by Modest Tchaikovsky, after a story by Pushkin. First performed at the Imperial Opera House, St. Petersburg, December 19, 1890. American *première*, in German, at the Metropolitan Opera House, March 5, 1910, and for the first time here in Russian at the New Amsterdam Theater, New York, on May 10, 1922. Like the same composer's *Eugene Onegin*, *Pique-dame* is based on a Pushkin text, the novelette, *Pikovaya Dama*, a model of narrative suspense and mounting dramatic impact. Merimée's translation of this Russian classic is virtually a French classic. As for the gambling motif which serves as psychological thread, it long remained a favorite device of Russian writers, notably Tolstoy and Dostoevsky. In preparing the libretto Tchaikovsky's brother Modest took some unavoidable liberties with the Pushkin original, but preserved the steady, unifying drive of Hermann's insensate gambling mania. Some of the music was originally written for an opera based on still another Pushkin tale, the adventure story, "The Captain's Daughter." Tchaikovsky abandoned that project after almost completing it.

CHARACTERS

HERMANN, *officer of the hussars*	*Tenor*	THE COUNTESS	*Mezzo-soprano*
COUNT TOMSKY, *his friend*	*Baritone*	LISA, *her granddaughter*	*Soprano*
PRINCE JELETSKY, *betrothed to* Lisa	*Bass*	PAULINE, *her friend*	*Soprano*
		THE GOVERNESS	*Mezzo-soprano*
CZEKALINSKY	*Tenor*	MASCHA, *a chambermaid*	*Soprano*
SSURIN	*Bass*		
TSCHAPLITZKY	*Tenor*	GUESTS, SOLDIERS, OFFICERS, PROMENADERS,	
NARUMOV	*Bass*	MASQUERADERS, ETC.	

CZEKALINSKY, SSURIN, TSCHAPLITZKY, NARUMOV } *Russian officers and noblemen*

The action takes place in St. Petersburg toward the end of the eighteenth century

ACT I

SCENE 1: *A Summer Garden on the St. Petersburg Promenade.* The central figure of *Pique-dame* is Hermann, a lieutenant of the hussars hopelessly in debt from constant gambling. Hermann has fallen in love with Lisa, a granddaughter of a mysterious old Countess, once the toast of St. Petersburg. From Tomsky Hermann learns that the Countess is the reputed possessor of a secret winning-card series wrested from a titled lover. Because of her luck at the tables she has been dubbed the Queen of Spades. Should the Countess reveal the formula to another lover, however, she will forfeit her life. Hermann's hopes of amassing a fortune revive and he resolves to force the secret from the Queen of Spades. Then he will make his fortune at cards and marry Lisa.

SCENE 2: *Lisa's Room.* Lisa has gathered her friends in her room, and soon Pauline joins her in a dreamy duet, after which Lisa sings a touching romanza, which suits her melancholy mood. All now take up a charming dance song of the steppes, which rises in ardor till the governess enters and reminds them it is time for bed. Lisa is to marry Prince Jeletsky, yet her thoughts keep reverting to the dashing young officer, Hermann. While she is alone, Hermann appears on the balcony, beckoning to her, but Lisa draws back till he vows to kill himself if she refuses to listen. In the midst of their troubled talk, the old Countess enters and scolds Lisa for staying up so late. Hermann, who has managed to hide himself in time, returns to his wooing when the Countess leaves. At length, Lisa gasps out: "I am yours!"

ACT II

SCENE 1: *A Masked Ball in the Home of a Nobleman.* Smartly clad officers mingle with brilliantly gowned ladies at this festive gathering. Prince Jeletsky is inquiring of Lisa why she appears so downcast, but Lisa remains silent. A divertissement in the pastoral style of eighteenth-century court entertainment now unfolds, relating how Chloë spurned the wealthy Plutus to marry the shy and penniless Daphnis, a parallel that is not lost on Lisa. Later when she meets Hermann, a passionate dialogue ensues at the end of which she agrees to a tryst in her room. Without suspecting Hermann's secret motive, Lisa gives him the key to the Countess' room, through which he must pass to reach hers.

SCENE 2: *The Countess' Bedchamber.* Concealed behind a curtain, Hermann awaits the Countess. At length, the Countess enters. In a wistful, nostalgic mood she recalls her youth, her brilliant conquests as a beauty, and sings a song from Grétry's opera, *Richard the Lionhearted.* Then she begins to doze off, but starts up in terror as Hermann steps from behind the curtain and implores her to divulge the wonder-working card sequence. The Countess is struck speechless with fright when Hermann, failing to get the secret by pleading, threatens her with a pistol. The Countess falls dead, and the coveted formula is lost forever. At this point Lisa enters the room and rushes to the Countess' side. She is crushed when she learns of Hermann's ruse and reproaches herself for having so foolishly been his accomplice. With her cry of "Murderer!" ringing in his ears, Hermann rushes off into the night.

ACT III

SCENE 1: *Hermann's Barracks.* Hermann is reading a letter from Lisa in which she expresses regret for her conduct and asks him to meet her at a place on the bank of the Neva River. Just then a funeral procession passes by and the Countess' ghost appears before Hermann. In great solemnity the ghost reveals the card formula as three, seven, and ace, in succession. Wild with joy, Hermann hurries to meet Lisa with the news.

SCENE 2: *On the Canal Bank Near the Winter Palace.* A prey to conflicting emotions, Lisa awaits Hermann on the quay. We now hear one of Tchaikovsky's most imaginative passages, Lisa's *scena* and arioso, as she waits for her card-crazed officer. "It will soon be midnight," she complains, "and Hermann is not here," and the distraught girl pours all her wretchedness into a magnificent song. "Ah, how worn out with sorrow I am," she sings to the silent night; "morning and night it crushes my heart like a heavy stone." At the stroke of twelve, Hermann appears, looking wildly jubilant, bursting with his ghastly secret. Spurred by his new hopes, Hermann talks now of eloping with her. The girl joins him in an ecstatic duet, which rises to feverish passion, but Lisa is again seized by despair as Hermann, wildly mumbling the card numbers, laughs at her pleas to abandon his mad designs. Hermann dashes off, and Lisa, in a frenzy of desperation, throws herself into the river.

SCENE 3: *At a Gambling House.* Officers are gathered around a faro table, Prince Jeletsky among them, as Tomsky sings a cheerful little song and the officers blend their voices in a kind of club anthem. Hermann enters, pale and shaken. Using the magic formula he begins to play, first placing 40,000 rubles on the three. He wins, and then doubles his stakes on the seven, and again wins. Only the Prince shows courage enough to continue opposing him. Meanwhile, Hermann philosophizes on the great gamble of life, in an aria of rich melodic appeal. "What is life?" he asks, seeking to lighten the tense mood of the moment and, voicing a devil-may-care credo, he cries out, "Life is like gambling; today I lose, tomorrow you lose!" Hermann now confidently stakes all his winnings on the next card, certain it will be the promised ace. In the breathless silence of the room, he turns up the card. It is not the ace, but the queen of spades! And again the ghost of the Countess appears to Hermann, grinning vengefully now. Hermann, hopelessly mad now, draws a dagger and kills himself.

THE RCA-VICTOR RECORDS
(Sung in Italian)

SCENE AND ARIOSO—L'ISTANT' È PRESSO ORMAI (It Is Near to Midnight) : *Irene Jessner,*
  Soprano, with Orch. 17559, 12"

SCENE FROM D'OYLY CARTE OPERA PRODUCTION

The Pirates of Penzance
(OR, THE SLAVE OF DUTY)

COMIC OPERA in two acts. Music by Sir Arthur Sullivan. Libretto by W. S. Gilbert. First performance (for copyright purposes only), Bijou Theater, Paignton, England, December 30, 1879. The next night it was performed in New York, Fifth Avenue Theater, whither Gilbert and Sullivan had gone for the ostensible purpose of staging an authorized version of *H.M.S. Pinafore*. Both performances had the original subtitle, *Love and Duty*. Initial showing in London, Opéra Comique, April 3, 1880, with the present subtitle, *The Slave of Duty*.

However, since *Pinafore* had already enjoyed a notable success in versions less authorized, it becomes obvious that the famous team had visited the United States in order to obtain some return from its popularity here. No reciprocal copyright agreement existing between Great Britain and the United States—a condition paralleled today between this country and Russia—it was possible for authors to realize profit on their works only if the manuscripts remained in their possession and were produced by themselves.

In any case, the *Pinafore* authorized version staged and somewhat successful, Gilbert and Sullivan soon got to work, while here, on still another operetta, which, as it developed, was *The Pirates of Penzance*. The work was a brilliant success. And to add to the tribulations of the authors (who had been having a time with the orchestra musicians), transcribers, copyists, and very real musical pirates haunted the performances of the piece, taking down as much of the work as they could. It was possible, in those days, to present some author's work without paying him a cent in royalty, provided that it was done "legally," that is, without stealing the actual manuscript. So, to circumvent, as much they could, the circulation of their operetta in presentations unprofitable to them, Gilbert and Sullivan decided to prepare a number of productions, rehearsing, altogether, four road companies. Thus the returns, quite sizable ones, were all their own.

Rayton Harb
England

CHARACTERS

RICHARD, *a pirate king*   *Bass*

SAMUEL, *his lieutenant*   *Baritone*

FREDERIC, *a pirate apprentice*   *Tenor*

MAJOR-GENERAL STANLEY, *of the British Army*   *Bass*

EDWARD, *a sergeant of police*   *Bass-Baritone*

MABEL, *General Stanley's youngest daughter*   *Soprano*

KATE
EDITH } *General Stanley's* — Zena —
ISABEL }   *daughters*   *Altos, Sopranos*

RUTH, *a piratical maid-of-all-work*   *Contralto*

CHORUS OF GENERAL STANLEY'S DAUGHTERS, PIRATES, POLICEMEN, ETC.

ACT I

SCENE: *A Rocky Seashore on the Coast of Cornwall.* As the curtain rises, groups of pirates are discovered, drinking and playing cards. Samuel, the pirate lieutenant, goes from one group to another, filling the cups. Frederic, an apprentice pirate, is seated in a despondent attitude. Ruth kneels at his feet.

With the closing notes of this chorus, the Pirate King congratulates his apprentice, Frederic, on having made the grade, and Frederic replies that he has done his best for the pirate band simply because it had to be, for he is "the slave of duty." He says that, when he was apprenticed to the pirates, it was entirely through an error, an error that he refuses to divulge because it would reflect on Ruth, the maid-of-all-work. She, however, tells the story, in the song "When Frederic Was a Little Lad": she stupidly apprenticed him to a pirate, instead of a pilot, as she had been ordered to do by his father.

When she has finished this disclosure, Ruth is comforted by Frederic. He tells the pirates of the dilemma he is in—for, though loving them all individually, he is such a slave of duty that as soon as his apprenticeship is up he must devote himself to their extermination. The pirates bemoan the fact that they don't seem able to make piracy pay. Frederic says that he knows why, and the Pirate King reminds him that—as he is not free from his indentures till twelve o'clock—he must tell them the fault that he sees. Frederic replies that they are too tenderhearted with their foes, particularly when they happen to be orphans, the pirates themselves all being orphans. Thus, the word has gone around, and everyone they attempt to pillage says he is an orphan. Ruth comes forward and asks what is to become of her. The Pirate King says that of course Frederic will take her with him when he leaves, and an amusing argument ensues. Frederic contends that, as he has never seen another woman, he does not know whether Ruth is good-looking or not. Ruth assures him that she is. As Frederic leans toward letting her stay with the pirate band, they endeavor to coax him to take her. Samuel says, "Yes, there are the remains of a very fine woman about Ruth." She is handed backward and forward, first to the Pirate King,

405

then to Frederic, until she finally remains with the latter. He, in bidding the pirates good-by, seeks to have them renounce their evil ways, but, in "Oh, Better Far to Live and Die," the Pirate King acquaints him with the impossibility of such a thing.

The Pirate King, Samuel, and all the pirates except Frederic leave the stage. Ruth enters and begs Frederic to allow her to stay with him. He questions her regarding her appearance, asking her to tell him quite frankly whether or not she is beautiful. She says that she would be deceiving him if she told him otherwise. At this moment a chorus of girls is heard in the distance. Frederic springs to the top of a rock to see who is approaching. He sees "by all that's marvelous, a bevy of beautiful maidens!" Ruth realizes that her deception has been discovered, and Frederic turns upon her bitterly for lying to him about her looks. He renounces her, and she leaves in despair. Frederic hides as the girls trip in, gaily singing "Climbing Over Rocky Mountain."

Kate, Edith, Isabel, and all the other girls who have now arrived on the scene are entranced with the beauty and apparent seclusion of this seaside spot. They mention the fact that their father, because of his age, has been left far behind. But Isabel says, "Oh, he will be here presently." The girls now decide to go in wading, and are in the act of taking off their shoes and stockings, when Frederic comes forward from the cave. He admits he is a pirate, and asks "Oh, is there not one maiden breast" who will rescue such a one as he? But none of the girls will marry him to reform him except, finally, Mabel, daughter of a major-general. She scolds her companions and bravely announces that she will save him. Then, in "Poor Wandering One," she offers him her heart. Frederic and Mabel make love, the other girls pretending not to notice. The pirates enter stealthily, and each conveniently embraces a girl for his bride. At this point Major-General Stanley enters and identifies himself in the song "Model of a Modern Major-General." Then he demands an explanation of what is transpiring. Samuel tells him that they intend to marry his daughters. The General does not recognize their uniform, and is startled to learn that they are the famous Pirates of Penzance. He says that he objects to pirates as sons-in-law, and the Pirate King—in turn—retorts that they object to major-generals as fathers-in-law, but that they'll waive the objection. Then the Major-General has an idea. He tells the pirates that he is an orphan, and asks them if they know what it means to be an orphan. The pirates are much disgusted, seeing their prey slip through their fingers in this fashion. There is an argument between the Pirate King and the General over a misunderstanding as they confuse the words "often" and "orphan." Then the Major-General addresses the pirates, explaining the situation in detail, and obtains permission to depart with his wards from the pirates' haven.

DARRELL FANCOURT
AS THE PIRATE KING

SYDNEY GRANVILLE
AS THE SERGEANT OF POLICE

ACT II

SCENE: *A Ruined Chapel by Moonlight.* Crumbling pillars and arches at the sides. Ruined Gothic windows at back. General Stanley is discovered seated pensively at the right, surrounded by his daughters; presently Mabel and Frederic join them. Mabel asks Frederic if he cannot in any way comfort her father. Frederic asks the General why he sits "in this draughty old ruin." The reply is that he has come to humble himself before the tombs of his ancestors in atonement for the lie he told the pirates—for he is not an orphan. Whereupon Frederic remarks that if the General has recently purchased the estate, those buried on it are not likely to be "his ancestors." The General answers that he does not know whose ancestors they are, but that he feels he is their descendant "by purchase." Frederic endeavors to console him, but is unsuccessful. The General learns that Frederic will lead an expedition against the pirates at eleven o'clock that night. He inquires if Frederic's followers, the policemen, have arrived, and the latter replies that they have and only await his orders. So the General expresses the desire to give them his blessing. The police enter, but they show great reluctance to leave, in "When the Foeman Bares His Steel."

Mabel tears herself from Frederic and departs, followed by her sisters, who try to console her. The General follows the police. Frederic remains alone and sits musing on his fate until interrupted by the appearance of the Pirate King and Ruth at a window. Instead of shooting him they explain that he is still bound to them, because having been born on February 29, he

407

has only served five, and not twenty-one years of his contract—counting only birthdays, of course. This situation seems to amuse all three to an extraordinary degree. Frederic exclaims that, on that basis, he must go with them, for "at any cost, I will do my duty." Then he is suddenly reminded that as a member of the pirate band, he must now divulge the truth about General Stanley, and he tells the Pirate King that the General only used the "orphan" story as a ruse to save himself and his daughters. "General Stanley is no orphan," he says. "More than that, he never was one!" Now the Pirate King assures them that his vengeance on General Stanley will be swift and sure. He and his pirates will attack the General's castle that very night. Frederic tries to dissuade him, but in vain. Ruth and the Pirate King depart, and Mabel enters, finding Frederic alone. He is determined to rejoin the pirates, and despite her pleading in the song "Ah, Leave Me Not to Pine," says farewell after promising to return for her in 1940, if he lives. Mabel, left alone, decides to be as dutiful as her lover and she addresses the sergeant of police, telling him how Frederic, who was to have led the police against the pirates, has once more joined his old associates. She says that she loves him all the more for his heroic sacrifice to duty. But, he has made himself her foe, so she will do *her* duty, and regard him in that light. She bids the police do theirs and departs. The policemen do not understand the situation. But their "course is clear." They must capture the pirates. The sergeant, joined by his men, bemoans their task of depriving erring fellow creatures of liberty, in the very amusing "A Policeman's Lot Is Not a Happy One."

The pirates are heard approaching, singing gaily "With Catlike Tread," and the police conceal themselves. Frederic sees a light inside and warns them that the General is coming. The General shows up in his dressing gown, for he "thought he heard a noise." Mabel and all the General's daughters enter, now, curious to know why he is up so late. The pirates and police struggle, the former winning. The General is promised swift death for his "orphan" lie, but the prostrate police ask the pirates to yield, "in Queen Victoria's name." They yield, and it is disclosed that the pirates themselves are not orphans but noblemen gone wrong. Everyone forgives everyone else, and the ex-pirates win the girls, after all.

THE RCA-VICTOR RECORDS
(Sung in English)

Complete Recording: *D'Oyly Carte Company; Dr. Malcolm Sargent, Cond.; under the personal direction of Rupert D'Oyly Carte. (The cast includes: Nellie Briercliffe, Nellie Walker, Dorothy Gill, Elsie Griffin, George Baker, Peter Dawson, Stuart Robertson, Derek Oldham, Leo Sheffield.)*

DC-6 (12916-12926), 11-12"
C-6 (9607-9617)

Gems: *Victor Light Opera Company, with Orch.*

36144, 12"
(In Album C-23)

408

Vandamm

ACT I—CATFISH ROW

Porgy and Bess

OPERA IN three acts. Music by George Gershwin. Text by Du Bose Heyward and Ira Gershwin, adapted from the play *Porgy* by Du Bose and Dorothy Heyward. Produced with an all-Negro singing cast, including Anne Brown, Ruby Elzy, Georgette Harvey, Todd Duncan, John W. Bubbles, Edward Matthews, and others, under the auspices of the Theatre Guild. First performance, Boston, September 30, 1935. First New York performance, Alvin Theater, October 10, 1935. With minor revisions and virtually the same cast the opera was revived by Cheryl Crawford, Majestic Theater, New York, January, 1942, after a two-week tryout at a summer theater in Maplewood, New Jersey, September, 1941. Alexander Smallens conducted all above performances, as well as the remainder of the engagements in both productions.

Porgy and Bess established overnight the standing of George Gershwin as a pioneer toward a new type of American opera. The sensationally successful play, *Porgy*, smelled of the soil and glowed with the rich primitive colors of American life. One of the most amazing things about George Gershwin's thoroughly amazing score is the fidelity with which it reflects and expresses and intensifies the dramatic elements of Du Bose and Dorothy Heyward's play. What is even more important is the fact that Gershwin wrote a work which not only marked a tremendous stride in his own development, but brought opera definitely and thoroughly down to earth.

The score of *Porgy and Bess* is filled with singable melodies, which appeal so strongly to the "man in the street" that he has no trouble humming them to himself. One of the vital qualities of any artistic work is that of universality, and this quality, frequently lacking in contemporary art, is present to an astonishing degree in Gershwin's music. For

409

Porgy and Bess

once the highbrow, the middle, and low come together in agreement upon music, and we have in *Porgy* a musical drama that gives every indication of being the first valid American folk opera.

The sensation of its first presentation, with lyrics by Du Bose Heyward and Ira Gershwin, sets by Serge Soudeikine, direction by Rouben Mamoulian, and with the distinguished conductor, Alexander Smallens, will not be soon forgotten.

CHARACTERS

PORGY	*Baritone*	CLARA	*Soprano*
BESS	*Soprano*	SPORTIN' LIFE	*Tenor*
CROWN	*Bass*	SERENA	*Soprano*
ROBBINS	*Baritone*		

NATIVES, HUCKSTERS, POLICEMEN, A CORONER, A DETECTIVE, AN UNDERTAKER,
BYSTANDERS, ETC.

The action takes place in and near Charleston, South Carolina

ACT I

SCENE: *Catfish Row.* The scene is laid in Catfish Row, a section of Charleston, South Carolina, formerly occupied by the aristocracy but now a Negro tenement. As the curtain rises, an evening in this little backwater of Negro life is revealed. There is impromptu dancing, and a mother sings a lullaby to her baby, the tuneful "Summertime," while among the men a red-hot game of dice is going on. Among the crap players are Robbins and Crown, a stevedore who is the great lover of the community. Crown quarrels with Robbins and attacks the latter, killing him in the subsequent fight. Crown escapes. Sportin' Life, the neighborhood high-liver, lover, and dope peddler, attempts to induce Bess, Crown's girl, to go to New York with him, but she refuses and, parted from Crown after his flight, seeks sanctuary in Porgy's room. Sportin' Life puts his philosophy of life in a devil-may-care song entitled "A Woman Is a Sometime Thing."

ACT II

SCENE 1: *Catfish Row in the Morning.* Fishermen are working about at odd jobs, and Porgy, a cripple who gets about in a goat-cart, is contented with his life with Bess, and sings a song of his complacence entitled "I Got Plenty o' Nuttin' " as well as a rousing duet with Bess in which they express their mutual love, "Bess, You Is My Woman Now." A buzzard flies over the court, and the bird of ill omen fills all the Negroes with premonitions of evil, which they express in the "Buzzard Song."

SCENE 2: *Kittiwah Island.* The scene changes to that of the Lodge picnic held on Kittiwah Island. One of the most entertaining features of the picnic is the singing and dancing of Sportin' Life, who testifies to his skepticism about spiritual things in the highly amusing song called "It Ain't Necessarily So." Unknown to anyone, Crown, who has fled after murdering Robbins, is in

410

Vandamm

ACT I—TODD DUNCAN AS PORGY

hiding on the island, and at an opportune moment appears, catching Bess alone and persuading her to stay with him there in his unsuspected retreat. A few days later she returns to Porgy's room, emotionally upset and delirious. She recovers, confesses that she has promised to join Crown when he comes out of hiding, but finally agrees that she loves only Porgy.

A bell sounds, giving warning of a hurricane. All the women are terrified, for their men are out fishing and in great danger. Clara particularly is thinking of her husband, who is far out at sea, and suddenly is convinced that he is in imminent danger. No one but Crown has the courage to go to his rescue, and Porgy and Bess sit together, certain that even so mighty a man as Crown could not survive the storm on the island. They are to be free of him at last. At this moment the door bursts open, and Crown enters. He ridicules Porgy for being half a man and rushes out to the rescue.

ACT III

SCENE: *Catfish Row at Night.* From Porgy's room Bess sings a "Lullaby." It is learned from Sportin' Life that Crown is still alive. Presently he appears on the scene and makes his way to Porgy's room. Porgy observes him as he is about to enter and, leaning out of his window, stabs him to death. The police cannot find out anything about the murder, but suspect Porgy and demand his presence at the inquest to identify the body. Porgy refuses to look at his victim and is dragged off to jail, and Bess sings the doleful "My Man's Gone Now." In confusion and distress, she is approached by Sportin' Life, who offers her dope and tries to persuade her to run away with him. He is at first unsuccessful, but leaves a package of dope on the step to tempt her. When he has departed she takes the package and carries it into her room. A week later, Porgy returns from jail in high spirits, bringing presents for all his friends. Presently he calls for Bess and she doesn't answer. He pleads for information as to her whereabouts and finally learns that, seduced by Sportin' Life, she has left for New York. Porgy asks how far it is to New York, and when he is told that it is a thousand miles away, he calls for his goat and cart and starts out undaunted on the road to find Bess.

THE RCA-VICTOR RECORDS
(Sung in English)

TODD DUNCAN AS PORGY

HIGHLIGHTS (Lullaby—Summertime and the Livin' Is Easy; My Man's Gone Now; Scene—Summertime and Crap Game; A Woman Is a Sometime Thing; I Got Plenty o' Nuttin'; Bess, You Is My Woman Now; Buzzard Song; It Ain't Necessarily So; Where Is My Bess?)
Lawrence Tibbett, Baritone; Helen Jepson, Soprano; Chorus and Orchestra; Alexander Smallens, Cond. (This recording was supervised by Gershwin.)
C-25 (11878-11881), 4-12″

GEMS: *Victor Salon Group; Jane Froman, Soprano; Felix Knight, Tenor; Nathaniel Shilkret, Cond.* 12334, 12″
(In Album C-29)

A SYMPHONIC PICTURE, FOR ORCHESTRA (Arr. Robert Russell Bennett)
Indianapolis Symphony Orchestra, Fabien Sevitsky, Conductor
DM-999 (11-8792-11-8794), 3-12″
M-999 (11-8789-11-8791)

SELECTIONS (Summertime; I Got Plenty o' Nuttin'; Bess, You Is My Woman Now; It Ain't Necessarily So)
Charlie Spivak and His Orchestra
SP-6 (20-1652-20-1653), 2-10″

SELECTIONS: *Raymond Paige and His Orchestra* 36379, 12″
(In Album G-28)

IT AIN'T NECESSARILY SO
A WOMAN IS A SOMETIME THING: *Paul Robeson, Bass, with Orch.* 26358, 10″

LULLABY
IT TAKES A LONG PULL TO GET THERE: *Paul Robeson, Bass, with Orch.*
26359, 10″

WHERE'S MY BESS?: *James Melton, Tenor; David Saperton, Bert Shefter, Duo Pianists* 11-9224, 12″

I GOT PLENTY O' NUTTIN': *Lawrence Tibbett, Baritone, with Orch.* 11-8860
(In Album M-1015)

Vandamm

ACT I—CRAP GAME

THE ROGUES DESERT IGOR'S ARMY

Prince Igor

OPERA IN a prologue and four acts. Music by Alexander Borodin. Libretto by the composer and Vladimir Stassov, based on *The Epic of the Army of Igor*, an old Russian chronicle. First produced at the Imperial Opera House, St. Petersburg, November 4, 1890. First performance in the United States, December 30, 1915, at the Metropolitan Opera House, New York City. Unfinished at the time of the composer's death, the opera was completed by Rimsky-Korsakov and Glazunov. Borodin had not written out the Overture, but Glazunov, who had often heard him play it on the piano, wrote the composition from memory and orchestrated it.

The popular theory that a musician, and, above all, a composer, is necessarily unsuited for practical affairs finds convincing rebuttal in the life and work of Borodin, for this man was one of the great scientific figures of his generation. Two of his chemical treatises have even become standard: *Researches upon the Fluoride of Benzol*, and *The Solidification of Aldehydes*. Moreover, Borodin was a professor of medicine and an early advocate of the emancipation of women. Equally fond of science and music, he chose the former for his career, remaining only a music lover until the age of twenty-eight, when he met Balakirev and began to devote all of his spare time to music. In that famous circle of "The Five"—Balakirev, Cui, Mussorgsky, Borodin, and Rimsky-Korsakov—Borodin was certainly one of the most richly endowed in musical originality. Because of his many professional commitments, Borodin left few compositions—among them, two symphonies, two string quartets, a number of songs and piano pieces, and his opera *Prince Igor*. All of these works, however, reveal remarkable rhythmic energy and melodic beauty. Though by no means a dramatic story, *Prince Igor* furnished Borodin splendid opportunities for effective treatment—the contrast of Russian and Oriental music, scenes of comedy, tragedy, and love, and the fiery dances of the Polovtsi. Unlike Mussorgsky, he was not highly skilled in dramatic utterance. Thus, the opera is written largely in a lyrical style, after the manner established by Glinka in *Russlan and Ludmilla*.

414

CHARACTERS

PRINCE IGOR	*Baritone*	KONTCHAKOVNA, *his daughter*	*Contralto*
JAROSLAVNA, *his wife*	*Soprano*	NURSE	*Soprano*
VLADIMIR, *their son*	*Tenor*	EROCHKA, *a warrior*	*Tenor*
PRINCE GALITSKY, *Igor's brother-in-law*	*Bass*	SKULA, *a warrior*	*Bass*
		OVLOUR	*Tenor*
KHAN KONTCHAK	*Bass*		

COURTIERS, PEASANTS, SOLDIERS, CITIZENS, TARTARS, POLOVTSIAN MAIDENS AND WARRIORS

The action takes place in medieval and semilegendary Russia

The Overture is permeated with Borodin's characteristic energy. After an impressive introduction, an allegro movement enters, impetuous with the vigor of a Russian folk dance. A phrase of the music associated with the Oriental Polovtsi is next heard briefly, followed by the beautiful, lyrical theme of Igor's aria, "No Sleep, No Rest," heard later in the second act. These themes are developed and repeated in spirited fashion, and the Overture ends in a jubilant mood.

PROLOGUE

SCENE: *The Market Place of Poutivle.* Prince Igor is about to start out on a campaign against the Khan of the Polovtsi. The people give him a rousing farewell. Suddenly an eclipse of the sun occurs. Frightened by the ill omen of this unnatural darkness, the people, joined by Igor's wife, the Princess Jaroslavna, beg him to postpone his departure. Undaunted, Igor entrusts the affairs of government to his brother-in-law, Prince Galitsky, and departs, accompanied by his son Vladimir. Two rogues, Skula and Erochka, reluctant to share the hardships of war, desert Igor's army and plan to take more agreeable service with Prince Galitsky.

ACT I

SCENE 1: *The Courtyard of Prince Galitsky's House.* There is feasting and carousing at Galitsky's. The Prince himself sings a wild, reckless song, expressive of his resolve to avoid a dull, dreary life. If he were governor he would give all a merry time, he boasts, for state and power are useless if they do not bring revelry. A group of young girls enter, bewailing the abduction of one of their friends. Their pleas for her return are so coldly mocked by the Prince, who boasts of being himself the abductor, that they leave, greatly frightened. Galitsky's followers, aroused by the prospect of adventure, shout that they will set him up as ruler in place of Igor.

SCENE 2: *A Room in the Palace of Prince Igor.* The Princess Jaroslavna is brooding over the absence of her husband and praying for news of his safety. She sings of her loneliness and hope in an intensely expressive aria—"Arioso of Jaroslavna." Her thoughts are interrupted by the entry of the group of frightened maidens, who appeal to her for protection from Galitsky. The Prince himself enters and bids them begone. They flee in terror. Jaroslavna upbraids her brother for his shameless conduct. When he taunts her for being cold and censorious, she reminds him that Igor's authority is legally invested in her. She commands him to release the abducted maiden and orders him from her sight. Scarcely has he left when the boyars enter, bringing word that Igor has met with defeat and is held captive with his son. The enemy is now approaching the city. Their loyalty aroused by this news of disaster, the boyars swear to defend their Princess and the city with their lives.

ACT II

SCENE: *The Camp of the Polovtsi.* Prisoner in the camp of the enemy, Prince Vladimir has fallen in love with Kontchakovna, the daughter of the Polovtsian chief. He now comes to serenade her. He tells her that Igor disapproves of their attachment, although her father favors it. Their meeting is cut short by the entrance of Igor, who begins soliloquizing on his unhappy condition. As his thoughts turn to his wife, he sings the beautiful melody first heard during the Overture, avowing: "My thoughts fly to you, oh, beloved; you alone will weep over my hapless fate!" Yet when Ovlour, a captive who is acting as guard, offers him a horse as a means of escape, Igor refuses, for he does not believe flight a fair way of treating his captor.

A moment later the chief of the Polovtsi, Khan Kontchak, approaches and greets Igor in the vigorous aria, "How Goes It, Prince?," in the course of which he asks why he appears so sad. When Igor pointedly refers to his loss of freedom, the Khan reproachfully reminds him he is his guest, not his prisoner, and even offers him one of his harem beauties. At length, the generous Khan promises Igor his freedom if he will agree never to fight the Polovtsi again. This Igor refuses to do, saying that if he were free he would bring a larger army and subdue them—frankness that the Khan admires. At his command, the Polovtsi slaves now enter and begin to sing and dance for Igor's entertainment. At first slow and languorous, their dance gradually develops to a climax of the most turbulent excitement. In rhythmic zest, rich melody, and exotic color, few concert numbers rival these dances in popularity.

ACT III

SCENE: *Another Part of the Camp of the Polovtsi.* The Polovtsian soldiers return, laden with spoils from their attack on Poutivle. Watching them, Igor is filled with pity for the misfortunes of his wife and people and now consents to flee. To aid him, Ovlour plies the soldiers with great quantities of wine as they divide their spoils. After a drunken orgy, the entire camp falls asleep. The chief's daughter has discovered the plot and comes to beg Vladimir not to leave. Her passionate entreaties so stir him that he is on the point of yielding when his father again arouses the sense of duty in him. However, when Igor gives the signal for the escape, Kontchakovna sounds an alarm and clings desperately to her lover until it is too late for him to flee. The Polovtsian soldiers rush in and are on the point of killing Vladimir for enabling his father to escape, when the chief enters. Sternly he forbids them to follow Igor or to slay Vladimir. He cannot help but admire Igor's bold dash for freedom, and, as he philosophically remarks, they may chain the young man to them by giving him a mate. This decision is, of course, most agreeable to both Vladimir and Kontchakovna.

ACT IV

SCENE: *Terrace of a Palace.* Jaroslavna stands on the terrace of her ruined palace, gazing over the once fertile plains, now barren from the ravaging of the hostile army. Her sorrow quickly gives way to joy at the unexpected arrival of her husband. As the reunited couple enter the great church of the kremlin at Poutivle, the merry rogues, Skula and Erochka, quickly switch their allegiance from Galitsky back to Igor and hurriedly set the town bell ringing to summon the people. Their villainy is forgotten in the great rejoicing that greets the rightful and justly beloved Prince.

THE RCA-VICTOR RECORDS
(Sung in Russian)

OVERTURE: *Sir Thomas Beecham, Bart., and the London Philharmonic Orchestra*   11-9666 & 11-9667, 2-12" (In Album M-1141)

General Platoff Don Cossack Chorus; Nicholas Kostrukoff, Dir. (Solo: Slepoushkin, Bass-Baritone)   11-9118, 12"

ACT I

PRINCE GALITSKY'S AIR—I HATE A DREARY LIFE: *Alexander Kipnis, Bass, with Orch.*   11-9285, 12" (In Album M-1073)

Feodor Chaliapin, Bass, with Orch.   1237, 10"

ACT II

HOW GOES IT, PRINCE?: *Feodor Chaliapin, Bass, with Orch.*   6867, 12"

POLOVTSIAN DANCES (Concert Version): *Leopold Stokowski and the Philadelphia Orchestra*   DM-499 (18444 & 18445), 2-12"   M-499 (15169 & 15170)

Princess Ida

(OR, CASTLE ADAMANT)

COMIC OPERA IN three acts. Music by Sir Arthur Sullivan. Libretto by W. S. Gilbert. First performance, Savoy Theater, London, January 5, 1884.

When late in 1883 a libretto for another collaboration with Sullivan was required of Gilbert, he made several suggestions, which were rejected by either Carte or Sullivan or both, and presently, reaching into an apparently bottomless reservoir of things he had dashed off or written seriously during the years, produced the blank-verse parody of Tennyson's *The Princess*. Not much work was necessary on this, excepting the converting of several speeches into song poems. And almost immediately Sullivan received the libretto of *Princess Ida*, which he set to music.

The score of *Princess Ida* is no less typical of Sullivan's gifts than any of the other operettas, yet Gilbert's libretto is not representative of his best, although the texts for the songs show the same excellent workmanship. Nevertheless, *Princess Ida* had its great success, being given at the Savoy for 246 nights running.

CHARACTERS

KING HILDEBRAND	Baritone
HILARION, *his son*	Tenor
CYRIL } *Hilarion's friends*	Tenor
FLORIAN }	Baritone
KING GAMA	Baritone
ARAC }	
GURON } *his sons*	Bass-Baritones
SCYNTHIUS }	
PRINCESS IDA, *Gama's daughter*	Soprano
LADY BLANCHE, *Professor of Abstract Science*	Contralto
LADY PSYCHE, *Professor of Humanities*	Soprano
MELISSA, *Lady Blanche's daughter*	Soprano
SACHARISSA }	
CHLOE } *girl graduates*	
ADA }	Sopranos, Altos

CHORUS OF SOLDIERS, COURTIERS, "GIRL GRADUATES," "DAUGHTERS OF THE PLOUGH," ETC.

De Bellis

MARTYN GREEN AS KING GAMA

ACT I

SCENE: *Pavilion in King Hildebrand's Palace.* There is an air of expectancy at King Hildebrand's Palace, for it is the day on which Princess Ida, the daughter of King Gama, should appear to meet Prince Hilarion, to whom she was betrothed twenty years before, when she was one and he only two years old. Soldiers and courtiers are discovered scanning the landscape, and debating whether or not the Princess will come.

King Hildebrand appears, and asks if Gama has yet been sighted, adding that if he does not come before sunset, bringing the Princess with him, "there's war between King Gama and ourselves." He hates the coming interview with Gama, who is twisted in body and warped in mind.

Gama is seen in the distance without the Princess. Hildebrand, puzzled, bids the best and the worst to be brought; the richest robes, the coarsest prison dress, for, as Gama brings the Princess or brings her not, so shall he have "much more than everything, much less than nothing."

Hilarion enters and sings in anticipation of his meeting with Ida. He is, however, uneasy because he has heard that she has forsworn the world, and, with a band of women, shut herself up within a lonely country house, there to study the deepest philosophies. His father vainly tells him that a reasonable man would be reconciled to the loss of such a wife.

The sons of King Gama approach and, having entered, sing of their valor. Gama introduces himself in a song, "If You Give Me Your Attention," that reveals his spiteful nature. After an exchange of anything but compliments, Gama informs Hildebrand that he has not brought the Princess, who refuses to leave her "University," having renounced mankind.

Gama tells the young men that, if they "humbly beg and humbly sue, most politely," the Princess might deign to look upon them. But Hildebrand retorts that, while they will make the attempt, Gama shall remain as hostage, and "should Hilarion disappear, we will hang you, never fear, 'most politely.'" Yet, Hilarion and his friends determine to try their fortune, Gama and his three sons being kept as hostages against their safe return.

ACT II

SCENE: *Gardens of Castle Adamant.* At Princess Ida's country home, the graduates of the Women's University are discovered seated at the feet of Lady Psyche, the Professor of Humanities. Their song is interrupted by the entry of Lady Blanche (Professor of Abstract Science), who proceeds to read the "list of punishments," after which Princess Ida approaches. She is welcomed as "Mighty maiden with a mission" and delivers her inaugural address, which takes the form of a tirade against Man, following which the curriculum for the day is reviewed. Lady Blanche is to lecture on Abstract Philosophy under three heads, "The Is, the Might Be, and the Must."

The Princess and the maidens pass on, leaving Lady Blanche to reflection and soliloquy. She goes off, and Hilarion and his two friends are seen climbing the wall. Having successfully negotiated the broken bottles adorning the top, they are highly diverted at having reached the jealously guarded precincts without detection. They find some academic robes left by the maidens, and these make such an effective disguise that they decide, on seeing the Princess approaching, to pose as three well-born maidens who wish to join the University. She questions them, and they manage to steer sufficiently clear of pitfalls to satisfy her as to their suitability. Together they lament the hollow pleasures of the world, and the Princess leaves them to meditate on the extraordinary fix into which they have been landed. Amid much merriment they decide to see the thing through, but their mirth is checked by the entrance of Lady Psyche, who is Florian's sister. There is only one way out and that is to let her into the secret.

This they do, and she informs them that the penalty, if they are discovered, is death. She is, nevertheless, very pleased to see them and tells them more about the objects of the University. She points her argument with the story of "The Ape and the Lady."

Meanwhile, Melissa, another of the girl graduates, enters unobserved and overhears them. She is, however, so fascinated on beholding a man for the first time that she readily agrees to keep the secret. A closer inspection begins to shake the girls' faith in the principles enunciated by Ida and, in the quintet that follows, the change of view is very pronounced. Melissa is left alone, and is presently joined by Lady Blanche, her mother, who has been attracted by the singing. She remarks how odd it is that of the three new "girls" two should be tenors, and one a baritone. Her suspicions are confirmed when she picks up the reticule dropped by one of them and finds that it contains not only scissors and needles, but . . . cigars! Melissa pleads with Lady Blanche, and reminds her that if she furthers Hilarion's scheme, Ida will marry him, and leave Blanche to "rule the roost."

When Lady Blanche has gone, Melissa sees Florian and urges him to fly. He is about to do so, taking her with him, when the luncheon bell is heard, and the Princess with Hilarion, Cyril, the staff and students appear; also "daughters of the plough," bearing luncheon. Having heard that the three new students know the court of King Hildebrand, the Princess, although affecting indifference, makes sly inquiries as to his son, Hilarion. The disguised youth answers cleverly, but unfortunately Cyril is taking too much wine and, after various rather dangerous interruptions, bursts into the "Kissing Song." It is at once discovered that they are men. The Princess, in panic, runs toward the rustic bridge that crosses the stream flowing through the grounds. Hilarion follows, endeavoring to explain; the Princess misses her footing and falls into the water. Hilarion springs in after her and brings her safely to shore, amid the plaudits of the assembled company. Ida, however, is furious at the trick which has been played and orders the arrest of the three young men, which command is carried out by the "daughters of the plough." Hilarion is bound, and the three are marched off.

At this moment Melissa rushes in and tells the Princess that an armed band is without the castle walls, demanding admittance in the name of King Hildebrand. As she speaks, the gate is battered down, and soldiers rush in; with them are the three sons of King Gama in chains. Hildebrand follows and tells the Princess that he has come to claim fulfillment of the vow which was made when she was a child, and that if she refuses, he will raze her castle to the ground. To the King's threat the three brothers, Arac, Guron, and Scynthius, add their entreaties, for Hildebrand has promised them that if he fails in his quest they will most certainly be hanged. He gives Ida twenty-four hours for her answer. The act closes with the Princess hurling defiance at the invader.

ACT III

SCENE: *The Outer Walls and Courtyard of Castle Adamant.* The Princess has decided to fight, and Melissa, Sacharissa, and the ladies are assembled, armed with battle-axes. The Princess enters, attended by Blanche and Psyche, and issues her instructions. Unfortunately, her theories break down in practice, and not one of the ladies is willing to perform the duties allotted to her. The fusiliers have not brought their rifles because they "might go off"; the band do not feel well and are therefore not present. Chloe and all the ladies enter and announce the approach of Ida's father, King Gama, and her brothers. Gama explains that Hildebrand is loath to war with women, and he has therefore sent the Princess' brothers to fight for her against Hilarion and his two friends. Gama tells Ida his punishment and the tortures he has endured, which consisted of having "nothing whatever to grumble at"; to his warped nature this being the worst that could be conceived. Ida is so moved by the tale of woe that she agrees to the contest's taking place. Disillusioned, she sings of the failure of her ambitions. The gates are opened, and soldiers with the three sons of Gama enter.

Hilarion, Florian, and Cyril are led in by the "daughters of the plough." They are still bound and wear their academic robes. Gama finds food for his mordant wit in their appearance, and goads them on for the fight. The fight takes place, Hilarion and his friends being victorious. The Princess begs them to stay their hands. She asks Lady Blanche if she can with dignity resign her post, in which case will she (Lady Blanche) take her place? This, of course, is just what Lady Blanche wants, and she takes the opportunity to indulge in a little abstract philosophy. So the Princess yields to Hilarion, Lady Psyche to Cyril, and Melissa to Florian. Lady Blanche is left to be the principal of the "University" and the opera ends in general joy.

THE RCA-VICTOR RECORDS

(Sung in English)

COMPLETE RECORDING: *D'Oyly Carte Company, Dr. Malcolm Sargent, Cond.; under the personal direction of Rupert D'Oyly Carte. (The cast includes: Muriel Dickson, Dorothy Gill, Alice Moxon, Nellie Briercliffe, Derek* *Oldham, Henry Lytton, George Baker, Stuart Robertson, Richard Watson, Darrell Fancourt, Edward Holland, Charles Goulding.)*

DC-20 (13304-13313), 10-12"
C-20 (11596-11605)

Le Prophète
(THE PROPHET)

OPERA IN five acts. Music by Giacomo Meyerbeer. Libretto by Scribe. First produced at the Paris Opéra, April 16, 1849. First performance in America in New Orleans on April 2, 1850. First performance at the Metropolitan, December 17, 1884; twice brilliantly revived—in 1918, with Enrico Caruso and Margarete Matzenauer, and in 1927, with Giovanni Martinelli and Mme. Matzenauer. The plot of Le Prophète is based on the uprising of the Anabaptists of the sixteenth century under the leadership of John of Leyden. In expressive power and adroit workmanship, Le Prophète is probably Meyerbeer's most artistic opera. The composer lavished great care upon the score and did not release it till he was satisfied with every measure. Contraltos have been especially grateful to Meyerbeer for providing them, in Fidès, with a role of vast opportunity for vocal and expressive display. Fidès' moving outburst, "Ah, mon fils!," rightly ranks among the finest arias of all time. As for the famous "Coronation March," it is still considered one of the great processional marches and is frequently used as such in Europe and America.

CHARACTERS

JOHN OF LEYDEN, The Prophet, chosen leader of the Anabaptists — Tenor

BERTHA, his fiancée — Soprano

FIDÈS, mother of John of Leyden — Mezzo-soprano

COUNT OBERTHAL, ruler of the domain about Dordrecht — Baritone

ZACHARIAS — Bass
JONAS — Tenor
MATHISEN — Bass

three Anabaptist preachers

ACT IV, SCENE 2—JOHN DENYING HIS MOTHER

NOBLES, CITIZENS, PEASANTS, SOLDIERS, PRISONERS

The action takes place in Holland and Germany at the time of the Anabaptist uprising in 1534

ACT I

SCENE: *A Suburb of Dordrecht.* Bertha, a subject of the domain of Count Oberthal, is betrothed to an innkeeper at Leyden named John. As she is required by law to have the Count's permission to marry, she has come with John's mother, Fidès, to request it. At the same time three somber Anabaptists arrive to exhort the people to revolt against the tyranny to which they are subjected. But the agitation they arouse ends with the appearance of the Count, who recognizes in one of the Anabaptists a former servant he had discharged for dishonesty. When Bertha makes her plea, the Count is so captivated by her beauty that, desiring her for himself, he orders the girl and John's mother cast into the dungeon of his castle.

ACT II

SCENE: *The Inn of Fidès in the Suburbs of Leyden.* Driven from the castle, the three Anabaptists enter the inn of Fidès. There, they see John and are at once struck with his resemblance to the portrait of King David in the Cathedral of Münster. Convinced that he would pass with the crowd for a reincarnation of the King, they urge John to become the leader of their movement. In reply he relates how in a dream he found himself being venerated by a vast throng of people in an immense cathedral. The Anabaptists seize on this dream as an added argument, but John again refuses because of his approaching marriage to Bertha.

Scarcely have the Anabaptists departed when Bertha, having escaped from the dungeon, rushes in and tells John of the Count's scoundrelly deed. Before he has time to conceal her, the Count enters with his soldiers, bringing Fidès as a prisoner. The Count swears that John's mother will be slain if he refuses to give Bertha up. John hesitates, but in the struggle loyalty to his mother ultimately prevails and he surrenders his betrothed. The released Fidès sings her gratitude in an aria of deep pathos, *"Ah, mon fils!"* ("Ah! my son")—a song in which the mother's proud exultation in the devotion of her son is sublimely expressed.

The Anabaptists now find it easy to persuade John to join them, for he has vowed to wreak vengeance on the Count. However, to assure the success of their plans, everyone, even his mother, must be made to believe that John is dead. Accordingly, some of John's clothes are stained with blood and left behind. Then, taking a solemn oath of secrecy, the conspirators depart.

ACT III

SCENE: *The Camp of the Anabaptists.* Easily persuaded that John is indeed the Prophet, the people have followed his leadership and risen against their oppressors. They now are encamped before the walls of Münster, where provisions are brought them by skaters. The Count is captured and reveals to John that Bertha has escaped and is now in Münster. The three Anabaptist leaders would put the Count to death at once, but John orders him spared—Bertha shall be his judge. Angered by John's assuming so much authority, the leaders now organize an attack of their own on Münster and meet with defeat. The disgruntled soldiers, threatening mutiny, are ready to murder John. But the bogus prophet succeeds in rallying the crowd to his support. By the force of his personality and the conviction of divine inspiration, he finally leads them to victory.

ACT IV

SCENE 1: *A Public Square in Münster.* Reduced to poverty, Fidès has come to Münster to beg. Meeting Bertha, she reveals to her that John is dead. Ignorant of the true state of affairs, Bertha assumes that John's death was caused by the insurgent Prophet, and on him she now swears vengeance.

SCENE 2: *The Münster Cathedral.* About to be crowned King, John is led to the ceremony in a procession of great pomp and brilliance into the church. As the procession advances, we hear the stirring strains of Meyerbeer's celebrated march. Fidès suddenly appears from behind a pillar and in a transport of joy greets the Prophet as her son. But John is forced to deny his mother, for to do otherwise would be to repudiate the divine origin ascribed to him as Prophet. However, to save her from execution, he pronounces Fidès insane and commands her to kneel before him. Then, standing over her with hands upraised, he bids the soldiers draw their swords and run them through his breast if this beggar woman should again affirm that she is the Prophet's mother. As the swords are ready to pierce John, the terrified mother cries out that he is not her son: she was deceived by her eyes made dim with age. Believing her cured of her mad obsession, all exclaim, "A miracle!" The Prophet has thus strengthened his power by this perilous meeting.

ACT V

SCENE 1: *A Crypt of the Palace.* At John's secret command, soldiers conduct Fidès to the dungeon of the palace. As they leave her there in the darkness, she exclaims, "O priests of Baal, where have ye led me?" (*"O prêtres de Baal"*), beginning a grand *scena* of the most elaborate Meyerbeerian proportions, well known as a concert aria under the title of "Prison Scene." Stricken with grief and shame by her son's denial of her, she cries out to heaven to strike him with its lightning; then suddenly relenting, prays that it have mercy on him. In a momentary interruption, an officer enters to announce the arrival of the Prophet. Greatly agitated, Fidès continues her stirring aria in a sudden surge of hope that a miracle will bring her son back to his senses.

Yet when John runs to her and throws himself at her feet, begging forgiveness, she assumes a severe manner, renounces him, and orders him away. Desperately he pleads with his mother, and finally succeeds in persuading her that he has been driven to violence and fraud to avenge Bertha's wrongs. Fidès, softening, forgives him, but only on condition that he return to Leyden. Fully repentant now, he gives her his promise to do so.

Presently they are joined by Bertha, whose joy at meeting her lover is short-lived, for at that moment a captain comes to announce to John that he has been betrayed—the Emperor's forces are storming the castle gates. Hor-

White JOHN AND FIDÈS

rified by this sudden revelation that the loathed Prophet and John are the same person, Bertha plunges a dagger into her heart and dies cursing her lover.

SCENE 2: *The Great Hall of the Palace.* After the Emperor's troops, led by the Count, have forced an entrance into the castle, John secretly orders the gates closed. When the Count, the source of all John's misfortunes, comes to him, saying, "You are my prisoner," John answers, "Nay, you are all my captives." With all hope of salvation gone, John now executes a plan of terrible revenge. A fire has been set which causes a terrific explosion. A wall falls and flames leap out on every side. Amid this scene of flaming destruction a frantic woman with wildly disheveled hair runs to John. "Mother!" he cries in anguish. Forgiving him all his wrongdoing, Fidès has come to share his fate. Mother and son die together, crying defiantly together, "Welcome, sacred flame!"

THE RCA-VICTOR RECORDS

(Sung in French)

ACT II

AH! MON FILS! (Ah! My Son!): *Sigrid Onegin, Contralto, with Orch.* 6803, 12"

ACT IV

MARCHE DU COURONNEMENT *(Marche du sacre)* (Coronation March): *Boston "Pops" Orchestra, Arthur Fiedler, Cond.* 10-1091, 10" (In Album M-968)

New York Philharmonic-Symphony Orchestra, Willem Mengelberg, Cond. 7104, 10"

ACT V

SCÈNE DE LA PRISON—O PRÊTRES DE BAAL (Prison Scene—O Priests of Baal): *Sigrid Onegin, Contralto, with Orch.* 7146, 12"

L·17 - 1963 - Wonderful - !!!
Palm Springs - Mar.·85

ACT IV—THE QUARTET

Rigoletto

OPERA IN four (originally three) acts. Music by Giuseppe Verdi. Libretto by Francesco Maria Piave, founded on Victor Hugo's play, *Le Roi s'amuse*. Produced, Teatro la Fenice, Venice, March 11, 1851; first performance in the United States, Academy of Music, New York, February 19, 1855. In present-day performances the two scenes of what is Act I in the original score are usually presented as separate "acts," thus making of *Rigoletto* a four-act opera.

Greatly desiring a new libretto for La Fenice, Verdi requested Piave to adapt Victor Hugo's play *Le Roi s'amuse* (*The King Amuses Himself*), which, in spite of its dubious morals, was recognized by the composer as possessing operatic possibilities. A libretto was soon written, the suggestive title being changed to *La Maledizione* (*The Curse*). A new work was desperately needed by the management of La Fenice, and dismay followed the flat refusal of the police to grant permission for the performance of a work in which a king was shown at such a disadvantage. It will be remembered that Venice was then in Austrian hands, and but a short time previously, 1848–49, there had been an Italian insurrection. At first, Verdi refused to consider any other plan, and the management was in despair. Help arrived from an unexpected quarter, for the Austrian police chief, Martello, was an ardent musical and dramatic enthusiast, and a great admirer of Verdi. He perceived that by substituting the Duke of Mantua for Francis I, and by changing the title to *Rigoletto*, the work could be presented without any material changes in the original dramatic situations. Verdi accepted this proposal. He went to Buseto, near his birthplace, and came back within six weeks with the completed musical score. The new work was a brilliant success, thus rescuing the management of the theater.

A remarkable feat of rapid composition, being written in less than forty days, *Rigoletto* still holds a firm place in the repertoire of all opera houses after three quarters of a century. Not without reason has it held this popularity, for Victor Hugo's drama, even with Piave's numerous alterations, makes a most effective opera libretto. Moreover, it supplies three characters of interest: the hunchback, Rigoletto, a vital centralizing dramatic figure who appeals to audiences and singers alike; the Duke, a brilliant tenor role and a debonair and cynical characterization; Gilda, the heroine, beloved by all coloratura sopranos. These characters have, indeed, been favorites with many of the greatest singers: Patti sang in the opera for the first time at New Orleans, February 6, 1861; Caruso made his North American debut singing the role of the Duke at the Metropolitan Opera House, New York, November 23, 1903; Ruffo first appeared in the United States as Rigoletto, November 4, 1912, at Hammerstein's Metropolitan Opera House, Philadelphia; and on November 18, 1916, occurred the triumphal first North American appearance of Galli-Curci when she sang the role of Gilda with the Chicago Opera Company. Musically, *Rigoletto* ranks with *Il Trovatore* and *La Traviata* as representing a second and higher stage in the composer's development. These compositions possess expressiveness of melody, variety of harmony, color and richness of orchestration, and subtleties in the drawing of character beyond his previous efforts.

CHARACTERS

RIGOLETTO, *a hunchback, jester to the Duke of Mantua*	*Baritone*	COUNT CEPRANO, *a courtier*	*Bass*
GILDA, *his daughter*	*Soprano*	COUNTESS CEPRANO, *his wife*	*Mezzo-soprano*
GIOVANNA, *her nurse*	*Mezzo-soprano*	MONTERONE, *a noble of the court*	*Bass*
DUKE OF MANTUA	*Tenor*	BORSA, *a courtier*	*Tenor*
SPARAFUCILE, *a hired assassin*	*Bass*	MARULLO, *a courtier*	*Baritone*
MADDALENA, *his sister*	*Mezzo-soprano*	CHORUS OF COURTIERS	

The action takes place at Mantua during the sixteenth century

ACT I

SCENE: *A Salon in the Ducal Palace.* After a short, ominous prelude the curtain rises and we behold a fete in progress at the Ducal Palace. Courtiers and ladies move gaily through the great ballroom. Through the large archway at the rear we can look into other luxurious apartments, all brilliantly lighted. Pages hurry to and fro. From an adjoining room come bursts of music and laughter. Amid all this bustle and gaiety and to a frivolous, lighthearted orchestral accompaniment the Duke enters with one of the courtiers, Borsa. He confides to him that he is pursuing an unknown beauty whom he has seen in church every Sunday during the past three months. He has followed her to her house in a remote part of the city, where, he has discovered, a mysterious man visits her every evening. At this moment a group of knights and ladies happen to pass by. "What beauties!" exclaims Borsa. "Ceprano's wife is the loveliest of all!" replies the Duke. His listener warns him that the Count might hear, but the Duke shrugs his shoulders indifferently and gives vent to his philosophy in the aria, *"Questa o quella"* (" 'Mid the fair throng"). The melody is smooth, it seems to float through the air, yet there is irony concealed beneath its gaiety.

The courtiers dance a minuet, accompanied by music, graceful and not inappropriately reminiscent of the minuet in *Don Giovanni*. The Duke dances with the Countess, closely watched, however, by Ceprano; the fervent manner in which he kisses her hand is not lost on the jealous husband, nor does it escape the court jester, the hunchback, Rigoletto. The Duke leads away the Countess, and Ceprano follows them, but not before the jester has launched a cutting taunt at the enraged Count.

Rigoletto forthwith saunters off, seeking other victims for his lord. As soon as he is out of sight he in turn becomes the object of similar jests. The gossip Marullo enters with the news that Rigoletto keeps a mistress and visits her every night. There are shouts of delight at the thought that the pander of the Duke's romances, Rigoletto himself, is now in love. The merriment is cut short by the re-entry of the Duke, followed by Rigoletto. The Duke is saying he would like to get rid of Count Ceprano so that he might have the beautiful Countess, and Rigoletto banteringly suggests that he run off with her. Then he mentions the possibility of prison for the Count, or exile, or beheading. This sarcasm of the misshapen jester disgusts even the Duke. Ceprano is boiling with rage at such boorish jesting and bids the courtiers, who likewise have smarted under Rigoletto's ribaldry, meet him the following night, then they shall have their revenge.

The festival music of the band on the stage supplies a flippant background to the badinage of this scene; then, while the Duke and Rigoletto continue their discussion, and the courtiers and Ceprano plot their revenge, the music grows to a climax, suddenly interrupted by the voice of someone outside, struggling for admission. A moment later the aged Count Monterone bursts in. His daughter has been dishonored by the Duke; now before the entire assembly he denounces that profligate ruler. The Duke at once orders his arrest; Rigoletto mocks him. Monterone, justly incensed with this injury doubled with insult, again reviles the Duke and, turning toward Rigoletto, cries, "As for you, serpent! You who can laugh at a father's anguish, a father's curse be on your head!" Monterone is led off by guards; the courtiers return to their festivities; but Rigoletto cowers, trembling with fright at Monterone's words.

ACT II

SCENE: *A Deserted Street.* A few somber chords are heard in the woodwinds. Then a subdued, rather suave melody in keeping with the scene—the end of a deserted street, sinister under the darkness of night. At the left, a small, humble-appearing house with a wall-enclosed courtyard; across the street, a very high wall, and beyond it a corner of Count Ceprano's palace.

Rigoletto, wrapped in his cloak, comes shambling down the street, but before he can turn in toward his house at the left he is accosted by an ominous black-robed figure, who offers his services, should they be desired, in putting rivals or enemies out of the way, charges reasonable. The hunchback does not need him now, but asks where he may be found. This assassin for hire tells his lodging, then departs, making known his name, Sparafucile.

Rigoletto stops meditatively at the doorway leading into the courtyard.

JAN PEERCE AS THE DUKE

429

Thus he soliloquizes, to music that varies with his shifting moods, in the dramatic aria *"Pari siamo"* ("We are equals"), a masterpiece of theater writing, and, understandably, a great favorite with baritones. He enters the courtyard at the moment that a young woman comes from the house. They embrace joyfully. "Gilda!" he exclaims; "Father!" she sighs in response. A cheerful orchestral melody accompanies their meeting. Knowing well the hazards of life with courtiers and Duke so near, and perhaps, the curse still ringing in his ears, he again for the thousandth time warns and solemnly enjoins her to remain strictly within the house and never to venture into the town. He even questions her to know if anybody has followed her to church; but Gilda, with some qualms of conscience, keeps silent regarding the stranger she has met there. To reassure himself further, Rigoletto calls the servant and briefs her, too, on matters of safety for his daughter.

Suddenly thinking he hears someone knock on the street door, Rigoletto hurriedly opens the door in the courtyard and goes out to look. The Duke has been loitering outside and, while Rigoletto is in the street, he quietly glides into the courtyard and throws a purse to the servant with a sign to keep silent. He hides himself. This action takes place to an agitated orchestral accompaniment, the frightened Gilda, unaware of his presence, murmuring, meanwhile, "Heaven! if he should suspect me!" Rigoletto must leave, and returns, saying, "My daughter, farewell!" "His daughter!" exclaims the Duke to himself, surprised at this revelation. "Farewell, O my father!" (*"Addio, mio padre"*) is Gilda's reply. Father and daughter then continue in a lovely duet, Gilda saying that they need not fear, for her mother, as an angel in heaven, is watching over them, while Rigoletto continues his charge to the servant, *"Veglia, o donna"* ("Guard her, woman").

As soon as Rigoletto has departed, the Duke, who, of course, is in disguise, comes from his hiding place. Gilda, alarmed, bids him begone; but he knows well how to calm her fears. He sings a gently swaying melody, *"E il sol dell' anima"* ("Love is the sun").

Soon Gilda is heard saying, as if to herself: "Ah! This is the dear voice of my dreams!"

Gilda desires to know his name; "Gualtier Maldè," he finally admits, adding that he is only a poor, struggling student. Then as he leaves they sing a tender farewell. Gilda remains pensive, dreaming of her lover, in the very popular florid air, *"Caro nome"* ("Dear name"). This melody, with delicate accompaniment and flute passages, is one of the most exacting of coloratura arias, calling for extraordinary skill if its *fioriture* are to be performed with the grace they demand.

While she is yet singing, conspiracy is at work, for under cover of night a band of masked courtiers, led by Ceprano, has come for vengeance. Rigoletto, unexpectedly returning, runs into them, and is much alarmed to find them in

R. Strohmeyer   ACT III—SAN FRANCISCO OPERA PRODUCTION

his neighborhood. His fears are somewhat calmed, however, when the courtiers declare that they are bent on stealing Ceprano's wife for their friend, the Duke. Rigoletto points out Ceprano's house, and offers help. They insist that he must be disguised, give him a mask, and then as if to fasten it securely, tie it with a handkerchief which they pass over the holes pierced for the eyes. Confused and blinded, Rigoletto holds the ladder against what he believes to be the wall surrounding Ceprano's house. By it the abductors climb over his own wall, enter his house, seize, gag, and carry away his daughter. Thus after a few minutes Rigoletto finds himself left entirely alone, holding the ladder. Becoming suspicious he tears off the mask. The door to his courtyard is open. On the ground he finds a scarf of Gilda's. Frantic with fear he rushes into the house. Gilda has disappeared. He staggers under this disaster which he has helped bring on himself. In agony, he cries out, *"Ah!—la maledizione!"* ("Ah, the curse").

ACT III

SCENE: *A Salon in the Duke's Palace.* At the back, large folding doors. On the walls, portraits of the Duke and the Duchess, an ideal duchess, for, like her portrait that looks mutely down upon her husband's philanderings, she makes no comment and does not enter into the action.

The Duke is very much upset; he has returned to Rigoletto's house and found it deserted, the bird flown. He laments his loss in a very effective aria, *"Parmi veder le lagrime"* ("Each tear that falls"), so effective that we nearly feel sorry for him!

Marullo and the courtiers enter with some amusing news. In a rousing chorus that has a most fascinating swing, they narrate their exploits of the previous night when they captured Rigoletto's "mistress."

The Duke is delighted with the details, laughing at the brilliant idea that made Rigoletto himself a party to the abduction. Knowing well that the woman in question is assuredly his latest inamorata, he is quite pleased when they inform him that they have brought her to the palace, and left her, in fact, in the very next room. He hurries to her.

No sooner has he gone than Rigoletto enters, pitifully striving to conceal his deep distress under a laughing exterior. "Poor Rigoletto," sing the courtiers, enjoying his discomposure at the loss of one they still believe to be only his mistress. The music is remarkably descriptive of Rigoletto's anxiety, as under the disguise of cynical indifference, singing "Tra-la-la," he searches furtively about the room for some evidence of Gilda's presence. A page enters to ask for the Duke; the courtiers tell him meaningly that his lordship cannot be disturbed now. The hunchback at once grasps the situation. "She must be here, in the next room!" he cries, then making no further attempt at concealment, he pleads, "Give me my daughter." He attempts to force an entrance, but the courtiers bar his efforts. Giving way to his feelings he rages among the Duke's followers.

The courtiers at first laugh at, then grow indifferent to, Rigoletto's plea, but their curiosity is again piqued as Gilda emerges from the Duke's apartment, runs to her father, and throws herself in his arms. Rigoletto orders the courtiers to go. Somewhat abashed, they leave the hunchback and his daughter together. Gilda tells him of the lover who followed her from church, in the plaintive aria, *"Tutte le feste"* ("On every festal morning").

Rigoletto does his best to comfort the girl, clasping her to his bosom with a tenderness and love that do much to atone for his vileness. "Weep, my child," he sings, to a melody of unusual beauty and pathos. Gilda replies, and their voices unite in a duet of most touching, exquisite loveliness—music that expresses in a wonderful manner the delicate, poignant tragedy of the scene.

By a singular chance, Count Monterone passes through the hall, being led to execution. He pauses before the Duke's portrait, exclaiming, "No thunder from heaven has yet burst down to strike you!" As he passes on, Rigoletto watches him grimly. Her father's stern demeanor frightens the girl, for he now swears a terrible vengeance on the Duke.

ACT IV

SCENE: *Sparafucile's Dwelling on the Deserted Banks of the Mincio.* An ancient inn, so ruined that one can see the broken staircase which leads to the loft, and even a couch within the loft itself. Near the inn is the river; beyond, the towers of Mantua reach toward the scudding clouds. Sparafucile is indoors, seated by the table, polishing his belt, unconscious that Rigoletto and his daughter are without, the latter dressed as a young cavalier, for it is her father's wish that she shall leave the city in disguise this very night.

He asks her if she still dreams of the Duke, and she confesses that she does cherish the student who came to her so full of romantic protestations. Thinking to cure her of this affection, he leads her toward the inn, so that she may peer through the dilapidated door and see the erstwhile "student" in his real character. The Duke, disguised as a soldier, enters the tavern and calls loudly for wine. While he is being served by Sparafucile, he sings one more song of the love of women. It portrays, clearly as words and music may, the indolently amorous young noble and his views of womankind, whom he charges, all and sundry, with his own worst failing, *"La donna è mobile"* ("Woman is fickle").

The murderous innkeeper, Sparafucile, brings the wine and then, as he goes out, knocks on the ceiling, a signal for his sister, Maddalena, to descend. This flirtatious, almost coarse, gypsy girl is the bait that has been used to lure the Duke to the inn. She is wise in the ways of men, and thus, for a time, laughingly evades the Duke's caresses.

The emotions of these four characters so widely different in sentiment are expressed in the wonderful quartet, *"Bella figlia dell' amore"* ("Fairest daughter of the graces").

In a most suave, ingratiating melody, the Duke sings to Maddalena, and Maddalena coquettishly replies. Observing all this, the heartbroken Gilda, concealed in the darkness outside, grimly remarks how lightly they speak of love, while the stern remarks of Rigoletto are added to the others. The voices, joined in simple though effective polyphony, mount to a splendid climax, one of the finest pieces of ensemble writing in all Italian opera.

Rigoletto then bids his daughter go with all speed to Verona, where he plans to follow. He forthwith summons Sparafucile and gives him half his assassin's fee; the remainder he will pay when the Duke's body is delivered, in a sack, at midnight. Sparafucile offers to throw the body in the river, but Rigoletto wishes that grim satisfaction for himself; he will return.

While these business transactions have been taking place outside, within the flirtation has grown more intimate. A storm gathers, and the Duke decides to stay the night at the inn. On Sparafucile's re-entry, he whispers to the girl that he will return to her soon, and ascends to the loft.

Even the professional coquette has fallen in love with the handsome Duke. Therefore, as soon as she is alone with her brother she suggests that he kill the hunchback rather than her Apollo. But the honor said to exist among thieves is, apparently, found among murderers too, for Sparafucile refuses to betray his employer. His sister pleads with such urgency, however, that finally he agrees that if another guest shall arrive before midnight, he will slay him instead of the Duke, so that Rigoletto will at least have a corpse for his money.

Meanwhile the storm has been drawing nearer, adding its terrors to those of the night. In spite of the darkness, Gilda has crept back to the inn, irresistibly drawn to the haunts of the man she loves. Thus it happens that, hearing this extraordinary agreement, she sees a way to save the life of her beloved and end her own sorrow.

The storm bursts in a sudden and overwhelming fury; the moaning of the wind, the long rush of the rain, the blinding lightning and crash of thunder are but outward symbols of the emotions of Gilda.Summoning up her disconsolate courage, she knocks at the door. Even the assassin seems startled that anyone should come at such a time. Sparafucile holds his dagger ready; Maddalena runs to open the door. Gilda enters. Between the lightning flashes her form is barely discernible. There is a quickly stifled outcry, then darkness and silence.

The storm's fury abates, though occasional lightning flashes illuminate the dreary scene. Rigoletto returns. He pays off the assassin and in return is given the sack with its gruesome contents. The murderer again offers to throw the body in the river; again the Jester claims this privilege. Left alone he gloats over his vengeance, then starts to drag the body toward the river. At that moment he hears a sound that makes his blood run cold. The Duke has awakened, and is again singing *"La donna è mobile."* Rigoletto trembles. Who, then, has he in the sack? He tears it open. A sudden flash of lightning reveals the form of Gilda. The unfortunate girl, wounded unto death, begs her father's forgiveness, singing with him a touching duet of farewell, *"Lassù in cielo"* ("There in heaven"). Rigoletto implores her not to leave him thus alone on earth. A little cry of pain, and Gilda falls back dead. "Ah! The curse!" sobs Rigoletto.

The music of Monterone's curse upon the Jester, who is now weeping over the corpse of his own despoiled daughter, thunders forth in the orchestra, an appalling triumph.

THE RCA-VICTOR RECORDS
(Sung in Italian unless otherwise noted)

COMPLETE RECORDING: *Piazza, Baritone; Lina Pagliughi, Soprano; Tino Folgar, Tenor; Salvatore Baccaloni, Bass; Olga de Cristoff, Mezzo-soprano; Aristide Baracchi, Baritone; Giuseppe Nessi, Tenor; Menni, Bass; Carlo Sabajno, Cond., with Chorus and Orchestra of La Scala, Milan*
DM-32 (12791-12805), 15-12"
M-32 (9525-9539)

ACT I
QUESTA O QUELLA ('Mid the Fair Throng) : *Jussi Bjoerling, Tenor, with Orch.*
10-1200, 10"

ACT II
MONOLOGO—PARI SIAMO! (Rigoletto's Monologue—Yon Assassin's My Equal) : *Leonard Warren, Baritone, with Orch.* 11-9413, 12"

IL NOME VOSTRO DITEMI (Tell Me Your Name) : *Lily Pons, Soprano; Giuseppe de Luca, Baritone; with Orch.*
17233, 12"
(In Album M-702)

È IL SOL DELL' ANIMA (Love Is the Sun) : *Jussi Bjoerling, Tenor; Hjoerdis Schymberg, Soprano; with Orch.*
11-8440, 12"

Rigoletto

Dupont
ENRICO CARUSO AS THE DUKE

Tito Schipa, Tenor; Amelita Galli-Curci, Soprano; with Orch.
1755, 12″
CARO NOME (Dearest Name): *Lily Pons, Soprano, with Orch.* 14203, 12″
(In Album M-329)
7383, 12″
Amelita Galli-Curci, Soprano, with Orch. 7655, 12″
Luisa Tetrazzini, Soprano, with Orch.
7883, 12″

ACT III
PARMI VEDER LE LAGRIME (Each Tear That Falls): *Jan Peerce, Tenor, with Orch.*
11-8926, 12″

Ferruccio Tagliavini, Tenor, with Orch.
12-0070, 12″
(In Album MO-1191)
18-0106, 12″
(Vinylite) (In Album VO-13)
Enrico Caruso, Tenor, with Orch.
11-8112, 12″
6016, 12″
(Acoustical Recording)
CORTIGIANI, VIL RAZZA DANNATA (Vile Race of Courtiers): *Leonard Warren, Baritone, with Orch.* 11-9413, 12″
TUTTE LE FESTE AL TEMPIO (On Every Festal Morning): *Lily Pons, Soprano, with Orch.* 7383, 12″

LEONARD WARREN AS RIGOLETTO

New York Times
JUSSI BJOERLING AS THE DUKE

ACT IV

LA DONNA È MOBILE (Woman Is Fickle):
Jussi Bjoerling, Tenor, with Orch.
4372, 10"

Enrico Caruso, Tenor, with Orch.
1616, 10"

Tito Schipa, Tenor, with Orch.
1099, 10"

QUARTET—BELLA FIGLIA DELL' AMORE
(Fairest Daughter of the Graces):
*Amelita Galli-Curci, Soprano; Louise
Homer, Contralto; Beniamino Gigli,
Tenor; Giuseppe de Luca, Baritone;
Metropolitan Opera Orch.*
10012, 12"

*Amelita Galli-Curci, Soprano; Flora
Perini, Contralto; Enrico Caruso,
Tenor; Giuseppe de Luca, Baritone;
with Orch.* 10000, 12"
(Acoustical Recording)

GIUSEPPE DE LUCA AS RIGOLETTO

GILDA AND RIGOLETTO

*Marcella Sembrich, Soprano; Gina Se-
verina, Contralto; Enrico Caruso,
Tenor; Antonio Scotti, Baritone; with
Orch.* 16-5001, 12"
(Acoustical Recording)
(In Album M-953)

*Noel Eadie, Soprano; Edith Coates,
Contralto; Webster Booth, Tenor; Arnold Matters, Baritone; London Philharmonic Orch. In English.*
36235, 12"

*Luisa Tetrazzini, Soprano; Josephine
Jacoby, Contralto; Enrico Caruso,
Tenor; Pasquale Amato, Baritone;
with Orch.* 15-1019, 12"
(Acoustical Recording)

436

ALBERICH'S PURSUIT OF THE NIBELUNGEN RING

Der Ring des Nibelungen
(THE RING OF THE NIBELUNGS)

DAS RHEINGOLD, DIE WALKÜRE, SIEGFRIED,
DIE GÖTTERDÄMMERUNG

A work without a parallel in the whole realm of music for grandeur and breadth of conception, the *Ring* occupied Wagner's ever-active mind for more than twenty-six years. While he was still a conductor at the Dresden Opera he had become greatly interested in the ancient Scandinavian, Germanic, and Icelandic sagas. There resulted a poem, *Siegfried's Death*, written in November, 1848. Then, while in exile, realizing that one drama would be inadequate for the proper presentation of so vast a legend, he wrote another poem as an introduction, named *Young Siegfried* (1851). Similarly, the following year, he prefaced this with *The Valkyrie* (*Die Walküre*), and this in turn with *The Rhinegold* (*Das Rheingold*). Wagner then set to work upon the music in the proper order of the dramas, and by 1857 had completed the score through part of the second act of *Siegfried* (originally *Young Siegfried*). By this time even the undauntable Wagner had, as he termed it, grown tired of "piling one silent score upon another," and he turned to what he considered the more practicable *Meistersinger* and *Tristan*. Not until 1869, encouraged by the patronage of the King of Bavaria, did Wagner resume work on *Siegfried*. The entire *Ring* was eventually finished, with the completion of the orchestration of *The Dusk of the Gods* (*Die Götterdämmerung*), originally *Siegfried's Death,* in 1874. Wagner termed his vast work a trilogy, considering *The Rhinegold* a preface to the story narrated in the three succeeding music-dramas, *Die Walküre, Siegfried,* and *Götterdämmerung.* Modern writers, however, regarding all four dramas as of equal importance, commonly refer to the series as a tetralogy.

No greater evidence of Wagner's ability as a dramatist can be found than the skill with which he has molded the old legends into a cohesive plot. A comparison of the sagas, beautiful as they are as poems, and Wagner's well-motivated drama is proof enough of this gigantic feat. Because of the order in which the text of the *Ring* was written, redundancies naturally occur; to remove them was a labor from which even this painstaking composer shrank. Into this mighty epic Wagner crowded a wealth of philosophical ideas. He cast his dramas into an alliterative form of verse, similar to that of the sagas, and through his fusion of music and verse, created an atmosphere of a remote age of myths and legends.

With the very opening of *Das Rheingold*—revolutionary as that magnificent opening must have been in its day—we realize that musically we are no longer in the world of *Lohengrin,* which preceded the *Ring* in time of composition. After long thought, Wagner had decided that if music drama was to progress beyond the classic scope of opera, it would be necessary to adapt to the theater the forceful method of thematic development perfected in the symphony by Beethoven. Only so was Wagner convinced that a fresh expressiveness could be obtained. An opera so written would no longer be opera, but "music drama," since, for Wagner, drama and music were conceived together, the melodies, harmonies, modulations, the very orchestration itself growing out of the moods and action of the drama. Wagner's music gains greatly in unity and psychological power through this use of "leading motives," which in the *Ring* are almost innumerable. A complete cataloguing and naming of all such motives was probably not contemplated by the composer. And certainly this is not necessary for the listener. Yet some knowledge of the more prominent themes does give added pleasure and understanding. For after repeated hearings and long acquaintance, the *Ring* assumes new beauties and reveals hitherto unnoticed details that often startle the attentive listener with their dramatic force and vividness.

In keeping with the magnitude of the trilogy, Wagner makes use of a gigantic orchestra, almost unprecedented in size. For special effects he introduced four of a family of instruments that he invented for the *Ring.* These instruments, now known as "Bayreuth tubas" or "Wagner tubas," are really a hybrid, uniting features of the French horn and trombone. Their timbre, of unusual nobility and pathos, is peculiarly suited to Wagner's purpose—that of intoning the leading motives of "Valhalla" and "The Wälsungs."

The *Ring*, as a whole, was first performed at Wagner's own theater at Bayreuth, on August 13, 14, 16, 17, 1876, as the crowning achievement of a lifetime of struggle. In the United States, the complete cycle was first performed at the Metropolitan Opera House, New York, March 4-11, 1889, performances of the individual dramas having been given at earlier dates.

An undertaking of such size has naturally enlisted the services of many of the world's greatest conductors and singers. At the first Bayreuth performances, 1876, Hans Richter was the conductor and Anton Seidl and Felix Mottl, assistants; while among the singers were Lilli Lehmann, Albert Niemann, and Amalie Materna. In 1896, Mme. Schumann-Heink sang the roles of Erda and Waltraute at Bayreuth. At the first performance of the entire *Ring* cycle at the Metropolitan Opera House, Anton Seidl was the conductor, and among the principals were Lilli Lehmann, Max Alvary, and Emil Fischer. The late Theodore Thomas was a Wagnerian pioneer in this country, in the days when it was heresy to play or like Wagner. Among the other great Wagnerian singers it is possible here to name only a few: Nordica, Ternina, Fremstad, Gadski, Eames, Homer, Jean de Reszke, Matzenauer, Van Rooy, Whitehill, and, among those of more recent times, Kirsten Flagstad, Marjorie Lawrence, Elisabeth Rethberg, Lauritz Melchior, Frida Leider, Friedrich Schorr, and Florence Austral. At the *Ring* cycle given at the Metropolitan Opera House in 1929, Mme. Schumann-Heink sang the role of Erda—the occasion for a triumphal return after many years of absence.

Panel By Hugo Braune
THE GODS ENTER VALHALLA

Painted By Echter
THE CAPTURE OF ALBERICH

439

Hans Makart THE THEFT OF THE RHINEGOLD

Das Rheingold
(THE RHINEGOLD)

MUSIC DRAMA in four scenes, prelude (*Vorabend*) to *Der Ring des Nibelungen*. Text and music by Richard Wagner. First produced, September 22, 1869, at Munich. First performance in the United States, January 4, 1889, at the Metropolitan Opera House, New York.

CHARACTERS

Gods		Goddesses	
WOTAN	*Baritone-Bass*	FRICKA	*Soprano*
DONNER	*Bass*	FREIA	*Soprano*
FROH	*Tenor*	ERDA	*Contralto*
LOGE	*Tenor*	The Rhine-maidens	
Giants		WOGLINDE	*Soprano*
FASOLT	*Bass*	WELLGUNDE	*Soprano*
	Bass	FLOSSHILDE	*Contralto*

Nibelungs (Gnomes)

ALBERICH	*Baritone*
MIME	*Tenor*

The action takes place during legendary times in the bed of the Rhine, at a mountainous district near that river, and in the subterranean caverns of Nibelheim

From the depths of the orchestra is heard a long-sustained tone, calm and motionless. After a time another is added and sustained with it; these tones will continue through the entire prelude. In the midst of this stream of sound, other tones soon become audible, moving slowly upwards. This upward motion continues steadily until it is transformed into a constant and overlapping series of gentle undulations. In time these undulations are imbued with a more fluid motion and rise gradually higher. The motion now grows more rapid, surging ever upwards, in great waves of tone, until the entire orchestra is participating in this onward-flowing movement. We are hearing a semblance of what we actually behold at the rise of the curtain— the depths of the mighty river Rhine.

Here, through the greenish twilight of the waters at the bottom of the river, the three Rhine-maidens sing their nonsensical and carefree song of *"Weia! Waga!"* as they playfully swim about. Their games are interrupted, however, by the crouching dwarf, Alberich, who approaches and attempts to make love to them. One by one, after urging him on with fair words, they laugh scornfully at the misshapen dwarf and swim away, eluding his grasp as he clambers over the rocks in an effort to catch one of them. Finally he remains gazing after the maidens in angry despair, thwarted in his attempt at love-making. But now the light of the sun begins to penetrate the waters and there is reflected from the pinnacle of one of the rocks a bright golden gleam. Against a shimmering accompaniment of violins we hear the motive of "The Rhinegold." The maidens, rejoicing in the radiance, sing their exultant song in praise of the gold.

On questioning them, the greatly interested Alberich learns that this gleaming substance is the Rhinegold of which the maidens are the guardians. Though valueless enough here, if forged into a ring, the gold would give the possessor unlimited wealth and power over gods and men. But in order to be able to forge such a ring, the owner must first renounce love. All this the chattering Rhine-maidens carelessly reveal. They have nothing to fear, for no being would ever renounce love, least of all this lecherous Alberich. Therefore, they swim about lightheartedly. The heedful Alberich, however, rapidly climbs up among the rocks. Thinking he is pursuing them, the maidens swim away, shouting in mock terror. Alberich renounces all love, seizes the gold, and disappears. The maidens follow in a vain attempt to catch the thief. The music rushes wildly downwards. The waters, bereft of the gold, are left in total darkness, a darkness that becomes like a dense cloud which in time dissolves into a light mist.

As the mist vanishes in the morning sunshine, a lofty mountaintop is revealed. On still another mountain peak in the distance, across the valley of the Rhine, is seen a mighty castle with towering pinnacles. From the orchestra is now heard the majestic "Valhalla" motive. As the day grows brighter, we behold Wotan, ruler of the gods, and his consort, Fricka, who are just awakening from sleep. The great castle, Valhalla (in German, *Walhalla*), has been built for the gods by the giants, Wotan having recklessly promised in payment the beautiful goddess of love, Freia. Even while his wife upbraids him for this rash promise, Freia rushes to them for protection against the giants, who follow, claiming their reward. Freia's cries for help bring her brothers, Froh and Donner, to the scene. Wotan is now faced with a dilemma. For it is this same Freia who keeps the golden apples that enable the gods to live in perpetual youth. Without her they will all grow old and perish. Yet Wotan has promised her to the giants, swearing to keep his word by the sacred runes of his spear. As guardian of the law through which alone the gods remain gods, he is compelled to respect his oath. With the hope that some substitute could be found acceptable to the giants in place of Freia, he has sent Loge, the tricky god of fire, over the earth to search for one. Just as the indignant giants are about to drag away the weeping goddess, Loge appears. This subtle diplomat announces that nowhere on earth has he found anyone who did not cherish youth and love. As he sings of the universal sway of love, the orchestra sounds the theme of Freia, glowing in great beauty. The giants seem triumphant.

In a rage Wotan turns to Loge—is this his promised help? Then Loge remembers the dwarf Alberich, who did forswear love and after stealing the Rhinegold and forging of it a ring, was now amassing a vast treasure in the lower world. The giants say that this treasure will be acceptable to them in place of the goddess, but, no longer trusting Wotan, they take Freia as hostage until they shall be paid. Bereft of her presence, the gods immediately grow pallid and weak. The mountaintop is shrouded in a mist. Wotan, lost in thought, finally resolves to descend to Nibelheim and wrest the treasure from Alberich. Preceded by Loge, he enters a cavern leading to the underworld. Sulphurous vapors arising from the cavern obscure the scene, and as they mount rapidly higher the theater seems to descend into the earth. The orchestra accompanies with a vividly descriptive passage, the leading motives of "Loge," "Gold," and "Flight" being beautifully woven into the symphonic web. In time a red glow shines from a distance, and the sound of hammering on innumerable tiny anvils grows louder, then recedes. The motive that now dominates the orchestra is associated both with the idea of a "Forge" and the "Nibelungs," who are the smithies.

As the clanging of anvils dies away we see a great subterranean cave— the abode of Alberich. Through the power of the Ring he has enslaved all the dwarfs of Nibelheim. Mercilessly he compels them to amass the treasures concealed in the bowels of the earth. Through the power of the Ring he has forced his brother dwarf Mime, a skillful craftsman, to forge for him a magic Tarnhelm that will enable the wearer to change his form or render himself invisible. Having thus made himself invisible, he now beats his slaves and the groveling Mime ferociously. Wotan and Loge approach. They flatter Alberich on his power and cunning and cleverly coax him to exhibit the magic of the Tarnhelm. At Loge's suggestion, he first transforms himself into a dragon. Loge pretends to be terrified and then says that he doubts Alberich's ability to turn himself into something very small, a toad, for instance. This, too, Alberich does—Wotan quickly puts his foot on the toad. Thus Alberich is captured, bound, and dragged back to the upper world.

On the mountaintop the enfeebled gods are still waiting in gloom and silence when Wotan and Loge return with the cowering dwarf. Alberich is forced to order his slaves to bring up from the underworld all his acquired wealth. Then he is compelled to part with the Tarnhelm and the Ring, the source of his power, for these Wotan wishes to keep for himself. Alberich trembles with rage at this loss. When he is released, he pauses before going away and utters a terrific curse upon the Ring. Let it bring death and destruction to whoever possesses it. Thus will the gods who have robbed him of his power be destroyed.

While the baleful motive of the "Curse" is still ringing in our ears, the giants now return with Freia. The treasures are heaped before her, since it is agreed that not until the goddess of Love is concealed by the gold will the giants give her up. Yet with all the treasure, and even the Tarnhelm added, Fasolt still sees Freia's eye shining through the pile. The Ring is needed, but this Wotan refuses to sacrifice. In a misty light, there suddenly rises from the mountain, Erda, the all-knowing, all-foreseeing goddess of the earth. With the utmost solemnity she warns him to surrender the Ring before dire calamities befall them all.

Wotan would detain her to learn more, but she sinks again into the earth, with a final cry of warning.

Shaken by her awesome prophecy of doom, Wotan casts the Ring on the heap. Freia is released, and the giants, starting away with their treasure, at once quarrel over the Ring. Fafner kills his brother, Fasolt—the curse on the Ring, its gold, and its power, is already at work. But the mountains still remain shrouded in murky clouds. These, Donner, god of thunder, summons to himself and, swinging his mighty hammer, disappears in a storm.

And now, gleaming in the light of the setting sun, Valhalla has become visible. Like a bridge across the valley a glowing rainbow has formed, and a theme of stunning power is now heard in the orchestra. Turning to Wotan, Froh urges him to make his way across this bridge, without fear.

The god, lost in contemplation of the castle, sings ecstatically of the promised safety and shelter of this new home. Bidden to join him on the trip to Valhalla, Fricka asks why he so names the castle. Enigmatically, Wotan replies that the future will explain the name.

As the gods proceed toward the bridge, Loge, remaining behind, looks after them and muses scornfully on the flaming end that awaits these proud gods glorying in their "overwhelming strength."

He follows the gods with sly unconcern. From the valley the Rhine-maidens are heard lamenting their lost gold: "Rhinegold! Rarest gold! . . . for thee now we implore. . . . O give us our glory again!" Wotan is annoyed by the sound of their plaint; at his command Loge calls down to them: "Ye in the water! Disturb us not. . . . If the gold gleams no longer upon you, then bask in the gods' augmented grandeur!" The gods laughingly turn again toward the bridge while the lamenting Rhine-maidens reply:

> *Rhinegold! Rarest gold!*
> *O might but again*
> *In the wave thy pure magic wake!*
> *What is of worth dwells but in the waters!*
> *Base and bad those who are throned above.*

Wotan halts for a moment as if seized by a mighty thought. From the orchestra there now thunders forth, in an impressive cadence, the motive of the "Sword"—the sword which the god hopes will bring him salvation. Then, while the gods continue their journey across the bridge to Valhalla, the theme of the "Rainbow" is heard, majestic and glowing in iridescent beauty.

THE RCA-VICTOR RECORDS
(Sung in German)

EXCERPTS (Arr. Stokowski) (Including Prelude, Rhine-maidens' Song, Alberich-Nibelungen Scene, Erda's Warning, Rainbow Music, and Entrance to Valhalla): *Leopold Stokowski and the Philadelphia Orchestra*
DM-179 (16594-16596), 3-12"
M-179 (7796-7798)

ERDAS WARNUNG—WEICHE, WOTAN, WEICHE! (Erda's Warning—Waver, Wotan, Waver!): *Kerstin Thorborg, Contralto, with Orch.* 17221, 12"
(In Album M-707)

Blanche Thebom, Mezzo-soprano, with Orch. 11-9795, 12"

EINZUG DER GÖTTER IN WALHALLA (Entrance of the Gods into Valhalla): *Leopold Stokowski and the Philadelphia Orchestra* 11-9230, 12"
(In Album M-1063)

Hugo Braune

WOTAN AND FRICKA
CONTEMPLATE VALHALLA

Die Walküre
(THE VALKYRIE)

MUSIC DRAMA in three acts; the "first day," of the *Ring des Nibelungen*. Text and music by Richard Wagner. First produced, June 26, 1870, at Munich. First performance in the United States, April 2, 1877, at the Academy of Music, New York.

CHARACTERS

BRÜNNHILDE	*Soprano*	WOTAN	*Baritone*
SIEGLINDE	*Soprano*	HUNDING	*Bass*
SIEGMUND	*Tenor*	THE EIGHT OTHER VALKYRIES	

ACT I

SCENE: *The Interior of Hunding's Dwelling.* The orchestral Prelude, one of Wagner's most descriptive passages, is a vivid portrayal of a tempest: the steady beating of the rain, the crash of thunder, and the hurried tread of a solitary man in flight through the forest.

The storm subsides, and the curtain rises, disclosing the interior of Hunding's dwelling—a curious abode of hides and crudely hewn timber, built around the stem of a great ash tree. A fire glows on the hearth. Suddenly the door opens, Siegmund appears, staggers weakly to the fireside, and falls exhausted before it, exclaiming, "Whoever may own this house, here must I rest!"

Sieglinde enters from another room, thinking she has heard her husband return. She is surprised to find a stranger lying at the hearth. At his request she hurries to bring him a draught of water. Siegmund revives, and they converse, finding a mysterious sympathy in one another. Siegmund would hurry away, for he has ever brought misfortune with him. Sieglinde replies that he can bring no further misfortune to this abode of unhappiness. He decides to wait for her husband, Hunding, who soon arrives. During the evening meal which Sieglinde prepares, Siegmund tells of his distressful life; how, when a boy, returning with his father, Wälse, from the chase, he found his home burned, his mother slain, and his twin sister vanished. This crime was done by the Neidungs, who from that time relentlessly pursued father and son. Then one day the elder Wälse himself disappeared. And now, wandering alone through the forest, Siegmund attempted to rescue a girl whose family were about to give her up to a hated lover, but overwhelmed by numbers, he was forced to flee. Thus it is that Hunding recognizes in him the enemy whom he and his kinsmen have been pursuing. Now, however, though weaponless in his enemy's house, Siegmund is his guest and therefore safe, under the ancient law of hospitality. With a threat as to what dawn will bring, Hunding retires for the night, preceded by Sieglinde.

Alone in the room, now entirely dark save for the glow on the hearth,

Franz Hanfstaengl   ACT I—SIEGLINDE AND SIEGMUND

Siegmund broods on his hapless fate. Then, as for a moment he thinks of the beautiful woman who showed him compassion, the motive of their love is heard in the orchestra. Lamenting that she should be the thrall of his enemy, he cries out, "Wälse, Wälse, where is thy sword?" for he remembers that his father had promised him a weapon whenever he should need it desperately. At this moment the fire on the hearth flickers up, and a ray of its light falls on the hilt of a sword plunged into the stem of the ash tree. Siegmund wonders what this gleam might be; then the glowing embers fade, and he lies down to sleep.

A moment later the door opens, and Sieglinde comes stealthily into the room. She whispers the information that she has put an opiate in her husband's evening draught in order that she might be able to reveal a weapon to the stranger. She now tells of her forced marriage to Hunding: how, while her kinsmen sat at the wedding feast a stranger entered the hall . . . an old man with one eye hidden by his hat, and the gleam of his single eye struck terror into the hearts of all except Sieglinde. Disdaining the assembly, the old man drew a sword from his belt and with a mighty swing thrust it deep into the trunk of the ash tree. There the sword remains, for though many have tried, the stranger decreed that only one, a great hero, should withdraw it. "Oh, that I might find that man," Sieglinde exclaims, "for in him also should I find the one who shall rescue me from my woe!"

Siegmund, holding Sieglinde in an ardent embrace, replies, "The man for whom the sword and the wife were decreed holds you in his arms!" Suddenly, the great door of the house swings open; Sieglinde starts back in fright, "Who went?" she cries. Siegmund, drawing her tenderly in his arms again, tells her that no one departed, but that spring entered. The beauty of the moonlit woods now pervades the room, and Siegmund, gazing rapturously upon Sieglinde, apostrophizes the spring night, singing the lovely melody well known as the "Spring Song."

In her rapture, Sieglinde answers: "Thou art the spring for which I have longed in frosty winter's spell. At thy first glance my pulses leaped. I knew that in thee all that lay hidden in my breast was awakened!" Tenderly Siegmund replies: "Oh, sweetest wonder! Woman above all! . . . What has entangled my heart now do I know! I stand and gaze upon thee in wonder!"

Sieglinde looks at Siegmund with increasing amazement as his features begin to awaken a memory of the past. She has seen herself reflected in the forest stream, and now when she looks upon Siegmund it is as if she regarded her own face. Siegmund replies that he has long had a dream image of her in his heart. In growing excitement Sieglinde asks, "Was Wälse thy father? Art thou a Wälsung!" On learning this, Sieglinde cries out ecstatically: "Struck then for thee was the sword! Now may I name thee, as thou hast ever been known and loved . . . Siegmund! So name I thee!"

ACT I—BAYREUTH PRODUCTION

Springing from Sieglinde's arms, Siegmund runs to the tree and places his hands upon the hilt of the sword that lies buried there, exclaiming, "Nothung! [Needful] so now I name thee, sword! come from thy scabbard to me!" With a powerful effort he draws out the sword and brandishes it before Sieglinde, who utters a cry of joy. "Siegmund of the Wälsungs stands before thee! As bridal gift he brings this sword. Let us fly from this house, into the laughing world of spring!" Embracing fervently, they rush forth into the forest to the accompaniment of a wildly pulsating passage in the orchestra.

ACT II

SCENE: *A Wild and Rocky Pass.* There is an agitated orchestral prelude descriptive of the flight of the Wälsungs through forest and mountains. After a time a new theme, "The Valkyries," enters proudly in the bass, for at the rise of the curtain, Brünnhilde, the favorite of Wotan's Valkyries, is seen. She is clad in battle array and stands on a cliff over a rock-strewn mountain pass. Wotan, also fully armed, comes up the pass and, addressing her, orders her to defend Siegmund in the coming struggle. The Valkyrie dashes up the rocky height, singing the battle cry of the Valkyries: "Ho-yo-to-ho!"

On reaching a high peak, she looks around her, then calls back to Wotan: "Take warning, Father, prepare yourself for strife; Fricka approaches stormily . . .

"I leave you to her, I prefer the fighting of heroes!" Resuming her wild cry, she disappears over the mountain.

Fricka is thoroughly enraged because of the illegal love of the Wälsung pair. *"So ist es denn aus, mit den ewigen Göttern?"* ("Have the eternal gods, then, come to this?"), she cries. The offended Hunding has prayed to her for justice, and as goddess of marriage she must punish the guilty. In vain Wotan tells why he became the father of these Wälsungs—how, enjoined from wresting the treasure from Fafner, he had hoped to raise a hero who of his own free will would recover the Ring and prevent its falling into the hands of Alberich. But Fricka demands righteousness, taunting Wotan with trying to deceive her with deep explanations: *"Mit tiefem Sinne willst du mich täuschen?"*

Siegmund must fall before Hunding, she warns, and Wotan, again compelled to uphold the law which gives him his power, reluctantly agrees.

As Fricka, proud in her triumph, departs, Brünnhilde returns to receive Wotan's further commands. She asks him the cause of his dejection. Wotan springs to his feet with an outburst of profound anguish: "Oh, infinite shame!" Frightened, Brünnhilde entreats him to reveal the source of his sorrow.

Wotan now dejectedly narrates to her the story of the heroes he has had gathered in Valhalla by his Valkyrie daughters. Brünnhilde asks, "Have we ever failed?" Wotan further divulges that the danger lies with Alberich's hosts, who in revenge for the loss of the Ring are working to overthrow the gods. In despair he exclaims: "Fade splendor of godhood! ... one thing only I await ... the downfall ... the end!" In the utmost bitterness he cries out: "Blessings on thee, Nibelung son! May thou inherit the empty pomp of the gods!"

"What must I do, then?" asks Brünnhilde in alarm. "Fight for Fricka," he replies. "Ah, but you love Siegmund, and him will I shield!" she counters. Again Wotan commands, "Siegmund must fall!" Brünnhilde, ever mindful

ACT II—WOTAN AND BRÜNNHILDE—BAYREUTH PRODUCTION

449

of Wotan's inmost will, exclaims: "I will shield him whom thou hast taught me to love!" Infuriated by this show of defiance, Wotan cries: "Dost thou scorn me? Siegmund shall fall! This be thy task!" He storms away up the mountain, leaving Brünnhilde confused and frightened. Dejectedly she takes up her weapons and enters a cavern overlooking the mountain pass.

A tumultuous orchestral passage now calls to mind the flight of the Wälsungs, and a moment later the young couple appear, faltering and exhausted. In her growing panic Sieglinde has run ahead of Siegmund and, despite her fatigue, is anxious to go farther ahead. But Siegmund lovingly calls to her, "Here rest awhile; Siegmund will guard thee safe." He overtakes her and embraces her tenderly while she gazes into his eyes. Then she starts away in sudden remorse, crying: "Away, away! Fly from the profane one!" Her mood suddenly changing, she confesses: "Within your arms I found all that had awakened my love!" Again she draws back overwhelmed with horror, pleading, "Leave me, lest I bring dishonor upon thee!" Siegmund exclaims: "Fly no farther! Nothung, my sword, shall pierce the enemy's heart!" Sieglinde does not hear him, for in her apprehension she believes Hunding and his kinsmen are approaching. In delirious terror, she cries out, then gazing vaguely about, whispers, "Where art thou, Siegmund?" For a moment she rests on his bosom, then starts up, exclaiming, "Hark! Hunding's horn . . . you fall . . . the sword is in splinters!" She sinks fainting in Siegmund's arms.

And now Brünnhilde emerges from the cavern. The ominous "Fate" motive and "Death Song" are heard, stern and ominous. "Siegmund," she calls, "look on me . . . the messenger of death to warriors! Wotan awaits thee in Valhalla!" Siegmund asks whom he will find in Valhalla. Brünnhilde answers: "Wotan . . . glorious heroes . . . wish maidens . . . but Sieglinde, no, she must remain on earth." Siegmund bids her greet Valhalla for him; he will not go where Sieglinde is not. In her astonishment Brünnhilde asks, "Dost thou prize Valhalla so lightly?" Siegmund raises his eyes to Brünnhilde in scorn. "Thou seemst fair and young, now I know thee hard and cruel. Feast on my distress!" Deeply moved, Brünnhilde asks to guard his bride. "None other than I shall shield her . . . may death unite us!" cries Siegmund, drawing his sword as if to run it through Sieglinde's heart. Brünnhilde, moved by such devotion, impulsively springs forward. "Stop! Ye both shall live, triumph shall be yours!" And so saying, she vanishes up the mountainside.

Siegmund remains lost in thought, as storm clouds gather over the mountaintop. Hunding's horn call is heard. Siegmund kisses the sleeping Sieglinde in farewell, then, calling a challenge, rushes after the enemy and disappears among the clouds. Sieglinde restlessly dreams of her home, her father, her mother, the ominous stranger, the house in flames. She awakens

ACT I—SIEGLINDE AND SIEGMUND—BAYREUTH PRODUCTION

in fright, calling, "Help, Siegmund!" She can see nothing but the dark clouds, through which are heard the voices of the combatants still seeking one another, and finally meeting on the summit of the mountain. As Sieglinde staggers toward them, there is a sudden flash of lightning, and she falls back. Brünnhilde's voice is heard urging Siegmund to attack Hunding. Yet even as Siegmund raises his sword, a ruddy glow in the clouds reveals Wotan stretching forth his spear; on it the sword is shattered. Hunding strikes the disarmed Siegmund dead, and Sieglinde, horrified, falls fainting. Brünnhilde leaps from the rocky cliff, snatches up the pieces of the broken sword, and, lifting Sieglinde before her on the saddle, vanishes down the gorge. Wotan, in grim dejection, turns upon Hunding: "Go, slave, tell Fricka that I have avenged her!" And at the god's gesture of contempt Hunding falls dead. Then, bursting into terrible wrath, Wotan cries: "But, Brünnhilde, the disobedient—vengeance upon her!" and disappears amid a turmoil of thunder and lightning.

ACT III

SCENE: *On the Summit of a Rocky Mountain.* One of Wagner's most stirring descriptive passages is heard at the beginning of this act—the famous "Ride of the Valkyries," picturing, with amazing vigor and realism, the wild neighing and rapid galloping of the magic steeds of the Valkyries as they dash through the storm to their retreat.

Their meeting place is the summit of a mountain, rocky and barren, with a dark cavern beneath its highest peak and a somber forest below. In

R. Strohmeyer   ACT II—SAN FRANCISCO OPERA PRODUCTION

the vast space beyond the precipitous edge of the mountaintop clouds are driven before a storm. On the uppermost peak four of the nine Valkyries stand, awaiting their sisters, whom they signal with their savage war cry, "Ho-yo-to-ho!" Two others answer the call as they arrive, galloping through the air on their steeds, fleet as the clouds, and wild as the lightning that plays about them. The six that have now arrived join in the war cry as they hear Roseweisse and Grimgerde approaching. They laugh wildly at their jests, then, seeing they are but eight, ask, "Where is Brünnhilde?" Suddenly Waltraute sees her coming, riding in terrifying haste and carrying not a warrior but a woman. All run forward to meet Brünnhilde. "Sister, what has happened?" they cry out in horror at her daring. Sieglinde, fully aroused now, urges Brünnhilde to escape. As for herself, she would rather be united in death with Siegmund. Brünnhilde, however, commands her to live, for she will be the mother of a child by Siegmund. Thrilled by the prophecy, Sieglinde now pleads for safety and protection. The Valkyries know of a place in the forest to the east where a dragon guards Alberich's Ring and where Wotan never goes. Sieglinde will be safe there. But no time must be lost, for the clouds grow darker and Wotan approaches. Brünnhilde urges Sieglinde: "Fly to the eastward! be brave to endure all ills . . . remember only: you bear in your womb the world's most glorious hero!" She gives her the splinters of Siegmund's sword, saying, "I saved these from his father's death field . . . he shall wield the sword reforged . . . Siegfried let him be called!" To the ecstatic melody of "Redemption Through Love," Sieglinde, who is deeply moved, replies: "O radiant wonder . . . farewell . . . I go to save the loved one for him we both loved . . . be blessed in Sieglinde's woe!" Sieglinde then hurries away. A moment later, Wotan, drawing near in the

452

lowering storm clouds, calls, "Stay, Brünnhilde!" The Valkyries cry out in terror, but generously conceal the recreant daughter in their midst. Wotan strides upon the scene, fiercely demanding, "Where is Brünnhilde?" The terror-stricken Valkyries try to evade his question. Sternly he commands: "Shield her not . . . Brünnhilde, come forth!" The warrior-maid comes slowly from among her sisters, saying meekly, "Here am I . . . pronounce my punishment." Wotan answers: "I will not chastise thee. . . . Thou art no longer a child of my will . . . no longer a Valkyrie!"

Brünnhilde anxiously asks, "Dost thou cast me off?" Wotan explains sadly: "No more will I send thee from Valhalla . . . thou art forever banished from my sight. Bereft of thy godhood, thou shalt be as other women . . . to be claimed by the first passing churl." The other Valkyries are loud in their lamentation. Wotan commands them to flee the spot forever, or share a like doom, and, still grieving, they ride quickly away. Wotan and Brünnhilde remain in silence, the Valkyrie prostrate before her father. Slowly she raises her head, and timidly asks: "Was it so shameful, what I have done, that my offenses are so sternly punished?" She whispers to Wotan the secret of the Wälsungs—no craven will come from that race. "Name them not, they are outcasts with thee!" cries Wotan. He decrees that she shall be chained in sleep, a wife for the first passing stranger who wakes her. "Let horrors ward off all but a fearless hero!" pleads Brünnhilde.

"Too much thou askest!" "Then crush out my life, but let me not suffer such shame!" Seized by a sudden inspiration, Brünnhilde implores: "Oh, enkindle a fire around this rock to sear the craven who dares approach!"

SET SVANHOLM AS SIEGMUND   JOEL BERGLUND AS WOTAN

Setzer
LOTTE LEHMANN AS SIEGLINDE

ROSE BAMPTON AS SIEGLINDE

Overpowered with emotion, Wotan turns eagerly toward her, raises her to her feet, and, gazing lovingly into her eyes, sings a poignant farewell to his favorite daughter. Brünnhilde sinks transfigured on Wotan's breast; then looks up into his face with deep emotion while he continues his tragic soliloquy in ever-growing anguish.

At length he places a long kiss on Brünnhilde's eyelids, and she sinks gradually into a deep slumber. Wotan lowers her onto a grassy mound overshadowed by a huge fir tree. He gazes sadly upon her, closes her war helmet, and covers her with her great shield. Then he moves slowly away, pausing to look back once again. Resolutely, he now goes to a large rock that juts from the summit of the mountain. Striking it with his spear, he summons Loge:

> *Loge, hear! Listen and heed!*
> *Appear, wavering spirit, and spread me thy*
> *Fire around this fell!*
> *Loge! Loge! Loge!*

As Wotan strikes the rock for the third time, flames pour forth and spread.

The music of Loge, god of fire and of deceit, flares upward with a roar, then assumes a constantly flickering form. As the flames surround Wotan, he commandingly directs them to encircle the mountaintop. Once again holding out his spear, he utters a spell:

> *He who my spear feareth*
> *Never shall cross this fiery wall.*

He casts one sorrowful glance at the sleeping Brünnhilde and turns slowly to depart. As he reaches the fire he again looks back, then disappears through the flames. Meanwhile, against the music of the "Fire," and the theme of "Brünnhilde's Sleep," the melody of "Wotan's Farewell" is heard, in deepest pathos. Next the motive of relentless "Fate" is sounded. Finally, only the "Fire" and "Brünnhilde's Sleep" motives remain, and tranquillity pervades the scene.

THE RCA-VICTOR RECORDS
(Sung in German)

EXCERPTS (Arr. Stokowski) (Including Portions of Act II, Ride of the Valkyries, Brünnhilde's Pleading, Wotan's Farewell, and Magic Fire Music of Act III): *Leopold Stokowski and the Philadelphia Orchestra; Lawrence Tibbett, Baritone*
DM-248 (16640-16643), 4-12″
M-248 (8542-8545)

ACT I

COMPLETE RECORDING: *Lotte Lehmann, Soprano; Lauritz Melchior, Tenor; Emanuel List, Bass; Vienna Philharmonic Orchestra, Bruno Walter, Cond.*
DM-298 (16933-16940), 8-12″
M-298 (8932-8939)

DER MÄNNER SIPPE SASS HIER IM SAAL (The Host of Kinsmen Sat in the Hall): *Lotte Lehmann, Soprano, with Orch.* 14205, 12″
(In Album M-329)

DICH SELIG FRAU HALT NUN DER FREUND (Then Here in His Arms Holds Thee That Friend): *Lauritz Melchior, Tenor; Vienna Philharmonic Orchestra, Bruno Walter, Cond.*
14204, 12″
(In Album M-329)

WINTERSTÜRME WICHEN (Siegmund's Spring Song): *Lauritz Melchior, Tenor; the Philadelphia Orchestra, Eugene Ormandy, Cond.* 2035, 10″

SIEGMUND HEISS ICH UND SIEGMUND BIN ICH (Siegmund, Victor, Henceforth Proclaim Me): *Lauritz Melchior, Tenor; Lotte Lehmann, Soprano; Vienna Philharmonic Orchestra, Bruno Walter, Cond.* 15817, 12″
(In Album M-633)

DU BIST DER LENZ (Thou Art the Spring): *Lotte Lehmann, Soprano; Vienna Phil-*

harmonic Orchestra, Bruno Walter, Cond. 15817, 12″
(In Album M-633)

Kirsten Flagstad, Soprano; the Philadelphia Orchestra, Eugene Ormandy, Cond. 1901, 10″

ACT II

COMPLETE RECORDING: *Lotte Lehmann, Soprano; Marta Fuchs, Soprano; Ella Flesch, Soprano; Margarete Klose, Contralto; Lauritz Melchior, Tenor; Hans Hotter, Baritone; Alfred Jerger, Baritone; Emanuel List, Bass; Berlin State Opera Orchestra, Bruno Seidler-Winkler, Cond.; Vienna Philharmonic Orchestra, Bruno Walter, Cond.*

DM-582 (16058-16067), 10-12″
M-582 (15506-15515)

HO-JO-TO-HO! (Brünnhilde's Battle Cry): *Kirsten Flagstad, Soprano, with Orch.* 1726, 10″

SO IST ES DENN AUS MIT DEN EWIGEN (The End of the Reign of the Gods);

DEINER EW'GEN GATTIN HEILIGE (Thine Eternal Spouse's Glory): *Kerstin Thorborg, Contralto, with Orch.*
17721, 12″
(In Album M-707)

ACT III

WALKÜRENRITT (Ride of the Valkyries): *Arturo Toscanini and the NBC Symphony Orch.* 11-9643, 12″
(In Album M-1135)

FEUERZAUBER (Magic Fire Music): *Leopold Stokowski and the Philadelphia Orch.* 15800, 12″

Jesús María Sanromá, Pianist
18153, 12″

ACT III–SIEGFRIED APPROACHES BRÜNNHILDE–BAYREUTH PRODUCTION

Siegfried

Music drama in three acts; the third work in the tetralogy *Der Ring des Nibelungen.*
Words and music by Richard Wagner. First performance, Bayreuth, Germany, August
16, 1876. American *première*, Metropolitan Opera House, New York, November 9, 1887.

CHARACTERS

SIEGFRIED	*Tenor*	FAFNER	*Bass*
MIME	*Tenor*	ERDA	*Contralto*
WOTAN	*Baritone or Bass*	BRÜNNHILDE	*Soprano*
ALBERICH	*Baritone or Bass*	FOREST BIRD	*Soprano*

ACT I

SCENE: *Mime's Cave in a Forest.* A dark, sinister orchestral prelude, built
largely from motives associated with Alberich and Mime, prepares us for the
opening of the first act. In a large cavern Mime has set himself up a smithy.
In this, his gloomy abode, he sits busily working at his anvil, soliloquizing
meanwhile on his unhappy lot and his musings, involving such matters as the
Golden Hoard, the hammering in the Nibelung smithshops, Servitude, and,
finally, the Ring. No matter how strong a sword he makes, the boy Siegfried
breaks it asunder. Yet he cannot succeed in welding together the fragments
of Siegmund's broken sword, "Nothung"; with that for a weapon Siegfried
could easily triumph over Fafner, who, transformed by the magic of the
Tarnhelm into a dragon, still guards the Ring. With his cunning, Mime could
then easily obtain the Ring from the unsophisticated Siegfried. And now,
that joyous youth enters from the sunlit woods, clad in his rude forest garb,
and leading a bear by a rope toward Mime. The dwarf runs in precipitous

haste to hide himself. Siegfried laughs, and then, having driven the bear off to the woods, demands his new sword from Mime. The dwarf timorously gives it to Siegfried, who shatters the weapon with one blow and complains of this "silly switch." Mime brings food as a peace offering; Siegfried, sprawling on a mossy couch, kicks the food aside—he will prepare his own meals. Why does he continue to come here, he asks, when he feels such a loathing for this groveling dwarf. Mime attempts to persuade him that it is because he is his father, and Siegfried scornfully refuses to believe him. Now he will have the truth, and he nearly throttles the dwarf in his endeavor to gain it. Mime finally confesses that the boy is the son of an unfortunate fugitive who, overwhelmed with sorrow, sought refuge here, and died in giving birth to him. Siegfried shows great emotion, then, fearing lest the crafty dwarf be deceiving him, demands evidence. Mime produces the fragments of Nothung. Siegfried, thrilled with the thought of owning his father's weapon, orders Mime to forge the pieces into a sword and runs back into the forest.

While the dwarf is still brooding over this impossible task, Wotan appears, disguised as a Wanderer. Mime is appalled at the one-eyed warrior towering above him, especially when the Wanderer carelessly touches the earth with his long spear and a soft roll of thunder follows. The dwarf vainly suggests to the Wanderer that he go elsewhere. The visitor insists on remaining; he will answer at the price of his life any three questions Mime can pro-

SIEGFRIED AWAKENS BRÜNNHILDE

pound. After successfully answering three riddles regarding the Nibelungs, the giants, and the gods, the Wanderer asks three himself at the same price. Mime successfully answers the first two regarding the birth of Siegfried and the Sword, but is terrified at the third: who will repair Nothung? This is the one thing Mime wishes to know, yet foolishly neglected to ask. Before the Wanderer departs, he generously refuses to collect his wager—Mime's head —but admonishes him to guard well his head, for it may become a prize of him who does not know fear—the forger of Nothung.

Mime remains a prey to the wildest imaginings, and when Siegfried returns he finds the dwarf hiding behind the anvil. When he asks for the reforged sword of his father, Mime replies by asking what would a sword avail him if he know not fear? Moreover, the dwarf says, the dying Sieglinde bade him teach her son to fear ere he ventured into the world. Siegfried is impatient to learn this mysterious thing. Has he never felt a strange trembling in the depths of the forest as night falls, asks the dwarf; then Mime will take him to the great dragon, Fafner; there Siegfried shall learn to fear. The youth is enthusiastic, but first he must have his sword. Mime is compelled to confess that it is impossible for him to forge the broken pieces. Siegfried then says he will himself reforge his father's broken weapon! In joyous excitement he files the pieces into powder, pours this into a crucible and places it on the forge. Then while he lustily blows the fire with the bellows, he sings for sheer youthful exuberance; the orchestra furnishes a wonderful picture of the fire as it flames up, casting off glowing sparks.

Mime realizes that the sword will now be forged—the Ring will fall into Siegfried's hands. While the youth continues with his task, singing, the while, the exciting "Forging Song," pouring the molten metal into a mold, plunging that into cold water, then hammering the newly formed blade on the anvil, Mime sets about to prepare a poisonous brew, for in his simple mind he has concocted an elementary plan: he will offer this brew to the boy as soon as he has slain the dragon, the thirsty youth will drink, and the Ring and its power will be Mime's! Siegfried brandishes his newly refashioned weapon and with one blow cleaves the anvil from top to bottom before the amazed and terrified Mime. The motives of "The Sword" and "Siegfried's Horn Call" rush into a jubilant prestissimo while the hero holds aloft the sword, shouting with glee.

ACT II

SCENE: *Fafner's Cave in a Deep Forest.* The orchestra plays another ominous prelude in which, against the shuddering of violins, is heard the theme of the giants, distorted to represent Fafner, the dragon. There also enter the motives of "The Curse," "The Ring," and that of "Annihilation." In the almost inklike blackness of night we scarcely are able to discern the

R. *Strohmeyer*   ACT I—SAN FRANCISCO OPERA PRODUCTION

author of that curse, Alberich, as he sits gloomily watching before Fafner's cave in the depths of the woods, still hoping to regain the Ring. Here arrives the Wanderer, accompanied by the lightning and thunder of a sudden storm. Alberich accuses the god of coming to interfere in the course of events, which Wotan denies, saying that it is only Mime who desires the Ring, not Siegfried or himself, and in proof of this suggests to Alberich that he should call the dragon and offer to save his life in exchange for the Ring. But Fafner, aroused from his tranquil slumber and warned of the approach of his doom at the hands of a youth, refuses to give up any of his hoarded treasure. "I lie and possess," he answers; "let me sleep." Then Alberich and the Wanderer go their separate ways, and as dawn creeps through the woodland, Mime and Siegfried approach. Now, says the dwarf, Siegfried shall learn to fear, but his prating of love and gratitude only awakens the boy's anger, and Mime slinks off muttering to himself, "Would that Siegfried and Fafner might kill each other."

Siegfried stretches himself out comfortably under a tree and, looking after the departing dwarf, exclaims that he is happy that Mime is no father of his. In the orchestra there is heard gradually rising, like a faint whisper, the wonderful music descriptive of the rustling sounds of the forest, the "Forest Murmurs." Siegfried begins his meditation, while the murmuring of the forest grows around him. He wonders about his father and his mother. Finally his attention is attracted by the song of a bird. He playfully tries to answer it on a reed. He decides he can do better on his horn, and sounds a rousing call. This awakens Fafner, who comes clumsily from his cave, and the youth, laughing at the sight, resolutely places himself in the dragon's path. In the battle that ensues, Siegfried, avoiding the lashing tail and venomous teeth, deftly plunges his sword into the monster's heart, and Fafner, though sorely wounded, admires the bravery of the young man, cautioning him, "He who led you blindly to do this deed surely plots for your death!" He sinks, dying, to the ground.

In withdrawing his sword, Siegfried receives a drop of the dragon's blood on his hand. Involuntarily he carries his hand to his lips. The result of having tasted the dragon's blood is that he can understand the song of the birds. The bird who sang for him before now tells him clearly of the Tarnhelm and the Ring. Siegfried enters the cave to search for these treasures. While he is gone, Alberich and Mime come forth from the hiding places, whence they have been looking on. Their bitter quarrel as to who shall claim the Ring is ended abruptly by the reappearance of Siegfried, who has innocently taken just those two things from the dragon's hoard. Alberich vanishes with a dark threat, and Mime, with seemingly fair words, tries to induce the young hero to partake of a supposedly refreshing drink. Siegfried, however, having tasted of the dragon's blood, can understand the significance of Mime's fawning deceit, and in a final burst of anger draws his sword and kills the dwarf, then drags Mime's corpse and also the body of the dead dragon into the cave. He soon emerges, and, exclaiming at the heat of the midday which sends the blood coursing through his head, throws himself down to rest under a tree. Looking up, he notices the bird twittering about with its "brothers and sisters," and is reminded that he has none.

His new-found friend tells him of a wonderful maiden who sleeps on a mountaintop girt round by protecting flames. With a shout of joy, Siegfried asks to be shown the way, and as the bird flutters off, he follows along the ground in eager pursuit.

The motive of the "Bird" dominates this scene. Mingled with it are heard the themes of "Fire," "Siegfried," his "Horn Call," and an often repeated impetuous passage expressive of Siegfried's youthful ardor. As the hero runs away, excitedly following the bird, the music swells to an exuberant climax and comes to a close with a brief passage that flutters captivatingly upward.

ACT III

SCENE 1: *A Wild Region*. A tempestuous orchestral prelude of unusual magnificence introduces the third act. The rhythm of "The Ride," and the motives of the "Distress of the Gods," "The Rhine," "The Fall of the Gods," "Alberich," "Sleep," "Fate," and "Wotan's Spear," all enter, with singular beauty and appropriateness. As we hear the mysterious harmonies of "Sleep," the curtain rises, revealing a savage, barren and rocky country, shrouded in obscurity. Wotan, the Wanderer, halts before a cave in the

mountainside, and with great solemnity invokes the goddess of the Earth.

The cavern begins to glow with a bluish light, and Erda slowly rises from the earth, her hair and garments shimmering as with hoarfrost. Dreamily she asks who wakens her. Wotan replies that he has come to her, the wisest of all beings, to learn her counsel. She wearily answers that her sleep is dreaming, dreaming that brings wisdom; but the Norns are ever awake, weaving the rope of fate from her knowledge; let him seek their counsel. Wotan, however, would not know the future; he would alter its course. Then Erda calls to mind that she once submitted to Wotan's will, bore him a daughter, the Valkyrie; why does he not seek the far-seeing Brünnhilde? The god informs her of the punishment that he has been compelled to inflict on the rebel warrior-maid; can he consult her who is no longer one of the gods? Erda is unwilling to counsel him who punishes the Valkyrie for having done his will; who, though he is a god and the upholder of truth, holds his sway through falsehood. She would return to her sleep. Wotan is resolved to accept his fate, to welcome his doom. The world, which in anger he had left to the Nibelung, he now bequeaths to the son of the Wälsungs. The splendid theme of "The Heritage of the World" is heard briefly in the orchestra. This hero, Wotan says, having gained the Ring, will awaken Brünnhilde, and she shall win the world's freedom. Gladly will Wotan yield to the eternally young. "Away, then," he says, "mother of all fear, to endless sleep, away, away!" Erda sinks into the earth.

Wotan awaits Siegfried, who appears with the approach of dawn and demands right of way from this stranger barring his path. Wotan questions him good-humoredly and learns of the death of Fafner. He asks, too, whence comes the sword, and Siegfried answers he has forged it from a broken weapon. "Who was it first made that sword?" pursues Wotan. Siegfried answers that he cares not since a broken weapon is useless until repaired. Wotan laughs, but Siegfried becomes insistent to know the way to the fiery couch of Brünnhilde, the bird that directs him having flown. Wotan confesses that the black ravens that always accompany him have frightened the bird away, and adds that although he has always loved Siegfried's race, he was once compelled to shatter the sword of that youth's father; now he bids him beware and not arouse his ire, lest the sword be again so shattered. Siegfried cries out for joy, thinking that he has discovered his father's enemy and thus his own. Wotan angrily bars the path with his spear. Siegfried severs the weapon with a mighty blow of Nothung, and hurries excitedly up the mountainside. Wotan turns gloomily away.

The themes of "Fire," "Sleep," and "Siegfried's Horn Call" blend in a magnificent tumult while flames rise up and obscure the scene from view.

SCENE 2: *The Valkyr Rock.* When the music and the flames subside, we again behold Brünnhilde still locked in her magic sleep on the desolate mountaintop. Siegfried approaches, wonderingly, and, seeing what he believes to be a sleeping knight in armor, raises the shield, removes the helmet, and cuts through with his sword the fastenings of the breastplate. This discloses Brünnhilde in woman's dress, and Siegfried starts back in dismay. Now for the first time, the hero is shaken with what he believes to be fear. He attempts vainly to arouse her from her sleep, and at last kisses her on the lips. This breaks the spell, and Brünnhilde slowly awakens, while we hear in the orchestra the luminous chords introducing Brünnhilde's rhapsodic greeting to the world.

She greets the sun, the light, the radiant day, and asks who wakened her. The youth gazing at her, transfixed with rapture, answers that it is Siegfried who has released her from the spell. Brünnhilde continues her apostrophe; then, in music of glowing fervor, they sing joyously together.

Siegfried tries to embrace her, but Brünnhilde springs up, repulses him, and flies in the utmost terror to the opposite side of the mountaintop. She cries out in fright and shame—no god's touch has she felt! Siegfried's ardor is unabated, and already the godhood in Brünnhilde is waning. She pleads gently with the hero, calling to mind happy days that are vanished. She implores him to go his way. But soon Siegfried's ardor arouses her own, and in a duet, in which the motive of "Love's Resolution" is heard in the orchestra, the two young people fall into each other's arms, and the music swells ecstatically, while the motive of "Love's Rapture" and that of Siegfried join in a final joyous outburst.

THE RCA-VICTOR RECORDS
(Sung in German)

EXCERPTS (Including Conclusion of Act I, Forest Murmurs Scene of Act II, Portions of Act III) : *Lauritz Melchior, Tenor; Rudolf Laubenthal, Tenor; Frida Leider, Soprano; Emil Schipper, Baritone; Rudolf Bockelmann, Baritone; Albert Reiss, Tenor; Maria Olszewska, Contralto; Nora Grühn, Soprano; Berlin State Opera Orchestra, Leo Blech, Cond.; London Symphony Orchestra, Albert Coates, Cond.; Robert Heger, Cond.; Vienna State Opera Orchestra, Karl Alwin, Cond.* DM-83 (13251-13260), 10-12″ M-83 (9805-9814)

EXCERPTS (Including Mime-Siegfried and Wanderer-Mime Scenes of Act I, Alberich-Wanderer, Siegfried-Fafner, and Alberich-Mime Scenes of Act II) :

SET SVANHOLM AS SIEGFRIED

Lauritz Melchior, Tenor; Friedrich Schorr, Baritone; Heinrich Tessmer, Tenor; Eduard Habich, Baritone; London Symphony Orchestra, Robert Heger, Cond.
DM-161 (17166-17171), 6-12"
M-161 (7691-7696)

EXCERPTS (Including Prelude to Act I, Complete Version of Act III Finale): Lauritz Melchior, Tenor; Florence Easton, Soprano; London Symphony Orchestra; Royal Opera Orchestra of Covent Garden, Robert Heger, Cond.
DM-167 (16590-16593), 4-12"
M-167 (7762-7765)

SYNTHESIS (Arr. Stokowski) (Including Forging Scene of Act I, Forest Murmurs of Act II, Siegfried-Brünnhilde Duet of Act III): Leopold Stokowski and the Philadelphia Orchestra; Fred-

erick Jagel, Tenor; Agnes Davis, Soprano   DM-441 (16423-16425), 3-12"
M-441 (14845-14847)

ACT I

NOTHUNG! NOTHUNG! (Forging Song): Lauritz Melchior, Tenor; the Philadelphia Orchestra, Eugene Ormandy, Cond.   2035, 10"

Ho-Ho! . . . SCHMIEDE, MEIN HAMMER (Hammer Song): Lauritz Melchior, Tenor, with Orch.   17725, 12"
(In Album M-749)
11-8678, 12"
(In Album M-979)

ACT II

WALDWEBEN (Forest Murmurs) (Concert Version): Leopold Stokowski and the Hollywood Bowl Symphony Orchestra   11-9418, 12"

LAURITZ MELCHIOR AS SIEGFRIED

GUTRUNE AT SIEGFRIED'S BIER

Götterdämmerung
(THE TWILIGHT OF THE GODS)

MUSIC DRAMA in three acts and a prologue, the fourth work in the tetralogy *Der Ring des Nibelungen*. Music and text by Richard Wagner. *Première*, Bayreuth, August 17, 1876. First performance in the United States, Metropolitan Opera House, January 25, 1888, with a cast including Lilli Lehmann as Brünnhilde, Albert Niemann as Siegfried, Adolf Robinson as Gunther, Auguste Kraus as Gutrune, Emil Fischer as Hagen, Rudolf von Milde as Alberich, and Sophie Traubmann, Marianne Brandt, and Louise Meisslinger as the Rhine Daughters. The conductor was Anton Seidl.

CHARACTERS

BRÜNNHILDE	*Soprano*	WALTRAUTE	*Soprano*
SIEGFRIED	*Tenor*	WOGLINDE	*Soprano*
ALBERICH	*Baritone*	WELLGUNDE	*Soprano*
HAGEN	*Bass*	FLOSSHILDE	*Mezzo-soprano*
GUNTHER, *chief of the Gibichungs*	*Bass*		*Soprano*
GUTRUNE, *his sister*	*Soprano*	THREE NORNS	*Mezzo-soprano*
HAGEN, *son of Alberich and half brother to Gunther*	*Bass*		*Contralto*

PROLOGUE

A brief though impressive orchestral prelude prepares us for the scene. In it are heard the themes of Brünnhilde's "Hail to the World," and "The

465

Rhine" in somber hues. "Fate" sounds darkly, and the curtain rises, showing the Valkyrie's rock, now shrouded in the obscurity of night. The three Norns, the Fates of Scandinavian mythology, sit gloomily winding the rope of destiny. As they speak of the fire which Loge, at Wotan's order, maintains around the mountain, the theme of the magic flames is heard, vague, like a distant glow in the orchestra. The first Norn, unwinding a golden cord and fastening it to the fir tree, recalls that once it was a joy to perform her task, sheltered by the branches of the mighty world-ash at the foot of which flowed the spring of wisdom. Wotan came to drink of the waters, she continues, giving in payment therefor one of his eyes; he tore a branch from the world-ash to make his spear. From that time the tree withered and fell in decay, and the spring became dry at its source. She then adds, "Sing, sister, for I throw you the rope . . . know you what next befell?" The second Norn takes the rope and, having fastened it to a rock, sings as she weaves. She tells how Wotan graved on his spear the runes of the treaties which gave him his power; how this weapon was shattered when the god opposed a young hero; how Wotan then commanded the warriors of Valhalla to destroy the world-ash. "What next is decreed?" she asks, throwing the rope to the other sister. The third Norn continues the narrative: In Valhalla Wotan and his heroes sit in state; around the castle is piled the wood of the world-ash. If that should be set afire, the gods will be destroyed. "Know you more?" she asks, throwing the rope back to the second Norn, who in turn throws it to the first, whose eyes are dimmed by sorrow. Wondering whether it is the dawn or the magic fire she sees, she asks what happened to Loge. The second Norn replies, telling how Wotan subdued Loge by means of his spear and bound him around Brünnhilde's rock. "Know you what then will befall?" she asks. The third Norn foresees that Wotan will plunge the broken pieces of his spear into the fire and then will cast the blazing spear into the heaped up boughs of the ash tree. "If you would know when this shall come to pass, give me the rope," cries the second Norn. The first Norn has it, however. "The night wanes," she sings, "I can grasp nothing more. I feel no longer the strands, the threads are broken. A dreadful sight overwhelms my senses; the Rhinegold that once Alberich stole, know you what came of that?"

The second Norn takes the rope again, fastening it to a rock. She cries in alarm, "The rope is breaking, cut by the rock! It is the curse of the Nibelung's Ring which gnaws at the strands! Know you what will hap?" The third Norn takes the rope. It is too slack, and as she stretches it, it breaks. The three sisters cry out in terror. They bind themselves together with the pieces of the broken rope. "Ended is eternal wisdom!" they lament, "the world shall hear our wisdom no more!" then sink into the earth to seek Erda, their mother.

Dawn begins to break, and the music swells into a fine climax developed

R. Strohmeyer   ACT II—SAN FRANCISCO OPERA PRODUCTION

on a theme associated with Brünnhilde, now a mortal. As the sunshine floods the mountaintop, the melody of Siegfried's horn call is heard, changed into a serious, heroic form, and Siegfried, in full armor, and Brünnhilde come out of the cave. *"Zu neuen Thaten"* ("To deeds of valor, I must send you forth!"), sings Brünnhilde. She has bestowed on him all the wisdom that she had known as one of the gods, yet thinks her gift too little. Siegfried replies passionately that though he may have been a poor scholar, he has learned well ever to remember her. She earnestly charges him not to forget the fire he crossed to win her and the love and faith they have vowed. "I must leave you here," Siegfried exclaims, "guarded by the fire. For all your runes I give you now this Ring won from a dragon." Joyfully Brünnhilde replies, "Take now my horse! Once he flew with me through the heavens, with me he lost his magic powers. Guard him well. Speak to him oft Brünnhilde's name!" Siegfried answers rapturously, "Upon your horse I shall fight, with your shield ward me, then shall I no longer be Siegfried, Brünnhilde's arm shall I be!" Brünnhilde calls upon the gods, "Apart, who can divide us? Divided—still we are one!" They unite in their ardent duet. Siegfried then leaps on Grane's back and rides quickly down the mountain. Brünnhilde stands watching him, as he disappears. At the moment of parting the motives of Siegfried and Brünnhilde are played brilliantly by the full orchestra, then as the music grows quieter Siegfried is heard joyfully sounding his horn call from the mountainside. Brünnhilde, standing far out on the cliff, catches sight of him again and waves delightedly before he finally vanishes from her sight. The long orchestral interlude known as "Siegfried's Rhine Journey" now is heard.

The motives of "Flight" and "The Decision to Love" enter in the orchestra, and then as the curtain falls, these motives are marvelously combined together with that of "The Magic Fire." At the moment of climax, there is a sudden change of key, the music associated with the Rhine enters, and in a burst of special magnificence, "The Adoration of the Gold" is combined with Siegfried's horn call, and "Gold." The music, growing quieter and more somber, is then pervaded by the theme of "The Ring," "The Gold," and "The Renunciation of Love." And now the music makes a transition into darker, more somber sounds and, presently, we hear the motive of Hagen.

ACT I

SCENE 1: *The Hall of the Gibichungs on the Rhine.* On the banks of the Rhine is the kingdom of the Gibichungs, of whom Gunther is the chief. He is now in consultation with his sister, the fair Gutrune, and his swarthy half brother, Hagen. The latter, while extolling their prowess, laments that neither Gunther nor Gutrune is as yet married. He tells Gunther of the sleeping goddess, Brünnhilde, who may be won only by a fearless hero capable of penetrating a wall of flames. Gunther would like to win Brünnhilde, yet he knows well that he cannot pass through the fire. Hagen then tells of Siegfried, the fearless hero who slew the dragon Fafner; he it is who might be persuaded to win Brünnhilde for Gunther. Moreover, Siegfried would be a worthy husband for Gutrune; should her beauty not succeed in winning his love, a magic potion will easily do so. Scarcely has this plan been devised when Siegfried arrives in his quest for adventure. He is welcomed effusively by Gunther. Then Hagen asks Siegfried if it is true that he rules the Nibelung treasure. Siegfried admits he had forgotten all about that. "Took you none of it?" asks the wondering Hagen. "Only this," replied Siegfried, pointing to the Tarnhelm, "this of which I know not the use!" Hagen explains to him the mystery of the Tarnhelm, then asks, "Was there nothing else?" "Only a Ring," Siegfried answers, "which now a glorious woman wears."

At this moment Gutrune enters the hall and advances to Siegfried, bearing a filled drinking horn. "Welcome to Gibich's house; as our guest take thou this drink!" she exclaims. Bowing to her kindly, Siegfried takes the drinking horn, which he holds before him meditatively. "If lost were all that you have taught me, one lesson I shall ne'er forget; this draught, the first my lips e'er tasted, Brünnhilde, I drink to you!" No sooner has he finished this magical draught of forgetfulness than he is fired with a sudden passion for Gutrune. When he learns that Gunther is unmarried, but desires for his wife a noble maiden who lives on a mountaintop surrounded by fire, he at once suggests that they go together to win her as a bride. They swear blood-brotherhood and set out immediately. Should they succeed, Siegfried shall be granted Gutrune's hand in marriage.

ACT III—BAYREUTH PRODUCTION

Hagen, now alone in the hall, broods over his sinister plan, while the orchestra supplies a background remarkable for its unmitigated gloom.

SCENE 2: *The Valkyr Rock*. The curtain is lowered for a few moments, while the orchestra continues playing in this mood of fateful brooding. When the curtain is raised we are again at the Valkyrie's rock. Brünnhilde is sitting at the mouth of the cave, contemplating Siegfried's Ring, which she covers with kisses as though lost in happy memories. Suddenly she is startled by a distant roll of thunder, then another, nearer. A Valkyrie is approaching. A cry is heard from the distance, "Brünnhilde! Sister!" Soon the Valkyrie reaches the mountaintop; it is Waltraute. Brünnhilde is so enrapt with her own felicity that she does not notice Waltraute's agitation, but asks her what lured her from Valhalla. Waltraute replies that serious matters bring her there. For the first time observing Waltraute's perturbed condition, Brünnhilde questions her. "Since Wotan bade you farewell," Waltraute answers, "no more has he sent the Valkyries to battle." She tells how he roamed, lonely and restlessly, over the world and returned to Valhalla, his spear shattered. How he then commanded his heroes to hew down the world-ash and pile the fragments about the castle. How he now sits in state surrounded by his warriors; ever silent and gloomy, no more does he eat of Freia's apples. The other gods sit near him in silent terror. He has sent his two ravens over the earth, continues Waltraute. Should they return with good tidings, the god will smile again. The Valkyries sit trembling at his feet. Waltraute tells how once in tears she clasped herself closely against Wotan's breast, then she hesitates as she continues, "Wotan's brooding broke, and his thoughts turned, Brünnhilde, to you!" And from the orchestra there is heard the motive of "Wotan's Farewell," a whisper of ineffable pathos, like a faint echo from a vanished day. Waltraute says that, sighing deeply, he murmured as in a dream that should the Ring be given back to the Rhine-maidens the gods and the world would be released from the curse. When Waltraute heard this she stole secretly away through the waiting ranks of silent warriors and came here, she confides. "End the grief of the gods!" she entreats, prostrating herself before her sister. Brünnhilde replies that she understands nothing, for Valhalla knows her no longer. "The Ring," cries Waltraute, "surrender it back to the Rhine!" "The Ring?" asks Brünnhilde in amazement, "Siegfried's bridal gift? Art thou mad?"

"Oh, hear me!" pleads the unhappy Waltraute. "The woe of all the world is caused thereby! Throw the Ring into the waters, so shall you end Valhalla's grief!" "You know not what this Ring is to me," cries Brünnhilde. "More than the wonder of Valhalla, more than the immortal pleasures of the gods! Siegfried loves me! Oh, that I could teach this rapture to you! . . . Go, then!" continues Brünnhilde, "to the gods in council arrayed, and say that never shall I give up love! Nor shall they steal it from me, though proud Valhalla fall!" Crying out in anguish, Waltraute mounts her steed and rides away in a storm cloud. Brünnhilde quietly contemplates the evening landscape, and the flames that glow in the distance at the foot of the mountain.

Suddenly the fire springs up brightly, a horn call is heard. "Siegfried!" exclaims Brünnhilde excitedly, "up, up, and be clasped in the arms of my god!" The flames mount higher and higher; suddenly there springs onto the mountaintop a strange figure. Brünnhilde shrieks in terror and cowers tremblingly, murmuring, "Who dares approach?" The stranger is, of course, Siegfried, transformed by the magic of the Tarnhelm into the likeness of Gunther. He claims Brünnhilde as his bride and, though she resists him, he quickly overpowers her, takes the Ring from her finger, and orders her into the cave. He then calls Nothung to witness his faithfulness to Gunther, whose wooing he is accomplishing.

ACT II

SCENE: *Riverbank Before the Hall of the Gibichungs.* Hagen is on watch outside of the hall of the Gibichungs. In the darkness there crouches near him the dwarf Alberich, his father. Urged on by Alberich, Hagen swears to recover the Ring before Siegfried learns of its power or is persuaded to restore it to the Rhine-maidens. Alberich goes his way as dawn approaches. Siegfried soon arrives, now in his natural form. After being greeted by Hagen and Gutrune, he tells how he penetrated the wall of flames; he adds that Gunther now follows with the bride there won for him.

Hagen mounts a rocky cliff overhanging the river near the hall, and blows a great cattle horn, which brings the vassals running. They ask, "Who is the foe?" He replies that Gunther comes bringing a wife and bids them make sacrifices unto the gods that the marriage might be blessed. He orders them to fill their drinking horns and, drinking freely, give honor due to the gods. The vassals laughingly answer that good fortune, indeed, greets the Rhine if Hagen, the grim one, makes merry. But Hagen, still grave, warns them to greet Gunther's bride; to be loyal to the lady; should she be wronged, swiftly to avenge her. Gunther's boat now approaches down the Rhine, and the vassals cheer wildly, "Hail! Welcome!" Gunther leads Brünnhilde ceremoniously forward, and the vassals, bowing respectfully, sing a stately welcome. Brünnhilde, however, has remained with downcast eyes, as one in a trance, but on hearing Siegfried's voice, she is startled with sudden amazement. Noting on Siegfried's finger the Ring which she believed was taken from her by Gunther, she divines that it was Siegfried who came to her on the mountaintop and, blazing forth in terrible anger, denounces him, and declares that she is his wife. Siegfried protests this, saying that he will swear that he has not betrayed Gunther. He asks on whose weapon he shall take oath. Hagen advances, saying that the oath may be taken on his "unsullied spear point." Siegfried, placing two fingers of his right hand upon the spear point, makes his solemn declaration. Brünnhilde rushes forward and strikes Siegfried's hand from the spear. "Holy spear!" she cries, "witness my eternal oath. I pray that he may perish by your point, for here he has sworn falsely an oath." The vassals in their astonishment call for the help of Donner. Siegfried tells Gunther to care for his "wild mountain maid" well; she is still bewildered and angry and knows not what she is saying. Then he takes Gutrune's hand and bids the vassals and their women follow into the hall for the feasting. The procession moves away, leaving only Hagen, Brünnhilde, and Gunther, all absorbed in gloomy meditation.

"What crafty thing lies hidden here?" mutters Brünnhilde to herself, lamenting the cruelty of the man who casts her aside after having accepted her love and wisdom. And she wonders who will bring a sword to sever her bonds. Hagen, coming near, whispers that she may trust him to avenge her. Turning toward him, Brünnhilde exclaims scornfully that he is no match for Siegfried, whereupon he questions her about any weakness the hero may have. He seeks some cunning way in which Siegfried may be made weak in Hagen's hands. And Brünnhilde, still rankling over her Siegfried's apparent deception, says, finally, that only his back is vulnerable, for although she worked all her wiles to cast a protection over him, she cast no spell over his back, knowing that he would never retreat from a foe, and thus never expose his weak point. "And there shall he be speared!" cries Hagen exultingly, and, turning toward Gunther, continues, "Up, noble Gibichung! Here

stands your warrior bride! Why so sad?" But Gunther responds with an outburst of grief at his dishonor; and Brünnhilde, turning upon him, exclaims
that low indeed has fallen the race that bore such faint heart as his. Gunther,
overwhelmed, complains that he, the betrayer, has been betrayed. And he
implores Hagen to help him. The latter realistically replies that nothing can
help, save Siegfried's death. And though Gunther is appalled at the thought,
remembering the oath of blood-brotherhood, Hagen insists that the oath has
been broken and calls for blood. The voices of the conspirators unite briefly
in a magnificent passage: Brünnhilde and Gunther call upon the gods to aid
their revenge, and Hagen mutters, "Alberich, father, again shall you be true
lord of the Ring!" The wedding procession of Siegfried and Gutrune comes
from the hall and is joined by Gunther and Brünnhilde. The joyful music of
the marriage feast sounds out brilliantly in the orchestra, but mingled with it
as a strange undercurrent is the ominous motive of "Revenge."

ACT III

SCENE 1: *A Wild, Wooded Valley on the Banks of the Rhine.* Again we are
at the banks of the Rhine, this time at a point where it flows through a woods.
In the waters swim the three Rhine-maidens, singing their fascinating song,
"Frau Sonne sendet lichte Strahlen" ("The sun sends rays of splendor").
They pause for a moment and listen as a hunting horn is heard, echoing in the
distance. Then joyfully splashing about in the water, they resume their song.

Again a horn call is heard, and the Rhine-maidens dive down into
the water to take counsel and await Siegfried, who, having lost his way in the
hunt, soon appears on the banks of the river. The Rhine-maidens rise to the
surface and call him by name. He asks where they have hidden his quarry,
the bear. They say they will tell if he will give them the Ring. They taunt him,
when he refuses, telling him that he should be more generous toward the
pleas of young maidens. But Siegfried replies that he could not part so easily
with his goods; his wife would not be pleased. Whereupon they make game
of him, teasing him about being henpecked, and with a final commentary on
his miserliness they dive down beneath the surface. Slightly disturbed by
their words, Siegfried calls to them, offering to give them the Ring. But when
the Rhine-maidens reappear they are much more solemn in both demeanor
and talk. He is told to keep his Ring, to guard it until he learns the awful
power it holds. Only then shall he be delivered from the curse of the Ring.

Siegfried thoughtfully replaces the Ring on his finger and asks the
Rhine-maidens to reveal what they know. In the somber tones of *"Schlimmes
wissen wir dir"* ("Evils await you"), they explain that the Ring is made of
gold that has been stolen from the Rhine, and that its maker laid a curse
upon it, dooming its possessor to death. Only the waters of the Rhine will
remove this evil power it has. Siegfried's retort is that he is as unmoved by

their threats as he was by their wiles. He says he was told of its curse by the dragon whom he slew, and that through the Ring he could win the riches of the world, which, he adds, he despises. In any case, he will not give it up. The Rhine-maidens, unable to make him do as they wish, remark on this self-esteeming young man who is so blind. And they add that this very day a woman shall inherit the treasure—a woman who will better do their bidding. With that they disappear.

The hunting party is heard, sounding the hunting horns and calling. Siegfried answers their call, and soon they appear—Hagen, Gunther, and a crowd of vassals. They put down their game and prepare for a repast. Siegfried says that he found no game—only "water fowl" who foretold his death. This gives Hagen a cue, and he asks Siegfried to tell them how he came to understand the song of birds. In the narrative *"Mime hiess ein mürrischer Zwerg"* ("Mime was a crabbed old dwarf"), Siegfried tells of his life with Mime, the forging of Nothung, the slaying of the dragon, the dragon's blood which enabled him to understand the song of birds, and the Ring and the Tarnhelm of which a bird told him. Hagen offers a drinking horn to Siegfried, saying that the mead will help rekindle his memory. Hagen has secretly put into the mead the juice of an herb. When the hero drinks it, the effects of the earlier potion which made him forget Brünnhilde are removed. Siegfried continues his story. He tells of the forest bird's promise to lead him to Brünnhilde, of his passing through the flames. He becomes more and more enraptured as he recalls the sleeping maiden he found, his awakening kiss, and how Brünnhilde's arms enfolded him. Gunther, rising in horror, cries, "What says he!" At this moment two ravens circle around over Siegfried.

"What do these ravens say?" demands Hagen. Siegfried turns to look. "Vengeance, they say to me!" cries Hagen. And with a fearful thrust he plunges his spear into Siegfried's back. Siegfried turns and raises his shield, intending to crush Hagen, but falls unconscious. Gunther and the vassals stand appalled, muttering, "What deed is this?" Hagen answers, "Falsehood do I avenge!" then walks gloomily away.

Gunther bends down sorrowfully at the side of the stricken man, surrounded by the sympathetic vassals. Siegfried, opening his eyes, whispers, "Brünnhilde! holiest bride!" The orchestra echoes the glowing music of Brünnhilde's awakening, as Siegfried addresses his last words to the absent Brünnhilde. Then he falls back lifeless. Sadly the body is lifted and carried in solemn procession to the Gibichungs' hall, while mists rising from the Rhine obscure the scene. But the music of Siegfried's death attains a height of tragic expression seldom equaled in opera. Contrasted with the ominous, relentless pulsating of the rhythm are the themes associated with the Wälsungs, Siegfried's parents, melodies of great simplicity, yet of most touching pathos. Then there gleams out the motive of "The Sword," brightly, but with a new breadth and solemnity. And now we hear the rhythm of "Death" swelling out in tones of overwhelming power and grandeur, soon to be joined by the motives of "Siegfried" and of "Siegfried's Horn Call," glorified in the most transcendent majesty. Then suddenly all the splendor of heroism fades, and again the music is veiled with grief. The motive of "Brünnhilde" is heard sorrowingly; the rhythm of "Death" persists, now somber-hued, and "The Curse" sounding darkly, the music subsides in the deepest gloom.

SCENE 2: *The Hall of the Gibichungs.* When the mists clear we find that the scene has changed to the hall of the Gibichungs. In the darkness the hall and the river beyond it are barely discernible. Gutrune is anxiously awaiting the return of the huntsmen, for she has been haunted by dreams of evil foreboding. Suddenly Hagen enters in agitation, and bids her prepare lights for her lord's return; then adds that Siegfried is dead, slain by a boar. The body is brought in; Gutrune falls fainting. Gunther would tend her, but she repulses him, and he reveals to her that it was Hagen who murdered her husband. Hagen, unashamed, approaches, claiming Siegfried's Ring. Gunther opposes him, they fight, and Gunther falls dead from a stroke of his brother's sword. Still undeterred, Hagen reaches for the Ring, but Siegfried's arm rises threateningly; Hagen recoils in horror, and the terror-stricken women shriek. At this moment Brünnhilde enters. "Silence your wailing!" she exclaims. "Children I heard whining the loss of their milk, yet heard I not lament worthy of the highest of heroes!" Gutrune rises in a sudden burst of passion: "Ah, Brünnhilde, you it was who for envy of me set the men against Siegfried." Brünnhilde gazes sadly at her and replies, "You were never wife of his. His troth he plighted me long ere he saw your face!" The unhappy Gutrune denounces Hagen for having brought the potion which caused Siegfried's forgetfulness.

Brünnhilde remains lost in deep contemplation, then, stirred with a sudden exaltation, she turns to the vassals and commands them to build up a mighty pile of logs by the river's edge; to kindle a fire high and bright, that in it may be consumed the body of the noblest of heroes! "Bring his steed," she continues, "that with me the horse may follow his lord." Then gazing on Siegfried's face, she sings, "Truer than he was none! None more faithfully held promises! Yet oaths and vows has he betrayed! Ye gods, guardians of all oaths, witness now my distress; behold your eternal disgrace. Wotan, hear me! On him, the hero who wrought your will, you laid the curse which fell upon you! Yet he must betray me, that all I might comprehend! Rest, then, god!" At a sign from Brünnhilde the vassals place Siegfried's body on the pyre, which is now completed. Brünnhilde takes from Siegfried's hand the Ring, and, looking at it thoughtfully, exclaims, "Rhine-maidens who so long have lamented the gold, take from my ashes the Ring! The fire which con-

Franz Hanfstaengl   SIEGFRIED AND THE RHINE MAIDENS

sumes me shall cleanse away the curse! Guard well, then, the gold!" She takes a firebrand from one of the men. "Fly home, ye ravens!" she cries; "tell Wotan what ye have here seen. And bid Loge hasten to Valhalla, for at last the day of the gods reaches its twilight!" So saying, she flings the torch upon the funeral pyre, which quickly breaks into flames, and Wotan's ravens, flying up from the riverbank, disappear in the distance.

Brünnhilde's horse is now led in. "Know you whither we go?" she asks. "There lies your master; would you follow him in the flames? In my heart flames, too, are glowing, fast to embrace him, with him forever made one—Siegfried, Brünnhilde greets you in bliss!"

She swings herself on Grane's back, and at her urging the horse leaps forward into the burning funeral pyre. The flames, growing constantly more violent, mount upward and overrun the hall, until the very building seems ablaze. The terrified Gibichung vassals draw back, huddled together in a corner. Suddenly the flames die down, the smoke drifts away, and the river

Rhine, having overflowed its banks, submerges the embers in an instant. The Rhine-maidens appear where last the pyre was seen blazing. Hagen, who has been anxiously watching, throws off his armor and plunges into the flood, shouting, "Back from the Ring!" Now for the last time, the motive of "The Curse" is briefly sounded. But the Rhine-maidens have recovered the Ring; then seizing Hagen, they drag him down into the depths. The Rhine returns to its normal course, and as the Rhine-maidens swim away rejoicing, the melody of their song is heard. Soon there enters with it the majestic theme of "Valhalla," while on the distant horizon is seen a red glow—Valhalla and its assembled gods and heroes are passing away in flames. Yet above these two themes is heard the ecstatic melody of "Redemption Through Love" swelling into a transcendent apotheosis; for though the gods be destroyed and though the gold be restored to its unsullied condition in the depths of the Rhine, there remains one power to govern the world—love.

THE RCA-VICTOR RECORDS
(Sung in German)

EXCERPTS (Including Prelude and Norn Scene; Greeting to Siegfried, Hagen's Watch, Waltraute's Narrative of Act I, Hagen and the Vassals, Oath Scene, and Finale of Act II, Portions of Act III) : *Florence Austral, Soprano; Walter Widdop, Tenor; Rudolf Laubenthal, Tenor; Ivar Andrésen, Bass; Emanuel List, Bass; Frederic Collier, Bass; Desider Zador, Bass; Arthur Fear, Bass; Göta Ljungberg, Soprano; Maartje Offers, Contralto; Noel Eadie, Soprano; Evelyn Arden, Contralto; Gladys Palmer, Contralto; Tilly de Garmo, Soprano; Kindermann, Soprano; Marker, Contralto; London Symphony Orchestra, Albert Coates, Cond.; Lawrence Collingwood, Cond.; Berlin State Opera Orchestra, Leo Blech, Cond.; Berlin State Opera Chorus*

DM-60 (Vol. 1) (13466-13473), 8-12"
(Vol. 2) (13474-13481), 8-12"
M-60 (Vol. 1) (9456-9462, 9486)
(Vol. 2) (9463-9469, 9487)

EXCERPTS (Arr. Stokowski) (Including Siegfried's Rhine Journey, Siegfried's Death Music, Brünnhilde's Immolation) : *Leopold Stokowski and the Philadelphia Orchestra; Agnes Davis, Soprano*

DM-188 (17144-17148), 5-12"
M-188 (7843-7847)

PRELUDE

ZU NEUEN THATEN (Did I Not Send Thee) : *Kirsten Flagstad, Soprano; Lauritz Melchior, Tenor; San Francisco Opera Orchestra, Edwin McArthur, Cond.*
17729, 12"
(In Album M-749)

SIEGFRIEDS RHEINFAHRT (Siegfried's Rhine Journey) : *Arturo Toscanini and the NBC Symphony Orchestra*
18318 & 18319, 2-12"
(In Album M-853)

Arturo Toscanini and the New York Philharmonic-Symphony Orchestra
14007 & 14008, 2-12"
(In Album M-308)

ACT I

ERZÄHLUNG DER WALTRAUTE (Waltraute's Narrative) : *Blanche Thebom, Mezzo-soprano, with Orch.* 11-9296, 12"
Kerstin Thorborg, Contralto, with Orch.
17222, 12"
(In Album M-707)

ACT III

SIEGFRIEDS ERZÄHLUNG (Siegfried's Narrative)
MIME HIESS EIN MÜRRISCHER ZWERG (Mime Was a Crabbed Old Dwarf)
IN LEID ZU DEN WIPFEL (In Grief to the Branches) : *Lauritz Melchior, Tenor; O. Helgers, Bass; with Chorus and Orch.* 7659, 12"

Robert le Diable

(ROBERT THE DEVIL)

OPERA IN five acts. Music by Giacomo Meyerbeer. Libretto by Eugène Scribe and Germain Delavigne. First performance at the Paris Opéra, November 21, 1831. American *première*, in English, at the Park Theater, New York, April 7, 1834; in French, at the same theater, July 2, 1845. First performance at the Metropolitan during the season of 1883–84, in Italian. The Paris production of *Robert le Diable* was such an overwhelming success that it made the fortune of the Opéra. The public was stirred by the brilliant enactment of romance, legend, and history, heightened by music of a powerful dramatic appeal. To the striking scenic effects were added sonorous orchestration, effective recitatives, and fiery arias and ensembles. In the excitement of the moment, the public overlooked the many glaring absurdities of the story. A new genre had arrived at the opera, for *Robert le Diable* had joined Auber's *La Muette de Portici* and Rossini's *Guillaume Tell (William Tell)* in founding the romantic school of early-nineteenth-century opera. The flamboyant hand of French romanticism was now on grand opera. Of interest, too, is the fact that *Robert le Diable* was the first opera of Meyerbeer's to be produced after his arrival in Paris. Amid traces of lingering Italian influence, the score shows strong indications of Meyerbeer's later style, which is thoroughly French of the period.

The action takes place at Palermo during the thirteenth century

Robert, Duke of Normandy, is really the son of the Devil by a mortal woman, the chaste Princess Bertha, of Normandy. Disguised and bearing the name of Bertram, the fiend follows his son about, constantly leading him into temptation in the hope of winning his soul for hell. The mother's good influence clings to Robert, however, in the form of a foster sister, Alice.

Banished from Normandy because of evil deeds inspired by Bertram, Robert has come to Sicily. There he falls in love with the beautiful princess, Isabella, and she with him. Bertram does his best to break up the romance. Through his wiles Robert is kept from attending the tournament, the winner of which may claim Isabella's hand. His chance to win her seemingly lost, Robert, ready to resort to unfair means, is led by Bertram to a ruined convent at midnight. There Bertram summons the ghosts of faithless nuns in a macabre and impressive invocation.

The ghosts dance about Robert in wild diabolical revelry. With a magical branch, Robert puts Isabella's guards to sleep and tries to make her submit to his will. But she pleads with him so earnestly, in the famous aria, *"Robert, toi que j'aime"* ("Robert, you whom I love"), that he breaks the branch and forfeits its supernatural aid. Once more Bertram tempts Robert, by trying to induce him to sign a contract yielding his soul. As a final argument, he reveals himself as Robert's father. The young man, overcome by despair, is about to sign. But Alice repeats the last words of his mother, warning him against the fiend. The signing of the pact is thus delayed till the clock strikes twelve. The spell is broken, and Bertram disappears to the nether regions. Isabella now appears in her bridal robes, waiting at the altar for the redeemed Robert.

THE RCA-VICTOR RECORDS
(Sung in Italian)

Evocazione—Suore, che riposate (Evocation—Ye Slumb'ring Nuns): *Ezio Pinza, Bass, with Orch.* 6710, 12"

ACT II, SCENE 2—LA SCALA PRODUCTION, MILAN

Roméo et Juliette
(ROMEO AND JULIET)

OPERA IN five acts. Music by Charles François Gounod. Libretto, after Shakespeare, by Jules Barbier and Michel Carré. First produced at the Théâtre-Lyrique, Paris, April 27, 1867. American *première*, in Italian, at the New York Academy of Music on November 15, 1867. A performance in English occurred on January 14, 1881, at the Park Theater in Brooklyn. First performance at the Metropolitan, in French (for the first time in America), December 14, 1891, with Jean de Reszke and Emma Eames in the title roles, and Édouard de Reszke as Friar Laurence. Mme. Eames and the brothers de Reszke had previously appeared together in performances of *Roméo et Juliette* at the Paris Opéra during the season of 1888–89. Mme. Eames, succeeding Adelina Patti in the role at the Paris Opéra, had made her world debut in opera as Juliet. Another historic American debut in the role was Geraldine Farrar's at the Metropolitan on November 23, 1906. Amelita Galli-Curci was the sensational new Juliet in the Metropolitan revival of 1922.

Though lacking the sustained inspiration of *Faust*, Gounod's *Roméo et Juliette* has an engaging quality of its own in its wealth of pretty tunes and graceful orchestral writing. Moreover, in its title roles it offers an irresistible appeal to tenors and sopranos of marked dramatic resource. For though the opera in no way measures up to the poetic sublimities of Shakespeare's original, it remains the most popular and practicable of the many operatic settings of Shakespeare's immortal love story. Bellini's *I Capuletti e i Montecchi* (1830) was the greatest of the *Romeo and Juliet* operas preceding Gounod's, and Zandonai's *Giulietta e Romeo* (1922) is the most recent. Comparisons between the libretto of Gounod's opera and Shakespeare's text are, of course, futile and unfair. The opera is, in any case, an adequate condensation of the action of the play. The main sequence is preserved, and if there are fewer words than in the original, there is, at any rate, the consolation of music that is sweetly sentimental and sometimes of a dazzling brilliance, as in Juliet's waltz song of the first act. Some of Shakespeare's minor characters have been eliminated, and one character has been added, the page Stephano. For those who know Shakespeare's lines, a reading of the English version of Barbier and Carré's libretto naturally yields a few surprises.

Roméo et Juliette

CHARACTERS

JULIET, *daughter of Capulet*	*Soprano*	PARIS, *Capulet's kinsman*	*Baritone*
STEPHANO, *page to Romeo*	*Soprano*	GREGORIO, *Capulet's kinsman*	*Baritone*
GERTRUDE, *Juliet's nurse*	*Mezzo-soprano*	CAPULET, *a Veronese*	
ROMEO, *a Montague*	*Tenor*	*nobleman*	*Basso Cantante*
TYBALT, *Capulet's nephew*	*Tenor*	FRIAR LAURENCE	*Bass*
BENVOLIO, *friend of Romeo*	*Tenor*	THE DUKE OF VERONA	*Bass*
MERCUTIO, *friend of Romeo*	*Baritone*		

GUESTS, RELATIVES, AND RETAINERS OF THE CAPULETS AND MONTAGUES

The action takes place in Verona in the fourteenth century

R. Strohmeyer — ACT I—SAN FRANCISCO OPERA PRODUCTION

ACT I

SCENE: *Ballroom in Capulet's House, Verona.* Capulet, a Veronese noble-man, is giving a masked ball in honor of his daughter Juliet's entrance into society. When the guests have gone to the banquet hall, Juliet lingers behind and gives expression to her girlish joy in the famous waltz song, *"Je veux vivre dans ce rêve"* ("Is the tender dream of youth"). All the girl's excitement in the festive surroundings throbs through the lilting arietta. She is about to leave when Romeo enters, having ventured with some of his comrades, all masked, into the house of their enemy. It is a case of love at first sight, but the meeting is cut short by the appearance of Juliet's hotheaded cousin, Tybalt. Recognizing Romeo through his mask, Tybalt denounces him as a member of the hated house of Montague. A general fight is averted

480

by the timely intercession of Capulet, who, loath to have the festivities spoiled, permits Romeo and his friends to depart in peace.

ACT II

SCENE: *Capulet's Garden; Juliet's Apartment Above.* Romeo has again braved the wrath of the enemy for another chance to see Juliet. Gazing up at her balcony, he now sings a lovely serenade, the famous cavatina beginning *"Ah! lève-toi, soleil! fais pâlir les étoiles"* ("Rise, O sun! make the stars pale"). Juliet appears on the balcony, and the two sing a beautiful love duet. Juliet's nurse calls for her, and the girl re-enters her apartment.

R. Strohmeyer

ACT III, SCENE 2—SAN FRANCISCO OPERA PRODUCTION

After a few moments she returns to bid Romeo good night. The tender scene is resumed as Romeo pleads with Juliet to linger awhile yet (*"Ah! ne fuis pas encore!"*). Taking up the melody, Juliet cautions her lover that someone may see them together (*"Ah! l'on peut nous surprendre!"*). The duet continues in this vein till Juliet bids Romeo good night and returns to her chamber. Romeo remains a few ardent moments to tell the evening breeze of his love.

ACT III

SCENE 1: *Friar Laurence's Cell.* The secret marriage of Romeo and Juliet takes place in the cell of Friar Laurence, who hopes that the union will reconcile the rival houses. Juliet then returns to her home.

SCENE 2: *A Street in Verona.* Romeo's imprudent page, Stephano, having

Wide World Studio   ACT V—METROPOLITAN OPERA PRODUCTION

come in search of his master, sings an impertinent song before the Capulet
house. This soon brings out Gregorio, angry at having been awakened. He
scolds the troublesome youth, and when he recognizes him as Romeo's companion of the previous night, a fight results. They are interrupted by Mercutio and Tybalt, who immediately join in the quarrel. Romeo enters and
tries to act as peacemaker, feeling that he cannot properly fight with the
relatives of his bride. His efforts are unsuccessful. The fight is resumed, and
Romeo's friend, Mercutio, is wounded. Believing him dead, Romeo is now
forced to avenge him. In the ensuing action he kills Tybalt, and for this he
is banished by the Duke of Verona.

ACT IV

SCENE: *Juliet's Room.* Having found a way into Capulet's house at the risk
of his life, Romeo has penetrated to the room of his bride. There he bids
her a tender farewell. After he has departed, Friar Laurence enters, to tell
the girl that it was Tybalt's dying wish that she marry Paris, and that the
wedding is now being arranged. Counseling the despairing Juliet to be
patient, he gives her a potion which he tells her to drink when the marriage
ceremony is about to take place. It will induce a deathlike trance for an
extended period. After that she may escape from her tomb and fly with
Romeo. The good priest leaves her. Soon Juliet sees her father and Paris
approaching. Quickly draining the contents of the phial, she grows faint
and appears to fall lifeless into Capulet's arms.

ACT V

SCENE: *Juliet's Tomb.* In the silent vault of the Capulets, Juliet lies on the bier, still in a trance. Having failed to receive Friar Laurence's message, Romeo forces in the door to gain one last glimpse of the bride he believes dead. Awed by the gloom and solemnity of the place, he bursts into an impassioned apostrophe to Juliet's tomb and hymns her beauty, still unsullied by the touch of death. He stoops to give Juliet a farewell embrace and then drinks a deadly poison. No sooner has he swallowed it than he is startled to behold signs of life in Juliet's body. But it is too late! The despairing lovers have time only to say farewell. Juliet draws a dagger concealed among her burial garments and stabs herself. Romeo and Juliet enter into their eternal sleep clasped in each other's arms.

THE RCA-VICTOR RECORDS

(Sung in French)

ACT I

VALSE—JE VEUX VIVRE DANS CE RÊVE (Juliet's Waltz Song—Is the Tender Dream of Youth): *Jeanette MacDonald, Soprano, with Orch.* 15850, 12"
Eidé Noréna, Soprano, with Orch.
14742, 12"
Eleanor Steber, Soprano, RCA-Victor Orchestra, Jean Paul Morel, Cond.
12-0526, 12"

HJOERDIS SCHYMBERG AS JULIET

ACT II

ROMEO'S CAVATINA—AH! LÈVE-TOI, SOLEIL! (Arise, Fair Sun!): *Richard Crooks, Tenor, with Orch.*
15542, 12"
(In Album M-585)
Charles Dalmores, Tenor, with Orch.
15-1013, 12"
(Acoustical Recording)
Jussi Bjoerling, Tenor, with Orch., Nils Grevillius, Cond. 12-0527, 12"

ACT III

QUE FAIS-TU (Dainty Dove): *Gladys Swarthout, Mezzo-soprano, with Orch.*
11-8280, 12"
(In Album M-925)

RICHARD CROOKS AS ROMEO

483

La Rondine

(THE SWALLOW)

OPERATIC COMEDY in three (originally two) acts. Music by Giacomo Puccini. Text by Giuseppe Adami, adapted from a German libretto by A. M. Willner and H. Reichert. First performance, Monte Carlo, March 27, 1917. First United States performance, Metropolitan Opera House, March 10, 1928, with Lucrezia Bori, Editha Fleischer, Beniamino Gigli, and Armand Tokatyan, Vincenzo Bellezza conducting. Revived at the Metropolitan, January 17, 1936.

While attending a light opera at Vienna in 1912, Puccini was approached by an Austrian publisher with a magnificent offer for a similar work. Then came the war, Austria and Italy were at arms, and Puccini lost all hope of ever receiving the $40,000 that had been offered. As completed, the opera differed from what had been originally planned, yet in the delicacy and lightness of the music as well as in the effective employment of waltz rhythms, it is possible to imagine something of Viennese influence—perhaps, also, emulation of Strauss' *Der Rosenkavalier*.

Not yet so well known as Puccini's earlier operas, *La Bohème* and *Madama Butterfly*, *La Rondine* reveals the composer, though in a lighter mood, still a master at writing pleasing melody.

CHARACTERS

RAMBALDO, *a wealthy Parisian banker*	Bass	RUGGERO, *son of an old friend of Rambaldo's*	Tenor
MAGDA, *his mistress*	Soprano	LISETTA, *maid to Magda*	Soprano
		PRUNIÈRE, *a decadent poet*	Tenor

DANCERS AT THE BAL BULLIER, STUDENTS, FLOWER GIRLS

The action takes place in Paris and the Riviera during the Second Empire

ACT I

SCENE: *The Salon of Magda's Paris Home.* In Magda's rather Bohemian salon in Paris Prunière remarks that old-fashioned love is due for a revival. Magda, recalling a youthful idyl, is greeted with the mocking laughter of her guests, and Prunière characterizes her as a swallow who will return home, after flying about in the land of romance. In any case, she is introduced to Ruggero, son of her lover Rambaldo's friend, and his ingenuousness and sincerity attract her strongly to him.

ACT II

SCENE: *The Bal Bullier.* Rambaldo and Ruggero have both gone to the Bal Bullier, and Magda, her curiosity about the youth still possessing her, follows them, in company with her maid, Lisetta. As expected, Magda falls in love with Ruggero, so much so, in fact, that she leaves Rambaldo quite suddenly and goes off with her new-found love, who by this time returns her affection.

LUCREZIA BORI AS MAGDA

ACT III

SCENE: *The Villa of Magda and Ruggero on the Riviera.* Although Ruggero and Magda are very happy in the illicit relationship they have known for some time, he secretly writes his mother, asking her permission to marry the girl. The mother is willing, but she makes the stipulation that the lady of his choice must be blameless. Whereupon Magda, with an attitude not untainted by irony, leaves Ruggero to his mother and some eligible convent lass, and wings her way back home, like the swallow, to her banker Rambaldo.

THE RCA-VICTOR RECORDS
(Sung in Italian)

ACT I

ORE DOLCI E DIVINE (What Hours of Sweetness Divine): *Lucrezia Bori, Soprano, with Orch.* 14615, 12″
(In Album M-405)

Saw this show Los Angeles. Winter 51.

The lousiest music & story I have ever seen & heard!
DON'T WASTE YOUR MONEY BUYING it TICKET !!

R. Strohmeyer
ACT II—SAN FRANCISCO OPERA PRODUCTION

Der Rosenkavalier
(THE CAVALIER OF THE ROSE)

"A COMEDY for music by H. von Hofmannsthal . . . music by Richard Strauss." Thus reads the title page of the score, an indication of the poet's importance. First produced, January 26, 1911, at the Royal Opera House, Dresden. First performed in the United States, December 9, 1913, at the Metropolitan Opera House, New York, with Frieda Hempel as the Princess, Margarete Ober as Octavian, Anna Case as Sophie, Otto Goritz as Baron Ochs, Hermann Weil as Faninal, and Carl Jörn as the Singer. Alfred Hertz conducted. A Metropolitan revival of November 17, 1922, offered in the cast Florence Easton, Maria Jeritza, Marie Sundelius, Paul Bender, Gustav Schützendorf, and Orville Harrold. Still later casts included Lotte Lehmann and Irene Jessner, as the Princess; Maria Olszewska, Jarmila Novotna, and Risë Stevens, as Octavian; Editha Fleischer, Eleanor Steber, and Nadine Conner, as Sophie; Emanuel List and Deszo Ernster, as Baron Ochs, and Kurt Baum and John Carter, as the Singer.

The questionable morals of Strauss' *Salomé* and the shockingly harsh dissonances of his *Elektra* may operate against their permanence in the repertoire, but all are agreed that *Der Rosenkavalier* is a lasting delight. The libretto, by one of the most prominent of contemporary Continental authors, is in itself a masterpiece, combining elements of the comedy of intrigue, the comedy of manners, a bit of farce, and satire, all held together by the blended humor and pathos of Hofmannsthal, the symbolist and poet. For this, Strauss has supplied thoroughly captivating music. Although, from a historical point of view, it is a bit of an anachronism, he has made frequent use of the ever-delightful waltz, securing thereby an inimitable atmosphere of lightness and romance.

While making use of innumerable leading motives, Strauss has revealed a wealth of beautiful straightforward melody, hitherto unsuspected of the composer of the great symphonic poems.

CHARACTERS

PRINCESS VON WERDENBERG		BARON OCHS AUF LERCHENAU,
(THE FELDMARSCHALLIN) *Soprano*		*her cousin* *Bass*

486

Der Rosenkavalier

OCTAVIAN, *a young boy, scion of a noble family* Mezzo-soprano

HERR VON FANINAL, *a parvenu* Baritone

SOPHIE, *his daughter* Soprano

MARIANNE, *Faninal's house-keeper* Soprano

VALZACCHI, *an intrigant* Tenor

ANNINA, *his accomplice* Contralto

A SINGER, A FLUTE PLAYER, A NOTARY, COMMISSARY OF POLICE, LACKEYS OF FANINAL, A MASTER OF CEREMONIES, AN INNKEEPER, A MILLINER, A NOBLE WIDOW AND THREE NOBLE ORPHANS, A HAIRDRESSER AND HIS ASSISTANTS, WAITERS, MUSICIANS, GUESTS, TWO WATCHMEN, KITCHEN SERVANTS, AND SEVERAL SUSPICIOUS APPARITIONS

The action takes place in Vienna, during the early part of the reign of Maria Theresa

Der Rosenkavalier begins with an orchestral introduction typical of Richard Strauss, yet sounding the mood of the work: impetuous, capricious, and witty. It grows to an impassioned climax ("parodied," according to Strauss' directions). The music then subsides to a mood of tranquillity mingled with tender yearning.

ACT I

SCENE: *The Princess' Bedroom.* Morning sunlight is streaming into the room as the very youthful Octavian kneels at the feet of the Princess von Werdenberg and declares a great love for her. She returns his passion, but alas, sounds, which the lovers believe to be her husband unexpectedly returning, disturb them. Octavian quickly conceals himself and puts on the dress of a lady's maid. Meanwhile the fears of the Princess are turned into amusement, for the person who arrives is the boastful and debauched Baron Ochs of Lerchenau. He noisily enters the room to ask the assistance of the Princess in his approaching marriage with Sophie Faninal. When Octavian, in his maid's disguise, has emerged from hiding, the observing Baron at once begins to flirt and invites "her" to supper with him. Meanwhile, the Princess has her usual morning interviews and is entertained by a flute player and an Italian tenor, and driven quite to distraction, besides, by the motley company of favor-seekers and tradesmen and the like.

The Baron leaves with the Princess a silver rose, which he requests her to have delivered to his bride, according to a custom of the day. He then departs, and in a moment of quiet and sadness the Princess meditates on her fading charms, and soon she will no longer be able to hold her lover. Octavian also goes, bidding her a tender farewell. When he has left, the Princess, suddenly remembering the rose, hurriedly sends a servant to him with it, for Octavian to deliver.

ACT II

SCENE: *Faninal's House.* All is excitement at the Faninal household, for Sophie is to marry a real notable, and now the ceremony of the presentation of the rose is to take place. Octavian enters, radiant in garments of white and silver. The music glistens and scintillates even as do the Knight of the Rose and the silver gage he bears. However, Sophie and Octavian are overwhelmed by each other and are able to speak only in the most hesitant fashion, for although they do not quite know it, they are already deeply in love.

Left alone for a moment, they suddenly confess their mutual affection, and forgetful of all else sing of the rapture of their love.

Through the earnest efforts of Valzacchi and Annina, a pair of scandalmongers, the Baron comes upon the young people, discovering them in each other's arms. In the subsequent duel Octavian slightly wounds the Baron's hand. Sophie, disgusted with the Baron's crude, blustering manner, refuses to marry him; but her father, seeing his social ambitions for a noble alliance broken, declares she shall marry the Baron or take the veil. Meanwhile Octavian has set his wits to work, assisted by the willing Annina, and now the Baron receives a note from the alleged waiting-maid of the Princess. The Baron thinks with delight of the dinner he is to have with "her."

ACT III

SCENE: *A Private Chamber in a Hotel of Questionable Repute in the Suburbs of Vienna.* Octavian, again in disguise as a maid, keeps the rendezvous at an inn. There such a host of tricks of Octavian's devising are played on the Baron that he believes himself mad. Faces appear from blank windows and trapdoors. Suddenly a woman with a horde of screaming children enters, claiming the Baron as husband and father! In the midst of this turmoil come the police, who arrest the Baron as a seducer of women. Faninal is furious to discover his prospective son-in-law in this brawl; Sophie renounces him. Upon the arrival of the Princess, the police withdraw, and Octavian reveals himself to the Baron in his usual male attire. The Baron begins to perceive how he has been duped, and is presently the butt of the mockery of everyone present. The Princess brings together the youthful lovers, and to the glowing music of the trio and finale expresses her sorrow and, lastly, her resignation at the loss of her youthful admirer, while Sophie and Octavian drink in their dreamlike bliss. The Princess takes her leave; the glittering music of "The Presentation of the Rose" returns in the orchestra, and Sophie and Octavian linger for a moment to tell one another yet again that their love is eternal. Then they also go. The room is empty and in semidarkness. An amusing, twittering melody darts up and down through the orchestra. The door opens, a little black servant boy runs in, picks up a handkerchief that Sophie has dropped, trips lightly out again. The curtain falls.

Der Rosenkavalier

THE RCA-VICTOR RECORDS
(Sung in German)

ABRIDGED RECORDING: *Lotte Lehmann, Soprano; Richard Mayr, Bass; Maria Olszewska, Contralto; Elisabeth Schumann, Soprano; Viktor Madin, Baritone; Anne Michalsky, Soprano; Hermann Gallos, Tenor; Bella Paalen, Contralto; Karl Ettl, Bass; William Wegnick, Tenor; Vienna State Opera Chorus; Vienna Philharmonic Orchestra, Robert Heger, Cond.*
DM-196 (17119-17131), 13-12"
M-196 (7917-7929)

ELEANOR STEBER AS SOPHIE

ORCHESTRAL SUITE (Arr. Antal Dorati): *Cincinnati Symphony Orchestra, Eugene Goossens, Cond.*
DM-997 (11-8786-11-8788), 3-12"
M-997 (11-8783-11-8785)

MICHAEL BOHNEN AS BARON OCHS

WALTZES (Orchestral): *The Philadelphia Orchestra, Eugene Ormandy, Conductor*
18390, 12"

WALTZES (Arr. Duo Piano): *Vitya Vronsky and Victor Babin, Duo Pianists*
13150

ACT II

HERR KAVALIER! (Finale—Letter Scene and Waltzes): *Alexander Kipnis, Bass; Else Ruziczka, Mezzo-soprano; with Orch.*
7894, 12"

LOTTE LEHMANN AS THE PRINCESS VON WERDENBERG

Ruddigore
(OR, THE WITCH'S CURSE)

COMIC OPERA in two acts. Music by Arthur Sullivan. Libretto by W. S. Gilbert. First produced at the Savoy Theatre, London, January 22, 1887. Though Gilbert regarded *Ruddigore* as one of his three best books, it was also the one that brought both him and Sullivan a long series of irritations. To begin with, while working on the new operetta, the collaborators were often at loggerheads over the question of precedence. Gilbert complained that Sullivan was giving it too much music, and Sullivan objected that he was giving it too little, that, in fact, the new work was "becoming a play with a few songs and some concerted music." Then, at the *première*, something almost blasphemous occurred, the booing of a Gilbert and Sullivan operetta, not too much booing, but enough to make producer, librettist, and composer anxious for the future. Cuts were speedily made in the lengthy score. A further misfortune soon befell the new work when George Grossmith, the Robin Oakapple, was hurried off to the hospital to undergo an operation for peritonitis. The jinx persisted, for a storm of protest now arose over the original title, *Ruddygore*. Sensitive souls quivered over its connotations of "bloody." Accordingly, the *y* became an *i*, but the issue still raged and friends continued to twit Gilbert about the title even in its bowdlerized form. "How's *Bloodygore?*" asked a friend of Gilbert's one day. "You mean *Ruddigore*," Gilbert replied. "Same thing," came the retort. "Indeed," said Gilbert. "Then if I say that I admire your ruddy countenance—which I do—it means that I like your bloody cheek—which I don't." As a matter of fact, Gilbert was so put out by the gibes and protests that he proposed altering the title to *Kensington Gore; or, Not So Good as the Mikado*.

Something even more serious threatened when the French press raised objection to Richard Dauntless' opening ballad, in which harmless fun is poked at the "Mounseers" (Monsieurs) and "Parley-voos" of the French navy. International friction was averted when Gilbert and Sullivan wrote to the editors of the Paris *Figaro* showing how "parley-voo" was used in the same good-natured way as "rosbif" and "goddam" in French comedies ridiculing the English. Actually, *Ruddigore* is an amiable burlesque of the blood-and-thunder melodrama that used to crowd the old English stage with elaborate spectacles of lurid crime. Sullivan supplied it with a stirring score, and Gilbert achieved one of his most fascinating mixtures of arrant absurdity and satiric merriment.

CHARACTERS

SIR RUTHVAN MURGATROYD, *disguised as Robin Oakapple, a young farmer* Baritone

RICHARD DAUNTLESS, *his foster brother, a man-o'-war's man* Tenor

SIR DESPARD MURGATROYD *of Ruddigore, a wicked baronet* Baritone

OLD ADAM GOODHEART, *Robin's faithful servant* Bass

ROSE MAYBUD, *a village maiden* Soprano

MAD MARGARET Soprano

DAME HANNAH, *Rose's aunt* Contralto

ZORAH, *professional bridesmaid*

CHORUS OF OFFICERS, PROFESSIONAL BRIDESMAIDS, VILLAGERS, AND GHOSTLY ANCESTORS

ACT I

SCENE: *The Cornish Fishing Village of Rederring, Showing the Harbor and Rose Maybud's Cottage.* The village boasts a subsidized corps of professional bridesmaids, but no weddings have occurred for at least six months. The village beauty, Rose, will have none of her many suitors, and the bridesmaids, fearful of losing their endowment, try to persuade Dame Hannah, Rose's aunt, to marry Adam, Robin Oakapple's aged servant.

Hannah, however, is pledged to eternal maidenhood. Years ago she was betrothed to a youth who wooed her under an assumed name. On the day they were to marry, she discovered that he was none other than Sir Roderic Murgatroyd, one of an accursed line. Hannah now tells the girls how her suitor's ancestor, Sir Rupert Murgatroyd, had employed his time in persecuting witches, and how one of his victims, in mortal agony at the stake, had laid this curse on him: "Each lord of Ruddigore, despite his best endeavor, shall do one crime, or more, once every day, for ever." The penalty for defying the curse is death by torture on the day the crimes cease, and each lord of Ruddigore has so died.

When Hannah chides Rose for not returning the love of "some gallant youth," Rose explains her difficulty. The youths of the village are bashful, and it would hardly become her to make advances. Rose, a foundling, bases her ideals on a book of etiquette which, together with a change of baby linen, was her sole possession when she was discovered in a plated dish cover suspended from the knocker of the workhouse door.

Robin enters to consult Rose on the predicament of a friend who is in love with a maid but is too diffident to tell her. Rose similarly wishes to ask his advice as to her friend, and they accordingly "consult" in a charming duet, without, however, mending matters.

Robin Oakapple is really Sir Ruthven Murgatroyd, but fearful of inheriting the title and the curse, he has fled his home and taken an assumed name. His younger brother, Despard, believing him to be dead, has succeeded to the title. Old Adam enters now and informs Robin that his foster brother, Richard, is home from the sea. This news is quickly followed by the entry of Richard himself. He kisses all the girls, spins them the yarn of the "Bold Mounseer," and dances a hornpipe as an appropriate climax.

Dick and Robin exchange greetings, and Robin, on being upbraided for being sad, tells his foster brother of his love for Rose, and of the shyness that prevents him from declaring it. Richard consults "the dictates of his heart," which tells him to speak up for his friend. Robin is overjoyed and sings a song, the burden of which is that, "If you wish in the world to advance . . . you must stir it and stump it, and blow your own trumpet."

Dick goes off on his self-imposed mission, but no sooner does he see Rose than his heart "dictates" once again, saying: "This is the very lass for *you*, Dick." He forgets Robin, and makes love on his own account.

Entering with the bridesmaids, Robin is astounded at the unexpected turn events have taken. Still, he has sworn to stand by Dick through thick and thin. Thus, while pretending to agree, he "gets his own back" by making many disquieting insinuations about the less respectable aspects of a sailor's life. This clever move turns the tables on Richard, and Rose forsakes him for Robin.

A new character is now introduced—Mad Margaret—whose mind has been unbalanced by the cruel treatment of Sir Despard Murgatroyd, the "Bad Baronet." She is actually trying to find Rose Maybud, of whom she is jealous, having heard that Sir Despard intends to carry her off as one of his daily "crimes." Rose tells her, however, that she need not fear, as she (Rose) is pledged to another. Despard Murgatroyd and his following of "Bucks" and "Blades" now appear. They are welcomed by the bridesmaids, who are tired of village swains, and are delighted with the swaggering newcomers in their gorgeous military uniforms.

Despard bewails his lot, for, being really thoroughly good, he is condemned to be thoroughly bad. He tries to balance his account of evil and good by getting his crime over the first thing in the morning, and then being good for the rest of the day. For example, in the morning he steals a child, and later in the day he builds an orphan asylum. Richard enters. To pay off his score against Robin, he reveals his secret to Despard, who is overjoyed to learn that he is not the real heir, for his elder brother is still living. They resolve to act without delay, for Rose and Robin, with the bridesmaids, have entered for the wedding ceremony. A lovely madrigal is sung, followed by a gavotte. The procession is about to start for the church, when Despard enters, and challenges Robin, claiming him as his elder brother, Sir Ruthven Murgatroyd, rightful heir to the baronetcy of Ruddigore. Robin cannot deny the fact, and Rose, in spite of Richard's blandishments, forsakes him, and offers herself to Despard. This offer is refused, for Despard, once again virtuous, keeps his vow to Margaret. Rose returns to Richard, and Robin, now the "Bad Baronet," falls senseless to the ground.

ACT II

SCENE: *Picture Gallery in Ruddigore Castle.* Round the walls are full-length portraits of the baronets of Ruddigore from the time of James I—the first being that of Sir Rupert; the last, that of the latest deceased baronet, Sir Roderic. Sir Ruthven and Adam enter melodramatically. They are greatly altered, Sir Ruthven looking guilty and haggard, and Adam filling the part of steward to such a wicked man. They hate the life, but there is no help for it, and they are trying to think of new crimes to commit. Adam suggests that as Richard has come to the castle with Rose Maybud to ask for Sir Ruthven's consent to their marriage, a really excellent crime would be to "poison their beer!" This is too much for Sir Ruthven, who has not yet reached the requisite state of "badness." Rose and Richard enter happily, and Sir Ruthven, thinking he has her in his power, threatens to cast her into a dungeon, and calls for assistance. He is foiled by Richard, who produces a small Union Jack, which even a "Bad Baronet" cannot defy. Rose pleads with Sir Ruthven, who yields to her, gives his consent, and allows them to leave unmolested.

The scene darkens. When it grows light again the pictures have become animated. A soft chorus of men's voices is heard as the ghosts of the ancestors step from their frames and march about, the last being Sir Roderic.

The ancestors reproach Sir Ruthven for having failed to fulfill the curse, and Sir Roderic sings an eerie song, "The Ghosts' High-noon." Sir Ruthven realizes who they are, and makes many weak excuses. For instance, he committed no crime on Monday because it was a Bank Holiday. On Tuesday he made a false income-tax return, on Wednesday he forged his own will, and so on. These misdemeanors do not satisfy the ghosts, who, after giving him a taste of the torture awaiting him if he fails to commit some real crimes, allow him one more chance. They command him to carry off a lady at once. Sir Ruthven consents, and the ghosts, having made him pardon them ("for having agonized him so"), return to their frames. The low, soft chorus is heard again, and the gallery assumes its normal aspect.

Sir Ruthven bids Adam go at once to the village and carry off a maiden. Despard and Margaret now appear. They, too, are changed, both being soberly dressed in garments of a formal cut. They run a National School, and Margaret is District Visitor. They have come to urge Sir Ruthven to abandon his wild courses. Despard points out that although Sir Ruthven has been a "Bad Baronet" for only a week, he is responsible, in the eyes of the law, for all the crimes committed by him, Despard, during the past ten years. This so appalls Sir Ruthven that he swears to reform.

Meanwhile Adam has returned, bringing with him Dame Hannah, who seizes the sword from a suit of armor on the wall, and makes for Sir Ruthven. In an agony of terror, he invokes the aid of his uncle, Sir Roderic, who once again steps from his picture.

Sir Roderic and Hannah, who were lovers before his death, ten years before, now recognize each other. Sir Ruthven is ordered by his uncle to leave them together. Hannah sings of her old love for him and bursts into tears, but at this moment Sir Ruthven rushes in excitedly, followed by all the other characters and the chorus of bridesmaids. An idea has occurred to him. Since a baronet of Ruddigore can die only through refusing to commit a daily crime, the refusal is tantamount to suicide. But suicide being itself a crime, Sir Roderic ought never to have died. This is all very satisfactory. Rose returns to her first love, Sir Ruthven, and Richard has to take Zorah, the chief bridesmaid, and the opera ends with a joyful chorus.

THE RCA-VICTOR RECORDS
(Sung in English)

COMPLETE RECORDING: *D'Oyly Carte Company; Dr. Malcolm Sargent, Cond.; under the personal direction of Rupert D'Oyly Carte. (The cast includes: Muriel Dickson, Nellie Briercliffe, Dorothy Gill, Alice Moxon, George Baker, Derek Oldham, Sydney Granville, Stuart Robertson.)*

DC-19 (13295-13303), 9-12"
C-19 (11510-11518)

Russlan and Ludmilla

OPERA IN five acts. Music by Mikhail Ivanovich Glinka. Libretto by Glinka and several collaborators, after the poem by Pushkin. First produced in St. Petersburg on December 9, 1842. The rambling libretto of Glinka's best-known opera was largely responsible for the dismal failure of the *première*. Pushkin himself was to have adapted the poem for operatic use, but he was slain in a duel before he began work on it. The libretto then circulated among Glinka's literary friends. When it again returned to him, it showed the collective surgery of five distinct personalities—K. Bakhturin, Nestor Kukolnik, Mikhail Gedeonov, N. Markevich, and a military man, Captain Shirkov. Glinka applied some finishing touches of his own. *Russlan and Ludmilla* proved a bitter disappointment to Russians who had been excited by Glinka's earlier opera, *A Life for the Tsar*. The patchwork fantasy of evil dwarfs, magically evoked storms, Tartar sorcerers, and mysterious abductions left the audience cold. Many even charged Glinka with desecrating the memory of Pushkin. And the music was another source of irritation. Here were strange new tricks of harmony and rhythm. Themes sounded exotic, barbaric, Oriental. For the public of 1842 this was harsh modernism indeed. Few suspected that Glinka's score would revolutionize Russian music. A fresh, national idiom was born in St. Petersburg that night, but only a handful of Glinka's friends hymned its coming. Indeed, so harsh was the reaction that the Grand Duke Mikhail Pavlovich punished offending officers by forcing them to attend performances of *Russlan and Ludmilla*. The opera is known to the outside world principally through its vital little Overture, though record collectors have long prized Feodor Chaliapin's version of Farlaf's famous "Patter Song," the Rondo.

CHARACTERS

SVIETOSAR, *Grand Duke of Kiev*	Bass	FARLAF, *a third suitor of Ludmilla*	Bass
LUDMILLA, *his daughter*	Soprano	GORISLAVA, *in love with Ratmir*	Soprano
RUSSLAN, *a knight in love with Ludmilla*	Baritone	FINN, *a sorcerer*	Tenor
		TCHERNOMOR, *a dwarf*	
RATMIR, *another suitor of Ludmilla*	Contralto	NAINA, *a fairy*	Mezzo-soprano

The action takes place in legendary Russia

The Overture follows classical patterns strictly. A tutti of fortissimo chords opens it, after which the chief theme (Presto, D major, 2-2) is sung by violins, violas, and flute. A lively passage for woodwinds, against pizzicato in the strings, follows. Then a folklike theme of lilting suavity is brought in by violas, cellos, and bassoon, in F major. The orchestra reviews it fortissimo, and a final melody is introduced, based on one of Russlan's arias. The material is worked over, and a rousing coda sets in. The whole-tone scale may be noted in a descending bass passage of the coda. This device Glinka used in the opera to depict the malign plotting of the gnome Tchernomor, thus foreshadowing the Wagnerian leitmotiv. Glinka's whole-tone innovation precedes Debussy's by half a century.

ACT I

SCENE: *The Court of Svietosar, Grand Duke of Kiev.* Three men have come to the court of Svietosar to sue for the hand of his daughter Ludmilla. They are the Russian knight, Russlan; the Varangian freebooter, Farlaf, and Ratmir, a wandering minstrel from the distant East. In the midst of the festivities surrounding their courtship, the lights suddenly go out and Ludmilla mysteriously disappears. This provides the anxious father with a way of settling the dispute: Ludmilla shall become the bride of the suitor who rescues her from the fiendish power that has spirited her away.

ACT II

SCENE 1: *The Cave of the Sorcerer Finn.* From the friendly sorcerer, Finn, who dwells in a cave, Russlan learns of Ludmilla's abduction by the dwarf Tchernomor. Moreover, he is cautioned against the machinations of the evil sprite, Naina, who is siding with the adventurer Farlaf in the contest for Ludmilla.

SCENE 2: *The Forest Dwelling of Naina.* Like Russlan, Farlaf is seeking the help of sorcery in his hunt for Ludmilla. If the valiant knight has his Finn, Farlaf has his Naina, who urges the unscrupulous suitor to bide his time. Let Russlan do the work of finding the Grand Duke's daughter, she counsels; then Farlaf will kidnap her all over again.

SCENE 3: *A Battlefield.* Guided by Finn's instructions, Russlan now finds himself in a field shrouded in mist. As the mist begins to lift, he stoops to pick up a lance, only to start back at the sight of a monstrous head lying on the ground. So powerful is the breathing of this awesome object that it gives rise to a violent tempest. Siegfried-like, Russlan lunges at the head with his lance and quells its roaring. As he steps back he discovers a magic sword, which the vanquished head divulges will help him overcome Ludmilla's gnomish abductor.

ACT III

SCENE: *Naina's Enchanted Domain.* Russlan now becomes a kind of Odysseus tempted by the wicked blandishments of a Russian Circe. Ratmir, one of Ludmilla's three suitors, has already succumbed to the charms of Naina's lovely companions. The same fate is about to overtake Russlan when his sorcerer friend, Finn, arrives and uses his magic powers to help him resist a bevy of sirens.

ACT IV

SCENE: *Tchernomor's Dwelling.* Russlan finally reaches Ludmilla's place of captivity. Fatigued by fear and hardship, the girl has fallen asleep, only to be awakened by Tchernomor on Russlan's arrival. Before he confronts the armed knight, the dwarf casts a spell of permanent sleep upon Ludmilla. In the duel that follows, Russlan defeats the evil gnome with the magic sword he had won from the monstrous head, and then tries to awaken the unconscious girl, but in vain.

ACT V

SCENE: *Same as Act I.* The obliging Finn again comes to the aid of his heartbroken friend. As all are despairing over the fate of the spellbound princess, the wizard fetches a gold ring from his store of magic objects and with it Russlan is enabled to break the trance. Having restored Ludmilla to her anxious father, Russlan has no need of claiming his reward, for the princess has already made up her mind.

THE RCA-VICTOR RECORDS
(Sung in Russian)

OVERTURE: *Indianapolis Symphony Orchestra, Fabien Sevitsky, Cond.*   17731, 12″
    Boston "Pops" Orchestra, Arthur Fiedler, Cond.   4427, 10″ (In Album M-554)

ACT II

FARLAF'S RONDO (Patter Song): *Feodor Chaliapin, Bass, with Orch.*   7704, 12″

ACT I, TABLEAU I—THE HALL OF THE MERCHANTS' GUILD

Sadko

OPERA IN seven tableaux; music by Nikolai Rimsky-Korsakov; text by the composer and V. I. Byelsky, after several variants of the legends concerning the eleventh-century min-strel-hero, Sadko.

First produced, January 7, 1898, at the Private Opera House, Moscow. Public hear-ings at St. Petersburg, spring, 1898, and February 8, 1901, Maryinski Theater. Portions have been sung in concert form in the United States, but the opera as a whole was first performed in America by the Metropolitan Opera Company, January 25, 1930, with Edward Johnson in the title role, Editha Fleischer as Volkhova, Gladys Swarthout as Nejata, and Rafaelo Diaz as the Hindu.

The ever-stormy North Sea that inspired Wagner in the writing of his *Flying Dutchman* also supplied Rimsky-Korsakov with a background for his sea music that figures prominently in *Sadko* as well as *Scheherazade* and other works. Wagner's won-derful sea music, of course, is profoundly subjective; Rimsky-Korsakov's, also very beautiful, is equally objective in character. In fact, Wagner's dictum regarding Men-delssohn, "A landscape painter in tones," might well be paraphrased for Rimsky-Korsakov, "A seascape painter in tones." His knowledge of the sea was intimate, for dur-ing a number of years he was an officer in the Russian navy. In his very interesting autobiography he even describes his visits to American ports; and he writes of the North Sea, in its wild, changeful moods, in a most entertaining manner.

In the legend of Sadko, Rimsky-Korsakov found material perfectly adaptable to his genius, which was always at its best in the treatment of nature, the fantastic, and the legendary. His interest in the pantheism and legends of his country, charmingly revealed in the fanciful *Snow Maiden*, was here offered a broader canvas for its expres-sion. The text, written by the composer with the aid of Byelsky, was taken from the several versions of the epic of Sadko; moreover, expressions and decorative and scenic details have been preserved exactly as they are in the old legends and songs. A youthful symphonic poem, *Sadko* was the basis of a ballet of that name danced in this country by Diaghilev's company in 1916.

Gray

ACT II, TABLEAU II—THE PORT OF NOVGOROD

Musically, *Sadko* is a thorough blending of the two contrasting styles that have persisted throughout the history of Russian opera: the lyrical manner of Glinka, and the declamatory style inaugurated by Dargomijsky. The thoroughly Russian flavor of the music is remarkable throughout the opera. For special effects other styles are contrasted with it: the vigorous and characteristically Scandinavian melody and harmonies of the song of the Viking merchant, the Oriental "Song of India," and the delightfully Italianate barcarolle of the Venetian. The opera is orchestrated in Rimsky-Korsakov's most glowing colors; one of the striking features of the orchestration is the clever imitation of the sound of the gusli by means of a combination of piano and harp. The gusli is a native Russian instrument that dates back to the most remote antiquity.

CHARACTERS

THE KING OF THE OCEAN — *Bass*

VOLKHOVA, *his favorite daughter* — *Soprano*

SADKO, *singer and gusli player at Novgorod* — *Tenor*

LUBAVA, *his wife* — *Mezzo-soprano*

NEJATA, *gusli player from Kiev* — *Contralto*

A VIKING ⎫

A HINDU ⎬ *foreign merchants*

A VENETIAN ⎭ — *Bass / Tenor / Baritone*

AN APPARITION, *a great hero in the garb of an old pilgrim* — *Baritone*

THE TWO ELDERS, *chiefs among the merchants of Novgorod* — *Tenor and Bass*

BUFFOONS — *Two Mezzo-sopranos, Tenor, and Bass*

CHORUS: MEN AND WOMEN, CITIZENS OF NOVGOROD; MERCHANTS OF NOVGOROD AND FOREIGN LANDS; THE COMPANIONS OF SADKO; THE DAUGHTERS OF THE KING OF THE OCEAN. BALLET: THE QUEEN OF THE OCEAN; THE BROOKS AND RIVERS, AND ALL THE MARVELOUS INHABITANTS OF THE REALM OF THE KING OF THE OCEAN. ACCORDING TO A NOTE IN THE SCORE, THE SEVEN TABLEAUX MAY BE PRESENTED IN THREE OR FIVE ACTS. IN THIS DESCRIPTION THE OPERA IS TREATED AS A WORK IN THREE ACTS

498

ACT I

TABLEAU I

SCENE: *Hall of the Merchants' Guild in Novgorod.* The members of the
merchants' guild of Novgorod sit at their richly laden tables in their sumptuous hall. They sing a lively song and praise the prosperity and freedom of
their own country, in which neither king nor soldier is the ruler, but the merchant. The two elders ask Nejata, singer and gusli player from Kiev, to sing
a song of old heroic times. When the singer has finished, the merchants applaud, then ask for a singer who will praise their own Novgorod. At this moment, Sadko appears, his gusli hung from his shoulder. He essays to comply
with their request, but he sings, rather, a song telling of his own strange ideas.
Novgorod, he says, is merely on a lake; he would have their ships carried to
the ocean, whence they could sail away and return with fortunes from all
the world. This Sadko would do and in doing become the richest in all
Novgorod. The merchants discuss his idea, but the elders are opposed to such
an innovation. Sadko, laughed at with scorn, bids the proud merchants farewell and departs with his gusli. The merchants continue their festivities and
are entertained with a comic song and a dance of buffoons.

TABLEAU II

SCENE: *A Bank of Lake Ilmen.* Clear summer night reigns over Lake Ilmen;
the crescent-shaped moon is sinking toward the horizon. Sadko approaches,
playing upon his gusli; he sings of his unhappiness and implores aid even
from the murmuring waters of the lake.

Gray

SKETCH FOR ACT I, TABLEAU I

Suddenly a breeze springs up, the waters are agitated, and a group of swans appear, coming from the distance. As they draw near they are transformed into young maidens; Volkhova, the Sea Princess, is among them. They have been fascinated by Sadko's singing, and at the request of the Princess Sadko sings them a dancelike song; the sea maidens dance away into the woods, and the Princess sits near the marveling Sadko, weaves him a garland, confesses her love for him, and claims him as her own. Dawn approaches, however, and, in parting, she promises Sadko that he will catch three golden fish in the lake; he will journey to distant lands; she, meanwhile, will await him faithfully for many a year, and he will come to her. Now her father, the mighty King of the Ocean, summons his daughters back to his realm. The sea maidens swim away over the lake and disappear, as the sun rises.

ACT II

TABLEAU I

SCENE: *Lubava's Room.* Lubava stands before the little window of her room, awaiting the return of her husband, Sadko. She sings despairingly. She has waited all night, and now the bell for matins is sounding. She fears that he has been moved by his ambition to seek adventure in distant lands, yet only yesterday he vowed his love for her, played for her his gusli, and sang his songs.

Then, suddenly seeing Sadko coming in the distance, she sings joyously and runs to meet him. As he enters, he thrusts her rudely aside. The song of the sea maidens is still ringing in his ears, nor can he forget it. The sound of a bell reminds him that, now the service is ended, people will be coming out from church; this is the time to make use of his secret. Pushing away the lamenting Lubava, he shouts, "Farewell!" and rushes away as one mad.

TABLEAU II

SCENE: *Novgorod, on the Shores of Lake Ilmen.* Ships lie at the quay. The merchants and people of Novgorod swarm around the merchants from foreign lands—Viking, Venetian, and Hindu. Among the crowd are two soothsayers. Nejata sits alone at one side, holding his gusli. With the song of the people are mingled the chant of pilgrims, the ribald ditties of the buffoons, and the voices of the two elders consulting the soothsayers. Sadko appears, and all greet him with derisive laughter. Saluting them respectfully, he declares that he knows a deep secret: fish of gold can be caught in Lake Ilmen. The elders laugh. That is no secret, they say; it is only a dream. Sadko wagers his head against all the wealth of the haughty merchants that he can prove his claim. A boat is launched, a net lowered. All await in hushed expectancy.

From the depths of the lake is heard the voice of the Sea Princess repeating her assurance. The net is raised, Sadko takes from it three golden fish, and is triumphantly acclaimed. He summons all adventurous young men to join him in his exploits. And while they are away preparing themselves, Nejata leads in the singing of the symbolic legend of the nightingale that became a great merchant.

Sadko and his followers return in gala attire, ready for the voyage, and he announces that he will restore the merchants their shops and goods—he desires only their ships. He asks three foreign merchants to sing of their own lands that he may decide to which he should go. First the Viking replies, singing of a rugged coast on which breaks a stormy sea, the swords and arrows of the Norsemen which spare not the enemy, Odin, their great god, and the sea, their destiny!

The people, with hushed voices, counsel Sadko not to visit that habitation of brigands. Next the Hindu sings his exotic lay, the celebrated "Song of India": India, land of incalculable gems, land where the maiden-faced Phoenix sings and hovers over the gleaming ocean, and the hearer forgets the world, as in a dream.

"Do not go there!" the people murmur. Now the Venetian sings a barcarolle, telling of his city, its wealth, its beauty—"Venice, Queen of the Ocean." Thither Sadko will go. Requesting the Novgorod merchants to care for Lubava, he bids her an affectionate farewell, and sets sail. Soon the ships disappear in the red glow of the sunset.

ACT III

TABLEAU I

SCENE: *Sadko's Ship*, The Falcon. Calm in mid-ocean. *The Falcon* slowly draws near; the other ships of his fleet pass by. *The Falcon* remains becalmed, and twilight falls over the sea.

Now, after twelve years, says Sadko, they are returning laden with gold and jewels, but they have not yet sacrificed to the King of the Ocean. Therefore sailors pour overboard great treasures. Still they remain becalmed. Another gift is desired. At Sadko's order, logs are cast into the water and all float away excepting Sadko's, which plunges directly to the bottom of the ocean. The sailors are overawed. A ladder is lowered, as Sadko has commanded, and that hardy mariner-minstrel, gusli in hand, descends to a plank that has been thrown overboard. Immediately a breeze springs up, and *The Falcon* sails away. Sadko, abandoned in mid-ocean, begins to play his gusli, and soon the Sea Princess is heard, calling. There is a sudden surging of the waters, and Sadko is drawn down into the deep. Clouds obscure the scene, and when they clear away we behold:

TABLEAU II

SCENE: *The Palace of the Sea King in the Ocean Depths.* Azure, iridescent, and transparent, rising in the dim, blue-green light at the bottom of the sea, is the palace of the King of the Sea. The King and Queen are on their thrones, Volkhova at her wheel, spinning seaweeds. The sea maidens are weaving wreaths of flowers, as Sadko appears. He greets the King and, at Volkhova's request, sings for him. In reward he is promised the hand of the Princess in marriage. Summoned by a blast of trumpets, there comes a great procession of wedding guests: the elder daughters of the King—the swift rivers; his nieces—the clear brooks; white water nixies; fish of gold and silver, and other wonders of the deep. The whale guards the entrance. All take their places according to their rank, and the marriage of Sadko and Volkhova is celebrated with song and dance. The clear brooks and little springs perform their lightly flowing divertissement; then follow the fish of gold and silver with their gayer movements. At the King's request, Sadko begins to play his gusli and sing; the inhabitants of the deep waters dance, gracefully, undulantly. Such is the charm of the minstrel's music that the King and Queen cannot resist joining the dance. Gradually the music and the movements of the dancers grow faster and faster, and, at length, become so frenzied that the waters of the ocean are stirred; a storm is raised on the surface of the sea and great ships are sunk. Suddenly an apparition of an old legendary hero appears, strikes the gusli from Sadko's hands, and the dance ends with a crash. The apparition speaks, saying that the reign of the King of the Ocean must end and that Sadko must return to Novgorod. Sadko and Volkhova seat themselves in a shell and are drawn away by sea gulls while the palace and all the court vanish in obscurity.

TABLEAU III

SCENE: *The Shore of Lake Ilmen.* The prelude pictures the voyage of Sadko and the Princess as they are drawn with lightning speed across the ocean.

In the gray light of early morning Sadko is seen asleep by the shore of Lake Ilmen, while around him rushes sway lightly in the breeze, and Volkhova watches over him, singing a lullaby.

Now the rosy light of dawn creeps over the waters of the lake. The Princess sings the sleeping minstrel a touching farewell, vanishes in a mist, and is converted into the mighty river Volkhova, flowing from Lake Ilmen to the sea. Thus will she be forever faithful to her singer, forever near his songs!

Lubava, still lamenting her husband, approaches the lake distractedly. Great is her happiness and amazement on finding Sadko; and he, awakening, greets her affectionately and joyfully. He believes the past years to have been a dream until he sees his fleet coming up the newly created river—an outlet to the ocean for Novgorod.

The people hurry from the city to welcome their singer. Even the Hindu, the Viking, and the Venetian, each singing the melody of his own land, join in the chorus of salutation. And Sadko, now happily reunited with his wife, leads in the hymn of praise for the hero of olden times who calmed the ocean's storm, and for Volkhova, the Princess, now become their river.

Carlo Edwards
GLADYS SWARTHOUT AS NEJATA

THE RCA-VICTOR RECORDS
(Sung in Russian unless otherwise noted)

ACT II

Song of the Viking Guest: *Alexander Kipnis, Bass, with Orch.* 11-9284, 12″
(In Album M-1073)
Feodor Chaliapin, Bass, with Orch. 6867, 12″

Song of India (*Chanson Indoue*): *Richard Crooks, Tenor, with Orch. Sung in French* 10-1093, 10″

Song of India (Orchestral): *Boston "Pops" Orchestra, Arthur Fiedler, Cond.* 4303, 10″

Wide World Studio   SCENE FROM METROPOLITAN OPERA PRODUCTION

Salomé

OPERA IN one act. Music by Richard Strauss. Text, Oscar Wilde's French poem, as translated into German by Hedwig Lachmann. First performance, Dresden, December 9, 1905. First American production, Metropolitan Opera House, January 22, 1907, in German, with Olive Fremstad, Marion Weed, Karl Burrian, and Anton van Rooy, in the leading roles, and Alfred Hertz conducting. There had been, prior to this performance, a dress rehearsal at which more than 2000 people were present. These two showings were the only ones given at the Metropolitan until January 13, 1934, the work being banned, apparently, because of the to-do. The 1934 performance, under Artur Bodanzky's direction, offered Göta Ljungberg, Dorothee Manski, Max Lorenz, and Friedrich Schorr in the cast. Later presentations at the Metropolitan have had Lily Djanel, Marjorie Lawrence, and Ella Flesch, as Salomé; Karin Branzell, as Herodias; René Maison, Frederick Jagel, and Arthur Carron, as Herod; Herbert Janssen and Julius Huehn, as Jokanaan.

Although between 1907 and 1934 there were no *Salomé* performances at the Metropolitan, the breach was filled by Oscar Hammerstein's company, which gave the work a triumphant word (in French) at the Manhattan Opera House with a cast including Mary Garden, Augusta Doria, Charles Dalmorès, and Hector Dufranne, Cleofonte Campanini conducting. This was the cast on January 28, 1909. Hammerstein repeatedly presented the opera, and his tradition was followed, after his retirement, by the Chicago Civic Opera Company.

More than once in his extraordinary career Richard Strauss has shocked the musical public. He administered the greatest shock of all, however, with the one-act opera *Salomé;* but it was the text and the action, rather than the music, which in this instance offended a certain section of the operagoing fraternity. Music suggesting the ecstasies of physical love is not in itself—removed from the subject, that is—offensive;

but the morbidity and sensual decadence of certain scenes in *Salomé*, which are accompanied by voluptuous sounds in the orchestra, touched with no gentle hand the sensibilities of operagoers in a more conservative day.

CHARACTERS

HEROD	*Tenor*	FIVE JEWS	{*Four Tenors* {*One Bass*
HERODIAS	*Mezzo-soprano*		
SALOMÉ	*Soprano*	TWO NAZARENES	{*Tenor* {*Bass*
JOKANAAN	*Baritone*		
NARRABOTH	*Tenor*	TWO SOLDIERS	*Basses*
		A CAPPADOCIAN	*Bass*
THE PAGE OF HERODIAS	*Mezzo-soprano*	A SLAVE	*Mute part*

The action takes place on a terrace of the palace of Herod, about A.D. *30*

The story of the opera deals with the passion of Salomé for Jokanaan (John the Baptist), who has been imprisoned by Herod Antipas, Tetrarch of Judea, because he had publicly reproached Herod for marrying his brother's wife, Herodias. Jokanaan is kept imprisoned in a cistern in the courtyard of Herod's palace. Salomé, passing by, hears the prisoner's voice as he foretells a great catastrophe. Infatuated with the voice, she asks the guards to let her see the prisoner. They obey unwillingly as they have orders to let no one see Jokanaan. When he is brought from the cistern Salomé is immediately possessed of a fierce desire for him, but her brazen advances are repulsed; Jokanaan curses her, comparing her unfavorably with her wicked mother, and counsels her to seek out the Lord and ask forgiveness for her sins. She begs stubbornly for kisses but the prophet refuses to let her touch him.

Narraboth, an officer in charge of the guard over Jokanaan, is in love with Salomé, and, hearing her passionate entreaty to the Apostle, is suddenly filled with despair and kills himself at her feet. Jokanaan descends into the cistern. At this moment Herod and his wife, with their court, appear. Herod, already distracted by troubles with the Jews, with his wife, and with a passion for Salomé, his stepdaughter, is deeply disturbed upon finding the dead body of the young soldier. He orders it removed and to soothe his tormented soul asks Salomé to drink from his cup, to eat with him, to show some sign of interest in him. She refuses. Jokanaan from his cistern is heard declaiming against the evils of Herod's family, and Herodias demands that Herod silence the prisoner and hand him over to the Jews for punishment. Herod is unwilling to do this because he rather fears Jokanaan. Again the voice of the prisoner resounds, foretelling the coming of the Saviour. When Herod asks who the Saviour might be, he is told by the Nazarenes that he has already come and that he has raised the dead and performed other miracles.

With fear added to his other troubles, Herod asks Salomé to dance, hoping to be distracted from his ominous forebodings. Salomé refuses until Herod promises to grant anything she will ask if she will dance for him.

Inspired with an evil thought, Salomé performs the seductive Dance of the Seven Veils.

When it is over she throws herself at the feet of Herod and then demands her fee—the head of Jokanaan, brought to her on a silver charger. Herod is horrified and offers her instead all his store of jewels and riches. Stubbornly Salomé insists that he keep his oath and give her what she wishes. Egged on by his wife, Herod finally acquiesces and orders Jokanaan beheaded.

The executioner, a giant Negro, descends into the well, and Salomé eagerly listens for the sound of the death stroke. Presently the head is brought to her on a great silver tray. In a hideous ecstasy compounded of amorousness, vindictiveness, satisfied revenge, and unsatisfied passion, Salomé fondles and kisses the lips of the dead man's head, singing wildly of his beauty and of her triumph.

Herod, suddenly revolted by the sadistic and insatiable passion of Salomé, tells his wife that her daughter is a fiend. Commanding that the lights be extinguished, he turns suddenly and orders his soldiers to kill Salomé. They instantly crush her to death beneath their shields.

THE RCA-VICTOR RECORDS
(Sung in French)

SALOMÉ'S DANCE (Dance of the Seven Veils): *Leopold Stokowski and the Philadelphia Orchestra* — 7259 & 7260, 2-12″

FINAL SCENE—SALOMÉ AND THE HEAD OF JOHN

TU N'AS PAS VOULU (Thou Wouldst Not Let Me Kiss Thy Mouth)

ET TA LANGUE, ELLE NE REMUE PLUS (Thy Tongue Speaks No More): *Marjorie Lawrence, Soprano; Pasdeloup Orch., Piero Coppola, Cond.* — 8682, 12″

OH, POURQUOI NE M'AS-TU REGARDÉ (Wherefore Didst Thou Not Look at Me?)

AH, J'AI BAISÉE TA BOUCHE (Ah, I Have Kissed Thy Mouth): *Marjorie Lawrence, Soprano; Pasdeloup Orchestra Piero Coppola, Cond.* — 8683, 12″

Apex

ACT III, SCENE 2—THE BACCHANALE

Echena

SAMSON AND DELILAH

Samson et Dalila
(SAMSON AND DELILAH)

OPERA IN three acts. Music by Camille Saint-Saëns. Libretto by Ferdinand Lemaire, based on the Biblical story in the Book of Judges. First produced at the Hoftheater, Weimar, December 2, 1877. American *première*, as an opera, at the French Opera House, New Orleans, January 4, 1893. First performance at the Metropolitan February 8, 1895, with Francesco Tamagno and Eugenia Mantelli in the title roles. In concert form the work had already reached New York's Carnegie Hall on March 25, 1892. A brilliant Metropolitan revival of *Samson et Dalila* was that of November 15, 1915, the opening night of the season. In the cast were Enrico Caruso, Margarete Matzenauer, and Pasquale Amato, with Giorgio Polacco conducting.

Though successful with his earlier operas, Saint-Saëns had trouble with his Biblical opera in his own country. Factional disturbances divided musical Paris at the time as a result of the revolutionary theories propounded by Wagner's operas. Saint-Saëns found himself grouped with the operatic left wing, although later he came to be regarded as an archconservative. Luckily, a powerful friend came to Saint-Saëns' aid, none other than Franz Liszt, who was known for his championship of ill-treated composers. Saint-Saëns was invited to Weimar, where Liszt was the ruling spirit, and *Samson et Dalila* was produced there, in German, with great success. Yet, Paris waited thirteen years before taking cognizance of an opera that was destined to become a hardy perennial of the French repertory. The performance occurred on October 31, 1890, at the Théâtre Eden. Two years later it was produced at the Opéra. *Samson et Dalila* has been frequently given in oratorio form because of the Biblical story and the profusion of choral music. As a work for the theater, it is the only one of Saint-Saëns' numerous operas to continue to hold the stage. Into this score the composer poured his best inspiration. Hebrew chants contrast vividly with the sensuous music of the pagan Philistines, and throughout the score one marvels at the facile workmanship. An Oriental atmosphere of warm moods and colors is evoked through the music of the Bacchanale, and in voluptuous appeal few operatic arias surpass Delilah's *"Mon coeur s'ouvre à ta voix"* ("My heart at thy sweet voice").

CHARACTERS

SAMSON, *a Hebrew leader*	*Tenor*	ABIMELECH, *Satrap of Gaza*	*Bass*
DELILAH, *a Philistine*		AN OLD HEBREW	*Bass*
temptress	*Mezzo-soprano*	MESSENGER OF THE PHILISTINES	*Tenor*
HIGH PRIEST OF DAGON	*Baritone*	CHORUS OF HEBREWS AND PHILISTINES	

The action takes place in Gaza, in Palestine, about 1150 B.C.

ACT I

SCENE: *A Public Square in the City of Gaza.* Before the rise of the curtain an invisible chorus of Israelites is heard bewailing their bondage and imploring Jehovah for release. At the rise of the curtain they are seen dimly, for it is early morning in a public square in Gaza, in the city of their conquerors. As they lament their servitude, Samson comes forward and in stirring tones urges his countrymen to arise and cast off the Philistines' yoke.

At first they continue their lamentations, but his fervent avowal of faith soon stirs them to action, and the Israelites exclaim: "It is the Lord who speaks through him! Let us follow Samson, and Jehovah be our guide!" Their ringing shouts now attract Abimelech, the Satrap of Gaza, who emerges from his palace with his bodyguard. He taunts the Israelites with the reminder that they are helpless. Of what avail their prayers to Jehovah? Did he befriend them in the day of battle? And Abimelech warns them: better

Wide World Studio   ACT I—METROPOLITAN OPERA PRODUCTION

R. *Strohmeyer*   ACT III, SCENE 2—SAN FRANCISCO OPERA PRODUCTION

turn to Dagon, the greatest of gods. This blasphemy moves Samson to declare himself the appointed leader of the Chosen People. The Israelites join him in singing a spirited battle hymn: "Arise, O Israel, and break asunder the chains that bind you! Let righteousness be victorious!"

Abimelech attacks Samson with drawn sword. Samson wrests the weapon from him and runs him through. The Satrap falls, calling for help. This is the signal for revolt, and the Israelites follow Samson in a sudden bid for freedom. When they have disappeared, the gates of the temple of Dagon swing open and the High Priest approaches with his attendants. Horrified at the sight of the murdered ruler, he calls down a curse on Samson, his people, and his God. The High Priest and his panic-stricken followers are forced to flee with the body of Abimelech as the victorious Hebrews return, chanting hymns of praise. It is Samson's hour of triumph.

Once more the gates of the temple of Dagon open. This time it is the seductively beautiful priestess, Delilah, who appears. While maidens bearing garlands of victory sing and dance, Delilah works her charm upon the hero. "I come to celebrate the victory of him who reigns in my heart," sings the priestly siren. An old Hebrew solemnly warns Samson. But, though he prays for divine power to resist the enchantress, the chosen leader is already vanquished. While the young girls continue their dance, Delilah sings to Samson her "Song of Spring," full of a sensuous appeal which is not lost on the stalwart rebel leader. Delilah returns to the temple with her dancing girls. As she goes, she casts an inviting glance at Samson, who gazes after her with longing.

ACT II

SCENE: *Delilah's House*. Night is descending upon the valley as Delilah, more sumptuously clad than ever, waits outside her dwelling for the approach of Samson. In a sensuous aria, *"Amour! viens aider ma faiblesse"* ("Love! come aid my weakness"), she calls upon love to come to aid her in gaining power over this man whom she really hates as the leader of a despised people.

The High Priest comes to Delilah, enjoining her not to fail in her purpose. After he has gone, Samson approaches to keep the rendezvous hinted at by Delilah in her "Spring Song." The powerful Israelite is still hesitant, but gradually his struggling sense of duty is overcome by temptation. For Delilah has begun to play on the man's emotions with a song of ravishing beauty, *"Mon coeur s'ouvre à ta voix"* ("My heart at thy sweet voice"), in which she pleads irresistibly that Samson remain with her. During this exquisite melody a storm has gathered, the swift pattering of the rain being suggested in the accompaniment. Delilah tries her utmost to persuade Samson to betray the secret of his miraculous strength. The growing fury of the

White   ACT III, SCENE 1—SAMSON TURNING THE MILL

Wide World Studio ACT III, SCENE 2—METROPOLITAN OPERA PRODUCTION

storm seems a symbol of the increasing turmoil of his feelings. Delilah alternately threatens and pleads. If he will not share his secret with her, she complains, he does not really love her. Though weakening, Samson still refuses, praying for strength. Seemingly in despair, Delilah runs into her house, crying out that he is a coward, that his heart is without love. Trembling with conflicting emotions, Samson raises his arms hopelessly to heaven, then hurries after her. The storm breaks over the scene in all its fury. As Philistine soldiers approach stealthily, Delilah appears at the terrace for a moment and summons them in. Samson is speedily overpowered.

ACT III

SCENE 1: *The Mill of Gaza.* Samson, slayer of thousands of the foe, is now helpless. Blinded, shorn of his long locks, and weighed down with chains, he slowly turns the mill that grinds corn for the Philistines. Out of the depths of his misery he calls upon the Lord for mercy. Near by his fellow countrymen sing: "For love of a woman he sold his power and made us captives!" Samson is led away.

SCENE 2: *The Temple of Dagon.* From the orchestra are heard soft chords and harp arpeggios, mild as the first glow of dawn which penetrates the temple of Dagon, crowded now with rejoicing Philistines. Repeating the dainty melody sung by the dancing girls in the first act, the Philistines sing the praises of the dawn which puts darkness to flight, and of love, which alone brings happiness.

As they finish singing, an oboe plays a weirdly exotic cadenza, and as the orchestra sounds a brisk dance rhythm, a group of dancers rush forward and begin a lurid bacchanal. The music, at times softly yet luxuriantly voluptuous, grows to a climax of frenzied, Oriental revelry.

The dance ended, Samson is led in by a child. All mock him with the cruelest scorn. Derisively, Delilah flings at him phrases of her former love song. Then all turn their attention to the morning sacrifice to the god Dagon, whom the High Priest and Delilah invoke in broad, canonic phrases. Meanwhile, Samson has directed that he be led between the two massive pillars that support the roof of the temple. Finally his unceasing prayers are answered, for he suddenly feels his old strength returning. While all are lost in the ecstasy of pagan worship, he seizes the pillars with a mighty effort, and as they crumble, the roof crashes to the ground, burying Samson with his enemies.

THE RCA-VICTOR RECORDS
(Sung in French unless otherwise noted)

ACT I

JE VIENS CÉLÉBRER LA VICTOIRE (I Come to Celebrate Victory): *Enrico Caruso, Tenor; Louise Homer, Contralto; Marcel Journet, Bass; with Orch.*   16-5003, 12″
(In Album M-953)
(Acoustical Recording)

PRINTEMPS QUI COMMENCE (Delilah's Song of Spring): *Sigrid Onegin, Contralto, with Orch.*   7320, 12″

ACT II

AMOUR! VIENS AIDER MA FAIBLESSE (Love! Come Aid My Weakness): *Gladys Swarthout, Mezzo-soprano, with Orch.*
14143, 12″

Marian Anderson, Contralto, with Orch. In English   18008, 12″

MON COEUR S'OUVRE À TA VOIX (My Heart at Thy Sweet Voice): *Gladys Swarthout, Mezzo-soprano, with Orch.*
14143, 12″

Sigrid Onegin, Contralto, with Orch.
7320, 12″

Marian Anderson, Contralto, with Orch. In English   18008, 12″

ENRICO CARUSO AS SAMSON

ACT III

BACCHANALE (Ballet Music): *Boston "Pops" Orchestra, Arthur Fiedler, Cond.*   12318, 12″
Leopold Stokowski and the Philadelphia Orchestra   6823, 12″

The Secret of Suzanne

(IL SEGRETO DI SUSANNA)

OPERA—OR INTERMEZZO—IN one act. Music by Ermanno Wolf-Ferrari. Book by Enrico Golisciani. First performance, Hofoper, Munich, December 4, 1909, in a German translation by Max Kalbeck. Initial American performance, March 14, 1911, in Italian for the first time, by the visiting Philadelphia-Chicago company, Metropolitan Opera House, with Mario Sammarco, Carolina White, and Francesco Daddi. Given by the resident Metropolitan Opera company, also in Italian, December 13, 1912, with Antonio Scotti, Geraldine Farrar, and Angelo Bada. Wolf-Ferrari's most successful work is *Il Segreto di Susanna*, considered an intermezzo in the same way that Pergolesi's *La Serva Padrona* is, because it is usually given in conjunction with some other, longer opera, or, perhaps, sandwiched between two such.

The charm of this piece is in its sprightly, vivacious score, the elegance of the orchestration, and the brightness of the musical mood, fitting perfectly, as they do, the spirit of the sparkling book itself.

CHARACTERS

COUNTESS SUSANNA	*Soprano* SANTE, *a servant*	*Silent role*
COUNT GIL	*Baritone*	

The action takes place in Piedmont, early in the nineteenth century

The Overture to *The Secret of Suzanne* is probably the high point of the score. It is a brief piece, lively and very melodious, and often heard in the concert hall.

SCENE: *The Home of Count Gil*. Recently married and, like all young newlyweds, very much in love and, understandably, a bit on the jealous side, Count Gil and Countess Susanna have a little tiff. It is really nothing very much, except that Gil's jealousy is rather trying. He suspects his wife of having a lover, because when he returns home, after his day's work or, perhaps, a little journey, he detects the odor of tobacco smoke about the house. The truth is that his wife is the smoker, not daring to puff away before her husband, who, she believes, would undoubtedly berate her.

To all his questioning she is, naturally, quite evasive, and that only serves to excite much more not only his curiosity, but, as you might expect, his jealousy. What can she be doing, he wonders. And being kept in ignorance of the actual state of affairs causes the Count, one fine day, to give way to his rage and break the furniture around the house.

Women's soothing powers are well known, and Susanna, you may safely wager, knows her own ability in that direction. She contrives, after some trying moments, to calm her husband, and counsels him to go to his club. The change will do him—and her—good, she suggests.

While he is away—in fact, almost as soon as he leaves—Susanna bids the servant Sante to fetch her cigarettes, and, like an inveterate, though ever so graceful, smoker, she indulges in her secret passion. However, Gil, who has been driven far enough, by now, to spy on his wife, has not gone to the club at all, but has decided to return and furtively look in through the windows. So imagine his surprise when, instead of seeing a man smoking, he beholds his own wife, all by her little self. So happy is he at the discovery that she is faithful, after all, that he forgets all about cigarettes and the propriety of women smoking. He rushes in gleefully and, amid a general air of good humor, joins his wife in a few puffs of contentment.

THE RCA-VICTOR RECORDS
(Sung in Italian)

Gioia, la nube leggiera (O Joy to Be Musing) : *Lucrezia Bori, Soprano, with Orch.*
14616, 12″ (In Album M-405)

Culver Service   LUCREZIA BORI AS SUSANNA

Wide World Studio   PROLOGUE—METROPOLITAN OPERA PRODUCTION

Simon Boccanegra

OPERA IN a prologue and three acts. Music by Giuseppe Verdi. Text by Francesco Maria Piave (later revised by Arrigo Boïto), founded on a Spanish drama by A. García Gutiérrez. First performance, Teatro la Fenice, Venice, March 12, 1857. First given in Boïto's revised version, Milan, March 24, 1881. United States *première*, Metropolitan Opera House, January 28, 1932, with Lawrence Tibbett as Simon, Giovanni Martinelli as Adorno, Ezio Pinza as Fiesco, Claudio Frigerio as Paolo, Paul Ananian as Pietro, Maria Müller as Maria. Tullio Serafin conducted.

Verdi himself looked upon the *première* of his work as a fiasco. Some others thought so, too, yet there were contributing circumstances—the tenor and baritone originally chosen for the roles of Simon and Gabriele were both ill and unable to appear; in addition, there was opposition from the audience, which, as the *Gazzetta di Venezia* described the occasion, behaved rudely, and created a disturbance, "such as could not possibly have been engineered by a public so proverbially courteous as that of Venice."

In any case, the press was almost unanimously favorable toward the work, its decline being blamed entirely on the indifference of the public.

Given at La Scala, Milan, March 24, 1881, with Boïto's revision of the libretto, besides Verdi's considerably altered score, the opera was eminently successful.

Not the most consistently expressive of Verdi's scores, the music of *Simon Boccanegra* yet contains many pages of true eloquence and dramatic power. Notable among these are Fiesco's prologue aria, *"Il lacerato spirito,"* which has become a standby of the recital hall; the *"Miserere,"* also in the prologue; the vivid finale of Act I; the duet between Simon and Fiesco in the last act. As for the libretto, it seems to be no better than average in quality of drama and motivation, despite Boïto's shrewd revisions.

CHARACTERS
PROLOGUE

SIMON BOCCANEGRA, *corsair in the*
   service of the Genoese
   Republic   *Baritone*
JACOPO FIESCO, *Genoese nobleman*   Bass

PAOLO ALBIANI, *gold-spinner of*
   Genoa   *Bass*
PIETRO, *Genoese commoner*   *Baritone*

SEAMEN, COMMONERS, FOLLOWERS OF FIESCO, ETC.

THE PLAY

SIMON BOCCANEGRA, *first Doge*
   of Genoa   *Baritone*
MARIA BOCCANEGRA, *his daughter,*
   known as Amelia Grimaldi   Soprano
JACOPO FIESCO, *known as Andrea*   Bass
GABRIELE ADORNO, *Genoese*
   nobleman   *Tenor*

PAOLO ALBIANI, *favorite courtier*
   of the Doge   *Bass*
PIETRO, *another courtier*   *Baritone*
A CAPTAIN OF THE ARBALISTERS   *Tenor*
AMELIA'S MAIDSERVANT   *Mezzo-soprano*

SOLDIERS, SEAMEN, COMMONERS, SENATORS, COURT OF THE DOGE, ETC.

The action takes place in and near Genoa, toward the middle of the fourteenth century
(N.B. Twenty-five years elapse between the Prologue and Act I.)

PROLOGUE

SCENE: *A Square in Genoa Before the Fiesco Palace.* Paolo and Pietro, together with other commoners, scheme to place the public favorite, the corsair Simon Boccanegra, on the Doge's throne. Simon arrives, his intention apparently being to enter the palace to seek news of Maria, Fiesco's daughter, with whom he has been carrying on a secret love affair. Apprized, however, of the commoners' plans, he accepts the honor, swearing fealty to the cause, having learned, too, that Maria is kept prisoner within the palace. As all depart, Fiesco, surrounded by his followers, emerges, and after a recitative in which he bids farewell to the palace, "haughty mound, chill sepulcher of my beloved one," he sings the celebrated bass aria, *"Il lacerato spirito"* ("My torn soul"), wherein he laments the death of his daughter Maria. The mourners leave, and Simon returns, unaware of her death, to see Maria. In an interview with Fiesco he is asked the whereabouts of the daughter born of the illicit union. Simon declares his ignorance and, after listening to the fiery vow of eternal enmity made by Fiesco, enters the palace on the latter's departure. Soon he emerges, aggrieved by the stunning discovery of Maria's demise. And in the midst of his grief the supporters return and proclaim him Doge.

ACT I

SCENE 1: *The Grimaldi Gardens on the Outskirts of Genoa.* Twenty-five years have elapsed. A young woman, Amelia Grimaldi, who is a supposed

Morton & Co. ACT II—SAN FRANCISCO OPERA PRODUCTION

orphan, lives under the protection of one Andrea, really Fiesco. She is actually the daughter of Simon Boccanegra and Maria, although this fact is unknown to either her or the fictitious Andrea. Her true name is, like her mother's, Maria, and as she gazes at the distant horizon, she sings an aria, *"Come in quest' ora bruna"* ("As in this dark hour"). Meanwhile, we learn that Fiesco, still detesting Simon, has joined Gabriele Adorno, a young nobleman who loves Amelia, in a conspiracy against the present Doge, who is, of course, Simon Boccanegra. Paolo, however, now comfortably installed in the graces of the ruler, has himself a desire to wed Amelia, but he is rebuffed, and therefore plots to abduct her.

Simon visits the Grimaldi home, there meeting Amelia, and soon discovers that she is his daughter. He reveals his identity to her, in turn swearing her to secrecy. Later, he tells Paolo to give up all hope of winning her, much to that suppliant's dismay.

SCENE 2: *The Council Chamber in the Doge's Palace.* In the council chamber the Doge, with his lawmakers, is attending to affairs of state, when a clamor is heard outside. As the sounds increase, Gabriele and Fiesco are brought before him, the former accused of having slain a certain Lorenzin, to whose home Amelia had been brought after her abduction. Amelia is also present, now, having been freed, and Paolo, fearing that his part in the deed will be discovered, attempts to escape. Simon, however, orders the doors barred.

In the heat of a strong passion, Gabriele exclaims that someone in a high place is responsible for the murder, and he hurls himself, sword in hand, at Simon, when Amelia gets between the two men. As the situation

517

gradually becomes calmer, thanks to Simon's impressive plea, he, suspecting Paolo, calls upon him to join all in placing a curse on the culprit. And this Paolo does, not without a visible nervousness. In the meantime, Gabriele and Fiesco, the latter not recognized by Simon, are put into temporary custody.

ACT II

SCENE: *The Doge's Quarters in the Ducal Palace.* The malcontent Paolo steals into the Doge's chamber, together with Pietro, and when the latter has left pours the contents of a poison vial into Simon's drinking bowl. Under escort of Pietro, who soon departs, Gabriele and Fiesco appear, and to the latter's query about where they are, Paolo answers, "In the rooms of the Doge, where I, Paolo, would talk with you." In their conversation, which is not to Fiesco's liking, Paolo urges him to stab Boccanegra. This Fiesco is loath to do, whereupon Paolo orders him back to his dungeon, meanwhile staying Gabriele. He plays on the young nobleman's jealousy, with the information that Amelia is in the palace. But not successful with those tactics, he threatens Gabriele with death unless he delivers the fatal blow.

Torn with doubts, Gabriele sings his aria, *"O inferno, Amelia qui!"* ("Oh, fury! Amelia here!"), right after Paolo's departure, and the lady in question herself presently appears. Gabriele accuses her of disloyalty, with which some stormy moments ensue, though later Amelia, unwilling to disclose her relationship to the Doge, begs Gabriele to hide, for she has heard a fanfare of trumpets announcing the arrival of her father. Gabriele conceals himself, and the Doge enters, reading a document. He greets his daughter lovingly, and in their talk he is informed that Gabriele is the man she loves, and she pleads for his life. The Doge, wearily falling into a chair, drinks the poisoned wine, while reluctantly agreeing to give Gabriele his freedom. The effect of the poison places the Doge in a stupor, and soon he is asleep. Gabriele rushes out, gazes at him a moment, then, unsheathing his dagger, is about to stab him, but again Amelia saves her father's life. Amelia does all she can to prove her innocence without revealing her secret, but finally when the Doge awakens he himself makes the disclosure, and Gabriele, throwing himself at the Doge's feet, asks his forgiveness, vowing to take up arms in his cause.

ACT III

SCENE: *Within the Palace.* The scene overlooks the illuminated city of Genoa. Great shouts come up from the crowds below, as they acclaim the victory of Boccanegra over his enemies. Paolo, instigator of the revolt, has been condemned to death, and as he is being led away, he confides to Fiesco that the Doge will die long before himself. The Doge, visibly failing from the effects of the poison, makes his appearance, preceded by a captain of the

Morton & Co.　　ACT I, SCENE 1—SAN FRANCISCO OPERA PRODUCTION

Arbalisters and a trumpeter. The captain addresses the multitude below from the balcony, telling them that it is the Doge's wish not to "offend with clamorous joy the heroes' death." The captain and the trumpeter depart, and Fiesco approaches the Doge, who complains of feeling a strange throbbing through his temples. In an apostrophe to the sea, he exclaims, "Why was not its cradle the corsair's tomb?" and Fiesco exultingly remarks that it would have been better so, for the pall of death is upon him. When Fiesco admits his identity, the Doge contentedly informs him that their old enmity is ended, for now, as he had been once asked to do, he consigns to Fiesco's paternal care the young Amelia, the granddaughter he had long ago sought. Fiesco's happiness at the discovery is soon changed to a tragic sadness, as he bemoans Simon's imminent death. Amelia and Gabriele enter, and in difficult whispers Simon tells her that she is of noble blood, for she is Fiesco's granddaughter. His last wish is that Gabriele be named his successor, and, before the awed gathering, he dies.

THE RCA-VICTOR RECORDS
(Sung in Italian)

ACT I
IL LACERATO SPIRITO (A Wounded Heart):
*Alexander Kipnis, Bass, with Chorus
and Orch.*　　　8684, 12"
　　　　　　　15820, 12"
(In Album M-633)

ACT II
GARDEN SCENE DUET
　RECIT.: DINNE ALCUN LÀ NON VEDESTI?
　(Tell, Did None E'er Come to See
　Thee?)
ARIA: FIGLIA, TAL NOME PALPITA (Daughter, at the Name I Thrill): *Rose*

Bampton, Soprano; Lawrence Tibbett, Baritone; with Orch.
　　　　　　　15642, 12"

ACT III
RECIT.: PLEBE, PATRIZI (Plebians and Patricians)
ARIA: PIANGO SU VOI (I Weep for You):
*Rose Bampton, Soprano; Lawrence
Tibbett, Baritone; Giovanni Martinelli, Tenor; Leonard Warren, Baritone; Robert Nicholson, Baritone;
Metropolitan Opera Chorus and Orch.*
　　　　　　　15642, 12"

Lande

ACT III, SCENE 2—TERESA'S MILL

La Sonnambula
(THE SOMNAMBULIST)

OPERA IN three acts. Music by Vincenzo Bellini. Libretto by Felice Romani. First produced at the Teatro Carcano, Milan, March 6, 1831, with Giuditta Pasta and Giovanni Battista Rubini creating the roles of Amina and Elvino. The great Maria Malibran was heard as Amina in an English version of the opera in London in 1833. *La Sonnambula* was first performed in America at the Park Theater, on November 13, 1835, in English. The first American performance in the original Italian occurred at Palmo's Opera House, New York, on May 13, 1844. Four years later, Bellini's sleepwalking opera underwent another change—as *The Room Scrambler*, a burlesque produced at the Olympic Theater of New York. Jenny Lind was long identified with the role of Amina, and so were Marcella Sembrich, Luisa Tetrazzini, Amelita Galli-Curci. Among the brilliant Metropolitan revivals of *La Sonnambula* was that of 1905, when Sembrich sang Amina; Caruso, Elvino; and Plançon, Rodolfo. In 1909 the Spanish soprano Elvira de Hidalgo caused a minor stir by walking barefoot during Amina's somnambulist wanderings. Lily Pons was largely responsible for keeping the opera in the repertory in the early 1930's, since when it has not been given at the Metropolitan. Earlier generations doted on this unpretentious little opera. By 1850 *La Sonnambula* figured seasonally in the repertory of most major opera houses of Europe, but for later generations the rising tide of Wagnerism diminished its vogue.

CHARACTERS

AMINA, *fiancée of Elvino*	*Soprano*	COUNT RODOLFO, *lord of the village*	*Bass*
ELVINO, *a wealthy peasant*	*Tenor*	ALESSIO, *a peasant, in love*	
LISA, *an innkeeper, in love*		*with Lisa*	*Bass*
with Elvino	*Soprano*	A NOTARY	*Tenor*
TERESA, *a milleress*	*Mezzo-soprano*	PEASANTS AND PEASANT WOMEN	

The action takes place in a Swiss village in the early nineteenth century

520

La Sonnambula

ACT I

SCENE: *A Village Square.* The betrothal of the charming Amina to Elvino is being merrily celebrated on the village green when a handsome stranger arrives, asking the way to the castle. As it is a considerable distance he decides to put up at the village inn for the night. The sight of these surroundings revives memories in the stranger that find their expression in the aria *"Vi ravviso"* ("As I view these scenes"). Night is approaching, and Amina's foster mother, Teresa, declares that it is time for all to go home lest the phantom that has lately been haunting the neighborhood appear. The people depart, and the stranger enters the inn. Elvino, remaining with Amina, reproaches her bitterly for her unseemly interest in the stranger. Her tears stop him, and he begs her forgiveness, saying that he is even jealous of the breeze that plays with her hair. The lovers then unite in a joyous duet of reconciliation.

ACT II

SCENE: *A Room at the Inn.* Lisa, the proprietress of the inn, stops at the stranger's door to see if he is comfortable, but when he starts to flirt with her she coyly slips away. As she does so, she drops her scarf. The stranger is stupefied at the unexpected sight that now confronts him: Amina calmly walks in through the window, saying, "Elvino, are you still jealous? I love only you." He realizes at once that she is walking in her sleep. Not knowing what do do in this most embarrassing predicament, he slips out the window. Meanwhile, Lisa has been peeping from an adjoining room. Herself in love with Elvino, and jealous of Amina, she runs off to inform the youth of his Amina's faithlessness. When she returns with Elvino and the villagers, Amina is soundly asleep in the stranger's bed. The luckless girl awakens with a start and runs, bewildered, to her lover. Though she protests her innocence, he thrusts her from him and rushes away. Amina is left to despair under the cold looks that meet her from all sides.

ACT III

SCENE 1: *In the Forest.* The stranger, it happens, is none other than Count Rodolfo, owner of the "haunted" castle. Believing that he alone can clear her good name, Amina goes to the castle with her mother. On the way they meet Elvino, and again they plead with him, only to be bitterly reproached. Elvino takes the betrothal ring from the girl's finger and departs.

SCENE 2: *An Open Field Near a Mill.* Elvino has transferred his affections to the now triumphant Lisa, and the two start out for the church. They are met by the Count, who assures Elvino of Amina's innocence, but Elvino refuses to listen and bids Lisa follow him. Again they are stopped, this time by Teresa, who, having heard of his proposed marriage, now shows Elvino Lisa's scarf, found in the Count's room. "Deceived again!" cries the perplexed bridegroom, wondering aloud if any woman is to be trusted. Once more the Count assures him of Amina's innocence. "But where is the proof?" asks Elvino. "There!" cries the Count suddenly, pointing to the roof of the mill. And there, to everybody's astonishment, Amina appears in her nightdress, carrying a lamp. It is plain to all that she is walking in her sleep. They watch her breathlessly for fear she will fall. She crosses the narrow, fragile bridge directly over the revolving water wheel and descends the stairs, singing to herself a tender, melancholy air in keeping with her plight. Overcome with mingled joy and chagrin, Elvino rushes to her. Amina awakens to find her lover kneeling at her feet. With a cry of delight, she raises him to his feet and falls into his arms. Amina now expresses her happiness in the brilliant but tender aria, *"Ah! non giunge"* ("Ah! he does not arrive"). Nothing now remains to mar their happy union. Even the mystery of the castle "ghost" has become clear, and Bellini's pastoral opera closes with general rejoicing.

JENNY LIND AS AMINA

THE RCA-VICTOR RECORDS
(Sung in Italian)

ACT I

Vi ravviso, o luoghi ameni (As I View These Scenes) : *Feodor Chaliapin, Bass, with Orch.* 1269, 10"

ACT III

Ah! Non credea mirarti (Could I Believe) : *Toti dal Monte, Soprano, with Orch.* 7198, 12"

The Sorcerer

GILBERT   SULLIVAN

COMIC OPERA in two acts. Music by Sir Arthur Sullivan. Libretto by W. S. Gilbert. First performance, Opéra-Comique, London, November 17, 1877. First American performance, Broadway Theater, New York, February 21, 1879. *The Sorcerer* followed *Trial by Jury* (1875), and as the latter is more of a cantata we may name *The Sorcerer* the first of the Gilbert and Sullivan operas. It was also the first production of the syndicate formed by Richard D'Oyly Carte. Although it may lack something of the practiced technique of the later Gilbert and Sullivan operas, *The Sorcerer* has a delightful freshness and easy flow. There is an abundance of fun and some charming music.

After the success of *Trial by Jury*, it occurred to Richard D'Oyly Carte that the team of Gilbert and Sullivan could be a gold mine, if handled with care and shrewdness. He forthwith communicated to the two men what plans he had, obtaining their promise not to write for anybody else, and immediately set about getting supporters for an idea he had. This was to establish a comedy theater for the presentation of works by British authors and composers, chief among whom were to be F. C. Burnand and Alfred Cellier, James Alberti and Frederick Clay, and, of course, Gilbert and Sullivan, whom he wished to inaugurate the new venture.

After some rebuffs he got together a group of backers early in 1877, formed the Comedy Opera Company, with himself at the head, and leased, for the envisioned productions, the Opéra-Comique. Sullivan, since *Trial by Jury*, had been occupied with a number of things, guest-conducting and composing songs, besides being principal of the newly established National Training School of Music (later to become the Royal College of Music), where he discharged his duties halfheartedly until his resignation.

In the meantime, Gilbert sent him the libretto for *The Sorcerer*, and Sullivan, although quite surfeited with many things, quickly set to work on the score.

CHARACTERS

SIR MARMADUKE POINTDEXTRE, *an elderly baronet* — Baritone
ALEXIS, *of the Grenadier Guards, his son* — Tenor
DR. DALY, *vicar of Ploverleigh* — Tenor
NOTARY — Bass
JOHN WELLINGTON WELLS, *of J. W. Wells & Co., Family Sorcerers* — Bass

LADY SANGAZURE, *a lady of ancient lineage* — Contralto
ALINE, *her daughter, betrothed to Alexis* — Soprano
MRS. PARTLET, *a pew-opener* — Contralto
CONSTANCE, *her daughter* — Soprano
CHORUS OF VILLAGERS

The action takes place in the village of Ploverleigh

ACT I

SCENE: *Before Sir Marmaduke's Elizabethan Mansion.* It is midday, and the villagers of Ploverleigh voice their joy at the betrothal of Sir Marma-

523

duke's heir, Alexis, to Aline, the only child of an equally aristocratic neighbor, the Lady Sangazure. There is one present, however, who does not share in the general joy. Constance, the daughter of Mrs. Partlet, the worthy pew-opener, is downcast and confesses to her mother that she loves (vainly, it seems) the vicar, Dr. Daly. On his appearance they withdraw, and Dr. Daly sings the notable ballad, "Time Was When Love and I Were Well Acquainted," in which he laments the days now gone, when, as a pale young curate, he had the adoration of the maidens of his flock. Mrs. Partlet, anxious to help Constance, comes forward and leads the conversation to the subject of marriage, but it is obvious from his replies that he looks on himself as a confirmed bachelor, and Constance is led away, sobbing, by her mother.

The vicar now turns to welcome Sir Marmaduke and Alexis in weighty language, and with a touch of allegory that pleases Sir Marmaduke, who is a great admirer of the school of stately compliment, and a stickler for "blue blood." He claims that his own family is directly descended from Helen of Troy, and is all for a marriage of pedigree, regarding love as a comparatively unimportant accessory.

Aline makes her appearance, and is greeted by the village girls. She acknowledges their good wishes, and her mother, Lady Sangazure, adds her congratulations. The men now welcome Alexis, and the lovers greet each other with ecstasy. Then follows a stately duet, "Welcome Joy, Adieu to Sadness," between Sir Marmaduke and Lady Sangazure, who were lovers in their young days. The stately gavotte measure is punctuated by their dreams of what might have been.

A notary has now arrived; all is prepared for signing the marriage contract. This done, Alexis and Aline are left together. Alexis does not agree with the views of his father, and, believing that men and women should be coupled in matrimony without distinction of rank, has done some propaganda work on the subject. So far, however, his ideas have been welcomed only by the humbler classes. His own happiness seeming assured, he reveals his scheme for making the whole village happy. He has engaged John Wellington Wells, a sorcerer, to administer secretly a love philter to all the others, which will first send them to sleep and, on their awaking, cause them to fall madly in love with the first person of the opposite sex they may see who has also drunk the potion. It has no effect on those already married.

Mr. Wells is introduced in the well-known patter song, "My Name Is John Wellington Wells," and then details are discussed. It is decided that the philter shall be placed in a large teapot which will be used for the "banquet" to follow. Mr. Wells then proceeds to his horrific Incantation, and after the Fiends have disappeared, the villagers return, make merry, and each drinks the enchanted tea. The act closes as the charm finally overcomes all present, save Alexis, Aline, and the Sorcerer.

ACT II

SCENE: *Same.* It is midnight, and the villagers are still lying where they have fallen. Mr. Wells, with a great sense of fitness, has had the more exalted members taken home and put to bed "respectably."

As the villagers wake, each falls in love with the first person of the opposite sex visible, Constance and the Notary making one couple.

Alexis is so pleased with his success that he urges Aline to join with him in drinking the philter, in order that nothing may be left to chance. She refuses, and they quarrel. The remaining characters begin to arrive: first Dr. Daly, the worthy vicar, who is puzzled because, in a village hitherto rather slow in the matter of marriage, he has suddenly had a request for hasty weddings from everyone—even Sir Marmaduke. Alexis is none too pleased when he finds that the philter has led the Baronet to fix on Mrs. Partlet, the pew-opener. Still, he must live up to his opinions, and there is a congratulatory quintet from those concerned. Mr. Wells, having caused the mischief, falls a victim to his own spell, for Lady Sangazure, entering, sees him and at once adores him. He, on the other hand, not having drunk the philter, does not reciprocate, and in an amusing duet endeavors to dissuade her. Without success, however, for she threatens to bury her woe in her family vault.

Aline, having pondered the matter, has decided to fall in with her lover's wish, and drinks the philter. Immediately afterwards, she catches sight of Dr. Daly and of course falls in love with him. He is delighted at his good fortune, but Alexis, coming in full of remorse, is astounded to find his embraces repulsed. Explanations ensue, and the vicar obligingly offers to quit the country and bury his sorrow "in the congenial gloom of a Colonial Bishopric."

This is not enough, for Aline is still under the influence of the philter, and no longer loves Alexis. They appeal to Mr. Wells, who reveals that there is one way only in which the spell can be revoked. Either he or Alexis must sacrifice himself to Ahrimanes. Argument ensues, and the issue is put to popular vote; John Wellington Wells loses and disappears into the earth to the sound of a gong.

All quit their temporary partners to rejoin their old lovers, and Sir Marmaduke, claiming Lady Sangazure, invites them all to another feast in his mansion.

THE RCA-VICTOR RECORDS
(Sung in English)

ABRIDGED RECORDING: *D'Oyly Carte Company, Isadore Godfrey, Cond.; under the personal direction of Rupert D'Oyly Carte. (The cast includes: Muriel Dickson, Nellie Briercliffe, Dorothy Gill, Anna Bethel, Alice Moxon, Darrell Fancourt, George Baker, Derek Oldham, Leslie Rands, Stuart Robertson)*
DC-21 (4503-4508), 6-10"
C-21 (4258-4263)

GEMS: *Light Opera Company with Orch.*
36147, 12"
(In Album C-23)

White   PROLOGUE—THE LEGEND OF KLEINZACH

The Tales of Hoffmann

(LES CONTES D'HOFFMANN)

FANTASTIC OPERA in three acts, with prologue and epilogue; music by Jacques Offenbach; text by Jules Barbier and Michel Carré, founded on a play by these authors, derived from three stories by E. T. A. Hoffmann. (Carré's name appears as co-librettist only in the first edition of the vocal score.) First produced, February 10, 1881, at the Opéra-Comique, Paris, the score revised and orchestrated, in part, by Ernest Guiraud. First performance in the United States, October 16, 1882, at the Fifth Avenue Theater, New York, by Maurice Grau's French Opera Company upon their first American appearance. Oscar Hammerstein's revival of the work—Manhattan Opera House, November 14, 1907—established it in this country. The cast, on that occasion, boasted Maurice Renaud, Charles Gilibert, and Charles Dalmorès in the principal male roles. First performance at the Metropolitan, January 11, 1913, with Umberto Macnez as Hoffmann, Adamo Didur as Coppélius, Dingh Gilly as Dapertutto, Léon Rothier as Dr. Miracle, Frieda Hempel as Olympia, Olive Fremstad as Giulietta, Lucrezia Bori as Antonia, and Jeanne Maubourg as Nicklausse.

Although Offenbach wrote many a successful *opéra comique*, this fantastic opera is now ranked as his masterpiece. Without being pretentious as music, the score has a delicacy, grace, and poetic feeling perfectly adapted to the fanciful imagination of Hoffmann's *Tales*.

Offenbach began his work in 1877, but before it was completed he became seriously ill. Believing it to be his finest piece of work, he was anxious to witness the first performance; unfortunately, he died, October 5, 1880, some four months before the work was first produced.

CHARACTERS

HOFFMANN, *a poet*	Tenor	COPPÉLIUS, DAPERTUTTO, AND
NICKLAUSSE, *his friend*	Contralto	MIRACLE, *a magician under*
	(or Baritone)	*various names* Baritone
		SCHLEMIL Bass
OLYMPIA, GIULIETTA, AND		SPALANZANI Tenor
ANTONIA, *the poet's loves*	Sopranos	CRESPEL Bass

PROLOGUE

SCENE: *Taproom of Luther's Tavern in Nuremberg.* The crowd of students in Martin Luther's Wine Cellar at Nuremberg sing the praises of the master of the tavern, but Hoffmann, who is among them, seems despondent. Upon the students' request for a song, however, he begins the weird "Ballad of Kleinzach," but soon wanders off into a song in praise of a beautiful woman. The students jest with him, saying that he is in love. He replies that he has given up all such matters, but will tell them of three of his own unfortunate love adventures. Each of the succeeding acts of the opera reveals one of these.

ACT I

SCENE: *A Physician's Drawing Room.* The famous scientist Spalanzani has what many consider a beautiful daughter, Olympia. She is, however, not really his daughter but a wonderful mechanical doll, made by the scientist and his friend, Coppélius. Hoffmann has seen this automaton through the window, and now comes to Spalanzani's house, ostensibly as his pupil, but really to make love to Olympia. Coppélius has persuaded him to wear a certain pair of spectacles with which to look at the girl. At an entertainment given by Spalanzani, Olympia sings her oddly mechanical coloratura song with its birdlike roundelays. At one point the song seems about to stop, a servant touches her shoulder, the sound of a spring is heard, and the song, Olympia's Aria, continues.

Hoffmann is so enraptured by her beauty and by her singing that he will not listen to his friend Nicklausse when he tries to enlighten him; and so carried away is he that when he tells the doll of his passion he believes she returns his affection, although she only says, "Yes, yes," whenever he happens to touch her shoulder. This odd couple begin a dance which grows faster and faster until Hoffmann falls to the floor in a swoon, thereby breaking his spec-

White

ACT II—THE BARCAROLLE

R. Strohmeyer   ACT I—SAN FRANCISCO OPERA PRODUCTION

tacles. Now Coppélius enters in a great rage, for Spalanzani has bought Olympia and paid for her with a worthless draft. In his anger, Coppélius breaks the priceless doll to pieces. Spalanzani and Coppélius quarrel, and the guests laugh at Hoffmann, whose first love has ended in disillusionment.

ACT II

SCENE: *Venice, the Gallery of Giulietta's Palace, Overlooking the Grand Canal.* Nicklausse sings with Giulietta the gently swaying, famous "Barcarolle." Hoffmann also is here, and in spite of Nicklausse's warning, he allows himself to become fascinated by Giulietta. This beautiful courtesan is really under the sway of the magician Dapertutto; for him she has stolen the shadow of her lover Schlemil, for him she now similarly sets out to ensnare Hoffmann in order to steal his reflection in a mirror.

Surprised by the jealous Schlemil, Hoffmann fights a duel with him, using Dapertutto's proffered sword. Schlemil is killed, and Dapertutto disappears. A moment later Giulietta passes in her gondola, leaning on Dapertutto's arm and singing a mocking song at Hoffmann. Thus, the second love affair ends in disappointment.

ACT III

SCENE: *A Room in Crespel's House, Munich.* Hoffmann is engaged to marry Antonia, daughter of Rath Crespel, at whose house we now see him. Antonia, like her mother before her, has a remarkably beautiful voice, and, also like her, is afflicted with consumption. Although singing gives his daughter great happiness, Crespel forbids her so taxing her strength since he knows it will be fatal to her. At first Hoffmann is delighted to hear her sing when alone with her, but after he has overheard a conversation between Crespel and Dr. Miracle and learns of the danger, he makes Antonia promise never to sing again. When, however, Crespel and Hoffmann have gone, Miracle, the evil genius that has haunted Hoffmann as Coppélius and as Dapertutto, returns, and, summoning the spirit of Antonia's mother, whom he has likewise killed, he persuades the girl to sing. Finally she falls exhausted, and when Hoffmann and Crespel return, she sinks dying in her father's arms. So ends in tragedy Hoffmann's third love story.

EPILOGUE

SCENE: *Taproom of Luther's Tavern.* The boon companions thank Hoffmann for his tales and take their leave. The Muse of Art now comes to console Hoffmann, and for a moment he is aroused to great ecstasy, then he falls, face forward, across the table—asleep? "Dead drunk," remarks one of the students in departing; but Stella, the girl who leans upon his arm, pauses, as she goes out, and throws a flower from her bouquet at Hoffmann's feet.

THE RCA-VICTOR RECORDS
(Sung in French unless otherwise noted)

ACT II

AIR DE LA POUPÉE—LES OISEAUX DANS LA CHARMILLE (Doll Song—The Birds in the Bushes): *Miliza Korjus, Soprano, with Orch. In German*   11921, 12"

ACT III

BARCAROLLE (Orchestral): *Leopold Stokowski and the Hollywood Bowl Orchestra*   11-9174, 12"
Sigmund Romberg and his Orchestra   11-9222, 12"
Victor Concert Orchestra   20011, 10"
Dick Leibert, Organist   27729, 10"
(In Album P-104)
BARCAROLLE—BELLE NUIT, O NUIT D'AMOUR (Beautiful Night, O Night of Love): *Jeanne Dessau, Soprano; Nancy Evans, Contralto, with Sadler's Wells Chorus and Orchestra. In English*   13824, 12"
Jarmila Novotna, Soprano, with Orch.   11-9263, 12"
Lucrezia Bori, Soprano; Lawrence Tibbett, Baritone; with Orch. In English   1747, 10"
DAPERTUTTO'S ARIA—SCINTILLE, DIAMANT (Sparkle, Diamond): *Leonard Warren, Baritone, with Orch.*   18420, 12"

GLADYS SWARTHOUT AS GIULIETTA

ACT IV

ROMANCE D'ANTONIA—ELLE A FUI, LA TOURTERELLE (Antonia's Romance—The Dove Has Flown): *Jarmila Novotna, Soprano, with Orch.*   11-9263, 12"

Lande

ACT III—METROPOLITAN OPERA PRODUCTION

Tannhäuser

OPERA IN three acts. Music and book by the composer. First produced, Hoftheater, Dresden, October 19, 1845. Initial American performance, Stadt Theater, New York, April 4, 1859, becoming the first of Wagner's operas to be given in the United States. It was *Tannhäuser* that inaugurated the German regime at the Metropolitan Opera House, when the work was presented there on November 17, 1884, with Auguste Kraus, Anna Slach, Anton Schott, Adolf Robinson, and Josef Kögel in the principal roles, the conductor being Leopold Damrosch. The so-called Paris version of the opera was first heard at the Metropolitan on January 30, 1889, featuring Lilli Lehmann as Venus; Anton Seidl conducted.

Among the celebrated artists who have appeared in *Tannhäuser*, either at the Metropolitan or at other New York performances, have been Amalie Materna, Nellie Melba, Johanna Gadski, Milka Ternina, Aïno Ackté, Berta Morena, Geraldine Farrar, Mariette Mazarin, Olive Fremstad, Maria Jeritza, Elisabeth Rethberg, Lotte Lehmann, Kirsten Flagstad, and Helen Traubel as Elisabeth; Olive Fremstad and Margarete Matzenauer were especially fine in the role of Venus; Max Alvary, Ernst Kraus, Heinrich Knote, Karl Burrian, Leo Slezak, Jacques Urlus, and Lauritz Melchior as Tannhäuser; Jean Lassalle, David Bispham, Anton van Rooy, Maurice Renaud, Fritz Feinhals, Friedrich Schorr, and Lawrence Tibbett as Wolfram; Emil Fischer, Robert Blass, Paul Bender, and Alexander Kipnis as the Landgrave.

The famous Paris *première* of *Tannhäuser* on March 13, 1861, was a failure, owing chiefly to Chauvinistic intrigue and interference. Only after an imperial order from Napoleon III, obtained through the good offices of the Princess Metternich, was the way cleared for its production at the Opéra. With typical enthusiasm, Wagner now found the opportunity to make certain revisions he had had in mind. These were principally concerned with lengthening the opening scene, laid in the mountain retreat of Venus, providing it with what is now sometimes called the "Parisian Bacchanale," while augmenting the dialogue between the goddess and the minstrel knight. In 1861, with *Lohengrin, Das Rheingold, Die Walküre*, a portion of *Siegfried*, and all of *Tristan und Isolde* already composed, Wagner was at the very top of his creative powers. However, despite the dramatic and musical excellence of the material and the previously proved effectiveness of the entire opera, it was received with much sarcasm and ill-feeling by the press and intelligentsia.

Further, the members of the fashionable Jockey Club had expected the ballet to take place in the second act, by which time—their leisurely dinners ended—they could repair to the opera house to absorb art in the comfortable manner. Wagner's opposition to any such suggestion, of course, was strong, and he left the dancing in the Bacchanale of the first act, where it best belonged. At any rate, after three nights, the opera was withdrawn. Paris did not hear it again until thirty-four years later, May 13, 1895.

All of Wagner's works for the stage possess either a legendary or historical foundation; Tannhäuser rests on both. According to medieval romance, the gods and goddesses of antiquity did not die, but took refuge in the underworld. Thus it was believed that the goddess of love, Venus, had established her court near the Wartburg beneath a mountain which came to be known as the Venusberg, there to prey upon the souls of men. The Landgraves who ruled in Thuringia were patrons of the arts and held contests of song. The minnesingers, a class of lyric poets and musicians, generally of noble birth, who sang of idealized love and beauty, were at their height in Germany from about 1150 to 1350 and often took part in such contests. Those appearing in the opera were actual characters. The historical Tannhäuser seems to have been too fond of the things of this world, and thus the legend arose concerning him that he had dwelt in the Venusberg. As treated by Wagner, the legend becomes symbolical of the struggle between the lower and the higher in human nature.

CHARACTERS

HERMANN, *Landgrave of Thuringia*	Bass	WALTHER VON DER			
TANNHÄUSER, *a minstrel knight*	Tenor	VOGELWEIDE			*Tenor*
WOLFRAM VON ESCHENBACH, *his*		BITEROLF		*minstrel*	*Bass*
friend and a minstrel		HEINRICH DER		*knights*	
knight	Baritone	SCHREIBER			*Tenor*
ELISABETH, *niece of the*		REINMAR VON			
Landgrave	Soprano	ZWETER			*Bass*
VENUS	Soprano or Contralto	A YOUNG SHEPHERD			Soprano

THURINGIAN NOBLES AND KNIGHTS, LADIES, ELDER AND YOUNGER PILGRIMS, SIRENS, NAIADS, NYMPHS, BACCHANTES

The action takes place in the vicinity of Eisenach at the beginning of the thirteenth century

Wagner himself wrote for the orchestra at Zurich an explanation of the meaning of the Overture. Greatly abridged, it runs as follows:

To begin with, the orchestra leads before us the Pilgrims' Chant alone; it draws near, then swells into a mighty outpour, and finally passes away. Evenfall; last echo of the chant. As night breaks, magic sights and sounds occur, a rosy mist floats up . . . the whirlings of a fearsomely voluptuous dance are seen. These are the "Venusberg's" seductive spells, that show themselves at dead of night. . . . Attracted by the tempting show, a comely human form draws nigh; 'tis Tannhäuser, love's minstrel. He sounds his jubilant "Song of Love" in joyous challenge, as though to force the wanton

ACT I, SCENE 2—METROPOLITAN OPERA PRODUCTION

witchery to do his bidding. Wild cries of riot answer him; the rosy cloud grows denser round him, entrancing perfumes steal away his senses.

In the most seductive of half-lights, his wonder-seeing eye beholds an alluring female form; he hears a voice that sweetly murmurs the siren call ... Venus herself it is. ... Then heart and senses burn within him: ... before the goddess' self he steps with that canticle of love triumphant, and now he sings it in ecstatic praise of her. ... The wonders of the Venusberg unroll their brightest before him; tumultuous shouts and savage cries of joy mount up ... in drunken glee bacchantes drive their raging dance and drag Tannhäuser to the warm caresses of love's goddess, who bears him where no step dare tread. ... A scurry, like the sound of the Wild Hunt, and speedily the storm is laid. Only a wanton whir still pulses in the breeze, a wave of weird voluptuousness ...

But dawn begins to break already; from afar is heard again the Pilgrims' Chant. As this chant draws closer ... as the day drives farther back the night, that whir and soughing of the air—which had erstwhile sounded like the eerie cries of souls condemned—now rises, too, to ever gladder waves; so that when the sun ascends at last in splendor, and the Pilgrims' Chant proclaims in ecstasy to all the world, to all that lives and moves thereon, Salvation won, this wave itself swells out the tidings of sublimest joy. ...

In the Paris version of the opera the Overture coalesces with the music of the opening scene, in the Venusberg. It is this version which nowadays is most often given.

ACT I

SCENE 1: *The Interior of the Venusberg.* The immense cavelike grotto, illuminated by mysterious multicolored lights, where Venus holds her court

Wide World Studio   ACT II—METROPOLITAN OPERA PRODUCTION

—the Venusberg. Here languorous youths, urged on by the enticements of nymphs, lead in a wild dance. Into their midst dash a throng of bacchantes who cause the dance to grow even more riotous. Satyrs and fauns appear from the clefts in the rock walls of the cavern and, running headlong after the nymphs, bring the dance to a tumult of frenzy. With the increasing madness of the dance, the music has grown to a climax of the wildest voluptuousness. The three graces vainly attempt to quell the riot. They awaken sleeping cupids, who fly above the tumult and shoot their arrows at the surging crowd below. Stricken with the pangs of love, the wounded take flight. The music subsides from its impassioned turbulence and, glowing with a wonderful, silvery iridescence, sinks into a profound calm. A rosy mist falls over the cave until only Tannhäuser, Venus, and the three graces are visible in the foreground. And now through the mist there appears a cloud picture of the abduction of Europa. From a remote portion of the grotto is heard the song of sirens.

The vision fades, and another is revealed: the soft glamour of the moon, Leda and the swan at a woodland pool. This vision also disappears, the graces withdraw, and Venus and Tannhäuser remain silent and motionless. The music dies away in a final languorous sigh.

Tannhäuser, beside the reclining Venus, starts up suddenly as from a dream. He has grown weary of the soft, sensuous life of Venus' court, and although the goddess of love herself uses all the fascinations in her power, each time he begins to sing his hymn in her praise he forgets his theme and tells of his longing for earth with its mingled joys and sorrows. When she finds that the allurements of herself or her realm avail nothing, the goddess threatens him, saying that on earth he will be scorned, an outcast among men. Tannhäuser replies that he trusts in Mary. At the name of the Blessed Virgin,

Venus and all her kingdom instantly disappear, and Tannhäuser finds himself standing in a valley near the Castle of the Wartburg.

SCENE 2: *The Valley of the Wartburg.* It is a bright spring morning; a shepherd plays on his pipe and sings merrily while near by can be heard the tinkle of his flock's bells; a band of pilgrims on their way to Rome pass by, singing their chant. Tannhäuser, shaken with emotion, falls on his knees in devout thankfulness. While he is yet kneeling, the sound of hunting horns is heard gradually drawing nearer, and soon the Landgrave and a party of minnesingers come along the path. They recognize Tannhäuser and greet him joyfully. When they ask where he has stayed for so long, he vaguely replies that he wandered far, that he is unhappy and would still continue his wanderings. Nor can all their entreaties and promises cause him to return to them, until the noblehearted Wolfram reminds him that here lives Elisabeth, and adds that she has sorrowed greatly since his departure. Deeply moved, Tannhäuser consents to remain.

ACT II

SCENE: *The Hall of Minstrels in the Wartburg.* The hall of the singers at the Wartburg is in readiness for a contest. Elisabeth enters, singing to it her joyful greeting, in the brilliant song, *"Dich, teure Halle"* ("Hail, hall of song").

Wolfram enters, conducting Tannhäuser to her. She is overjoyed, but modestly refrains from revealing her happiness too openly. When she asks where he has been so long, he again vaguely says that he wandered in a distant land, only by a miracle did he escape; and, he adds, it was she who caused him to return. They sing a duet in praise of this power which has reunited them, then Tannhäuser leaves to prepare for the contest. Elisabeth's uncle, the Landgrave, enters and informs her that he will offer her hand to the singer she crowns as victor in the contest. At this moment a trumpet fanfare announces the arrival of the time appointed; a hurrying figure, as of pleasant agitation, is played by the strings; then a broad, magnificent march theme is announced. Elisabeth and the Landgrave welcome their guests as they enter. The chorus of voices singing, "Hail, bright abode, Landgrave Hermann, hail!" swells in power and brilliance even as the number of those assembled constantly grows. Finally, when the hall is filled with the nobles, the march comes to a dazzling close.

The Landgrave addresses them in welcome—*"Blick' ich umher"* ("Gazing on this fair assembly")—states the theme of the contest, "Love," and pages collect lots to determine the beginner. The minnesingers hymn the praises of virtuous love.

Tannhäuser, growing more and more agitated, replies to each of them,

Wide World Studio   ACT III—METROPOLITAN OPERA PRODUCTION

singing of the delights of merely sensual passion. Finally, inspired by some unnatural force, he bursts into his hymn in praise of Venus: those who know her not know not love! The women hurry from the hall as from a place unholy; the men, drawing their swords, rush at Tannhäuser. Elisabeth, though heartbroken at her betrayal, throws herself before him, and pleads that they allow him to seek heaven's forgiveness. The Landgrave consents on condition that Tannhäuser will seek pardon from the Pope. A group of younger pilgrims are heard singing as they start on their journey to Rome. Stricken with remorse, Tannhäuser rushes out to join them.

The Prelude to Act III, described in the score as "Tannhäuser's Pilgrimage," combines several themes, including the theme of Penitence, that of Elisabeth's intercession, and the one symbolizing Tannhäuser's suffering. These are the main elements of the music, although we hear also references to the themes of Repentance, the Pilgrims' Hymn, and two others.

ACT III

SCENE: *The Valley of the Wartburg*. In the valley of the Wartburg stands a crucifix; before it Elisabeth, arrayed in white, kneels in prayer. From a distance is heard the song of returning pilgrims, gradually drawing nearer.

Elisabeth rises and scans them in the greatest anxiety as they pass by and disappear in the distance. *He* is not among them. She sinks once more before the crucifix and in the greatest agony of soul sings the affecting prayer.

Wolfram has been standing at a distance, sorrowfully watching, and when Elisabeth rises and starts to return to the castle, he gently asks if he may not accompany her. By her gesture she declines. Meanwhile night has fallen over the valley and the evening star glows on high. Thinking of Elisabeth, Wolfram sings a wonderfully expressive apostrophe to the star, accompanying himself on his minstrel's harp.

A gloomy motive is heard in the orchestra, and Tannhäuser appears, haggard and weary. In a broken voice he asks of Wolfram the way to the Venusberg. Wolfram recoils in mingled horror and pity. He urgently questions Tannhäuser, who then tells of his pilgrimage: how he suffered every privation and hardship over dangerous mountains and rock paths; how he prostrated himself before the Pope, and in deepest contrition confessed his sin, only to be told that pardon and salvation can never be for him, so long as the papal staff is barren of leaves.

He fled from Rome in despair. Now, without hope of salvation, he seeks forgetfulness at the Venusberg. A ruddy glow illuminates the recesses of the mountain; the song of the sirens and the voluptuous music of the Venusberg are heard; Venus appears, holding out her arms to welcome Tannhäuser. Wolfram pleads with him, but the minstrel spurns his entreaties. At this moment when Venus seems to have won her prey, Wolfram recalls to Tannhäuser the name "Elisabeth." The knight stands as if spellbound. Recognizing her defeat, Venus vanishes with all her magical companions. Bells are heard tolling, for Elisabeth has died during the night, and now the mournful music of her funeral train draws near. As the procession of mourners enters the valley carrying the bier, Tannhäuser, broken with grief and exhaustion, sinks dying beside Elisabeth. As his soul takes its flight, the second band of pilgrims arrives. They carry the papal staff which has brought forth green leaves—a miracle revealing that Tannhäuser has been pardoned.

THE RCA-VICTOR RECORDS
(Sung in German unless otherwise noted)

EXCERPTS (Including: Overture, Venusberg Music, Prelude to Act III) : *Leopold Stokowski and the Philadelphia Orchestra, with Women's Chorus*
DM-530 (16159-16163), 5-12"
M-530 (15310-15314)

ACT I

DIR TÖNE LOB! (Tannhäuser's Hymn to Venus—All Praise Be Thine!) : *Lauritz Melchior, Tenor, with Orch.*
17726, 12"
(In Album M-749)
11-8676, 12"
(In Album M-979)

ACT II

DICH, TEURE HALLE (Hail, Hall of Song) : *Helen Traubel, Soprano, with Orch.*
17268, 12"

Kirsten Flagstad, Soprano, with Orch.
14181, 12"

Elisabeth Rethberg, Soprano, with Orch.
15818, 12"
(In Album M-633)

Johanna Gadski, Soprano, with Orch.
18142, 12"
(In Album M-816)
(Acoustical Recording)

FESTMARSCH—EINZUG DER GÄSTE (Grand March — Entrance of the Guests) :

Boston "Pops" Orchestra, Arthur Fiedler, Cond. 12448, 12"
(In Album M-569)

BLICK' ICH UMHER (Gazing on This August Assembly) : *Friedrich Schorr, Baritone, with Orch.* 7426, 12"

Joel Berglund, Baritone, with Orch. 12-0185, 12"

ACT III

PILGERCHOR (Pilgrims' Chorus) : *Victor Male Chorus, with Orch. In English* 20127, 10"
Lew White, Organist 36212, 12"

ELISABETHS GEBET (Elizabeth's Prayer) : *Kirsten Flagstad, Soprano, with Orch.* 8920, 12"

O DU MEIN HOLDER ABENDSTERN (Evening Star) : *John Charles Thomas, Baritone, with Orch.* 15818, 12"

(In Album M-633)
7605, 12"

Joel Berglund, Baritone, with Orch. 12-0185, 12"

Lawrence Tibbett, Baritone, with Orch. 8452, 12"
11-8862, 12"
(In Album M-1015)

Reinald Werrenrath, Baritone, with Orch. In English 6563, 12"

Raya Garbousova, Cellist, with Piano 11-8870, 12"
(In Album M-1017)

Pablo Casals, Cellist, with Piano 6620, 12"

Charles Courboin, Organist 1968, 10"

ROM' ERZÄHLUNG (Rome Narrative) : *Lauritz Melchior, Tenor, with Orch.* 17727, 12"
(In Album M-749)
11-8677, 12"
(In Album M-979)

Set Svanholm, Tenor, RCA-Victor Orchestra, Frieder Weissmann, Cond. 12-0528, 12"

KIRSTEN FLAGSTAD AS ELISABETH

Apex   ACT II, SCENE 2

Thaïs

OPERA IN three acts. Book, in prose, by Louis Gallet, after the novel by Anatole France. First performed at the Paris Opéra, March 16, 1894. American *première*, at Oscar Hammerstein's Manhattan Opera House, New York, on November 25, 1907, with Mary Garden and Maurice Renaud in the chief roles. First Metropolitan performance, February 16, 1917, with Geraldine Farrar as Thaïs and Pasquale Amato as Athanaël. Massenet wrote *Thaïs* for the lovely Sibyl Sanderson, just as he had written *Esclarmonde* for her five years before. The California soprano was a sensation in the role, thanks mainly to her dazzling beauty. But for power and glow of interpretation, the singer inseparably linked with the part is Mary Garden, who triumphantly launched her American career with *Thaïs*. In this opera Massenet is perhaps at his best as operatic craftsman. The patterns are clear and precise, and the moods of religious fervor and romantic ecstasy are deftly contrasted and blended. Both in the vocal and in the instrumental writing the score pulses with drama and passion. In the "Meditation," moreover, it boasts an orchestral interlude of haunting appeal.

CHARACTERS

THAÏS, *a courtesan*	*Soprano*	PALEMON, *an old monk*	*Bass*
ATHANAËL, *a monk of the*		ALBINE, *an abbess*	*Mezzo-soprano*
Cenobite Order	*Baritone*	CROBYLE, *a slave*	*Soprano*
NICIAS, *a young Sybarite*	*Tenor*	MYRTALE, *a slave*	*Soprano*

MONKS, NUNS, CITIZENS, SERVANTS, DANCERS, ETC.

The action takes place in Egypt in the early Christian era

538

ACT I

SCENE 1: *Cenobite Dwellings Near the Nile.* At a time when Alexandria is wrapped in luxury and profligacy, Thaïs, a priestess of Venus, is recognized as the most beautiful of women. Athanaël, a Cenobite monk who has been to the city in an effort to preach the gospel, returns to his devout associates with strange stories of Alexandria's wickedness. At night his sleep is troubled by a vision of Thaïs, posing in the Alexandrian theater before a great throng noisily applauding her beauty. Awaking with a start, he is determined to save her. Against the advice of the aged monk Palemon, he sets out upon his mission.

SCENE 2: *Nicias' House in Alexandria.* In Alexandria, Athanaël finds a friend of his unregenerate days named Nicias, whose palace occupies a commanding situation. Nicias greets his old friend with courtesy, but is moved to laughter at his whimsical resolve to reform the lovely Thaïs, upon whom Nicias himself has squandered a fortune. Willing to help for old times' sake, however, he commands his household slaves to array Athanaël in rich robes, concealing his monkish habit. When at last Thaïs herself arrives she is at first repelled, then intrigued by this austere visitor. Athanaël tells her that he has come to bring her to the only true God, whose humble and devout servant he is. Thaïs' reply is flippantly pagan—she believes only in the joy of living. But she is none the less impressed. Athanaël leaves, horrified, as Thaïs begins to disrobe, to pose as Venus.

ACT II

SCENE 1: *Thaïs' House.* In her room lies Thaïs. The floor is carpeted with precious rugs from Byzantium. The air is laden with the exotic perfumes of flowers in vases of agate . . . incense burns before a statue of Venus. Yet Thaïs is wearied of the world and her luxury. The words of the strange monk haunt her memory. She fears that beauty and happiness will quickly fade. Taking a mirror, she contemplates herself, and begs it to assure her that she shall be forever beautiful. *"Dis-moi que je suis belle"* ("Say that I am lovely"), she sings with fervid longing. At this moment Athanaël enters. He speaks to her of life everlasting, of the eternal beauty of the spirit. Thaïs tries at first to triumph over him with her allurements, then succumbs to fear. The righteous Athanaël leaves, declaring, "On thy threshold till dawn I shall await thy coming!" The curtain falls, but the orchestra continues playing with the famous "Meditation," symbolical of the conversation of Thaïs. To a harp accompaniment, a solo violin plays a melody of haunting sweetness.

SCENE 2: *Before Thaïs' House.* True to his word, Athanaël waits before Thaïs' house. From another house near by come the sounds of revelry. Toward dawn, Thaïs appears, worn and repentant after a sleepless night of torment, ready now to follow this holy man into the wilderness. She leaves everything behind, begging only for a small statue of Eros—love himself, for, she says, love has long been a rare visitor among men. She asks to take the statue along to set up in some monastery as an emblem of the love celestial. Athanaël listens patiently until she remarks that this was a gift from Nicias. He then seizes the statue and casts it to the ground, shattering it into a thousand fragments. They enter her palace to destroy the treasures, relics of pagan revels. Thaïs accepts this sacrifice without protest. As soon as they have gone, Nicias appears. Having won heavily at the games, he orders dancing, wine, and music. When Thaïs and the stern monk return, they are greeted by a scene of wanton revelry. This quickly changes to a near riot, for the companions of Nicias are grumbling at the threatened loss of Thaïs. And they are furious at Athanaël, for in his zeal he has set fire to her palace. The crowd is about to seize and kill the monk. To save him, Nicias throws gold coins among the assailants. As the people scramble for the money, Athanaël and Thaïs escape toward the desert and a life of worship and repentance.

ACT III

SCENE 1: *An Oasis in the Desert.* Tortured by thirst and weary from her long journey across the desert, Thaïs nearly faints. Yet, the journey is almost over. The monk drives her on remorselessly, bidding her "mortify the flesh," and she goes willingly. Finally she staggers from weakness, and Athanaël,

Wide World Studio
BALLET FROM ACT II, SCENE 2—METROPOLITAN OPERA PRODUCTION

Wide World Studio
ACT III, SCENE 3—THE DEATH OF THAÏS—METROPOLITAN OPERA PRODUCTION

moved to pity, allows her to lie down while he bathes her feet and gives her fruit and water from the oasis at which they have arrived. Thaïs now seems a new person, raised beyond the dominion of flesh to a great spiritual exaltation. She rejoices when the Abbess Albine and the White Sisters come to lead her to a cell in a near-by convent. Thaïs has found the peace for which her soul secretly craved. But now it is Athanaël whose soul is troubled.

SCENE 2: *The Cenobite Dwellings Near the Nile.* Back among the brethren of the Cenobite camp, Athanaël is compelled to confess to the aged Palemon that he has saved Thaïs at the cost of his own soul. Raging passionately at himself, he struggles to cast from his mind the memories of his human weakness, of her intoxicating beauty. He longs for Thaïs. In his sleep, a vision comes to him of the courtesan, lovely, confident, mocking, as he first beheld her in Alexandria. Then the vision changes. Her face is aglow with the fervor of religious ecstasy as she lies dying in the convent. With a cry of terror he awakens and rushes out into the darkness.

SCENE 3: *The Garden of the Monastery.* Thaïs, worn with severe repentance and self-denial, is dying, surrounded by the White Sisters, who respectfully withdraw when Athanaël enters. Utterly distraught, the monk implores Thaïs to return to Alexandria. There they shall live happily, for all that he has taught her is false. The ecstatic music of the "Meditation" surges again from the orchestra, and now Thaïs, heedless of the words of Athanaël, sings of the gates of heaven opening before her . . . the smiles of angels . . . the beating of celestial wings. Suddenly she falls back dead, and Athanaël, anguished by a frightful remorse, cries out in despair.

THE RCA-VICTOR RECORDS
(Sung in French)

New York Times
HELEN JEPSON AS THAÏS AND
JOHN CHARLES THOMAS AS ATHANAËL

ACT II

MÉDITATION (Intermezzo): *Boston "Pops" Orchestra, Arthur Fiedler, Cond.*
11887, 12″

Mischa Elman, Violinist, with Piano
11-8950, 12″

Fritz Kreisler, Violinist, with Piano
6844, 12″

Charles R. Cronham, Organist
35858, 12″

ACT III

MORT DE THAÏS—TE SOUVIENT-IL DU LUMINEAUX VOYAGE (Death of Thaïs—Dost Remember the Luminous Voyage): *Dorothy Kirsten, Soprano; Robert Merrill, Baritone; with Orch.*
11-9792, 12″

TOSCA AND SCARPIA

Tosca

OPERA IN three acts. Music by Giacomo Puccini. Libretto by Giuseppe Giacosa and Luigi Illica, after Victorian Sardou's play, *La Tosca*. First performance, Teatro Costanzi, Rome, January 4, 1900. United States *première*, Metropolitan Opera House, February 4, 1901. In this country the heroine's role has been sung by such famous artists as Milka Ternina, Emma Eames, Olive Fremstad, Maria Labia, Carmen Melis, Geraldine Farrar, Lina Cavalieri, Emmy Destinn, Mary Garden, Claudia Muzio, Maria Jeritza, Lotte Lehmann, and Grace Moore. The tenor role of Mario Cavaradossi was a favorite not only of Caruso's and, incidentally, one of his best, but also of such singers, all heard here, as Giuseppe Cremonini, who sang it when the opera was first produced at the Metropolitan, Giovanni Zenatello, Alessandro Bonci, Giovanni Martinelli, Beniamino Gigli, Giacomo Lauri-Volpi, Mario Chamlee, Galliano Masini, Richard Crooks, Jan Peerce, James Melton, and Charles Kullman. As for the compelling part of Baron Scarpia, Antonio Scotti became almost inseparably related to it, and Maurice Renaud was believed to be by many the greatest of its interpreters. Also effective in the part were Vanni Marcoux, Giuseppe de Luca, Pasquale Amato, Jean Périer, and others. The place of honor with respect to embodying the amusing Sacristan seems to go to the celebrated bass, Charles Gilibert.

This gruesome tragedy by Sardou at first seems scarcely suitable for musical treatment. Yet such was Puccini's genius for the theater that his score is not only equal to the demands of the action, but it adds also to the tensely dramatic atmosphere, and is in excellent taste. Moreover, at every opportunity for lyrical expression the composer has given his typical sensuous melodies.

CHARACTERS

FLORIA TOSCA, *a celebrated singer*	*Soprano*	A SACRISTAN	*Baritone or Bass*
MARIO CAVARADOSSI, *a painter*	*Tenor*	SPOLETTA, *a police agent*	*Tenor*
BARON SCARPIA, *chief of police*	*Baritone*	SCIARRONE, *a gendarme*	*Bass*
CESARE ANGELOTTI, *a political plotter*	*Bass*		

A JAILER, A SHEPHERD BOY, AN EXECUTIONER, ETC.

The action takes place in Rome, in 1800, during a particularly seething period of political intrigue

ACT I

SCENE: *The Church of Sant' Andrea della Valle.* As the curtain rises, three somber chords are thundered out by the orchestra, and we behold the high-vaulted interior of the church of Sant' Andrea. Angelotti enters, pale, disheveled, panic-stricken, in prison garb. He barely has time to conceal himself before the Sacristan appears, going about his duties. A moment later Cavaradossi appears, returning to work. He has been painting a fair-haired, blue-eyed Madonna, using for his model an unknown worshiper in the church whose beauty has impressed him. He is unaware that she is the sister of his friend, Angelotti, and anyway his interest is purely artistic. Drawing from his bosom a miniature of his beloved, the dark-eyed Tosca, he sings of the strange manner in which the various features of her loveliness blend into a harmonious whole, *"Recondita armonia"* ("Strange harmony").

The Sacristan goes, after a covetous glance at Cavaradossi's lunch basket. A moment later the wild-eyed Angelotti appears, relieved at finding his old friend, who promises him aid in escaping. Tosca is heard calling outside for her "Mario." Cavaradossi gives the fugitive a few hurried directions, and Angelotti disappears, taking with him a woman's dress left as a disguise for him by his sister.

Tosca enters. The temperamental singer is angry at Mario's delay in admitting her and is suspicious, having heard voices. The painter quiets her jealous fancies, and they arrange to meet that evening. Tosca leaves, and Mario goes to aid Angelotti further his escape.

The members of the choir enter, hurriedly preparing for a festival to celebrate Napoleon's defeat. Their excitement is suddenly hushed at the entrance of Scarpia, the dreaded chief of police. The escaped prisoner has been traced to the church. A fan is discovered belonging to Angelotti's sister, and overlooked by the prisoner in his haste. Tosca, still doubting her lover, returns to church under some trivial pretext. She is greeted not by Mario, but by Scarpia, who approaches her courteously. Flatteringly saying that she comes to church devoutly, to pray, not like other women who come

Castagneri

ACT I—THE CHURCH OF ST. ANDREA

to distribute their favors, Scarpia arouses her jealousy by showing her the fan. Tosca becomes greatly excited and leaves the church, weeping. Scarpia orders three of his agents to follow her. The cardinal and a great procession now enter the church, advancing toward the High Altar, and a *"Te Deum"* is sung. The voices of the choir mount in sacred song, and Scarpia, kneeling in mock devotion, can be heard muttering to himself while he gloats over the anticipated destruction of his rival and the moment when Tosca shall be his own. At this thought he joins with the final magnificent outburst of the choir.

ACT II

SCENE: *Scarpia's Apartment in the Farnese Palace.* Scarpia restlessly awaits news of his prey—Cavaradossi and Angelotti. Hearing Tosca's voice in the Queen's apartment near by, he sends a message to her, saying that he has received word of her lover. This, he knows, will be bait enough for Tosca, tormented as she is with jealousy; again Scarpia rejoices at the thought of his conquest. Yet a moment later he is angered, for Spoletta, his agent, brings word that Angelotti cannot be found. He is quickly consoled, however, on hearing that Cavaradossi has been captured. The painter, when brought in, refuses to divulge Angelotti's hiding place. Accordingly he is consigned to the torture chamber—just as Tosca appears. Scarpia greets her with an exaggerated courtesy, and bluntly tells her that her lover is in the next room being tortured; for each refusal the pain-producing instrument is tightened. Tosca trembles with anxiety, and Scarpia sadistically opens the door so that she may hear Mario's stifled cries. The artist urges her to reveal nothing. Scarpia bids her look at her lover; one glance, and Tosca cries out in horror; even the hardened Spoletta is appalled at the abominable proceedings. The ever-augmented pain brings a suppressed cry from Mario; Tosca can endure this no longer and tells Scarpia where Angelotti is hidden. Cavaradossi is then brought in, still racked with pain, near fainting. Suddenly word comes that the reported defeat of Napoleon was a mistake; he was really the victor. Scarpia stands abashed, but Mario, in spite of his weakness and Tosca's whispered admonition to remain silent, gives a shout of victory. The enraged official orders Cavaradossi to prison and death.

When Mario has been taken away, Scarpia begins his cruel love-making; he has long adored Tosca, has sworn to possess her; he will brook no refusal. Her spirit crushed, Tosca weeps for shame and sings her famous plea, *"Vissi d'arte"* ("Love and music"). She has devoted her life to art and love, has gone regularly to church and been generous in bestowing charity; how can she deserve this cruel treatment?

Scarpia replies to her impassioned prayer cynically, and at last in desperation Tosca says that she will yield to his unholy demand if he will rescind the order of execution and write a passport giving Mario and herself safe-conduct to leave the country.

Scarpia is overjoyed. He informs her that a mock execution will be necessary, summons Spoletta for a moment to give him some secret instructions, then turns to his desk to write the required papers. Meanwhile Tosca surreptitiously takes from the table a sharp knife and conceals it. Scarpia advances toward her, overpowering in his triumph. He takes her in his arms; Tosca drives the knife into his body, and he falls lifeless. With grim reverence, she extends the corpse upon the floor, places lighted candles at the head and a crucifix on the bosom, crosses herself, and steals noiselessly away.

R. Strohmeyer
ACT I—THE CHURCH OF ST. ANDREA—SAN FRANCISCO OPERA PRODUCTION

Louis Melançon
ACT I—METROPOLITAN OPERA PRODUCTION WITH PIA TASSINARI AND FERRUCCIO TAGLIAVINI

ACT III

SCENE: *The Terrace of Castel' Sant' Angelo.* Mario is brought out from his cell to the terrace of the castle of Sant' Angelo. The city is still in darkness although the sound of sheep bells on the distant hillsides and the clanging of the great bells in the church tower announce the approach of dawn. Told that he has only one hour to live, Cavaradossi sings a touching farewell to his dreams of art and to his beloved, recalling their former meetings on starlit nights in quiet gardens, *"E lucevan le stelle"* ("The stars were shining").

He is suddenly startled by the arrival of Tosca. She tells him of the death of Scarpia, and he commends the gentle hands that struck the blow, even though regretting that they should have had to be soiled with the blood of such a scoundrel. The soldiers come, the shots of the supposedly mock execution are fired, and Mario falls. Tosca, waiting till the firing party has gone, bids him rise—"Now, Mario, all is safe." He does not answer. She rushes to him, stunned by the knowledge that Scarpia has tricked her. Mario is dead. She throws herself on the body in an agony of grief. Spoletta and the soldiers approach to seize her as Scarpia's murderer. Before they realize her intention she evades them, quickly climbs the parapet of the castle, and leaps to freedom and death.

Tosca

THE RCA-VICTOR RECORDS
(Sung in Italian)

COMPLETE RECORDING: *Maria Caniglia, Soprano; Beniamino Gigli, Tenor; Armando Borgioli, Baritone; Ernesto Dominici, Bass; Giulio Tomei, Bass; Nino Mazziotti, Tenor; Gino Conti, Bass; Anna Marcangeli, Soprano; with Chorus and Orchestra of the Royal Opera, Rome, Oliviero de Fabritiis, Cond.*

DMC-109 (DM-539) (Vol. 1)
(16092-16098), 7-12″

(DM-540) (Vol. 2)
(16099-16105), 7-12″

MC-109 (M-539) (Vol. 1)
(15611-15617)

(M-540) (Vol. 2)
(15618-15624)

ACT I

RECONDITA ARMONIA (Strange Harmony):
Jussi Bjoerling, Tenor, with Orch.
4372, 10″

James Melton, Tenor, with Orch.
10-1357, 10″

Enrico Caruso, Tenor, with Orch.
11-8569, 12″

RICHARD CROOKS AS CAVARADOSSI

TE DEUM: *Lawrence Tibbett, Baritone; Metropolitan Opera Chorus and Orch.*
8124, 12″
11-8861, 12″
(In Album M-1015)

LOVE DUET: *Florence Quartararo, Soprano; Ramon Vinay, Tenor; RCA-Victor Orchestra, Jean Paul Morel, Cond.*
12-0531, 12″

ACT II

CANTABILE DI SCARPIA (Scarpia's Air):
Antonio Scotti, Baritone, with Orch.
18142, 12″
(In Album M-816)
(Acoustical Recording)

VISSI D'ARTE (Love and Music): *Licia Albanese, Soprano, with Orch.*
11-9115, 12″

ACT III

È LUCEVAN LE STELLE (The Stars Were Shining): *Jussi Bjoerling, Tenor, with Orch.* 4408, 10″

James Melton, Tenor, with Orch.
10-1357, 10″

Jan Peerce, Tenor, RCA-Victor Orchestra, Erich Leinsdorf, Cond.
MO-1250 (12-0498-B)
VO-22 (18-0176-B)

ANTONIO SCOTTI AS SCARPIA

Pleasant — some very pleasant passages. 2-29-4

ACT I—METROPOLITAN OPERA PRODUCTION

La Traviata
(THE STRAYED ONE)

OPERA IN three acts. Music by Giuseppe Verdi. Libretto by Francesco Maria Piave, after Alexandre Dumas' *La Dame aux camélias*. First performance, Teatro la Fenice, Venice, March 6, 1853. First performance in the United States, Academy of Music, New York, December 3, 1856. Initial hearing at the Metropolitan, November 6, 1883, with Marcella Sembrich as the heroine, Violetta. A prima donna's opera, *La Traviata* has had in the role of Violetta, through the years, a brilliant company of interpreters, including Adelina Patti, Marietta Piccolomini, Angiolina Bosio, Christine Nilsson, Anna de La Grange, Nellie Melba, Rosina Storchio, Luisa Tetrazzini, Amelita Galli-Curci, Lucrezia Bori, Claudia Muzio, Rosa Ponselle, and, more recently at the Metropolitan, Licia Albanese and Bidu Sayao. The Alfredos have been no less distinguished, the listing being headed by Enrico Caruso and Alessandro Bonci. In later seasons there have been Beniamino Gigli, Giacomo Lauri-Volpi, Jan Peerce, and Ferruccio Tagliavini, all Metropolitan Alfredos. The part of the elder Germont, though scarcely pleasing to its creator, Felice Varesi, has been held in high esteem by baritones of a later day, what with the lyrical opportunities provided in the second act. One of the greatest impersonations of the father, we are told, was that by Maurice Renaud, who appeared in the opera with Nellie Melba at Hammerstein's Manhattan Opera House during the winter of 1907. Subsequent elder Germonts have been sung by Giuseppe de Luca, Lawrence Tibbett, and Leonard Warren, among others.

When first produced, *La Traviata* was a failure. This has been ascribed to a variety of causes. One of these was the fact that, being based on a then contemporary drama and performed in the costumes of that day, it dazed an audience accustomed to operas given in the garb of older times. Further, the leading tenor, Graziani, was hoarse; Varesi, the baritone, scarcely extended himself, since he disliked the role; the soprano, Signora Donatelli, an excellent singer, looked like anything but a consumptive, with her generous proportions, and her dying scene in the last act, consequently, excited the audience to loud laughter.

On May 6, 1854, a little over a year later, *La Traviata* was given in the same city, Venice, though at another theater, the San Benedetto, and there, with the men wearing costumes of the period of Louis XIII, it gained the success it had deserved from the start. The Violetta of that performance, Signora Spezia, was easy to look at and, paradoxically

549

enough, believable as a victim of tuberculosis; the tenor, Landi, proved most satisfactorily in voice, and the baritone, Coletti, made it apparent to all that he enjoyed his work.

La Traviata has since earned a stellar place in almost every opera company's repertoire. In that respect it may be said to be a rival of the same composer's *Aïda* and *Rigoletto*. Perhaps one of the greatest modern performances of *La Traviata* was that produced in concert form for a broadcast of the National Broadcasting Symphony, under the direction of Arturo Toscanini, during the 1946–47 season. The principals, on that occasion, were Licia Albanese, Jan Peerce, and Robert Merrill, all of the Metropolitan.

CHARACTERS

VIOLETTA VALERY, *a courtesan*	*Soprano*	GASTONE DE LETORIÈRES	*Tenor*
FLORA, *Violetta's friend*	*Soprano or Mezzo-soprano*	MARQUIS D'OBIGNY	*Bass*
		DR. GRENVIL	*Bass*
ALFREDO GERMONT, *Violetta's lover*	*Tenor*	GIUSEPPE, *Violetta's servant*	*Tenor*
GIORGIO GERMONT, *his father*	*Baritone*	ANNINA, *Violetta's confidante and maid*	*Soprano*
BARON DOUPHOL, *a rival of Alfredo*	*Baritone*		

LADIES AND GENTLEMEN, MASQUERS, SERVANTS

The action takes place in Paris and environs circa *1840 (sometimes 1700)*

The Prelude begins with very soft tranquil harmonies, high in the strings, similar to the Prelude to the scene of Violetta's death, Act III. There follows a haunting melody, passionate, yet sentimental—the melody of the heroine's parting in the second act. This melody is repeated by the violoncellos while the violins play embroidery above. At the close the music fades gently away, making all the more striking the contrast with the brilliant music of the opening scene.

ACT I

SCENE: *A Salon in Violetta's House.* Violetta's elaborately furnished salon is the meeting place of the gayer element of Parisian life. Tonight an unusually lively entertainment seems to be taking place. Alfredo Germont is introduced to Violetta as another of her admirers, and at her request he sings a jovial drinking song, *"Libiamo ne' lieti calici"* ("A bumper we'll drain"), in which Violetta and the guests join. The energetic rhythm and lively melody of this number cause it to be ranked high among operatic drinking songs.

Music is heard from the adjoining ballroom, toward which the guests proceed. Violetta is seized by a sudden faintness, an ominous forewarning of consumption, but at her request the guests continue into the ballroom; Alfredo, however, remains behind. Violetta cannot quite understand why a young man of such evidently good standing should be concerned with her—a mere butterfly. He confesses that he loves her, has loved her since the day when first he happened to see her a year ago. At first Violetta thinks his protestations mere banter; when she begins to realize their seriousness she is profoundly moved and begs him to go ... she is unworthy, he must forget her.

ACT III—SAN FRANCISCO OPERA PRODUCTION

Alfredo's tender confession of love and Violetta's nervous response are beautifully expressed in their duet, *"Un dì felice"* ("Rapturous moment").

The rosy light of dawn begins to penetrate the curtained windows. The guests take their leave; Alfredo follows. Violetta is left alone in the room, which is now in disorder and tawdry under the growing daylight.

She meditates on the night's happenings, saying to herself, in recitative, "How strangely those words have moved me."

Then singing a hesitant but most expressive little air, *"Ah, fors' è lui"* ("The one of whom I dreamed"), she continues to speculate on the possibilities of this new situation.

An instant later she becomes suddenly transformed, for, thinking that her dreams are hopeless, she begins a dazzling coloratura aria, singing, *"Sempre libera"* ("Ever free"), in which she rather gives the impression that she will no longer squander her days in the pursuit of pleasure, now that a new interest has entered her life.

ACT II

SCENE 1: *A Country House Near Paris.* Violetta and Alfredo have been living a life of idyllic happiness in a little country house near Paris. Poetical young man that he is, Alfredo is enraptured at having found in Violetta a true mate. Singing a very melodious aria, *"De' miei bollenti spiriti"* ("Wild my dream of youth"), he tells of his contentment in this haven of peace and love, and contrasts it with his own turbulent youth.

The practical affairs of life, however, recall him from his amorous dreams; for the maid enters, and upon questioning her, Alfredo learns that Violetta has secretly had all her jewels sold in order to keep this secluded home. He is much ashamed on thus suddenly realizing his position, and hurries to the city to obtain funds.

Violetta enters; no more is she the painted courtesan of the city, but a gracious, modest young woman. On reading an invitation to a party at the home of a former friend, Flora, she smiles in refusal; such things do not interest her now. Presently Alfredo's father appears and makes himself known. He is none too polite in his greetings, for he has been greatly distressed at what he conceives to be his son's boyish entanglement. Violetta maintains such dignity, however, that he is soon charmed and abashed, especially when he learns that, far from being dependent upon Alfredo, she has sold her property to support him. Thus abandoning his former attitude, he throws himself wholly on her mercy. Alfredo has, it seems, a younger sister, whose marriage to a nobleman will be jeopardized if this scandalous *mésalliance* continues in the Germont family. Violetta at first refuses to give up her lover, then, as the father continues to plead, she begins to realize that her union with Alfredo will ultimately react to his disadvantage. She finally yields, singing through her tears, *"Dite alla giovine"* ("Tell your daughter"), a moving song in which Violetta renounces all claim to Alfredo for the sake of his sister. Violetta continues, saying, "Now command me." Germont answers, "Say you do not love him." She replies, "He'll not believe me." Violetta thinks of a plan; but she is shaken with sobs and pleads for consolation; she will need courage in order to go through with her resolve. The father comforts her tenderly, then leaves.

The music of this scene represents Verdi at his best. The melodies are lovely, very appropriate to the situation and characters and the changing sentiments of the text.

As soon as Germont has gone, the unhappy Violetta writes a note of farewell to Alfredo and makes ready to leave for Paris. Alfredo returns, and is mystified by her confusion. His father has written him a stern letter demanding an interview—Alfredo expects him at any moment. Not even suspecting that Violetta and his father have ever met, he believes that the charm of her bearing and personality will cause the elder Germont to relent. Violetta begs to be excused for a time, saying that she will return and throw herself at his father's feet, he will forgive them, they will then be happy forever! But before she goes out she questions Alfredo with such extreme anxiety, "Do you love me? Do you truly love me?" and says "Farewell" with such tenderness that her lover is deeply moved.

In a very few moments a servant comes with a note for Alfredo. It is in Violetta's handwriting. He tears it open, staggers as he realizes its meaning. His father has entered unobserved, and tries to console his son by recalling their home, singing, *"Di Provenza il mar"* ("Thy home in fair Provence"). In spite of the declaration of critics that it is trite and inappropriate, an ex-

R. Strohmeyer ACT II—SAN FRANCISCO OPERA PRODUCTION

ample of Verdi in a weaker moment, this melodious aria remains one of the most popular in the opera.

The father appeals in vain to Alfredo to return to his home. Gazing vaguely about the room, Alfredo notices Flora's letter and on reading it concludes that, having abandoned him, Violetta will make her plunge back into a life of gaiety at Flora's fête. Burning with anger and jealousy, he rushes out to seek revenge.

SCENE 2: *A Gallery in Flora's Parisian House.* The scene changes. Festivities are being held in the richly furnished and brightly lighted salon in Flora's palace. The first feature of the entertainment is a masquerade. The music ripples along with the utmost frivolity; gypsies appear and contribute to the gaiety with their jangling tambourines and a little byplay at fortune-telling. They are followed by another group dressed in Spanish costume who sing a festive song of matadors.

To this party now comes Alfredo, who remarks with assumed indifference that he knows nothing of Violetta's whereabouts. The primary feature of the entertainment being gambling rather than dancing, he joins the game, and, oddly enough, is extremely lucky in his winnings. When Violetta arrives, leaning on the arm of Baron Douphol, she is shocked at seeing Alfredo. Pretending not to notice her, Alfredo remarks, "Misfortune in love brings luck at cards." The Baron is plainly disturbed by Alfredo's presence, cautions Violetta not to speak to him, then goes over and joins the game. Again Alfredo wins; angry words follow between Alfredo and the Baron that threaten to lead to a duel. The tension is relieved, fortunately, by a servant's announcement that the banquet is ready. All withdraw to the adjoining salon.

Violetta returns immediately, followed by Alfredo, whom she has asked to see privately. She begs him to leave the house at once, thus he will avoid further trouble. He will go only on one condition—that she come with him. Though her heart is breaking, she remembers her promise to the elder Germont and says she cannot—she is bound. "To whom?" questions Alfredo anxiously, "To Douphol? then you love him!" With a painful effort she replies, "Yes!" Trembling with fury, Alfredo flings wide the doors and calls back the astonished guests. Before them all he denounces Violetta, and shouting, "I call on you to witness that I have paid her back!" he flings a purse at her feet. She sinks fainting in the arms of Flora. All are shocked at Alfredo's outrageous conduct. Germont enters at this moment and denounces his son. As the curtain drops, the Baron challenges Alfredo to a duel.

ACT III

SCENE: *Violetta's Bedroom.* Violetta is now a mere shadow of her former self, for her unhappiness has greatly aggravated her illness. Although the doctor reassures Violetta, he whispers to the faithful maid that her mistress has not long to live. Left alone, Violetta reads a letter she has received from Germont; meanwhile the orchestra whispers touchingly a strain of the first duet of the lovers:

You have kept your promise. The duel took place, and the Baron was wounded, but is improving. Alfredo is abroad. I myself have revealed your sacrifices to him. He will return to implore your pardon. I also shall come. Hasten to recover; you deserve a bright future.—Giorgio Germont.

"Too late!" is her comment in a hollow voice. Then she rises, saying, "I've trusted, and waited, but alas, he comes not!" She pauses to look at herself in the mirror. "Oh, how I'm faded, and the doctor said that I would soon recover, but this faintness tells plainly all is hopeless." She continues, singing a beautiful and pathetic farewell to this "fair world of sorrow," *"Addio del passato"* ("Farewell to the past"). The melody, of a fragile delicacy like the wasted heroine herself, rises at its close to clear high tones of poignant loveliness as she exclaims, "All is ended."

A moment later the door opens, and Violetta is soon in her lover's arms. In contrition Alfredo begs forgiveness; it is at once joyfully granted. Violetta's health seems to return with her happiness; even Alfredo is for a moment deceived. They plan a bright future in the quiet country life in which they first found happiness, as they sing *"Parigi, o cara"* ("Far from gay Paris"). The joy of the meeting has been too much; soon she collapses, and Germont enters with the physician. The father blames himself for having brought all these sorrows on his son and Violetta, and again the melody of the lovers' duet is heard, whispered by the violins in ethereal, tremulous beauty. Violetta no longer feels pain; she rouses herself with an unnatural return of strength and cries, "I live! I have again returned to life!" With this she falls back upon the couch—dead.

DOROTHY KIRSTEN AS VIOLETTA

LAWRENCE TIBBETT AS GERMONT

THE RCA-VICTOR RECORDS
(Sung in Italian)

COMPLETE RECORDING: *Anna Rosza, Soprano; Olga de Franco, Soprano; Alessandro Ziliani, Tenor; Luigi Borgonovo, Baritone; Giordano Callegari, Tenor; Antonio Gelli, Baritone; Arnoldo Lenzi, Baritone; with Chorus and Orchestra of La Scala, Milan, Carlo Sabajno, Cond.*
DM-112 (12870-12882), 13-12"
M-112 (11105-11117)

PRELUDE: *Arturo Toscanini and the NBC Symphony Orchestra* 18080, 12"
11-9233, 12"
(In Album M-1064)

ACT I

BRINDISI—LIBIAMO, LIBIAMO NE' LIETI CALICI (Drinking Song—A Bumper We'll Drain): *Anna Rosza, Soprano; Alessandro Ziliani, Tenor; Chorus and Orch. of La Scala* 12832, 12"

UN DÌ FELICE ETEREA (Rapturous Moment): *Licia Albanese, Soprano; Jan Peerce, Tenor; with Orch.*
11-9290, 12"
(In Album M-1074)

Amelita Galli-Curci, Soprano; Tito Schipa, Tenor; with Orch.
1754, 10"

AH! FORS' È LUI (The One of Whom I Dreamed);
SEMPRE LIBERA (I'll Fulfill the Round of Pleasure): *Licia Albanese, Soprano, with Orch.* 11-9331, 12"

Helen Jepson, Soprano, with Orch.
15819, 12"
(In Album M-633)

Marcella Sembrich, Soprano, with Orch.
18140, 12"
(In Album M-816)
(Acoustical Recording)

Georg
AMELITA GALLI-CURCI AS VIOLETTA

Frieda Hempel, Soprano; Pasquale
Amato, Baritone; with Orch.
(Acoustical Recording) 15-1020, 12"

DI PROVENZA IL MAR (Thy Home in Fair
Provence): Robert Merrill, Baritone,
with Orch.   11-9794, 12"
John Charles Thomas, Baritone, with
Orch.   15680, 12"
(In Album M-645)
7605, 12"
(In Album M-329) 14205, 12"

Giuseppe de Luca, Baritone, with Orch.
7086, 12"

AH SÌ! CHE FECI! (What Was I Doing?):
Anna Rosza, Soprano; Olga de
Franco, Soprano; Alessandro Ziliani,
Tenor; Luigi Borgonovo, Baritone;
Antonio Gelli, Baritone; Chorus and
Orch. of La Scala   12832, 12"

AH! FORS' È LUI (Only): Lucrezia Bori,
Soprano, with Orch.   7438, 12"

SEMPRE LIBERA (Only): Lucrezia Bori,
Soprano, with Orch.   11-8569, 12"

ACT II

DE' MIEI BOLLENTI SPIRITI (Wild My
Dream of Youth): Jan Peerce, Tenor,
with Orch.   11-8926, 12"

AH! DITE ALLA GIOVINE (Ah! Say to Thy
Daughter)

IMPONETE (Now Command Me): Licia
Albanese, Soprano; Robert Merrill,
Baritone; with Orch.   11-9175, 12"

JOHN CHARLES THOMAS AS GERMONT

ACT III

PRELUDE: Arturo Toscanini and the NBC
Symphony Orchestra   18080, 12"

Arturo Toscanini and the New York
Philharmonic-Symphony Orchestra
11-9233, 12"
(In Album M-1064)

ADDIO DEL PASSATO (Forever I Must Leave
Thee): Licia Albanese, Soprano, with
Orch.   12-0014, 12"

PARIGI, O CARA, NOI LASCEREMO (Far From
Gay Paris): Amelita Galli-Curci, So-
prano; Tito Schipa, Tenor; with
Orch.   1754, 10"

Lucrezia Bori, Soprano; John McCormack, Tenor; with Orch.
15-1009, 12"
(Acoustical Recording)

ELEANOR STEBER AS VIOLETTA

FINALE—D'OYLY CARTE OPERA PRODUCTION

Trial by Jury

"Dramatic Cantata" in one act. Music by Arthur Sullivan. Libretto by W. S. Gilbert. First produced at the Royalty Theatre, London, March 25, 1875. Of all the Gilbert and Sullivan operettas, *Trial by Jury* is the only one without dialogue. Lasting less than an hour, it usually serves as curtain raiser on a double bill. For those who love sparkling melody and lighthearted spoofing *Trial by Jury* is an uninterrupted delight. Apart from that, it is important as the work that marked the first success of one of the great collaborations of musical history. In 1868 Gilbert had published a "burlesque opera" with the title *Trial by Jury*. Carl Rosa, a producer and composer, proceeded to set it to music for his wife, the singer Mme. Parepa-Rosa. But she died shortly after, and Rosa returned the book to Gilbert. At this point another composer-impresario stepped into the picture, a man named Richard D'Oyly Carte. It so happened that D'Oyly Carte needed a curtain raiser for his production of Offenbach's *La Périchole* at the Royalty. Knowing Gilbert's work, he asked him to furnish a libretto, which turned out to be a new version of the same *Trial by Jury* published a few years before. D'Oyly Carte was delighted with the book and promptly saw the great possibilities of Gilbert and Sullivan as a team. To his biographer Arthur Lawrence, Sullivan later related the details of the crucial meeting:

"It was on a very cold morning, with the snow falling heavily, that Gilbert came round to my place, clad in a heavy fur coat. He had called to read over to me the MS of *Trial by Jury*. He read it through, and, it seemed to me, in a perturbed sort of way, with a gradual crescendo of indignation, in the manner of a man considerably disappointed with what he had written. As soon as he had come to the last word he closed up the manuscript violently, apparently unconscious of the fact that he had achieved his purpose so far as I was concerned, inasmuch as I was screaming with laughter the whole time."

The operetta proved perhaps the greatest hit of the London season. Londoners went about humming and whistling the tunes and chanting its gaily preposterous thrusts at the formidable institution of the English court system.

557

Trial by Jury

CHARACTERS

THE LEARNED JUDGE	*Baritone*	FOREMAN OF THE JURY	*Bass*
COUNSEL FOR THE PLAINTIFF	*Tenor*	USHER	*Baritone*
THE DEFENDANT, EDWIN	*Tenor*	THE PLAINTIFF, ANGELINA	*Soprano*

CHORUS OF JURYMEN, BRIDESMAIDS, BARRISTERS, ATTORNEYS, ETC.

SCENE: *A Court of Justice.* The curtain rises on a chorus of barristers, attorneys, and jurymen with ushers. The chorus, in a sturdy song, makes known the course of events:

> *For, today, in this arena,*
> *Summoned by a stern subpoena,*
> *Edwin—sued by Angelina—*
> *Shortly will appear.*

The Usher, having marshaled the jurymen into the jury box, gives them the judicial counsel to heed the plaintiff, "The Broken-hearted Bride," and not "The Ruffianly Defendant," for,

> *From bias free, of every kind,*
> *This trial must be tried.*

The Defendant appears, asking, "Is this the Court of the Exchequer?" and is greeted with scorn: "Monster, dread our damages!" The Defendant explains that happiness with the Plaintiff having palled, he became "Another love-sick boy." The Jury admit that once they too were like that, but have since grown respectable and have no sympathy for the Defendant. The Usher orders silence, for the Judge approaches. The chorus greets him with churchly song, "All hail, great Judge!"

Having thanked them, the Judge proceeds to relate how he reached his exalted station. When young, he confides, he was an impecunious lawyer:

> *So he fell in love with a rich attorney's*
> *Elderly, ugly daughter.*

The attorney turned plenty of cases over to him, and when he had grown "rich as the Gurneys" he threw over the "elderly, ugly daughter." But now he is a Judge ("it was managed by a job"), and ready to try this breach-of-promise case.

At the Judge's order, the Usher now swears in the jury and summons the Plaintiff, Angelina. The bridesmaids enter as her escort. While they are singing, the Judge sends a "mash note" to the first bridesmaid by the Usher, but when Angelina sings her graceful air, he shifts his attention to her. He even admits that he never saw "so exquisitely fair a face." For their part, the jurymen profess great admiration for the bridesmaids and again address the Defendant as "Monster." The Counsel for the Plaintiff makes his appeal to the jury, telling how the Defendant

> *. . . deceived a girl confiding,*
> *Vows, et cetera, deriding.*

And when the Plaintiff wished to name the day, he left her—

> *Doubly criminal to do so,*
> *For the maid had bought her trousseau!*

Counsel and jurymen join in rallying the Plaintiff with the words, "Cheer up!" while she sighs, "Ah me!" in mock operatic style. The Plaintiff reels as if to faint and falls sobbing on the Foreman's breast, but when the Judge approaches she leans on him instead. Edwin now attempts to defend himself against the charge of "Monster," observing that

> *Of nature the laws I obey,*
> *For nature is constantly changing.*

In conclusion, he volunteers that,

> *If it will appease her sorrow,*
> *I'll marry this lady today,*
> *And marry the other tomorrow!*

This seems reasonable to the Judge, but the Counsel, on referring to his books, finds that to marry two wives at a time is a serious offense, "Burglaree!" This dilemma is discussed in a splendid burlesque of an Italian opera sextet. The Usher having restored silence in court, Angelina proves her loss. Crying "I love him," she embraces the Defendant, and then adds:

> *Oh, see what a blessing, what love and caressing*
> *I've lost, and remember it, pray,*
> *When you, I'm addressing, are busy assessing*
> *The damages Edwin must pay.*

The Defendant counters by saying that he is a bad lot, given to liquor, he's sure he would beat her, and that she couldn't endure him very long; the jury should remember this when assessing the damages. These conflicting statements are developed in a dramatic ensemble. The Judge accordingly suggests that they make the Defendant "tipsy" and see if his assertions are true. But to this proposition all save the Defendant object. The Judge is now furious, for he is in a hurry to get away. So he settles the case quickly by declaring that he'll marry Angelina himself! And thus the "trial" ends in a mood of general rejoicing, while the Judge makes his concluding comment:

> *Though homeward as you trudge,*
> *You declare my law is fudge,*
> *But of beauty I'm a judge.*

To which all reply:

> *And a good judge, too!*

Trial by Jury

THE RCA-VICTOR RECORDS
(Sung in English)

COMPLETE RECORDING: *D'Oyly Carte Company; under the personal direction of Rupert D'Oyly Carte. (The cast includes: Winifred Lawson, Leo Sheffield, George Baker, Derek Oldham, Arthur Hosking)*   DC-4 (12901-12904), 4-12″   C-4 (9314-9317)

SYDNEY GRANVILLE AS THE JUDGE

Inquirer Photo ON BOARD TRISTAN'S SHIP—HERBERT GRAF PRODUCTION

Tristan und Isolde
(TRISTAN AND ISOLDE)

OPERA IN three acts. Music and book by Richard Wagner. First performed at the Hof-und-National-Theater, Munich, Germany, June 10, 1865. American *première* at the Metropolitan Opera House, December 1, 1886, with Anton Seidl conducting, and Albert Niemann and Lilli Lehmann in the title roles. In Seidl's revival of November 27, 1895, Jean de Reszke, Lillian Nordica, and Edouard de Reszke appeared for the first time as Tristan, Isolde, and King Mark. When Arturo Toscanini first directed the opera at the Metropolitan, Karl Burrian was the Tristan and Johanna Gadski the Isolde. *Tristan und Isolde* was, of course, one of the repertory victims of the First World War. On its return to the repertory on November 20, 1920, an English translation was used, the company reverting to the German original only a year later.

Tristan und Isolde is romantically supposed to enshrine Wagner's love for Mathilde von Wesendonck, the beautiful wife of a wealthy silk merchant of Zurich who helped Wagner through one of his many financial crises. Wagner was ardently in love with his friend's wife. Since circumstances prevented any real development of the romance, the theory is that *Tristan und Isolde* is the memorial of a tragically unfulfilled passion. Whether such was the sequence of events or not, it is hard to say. Certainly Wagner's feelings for the lovely Mathilde added fervor and intensity, and perhaps pain, to the process of composition. For like Tristan, he suffered the anguish of loving the hopelessly unattainable.

Among all the stories that have been told of unhappy love, a few, handed down for generations, seem well-nigh immortal. Among these is the legend of Tristan and Isolde. This story has been narrated in a variety of forms by poets from medieval times to the present. In the poetic versions of Gottfried von Strassburg, Matthew Arnold, and Swinburne the drinking of the love potion is a purely accidental affair. Thus Tristan and Isolde are made innocent victims of their love. Omitting the love potion, Tennyson makes the passion between the two a guilty, conscious one. With Wagner, Tristan and Isolde are in love before the drinking of the potion, which serves primarily as a way of removing the ethical restraints of the lovers.

Writers on aesthetics are fond of pointing out that *Tristan und Isolde*, with little of the complexity and violent action of the *Ring*, more closely approaches the condition of a perfect music drama. Yet this minimum of outward action in *Tristan und Isolde* may prove a stumbling block. Few works for the lyric stage are so highly charged with drama, but it is an inward, psychological drama, intensely absorbing and profoundly moving. Wagner was at the summit of his powers when he brushed aside the half-finished *Ring* to write this more practical music drama. How "practical" it proved is illustrated by the fact that at Vienna, after more than fifty rehearsals, the work was abandoned as impossible! With time, however, Wagner's impassioned score won the recognition it deserved. This tense, feverishly glowing music is built from a wealth of leading motives, flowing together in an irresistible unity and forming a continuous commentary on the action. But since these motives are themselves so largely subjective in character and associated with emotions or states of mind, the names given them are merely convenient labels of identification. Following closely every changing mood of the drama, this fervid music grows in intensity as the tragedy unfolds, attaining an almost unbearable poignancy and beauty of passionate expression in the last act. The music drama closes with Isolde's magnificent scene, the famous "*Liebestod*," or "Love Death," a title first applied to it by Franz Liszt.

CHARACTERS

TRISTAN, *a Cornish knight, nephew of King Mark*	*Tenor*	MELOT, *one of King Mark's courtiers*	*Tenor*
KING MARK OF CORNWALL	*Bass*	BRANGÄNE, *Isolde's friend and attendant*	*Soprano*
ISOLDE, *Princess of Ireland*	*Soprano*		
KURVENAL, *Tristan's servant*	*Baritone*		

A SHEPHERD, A STEERSMAN, A SAILOR LAD; CHORUS OF SAILORS, KNIGHTS, AND MEN-AT-ARMS

The action takes place during legendary times, at sea, in Cornwall, and in Brittany

LEGENDARY EVENTS PRECEDING THE MUSIC DRAMA

Isolde, Princess of Ireland, was betrothed to Sir Morold, slain by Tristan in the war against Cornwall. This heartless adversary had sent the head of the slain warrior back to the Princess, who discovered in it a splinter of steel from the sword of her lover's murderer.

Tristan, however, had also been gravely wounded in the fight, and his wound would not heal. Having learned that the Princess of Ireland was skilled in magic balms and potions, he disguised himself, assumed the name of Tantris, and went to Ireland to seek her aid. Moved by his suffering, Isolde tended him without suspecting his identity. Then, one day, she was horrified to discover that she had been sheltering Sir Morold's slayer, for the splinter of steel exactly fitted a notch in the stranger's sword. Seized with a desire for revenge, she raised the weapon to kill the stricken man. At that moment their eyes met. Powerless against the piteous appeal of his glance, she let fall the sword and, concealing the secret of his identity, continued to tend him. The knight recovered and departed with many declarations of gratitude.

Tristan soon returned, however, this time under his true name, as an emissary to seek the hand of Isolde for his uncle, King Mark. Her parents assented, believing, as did Mark, that this alliance would end the long strife

ACT II—ISOLDE GIVING THE SIGNAL—COLOGNE FESTIVAL PRODUCTION

between Ireland and Cornwall. Grieving bitterly, for she secretly loved Tristan and believed that he loved her, Isolde was compelled to follow the knight to Cornwall. Such was the chain of events traditionally supposed to have taken place before the beginning of the music drama.

The Prelude to *Tristan und Isolde* is one of Wagner's most impassioned compositions. Built marvelously from a few brief themes which will be of prominence during the course of the action, it begins with a mere whisper, like a sigh of deepest yearning. Played by the cellos, this motive is known as "The Confession to Love." The effect of this is heightened by the poignant interrogation of the "Desire" theme which immediately follows. After a reiteration there enters the eloquent motive of "The Glance," expressive of the origin of the mutual passion of Tristan and Isolde. This is followed by the suave motive of the "Love Philter." There now begins a gradual crescendo in which the theme of "Deliverance by Death" is heard, growing to a climax of overpowering vehemence. The tumult of emotions finally subsides, and as the music ends in a mood of expectancy, the curtain rises. The Prelude is often joined to the *"Liebestod"* as a single concert-hall unit.

ACT I

SCENE: *The Deck of a Ship.* On board Tristan's ship a magnificent pavilion has been erected to house Isolde. From above, in the masthead, a sailor sings of his "Irish maid, wild and amorous maid," a song that only increases Isolde's unhappiness. The ship is now nearing Cornwall, and the Princess is growing indignant at Tristan's persistent refusal to see her. She has grown desperate at the thought of the loveless marriage that awaits her. Her maid, Brangäne, suggests that with the aid of a magic potion she can win the love of King Mark after she is married to him. Isolde bids her bring the casket containing the potion. From it she selects, not the love philter, but a swift death-bringing poison. Isolde commands the maid to prepare a draught. Vengeance and a speedy end to her sorrows are her aim, for she will die and Tristan with her!

She summons Tristan, and at first declares to him that she has resolved to avenge her murdered lover, Morold. Tristan boldly offers her his sword; he is ready to die. Isolde now relents, explaining that she ought not to deprive her husband-to-be of his most trusted knight. She suggests that as a pledge of peace, they drink a cup of reconciliation and forgetfulness. While outside the sailors shout joyfully as the ship approaches land, the trembling Brangäne sets about preparing the drink. Isolde presents the cup to Tristan, who resolutely grasps it. He has divined her intentions and is glad thus to end the grief which oppresses his heart. He drinks, but before he has finished Isolde snatches the cup from his hands and drains it, to the dregs. Their plans go amiss, however, for Brangäne, reluctant to see her mistress die, has substituted the love potion for the poison. Overcome with emotion, the lovers gaze longingly at one another, and then sink into each other's arms, as a great shout outside announces the arrival of the ship at Cornwall.

ACT II

SCENE: *A Garden Before Isolde's Chamber.* Isolde is waiting impatiently before her dwelling. The King has gone on a hunt, and through the soft air of this lovely summer night the sound of the hunting horns can be heard, growing fainter in the distance. Brangäne is fearful lest the hunt be merely a ruse, planned by Melot, who she thinks suspects the true state of affairs. Heedless of the admonition, Isolde, by extinguishing the torch burning at her doorway, gives the signal for Tristan to come. Then, excitedly, she waves her scarf to her approaching lover. While Brangäne watches from the tower, singing a song of warning at the approach of day, the lovers rapturously embrace, oblivious of all but their love. They sing of this love in ecstatic outbursts, appealing to the soft night to delay the dawn that will bring sorrow and separation. *"O sink' hernieder, Nacht der Liebe!"* ("Descend upon us, O night of love!"). They sing, too, of death, which would bring freedom, and of their complete felicity. As their ecstasy reaches a fevered pitch, Brangäne utters a piercing cry of warning. Kurvenal rushes in, shouting, "Save yourself, Tristan!" It is too late! The King enters with his courtiers and Melot. Deeply grieved that he should have been betrayed by his beloved knight and nephew, the King reproaches Tristan in poignant tones. Melot rushes at Tristan with drawn sword. Tristan pretends to respond to the attack of his treacherous friend, but, letting his sword fall, receives the fatal thrust.

Culver Service

OLIVE FREMSTAD AS ISOLDE   LAURITZ MELCHIOR AS TRISTAN

ACT III

SCENE: *A Castle Garden*. An orchestral prelude wondrously pictures the
desolation of Tristan's castle, his prolonged suffering, and the wide expanse
of the ocean. The scene shows the garden of Tristan's ancestral castle in
Brittany. It is situated on a rocky cliff overlooking the sea. A shepherd who
is on watch looks over the wall and asks Kurvenal about Tristan. Refusing
to disclose the cause of his master's distress, Kurvenal orders the shepherd
back to his watch and instructs him to play a lively melody the moment he
sees a ship. After scanning the sailless horizon, the shepherd begins a plaintive melody on his reed pipe as he gradually disappears down the cliff.
Tristan awakens, and upon hearing the mournful tune cries out dejectedly,
"Ever the sorrowful melody!" At the sound of Tristan's voice, Kurvenal is
overjoyed. "Life returns to my Tristan!" he exclaims. Still only half conscious, Tristan asks, "Where am I?" Kurvenal assures him that he is in
Kareol, in his own castle, surrounded by his faithful followers. But Kurvenal's reassuring words fail to awaken Tristan's memory. He knows not
whence he came nor whither he goes, for he longs now only for death. In
oblivion he will be once more united to Isolde. When Kurvenal assures him
that he has sent for her, Tristan becomes still more excited and delirious.
He now works himself up into a frenzy of anticipation, even believing that
he sees the ship bringing his beloved. Then the mournful tune of the shepherd's pipe is heard again, and Tristan, exhausted by his fevered imaginings,
falls back in despair, as though lifeless. Kurvenal, fearing him dead, bends
over to hear his breathing.

While Tristan slowly revives, a feverish vision of Isolde comes to him, and we hear the motives of "Desire" and "Love's Peace" in the orchestra. Again he is convinced his beloved is approaching. This time he is not deceived, for as he exclaims, "The ship! Isolde's ship!" the shepherd begins a lively tune. Kurvenal runs to the watchtower and describes the approach of the vessel while Tristan listens in mounting agitation from his couch. For a moment, when the ship is hidden behind the cliff, Tristan is alarmed, for the rocks there are treacherous. "Who is the helmsman," he cries, "some accomplice of Melot's? Do you also betray me? Do you not yet see her? All is lost then!" A moment later the ship comes into view. Isolde is on the deck, waving to them. In a delirium of joy, Tristan sends Kurvenal to meet her.

Alone now, Tristan tosses on his couch in growing restlessness. Soon he raises himself, tears the bandage from his wound, and staggers forward to meet Isolde. He hears her voice, and his dazed mind thinks of it as the light of the torch which once summoned him to her. "Do I see the light?" he cries. Having overtaxed his vanishing strength, he sinks dying into the arms of his beloved, with a final, heart-rending gasp, crying, "Isolde!" In despair Isolde calls to him, but in vain; he cannot return even for the one hour she pleads for. Distractedly she cries out that she will heal his wounds, and then, realizing that he is forever silent, she falls unconscious.

The shepherd hurries in and calls softly to Kurvenal that another ship has come. Recognizing it as King Mark's and believing that the sovereign has come to attack Tristan's castle, Kurvenal summons his men to its defense. Brangäne is heard, calling her mistress from a distance. Melot, too, approaches, and Kurvenal, rushing at him, savagely strikes him down as he enters the gate. Having thus avenged his master, Kurvenal attacks the others of the King's retinue. Brangäne rushes in to tend Isolde, and Kurvenal, gravely wounded, totters toward his master. With his dying breath, he entreats, "Chide me not, O Tristan, if I try to follow you!"

King Mark is stunned by the death of Tristan, once his most faithful of knights. Frantically, he calls, "Awake, and hear my grief!" Brangäne, having revived Isolde, pleads for forgiveness, saying that she has told the King of the love potion. Mark muses sorrowfully: "When I understood what I had failed to grasp before, how glad I was to find that my friend was blameless! So to unite you, I hurried with flying sails. . . . Yet I only added to the harvest of death; error increased our woe!" Brangäne asks pleadingly, "Do you not hear, Isolde?" And now the *"Liebestod"* ("Love Death") begins. She imagines Tristan to be living, transfigured, as the exultant avowal of a deathless love rises to her lips—*"Mild und leise wie er lächelt"* ("Mild and softly he is smiling"). At first somber, then transformed, growing ever lighter, the magnificent song continues. As Isolde becomes more and more carried away by her vision, the theme of "Ecstasy" enters, constantly growing more agitated, swelling toward a climax, only to begin anew. Isolde exclaims: "Hear you not . . . round me flowing . . . growing nearer . . . clearer . . . the wondrous melody?" The music, having reached its summit of passion, seems to burst in shattering glory, then melt away in deepest calm, while Isolde breathes her last: "In the billowy waves, in the resonant harmony, in the life breath of creation, drink deep and drown in the dreamless sleep, purest bliss!" As though glorified, Isolde sinks into the arms of the faithful Brangäne and dies upon Tristan's body. King Mark raises his arms in blessing over the dead.

THE RCA-VICTOR RECORDS
(Sung in German)

SYMPHONIC SYNTHESIS (Including: Prelude, *Liebesnacht, Liebestod*) : *Leopold Stokowski and The Philadelphia Orchestra*
> DM-508 (16232-16236), 5-12"
> M-508 (15202-15206)

ACT II

LIEBESNACHT—ISOLDE! TRISTAN! GELIEBTER (Love Duet—Isolde! Tristan! Beloved!) : *Kirsten Flagstad, Soprano; Lauritz Melchior, Tenor; San Francisco Opera Orchestra, Edwin McArthur, Cond.*
> DM-671 (18477 & 18478), 2-12"
> M-671 (16238 & 16239)
> 11-8674 & 11-8675, 2-12"
> (In Album M-975)
> 15838 & 15839, 2-12"
> (In Album M-644)

Frida Leider, Soprano; Lauritz Melchior, Tenor; with Orch.
> 7273 & 7274, 2-12"

BRANGÄNES WARNUNG (Brangäne's Warning) : *Blanche Thebom, Mezzosoprano, with Orch.* 11-8928, 12"

Kerstin Thorborg, Contralto, with Orch.
> 17223, 12"
> (In Album M-707)

ACT III

LIEBESTOD—MILD UND LEISE (Isolde's Love Death—Mild and Softly) : *Arturo Toscanini and the NBC Symphony Orchestra; Helen Traubel, Soprano*
> 11-8666, 12"
> (In Album M-978)

Alfredo Valente
HELEN TRAUBEL AS ISOLDE

Kirsten Flagstad, Soprano; San Francisco Opera Orch., Edwin McArthur, Cond. 15840, 12"
> (In Album M-644)

Castagneri   ACT IV, SCENE 1—THE RAMPARTS OF ALIAFERIA

Il Trovatore
(THE TROUBADOUR)

OPERA IN four acts. Music by Giuseppe Verdi. Libretto by Salvatore Cammarano (completed after his death by Bardare), after a play by Antonio García Guitiérrez. First performance, Teatro Apollo, Rome, January 19, 1853. Metropolitan *première*, November 26, 1883, with Alwina Valleria as Leonora, Zelia Trebelli as Azucena, Roberto Stagno as Manrico, Giuseppe Kaschmann as Count di Luna. An important revival took place at the Metropolitan under the direction of Arturo Toscanini, February 20, 1915, with Emmy Destinn, Margarete Ober, Giovanni Martinelli, Pasquale Amato, and Léon Rothier as the chief artists.

Ever since its first production, *Il Trovatore* has ranked as one of the most popular of operas. And it has good reason to be, for its music is melodious and its action swift. The plot, it is true, is overmelodramatic and not so very clearly expressed, yet the irrepressible verve of the master's music sweeps all else before it; even without knowing the story one can feel the forceful surge of many of the scenes. *Il Trovatore* is, indeed, a triumph of the composer's uncanny skill in expressing the dramatic; here, at times, on a mere dance rhythm, such as a waltz or mazurka, he develops melodies of passionate beauty and dramatic appropriateness. *Il Trovatore* preaches no moral and cloaks no philosophy; it aims only at telling an exciting story of a gypsy's vengeance, and in that it succeeds admirably.

In fact, *Trovatore* succeeds too well. Its melodies have been played and sung in every conceivable arrangement until their spontaneity has largely been worn away. Particularly is this true of the remarkable ensemble known as the *"Miserere,"* but heard so often that if we do not pause to give it thought we are likely not to appreciate fully its excellent qualities. The fact that it is still effective is in iself a tribute to Verdi's genius, and, when sung by great artists, it still is wonderfully thrilling.

A "high C" that Verdi never wrote in the tenor aria, *"Di quella pira"* ("Tremble ye tyrants") has been the cause of much argument. Yet it has been sung for so many operatic generations that it has become a firm tradition.

568

Il Trovatore

CHARACTERS

LEONORA, *a noble lady of the court of a princess of Aragon* — Soprano

AZUCENA, *a wandering Biscayan gypsy* — Contralto

INEZ, *Leonora's attendant* — Soprano

MANRICO, *a young chieftain under the Prince of Biscay, of mysterious birth, and in reality a brother of the Count di Luna* — Tenor

COUNT DI LUNA, *a powerful noble of the Prince of Aragon* — Baritone

FERRANDO, *a captain of the guard, and under di Luna* — Bass

RUIZ, *a soldier in Manrico's service* — Tenor

AN OLD GYPSY — Tenor

A MESSENGER, A JAILER, SOLDIERS, NUNS, GYPSIES, ATTENDANTS, ETC.

The action takes place in Biscay and Aragon, in the middle of the fifteenth century

EVENTS PRELIMINARY TO THE OPERA

The old Count di Luna, now long since dead, had two sons of almost the same age. One night, while they were still infants, asleep under a nurse's charge, a gypsy hag who had stolen unobserved into the old Count's castle, was discovered bending over the cradle of the younger child. She was instantly driven away, yet because the child grew wan and pale afterwards she was believed to have bewitched it. She was caught and after the fashion of the times burned to death at the stake.

Her daughter Azucena, then a young gypsy woman with a child of her own, witnessed the execution. She swore vengeance. The following night she crept into the castle and stole the younger child of the Count from its cradle. Then she hurried back to the scene of the execution, where the fire that had consumed her mother still raged. She intended to throw the Count's child into it, thus securing her vengeance. Blind, half crazed with the horror of the sight she had witnessed, she hurtled into the flames *her own child*. Her vengeance temporarily thwarted, Azucena fled with the Count's child and rejoined her gypsy tribe. She revealed her secret to no one, brought the infant up as her own son, and though she has grown to love him, still cherishes the thought that through him she may wreak vengeance upon his family. When the opera opens this child has grown up, known by the name of Manrico, the Troubadour. Azucena has become old and wrinkled, but still thirsts for vengeance, and the old Count has died, leaving his elder son, the Count di Luna appearing in the opera, sole heir to his title and possessions.

ACT I

SCENE 1: *Vestibule in the Palace of Aliaferia.* The retainers of Count di Luna are keeping guard in an outer chamber of Aliaferia Palace. The captain of the guard, Ferrando, passes away the time with a story of the gypsy who was burned for casting a spell on one of the children of the former

Count, and of her daughter, who for vengeance stole the present Count's brother and is believed to have burned him to death at the place of her mother's execution. He relates his tale, while singing a markedly rhythmical melody, expressive of the weird horror of his narrative, *"Abbietta zingara"* ("Despicable gypsy"). A clock strikes midnight, and the retainers, already frightened by the gruesome tale, rush out in terror.

SCENE 2: *The Gardens of the Palace.* In the gardens of the palace the fair Leonora strolls with her attendant and companion, Inez. To her she confides her interest in an unknown knight, victor at a recent tourney. She knows that her love has been requited, for the hero has since serenaded her. Thus it is that they refer to him as *"Il Trovatore"* ("The Troubadour"). She tells of his serenade and the emotions it has awakened, in an aria of unusual beauty and expressiveness, *"Tacea la notte placida"* ("Peaceful was the night").

Leonora's companion speaks of an evil presentiment, and begs her lady to forget her hero, but Leonora cannot.

The ladies enter the palace just as the Count di Luna comes into the garden. He has barely appeared before the voice of the Troubadour is heard from a near-by clump of bushes, singing his serenade. Leonora again comes out of the palace. Mistaking the Count in the shadows of the trees for her Troubadour, she hurries toward him. At that moment the moon happens to emerge from behind the dense clouds that are hurrying across it. Leonora then realizes her mistake, sees the Troubadour, and rushes to him declaring her love for him. The Count is in a terrible rage, and demands to know the intruder's identity. Unmasking, the Troubadour reveals himself as Manrico, a follower of the Prince of Biscay, and thus proscribed in Aragon. Unable to restrain their jealousy, the two men draw their swords and rush away to fight a duel. Leonora falls fainting.

ACT II

SCENE 1: *A Ruined House at the Foot of a Mountain in Biscay.* Dawn at a gypsy camp in the Biscay Mountains. A ruined house. In it a bright campfire; groups of gypsies scattered about. Azucena hovers near the fire; Manrico, at a distance, holding his sword, at which he looks thoughtfully.

As the daylight grows brighter the gypsies bestir themselves about their duties; working at the forges they swing their hammers and bring them down on the clanking metal while they lustily sing the famous "Anvil Chorus."

The aged Azucena has been gazing abstractedly at the blaze of the campfire. When the gypsies pause to rest a moment from their labors, she begins to sing, as to herself, of the vision that plagues her memory as she watches the blaze. The gypsies draw near and attentively listen to her song,

Castagneri

THE CONVENT NEAR CASTELLOR

a melody perfectly in keeping with the character of this wild gypsy woman and of the harrowing scene she describes, *"Stride la vampa"* ("Flames soaring upward").

When she has finished, the gypsies depart, the echoes of their song becoming fainter and fainter from down the mountains. Azucena is still trembling with the horror of the memory she has revived, still seems to hear the command, "Avenge thou me!" As in a trance, not realizing what she is saying, she continues her narrative, describes her attempt at revenge and her frenzied error when she destroyed her own child instead of her enemy's.

The story sets Manrico thinking. "I'm not your son, then. Who am I?" The gypsy woman, with a quick instinct for prevarication, avoids the question, claiming him as her son. She changes the subject by reminding him how she had nursed him back to life after the almost fatal wound he had received in the battle between the forces of Biscay and Aragon, at Petilla. The enemy forces were led at that battle by the Count di Luna, whom a short time before Manrico had overcome in a duel. Why, asks the gypsy, did he spare the Count's life?

Manrico replies, in a melody, smooth and flowing, yet with a certain martial vein, saying that the foe lay at his mercy, and his sword was raised to strike the fatal blow, when he seemed to hear a voice from heaven, crying, "Do not strike!" This is all expressed in the aria *"Mal reggendo all' aspro assalto"* ("At my mercy lay the foe").

The music grows more agitated as Azucena with the utmost vehemence urges her supposed son never to allow this enemy to escape again, but to kill him without hesitation. This leads to a powerful, intensely rhythmic climax, in which both voices are strikingly blended.

Ruiz enters with a message from the Prince of Biscay, ordering Manrico to take command of the defense of the castle Castellor, also informing him that Leonora has believed reports of Manrico's death at the battle of Petilla, and is about to take vows at a convent. Manrico hurries away in spite of Azucena's protests.

SCENE 2: *The Cloister of a Convent Near Castellor*. Count di Luna has determined that before Leonora assumes her vows he will carry her away by force, and has come here with a body of troops. While they lurk outside the chapel, the Count thinks of the happiness that will soon be his, singing, *"Il balen del suo sorriso"* ("The glow of her smile").

The Count's aria is so effective that one tends to forget his character and feel sorry for him. The nuns are heard singing within their convent, while outside Ferrando and the Count's retainers give vent to a variety of exclamations.

The nuns issue from the convent, conducting Leonora to the chapel where the ceremony is to take place. Leonora pauses to bid farewell to her faithful attendant, Inez, then turns to enter the chapel. The Count and his followers now rush forward, and the women draw back in terror. At this moment Manrico appears with his soldiers, and with their aid wards off the baffled Count and his troops, and rescues his beloved.

ACT III

SCENE 1: *A Military Encampment*. The Count di Luna has laid siege to Castellor, whither Manrico has taken Leonora. The soldiers of the Count are about to attack, and they sing a rousing chorus telling of their hopes of winning fame and booty when they capture the castle. They march away singing their stirring war song, and their voices grow softer as they disappear in the distance.

Azucena, in her anxiety to see her son, has attempted to get through the besieging forces. She is captured and brought before the Count as a possible spy. Questioning brings out the story of her past and her connection with the episode of the Count's childhood. Ferrando swears she is the murderess of di Luna's long-lost brother. Azucena, in her extremity, cries out the name of Manrico, and the Count, on finding that she claims the Troubadour as her son, vows upon her a double vengeance. She is bound and dragged away.

SCENE 2: *A Hall Adjoining the Chapel of Castellor*. Within the stronghold of Castellor, Manrico and Leonora await the hour appointed for their mar-

Castagneri   ACT I—THE GARDENS OF ALIAFERIA

riage. Their happiness is troubled, however, by the fear that the Count di Luna may soon attack the castle. Thus it is that Manrico attempts to quiet Leonora's alarm, singing an aria of his devotion to her, *"Ah! sì, ben mio"* ("Ah, yes, beloved").

As he finishes this declaration of love the solemn music of the organ in the adjoining chapel announces the beginning of the ceremony. Manrico takes his bride's hand to lead her to the altar. At that very moment Ruiz enters with the news that Azucena has been captured by the besiegers. Already fagots are being heaped together, for she is to be burned at the stake as was her mother. Delay would be fatal. Manrico drops Leonora's hand, draws his sword, and, while his soldiers are being summoned, gives vent to his rage and horror in a famous aria—a tour de force for operatic tenors—*"Di quella pira"* ("Tremble, ye tyrants").

He then rushes away to the rescue, followed by his soldiers.

ACT IV

SCENE 1: *A Wing of the Palace of Aliaferia; a Dungeon Tower, Showing a Barred Window.* Defeated by Count di Luna and his forces, Manrico has been taken captive and cast into the dungeon tower of Aliaferia, where Azucena has already been chained. Outside of these frowning battlements Leonora lingers, for on this clouded night she has come with a despairing hope of saving her lover. She wears a poisoned ring so that if need be she can take

ACT IV, SCENE 2—METROPOLITAN OPERA PRODUCTION

her own life. Her thoughts turn toward Manrico, and she sings a poignantly expressive melody declaring her hope that love may even penetrate into his dungeon, *"D'amor sull' ali rosee"* ("Love, fly on rosy wings").

Within the tower voices begin a solemn chant of *"Miserere,"* praying for heaven to have mercy on the soul of him about to perish. Meanwhile a deep-toned bell tolls out the announcement of Manrico's impending doom.

The mournful ecclesiastical chant, and the tolling knell sounding from the tower across the blackness of the night, fill Leonora with terror; while the orchestra accompanies with shuddering chords in slow but irresistibly reiterated rhythm, like the approach of doom, she sings of her fears.

From his prison the Troubadour, seemingly unconscious of all that is taking place around him, sighs forth his plaint,*"Sconto col sangue mio"* ("Paid with my blood"). And he closes his song with the words "Do not forget me! Leonora, farewell."

While the voices resume their chant and the bell continues tolling, Leonora exclaims that she can never forget him; that she will save his life with the sacrifice of her own.

Then Manrico resumes his song. To it the voices of the chanting priests supply a funereal background, and interwoven with it is the cry of Leonora; a marvelously impressive ensemble.

The Count enters, Leonora begs mercy for Manrico, but he refuses, gloating over his triumph. As a last resource she offers to marry the Count if her lover may go free. So great is di Luna's passion for Leonora that he agrees. While he is giving orders to one of the guards, Leonora swallows the poison she has concealed in her ring, muttering to herself that his prize will be a cold and lifeless bride.

SCENE 2: *A Gloomy Dungeon.* In the gloom of their prison Manrico and Azucena await execution. The gypsy pictures to herself the horror of the flames leaping around herself even as they did around her mother. She falls overwhelmed with terror, and Manrico tries to comfort her. Azucena replies, singing a serious melody, tranquil yet with an undercurrent of agitation. Manrico reassures her, softly urging her to rest. Then thinking of the happy days that are past, Azucena meditates nostalgically, as in a dream, *"Ai nostri monti"* ("Home to our mountains").

Again Manrico tries to comfort her, then their voices are heard together, while Azucena falls asleep, still thinking of her gypsy home. Thus closes in reposeful beauty this justly beloved duet.

Leonora enters with news of Manrico's freedom. His joy, however, is turned to desperation as he learns the price to be paid. In a sudden frenzy he accuses Leonora of betraying his love. At this moment the poison begins to claim its victim. Leonora sinks to the floor at Manrico's feet, in a death agony. The lover, who now realizes the full extent of her sacrifice, is all contrition and pleads for forgiveness. The Count suddenly appears, pausing on the threshold. Leonora confesses to the Troubadour that she prefers death in his presence than life as another's bride. Then she sinks lifeless to the ground.

Perceiving that Leonora has cheated him, di Luna orders Manrico to instant execution, and drags Azucena to the window to witness the death of her son. The old gypsy is crazed with excitement, blind to the external world. "It is ended," the Count exclaims when the executioner's work is done.

"He was your brother!" she shrieks. "You are avenged, O mother!" Then she falls lifeless.

The Count, overwhelmed with horror, exclaims, "And still I live!"

LOUISE HOMER AS AZUCENA   LEONARD WARREN AS COUNT DI LUNA

Il Trovatore

THE RCA-VICTOR RECORDS
(Sung in Italian unless otherwise noted)

COMPLETE RECORDING: *Maria Carena, Soprano; Irene Minghini-Cattaneo, Mezzo-soprano; Aureliano Pertile, Tenor; Apollo Granforte, Baritone; Bruno Carmassi, Bass; Olga de Franco, Soprano; Giordano Callegari, Tenor; Antonio Gelli, Baritone; with Chorus and Orchestra of La Scala, Milan, Carlo Sabajno, Cond.*

DMC-103 (DM-106) (Vol. 1)
          (13379-13386), 8-12″
   (DM-106) (Vol. 2)
          (13387-13393), 7-12″
MC-103 (M-106) (Vol. 1)
          (11040-11047)
   (M-106) (Vol. 2)
          (11048-11054)

TACEA LA NOTTE: *Florence Quartararo, Soprano, RCA-Victor Orchestra, Jean Paul Morel, Cond.*   12-0530, 12″

ACT II

CORO DEI GITANI (Anvil Chorus or Gypsy Chorus): *RCA-Victor Choral and Orch., Robert Shaw, Cond.*
          11-9294, 12″
Victor Mixed Chorus, with Orch. In English   20127, 10″
Arthur Pryor's Band   19879, 10″

IL BALEN DEL SUO SORRISO (Tempest of the Heart);

RECITATIVE: QUAL SUONO! (That Ringing);

ARIA: PER ME ORA FATALE (That Passion That Inspires Me): *Leonard Warren, Baritone, with Orch.*   11-9956, 12″

MAL REGGENDO ALL' ASPRO ASSALTO (At My Mercy Lay the Foe): *Louise Homer, Contralto; Giovanni Martinelli, Tenor; with Orch.*   8105, 12″

NUNS' CHORUS: AH! SE L'ERROR T'INGOMBRA (Ah! Mid the Shades of Error): *Leonard Warren, Baritone; RCA Victor Choral, Robert Shaw, Choral Director, with Orch.*   11-9956, 12″

ACT III

AH! SÌ, BEN MIO, COLL' ESSERE (The Vows We Fondly Plighted): *Jussi Bjoerling, Tenor, with Orch.*   2136, 10″

DI QUELLA PIRA (Tremble, Ye Tyrants): *Jussi Bjoerling, Tenor, with Orch.*
          2136, 10″
Giovanni Martinelli, Tenor; Metropolitan Opera Chorus and Orch.
          8109, 12″

MISERERE—AH! CHE LA MORTA OGNORA (Pray That Peace May Attend a Soul): *Zinka Milanov, Soprano; Jan Peerce, Tenor; Victor Chorus and Orch.*   11-8782, 12″
Rosa Ponselle, Soprano; Giovanni Martinelli, Tenor; Metropolitan Opera Chorus and Orch.   8097, 12″
Frances Alda, Soprano; Enrico Caruso, Tenor; Metropolitan Opera Chorus and Orch.   8042, 12″
(Acoustical Recording)

AI NOSTRI MONTI (Home to Our Mountains): *Kerstin Thorborg, Contralto; Jan Peerce, Tenor; with Orch.*
          11-8782, 12″
Louise Homer, Contralto; Giovanni Martinelli, Tenor; with Orch.   8105, 12″
Ernestine Schumann-Heink, Contralto; Enrico Caruso, Tenor; Metropolitan Opera Chorus and Orch.   8042, 12″
(Acoustical Recording)

GIOVANNI MARTINELLI AS MANRICO

Bertolozzi

THE ARENA DI VERONA

Turandot

OPERA IN three acts. Music by Giacomo Puccini. Libretto by Giuseppe Adami and Renato Simoni, after a *fiaba* by Carlo Gozzi. First performance, Teatro alla Scala, Milan, April 25, 1926, with Rosa Raïsa as Turandot, Maria Zamboni as Liù, Miguel Fleta as Calaf, and Giacomo Rimini as Ping, and Arturo Toscanini conducting. The initial United States production took place at the Metropolitan Opera House, November 16, 1926, with Maria Jeritza, Martha Attwood, Giacomo Lauri-Volpi, and Giuseppe de Luca.

Unfortunately, Puccini died before completing this opera. The last part of Act III, beginning with the final duet between Turandot and Prince Calaf, "*Principessa di Morte*," was completed by Franco Alfano from sketches left by Puccini. When this place was reached, at the first performance, Toscanini made an abrupt ending and, turning to the audience, remarked simply, "At this point the Master laid down his pen."

In *Turandot* Puccini advanced beyond any of his previous work in harmonic subtlety, orchestral coloring, and choral writing, even introducing polyphony. Yet in its wealth of melody the opera is distinctly Puccinian.

CHARACTERS

PRINCESS TURANDOT	*Soprano*	PING, *the Grand Chancellor*	*Baritone*
THE EMPEROR ALTOUM, *her father*	*Tenor*	PANG, *the General Purveyor*	*Tenor*
TIMUR, *dethroned Tatar King*	*Bass*	PONG, *the Chief Cook*	*Tenor*
PRINCE CALAF, *the Unknown*		A MANDARIN	*Baritone*
Prince, Timur's son	*Tenor*	THE PRINCE OF PERSIA	*Baritone*
LIÙ, *a young slave girl*	*Soprano*	THE EXECUTIONER	*Baritone*

The action takes place in Peking during legendary times

ACT I

SCENE: *The Walls of the Great Violet City of Peking.* Amid the confusion of the listening crowd that has gathered at the Imperial Palace, an old man

577

makes his way, supported and guided by a young slave girl, Liù. Suddenly a youth hurries toward them from the crowd. Their whispered conversation reveals that the old man is the dethroned Timur, King of the Tatars, the youth, his son, Calaf, called the "Unknown Prince." Soon there is a movement of agitation in the crowd, because the Prince of Persia, attempting to solve Turandot's riddles, and failing, as all others have done, is now being led to execution. For the Princess Turandot, as a mandarin has previously announced, has decreed that whosoever would win her hand must solve three riddles, and, failing, suffer death. The people, moved by the youthfulness of the Persian prince, cry for mercy. But Turandot, when she appears upon the balcony, silences them by the mere sight of her matchless beauty. The thud of the executioner's ax is heard, then the head of the Persian prince is seen, raised on a pike over the city gates.

The Unknown Prince is greatly thrilled by the beauty of Turandot. Forgetting her cruelty and heedless of the prayers of his father and Liù, and of the warnings of the ghosts of Turandot's executed lovers, and unmindful of the counsels of the three court officials, Ping, Pang, and Pong, he determines to brave the Princess' enigmas. In token of which he sounds the great gong that hangs at the palace gate three times, calling out the name of the Princess.

ACT II

SCENE: *A Pavilion in the Palace.* Accordingly there assembles a multitude of great personages on the staircase that leads to the Imperial Palace. Turandot, coming before them, tells of her grandmother, the chaste Princess Lo-u-ling, who, ravished by the invading Tatars, died most unhappy. To avenge her ancestor's wrongs, Turandot has meted out a cruel fate to all who would be her suitors. She turns to the Unknown Prince, and propounds her direful enigmas. One by one the Unknown Prince answers them, boldly and correctly; he is greeted by shouts of joy from all except Turandot. The Princess, dismayed, begs to be saved from the stranger; but her father, Emperor and guardian of the law, decrees that her word must be held sacred. Turandot therefore pleads with the conqueror for her freedom, and he, answering, says that he will indeed release her from her vow and give up his life even as though he had failed in the trial, should she be able to learn his name ere the morrow.

ACT III

SCENE: *The Palace Gardens Near Turandot's Apartments.* Thus it comes about that during the entire night heralds search through all the city, but none they find who can rightly name the Unknown Prince. Someone then whispers that an old man and the girl Liù had been seen with him. They are brought to the palace, but Liù cries out that she alone knows the Prince's name, and then, fearing she may reveal the secret during the tortures to which she will be subjected, she quickly seizes a dagger from one of the soldiers and plunges it into her heart. Turandot is troubled—what moved the girl to such self-sacrifice? The Prince, reproaching Turandot, clasps her passionately. Thus is the Princess vanquished, and she confesses that she loves the Unknown Prince. He likewise says that such is his love that he would be happy to die for her, and reveals his name. Knowing him to be the enemy Tatar prince, Turandot again becomes proud and unattainable. Dawn now approaching, she leads him to the palace to announce her victory and his doom. At the throne of the great Emperor she cries out that she has learned the stranger's name; then looking at Calaf, she is shaken by a strange emotion, and murmurs, "His name is Love!" And the multitude that has assembled sings for joy.

Culver Service
MARIA JERITZA AS TURANDOT AND GIACOMO LAURI-VOLPI AS CALAF

THE RCA-VICTOR RECORDS
(Sung in Italian)

ACT III

NESSUN DORMA (None Shall Sleep): *Jussi Bjoerling, Tenor, with Orch.*   10-1200, 10"

Werther

Lyric drama in four acts. Music by Jules Massenet. Libretto by Édouard Blau, Paul Milliet, and Georg Hartmann, based on Goethe's short novel, *Die Leiden des jungen Werthers (The Sorrows of Young Werther)*. First produced, in German, at the Hofoper, Vienna, February 16, 1892, with a cast headed by Ernest van Dyck and Marie Renard. First performance in Paris, in French, January 16, 1893. American *première* at the Metropolitan Opera House, April 19, 1894, with Jean de Reszke and Emma Eames. Two important debuts occurred in the Metropolitan revival of November 16, 1909, at the company's New Theater. Edmond Clément made his American debut, and Alma Gluck appeared for the first time in opera anywhere. Although one of the less popular of Massenet's many operas, *Werther* contains some of its composer's most imaginative pages. The melodies are bright and fresh, and the orchestral writing is colorful and expressive. The romantic story appealed strongly to Massenet's susceptible nature, though it has been suggested that he wrote *Werther* to show that he could portray a virtuous woman—Charlotte—in music. Friends had complained to him that all his heroines were courtesans.

The action takes place in Germany in 1772

Surrounded by her brothers and sisters, Charlotte is preparing the noonday meal. Werther, a serious-minded young man, comes to the house with Albert, who is betrothed to Charlotte. Werther promptly falls in love with his friend's fiancée. The girl returns his affection, but feels it her duty to marry Albert, to keep a promise made to her dying mother. She begs Werther to leave the village. At Christmastime Werther returns and visits Albert and Charlotte, who are now maried. The familiar household fills him with joy. Noticing a volume of Ossian's poems, he begins to read one of the poet's nostalgic chants. But as he sings, the poem becomes an expression of his own despairing love. The aria, *"Pourquoi me réveiller?"* ("Why awaken me?"), is filled with warm beauty and passionate intensity.

The song deeply affects Charlotte. Realizing that her secret love for Werther remains unchanged, she entreats him to go away forever. Later, a servant brings a letter for Albert from Werther, saying that he is about to go on a long journey, and requesting the loan of Albert's pistols. Charlotte reads the letter, and, greatly worried, hurries at midnight through a blinding snowstorm to Werther's dwelling. There she finds him mortally wounded, by his own hand. As Werther dies in her arms, Charlotte, overcome with grief, collapses. Outside, in ironic contrast, bells peal joyfully and children sing Christmas carols.

THE RCA-VICTOR RECORDS
(Sung in French)

ACT III

Pourquoi me réveiller? (Why Awaken Me?): *Richard Crooks, Tenor, with Orch.*
10-1093, 10″

SKETCH FOR ACT I BY GIANNI VAGNETTI

William Tell
(GUILLAUME TELL)

OPERA IN four acts. Music by Gioacchino Rossini. Libretto by Étienne de Jouy and Hippolyte Bis, after the play by Schiller. First performance, Paris Opéra, August 3, 1829. First American performance, New York's Park Theater, in English, September 19, 1831, preceded by the opera *Cinderella* and followed by a farce *'Twas I*. The work was presented in French at the Théâtre d'Orléans, New Orleans, December 13, 1842. Given also in French at the Park Theater, New York, June 16, 1845. Produced in Italian, Academy of Music, New York, April 9, 1855, and at the same theater in German, April 18, 1866.

William Tell obtained its initial hearing at the Metropolitan Opera House in German, November 28, 1884, with Adolf Robinson as Tell, Udvardi as Arnold, Josef Kögel as Walter, Josef Staudigl as Gessler, Marie Schröder-Hanfstängel as Mathilde, and Marianne Brandt in the minor part of Tell's wife, Hedwig.

During a supplementary season of operas given by a visiting company at the Metropolitan, Francesco Tamagno sang the role of Arnold in an Italian-language production, this in the spring of 1890. Italian has since been the language of all presentations at the Metropolitan. Among the later Metropolitan Arnolds have been Giovanni Martinelli and Giacomo Lauri-Volpi; the part of William Tell has been sung by Mario Ancona and Giuseppe Danise; the Walter has been embodied by Édouard de Reszke, José Mardones, Ezio Pinza, and Léon Rothier; Gessler has had such interpreters as Pol Plançon, Adamo Didur, and Pavel Ludikar. At Libia Drog's American debut there, November 21, 1894, the artist forgot her lines, having worked on the part only two days, and broke down completely, leaving the opera without a prima donna. Further Metropolitan performances that season offered Lucille Hill in the role of Mathilde, and, later, it was sung by Rosa Ponselle, Elisabeth Rethberg, and Editha Fleischer.

William Tell is one of the longest operas in existence. It has been customary to cut a good deal of the work for anything like a comfortable evening's presentation. The uncut version had been tried in Paris in 1856, and it is said that it ran from 7 P.M. until one in the morning. It is known that after fifty-six performances of the work in all five acts, the director of the Paris Opéra ordered it shortened to three by omitting the third and fusing together the fourth and fifth. Also, for some time, only Act II of *William Tell* was presented there, permitting it to serve some other work as a curtain raiser. In passing, Rossini was once informed that the second act of *William Tell* was to be given on a certain evening. His characteristic retort was, "What, the whole of it?"

Oddly enough, although Rossini composed the score to this opera while at the high noon of his creative powers, he did not write again a work for the lyric theater. The mystery surrounding this thirty-nine years' abstinence has never been solved, although many—and varied—have been the explanations supplied, or invented.

A strongly vivid, typically Rossinian score—though, naturally, in much more dramatic vein than that of his well-known *Barber of Seville*—*William Tell* has not been given with consistency by American opera companies. The principal roles—especially that of Arnold—are by no means a sinecure, yet one knows of other equally difficult roles in other operas, whose popularity has not waned, in spite of taxing vocal demands.

CHARACTERS

WILLIAM TELL			Bass
ARNOLD	Swiss patriots		Tenor
WALTER FÜRST			Bass

MELCTHAL, *Arnold's father* — Bass
GESSLER, *Governor of Schwitz and Uri* — Bass
RUDOLPH, *captain of Gessler's bodyguard* — Tenor

RUODI, *a fisherman* — Tenor
LEUTHOLD, *a shepherd* — Bass
JEMMY, *William Tell's son* — Soprano
HEDWIG, *Tell's wife* — Soprano
MATHILDE, *Gessler's daughter and a princess of the House of Hapsburg* — Soprano

PEASANTS, KNIGHTS, PAGES, LADIES OF THE TRAIN OF MATHILDE, THREE BRIDES AND THEIR BRIDEGROOMS, HUNTERS, SOLDIERS, AND GUARDS

The action takes place in Switzerland during the fourteenth century

The Overture is probably the best-known fragment of the opera's score today. Melodious, rhythmically vivid, dramatically contrasting, it is played, especially in this country, day in and day out on the radio and, it seems, everywhere else, not excluding the symphony programs. It is, rather, a miniature symphonic poem of Switzerland, picturesque and, one should imagine, programmatically suggestive.

ACT I

SCENE: *William Tell's Chalet on the Shores of Lake Lucerne.* The despotic rule of Governor Gessler has increasingly inflamed the spirit of the Swiss, and in this opening scene Tell, in an aside, points a contrast between the young fisherman Ruodi, who blithely sings of love, and himself, tortured by his country's oppression. The people gather, on signal from a horn, and presently preparations get under way for the celebration of three marriages by the beloved patriarch, Melcthal, Arnold's father. Arnold, Mathilde's suitor, aggrieved by the difficulties that surround his courtship of Gessler's daughter, speaks with Tell, who—always furiously patriotic—recites Gessler's crimes. He, therefore, asks Arnold's aid in overthrowing the tyrant. Arnold's reluctance, natural under the circumstances, is misunderstood by Tell, but after some explanations the patriot gets Arnold's word to support the rebels' cause.

In the mountains near by the horns of Gessler's hunting party are heard, as an ominous portent. Meanwhile, Melcthal joins the three young couples in marriage, and gaiety takes possession of the scene, until the old shepherd Leuthold rushes in, seeking protection from Gessler. It seems that one of the despot's soldiers, in a sportive mood, has attempted to abduct Leuthold's young daughter, whereupon he received, for his pains, the father's ax in the middle of his skull. Leuthold begs Ruodi to ferry him over to safety on the other side of the lake, but the latter refuses, giving as his excuses the dangers present in the jagged underwater rocks and the strong current. The soldiers in search of Leuthold are heard approaching, and Tell impulsively springs into the boat, ordering Leuthold to jump in after him, and they set out for the opposite shore.

When the soldiers arrive they become furious at the escape of their quarry, and Melcthal, having defied their captain, Rudolph, is carried off under arrest.

ACT II

SCENE 1: *A Pine Forest on the Heights of Rütli.* Mathilde has caught a glimpse of Arnold during the hunt and thinks that if he has spied her, he, too, will come to this spot, and he does. But, awaiting him, she sings a brilliant coloratura aria, *"Sombre forêt"* ("Somber Forest"), in which she tells of her much greater preference for an idyllic, if simple, life with Arnold, over the manifold luxuries of the court. When Arnold arrives, the two lovers sing a duet protesting eternal love, while deploring the evil fortune that keeps them apart. Mathilde makes a quick exit when she hears the sounds of people approaching, and the newcomers, William Tell and Walter Fürst, are somewhat suspicious of Arnold, at first, having recognized Gessler's daughter. In any case, they reveal to him that his father has been slain by Gessler, and it can be easily guessed that from now on only vengeance can motivate the young man. The three patriots now swear allegiance to their cause, and Arnold is urged to be present that night at a gathering of all the partisans.

SCENE 2: *The Gathering of the Cantons in a Hidden Wood.* The men of Unterwald, those of Schwitz and of Uri, arrive stealthily at this forest meeting spot. Tell and Walter greet them, and the furtiveness of the occasion is emphasized by the deft music of Rossini. Tell inspirits all about him with the intensity of his speech, and in a compellingly dramatic sequence all clasp hands and swear to down the tyrant, invoking, at the same time, heaven's wrath on any traitor among them.

ACT III

SCENE 1: *A Ruined Chapel in the Grounds of the Governor's Palace at Altdorf.* Arnold and Mathilde meet in the ruined chapel. He informs her of his father's execution, ordered by her own father, and sings a song of farewell to dreams, in the aria *"Pour notre amour"* ("For our love"). Mathilde, for her part, promises ever to remember him and anxiously cautions him to escape.

SCENE 2: *The Market Place of Altdorf.* In the market place of Altdorf, Gessler has caused to be erected a banner with his coat of arms. Topping that is his own hat, to which, by express order, all must bow. Addressing the throng, Gessler remarks on the hundred years of Austrian rule, and he orders the people to celebrate the occasion with dancing and festivity. A number of ballets and a soldiers' march take the center of the action, which is interspersed with occasional outbursts of song by the chorus.

All who pass the Gessler coat of arms and hat bow in obeisance. However, Captain Rudolph notices that William Tell is not one of these. He remains, in fact, boldly erect. The patriot, who is with his young son, Jemmy, is arrested and brought before the governor, Tell, however, bidding Jemmy to go home and bring the message to his mother that all the beacons are to be lighted in the mountains—the signal that the moment of liberation has come.

Gessler, believing that he may further increase his pleasure by humbling Tell, orders him, fine archer that he is, to split with one of his bows an apple placed on Jemmy's head. For only a moment Tell pleads with Gessler, but on hearing the tyrant's order that Jemmy be put to death he says that he will do as Gessler asks. He takes two arrows, secreting one in his clothes, and after some anxious moments, a prayerful look to heaven, and a gathering of spiritual forces, aims, and splits the apple in two. When Jemmy rushes up to him in tearful joy, Tell embraces him, but as he does so the second arrow drops to the ground. To Gessler, who queries him about it, he says that had he failed and injured his son, he would have sent the second missile straight to Gessler's heart, whereupon Gessler gives a furious command for Tell's arrest.

ACT IV

SCENE 1: *Before Melcthal's House.* Arnold comes to his father's house, saying that he cannot cross the threshold, deciding, instead, to deliver an apostrophe to his father and his own joyous childhood days, in the aria *"Asile héréditaire"* ("Ancestral home"). When he has ended this song, cries of "Vengeance" are heard, and people stream in, telling him of Tell's imprisonment and exhorting him and all patriots to take up arms for the rescue.

SCENE 2: *The Shores of Lake Lucerne.* Grieving over her husband and her son, Hedwig is soon comforted with the joyous cries of Jemmy, who has been brought thither by Mathilde. From her Hedwig learns that Tell has escaped and is at that moment on the lake, over which a storm is brewing. At this Jemmy rushes out to call the patriots. Against storm music in the orchestra Tell appears, safe and sound, and exceedingly thankful that he is again with his dear ones. He discovers that his son has been shrewd enough, while setting fire to the house as a signal to the patriots, to save his father's bows and arrows, and exultantly calls for them. Gessler, on the hunt for Tell, appears on the rocks above, and Tell, fitting an arrow to his bow, takes aim and kills the tyrant forthwith. All is jubilation, now, and Arnold, together with other patriots, rushes in with the news that the castle has fallen. The opera closes with a rousing invocation to freedom.

THE RCA-VICTOR RECORDS

OVERTURE: *Arturo Toscanini and the NBC Symphony Orchestra*
>> DM-605 (2203 & 2204), 2-10"
>> M-605 (2020 & 2021)

Boston "Pops" Orchestra, Arthur Fiedler, Cond.
>> DM-456 (4570 & 4571), 2-10"
>> M-456 (4393 & 4394)

Victor Symphony Orchestra, Rosario Bourdon, Cond.
>> 20606 & 20607, 2-10"

ACT I

DANCE—PASSO A SEI (Dance in Six):
Arturo Toscanini and the NBC Symphony Orchestra 11-9069, 12"
>> (In Album M-1037)
>> 18-0008, 12"
>> (Vinylite) (In Album V-2)

A. Bauer   WILLIAM TELL

De Bellis

ACT II—"I HAVE A SONG TO SING, O!"—D'OYLY CARTE OPERA PRODUCTION

The Yeomen of the Guard

(OR, THE MERRYMAN AND HIS MAID)

COMIC OPERA in two acts. Music by Sir Arthur Sullivan. Libretto by W. S. Gilbert. First performance, Savoy Theater, London, October 3, 1888, where it ran for 423 consecutive nights. First New York performance, Casino Theater, October 17, 1888.

Sullivan's friends disapproved of his devoting himself to "trifles" like the pieces he had been doing with Gilbert, and particularly because it would be expected of Sir Arthur Sullivan, knighted for his musical talents, to compose serious works. These urgings had been going on for some time, ever since his knightly honors, in fact, and no less a musical authority than George Grove had written in his famous *Dictionary of Music and Musicians*, "Surely the time has come when so able and experienced a master of voice, orchestra, and stage effect . . . may apply his gifts to a serious opera on some subject of abiding human or national interest."

The two partners, probably because of such declarations and Sullivan's understandable ambitions, had a slight difference, Sullivan refusing to do any more comic operas. But it took careful handling by Gilbert to convince Sullivan that, as a team, they were pretty important creators, and that their joint works had every chance of becoming classics of their genre.

Be all that as it may, Gilbert had been working on a libretto which was not altogether of the type he had previously written, that is, he created some difficulties for himself by not adhering to the same pattern, wondering whether or not the story would prove to be too serious, finding it hard work to get to the comic scenes. In the meantime, he changed the title of the libretto several times (finally fixing on *The Yeomen of the Guard; or, The Merryman and his Maid* about a week before the opening). And after due consideration, Sullivan began to compose in July, 1887, but getting scarcely anything done until the latter part of August, 1888, when he knuckled down in earnest.

586

CHARACTERS

SIR RICHARD CHOLMONDELEY, *Lieutenant of the Tower*	*Bass*	WILFRED SHADBOLT, *head jailer*	*Bass*
		THE HEADSMAN	*Silent Role*
COLONEL FAIRFAX, *under sentence of death*	*Tenor*	ELSIE MAYNARD, *a strolling singer*	*Soprano*
		PHOEBE MERYLL, *Sergeant Meryll's daughter*	*Contralto*
SERGEANT MERYLL, *of the Yeomen of the Guard*	*Baritone*		
		DAME CARRUTHERS, *housekeeper to the Tower*	*Contralto*
LEONARD MERYLL, *his son*	*Tenor*		
JACK POINT, *a strolling jester*	*Baritone*	KATE, *her niece*	*Soprano*

CHORUS OF YEOMEN OF THE GUARD, GENTLEMEN, CITIZENS, ETC.

The action takes place in London during the sixteenth century

ACT I

SCENE: *The Tower Green.* Colonel Fairfax, a man of science, but formerly a soldier of great and dashing bravery, is confined in the Tower of London. He is under sentence of death as a sorcerer. Although he has long been a student of alchemy, Fairfax is still young and handsome, and Phoebe has lost her heart to him, for she sees him occasionally taking exercise on the Beauchamp Tower.

As the curtain rises the unhappy girl is discovered sitting at her spinning wheel, sighing over her hopeless love for the prisoner, and she sings a wistful air, "When Maiden Loves." Wilfred Shadbolt, head jailer and assistant tormenter, is greatly put out, for Phoebe will have none of him, though before the arrival of Fairfax she had not been so averse to his attentions. Dame Carruthers, the housekeeper to the Tower, believing Fairfax to be guilty, resents Phoebe's praise of him and her criticisms of the Tower. The Dame was born in the old Keep, and the Tower is very dear to her; she leaves no doubt of her sentiments in the noble air, "When Our Gallant Norman Foes." Sergeant Meryll, of the Yeomen of the Guard, is saddened by the thought of the approaching execution of Fairfax. He greatly admires Fairfax for his brilliant career as a soldier, and not even the imminent arrival of his son, Leonard Meryll, can raise his despondent spirits, though there is a hope that Leonard may bring with him a reprieve from court for Fairfax. Leonard arrives even while Phoebe and her father are discussing the sad case of the unfortunate prisoner; there is no reprieve. None saw him enter, and the unheralded coming gives Sergeant Meryll an idea. "Give me the dispatch," he says . . . "lie hidden for a space." Leonard does so willingly, for Fairfax was once his great friend. A moment later Fairfax passes by, under guard, on his way to the Cold Harbour Tower to await his end in solitude. He sees and recognizes Sergeant Meryll and bids him cheer up; as a soldier, he says, he knows how to die. If life is a boon, he says, death must inevitably come too soon. Phoebe and her father are overcome with emotion and leave him. Fairfax asks the

De Bellis

DARRELL FANCOURT AS SERGEANT MERYLL

Lieutenant of the Tower to grant him a favor. He is, he says, imprisoned as a result of the machinations of his cousin, Sir Clarence Poltwhistle—a greedy fellow to whom the Fairfax estates must naturally fall, if Colonel Fairfax should die unmarried. Fairfax's request is therefore that the Lieutenant shall find him a woman willing to go through a form of marriage with him: her dower shall be Fairfax's name and a hundred crowns. Since he is to be executed in an hour's time it should be easy enough to find someone. As Fairfax moves on his way there is laughing and shouting, and a roistering throng of men and women, pursuing a wandering jester and a merrymaid, appear. The jester, Jack Point, and the girl, Elsie Maynard, are both more than a little terrified, for the crowd, in demanding entertainment, threaten to throw them into the river if they do not come up to expectations. They sing them the "singing farce of the Merryman and his Maid," and are about to be mobbed by the less appreciative members of the audience when the Lieutenant reappears from the Cold Harbour Tower. The crowd is dispersed, and the Lieutenant, learning all about Elsie and Jack Point, suggests to Elsie that she be Fairfax's bride for the short hour he has to live. The hundred crowns which she is to receive first tempt and then persuade her. She is led blindfold to the cell where Fairfax and his confessor await her. While she is gone Point, in the song "I've Jibe and Joke," explains his calling of a jester, and he is engaged by the Lieutenant as his jester. Then Elsie returns and reflects on her married state and the fact that she will be a widow in an hour. Phoebe enters with Sergeant Meryll, who remains in the background, unobserved. Finding Wilfred alone, she determines to get the keys of Fairfax's cell from him. Exerting all her charms and flattering Wilfred, she compliments him on his jollity and wit, though he is in truth the heaviest-minded dolt. Slyly she takes the keys from his belt and hands them to her father, who disappears immediately. Whilst her father is away she sings a tempting little ditty, "Were I Thy Bride." As she begins the last verse the keys are pushed back into her hand by her father, and she cleverly puts them back on Wilfred's belt. She runs off, and Wilfred wanders away, bewildered and happy.

No sooner has he gone than Sergeant Meryll and Fairfax appear from the Tower. Fairfax has shaved off his beard and has put on the dress of a Yeoman of the Guard. He is to pose as the Sergeant's son, Leonard. Sergeant Meryll presents his "son" to the assembled Yeomen, who cheer him to the echo. Phoebe, too, welcomes this "brother" far more lingeringly and ecstatically than might be considered perfectly natural. Then while "brother and sister" are greeting one another the bell of St. Peter's begins to toll, and crowds surge around to witness the execution of Fairfax. Fairfax (disguised as Leonard) and two other Yeomen are ordered to fetch the prisoner, but are back in a moment; the prisoner has escaped!

ACT II

SCENE: *The Tower Green by Moonlight.* Two days have elapsed. Jack Point is now in a quandary. He has agreed to Elsie's marrying the imprisoned Fairfax because he was assured that Fairfax would die within the hour. Now that Fairfax has escaped Elsie is still a married woman, and Jack Point cannot himself marry her. He conceives a plan, however. With the dazzling bribe of a free schooling in the trade of a jester, he persuades Wilfred to help him in his scheme. They move off mysteriously. Meanwhile Fairfax has learned of the identity of the woman whom he married and, finding her most appealing, resolves to woo her and thus test her fidelity. A shot from the tower sets everyone agog, and an excited crowd quickly gathers. Wilfred and Point both appear with an air of importance. Wilfred almost convincingly asserts that he has had a desperate struggle with Colonel Fairfax, whom he caught trying to escape, and therefore shot him. Fairfax, apparently out of the way, Jack Point may now ask Elsie to marry him. But the disguised Fairfax, rather enjoying himself in the role of Leonard, remarks that "A man who would woo a fair maid" should be equipped with more than a bag of tricks. Elsie admits to the supposed Leonard Meryll that she loves him, when there is an interruption. A pardon for Fairfax has arrived, and simultaneously comes news that Fairfax, quite alive, is returning to claim his bride. Poor Elsie is distracted: she must follow Fairfax, though her heart is elsewhere. There is much musical analysis of love.

Fairfax enters, and Elsie comes forward with bowed head, lamenting her cruel fate. She looks up and with a start she sees that "Leonard" and Fairfax are one and the same. With a cry of joy she falls into his arms, amid general rejoicing. Meanwhile Dame Carruthers has forced Sergeant Meryll into a proposal, and Phoebe Meryll is promised in marriage to the uncouth Wilfred.

The final scene is one of general gaiety—only Jack Point is left without a mate—and still singing the refrain "Heighdy, heighdy! Misery me, lacka-daydee! . . . for the love of a ladye!" he falls insensible at the feet of the now happily united couple.

THE RCA-VICTOR RECORDS
(Sung in English)

COMPLETE RECORDING: *D'Oyly Carte Company, Dr. Malcolm Sargent, Cond.; under the personal direction of Rupert D'Oyly Carte. (The cast includes: Nellie Briercliffe, Dorothy Gill, Winifred Lawson, Elsie Griffin, Derek Oldham, George Baker, Henry Millidge, Walter Glynne, Peter Dawson, Arthur Hosking, Leo Sheffield)*

DC-17 (13284-13294), 11-12"

C-17 (11220-11230)

GEMS: *Light Opera Company, with Orch.*

36145, 12"

(In Album C-23)

De Bellis

SYDNEY GRANVILLE AS WILFRED SHADBOLT AND MARJORIE EYRE AS PHOEBE MERYLL

Appendix

LISTED below are the RCA-Victor recordings from operas and certain operettas not included in the main body of *The Victor Book of Operas*.

ALEKO (Rachmaninoff)
THE MOON IS HIGH IN THE SKY: *Feodor Chaliapin, Bass, with Orch. In Russian*
14902, 12″

ALESSANDRO (Handel)
LUSINGHE PIÙ CARE (With Artful Beguiling): *Lily Pons, Soprano; Renaissance Quintet. In Italian*
2151, 10″
(In Album M-756)

ARLÉSIANA, L' (Cilèa)
LAMENTO DI FÉDERICO (Frederick's Lament): *Ferruccio Tagliavini, Tenor, with Orch. In Italian*
12-0071, 12″
(In Album MO-1191)
18-0107, 12″
(Vinylite) (In Album VO-13)
Richard Crooks, Tenor, with Orch. In Italian
15544, 12″
(In Album M-585)

ATALANTA (Handel)
CARE SELVE (Come, Beloved): *Rose Bampton, Contralto, with Piano. In English*
7746, 12″

ATTILA (Verdi)
TE SOL QUEST' ANIMA (To Thee My Heart Belongeth): *Elisabeth Rethberg, Soprano; Beniamino Gigli, Tenor; Ezio Pinza, Bass; with Orch. In Italian* 8194, 12″

BEGGAR'S OPERA, THE (John Gay—Pepusch)
SELECTIONS: *Alys Brough, Ruby Gilchrist, Aubrey Mildmay, Sopranos; Linda Grey, Constance Willis, Contraltos; Bruce Flegg, Tenor; Joseph Farrington, Roy Henderson, Michael Redgrave, Baritones; with Orch.; Michael Mundie, Cond.*
DM-772 (17960-17965), 6-12″
M-772 (17948-17953)

BELLE HÉLÈNE, LA (Offenbach)
OVERTURE: *Boston "Pops" Orchestra, Arthur Fiedler, Cond.* 11-9026, 12″

BOCCACCIO (Suppé)
HAB' ICH NUR DEINE LIEBE (Had I Only Your Love) (Act I): *Elisabeth Rethberg, Soprano, with Orch. In German*
7415, 12″

BOHEMIAN GIRL, THE (Balfe)
GEMS: *Victor Light Opera Company, with Orch.* 35819, 12″

BRONZE HORSE, THE (Le Cheval de bronze) (Auber)
OVERTURE: *London Philharmonic Orchestra, Constant Lambert, Cond.* 12511, 12″

CAÏD, LE (Thomas)
AIR DU TAMBOUR-MAJOR (Air of the Drum-Major): *Pol Plançon, Bass, with Orch. In French*
18143, 12″
(Acoustical Recording) (In Album M-816)

CAPONSACCHI (Richard Hageman)
ARIA—THIS VERY VIVID MORN (Act I);
LULLABY (Act III): *Helen Jepson, Soprano, with Orch. In English* 14183, 12″

CENERENTOLA, LA (Cinderella) (Rossini)
OVERTURE: *Arturo Toscanini and the NBC Symphony Orchestra* 11-9068, 12″
(In Album M-1037)
18-0007, 12″
(Vinylite) (In Album DV-2)
SCENE AND RONDO FINALE—Act II—NACQUI ALL' AFFANDO (I Was Born to Suffer): *Rose Bampton, Soprano, with Orch. In Italian*
18217, 12″

591

CÉPHALE ET PROCRIS (Grétry)
AIRS DE BALLET: *Chicago Symphony Orchestra, Désiré Defauw, Cond.*   11-8825, 12"
CYDALISE ET LE CHÈVRE-LIED (Pierné)
MARCHE DES PETITS FAUNES (Entrance of the Little Fauns): *Boston "Pops" Orchestra, Arthur Fiedler, Cond.*   4319, 10"
DAME BLANCHE, LA (Boïeldieu)
OVERTURE: *Boston "Pops" Orchestra, Arthur Fiedler, Cond.*   11-9569, 12"
DAUGHTER OF THE REGIMENT, THE (Figlia del Reggimento) (Donizetti)
PER VIVER VICINO A MARIA (To Be Near Her): *John McCormack, Tenor, with Orch. In Italian*   15-1015, 12"
(Acoustical Recording)
DUE FOSCARI, I (The Two Foscari) (Verdi)
O VECCHIO COR, CHE BATTI (My Beating Heart): *Pasquale Amato, Baritone, with Orch. In Italian*   15-1005, 12"
(Acoustical Recording)
ENFANT PRODIGUE, L' (Debussy)
RECITATIVE AND AIR DE LIA—L'ANNÉE EN VAIN (The Years Roll By): *Dorothy Maynor, Soprano; the Philadelphia Orchestra, Eugene Ormandy, Cond.*   17698, 12"
Rose Bampton, Contralto; with Piano   7746, 12"
ÉTOILE DU NORD, L' (The Star of the North) (Meyerbeer)
LÀ, LÀ, LÀ, AIR CHÉRI (Grand Air of Catherine): *Amelita Galli-Curci, Soprano, with Orch. (2 Flute Obbligati)*   7655, 12"
FAIR AT SOROTCHINSKI, THE (Mussorgsky)
GOPAK (Hopak): *London Symphony Orchestra, Albert Coates, Cond.*   11443, 12"
FLEDERMAUS, DIE (The Bat) (Johann Strauss)
OVERTURE: *Boston "Pops" Orchestra, Arthur Fiedler, Cond.*   12-0189, 12"
Paris Conservatory Orch., Bruno Walter, Cond.   13688, 12"
(In Album M-805)
Victor Symphony Orch., Nathaniel Shilkret, Cond.   35956, 12"
Marek Weber and His Orch.   36226, 12"
MEIN HERR MARQUIS (Laughing Song): *Miliza Korjus, Soprano, with Orch. In Spanish*   11-8579, 12"
CSARDAS: KLÄNGE DER HEIMAT (Had I Only Your Love): *Elisabeth Rethberg, Soprano, with Orch. In German*   7415, 12"
Vienna Boys Choir, with Piano. In German   1911, 10"
(In Album M-561)
BRÜDERLEIN UND SCHWESTERLEIN (Brothers and Sisters We): *Vienna Boys Choir; with Piano. In German*   1911, 10"
(In Album M-561)
TIK-TAK POLKA: *Boston "Pops" Orch., Arthur Fiedler, Cond.*   10-1205, 10"
(In Album M-1049)
DU UND DU—WALTZER (You and You—Waltz): *Vienna Philharmonic Orch., Erich Kleiber, Cond.*   11-8361, 12"
(In Album M-907)
Chicago Symphony Orch., Frederick Stock, Cond.   1481, 10"
Marek Weber and His Orch.   26514, 10"
(In Album P-14)
Dick Leibert, Organist, with His Orch.   27525, 10"
(In Album P-81)

FLORIDANTE (Handel)
ARIETTA—ALMA MIA (My Beloved): *Richard Crooks, Tenor, with Piano. In Italian*   2175, 10"
(In Album M-846)
Lily Pons, Soprano; Renaissance Quintet. In Italian   2151, 10"
(In Album M-756)
Ezio Pinza, Bass, with Piano. In Italian   17914, 12"
(In Album M-766)

DÉSERTEUR, LE (Monsigny)

ADIEU, CHÈRE LOUISE (Farewell, dear Louise): *Maggie Teyte, Soprano, with Orch.*
In French   10-1371, 10″

(In Album MO-1169)

GAZZA LADRA, LA (The Thieving Magpie) (Rossini)

OVERTURE: *Arturo Toscanini and the NBC Symphony Orch.*   11-9067, 12″

(In Album M-1037)

18-0006, 12″

(Vinylite) (In Album V-2)

Boston "Pops" Orch., Arthur Fiedler, Cond.   13751, 12″

GERMANIA (Franchetti)

FERITO PRIGIONIERO (A Wounded Prisoner): *Pasquale Amato, Baritone, with Orch.*
(Acoustical Recording) 15-1005, 12″

GOYESCAS (Granados)

INTERMEZZO: *Boston "Pops" Orch., Arthur Fiedler, Cond.*   12429, 12″

(In Album M-554)

Pablo Casals, Cellist, with Piano   6635, 12″

QUEJAS O "LA MAJA Y EL RUISEÑOR" (No. 4 of Piano Version): *José Iturbi, Pianist*
11562, 12″

GUARANY, IL (Gomes)

OVERTURE: *Boston "Pops" Orch., Arthur Fiedler, Cond.*   11-9112, 12″

GENTILE DI CUORE (Gentle of Heart);

BALLATA—C'ERA UNA VOLTA UN PRINCIPE (There Was Once a Prince): *Bidu Sayao,*
Soprano, with Orch. In Italian   11561, 12″

ITALIANA IN ALGERI, L' (Rossini)

OVERTURE: *Arturo Toscanini and the New York Philharmonic Symphony* 11-8511, 12″

(In Album M-825)

14161, 12″

IVAN THE TERRIBLE or THE MAID OF PSKOV (Rimsky-Korsakov)

PRELUDE TO ACT III—HUNT AND STORM MUSIC: *Leopold Stokowski and the Phila-*
delphia Orch.   17502, 12″

(In Album M-717)

JOCELYN (Godard)

BERCEUSE—CACHÉS DANS CET ASILE (Angels Guard Thee): *Richard Crooks, Tenor,*
with Orch. In English   8421, 12″

John McCormack, Tenor; Fritz Kreisler, Violinist; with Piano. In English
8032, 12″

(Acoustical Recording)

Charles R. Cronham, Organist   35828, 12″

Dick Leibert, Organist   27727, 10″

(In Album P-104)

KISS, THE (Hubička) (Smetana)

CRADLE SONG (*Ukolebavka*): *Jarmila Novotna, Soprano, with Orch. In Czech.*
11-9153, 12″

KOANGA (Delius)

LA CALINDA: *The Hallé Orchestra, Constant Lambert, Cond.*   11-8644, 12″

LIGHT CAVALRY (Suppé)

OVERTURE: *Boston "Pops" Orchestra, Arthur Fiedler, Cond.*   11-9954, 12″

LOMBARDI, I (Verdi)

QUAL VOLUTTÀ TRASCORRERE (With Sacred Joy): *Elisabeth Rethberg, Soprano; Benia-*
mino Gigli, Tenor; Ezio Pinza, Bass; with Orch. In Italian   8194, 12″

Frances Alda, Soprano; Enrico Caruso, Tenor; Marcel Journet, Bass; with Orch.
In Italian   16-5002, 12″

(Acoustical Recording) (In Album M-953)

POLONAISE—QUELLE IVRESSE BONHEUR SUPRÊME (With Sacred Joy): *Blanche Arral,*
Soprano, with Orch. In French   15-1016, 12″

(Acoustical Recording)

MAY NIGHT (Rimsky-Korsakov)
SLUMBER SONG: *Irene Jessner, Soprano, with Orch. In French*   17559, 12″

MEFISTOFELE (Boïto)
L'ALTRA NOTTE IN FONDO AL MARE (Last Night in the Deep Sea): *Licia Albanese,*
   Soprano, with Orch. In Italian   11-9848, 12″

MERRY MOUNT (Howard Hanson)
'TIS AN EARTH DEFILED: *Lawrence Tibbett, Baritone, with Orch. In English*   7959, 12″
   11-8932, 12″
   (In Album M-1015)

MERRY WIVES OF WINDSOR, THE (Nicolai)
. OVERTURE: *Boston "Pops" Orch., Arthur Fiedler, Cond.*   12533, 12″
   BBC Symphony Orch., Adrian Boult, Cond.   11836, 12″

NATOMA (Victor Herbert)
SELECTIONS (Habañera, Vaquero's Song, Natoma Theme, Dagger Dance, Finale):
   Victor Salon Orch., Nathaniel Shilkret, Cond.   9907, 12″
   (In Album C-11)
   DAGGER DANCE: *Boston "Pops" Orch., Arthur Fiedler, Cond.*   11932, 12″

OIES DE FRÈRE PHILIPPE, LES (Dourlen)
JE SAIS ATTACHER DES RUBANS (I Know How to Put On My Ribbons): *Maggie Teyte,*
   Soprano, with Orch. In French   10-1370, 10″
   (In Album MO-1169)

ORPHEUS IN HADES (Offenbach)
OVERTURE: *Detroit Symphony Orch., Karl Krueger, Cond.*   11-8761, 12″
   London Philharmonic Orch., Constant Lambert, Cond.   12604, 12″

PARTENOPE (Handel)
SE MIA GIOIA (You Are My Joy): *Richard Crooks, Tenor, with Piano. In Italian*
   2176, 10″
   (In Album M-846)

PAUL ET VIRGINIE (Victor Massé)
CHANSON DU TIGRE (Song of the Tiger): *Jeanne Gerville-Réache, Contralto, with*
   Orch. In French   15-1008, 12″
   (Acoustical Recording)

PHILÉMON ET BAUCIS (Gounod)
AU BRUIT LOURD DES MARTEAUX (Vulcan's Song): *Marcel Journet, Bass, with Orch.*
   In French   15-1003, 12″
   (Acoustical Recording)

REINE DE SABA, LA (Gounod)
PRÊTE-MOI TON AIDE (Lend Me Your Aid): *Enrico Caruso, Tenor, with Orch. In*
   French   15732, 12″

RIENZI (Wagner)
OVERTURE: *Boston "Pops" Orch., Arthur Fiedler, Cond.*
   DM-569 (13844 & 13845), 2-12″
   M-569 (12447 & 12448)
   Leopold Stokowski and the Philadelphia Orch.   6624 & 6625, 2-12″

RINALDO (Handel)
LASCIA CH' IO PIANGA (Leave Me to Languish): *Gladys Swarthout, Mezzo-soprano,*
   with Piano. In Italian   16778, 12″
   (In Album M-679)

ROBIN HOOD (Reginald de Koven)
OH, PROMISE ME: *Nelson Eddy, Baritone, with Orch.*   4370, 10″
   (In Album C-27)
   Jesse Crawford, Organist   20663, 10″

ROI D'YS, LE (Lalo) (The King of Ys)
OVERTURE: *San Francisco Symphony Orch., Pierre Monteux, Cond.*   11-8489, 12″
AUBADE—VAINEMENT, MA BIEN AIMÉE (In Vain, My Beloved): *Richard Crooks, Tenor, with Orch. In French*   15543, 12″
(In Album M-585)
15821, 12″
(In Album M-633)

ROSE ET COLAS (Monsigny)
LA SAGESSE EST UN TRÉSOR (Wisdom Is a Treasure): *Maggie Teyte, Soprano, with Orch. In French*   10-1369, 10″
(In Album MO-1169)

ROUSSALKA, THE (The Mermaid) (Dargomijsky)
MILLER'S ARIA (Act I): *Alexander Kipnis, Bass, with Orch. In Russian.*   11-9286, 12″
(In Album M-1073)
Feodor Chaliapin, Bass, with Orch. In Russian   7704, 12″
MAD SCENE AND DEATH OF THE MILLER (Act III): *Feodor Chaliapin, Bass; Pozemkovsky, Tenor; with Orch.*   11-8695, 12″

SCALA DI SETA, LA (The Silken Ladder) (Rossini)
OVERTURE: *Arturo Toscanini and the BBC Symphony Orch.*   15191, 12″
11-8510, 12″
(In Album M-825)

SCHÖNE GALATHEE, DIE (The Beautiful Galatea) (Suppé)
OVERTURE: *Boston "Pops" Orchestra, Arthur Fiedler, Cond.*   11-9494, 12″

SCHWANDA (Weinberger)
POLKA AND FUGUE: *Minneapolis Symphony Orchestra, Dimitri Mitropoulos, Cond.*   12-0019, 12″
Minneapolis Symphony Orchestra, Eugene Ormandy, Cond.   7958, 12″
11-9225, 12″
(In Album M-1062)
Vitya Vronsky and Victor Babin, Piano Duo   11-8189, 12″

SEMIRAMIDE (Rossini)
OVERTURE: *Arturo Toscanini and the New York Philharmonic Symphony*
DM-408 (18440 & 18441), 2-12″
M-408 (14632 & 14633)
11-8512 & 11-8513, 2-12″
(In Album M-825)
BEL RAGGIO LUSINGHIER (Beautiful Flattering Ray) (Act I): *Rose Bampton, Soprano, with Orch.*   18217, 12″

SERVANTE MAÎTRESSE, LA (Pergolesi)
AIR DE ZERBINA (Zerbina's Aria): *Maggie Teyte, Soprano, with Orch. In French*   10-1369, 10″
(In Album MO-1169)

SIGNOR BRUSCHINO, IL (Rossini)
OVERTURE: *Arturo Toscanini and the NBC Symphony Orch.*   11-9069, 12″
(In Album M-1037)
18-0008, 12″
(Vinylite) (In Album V-2)

TABLEAU PARLANT, LE (Grétry)
VOUS ÉTÌEZ, CE QUE VOUS N'ÊTES PLUS (You Are No Longer What You Once Were):
Maggie Teyte, Soprano, with Orch. In French   10-1371, 10″
(In Album MO-1169)

TALE OF THE INVISIBLE CITY OF KITEZH, THE (Rimsky-Korsakov)
THE BATTLE OF KERSHENETZ: *Boston Symphony Orchestra, Serge Koussevitzky, Cond.*   18410, 12″
(In Album M-870)

TALE OF TSAR SALTANA, THE (Rimsky-Korsakov)
MARCH (Introduction to Act II): *San Francisco Symphony Orch., Pierre Monteux, Cond.* 11-8384, 12"
(In Album M-920)
FLIGHT OF THE BUMBLEBEE (Act III): *Jascha Heifitz, Violinist, with Piano* 1645, 10"
Alexander Brailowsky, Pianist 11-9009, 12"

TROYENS, LES (The Trojans) (Berlioz)
CHASSE ROYALE ET ORAGE (Royal Hunt and Storm) (Act III)
MARCHE (March) (Act III): *Sir Thomas Beecham, Bart., and the London Philharmonic Orchestra*
11-9667 & 11-9668, 2-12"
(In Album M-1141)

TSAR'S BRIDE, THE (Rimsky-Korsakov)
MARTHA'S ARIA (Act II): *Miliza Korjus, Soprano, with Orch. In German* 12021, 12"

VIDA BREVE, LA (Falla)
VIVAN LOS QUE RIEN (He Who Laughs Lives): *Lucrezia Bori, Soprano, with Orch. In Spanish* 14615, 12"
(In Album M-405)
SPANISH DANCE No. 1: *St. Louis Symphony Orch., Vladimir Golschmann, Cond.*
11-8592, 12"
Fritz Kreisler, Violinist, with Piano 1891, 10"

XERXES (Serse) (Handel)
LARGO—OMBRA MAI FU (Oh, Lovely Tree): *Enrico Caruso, Tenor, with Orch. In Italian* 8806, 12"
Boston "Pops" Orch., Arthur Fiedler, Cond. 11887, 12"
Archer Gibson, Organist 35972, 12"

ZAMPA (Hérold)
OVERTURE: *Boston "Pops" Orchestra, Arthur Fiedler, Cond.* 13647, 12"

ZAZÀ (Leoncavallo)
ZAZÀ, PICCOLA ZINGARA (Zazà, Little Gypsy): *John Charles Thomas, Baritone, with Orch. In Italian* 15859, 12"
Robert Merrill, Baritone, RCA-Victor Orchestra, Jean Paul Morel, Cond.
12-0450, 12"
(In Album M-645)

ZÉMIRE ET AZOR (Grétry)
ROSE CHÉRIE (Beloved Rose): *Maggie Teyte, Soprano, with Orch. In French*
10-1370, 10"
(In Album MO-1169)
LA FAUVETTE AVEC SES PETITS (The Warbler with Her Little Ones): *Lily Pons, Soprano, with Renaissance Quintet. In French* 2149, 10"
(In Album M-756)

ZIGEUNERBARON, DER (The Gypsy Baron) (Johann Strauss)
OVERTURE: *Boston "Pops" Orchestra, Arthur Fiedler, Cond.* 12-0188, 12"
London Symphony Orch., Bruno Walter, Cond. 13689, 12"
(In Album M-805)
SWEETHEART WALTZ (My Darling or Treasure Waltz): *International Concert Orch.*
36127, 12"
Dick Leibert, Organist, with His Orch. 27525, 10"
(In Album P-81)
LOVE CAN BE DREAMED; MINE ALONE; OPEN ROAD: *John Charles Thomas, Baritone, with Orch. In English* 16184, 12"

3-11-74 WED - Falstaff
3-18-74 WED - Cav. Rust. o Paliacci

2-19-85 P/S - Eugene Onegin
3   85 P/S - Rigoletto